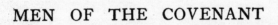

MEN OF THE COVENANT

ALEXANDER HENDERSON.

From the Fordel Portrait.

Men of the Covenant

by

ALEXANDER SMELLIE, M.A., D.D.

"Who through faith subdued kingdoms . . ."   HEB. xi, 33.

THE BANNER OF TRUTH TRUST

1960

Copyright by W. A. and J. A. Smellie

Portraits and Illustrations by A. Scott Rankin
and E. A. Pike

First Published by Andrew Melrose .	*November*	1903
Second Impression	*December*	1903
Second Edition	*June*	1904
Fourth Impression	*December*	1904
Cheap Edition (5000 Copies) at 2s. 6d.	*October*	1905
Edition de Luxe (920 Copies), with additional matter and New Illustrations in Two Volumes, 31s. 6d. net	*January*	1909
Seventh Edition, with additional matter and Illustrations as in Edition de Luxe	*August*	1909
Popular Edition (5400 Copies), 2s. 6d.	*January*	1911
Memorial Edition	*November*	1924
Tenth Edition (facsimile of seventh edition) published by The Banner of Truth Trust	*March*	1960

PRINTED IN GREAT BRITAIN BY OFFSET LITHOGRAPHY BY
BILLING AND SONS LTD., GUILDFORD AND LONDON

IN DEAR MEMORY OF

F. E. S.

A CHILD WHOM GOD LEADS

IN GREEN PASTURES

AND BESIDE THE STILL WATERS

PREFATORY NOTE TO THE FIRST EDITION

———◆———

IN the march of years, the heroisms of the past, its agonies and triumphs, fade very quickly into a mist of indistinctness. New events, new debates, and new achievements come crowding in, until their predecessors are well-nigh forgotten. That is why this book has been written. It seeks to recall a notable period, and to summon from the shadows which begin to gather about them some stalwart and noble figures in whose fellowship it is good to linger. I have addressed myself to ordinary readers, who have not the opportunity or the leisure to consult for themselves the pages of James Kirkton and Robert Wodrow, of Patrick Walker and Alexander Shields, of Dr. Osmund Airy and Dr. Hay Fleming. Where the portrait at full length is unattainable, the miniature or the pencilled sketch may have its place and use. Surely we, in our time, ought to know, and, knowing, to praise famous men, and women not a whit less famous—those men and women who, in Mr. Kipling's phrase,

> put aside To-day
> All the joys of their To-day,
> And with toil of their To-day
> Bought for us To-morrow.

The twenty-eight years of the Persecution, whilst they have an absorbing and manifold interest, are set with snares and pitfalls; and the pilgrim through them, when he seeks to shun the ditch on the one hand, is ready to tip over into

the mire on the other.   I do not doubt that errors have crept
into my recital; and, indeed, I make no shadow of claim to
the fulness and certitude of the expert.   But I think I can
say that I have done what I could to acquaint myself with
the theme which I have striven to expound.

Some may complain that the atmosphere of these chapters
is too Whiggish, and that they scarcely so much as try to
understand and appreciate the Cavalier.   I can but plead
that to me it seems evident that the Covenanter, in the main,
was incontestably right; although I hope that I have never
been conspicuously unfair to his opponent.   And, when Mr.
Lang and Mr. William Law Mathieson—in whose footsteps
Mr. J. H. Millar has but yesterday been following—have
recently done so much to glorify those who upheld the Royal
prerogative and the Episcopal rule, perhaps one, who only
wishes that he knew how to speak their great language, and
who holds them in admiration for their shining gifts, may
present his humbler brief on behalf of the dogged fighters for
freedom in Church and State.   This was done for a former
generation by writers like James Dodds and George Gilfillan.
But their books are not easily to be procured to-day; and,
since they were penned, facts have been brought to light
which help in the elucidation of the drama. . . .

November 1903.

PREFATORY NOTE TO THE *EDITION DE LUXE*

I HAVE little to add to these sentences, which were penned five years ago. The book they prefaced then has been kindly and even generously received; and I am glad to think that it may have done something to keep in memory those "starry gentlemen," the Scottish Covenanters.

In preparing a fresh edition, I have been helped by not a few recent volumes that treat of the period—by Mr. G. M. Trevelyan's *England under the Stuarts*; by Professor Sanford Terry's scholarly books on *The Pentland Rising* and *John Graham of Claverhouse*; by Dr. Willcock's admirable biography, *A Scots Earl*; by Mr. Lang's *Sir George Mackenzie, His Life and Times*—a volume as fair and frank as it is learned and full; and, most of all, by Dr. J. King Hewison's great treatise on *The Covenanters*—a treatise which covers the entire field and seems to leave no word unsaid. First and last, I owe much to a multitude of benefactors. My very special thanks, however, are due, and are heartily given, to the two artists who have illuminated these pages with a galaxy of delightful pictures; readers of them will agree that the work of Miss Pike and Mr. Scott Rankin is beyond praise. And I am so deep in my Publisher's debt that I can discover no language that will properly express my obligation; it was he who conceived, and he who has carried out, the idea of this *Edition de Luxe*, in which you see on Japanese vellum the presentments of men and women *who wandered in deserts, and in mountains, and in dens and caves of the earth.*

A. S.

October 1908.

ix

CONTENTS

ILLUSTRATIONS

ILLUSTRATIONS XV

AN OUTLINE OF SCOTTISH CHURCH HISTORY*

FROM THE REFORMATION TO 1688

1528 Patrick Hamilton, the first Reformer, martyred. Popery prevails everywhere in Scotland except for the presence of many Lollards in the South-West.

1542 Death of James V. The infant Mary Stuart becomes Mary Queen of Scots at the age of one week.
Assisted at first by the patronage of the Regent, the Earl of Arran, and especially by the preaching of George Wishart, (martyred 1546) the Reformation makes progress.

1547 John Knox, called to the ministry, is captured by French forces and made a galley slave. Restored to freedom in 1549. He preaches in England till 1554.

1554 Arran resigns regency to the French Queen-mother, Mary of Guise, a strong Roman Catholic.
Accession of Mary Tudor to English throne leads to flight of certain Protestant preachers to Scotland.

1555-6 Knox visits Scotland, then returns to Geneva.

1557 Protestant Scottish nobility draw up *The First Covenant* and become known as "Lords of the Congregation." They enter into alliance with the Protestant English Government of Queen Elizabeth in 1560. This leads to the expulsion from Scotland of French military forces which had been assisting in the attempted suppression of the Reformation since 1547.

* Drawn up by the publishers for inclusion in the 1960 reprint of this book as an aid to those who are unfamiliar with the background of the period.

1559 Knox returns to Scotland.

1560 Scottish Parliament under guidance of Knox declares the
Reformed Faith to be the national religion. The Scots
Confession is approved and Popery condemned. The
General Assembly of the Reformed Church of Scotland
meets for the first time (Dec. 20, 1560).

1561 The young Queen Mary Stuart returns to Scotland after a
Roman Catholic upbringing in France, and assumes the
reins of government. She attempts to revive the interests
of her faith by gaining the favour of the nobility.

1567 Mary's conduct and unprincipled marriage relationships
alienate the nation and lead to her abdication. Her infant
son proclaimed James VI of Scotland.
The nation governed by regents till 1578. The Protestant
Regent, the Earl of Moray, assassinated in 1570 (Jan. 23).
Morton, Regent from 1572-8, attempts to remove the
freedom and independence of the Church of Scotland by
introducing " Tulchan Bishops " into her government.

1574 The Church, leaderless since the death of Knox in 1572, is
revived by the return of Andrew Melville from the Continent.

1578 James VI, aged twelve, begins to exercise his monarchy
and governs through unprincipled courtiers. The Court
and Church engage in a struggle which continues till 1638
over the right of the Church to govern her affairs inde-
pendently of the civil powers. (James's hostility to
Presbyterianism arose from his ambition to be regarded as
head of the Church. He aimed to retain the pre-Reforma-
tion episcopal organization (without the Roman faith) and
by means of bishops to control the Reformed Church and
her General Assemblies. In the next century the Stuarts
attempted to overthrow the whole Presbyterian
constitution.)

1580 The Protestant leaders pledge themselves to support the
Reformed doctrine and discipline in *The National Covenant*.

1584 *The Black Acts.* The Court party predominating, Parliament overturns the independence of the Church by ordaining that no ecclesiastical assembly is to be held without the King's consent and that all ministers are to acknowledge the bishops as their ecclesiastical superiors.

1592 The legislation of 1584 repealed and the Presbyterian discipline re-established. James, controlled temporarily by the force of public opinion, professes to be a true Presbyterian.

1596 The National Covenant renewed. A revival of religion and a remarkable General Assembly at Edinburgh. (This was sunshine before a storm and proved to be the last true General Assembly till 1638.)

1603-18 James VI (James I of England from 1603) establishes bishops by royal authority, packs and bribes General Assemblies, exiles the leading Presbyterians and by the Articles of Perth (1618) seeks to conform Scottish worship to the pattern of the Anglican church.

1625-30 This dark period broken by a series of powerful revivals, particularly under the preaching of David Dickson at Irvine, Robert Blair in Ireland, and John Livingstone at Kirk of Shotts—where about 500 people ascribed their conversion to one sermon (June 21, 1630). " One of the largest manifestations of the Spirit that hath been seen since the days of the apostles." Charles I, who succeeded to the thrones of England and Scotland in 1625, pursues his father's anti-Presbyterian policy with renewed vigour, spurred on by Archbishop Laud.

1637 Charles attempts to introduce a liturgy composed by Laud into the Church of Scotland. It is rejected in Edinburgh and throughout the country.

1638 The National Covenant renewed, amidst great excitement, in Edinburgh (Feb. 28). The people stirred against " Arminianism, popery, and despotism " and the King is compelled to allow a free General Assembly to meet. The independence of the Church is re-asserted. Charles attempts to subdue Scotland by force but is defeated in the *First and Second Bishops' Wars* (1639-40).

1642 *The Civil War* commences in England. The predominantly Puritan Parliament seeks aid from Scotland and by *The Solemn League and Covenant* (1643) the English Puritans and Scottish Presbyterians pledge their nations to uniformity in religion according to The Word of God.

1645 Royalist army defeated at *Naseby* by Parliamentary forces. Disagreement on how the defeated King should be treated occasions a breach in the English-Scottish alliance. In *Second Civil War* (1648) Scots fight for King against Parliament. (The Scots had no objection to monarchy as such; they strongly resented Charles's execution in 1649, and immediately declared his son, Charles II, the lawful successor to the throne.) The English army, under Cromwell, invades Scotland and obtains victory over the Scots at *Dunbar* (1650).

1651 The Scots crown Charles II at Scone, but at *Worcester* are again defeated by Cromwell, and the country remains largely under English control for next nine years. (Despite internal divisions and the interference of Cromwell, the Church of Scotland enjoyed a period of spiritual prosperity —" piety was both more intense and more widely diffused than it has ever since been in Scotland "—T. McCrie.) Students trained by Dickson in Edinburgh and by Rutherford at St. Andrews.

1660 Charles II, an exile since *Worcester*, is restored to the throne of England and Scotland after the death of Cromwell (1658). He throws off his former allegiance to the Scottish Presbyterians and packs the Scottish Parliament with his own supporters. An act is passed recognizing the King's authority in matters both civil and ecclesiastical and soon prelacy (the government of the Church by bishops) is re-established by law. The Church of Scotland thrown into a furnace of 28 years' persecution.

1662 400 ministers ejected from their churches.   At Edinburgh all ministers required to comply with the new order of things or leave the city and desist from preaching.

1663 Ejected ministers begin preaching in the open-air at " field-meetings."   The government attempts to suppress them by fines and military force.

1666 Increasing oppression provokes an unpremeditated rising amongst the " Covenanters " (the term by which those who adhered to the old Presbyterian principles became known) in Galloway, but their ill-equipped forces overcome at *Rullion Green* (November 28).   This event followed by many executions and gives excuse for greater persecution— " the first time Scotland ever endured so much cruelty " (Kirkton).

1669 *An Act of Indulgence* promises relief (on certain conditions) to ministers who could not conform to the established order. Some accept this relief but the more resolute Covenanters refuse it.   This divides the Presbyterians into the " indulged " and the " non-indulged."

1670 " Field-meetings " made treasonable and preaching at such a meeting becomes a capital offence.   Nevertheless these meetings rapidly increase.   About this time arms begin to be carried for self defence and " field-meetings " begin to develop into " armed conventicles."
" Through unrelenting persecution these decent congregations were transformed into what their persecutors had at first falsely asserted them to be—battalions of armed men, resolved to defy opposition, and prepared to take the field against their aggressors."   (T. McCrie.)

1679 The Covenanters rise in Galloway, condemn all the proceedings of the government since 1660, and defeat the government's forces at the battle of *Drumclog*.   But they fail to take Glasgow and become divided over their attitude towards those who had accepted *the Indulgence* and towards King Charles.   The extreme party begins to maintain that the King, by breaking his coronation oaths (made to the Presbyterians at Scone in 1651) and by assuming ecclesiastical powers, had forfeited all right to the civil obedience of his subjects. The Covenanters, disheartened by the divisions amongst their leaders, are overcome by superior numbers at *Bothwell Bridge.*

Cameron and Cargill, leading the party which disowned civil allegiance, continue field-preaching; the former is killed at *Ayrsmoss* (July, 1680) and the latter executed in Edinburgh (July, 1681). "The subsequent period down to 1688 exhibits little more than a series of executions, civil and military, differing from each other only in their degrees of horror and atrocity." (T. McCrie.)

1684-85 "*The Killing Times*"—the hottest period of persecution. Common soldiers are empowered to put suspected persons to death without trial.

Charles II dies (Feb. 1685) and is succeeded by his Roman Catholic brother, James II.

A daring remnant, led by James Renwick, continues to outbrave the government by continuing to hold "field-meetings."

1688 Renwick captured and martyred.

"*The Glorious Revolution*" in England leads to the flight of James II and the accession of the Protestant William and Mary. The Church of Scotland is restored to her spiritual freedom and liberty.

(Since 1660 some 18,000 had suffered for their allegiance to The Word of God and to Christ as the only Head and Lawgiver of the Church.)

MEN OF THE COVENANT

PROLOGUE.

THE Covenanters were the men and women who uttered the strongest convictions of their souls in two great documents of the seventeenth century, a heroic period in the history of Britain. One of these documents is the National Covenant of Scotland, as it was recast and sworn in 1638. The other is the Solemn League and Covenant, similar in aspiration, but wider in geographical scope, being designed to embrace England and Ireland as well as the smaller country north of the Cheviots and the Solway. In this book there is no intention of depicting the events and persons of the days in which these famous confessions sprang into existence. It begins with the *Annus Mirabilis* of the Restoration, when the National Covenant was two-and-twenty springtimes old, and when some who were prominent in commending it to their fellows 'had passed from the scene of their earthly battle. Its concern is with the characters, the doings, and the sorrows of their immediate successors, who coincided with them in intellectual belief and in religious enthusiasm. It will attempt, once more, to describe the features of an age when, in Scotland, the conflict was even more keenly waged, and the tragedy had become painfuller and more lurid. But, if we are to understand the later epoch, it will be necessary at the outset to recall a few of the incidents in the earlier.

For years the Scottish people had been familiar with the practice of covenanting. By a kind of spiritual instinct they had turned to it, so soon as the First Reformation brought them freedom from the darknesses and enslavements of mediævalism. After long slumber they were at last awake, and the morning was the gladdest in their history.

> Hay! now the day dallis,
> Now Christ on us callis,
> Now welth on our wallis
>   Apperis anone :
> Now the Word of God regnes,
> Quhilk is King of all kingis,
> Now Christis flock singis,
>   The nycht is neir gone.

And one device by which the enfranchised men gave expression to the joy that was surging within them, and to their firm determination never to let it go, was found in the vows they registered, the " Godly Bands " they wrote and subscribed, pledging themselves to continue faithful to their heavenly Lord and to His Kingdom in their native land. Sometimes the Bands were private and personal, each the oath sworn by a single soldier in the Holy War that, through time and eternity, he would remain by his Captain Christ and by the cause to which he had surrendered himself. " I here," a lady of the Covenant declared, " give my hearty consent, Lord Jesus, to Thy coming in and taking possession of my soul, and to Thy casting out of everything there that stands in opposition to Thee. I desire to take Thee for my All, to be ruled and governed by Thee, acquiescing to whatsoever shall be Thy way of dealing with me. Give me Thyself, and this shall be all my desire." Many such attestations and contracts, couched in terms of the profoundest intimacy, and quivering with a devotion that will not hide, might be quoted. For the lonely flight of the individual spirit to God's breast, its own abode, has numerous illustrations in the Scottish religion of the sixteenth and seventeenth centuries; and nothing is more unjust to the facts of the case than to portray that religion as one merely of rigid and untender dogma. If its face seemed hard and severe, the tears were never far from its eyes, and its secret heart was the shrine of love and fire.

But frequently the Covenants, earlier as well as later, were public, signed by a multitude of hands, and concerned with the prosperity and health of the commonwealth at large. There was, for example, the Band of 1557, entered into by the Lords of the Congregation—noblemen like Argyll and Glencairn and Morton and John Erskine of Dun, who had espoused the tenets of Protestantism, and who desired to see the Reformation spread itself throughout the country. A decade later, when Queen Mary was a prisoner in Loch Leven Castle, and when the General Assembly was meeting in Edinburgh, those peers, barons, and commissioners of towns, who were members of the high court of the Church, to the number of eighty, agreed to certain Articles, and appended their names to the agreement. They were to destroy the mass and the monuments of idolatry; to set up the true religion through the whole realm; to increase the stipends of the ministers, and improve the schools and colleges, and ease the poor of the teinds; to punish crime and offences, and to defend the young prince, training him in the fear of the Lord. Better still, they consented and offered to "reforme themselves according to the Booke of God." In January 1581, rather more than eight years after Knox had finished his travail, John Craig, once his colleague in St. Giles, a man with a biography as full of colour and a courage as dauntless as his own, drew up a Covenant which had a greater renown than any of its predecessors—"The King's Confession," as it is generally called. In trenchant language it condemned the false teachings and corrupt practices of Roman Catholicism. It "wes the touchstone," as the historian Row affirms, "to try and discern Papists from Protestants." But it was as eager to avow the attachment of its subscribers to their ruler, so long at least as he reigned wisely and as God's vicegerent should. With their "geyr, bodyes and lyves," they protested and promised that they would help the King's Majesty, "in the defence of Christis Evangell, libertie of owre cowntrey,

ministration of justice, and punishment of iniquitie, as we
desyre owre God to be a strong and mercyfull Defender to
us, in the day of owre death, and coming of owre Lord Jesus
Christ." These two notes—the resolution to preserve the
Church pure from error, and the avouchment of the subject's
allegiance to his prince—were to be rung out again and
again by the Covenanters of subsequent years.

Thus the men and women of the newer generation were
only repeating a habit of their ancestors when they bound
themselves, in clearly worded and uncompromising written
engagements, to venture and achieve and suffer their uttermost for that which they believed to be the truth committed
to them by God.

When we enter this new generation, it is inevitable that
we should make our initial pilgrimage to the churchyard of
the Greyfriars, in Edinburgh.

Charles the First was in some respects the best of the
Stuarts. He was free from the childishness of his father—
that pompous and solemn father, who was "deeply learned,
without possessing useful knowledge; a lover of negotiations,
in which he was always outwitted; fond of his dignity, while
he was perpetually degrading it by undue familiarity;
laborious in trifles, and a trifler where serious labour was
required; the wisest fool in Christendom." He had none of
the ribald license of the son who followed him on the throne,
nor of the saturnine malignity of the other son who had
scarcely grasped the reins of power when he was compelled
to lay them down. But less than either James the Sixth or
Charles the Second he understood how to govern his people.
To the last degree he was opinionative and despotic. He
would not bate a jot of his divine right. Never for a
moment was he disposed to listen to the voices of sound
reason and popular liberty. In Scotland especially, he rode
roughshod over the convictions of his subjects, even although,
with a persistent and pathetic loyalty, they were ready to
shed every drop of their blood in his defence. Matters
reached a crisis on that historic Sabbath, the 23rd of July in

1637, when the new liturgy, which the King and Archbishop Laud had gifted to a nation thirled to Calvinistic Presbyterianism, was to be read in the church of St. Giles. Dean Hanna was not permitted to use the " Popish-English-Scottish-Mass-Service Book "; he, and Bishop Lindsay, and the authorities in London and Canterbury, had not calculated on Jenny Geddes and Mrs. Mein and their compeers. At last the Scots were in a white heat of indignation.

"Are we so modest spirits," writes Robert Baillie —and he was himself among the more pliable of the ministers of the Kirk—" and are we so towardly handled, that there is appearance we shall embrace in a clap such a mass of novelties ? " The one plea which may be urged for the sovereign and "little Laud" is that they had a totally inadequate conception of the intensity of religious feeling in Scotland ; they lived in a fool's paradise, like the French officer in Alphonse Daudet's story, who, up to the very day when the Germans entered Paris, dreamed that it was Prussia which was going down in the cataclysm of 1870. Lord Clarendon tells us how profoundly indifferent the English people and their leaders were in those years to everything which happened on the farther side of the Tweed. " When the whole nation was solicitous to know what passed weekly in Germany and Poland and all other parts of Europe, no man ever inquired what was doing in Scotland, nor had that kingdom a place or mention of one page of any gazette." It was a silly and culpable ignorance, and the awakening was to be swift and stern.

For it was out of the peril in which the Scottish nation found itself that there came the renewal of the National Covenant. Two men, whose names are written bright across the annals of the time, planned this renewal: Archibald Johnston of Wariston, the young advocate of the Edinburgh courts, and Alexander Henderson, foremost and most statesmanlike of the Presbyterian clergymen of the day. Between them they framed the momentous charter. It consisted of three portions. The first was a reproduction of that older Covenant, the King's Confession of 1581 ; the second enumerated the various Acts of the Scottish Parliament, which condemned Popery and confirmed the privileges of the Reformed Church; the third was a grave and emphatic protest against those alien modes of worship which had provoked the present troubles. Wariston was author of the second portion, Henderson of the third.

We may hearken to the accents of this Magna Charta of offended Presbytery. "Because," its writers say, "we plainly perceive, and undoubtedly believe, that the innovations and evils contained in our supplications, complaints, and protestations, have no warrant of the Word of God, are contrary to the articles of our Confession, to the intention and meaning of the blessed Reformers of religion in this land, to the above-written Acts of Parliament; and do sensibly tend to the re-establishing of the Popish religion and tyranny, and to the subversion and ruin of the true Reformed religion, and of our liberties, laws, and estates: therefore, from the knowledge and conscience of our duty to God, to our King and country, without any worldly respect or inducement, so far as human infirmity will suffer, wishing a further measure of the grace of God for this effect, we promise and swear, by the great name of the Lord our God, to continue in the profession and obedience of the foresaid religion; and that we shall defend the same, and resist all these contrary errors and corruptions, according to our vocation, and to the uttermost of that power that God hath put in our hands, all the days of our life." Here is a trumpet which gives no uncertain sound. But the Covenanters were careful, also, that there should not be the slightest diminution in the reverence they yielded to the monarch. "On the contrary," they assert, "we promise and swear that we shall, to the uttermost of our power, with our means and lives, stand to the defence of our dread sovereign." Surely it was a criminal shortsightedness which drove into opposition citizens so leal.

In the churchyard of the Greyfriars, where once the monastery of the Franciscans had stood, a new restingground of the dead in Henderson's time and Wariston's, although already it held the grave of George Buchanan, the

Covenant was signed. It is to-day a romantic spot in the most romantic town in the world; two centuries and a half ago it must have been even more picturesque, for from its slope the view was unbroken over the wide space of the Grassmarket to the crags of the Castle. But the crowds who gathered to it, on this 28th. of February 1638, had neither the leisure nor the inclination to admire their natural surroundings. They came from every Lowland county of Scotland, and there were not wanting representatives from the remoter shires beyond the Tay. It is said that there were sixty thousand persons in all; unconsciously the number was, perhaps, somewhat exaggerated. The great nobles, the lesser barons, the ministers, the burgesses, the common people—from early morning they had been hurrying to the chosen meeting-place. At two o'clock in the afternoon, inside the church, the solemnity commenced. The Earl of Loudoun, famed for his eloquence, addressed the densely packed congregation. After him, Alexander Henderson offered up fervent prayer. Then Archibald Johnston lifted the "fair parchment above an elne in squair," which sometimes has been designated "the Constellation upon the back of Aries," for it was on a splendid ramskin that the Covenant had been inscribed. He read its contents distinctly and firmly, so that all could hear. When this was done, the Earl of Rothes called for objectors; but who in the ardent multitude had come to object? Then, in every corner of the church, right hands were uplifted, and the oath to keep the bond was sworn, and many cheeks were wet with weeping. The process of subscribing followed; inside the walls it went forward hour after hour. Some wrote after their autograph, "Until death." Some "did draw their own blood and used it in place of ink." When, at length, the ramskin was carried out to the churchyard, evening had set in after the short spring day. But the people, waiting there excited and expectant, could not be satisfied until many of them too had appended their names. There are flat tombstones close beside the building, on one or other of which the parchment must have been spread. It was "neir eight" ere the work was over and the crowds dispersed.

And this was simply the first step. When the transaction in Greyfriars was ended, the Covenant had still thousands of adherents to win; in a few weeks it became very apparent that it was indubitably the symbol of the nation's will. Noblemen and gentlemen conveyed copies of the pregnant deed from district to district, from town to town, from village to village. The ministers explained and commended its sentences from well-nigh all the pulpits of the land. Virtually the whole of Scotland signed it, the two notable exceptions being the Episcopal capital of St. Andrews and the city of Aberdeen—Aberdeen, which the young Marquis of Montrose, soon to be protagonist for the King, vainly attempted to coerce into acquiescence. Those on the other side stood aghast at the triumphant march of the movement; now and then they tried to disparage it, as if it had no real spontaneity, but was fed and fostered by domineering leaders. "If you knew," one of these opponents wrote, in April, to a friend at Court, "what odd, uncouth, insolent, and ridiculous courses they use to draw in silly, ignorant fools, fearful fasards, women and boys, I can hardly say whether it would afford His Majesty more occasion of laughter or anger." But the uprising was no product of compulsion and imperious management. It was the unforced and resolute answer of the Scottish race to Canterbury and Whitehall.

The answer was one in which patriotism and religion were blended. It was the protest of an indomitable people against the curtailment of political right and freedom, too dear to lose. It was the declaration, also, on the part of a Church, which loved intelligently its own simplicities of creed and worship, that it could not tolerate the imposition of forms which it hated, and from which, not so long before, it had by a mighty effort emancipated itself. Scotland was heartily willing to acknowledge Charles, to fight his battles, and to give him her unstinted allegiance; but he must not filch from her either her civic liberty or her spiritual birth-

ANNE, MARCHIONESS OF HAMILTON.

After a Painting by George Jamesone.

right. If he touched these treasures, he would find her humour "thwarteous" indeed, and he was certain to confront a will yet more decided than his own.

The outlook for the King's party did not brighten as the months wore on. When we halt next, in the Cathedral of Glasgow, to watch the doings of the Assembly which held its meetings within the stately shrine, we discover that the cause of Presbytery has advanced by leaps and bounds.

For a full month, from the 21st of November to the 20th of December, in the same year which witnessed the signing of the Covenant, the Glasgow Assembly was in session. Charles had most reluctantly granted the ministers his permission to come together; so long as he was able he fought against the request of the nation. Through the whole of summer and autumn one obstructive device after another was grasped at by the Court; up to London and back to Edinburgh the Marquis of Hamilton, who was the King's delegate, had journeyed time after time. But nothing except the Assembly would please the people; and in the end the sovereign gave way. In August, letters of direction were sent by the leaders in Edinburgh to the fifty-three Presbyteries of the country, and even to all the Kirk-Sessions, containing explicit instructions as to the representatives who ought to be elected; as far as might be, the tares must be excluded from the wheatfield of Christ. At length everything was ready. There were one hundred and forty-four ministers and ninety-six lay members, some of these last the highest noblemen in the land—Rothes, and Lothian, and Cassillis, and Eglintoun, and Montrose, and Wemyss, and Home. And besides those who were thus commissioned to speak and act, we must think of the vast concourse of interested spectators; during the four weeks when the Assembly was busy at its epoch-making tasks, Glasgow had a great addition to its resident population of twelve thousand souls. No one gives us a more lifelike account of the occurrences of these weeks than Robert Baillie, the vivacious letter-writer of the Covenant; and the trouble occasioned by the throning crowds is among the themes on which he descants. "The Magistrates, with their toun guard, the noblemen, with the assistance of the gentrie, whyles the Commissioner in person, could not get us entrie to our roomes, use what force, what policie they could, without such delay of tyme and thrumbling through as did grieve and offend us." Nor were the manners of the onlookers all that could be wished. "It is here alone," the minister of Kilwinning is constrained to confess, "where, I think, we might learn from Canterburie, yea, from the Pope, from the Turkes or pagans; at least their deep reverence in the house they call God's ceases not till it have led them to the adoration of the timber and stones of the place. We are so farr the other way that our rascals, without shame, in great numbers, make such dinn and clamour in the house of the true God, that, if they minted to use the like behaviour in my chamber, I could not be content till they were down the stairs." Now and then, it was a sadly turbulent auditory which the High Church housed that memorable winter.

Two figures are prominent in the story of the meeting. One is the Moderator, Alexander Henderson, of Leuchars. Until he was upwards of fifty years of age, he was the studious and hard-working minister of his quiet country parish. It was the urgency of the national crisis which drew him from obscurity. But, when he stepped into the arena of public affairs, his commanding powers and unfailing sagacity made him the helmsman of the Church. He was little of stature, with a pensive face; one would scarcely guess from the exterior of the man what wisdom and what courage resided within. "Every knight," said Tristram of Arthur, "may learn to be a knight of him;" and Dickson, and Rutherfurd, and Cant, and Rollock had the same tribute to pay to Henderson. He was, Baillie wrote, " incomparably the ablest man of us all for all things." "In every strait and conflict"—it is Professor Masson's witness—"he had to be appealed to, and came in at the last as the man of supereminent composure, comprehensiveness, and breadth of brow." We do not wonder that, necessarily and unani-

mously, he was summoned to the presidency of the Glasgow
Assembly.

The other figure is different. It is that of the Royal
Commissioner, the Marquis of Hamilton. His portrait has
been drawn for us by the friendly hand of Bishop Burnet;
and, even when we have allowed for the partialities of an
apologist, it remains a courtly and gracious portrait. " An
unclouded serenity dwelt always on his looks, and discovered
him ever well-pleased;" "one advantage he had beyond
all he engaged with in debating, that he was never fretted
nor exasperated, and spake at the same rate without clamour-
ing or eagerness;" his tones, like those of Christina Rossetti's
Princess, were

> modulated just so much
> As it was meet:

and these were valuable assets in the envoy who was sent
to propitiate the militant theologians of his native country.
A clinging pathos, too, haunts the person of the ill-fated
soldier, who, in March of 1649, somewhat more than ten
years after his experiences in Glasgow, laid down his head
on the block for his kingly master. On the scaffold he bore
himself as bravely as Charles himself had done six weeks
previously: "when he was desired to change the Posture he
stood in, since the Sun shined full in his Face, he answered
pleasantly, ' No, it would not burn it, and he hoped to see a
brighter Sun than that very speedily.'" But, with all his
winning qualities, there was nothing impressive about the
Marquis. His abilities were superficial. He had neither
much depth of character nor much strength of will; his
mother, one of the most zealous ladies of the Covenant, was
endowed with immeasurably more spirit than her son. It
might have been predicted beforehand that, in conflict with
Alexander Henderson, the Commissioner was destined to
defeat.

The defeat came a week after the Assembly met. On
the morning of the 28th of November, the King's spokesman,
who had been challenging the conduct of the members ever
since they convened, addressed them for the last time. He

objected to the presence of the lay elders, the influence of
many of whom Charles greatly dreaded: were they all, he
asked sarcastically, "fit to judge of the high and deep
Mysteries of Predestination, of the Universality of Redemption, of the Sufficiency of Grace given or not given to all
men, of the Resistibility of Grace, of total and final Perseverance or Apostasie of the Saints, of the Antelapsarian or
Postlapsarian Opinion, of Election and Reprobation?" Still
more explicitly, he denied the right which the Assembly
claimed, and which it was resolved to exercise, of passing
sentence on the Bishops: the citations, commanding the
prelates to appear at its bar, had been read in the pulpits of
the country, "which is not usual in this Church"; and,
moreover, men pledged to the assertions of the Covenant
never could deal fairly with the representatives of Episcopacy
—"who ever heard of such Judges as have sworn themselves
Parties?" If the dogged Presbyterians in front of him
intended to persevere in their determination, the Commissioner
declared with tears, tears which "drew water from many
eyes," that he must leave the Assembly, and must pronounce
it dissolved and its enactments invalid and worthless. Yes,
the Moderator replied, unruffled and tranquil, they had no
choice but to remain until their duty was done. So the
Marquis passed out of the Cathedral, and next day issued
his proclamation, ordering every person who was not resident
in Glasgow to depart from the city within twenty-four hours.

But, unperturbed by the proclamation, the members of
Assembly sat on, and pursued their work to its completion.
The victory in the duel rested with Henderson—Henderson,
"who went all this while for a quiet and calm-spirited man,"
Laud wrote in a letter of condolence to Hamilton, "but who
hath shewed himself a most violent and passionate man, and
a Moderator without Moderation." The walls of Jericho, as
this intrepid Joshua of the Scottish Church phrased it, were
pulled down with a thoroughness which satisfied the Israel
of the Covenant. The Acts of previous Assemblies, ratifying
Episcopacy, were annulled. The Service Book, and the
Canons, and the Court of High Commission, and the Articles

of Perth, were swept away. Eight of the Bishops were excommunicated, and the other six were deposed or suspended. The National Covenant was confirmed. On the ruins of the Prelacy, which Scotland found so distasteful, the fabric of Presbyterianism rose again fair and strong.

Close upon five years have passed—years crowded with stirring events, with plots and counterplots, with rumours of battle and actual unsheathings of the sword. When we pause next in our hasty survey, the English Civil War is in progress, and King Charles and his Parliament have abandoned their wordy quarrels for "strenuous trump and drum." The time is Monday, the 25th of September 1643, and the place is St. Margaret's Church at Westminster.

There and then the Solemn League and Covenant was sworn, by two hundred and twenty members of the House of Commons, and by the divines of the great Westminster Assembly, which had now been deliberating for nearly three months. The Solemn League and Covenant—and what was it? Robert Burns sings its eulogy, when he declares that it "sealed Freedom's sacred cause." Henry Hallam summarises its contents in one long sentence, which yet is admirably clear: "The Covenant consisted in an oath, to be subscribed by all persons in both kingdoms, whereby they bound themselves to preserve the Reformed religion in the Church of Scotland, in doctrine, worship, discipline, and government, according to the Word of God and practice of the best Reformed Churches; and to endeavour to bring the Churches of God, in the three kingdoms, to the nearest conjunction and uniformity in religion, Confession of faith, form of Church government, Directory for Worship, and catechising; to endeavour, without respect of persons, the extirpation of Popery, Prelacy, and whatsoever should be found contrary to sound doctrine and the power of godliness; to preserve the rights and privileges of the Parliaments, and the liberties of the kingdoms, and the King's person and authority in the preservation and defence of the true religion and liberties of the kingdoms; to endeavour the discovery of incendiaries and malignants, who hinder the reformation of religion and divide the King from his people, that they may be brought to punishment; finally, to assist and defend all such as should enter into this Covenant, and not suffer themselves to be withdrawn from it, whether to revolt to the opposite party, or to give in to a detestable indifference and neutrality." Once we have mastered Hallam's sentence, we understand the aims of the Solemn League.

It takes in a wider area than its forerunner, the National Covenant of Scotland. It is anxious for the spiritual prosperity of England and Ireland, no less than for the welfare of their Northern neighbour. And how has the enlargement of horizon come about? The explanation is not difficult to find. It is due to the ill success which, in the opening months of the War, attends the Parliamentary armies. Reverse after reverse has fallen on their standards. The clouds are massed ominously overhead. It is time, the chiefs in London think, to appeal for aid to the Scots. So a deputation goes to the Convention of Estates in Edinburgh and to the General Assembly in St. Andrews—four members of it from the Commons, of whom young Sir Harry Vane is the best known, and two members from the divines in King Henry the Seventh's Chapel, Stephen Marshall and Philip Nye. Their petition is successful. They secure that Scotland shall not hold aloof from the strife, and shall not attempt to mediate between Royalist and Roundhead, but shall in effective fashion stretch out a hand of succour to the struggling forces of the Parliament. But there must be a formal treaty between the nations. The deputies—Philip Nye, the stout Independent, foremost in the argument—would prefer it to be purely political, occupying itself with nothing more than the liberties of the kingdoms; but the Scots, with whom the affairs of the soul and the interests of the cause of God bulk biggest, want something deeper. "The English were for a civil league, we for a religious covenant," writes Robert Baillie. The suppliants from London have to yield the point; and Alexander Henderson—always, like William of Deloraine, "good at need"—draws up the bond.

This bond it is, with a few emendations, which is sworn in St. Margaret's, sworn afterwards throughout the length and breadth of England, as well as in the Scotland where such Covenants have their native air and most congenial home.

Looking at the Solemn League and at its Scottish predecessor, what judgment shall we pronounce upon them? It will be strange if we do not admit that the ends which they sought were sublime and sacred. Above all things else, their framers desired the victory of true religion in the land. No doubt, it was one particular variety of religion which most of these high-thoughted men were eager to have rooted and grounded among their fellow-citizens—the variety which we know as Calvinistic Presbyterianism. The Solemn League may not insist, in so many words, that this shall be the system of dogmatic faith and Church government to be accepted by England and Ireland; but it was the well-defined goal towards which Henderson and his comrades panted with zealous hearts. It was no unworthy goal. The Genevan creed has bred a glorious multitude of stalwart natures. The Presbyterian Church has been a hearth at which many heroes and saints have gained an enriching nurture. For few grander purposes have men ever banded themselves than for the realisation of the Covenanting ideal. But an oath so lofty, if it is to be valid, must always be voluntary. It must utter the conviction of each person who swears it. It must not be imposed on dubious and wavering souls, and far less on souls unfriendly and hostile. This was one respect in which the Covenanters erred, one mistaken course which sowed seeds of weakness in their dedicated ranks. So hungry they were for uniformity in spiritual things—so anxious to see fulfilled the high aspiration of Sir David Lindsay of the Mount,

> *Habitare fratres in unum*
> Is a blissful thing;
> One God, One Faith, One Baptism pure,
> One Law, One Land, One King!—

that they were prepared to coerce their countrymen, if these should be unwilling, into nominal agreement with themselves.

The method was wrong; there is none to-day who will be its advocate; and yet the men themselves were crusaders of Jesus Christ. They wished to have Him enthroned over the country which they loved with more than the patriot's affection. It was His crown which was the oriflamme of their holy war. For His inalienable rights they counted no peril too hazardous and no sacrifice too great.

It is easy to accuse them of want of tolerance. We do not pledge ourselves now to "the extirpation" of any form of religious belief; our minds are too hospitable and catholic. But, with one or two inspiring exceptions, the men of the seventeenth century, whatever their opinion and Church, showed none of the modern comprehensiveness. Oliver Cromwell had it among the Independents, and Jeremy Taylor amongst Episcopalians, until he rose to be Bishop of Down and Connor, and in his day of power dismissed six-and-thirty Presbyterian ministers from their parishes; but how many agreed with them? The *Liberty of Prophesying* was published four summers after the solemnity in St. Margaret's. It advocated the admission to Christian fellowship of every one who from the heart could repeat the Apostles' Creed. It suggested no more stringent and elaborate test. Few forget the beautiful apologue with which it concludes: how, one evening, Abraham sat at his tent door, waiting to entertain strangers, and saw coming to him a weary old man, who was a hundred years of age; how he provided supper for him, but, when the wayfarer asked no blessing on his meat, and acknowledged himself a fire-worshipper, the patriarch in his zeal thrust him out of the tent, and exposed him to all the evils of the darkness; how then God rebuked Abraham —"I have suffered him these hundred years, although he dishonoured Me; and couldst not thou endure him for one night, when he gave thee no trouble?"—and so Abraham fetched the stranger back, and lodged him kindly, and lavished on him the wisest instruction. The Covenanters would have detected in the apologue a "detestable indifference and neutrality"; but so would nine out of every ten of their compatriots; the era of broad-mindedness had not

GEORGE GILLESPIE.

From the Portrait in New College, Edinburgh.

dawned when they climbed their uphill road. And, after all, there is something to be urged on behalf of their peremptory assertion of principle. Persecution is indefensible and shameful. It is both a blunder and a sin. But men should be fully persuaded in their own minds, and ready to give a sufficient reason for the faith which is in them. There is a poor and pitiful tolerance as well as a tolerance which is magnanimous and Godlike; a pseudo-charity which is not careful to search out the truth, that it may rejoice in it; a shallowness and a cowardice which are destitute of convictions of any sort, and too nerveless to say, " Stand thou on that side, for on this am I."

Nothing should commend the adherents of the Covenant to the children of the twentieth century more than their wisely balanced love of freedom. They were invincible haters of despotism. There were prerogatives of Parliament and of the people which they would surrender to no one. They could not find room in their polity for a tyrant. But, on the other hand, they kept, as we have seen, an unbounded loyalty for the monarch who respected their native and proper rights. Not serfs and feudal vassals, but constitutional subjects—that is what they aspired to be. The King's person and authority shall be jealously preserved, they said, if in his turn he preserves the true religion and the liberties of the commonweal. In the Scotland of that day, however it might be in England, there was nowhere any craving for a republic; there was a universal and even a passionate anxiety to guard the name and fame of Charles. It was he who squandered a heritage of devotion and obedience which he might have retained to his latest hour. It was because he was a rebel against justice and law that he drove into rebellion those who would have spent their lives to promote his good.

Beside two deathbeds we may take our stand for a few minutes, our heads bent in reverence. They are the death-beds of those to whose wisdom and courage and Christliness the distracted Scotland of the time owed an inexpressible debt, and whose absence from her struggle will leave her crippled and poor.

In the spring months of 1637, when he was himself a prisoner in Aberdeen, Samuel Rutherfurd wrote to Alexander Henderson: "As for your case, my reverend and dearest brother, you are the talking of the North and South, and looked to as if you were all crystal glass; your motes and dust will soon be proclaimed, and trumpets blown at your slips. But I know you have laid help upon One that is mighty." *All crystal glass* Henderson was to the friends of the Covenant; although he had little liking for the excitements of public business, and would have preferred the scholar's life of seclusion with his books and the preacher's of devotion to the shepherding of his flock. It was the compulsion of conscience and of his Master which drove him forth, as he said in the preface to one of his sermons, from "soliloquies and contemplations" to "debates and controversies," to "act things which he never determined nor so much as dreamed of." But without him the Church must have been deprived of the strongest of her leaders, and the prelacy she hated might have been foisted upon her despite her loudest protestations that she would have none of it. When the hot wind of the desert smote her, and threatened to smother and engulf her in the choking death it brings, this was the man who was as the shadow of a great boulder in a weary land.

He had himself begun as a prelatist. After spending some winters in teaching philosophy in St. Andrews, he had been thrust in 1612, when he was a man of nearly thirty, upon the unwilling parish of Leuchars. On his ordination day he found the door of the church nailed against him, and he and his brother-clergymen were forced to break into the building by one of the windows. But, a few years later, he went in disguise to hear Robert Bruce preach, being drawn to him, as Augustine was at first to Ambrose, simply by the fame of his oratory; and Bruce became the messenger of God to him. The very text, pronounced with the slow and deliberate emphasis which was the preacher's manner, was a sword-thrust: *Verily, verily, I say unto you, He that entereth not by the door into the sheepfold, but climbeth up some other way, the same is a thief and a robber.* It seemed to the listener as if Christ were in the pulpit, searching him with reproachful eyes, and reproving him in the accents of a righteous Judge for his intrusion into a sphere to which he did not belong. This was the hour when Alexander Henderson's sleeping soul sprang into life and vigour. He returned to Leuchars another man, penitent, believing, dedicated to the Lord Who had. made him aware of his sin, and filled with ardour for the Presbytery he had opposed and despised. Year after year passed in the steadfast perform-ance of his unassuming ministry, and in the accumulation of that rich and varied learning which God was yet to turn to manifold use. Only once, in the Perth Assembly of 1618, when the obnoxious Articles were enacted which imposed kneeling at the Communion, the private celebration of the Sacraments, episcopal confirmation, and the observance of holy days, was the silence of the long time of waiting broken ; and one brave voice was lifted against the overbearing wishes of the King. But in the fateful weeks which preceded the signing of the Covenant in Greyfriars, the needs of the country impelled Henderson to take farewell of his restful Nazareth ; and henceforth, through the nine years that were left to him, there was to be no pause of leisure and calm. Whether it was as the counsellor of the Tables in Edinburgh, or as the author of the Covenants, or as moderator of three General Assemblies, or as commissioner to the divines at Westminster, he was, as Clarendon tells us, "the principal engine by which the whole nation was moved," and never again was he allowed to escape to the sheltered and "sunny side of the brae."

If we ask how he came to wield so paramount an influence, his own personality is the answer. Since Knox's death and Andrew Melville's, he stood forth as the most distinguished son of the Scottish Church ; and probably he was not inferior to either of his stately precursors. Beneath the plainness of his appearance, for he was short in figure and there was nothing striking in his looks, he carried a capacious soul. His speech, whether in preaching or in debate, was singularly weighty. To his auditors it appeared as if he never left any word unsaid which the occasion demanded; and this was true even when he had to declare his opinion on the spur of the moment, and with no breathing-space for reflection. His culture, too, was massive and full. Those years of retirement in the Fifeshire village, consecrated to patient research and brooding thought, bore the noblest harvest. They fashioned him into a theologian who was equipped at every point, and a scholar who, in the endless discussions of the period, seldom met his match. But, more prevailing than his sagacity and his erudition, was his holiness. Men recognised that conscience governed all his decisions and actings—a conscience enlightened by God's Word and Spirit. They felt that he was without a trace of self-seeking. They honoured him as one who loved Christ first and masterfully, and in whom they beheld the reflection of Christ's image. It was not strange that they trusted him without reserve.

An especial and wistful interest clings to Henderson's relations with Charles the First. When the King was in Edinburgh in 1641, he went more than once to hear the preacher who, as president of the Glasgow Assembly, had effectually curbed his own tyrannical designs against the Kirk. He could not but acknowledge the honesty and dignity and power of his antagonist. He selected him, indeed, for one of his chaplains; and on different mornings and evenings, within the palace of Holyrood, the Covenanting minister conducted family worship; and the two, the Stuart sovereign and the subject whose heart was so humble and so regal, knelt together at the throne of God. Five years afterwards, they met again. Charles's sky was overcast with the heaviest clouds. The Civil War had led him and his Cavaliers from disaster to disaster. He was a fugitive in the camp of the Scots at Newcastle. He desired that Mr. Henderson should be summoned to confer with him about the thorny questions of Church government. And, although the sickness was on him which was to issue soon in his death, Henderson hastened from London at the bidding of the monarch; and they talked frequently and earnestly of Presbyterianism and Episcopacy—which might be the will of God, and which was suited to the genius of the Scottish people. They did not agree, but neither did they quarrel. Henderson, says Mr. Hill Burton, was "true throughout to his cause, and true without violence or arrogance"; he was "respectful but not servile." When he parted from his opponent, it must have been in pity more than in anger. Is it not a sign of grace in Charles that he saw and confessed the worth of one who was as manly as he was godly? It was his tragic weird that he had few advisers so sagacious and good.

That was in the summer of 1646. It was the middle of July when Henderson left his lodging in Newcastle and took ship to Leith. He was ill and suffering, and he yearned to be at home. On the 16th of August, the last call came. His friends had dreaded it, and had prayed that it might be delayed yet awhile; they feared for the Church and the realm when both should be without him. But to himself the end was sweet and kind, as it was to St. Francis, round whose couch the Little Brothers sang the canticle, "Praise be to my Lord for our sister, the death of the body!" "Never schoolboy more longed for the breaking-up," Henderson cried, "than I do to have leave of this world." It was release, emancipation, harbour after the climbing waves and the open sea.

The other deathbed is that of George Gillespie.

He ran his course more rapidly than Henderson; for he was but thirty-five years of age when his wife said to him, "The time of your relief is near and hard at hand," and he answered her, "I long for that time. Oh, happy they that are there!" And he is worthy to stand beside the older man, a fit helper and squire of that consummate captain. From his boyhood his zeal for Presbytery had been conspicuous. It had kept him out of a pastoral charge of his own, until the events of 1638 sapped the authority of the Bishops, and the parishioners of Wemyss made supplication that he might be their minister. But already, young as he was, he had won his laurels. While he was tutor in the family of the Earl of Cassillis, he had published *A Dispute against the English Popish Ceremonies*, which filled the Privy Councillors with such indignation that they had it burned in the Edinburgh streets, and which extorted from Robert Baillie, who would have walked more quietly himself and therefore "misliked much of the matter," a tribute of marvelling admiration for the abilities of the writer: " I think," he averred, " he may prove amongst the best wits of this isle." The forecast was abundantly fulfilled. Gillespie was among the youngest members of the Westminster Assembly, and among the shrewdest and most eloquent. The story has often been told of how in debate he vanquished John Selden, the champion of the Erastian party and one of the supreme scholars in Christendom, sweeping away by a single speech, as his mortified adversary admitted, "the learning and the labour of ten years of my life"; and of how, after he sat down, and his friends had possessed themselves of his notebooks, in the hope of discovering the outline of his arguments, they found nothing on the page but the *cri du cœur*, again and again repeated, *Da lucem, Domine!* Out of his encounters with the Erastians came Gillespie's crowning book, with its quaint title of *Aaron's Rod Blossoming* —a vindication of the rights of the Lord Jesus Christ to govern, by His own laws, the Church which He purchased for Himself with His blood. Had he lived, the Covenant would have had no man-at-arms more alert and more unyielding.

But the blade was too keen for the scabbard, and his frail body was wearing itself out. In December 1648, George Gillespie lay dying in his native town of Kirkcaldy. "The time that I have had in the exercise of the ministry," he said, "is but a moment." "Yes!" a friend replied, "but your moment hath exceeded the grey heads of others." Rutherfurd came to see him. "Would not Christ be a welcome guest to you?" Mr. Samuel asked; and immediately he had the answer, "The welcomest guest that ever I saw." Another spoke of his faithfulness, and of the sure and ample reward to which he was going; but to Gillespie the King was always better than the kingdom. " I think it reward enough," he responded, " that ever I got leave to do Him any service." He was like that unnamed Huguenot who, himself sorely stricken, lifted the curtain of Coligny's litter, as the Admiral was being carried, wounded in three places, from the calamitous field of Moncontour, and exclaimed, with shining countenance and a catch in his voice, " Si est ce que Dieu est très doux," *Surely God is good to Israel.* George Gillespie wore the true servant's title; because he never, " for his Lord's gifts, how rich soe'er, his Lord Himself forgot."

Round a scaffold, in the Edinburgh market-place, between the Mercat Cross and the Tron Church, a great multitude is gathered. It is a May afternoon in 1650, and the people have come out to witness the execution of James Graham, Marquis of Montrose, and to hear his last words. In reality they hear nothing; the sufferer is allowed to address himself only to those who stand closest to him, immediately under the gallows thirty feet high. But they see him die with undismayed face, and with that gay and proud bravado which has always marked " the finest gallant in the realm." And then the whole crowd " gave a general groan; and it was very observable that even those who at first appearance had bitterly inveighed against him could not now abstain from tears."

What has brought the Marquis of Montrose, while he is yet in the early prime of his manhood, to this grim scaffold covered with the black cloth?

It is impossible to linger over the incidents of his career, although few histories have such extraordinary fascination. We have seen him with his peers signing the National Covenant in the Greyfriars, and attempting afterwards to school the men of Aberdeen, " that unnatural town," into acquiescence with its terms. To the end he protested his fidelity to the purely Scottish Covenant; it was the Solemn

League, he said, which angered him, because it pledged the subjects of the State, under cover of religion, to wrest the regal authority from their King. But his attachment to the popular side never could have been deep; by the summer of 1640, when Charles and the Scots were at war, and when he was himself an officer amongst the Presbyterians, he was in correspondence with the sovereign. Was it because he was displeased that Alexander Leslie had received the supreme command in the army? Or was it that the King, who had not given him at first the notice and regard which he thought due to his quality, was manifestly disposed now to cultivate his friendship? Or was it that he was indignant at the larger respect shown by the Covenanters to Argyll, his hereditary rival?—"The people looked upon them both," Lord Clarendon writes, "as young men of unlimited ambition, and used to say that they were like Cæsar and Pompey: the one would endure no superior, and the other would have no equal." Perhaps there was a mingling of all three motives, although the last may well have been the strongest; for Montrose never loved Argyll, and could not brook that he should outdistance him in the race. One way or another, it befell that soon King Charles had not a doughtier champion than James Graham.

Not a doughtier; for what an astonishing soldier he proved himself! In the records of war, there are few leaders of a guerilla campaign who have achieved so much, or whose brows better deserve to be encircled with the victor's wreath. At a time when, in England, the Royalist cause was travelling rapidly downward, he gained for it in Scotland, with his Highlanders and Irishmen, one amazing success after another. At Tippermuir, the onset of the mountaineers was irresistible, and at night three hundred Covenanters lay stark on the field. At the Bridge of Dee, his men gave the Gordons, by and by to be allies and not foes, "the broadsword and the butt-end of their muskets," and drove them in headlong flight into the streets of Aberdeen. At Inverlochy, he humbled all the glory of his great antagonist, and fifteen hundred of the clansmen of

JAMES GRAHAM, MARQUIS OF MONTROSE.

After the Portrait by Honthorst, 1649.

Argyll were slain either in the battle or in the relentless pursuit which went on for nine long miles. At Auldearn, at Alford, at Kilsyth, each master-stroke following hard after its fellow, the best soldiers whom the Scottish Estates could send against him were mowed down in battalions, and massacred without ruth or regret. Into ten or eleven months in 1644 and 1645, Montrose crowded marches and surprises and triumphs sufficient to last most generals for a lifetime. But then the end came. At Philiphaugh, in September of the later year, in a district which had no love for the cause he maintained, and in which his patrols and scouts could glean little news beforehand, he met David Leslie and was hopelessly routed. James Graham indisputably had won the right to make the noble boast of Sir Peter Harpdon in the poem—

> I like the straining game
> Of striving well to hold up things that fall.

But, with whatever preternatural skill the chivalrous game is played, the unavoidable doom descends at last.

For rather more than four years he was in exile on the Continent, in Norway and the Netherlands; and then at the bidding of the Second Charles—because, in the interval, the First had fought his last and kingliest fight—he returned to Scotland, to make one endeavour more in defence of that discredited Stuart name whose bravest standard-bearer he was. But his new master was of meaner nature than the old. By the juggling and subterfuge of his conduct he acted the traitor towards his good ally. He was parleying with the Covenanters, all the while that he encouraged their opponent with valiant and unreal promises; he did not deserve a follower so steadfast. It was to death that Montrose had sailed, death in which shame and glory were strangely united. At Carbisdale, in the Kyle of Sutherland, he was defeated by Colonel Strachan, and, after wandering in disguise through the wilds of Assynt, he was made prisoner at Ardvreck Castle. They sent him south to Edinburgh, where he was loaded with a hundred unmerited insults, bearing himself through all the ignominy with the half-contemptuous courage which friends and foes knew so well. At length—and, after the blows he had inflicted and the damage he had done, he could expect nothing else— they condemned him to the gallows of which we have had a glimpse. He arrayed himself for it as he would have done for his wedding. John Nicoll, the notary-public, was among the eye-witnesses, and this is what he saw: "In his doun going fra the Tolbuith to the place of execution, he was verrie rychlie cled in fyne scarlet, layd over with riche silver lace, his hat in his hand, his goldin hat-ban, his stokingis of incarnet silk, and his schooes with their ribbenes on his feet, and sarkis provydit for him with pearling about; above ten pund the elne. All these war provydit for him be his friendis; and ane prettie cassik put upone him, upone the scaffold, quhairin he was hangit. To be schoirt, nothing was heir deficient to honour his pure carcage, moir beseiming a brydegroom nor a criminall." And thus his death was in consonance with his life; for, to quote Lord Clarendon again, "He was not without vanity; but his virtues were much superior, and he well deserved to have his memory preserved and celebrated among the most illustrious persons of the age."

One could wish that Neil Macleod of Assynt had surrendered to the kindlier impulses of his soul, and had permitted his princely captive to escape. Assuredly one could wish that Lord Lorne had kept away from the balconies of Moray House, when the cart that carried the Marquis, bareheaded and bound to his seat, was driven up the slope of the Canongate. One almost reverences Bishop Wishart, otherwise by no means very admirable, for his unconquerable affection to his dear patron, *Jacobus Montisrosarum Marchio*; it was his little book of *Montrose's Deeds* which the executioner fastened round the sufferer's neck on the scaffold; and are they not fine lines which close his elegy over his stricken hero?—

Verus amor nullis fortunæ extinguitur undis;
Nulla timet fati fulmina verus amor;
Immortalis amor verus manet, et sibi semper
Constat, et æternum, quisquis amavit, amat.

Yet we cannot forget that there are disfiguring blots on James Graham's escutcheon. In many of the features of his character he was a Mediæval knight, who might have stepped out of the chapters of Sir Thomas Malory; but there was that about him, too, which was far from knightly. The cavalier's ideal of Honour has been resolved into the four constituents of Courage, Loyalty, Truthfulness, and Compassion. In the first two qualities the Marquis was resplendent; the third we may imagine lacking, when we recall his desertion of the Covenanting ranks for those of the King, until we recollect that in this he answered the summons of his real predilections; but of the fourth, the quality of mercy, the grace of compassion, he showed scarcely a trace. When the blameless King of romance has beaten his enemies, he takes their dead bodies, and these he "did do balm and gum with many good gums aromatic, and after did do cere them in sixty fold of cered cloth of Sendal, and laid them in chests of lead, because they should not chafe nor savour; and upon all these bodies were set their shields with their arms and banners." No such gleams of human feeling illumine the story of Montrose's campaigns. His victories were followed by a carnage which was frightful. He does not appear to have imposed any check on the sanguinary vindictiveness of the rough hillmen whom he captained. We pity his sore tragedy; we kindle at the recollection of the markman safe and sure, "whom neither force nor fawning could unpin"; but, if he had been cast in a gentler mould, the great Marquis would have been greater still.

Seven months have gone. It is the New Year's Day of 1651. We are in the Parish Church of Scone, spectators of an event no less memorable than the coronation of His Majesty, King Charles the Second. Robert Douglas has preached "a very pertinent, wise, and good sermon" from a text in the Second Book of Kings: *And he brought forth the King's son, and put the crown upon him, and gave him the testimony; and they made him King, and anointed him;*

*and they clapped their hands, and said, God save the King!
And Jehoiada made a covenant between the Lord and the King
and the people, that they should be the Lord's people.* He has
spoken some home-truths about the bounds and limits of the
monarch's power : how he must not use his strength unduly,
or break his contract with his subjects ; how, if he does,
they will be amply justified in resisting his despotism.
Charles, we are told, listens " with all appearance of interest."
The Covenants, National and Solemn League, are read to him
next, and sworn by his lips, and subscribed by his hand.
And now Archibald, Marquis of Argyll, places the crown on
the young man's brow—he will not see his twenty-first
birthday for five months yet ; and he is presented to receive
the homage of his nobles and people. The Earl of Crawford
and Lindsay gives him the sceptre, while Argyll conducts
him to the throne, or chair of state, which has been erected
some six feet above the floor of the church. As he installs
him, the Marquis pronounces the words : " Stand and hold
fast from henceforth the place, whereof you are the lawful
and righteous heir by a long and lineal succession of your
fathers, which is now delivered unto you by authority of
Almighty God." After which Robert Douglas has some
additional counsels and warnings to give, and the 20th
Psalm is sung, and the apostolic benediction ends the
service.

It is not a transaction on which we can look back with
joy or pride. Seldom in history has there been a more
conspicuous example of " faith unfaithful." Both the prince
and the leaders of the Covenant were, in this instance,
unpardonably in the wrong. Robert Douglas was a man of
public spirit and of profound religion ; but when one asks
whether Alexander Henderson, whose lips had been stilled
in death nearly five years before, would have helped
Charles the Second to his kingdom, the answer must
be, No.

Very keenly the Scots had resented the execution of
Charles the First. It snapped the ties which united them
with the Parliament of England. With few exceptions, it

made them the adherents of the martyred sovereign's son.
Within a week of his father's death they proclaimed him,
in Edinburgh, "King of Great Britain, France, and Ireland."
Twice over, in the months which succeeded, they sent
embassies across the German Ocean to treat with him. At
first he and they could not come to terms. It was hard for
him, being what he was, to promise obedience to the Covenants.
It was hard, though it should have been infinitely harder,
to part with Montrose, whom the Scottish Parliament had
outlawed and the Scottish Assembly had excommunicated.
There were Royalist noblemen in his retinue who urged him
to resist demands so drastic. There was the Queen Mother,
of more decided character than himself, who sent message
after message, adjuring him never to trammel himself with
vows and oaths repugnant to them both, and never to
abandon the followers whose sympathies were identical with
his own. Moreover, he had the hope that among the Irish
Catholics, rather than among dour and precise Presbyterians,
he might find the deliverers he needed. So the Commissioners, to their great "discomfort and grief," had to
kiss his hands and say their farewells. "It were all the
pities in the world bot he were in good companie," wrote
Robert Baillie, who was one of them. "He is one of the
most gentle, innocent, well-inclyned Princes, so far as yet
appears, that lives; a trimme person, and of a manlie
carriage; understands prettie well; speaks not much:
Would God he were amongst us!"

But Oliver Cromwell and his soldier-saints soon dispelled
the vain dream of help from Ireland; and, when the Scots
returned, Charles was willing to promise them all. We
have seen how, playing a double part with that cool heart-
lessness of which afterwards he was to furnish many proofs,
he had meanwhile sent his best paladin to a cruel death:
what price would he not pay to win back his throne?
Then, in June 1650, he embarked at Harslaerdyck. On
the 23rd of the month, outside the mouth of the Spey, he
swore that, in every clause and syllable, he would keep the
Covenants. John Livingston, who was among the repre-

sentatives of the Kirk, heard, indeed, that "the King is minded to speak some words, that his oath should not import any infringeing of the laws of England." But he was at once answered that not a single modifying expression would be tolerated; and he "performed anything that could have been requyred, yet without any evidence of any real change of heart." And why did men, to whom the fear of the Lord was the beginning of wisdom, countenance the hollow mockery and an imposture so fateful and perilous? Why did they, as Livingston phrases it, "take the plague of God to Scotland"? If Charles's honesty was gone, theirs for the moment was sacrificed too.

There is no room here to recount the crookednesses which ensued. At the bidding of his monitors he confessed his sorrow for his father's errors and his mother's idolatry. His life became a weariness, so continually and so closely he was watched. Perhaps, in heart, he rejoiced as much as Oliver did over the rout of the Covenanters at Dunbar, although he declared, in sentences veneered with piety, that "the stroake and tryal is very hard to be borne." Once he made an effort to extricate himself from his bondage—the futile effort which is known in Scottish history as "the Start." We can scarcely wonder that, through all his subsequent life, his hostility against Kirk and Covenant was of the most unforgiving sort. Then came the Coronation scene at Scone, and afterwards, for eight months, he had the simulacrum of royalty; until Worcester fight dissolved the thin phantom, and again Charles was in exile.

The lover of the Covenanters longs with his whole soul that they had not demeaned themselves to traffic with the godless prince. Loyalty prompted them; but they knew that he was unworthy of their loyalty. He gave them his solemn and reiterated assurances that not only had he "the honour and civil liberties of the land to defend, but religion, the Gospel, and the Covenant, against which Hell shall not prevail"; but they felt that in the assurances there was no single grain of truth. They were angry with Cromwell and his doings; but their anger should never have conducted them to this heart-wounding hypocrisy. It is a chapter which their friends would fain erase from their radiant and quickening annals. For, if the crimes of the bad are certain to yield a plentiful harvest of evil, the crimes of the good are unspeakably more mischievous and mournful.

The retribution came quickly. In large measure, it was because of these dallyings and intrigues with Charles that the Covenanting ranks were for many years to be cleft asunder by a melancholy quarrel—the quarrel between Resolutioner and Remonstrant or Protester. The trouble reached its height in the General Assembly of 1651, held at St. Andrews and Dundee. There the Resolutioners were in the ascendant, and nothing would content them but the deposition of their three most active opponents—James Guthrie of Stirling, Patrick Gillespie of Glasgow, and James Simpson of Airth. If the Presbyterian Church had gained a King, "whose word no man relied on," it was sending adrift some of its most valiant sons. The exchange tended wholly to its own impoverishment and loss.

"In large measure," the strife arose out of the entanglement with "the chief Malignant." Yet it had its roots further back, and a momentary retrospect becomes necessary. In the closing hours of 1647, within the walls of Carisbrooke Castle, Charles First had been closeted with certain Scottish noblemen, and had signed with them the bargain which history designates "the Engagement." It promised, on the King's side, that the Solemn League and Covenant should be confirmed by Parliament, and that Presbytery should be established in the country for a period of three years, at the end of which term a definite settlement of the religious question was to be made. On the other side, there were stipulations that the Covenant should not be forced upon those who did not like it, and that within the Royal Household the Episcopal forms of worship should remain unchallenged. It was in consequence of this bargain that the Duke of Hamilton, whom, as Marquis, we saw contending with the Glasgow Assembly, led into England on his master's behalf that army of "raw and undisciplined troopers," on which Cromwell inflicted the bitterest chastisement at Preston. But the Church never approved the Engagement, nor did the stricter of the Covenanting peers, who, after Hamilton's hapless venture, found themselves again at the helm of affairs. So, early in 1649, the Act of Classes was passed. It was an endeavour to bar the Canaanite outside the house of the Lord. It declared that there were persons who had unfitted themselves for occupying places of trust and power—four classes of them, of whom the thoroughgoing Royalists and Episcopalians were one, and the lukewarm Covenanters who had promoted the Engagement were another. For life, for ten years, for five years, for two years, these classes were to be excluded from office. And thus, as one of the Puritan statesmen who defended the Act put the matter in a vigorous metaphor, the teeth of the Malignants were broken.

But dragons' teeth have a troublesome habit of reappearing, sometimes in aggravated size and terribleness. Scarcely had the Act of Classes become law, when Scotland heard, with a shudder, that the King had gone to his doom. The negotiations with his son followed, and Cromwell's invasion, and the catastrophe of Dunbar. The Scottish Parliament took fright. Desirable as it might be to enlist in the service of the country those alone whose shields, like that of Edmund Spenser's hero, were formed of one diamond, "perfect, pure, and clean," there was clamant need that the regiment of her defenders should be largely and immediately reinforced; and new helpers could not be found except among the men who had been tainted and disqualified so brief a time before. The Parliament determined to welcome these men back. In June 1651, it rescinded the Act of Classes, and the Assembly of the Church, meeting in the next month, ratified the decision of the legislators. It framed its "Publick Resolutions, for bringing in the Malignant party first to the army and then to the judicatories." There were some who protested, however, clinging fast to the older and austerer method of fighting God's battles with none but God's soldiery. They had short shrift, as we have noted, from

OLIVER CROMWELL.

From the Painting by Samuel Cooper, in Sidney Sussex College, Cambridge.

their brethren. These were the Protesters, or Remonstrants; and those who carried things their own way and deposed the dissentients were the Resolutioners.

When Charles, the roof and crown of Malignancy itself, had been rehabilitated and enthroned, it was inevitable that some such relaxation as that adopted by Parliament and Assembly should come. It will be granted, too, that, in the parlous state of the nation's fortunes, the Resolutioners had cogent reasons to allege in their defence; it was difficult to reject good fighters merely because they abhorred the Covenant or held fellowship with men who did. But the Protesters could claim the greater consistency. The cause committed to them was sacred even more emphatically than political, and they felt that its lustre would be tarnished if they intrusted it to unworthy hands; only His reproachless servants should bear the vessels of the King of kings. They might not be careful enough to speak the truth in love; Samuel Rutherfurd and Patrick Gillespie were but too human in the hotness of their tempers; but theirs was the better part, the more straightforward policy, the higher road. And if the Assembly condemned them, they had but to turn to their congregations, and they were surrounded by disciples and friends. So lamentable the breach became that the Church was practically rent in two; and for too long a period the Protester had communion with none but the Protester, the Resolutioner simply with his fellow-Resolutioner. Ephraim distrusted Judah, and Judah vexed Ephraim.

The divergence revealed itself in other matters than the discussion of military and civic appointments. A Resolutioner —Robert Douglas, or Robert Blair, or Robert Baillie, or David Dickson—preached and conducted public worship in a mode distinguishable from that favoured by some in the rival party. He was more methodical and systematic, colder and statelier, than the evangelic and enthusiastic Protester. Baillie, for instance, had scant patience with the "few headie men who waste our Church." Trained in the orthodox school of Dutch divinity, having spent his youth in doing battle against Arminians and Antinomians, he entertained a wholesome dread

C

of all novelties in pulpit or pew.　Speaking of Andrew Gray
of Glasgow, he says : " He has the new guyse of preaching,
which Mr. Hew Binning and Mr. Robert Leighton began, con-
temning the ordinarie way of exponing and dividing a text, of
raising doctrines and uses ; bot runs out in a discourse on
some common head, in a high, romancing, unscriptural style,
tickling the ear for the present, and moving the affections in
some, bot leaving, as he confesses, little or nought to the
memorie and understanding."　Even the tones of voice which,
as it seemed to him, the Protester assumed as evidence and
expression of his devoutness, offended our staid and custom-
bound divine.　" The man's vehemencie in his prayer, a strange
kind of sighing, the like whereof I had never heard, as a
pythonising out of the bellie of a second person, made me
amazed."　Robert Baillie himself, learned, good, honourable,
never offended against the proprieties, nor was much troubled
with " vehemencie."

　　Shall we take an illustration of the varying accents of
Resolutioner and Remonstrant ?　Here are some sentences
from *The Sum of Saving Knowledge,* a little book which is
no ignoble sample of the more precise and less impassioned
theology.　" Let the penitent desiring to believe reason thus :
What doth suffice to convince all the elect may suffice to convince me also ; but what the Spirit has said suffices to convince
the elect world ; therefore what the Spirit hath said serveth to
convince me thereof also.　Whereupon, let the penitent desiring to believe take with him words, and say heartily to the
Lord, ' Seeing Thou sayest, *Seek ye My face,* my soul answereth
to Thee, *Thy face will I seek.*　I have hearkened unto the offer
of an everlasting covenant of all saving mercies to be had in
Christ, and I do heartily embrace Thy offer.　Lord, let it be a
bargain.'　Thus may a man be made an unfeigned believer in
Christ."　It may be irrefragable ; but is it not too icily regular,
too statuesque and syllogistic ?　The soul in its agony craves
something simpler, more vital, fuller of the strong consolations
of God.　But now let us hearken to Hew Binning, the Protester, on whose " new guyse of preaching " Baillie looked with
a frown.　" He that is in earnest about this question, *How*

shall I be saved? I think he should not spend the time in reflecting on and examination of himself, till he find something promising in himself, but from discovered sin and misery pass straightway over to the grace and mercy of Christ, without any intervening search of something in himself to warrant him to come. There should be nothing before the eye of the soul but sin and misery and absolute necessity, compared with superabounding grace and righteousness in Christ; and thus it singly devolves itself over upon Christ, and receives Him as offered freely. I know it is not possible that a soul can receive Christ, till there be some preparatory convincing work of the law; but I hold that to look to any such preparation, and fetch an encouragement or motive therefrom to believe in Christ, is really to give Him a price for His free waters and wine. It is to mix in together Christ and the law in the point of our acceptation." Who is not conscious, when he reads the words, that he is moving in a diviner air? The sentiment is the same as before. But formerly there was a dissonance in uttering it which grated on the ear, and almost made the music of the Gospel harsh. Now the speaker feels no down-dragging influences in his Calvinism; he does not measure his syllables lest he should render the grace of God too large and too accessible; he soars away and aloft, like the lark,

> Up in the glory, climbing and ringing;

or like the angel of Bethlehem, throbbing with uncontrollable gladness as he publishes his message, *Behold, I bring you good tidings of great joy, which shall be to all people.*

There is a final picture at which we must glance. It is the picture of two personalities that confront each other. Their attitude is that of antagonism. Their tempers are incompatible. They are for the most part in undisguised and open strife. The personalities are those of the Covenanter and Oliver Cromwell. "The late Usurper": it was the Covenanter's customary name for the great God-fearing Englishman, after that September day in 1658, when, trusting in the promises which are *Yea and Amen in Christ Jesus,* the Lord Protector passed from the world which he had vastly enriched.

We need not wonder at the alienation, however we must lament its vigour and sharpness. "The English Government of Scotland," says Dr. Samuel Gardiner, "was a good example of the government which fails, in spite of its excellent intentions and excellent practice, simply because it pays no heed to the spirit of nationality." Cromwell stood in many respects at an opposite pole of thinking from the Scots. He was a soldier; and they began to dread that tremendous engine of conquest, the Army of the Parliament, which his genius had designed and compacted, and which menaced their independence more overwhelmingly than Charles had ever been able to do. He was a statesman; but he felt none of their stubborn loyalty towards a King, who had perversely thrown away his right to rule; and they could never forgive the regicide, even if they saw clearly enough the ineradicable faults of the prince whom he helped to lead to the block. He was a man of religion; but they differed radically from him. Oliver signed the Solemn League, it is true; but in his eyes the bond was not the sacred and awful symbol which it was to Presbyterian Scotsmen. He was an Independent; he was in favour of a far wider catholicity and toleration than they could abide; he permitted the growth in his regiments, and by and by in the Commonwealth, of all manner of Sectaries. It was scarcely surprising that they scowled on him, and fought against him, and counted him an enemy rather than a friend. When we recall Dunbar drove, and the subsequent marches and countermarches of the Ironsides through a subjugated country; the forcible dismissal, too, of the General Assembly of 1653, vexed and noisy with the strife of tongues, and the refusal in succeeding years to sanction the meeting of the supreme court of the Church: we comprehend why Scotland disliked the Puritan captain. Her distrust is more intelligible than that of some others. It has been pointed out that the English peasant of our day, although his ancestors were against the King, and helped in the execution of Cromwell's stern policy, abhors "Old Noll" as if he were an ogre. "Where traces of desecration are visible in a church, where a shattered wall is all that remains of a stately home hallowed by the presence of Gloriana, where an ancient door shows the pattern of bullet-marks," Hodge will have it that the mischief is due to the commander and ruler who raised England to the first rank among the nations of Europe. The Scot of the seventeenth century, although his persevering opposition cannot be justified, had more of reason on his side.

There were exceptions, no doubt. In the West, Colonel Strachan and a little company of his followers joined Oliver. Patrick Gillespie sometimes prayed publicly for the Protector. Dumbartonshire and Wigtown accepted the Tender of Union with England with a degree of enthusiasm, as being "the excellent blessing of God, who by a long-continued series of providences seems to hold out this to be His great design for the common good of the people of this island." After the Union, belated and yet premature, was proclaimed at the Mercat Cross of Edinburgh in the Maytime of 1654, and after General Monck had been feasted at a banquet which was "sex dayis in preparing, quhairit the bailleis did stand and serve the haill time," a few Scotsmen sat in Cromwell's Parliaments. But the country as a whole was unfriendly; and the Church, hating that motley troop of sects she saw overspreading England, was more critical still. "As for the Kirkmen and their vassals," we read in a Newsletter sent from Edinburgh on the 27th of December 1651, "they retain their old rugged Obstinacie and currish behaviour."

Yet the strong and stable discipline of Cromwell was an untold blessing to these censorious Kirkmen. The Scotland of the years of the Commonwealth had its grave moral blemishes. There were prominent and repulsive national sins, then as now. There was no little superstition, as we may learn from the hideous story of how the witches were persecuted and done to death. But, side by side with the unlovelier features of the period, there were the blossom and the fruitage of genuine religion. "Then," writes good James Kirkton, "was Scotland a heap of wheat set about with lilies, uniform, or a palace of silver beautifully proportioned; and this seems to me to have been Scotland's high noon." On a later page, he expands and explains his panegyric of the golden season, round which the shades of the prison-house closed all too early. "At the King's return every paroche hade a minister, every village hade a school, every family almost hade a Bible, yea, in most of the countrey, all the children of age could read the Scriptures. Every minister was obliedged to preach thrice a week, to lecture and catechise once, besides other private duties wherein they abounded, according to their proportion of faithfulness and abilities. None of them might be scandalous in their conversation, or negligent in their office, so long as a presbytrie stood; and among them were many holy in conversation and eminent in gifts. In many places the Spirit seemed to be powred out with the Word, both by the multitude of sincere converts, and also by the common work of reformation upon many who never came the length of a Communion; there were no fewer than sixty aged people, men and women, who went to school, that even then they might be able to read the Scriptures with their own eyes. I have lived many years in a paroche where I have never heard ane oath, and you might have ridde many miles before you had heard any. Also you could not for a great part of the countrey have lodged in a family where the Lord was not worshipped by reading, singing, and publick prayer. No body complained more of our church government than our taverners, whose ordinarie lamentation was, their trade was broke, people were become so sober." And the man who, more than any other, helped to secure for the land this Sabbatism of godliness was misunderstood, resisted, denounced. It is one of those pitiful and poignant contradictions of which history provides many an example.

CHAPTER I.

HOW THE KING CAME HOME.

ENGLAND and Scotland forgot themselves in an ecstasy
of sheer delight, when Charles the Second, now thirty
years of age, landed at Dover, and made his progress to
Whitehall. There had been tiresome negotiations beforehand;
but they might have been forborne, for the event proved that
they were needless. "It is my own fault," the King laughed,
"that I did not come back sooner." From London Bridge to
his palace gates the procession advanced through what Evelyn
calls "a lane of happy faces." Charles saw little else than
the waving of scarfs and the flashing of rapiers, and, behind
these, the laughter and tears of his subjects: "the ways
strewn all with flowers, bells ringing, steeples hung with
tapestries, fountains running with wine, trumpets, music, and
myriads of people flocking; and two hundred thousand horse
and foot brandishing their swords, and shouting with inexpressible joy." In such a carnival of gaiety, on this 29th of
May 1660, birthday as well as Restoration day, the monarch,
long discrowned, seated himself again in the home of his
fathers.

Can we catch the likeness of the man who was welcomed
so deliriously?

His outward features were not attractive. "Until near
twenty," one of his friends says, "the figure of his face was
very lovely; but he is since grown leaner." And not leaner
merely but grimmer, sombre and forbidding. Merry: that is
the adjective which is the Second Charles's property; but in
his gaunt visage there was "neither joy nor love nor light."

39

He avowed it himself. "But I'm the ugly fellow!" he sighed, as he stood before his portrait. His skin was as brown as if he had been born under a tropical sun. "Of a tall stature and a sable hue," Andrew Marvell pictures His Majesty ; and Bishop Burnet, who, to be sure, had no fondness for him, tells us that he resembled the Emperor Tiberius, *tristissimus ut constat hominum.* It is conceivable that the Bishop intended his readers to carry the comparison further, into more essential qualities of mind and soul. And the exercise would not be difficult or recondite.

The King has been summarised as a compendium of all the vices. The verdict is pitiless ; but it cannot be deemed too harsh. Yet there were broken fragments of a better nature to be seen here and there, in the corners of his strange personality—a nature which never had much opportunity of asserting itself, and which was stifled more and more under its owner's incorrigible idlenesses and sins.

It is to his credit that he was a lover of the open air, physically alert and athletic. In Sir Robert Moray's charming letters to Lauderdale, we get many peeps at the prince when he was in the prime of his vigour. He is constantly in the saddle. One day he rides fourteen miles to dinner with Lord Herbert. On another day he covers no less than sixty miles, rising with the summer dawn, and returning to transact business at midnight. Or again, when the statesman wants to discuss some question of politics, he is out with the hounds, and nobody is sure when he will return. Claverhouse, too, had the same experience twenty years later. When he wished to escape from London to his harrying of the Covenanters in the Western shires, his dilatory master detained him. "I walked nine miles this morning with the King," he informed a correspondent in 1683. "The heaven above," and "the road below," and "the bed in the bush with stars to see"—Charles could have appreciated our modern wanderer's satisfaction with these wholesome joys. His friends declared that he would have preferred angling and a life in the country to all the punctilios of Whitehall. Scottish history would have been

CHARLES II. AS A BOY.

From a Painting by Van Dyck.

a calmer and sweeter record if the preference had been granted.

In his earlier and more Spartan years, before the luxuriousness first of Paris and then of London had softened and spoiled him, he had plenty of soldierly courage. At Worcester, he demeaned himself as a true commander of men, and his tenacity and spirit were in bright contrast to David Leslie's curious irresolution. "God preserve him!" one of the Royalists cried, "for a more gallant prince was never born." And then, when the ruinous fight was over, what an indomitable gaiety he flung into all those adventurous hazards which were its sequel! After he had been dressed at Whiteladies in an old leathern doublet, and breeches of coarse green cloth, and grey stockings much darned about the knees, and a steeple-crowned hat, Richard Penderel cut his hair short and trimmed it in the country fashion; "and the King was pleased to take notice of Richard's good barbering, so as to prefer his work before my Lord Wilmot's." In the branches of the Boscobel oak, when "far below the Roundhead rode and hummed a surly hymn," he fell fast asleep in the arms of the officer who was his sole companion; and the sleep was so unperturbed and sound that his comrade had to pinch him before he could be brought back to consciousness. At the inn in Bridport, he encountered Colonel Haynes's regiment of Ironsides, fifteen hundred strong, preparing to embark for Jersey; and for a round hour, with a smiling face and many merry sallies of humour, he stood in the yard, conversing with one and another of his inexorable enemies. Two days before his perils ended, and he sailed from Brighton to Fécamp, he was mistaken for a Puritan, so complete was his disguise, and nobody could be more desirous than he to play the part just then; and so, when the man who had committed the error slipped in his speech into an involuntary oath, the pseudo-pietist reproved him most gravely: "Dear brother," he said, "swear not, I beseech thee." A fortitude so intrepid, so indefatigable, so debonair and lightsome, when the outlook was as black as it could be, captivates us whether we will or no, and is a powerful plea on Charles's behalf.

He was an admirable talker, brimful of repartee and shrewdness and sparkle. A hundred instances of his cleverness have been commemorated, and they show what a nimble intellect played behind the uninviting face. "Was it not a pretty pass," asks Miss Guiney in that *tour de force* of adroitest advocacy, *An Inquirendo into the Wit and Other Good Parts of His Late Majesty King Charles the Second*— "was it not a pretty pass, between the monarch and his impregnable Quaker who wanted a charter? Penn came to his first audience with his hat, on the principle of uncon-vention and equality, firmly fixed upon his brows. Presently the King, having moved apart from his attendants, in his gleaming dress, slowly and ceremoniously bared his head. 'Friend Charles, why hast taken off thy hat?' 'Because it has so long been the custom here,' said the other, with that peculiar lenient smile of his, 'for but one person to remain covered at a time.'" His dexterity never forsook him. It taught him how to adapt his conversation to every circle. He could be "a gracious youth" to Robert Baillie, and more vulgar than the most unblushing with courtiers like the Earl of Rochester. Among the bishops he was a scholar, and among the sportsmen at Newmarket he had no thought nor speech for anything but the excitements of the race. "Such ability and understanding has Charles Stuart," one of his intimates said to him in a jest as pointed as it was kind, "that I do long to see him employed as King of England."

There could not be a doubt of the ability. People re-marked what a competent judge of men he was; he read the place-hunters who thronged his corridors with unerring skill, and he had an insight as penetrating into the position of the political factions. If he could not claim book-learning, he honoured it in others, being interested especially in science. It was he who founded the Royal Society, and who established the Observatory at Greenwich. To moral excellence as well as to intellectual gifts he threw approving glances and hearty words; he saw and commended the better way, while he

followed the worse. Thus he promoted Thomas Ken, the
saintly Fellow of Winchester College and Prebendary of its
Cathedral, to the bishopric of Bath and Wells, for no other
reason than that the brave man had once rebuked him for
the gross irregularities of his conduct. He had his fleeting
visions of righteousness and transient impulses towards the
higher life. It is wholly pleasant, too, to see the constancy
of his love for his child-sister, Henrietta of Orleans. "To
my deare deare Sister" he wrote letters of beautiful affection.
"Pour l'avenir, je vous prie, ne me traitez pas avec tant de
ceremonie, en me donnant tant de 'majestés,' car je ne veux
pas qu'il y ait autre chose entre nous deux, qu' amitié."
And nothing but unbreakable friendship there was until the
hour of her too early death.

But, despite his "great talents and great chances and, in a
sense, great qualities," Charles was a bad ruler and a bad
man. In everything except physical exercise, he was irre-
coverably lazy. "When anything is to be done by the King's
own hand," his Chancellor once complained, "we must be
content to wait, he being brought very unwillingly to the
task, which vexes me exceedingly." The stinging satire,
which Marvell put into his mouth, depicted His Majesty's
aims with too much accuracy—

> I'll have a fine pond, with a pretty decoy,
> Where many strange fowl shall feed and enjoy,
> And still in their language quack, *Vive le roy!*

And, under the easy temper, there was a mind governed by
selfishness. He appears to have been incapable of steadfast
comradeship. We have learned how he abandoned Montrose
to his fate, because at the moment he was trafficking with
the Covenanters; and the remorseful letter he sent to the
dead chieftain's son expressed a penitence which was forgotten
almost as soon as it was uttered. The Marquis of Ormonde,
who sacrificed himself to uphold his master's cause in Ireland,
gained from him nothing but the wintriest acknowledgments.
He wearied of that most devoted cavalier, Edward Hyde,
Lord Clarendon; and the man to whom he owed his throne
left the court in disgrace. It was a hateful ingratitude;

and the royal libertinism was even worse. Mistress was added to mistress, and each won the loftiest rank for her children; centuries instead of months separated Charles's palace from Oliver's. These astute temptresses grew rich on the nation's money, and he never sought to put boundaries to their cupidity. He starved the Navy, to find dresses and jewels for the Countess of Castlemaine and the Duchess of Portsmouth and Miss Nell Gwyn. In truth, he had no vestige of pride in the good name of his country. By a humiliating treaty, which he dared not divulge except to one or two, he became the paid servant of Louis of France. He made war on Holland, and plunged Britain into a succession of defeats such as she had never before experienced. But the national shame brought no shadow of distress or regret over his careless heart. He spent a long evening hunting moths with his associates while the guns of the Dutch were thundering off Chatham. In warp and in woof his character was bohemian. "He minded nothing but pleasures," Samuel Pepys confesses with a sigh.

The secret was that he had no religion. His father, obstinate and formal as he showed himself, was devout; but the son was a stranger to the life of the soul. He "floated upon that new tide of politeness" which surged in with the Restoration, Mr. G. K. Chesterton pleads in some apologetic paradoxes; he was "perfect in little things"; he "could not keep the Ten Commandments, but he kept the ten thousand commandments." But politeness is a poor substitute for the grace of God, and courtesy has sometimes been divorced from goodness. At the first glance it seems curious that, under the sway of a man without vital faith, there should be much persecution. But the King had counsellors whose Anglican-ism was of a determined sort; and he himself, deciding all spiritual problems by the canons of etiquette, was accustomed to protest that "Presbytery is no religion for a gentleman." In truth, those who hunt after the treasures of Egypt are not always lenient and forbearing; as likely as not, they are impatient with any Moses who rejects their prizes and prefers the reproach of Christ. It was so with this representative

of the Stuarts. He hated vehemence and ardour wherever
he found them, and he hated them most in the sphere of
religion. His was the scourge not of the bigot but of the
sceptic; he cared not a farthing himself "what the sects
might brawl"; but the freethinker's lash can be as merciless
as the inquisitor's. Negatives describe him best; nothing
pure, nothing serious, nothing worthy, nothing divine, is to
be discovered in Charles the Second. They are scathing
sentences with which Dr. Osmund Airy concludes his great
monograph: "His guide was not duty; it was not even
ambition: but his guide was self; it was ease, and amusement, and lust. The cup of pleasure was filled deep for
him, and he grasped it with both hands. But pleasure is
not happiness. There is no happiness for him who lives
and dies without beliefs, without enthusiasms, and without
love."

Such was the King, and he brought with him a new era.
It was livelier, more jocund, more boisterous, than the old.
It had music in it, and dancing, and play-going, and all the
hurry and hilarity of Vanity Fair. But the massiveness, the
spiritual magnificence, the militant saintliness of Cromwell's
time had disappeared. Puritanism was not dead; but it
walked in the shadow and spoke in whispers. It worked on
as an unobtrusive leaven; it did not peal forth its doctrines
and commandments any more. The men who had revolted
against the stringent regimen of the Ironsides had their
summer of opportunity. The men who had worn a mask of
gravity threw off the troublesome disguise and decked themselves in the rainbow colours they loved. Revelry and
ribaldry; drinking and dicing; intrigue and adventure;
those sins of the flesh and the spirit which, in Stephen
Phillips's phrase, are "agony shot through with bliss"—these
filled their days and nights. To one famous survivor of the
Protectorate, sitting in solitude and blindness, the England
of Charles was no longer a puissant nation rousing herself
from sleep and shaking her invincible locks, but a province
of Belial, than whom a spirit more lewd fell not from
heaven.

In courts and palaces he also reigns,
And in luxurious cities, where the noise
Of riot ascends above their loftiest towers,
And injury and outrage ; and, when night
Darkens the streets, then wander forth the sons
Of Belial, flown with insolence and wine.

Yet the mass of the English people was probably
untainted by all the brilliancy and irreligion. If the ruling
and fashionable classes were corrupt, the bulk of the citizens
in the towns, and the farmers and cottagers in the country,
retained sobriety and sense. This was even more emphatically
true of Scotland. It clung to its Presbyterianism. The
population of the Lowland counties was unhurt by the lax
moralities of the leaders in society and legislature and camp.
The plodding and insistent Scot stood like a rock, and refused
to modify his convictions. He heard of the wild doings in
the South ; he saw them enacted, on a smaller scale, in
Holyrood House and the High Street of Edinburgh ; there,
a fortnight before his entry into London, Charles had been
proclaimed "with all solemnities requisite, by ringing of
bellis, roring of cannounes, touking of drumes, dancing about
the fyres, and using all uther takins of joy for the advancement and preference of their native King." But the finery,
the extravagance, the hard drinking, the iridescent vice, only
stirred the Scot, ninety-nine times out of the hundred, into
sorrow of soul. They failed to capture him by their
enchantments.

None the less, he was a zealot in his loyalty. Occasionally he gave mental harbourage to fantastic legends, which
told how the very plants and animals exulted along with
him. On the citadel of Perth the arms of the Commonwealth
had been carved ; but, when the King returned, a thistle, the
proud and rugged emblem of the North, grew from the wall
and hid the alien insignia. Still more marvellous is that
history of the leal swans of Linlithgow, which may be read
in the *Mercurius Caledonius* of Friday, January 25th, 1661.
"At the town of Linlithgow His Majesty hath a palace upon
the skirt of a most beautiful lake ; and this same lake hath
been ever famous for the number of swans that frequented

it. But when this Kingdom, as England, was oppressed with
usurpers, they put a garrison in this palace of His Majesty's,
which no sooner done but these excellent creatures, scorning
to live in the same air with the contemners of His Majesty,
they all of them abandoned the lake, and were never seen
these ten years, till the 1st of January last. When, just
about the same time of the day that His Majesty's Commissioner entered the Parliament House and sat in the chair of
state, did a squadron of the royal birds alight in the lake;
and, by their extraordinary motions and conceity interweav-
ings, the country people fancied them revelling at a country
dance, for joy of our glorious Restoration." When thistles
and swans were thus aggressively Carolean, men and women
would have scorned to lag behind.

Those were tales, no doubt, born in the breasts of the
Malignants. But sober Presbyterians were as frank in their
welcome. Here and there, among the Protesters, some might
be in sore perplexity about Charles Stuart; since 1650, they
could not credit him with virtue or principle or grace. But
these, too, deep as their disappointment was with the man,
were prepared to obey the monarch. And most of their
brethren were unfeignedly cordial. In the last weeks of
1659, before he commenced his great march on London—
the march which was the beginning of the Restoration—
General Monck had summoned the Scottish shires and burghs
to send their delegates to confer with him in Edinburgh.
He acquainted them with his plans. He was going South,
he said, "to assert and maintaine the liberty and being of
Parliaments, our antient constitution, and the freedome and
rights of the people of these nations from arbitrary and
tyrannicall usurpations upon their consciences, persons, and
estates; and for a godly ministry." Nothing was avowed in
the diplomatic speech about bringing back the King. But
his listeners understood how the tides of sentiment were
running; and they bade Monck God-speed, expressing themselves "well satisfied with his Lordshipp's engagement."
Their attitude was typical. Scotland, it has been explained,
had chafed under the domination of Cromwell: it was anti-

national; it was military; it was sectarian. Many an eager thought she had cast over the narrow seas to the banished prince. Next to her religion, she loved the house of Stuart; just as the Vendéans of the next century fought first for their faith and then for the white flag of their sovereign. In 1660, Charles had no subjects more firmly rooted in their fealty than the sons and daughters of the Kirk. It was his own fatuity which transformed numbers of them into foes.

Too quickly the fatuity was revealed; and yet there was something else than short-sightedness, something calculated and intentional, in the rude treatment he measured out to the Covenanters. For long he had cherished a personal grudge against them. He meant to have his revenge on those who, ten years before, had held him in a pupillage he abhorred. During his sojourn in Scotland in 1650 and 1651, he had been a virtual prisoner, debarred from a share in the government, unable to dispose or order anything, cut off from intercourse with his favourites and friends. Sentinels had been stationed round his lodgings at night. Spies had watched his words and actions. In the churches on the Sabbath, and during the week in the houses where he stayed, he listened to discourses, frank to a degree, in which denunciation was poured on his father, his mother, and himself. Tradition has it that once he was condemned to hearken to six of these unpalatable sermons in succession. His amusements were curtailed and scrutinised. His very looks and gestures were made the topic of criticism. He fancied, he said, that he ought almost to apologise for having ever been born. The memory of these irksome experiences, and of all that excess of zeal, was written indelibly on his mind. It bred within him a positive hostility to the Scottish Church. When he returned to his throne, Charles was determined to show no countenance to the religion that had so dogged his footsteps and abridged his delights.

No doubt, the vigilance had been too assiduous, the espionage too vexatious and meddlesome. But the punishment was utterly to outweigh the offence. As in England so on the other side of the Tweed, the worst men came to the front with the advent of the King—men who always had been hostile to Presbytery, or who had hitherto pretended an acquiescence which they did not feel, or who, although they were children of Covenanters, were fired by few of their fathers' ideals. Under their misrule all manner of contumely was to be heaped on beliefs which were dearer than life to multitudes in the nation. Was it astonishing that, in such circumstances, the cords which linked the people with the monarch were loosened and, frequently, were snapped outright? No other issue was possible. When a ruler derides and wounds those aspirations which are most prized by his subjects, the divinity that hedges him round soon fades away.

CHAPTER II.

THE DRUNKEN PARLIAMENT.

AT the Restoration Lowland Scotland continued essentially Presbyterian. Why, it may be asked, was Presbyterianism practically so helpless from the moment that Charles took the management of affairs? The rulers he chose for his northern dominion, rulers with all his own dislike of religion, mounted to power with scarcely so much as a protest on the part of the people. It seems singular that the transition should be made so smoothly. Hitherto Presbytery had been queenly and forceful. Her sceptre had swayed rich and poor, merchant and soldier, old and young. She had moulded creed and conduct. She had given to the citizens the priceless boon of good education. She had fought successfully against the encroachments of royalty. She had schooled the unruly nobles into apparent decorousness. She had leavened the rank and file of the nation with the truths she taught and the enthusiasms she inspired. Yet the diadem passed from her, as it were in a night. In 1660 Charles did what he pleased with the Church of Scotland; and the old remonstrances and defiances, if they were heard, were but feeble and futile.

But there were reasons for an impotence so remarkable.

One of them, probably the most operative, was that the Church was no longer a unity. Mournful divisions played havoc with her strength. To Resolutioner and Protester the cardinal verities were the same, and there was comparatively little to drive them into antagonism. But they were too apt to concentrate their debates and energies on their disagreements and not on their concords. The Resolutioner regarded his neighbour as a precisian; the Protester saw in his co-religionist a latitudinarian who might join hands with the enemy. Here was an "infatuating and ruining distemper," which intruded into Synod and Presbytery and Kirk-Session; and the very homes were pre-eminently fortunate which were not embittered by its poison.

It must be granted, also, that the Covenanters had failed to gain the affection of numbers of the men of position and title. They had their "princes of the chariot," and these were not few; but the larger proportion of their adherents came from the middle class and from the peasantry. Many of the nobles were hostile. Earls and barons and knights, with lives which were only too ungoverned and rough, and private sins that they wished to keep undisturbed, resented the faithfulness of the Church's rebukes and the supervision she tried to exercise over their households and manners. During her halcyon days they yielded an outward submission; but, with the King's star in the ascendant, they could discard their pretended meekness and could flout their instructress.

There was a third source from which trouble flowed to the Kirk. It was the desperate poverty of the ruling families in the country. In 1654, Robert Baillie writes with pitiful emphasis of "our wracked Nobilitie." "Dukes Hamilton, the one execute, the other slaine, their state forfault"; "Huntlie—there is more debt on the House nor the land can pay"; "Dowglass and his sonne Angus are quyet men, of no respect"; "Marschell, Rothes, Eglinton and his three sonnes, Craufurd, Lauderdaill, and others, prisoners in England, and their lands sequestrate or gifted to English sojours"; "Balmerinoch suddenly dead, and his sonne for publict debt keeps not the causey":—thus, from one depressing item to another, the black catalogue moves on. But the Restoration brought to these impoverished lords the chance of escape from their bankruptcy. It offered them forfeited estates and places of consequence. We may be sorry, but we cannot be surprised, that some of them were quick to accept the glittering bribe. For a handful of silver,

silver that was urgently needed, they abandoned a Church for
which they had never entertained any profound regard.

So it came about that Presbytery, whose trumpet had
blown such far-sounding blasts, triumphant and admonitory,
was all but silent at the crisis when her adversaries prevailed.
Their victory was indisputable. For a few months in the
autumn of 1660, Charles ruled Scotland through the old
Committee of Estates. But, on the New Year's Day of 1661,
a Scottish Parliament met in Edinburgh. Nine years had
passed since a similar meeting; and the men who assembled
at the King's call—seventy-seven nobles, fifty-six lairds, and
sixty-one commissioners of burghs—were vastly different from
their predecessors. They had been carefully selected, so that
obnoxious members might be excluded; the House could be
trusted to prove itself a pliant instrument. Before this fateful Parliament rose, on the 12th of July, it had turned
Scottish history into new channels, as momentously as when
Cyrus changed the course of the Euphrates on the night
that he and his Persians captured Babylon.

The Commissioner of Charles, who directed the Parliament, and whose name stands in the forefront of public
affairs for a year or two, was John, Earl of Middleton. He
was one of those soldiers of fortune, who occupied themselves
too busily in national concerns, and who were for the most
part without either human pity or religious faith. He had
carved his way to office by his military ability. Originally
poor, he sought distinction in foreign service; and we hear
of him as " a pikeman in Colonel Hepburn's regiment in
France." Returning to his own country, he was " so zealous
anent the Covenant that, when he took it and held up his
right hand, he wished that that right arm might be his
death," if ever he should forget his vow. It was under the
Blue Banner that he fought in the campaigns of 1644 and
1645, and David Leslie had not many subordinates whom he
held in greater esteem. But then he veered round. When
Charles was in Scotland in the months preceding Worcester,
Major Middleton was his close friend. Throughout the
reign of the Commonwealth, he missed no opportunity of

striking a blow for the absent prince. He commanded the moss-troopers who for a time kept the flame of revolt blazing in the Highlands; but, in July 1654, at Dalnaspidal, near the head of Loch Garry, he was overtaken and beaten by Colonel Morgan. Now, when Puritanism was shorn of her pride, Middleton became a peer of the realm and the King's representative in Scotland.

He was a fearless officer, and he had gone cheerfully through perils and imprisonments for his sovereign. For proof of it, we may linger over the story of the campaign, always desperate, which had such an untoward close at Dalnaspidal. Under a thousand discouragements he had borne up valorously to the last. The rising had been in progress for eight or nine months, before Charles sent him from his retreat in Holland to shape its course and to be first among those fiery chieftains who each aspired to the leading place. Previous to his arrival it was a Lowland nobleman, William Cunningham, the Earl of Glencairn, who in name had been the commanding officer; but Glencairn's suzerainty was hotly challenged by the Highland Lords, Lorne and Kenmure and Glengarry. By and by the first of these "went away in a great rage," swearing that he would rather lose his life than submit for a day longer to a man whom he distrusted. Lord Balcarres soon followed his example, and hastened to Paris to pour his querulous jealousies and suspicions into the ears of the Queen Mother and the King. Charles was in despair. "The enemy," he told his ill-assorted lieutenants, "more depends upon the divisions and animosities among you than upon his own strength." Those were the jarring discords which Sir John Middleton, as he was then, had to weld into something like unity; and, if he had a very partial success, he managed to accomplish more than any one else could. For many weeks his own cheerfulness breathed a new hope into his little army. He thought that, if he could but coax his royal master across the seas, the King's presence would render victory sure. "Your Majestie," he wrote, "will meet with no such desperat game as be manie is represented." Indeed, had Lilburn,

dilatory and hesitating, remained at the head of the forces
which Cromwell had stationed in Scotland, Middleton might
have been for a considerable period a sufficiently troublesome
antagonist.   But Monck, a captain made of sterner stuff,
was set free soon from his work on the Continent.   From
the Forth and the Tay he marched steadily northward.
Over a boggy and hilly country he kept the Royalists moving
from one camping-ground to another, until they were exhausted and weary.   Then he sent forward Colonel Morgan,
and the unavoidable defeat ensued, and Middleton had to
seek refuge with the Macleods in Skye.   Charles's general
had fought a losing battle; but he fought it with skill and
audacity and stubbornness, and he extorts our admiration.
But the man who could use his sword and musket to good
purpose, and who understood how to manipulate others as
headstrong as himself, was too violent, too arbitrary, too
revengeful, to be a wise civil governor.   He had a temper
which would not bear opposition.   His tastes were coarse,
and his habits, even in an age not over-nice, were noticeably
gross and brutish.   He was seldom sober, and rarely away
from his boon-companions.   "It was a mad roaring time, full
of extravagance," Gilbert Burnet writes, "and no wonder it
was so, when the men of affairs were almost perpetually
drunk."   The Commissioner's judgment was beclouded, and
his passions inflamed, and his heart hardened, by constant
dissipation.

As for living belief, he did not know what it meant.
Robert Wodrow has a story which shows him a freethinker,
in whom bluster and superstition were commingled.   In
Hamilton's army in 1648, the minister of Eastwood narrates,
Middleton had for bosom-friend a certain Laird of Balbegno,
the neighbour of his family in Kincardineshire.   It was
within a week of the fight at Preston, and the two were
talking of the risks in front.   "If there is a battle,"
Middleton suggested, "what if we are killed? what will
become of us?"   "No matter!" the other answered, "we
shall be free from our vexations hereaway."   But his
comrade was not wholly convinced that we "drink of Lethe

at last and eat of lotus." "What if there is a future world,"
he retorted, "and a future life?" It was an empty fable
of the ministers, Balbegno replied; and Middleton professed
his sympathy. "But suppose," he went on, "that things
should turn out otherwise?" So they made a compact that,
if one died, he should return, if that were possible, from the
land of mystery, to inform the survivor of what he discovered
there. At Preston Balbegno fell. For awhile Middleton
forgot the bargain, until, one night, he was sitting alone,
a captive, in the Tower of London. Two sentinels guarded
his room. He had been listlessly turning over the pages
of a Bible which he had found in the chamber, "for what
end he knew not, it having been so little his custom," when,
lifting his head, and looking to the door, he saw a man
standing in the shadow. "Who is there?" he asked, and
the answer came, "Balbegno." "That cannot be," he
declared, "for I saw Balbegno buried after he was slain in
battle." But the ghostly visitor glided forward, and
reminded him of their agreement, and caught his arm. The
hand laid in his, Middleton told afterwards, "was hot and
soft, just as it used to be, and Balbegno in his ordinary
likeness." "I am permitted to stay one hour," the apparition said; "so let us sit down, and put your watch before
us." In the weird interview the prisoner learned many
things: how he should escape from his dungeon; how the
King was to be restored; how, at Court, favour and honour
awaited him; but how, at length, the sunshine was to be
clouded over with calamitous eclipse. Then, when the hour
was done, Balbegno rose, and took his leave, and lingered
for an instant amongst the shadows at the door, and so
disappeared.

This was the man who guided Scotland—bold in the
din of the fight, and true to his King, but not a Happy
Warrior, unbelieving, boorish, roystering. Others of kindred
temperament helped him. The Earl of Glencairn, his
comrade in the campaign of seven years before, was
Chancellor; and he was Royalist to the backbone. Sir
Archibald Primrose filled the office of Clerk-Register; his

were the shrewdest intellect and the cleverest tongue in the Parliament House; he "had an art of speaking to all men according to their sense of things, and so drew out their secrets while he concealed his own, for words went for nothing with him." The King's Advocate was Sir John Fletcher, in whose veins was none of the milk of kindness; "he hated all mild proceedings, and could scarce speak with decency or patience to those of the other side." It mattered little that Lord Crawford, who was earnest in his Presbyterianism, was Treasurer; his advice was overborne by the clamours of the rest. Within a few years the Commissioner, drugged by the sweets of power as well as by fiery liquors, was to cross swords with a man keener-eyed and stronger-willed than himself, and was to be worsted in the duel;— Balbegno's gloomier auguries were fulfilled as surely as his gladsomer predictions. But, until that moment of disaster, Middleton and his allies might do whatever they chose.

They made abundant use of their chances. During its session of six and a half months, the Parliament of 1661 passed no less than three hundred and ninety-three Acts. It would have been extraordinary if, in so long a list, there were not some beneficent measures. It is curious to note that means were adopted to safeguard the observance of the Sabbath, and to prevent profane swearing and excessive drinking: now and then Satan discloses himself as the unexpected reprover of sin. But Middleton's first session is remembered by other achievements than these. Its "great design and business was to make the King absolute." To reach this end, the framers of the laws had to "demolish the outworks and bulwarks of the Church, and to blow up her government itself." Their aim was to re-establish despotism and to destroy Presbytery. They "plunged on," Professor Masson says, "legislating in their own way, as if in iron boots and with iron flails, tramping and thrashing a space clear for the erection of Nebuchadnezzar's image." Some of them were amazed at themselves when they recalled their proceedings in subsequent years. Sir Archibald Primrose, in his moments of candour, would confess to

THE OLD PARLIAMENT HOUSE OF EDINBURGH.

Burnet that he thought he was "as one bewitched" when he sat down to draft his bills and acts, "for, not considering the ill use might be made of them afterwards, he drew them with preambles full of extravagant rhetoric, reflecting severely on the proceedings of the late times, and swelled them up with the highest phrases and fullest clauses he could invent." England had to mourn the illegalities of its statesmen in those months of the King's return; and its best citizens looked on in surprise and anger while many of their liberties were narrowed, and some of their rights were stolen away. But England would not have endured the irrational and unchecked absolutism by which Scotland was reduced to bondage. And the pity of it was that the chains were forged and fastened by Scotland's unworthy sons.

There were no boundaries to the powers with which they invested the King. Their earliest proceeding was to construct an Oath of Allegiance—an Oath in which every jurisdiction except that of His Majesty was renounced. Its terms said nothing about Charles's right to interfere with the Church; the omission and the ambiguity were deliberate, for meanwhile it seemed prudent to veil some of the tyrannies which the future would bring to light. But, under cover of its clauses, the authors of the Oath intended to violate the domain of conscience and to attack the household of Christ. In coming years it was to be an effective weapon of persecution; the fidelity of men and women to the Crown was to be tested by their willingness to swear its sentences; and if they had any scruples, no mercy was shown. Further still the Parliament went in subservience to the sovereign. It decreed that he alone could choose his officers of State, his Privy Councillors, his Lords of Session; that he alone could call and hold and prorogue and dissolve all conventions and meetings; that he alone could enter into leagues and treaties; that he alone could proclaim peace or war: his was to be the voice of a god rather than that of a man. The members set apart the 29th of May, the day of the Glorious Return, "to be for ever an holy day unto the Lord." Its opening hours were to be consecrated to

prayer, preaching, thanksgiving, and praise; its afternoon
and evening were to be spent "in lawful divertisements
suitable to so solemn an occasion." We can perceive to
what license the gates were unbarred by this statute, and
why it staggered the friends of the Covenant, who kept their
garland of sanctity for God's Sabbath, and cherished an
invincible mistrust of man-made festivals. One consummate
folly placed the copestone on the Parliament's excess of
loyalty. It voted Charles an annual grant of £40,000
sterling, and thus exhausted the resources of a nation which
required every penny of its money. Four years later, the
Earl of Tweeddale, a nobleman with some love for his
country, wrote that a Dutch invasion would be for Scotland
a much less serious evil than the smallest increase in the
taxation of the people. But Middleton and Glencairn and
Sir Archibald Primrose were dominated by other ideas. For
the benefit of their royal and wasteful master they would
pauperise the whole community. As James Kirkton described
it, "they installed their King a sort of Pope."

But what filled many hearts with sharper sorrow than
this servility towards the monarch was the treatment meted
out to the Church. In decision after decision, Parliament
heaped insult on the Covenant. It annulled the proceedings
of the Convention of Estates, which had sworn the Solemn
League. It protested that the great bond, "which had in
Scotland universal respect next to the Scripture," was
without public and permanent obligation. Then, growing in
hardihood, the leaders had recourse to a master-blow. By
a general Rescissory Act, carried on the 28th of March
after a single debate, they revoked "the pretendit Parliaments
keept in the yeers 1640, 1641, 1644, 1645, 1646, 1647,
and 1648, and all acts and deids past and done in them,"
declaring "the same to be henceforth voyd and null." When
the notion was mooted first, it seemed too big, too venturesome, a goal too desirable for attainment. It "appeared so
choking that it was laid aside." But, when one drastic
measure after another secured a glib consent, Middleton
returned to the darling scheme. The Clerk-Register was

sick; but King Charles's deputy wrote him a letter, beseeching him to frame the monstrous statute without delay. "Now," he said, "I am more concerned in this than I was ever in a particular. The speedy doing is the thing I propose as the great advantage." So let the bill be in readiness by ten o'clock to-morrow forenoon, to go before the Lords of the Articles—the Cabinet, as it were; and in the afternoon it could be brought into Parliament, and passed there and then. The clever and compliant draftsman did as he was enjoined; but he thought it was a piece of useless labour—"so ill-grounded that, when it came to be considered, it must certainly be laid aside." He was mistaken. Middleton carried everything before him, hurrying the Act through a nerveless and recreant House, although even in it there were notable dissentients, like the Duke of Hamilton and Lord Crawford. And what did he gain by his extraordinary *coup de main*? The cancelling of everything that successive legislatures, in which the Presbyterian element predominated, had effected for the Church. The right to pronounce disloyal and traitorous those who should still assert their attachment to the flag of the Second Reformation. The construction of a high road by which the Bishops might ride back triumphant. Indeed, the Commissioner would have pushed on immediately to the creation of his hierarchy; but astute Sir Archibald Primrose counselled a pause. "Bring the Bishops in," he advised; "let it be done surely, but let it likewise be done slowly"; and for the time the wary lawyer won his point with his more headstrong chief. But, whenever the Act Rescissory had received the imprimatur of Parliament, the end was in sight. It could not be many months until the mitre and lawn sleeves of the prelate displaced the modest Geneva gown of the minister.

These were the doings of the Drunken Parliament, as it has been nicknamed ever since. For, often, it was when they were stupefied by their carousals that the senators determined on their revolutionary enactments. They robbed the nation of its liberties; they checked its social progress; they did

what they could to stifle its religious life; and their sorry
victory was procured, when wine had stolen from them brain
and conscience and patriotism and most things worth the
keeping.   Bishop Burnet's epithets are not too severe: it
was "a mad roaring time."

One day, when these melancholy events were happening,
David Dickson, who had been minister in Irvine and was now
Professor in Edinburgh, and who wrote some verses not yet
forgotten—*O Mother dear, Jerusalem!*—went to expostulate
with the Earl of Middleton.   But the King's Commissioner
was hugely offended.   He told his monitor that he was
deluding himself if he thought to overawe him; he was no
coward to tremble before a priest.   "For three-and-twenty
years," the old man replied, "I have known that you are no
coward, ever since the Brig o' Dee in the June of 1638."   It
was a home-thrust; for, in that past midsummer, Middleton's
sword had been unsheathed in defence of the Covenant.   The
Earl had no answer; and the minister pleaded with him to
pay regard, if not to the Presbytery, at least to those forty-
two members of Parliament who had dared to oppose the
Rescissory Act.   "And, my Lord," he added, "I would put
you in mind of that deep exercise of soul, under which you
lay in St. Andrews in 1645, when you were sick and in
hazard of death."   "What!" Middleton sneered, "do you
presume to speak to me of a fit of fever?"   So, pained to
the heart, David Dickson turned and left the room.

The night was to grow darker—moonless, starless, hopeless—before there was a streak of day.

CHAPTER III.

A DEATHBED IN ST. ANDREWS.

THE Drunken Parliament did something more than pass laws which were fraught with mischief and misery. It determined to send to a violent death the leaders in the Protesting section of the Church, the men whose advocacy of the Covenant was most unfaltering and outspoken. Four of these leaders were marked for execution—Samuel Rutherfurd; the Marquis of Argyll; James Guthrie; and Archibald Johnston, Lord Wariston. The first and the last of the four eluded the doom intended for them: the one because the finger of God beckoned him, before his enemies could accomplish their purpose; the other because he contrived to hide himself until Middleton's power was vanishing, although in this instance the scaffold was merely postponed, and the infliction of the sentence came at the hands of those who had ousted the Commissioner from his place. As for the Marquis and the minister of Stirling, they were crowned at once with the thorny crown which the Parliament had twined for their brows.

Ever since the Restoration Samuel Rutherfurd must have guessed the punishments which his enemies designed for him. Three months after Charles's return, the Committee of Estates in Edinburgh issued a proclamation, worthy in its rage and impotence of the angriest of the Popes. It decreed that all copies of the *Lex Rex* which could be found should be gathered before the middle of October, and burned at the Mercat Cross in the capital and at the gates of the New College in St. Andrews. The thing was duly done; but,

D

"full of seditious and treasonable matter" as the *Lex Rex* was announced to be, its teaching lives to this hour. It is the plea of the Covenanters for the majesty of the people; for the truth that the law, and no autocrat on the throne, is king; for the creed that limitless sovereignty is the property of God alone. The Stuart monarch could not check the advance of these principles by bonfires in the streets of Edinburgh and St. Andrews. Much of the book, it has been said, is "the constitutional inheritance of all countries in modern times."

Through forty-four chapters, or "Questions," Rutherfurd develops his argument. The book, says Dr. Hume Brown, is "tediously pedantic"; and no doubt it is so, if one should attempt to read it in its entirety. There are too many minute details, and the hard and syllogistic method of the debater is overmuch in evidence. But, every little while, the underlying enthusiasm mounts to the surface, and refuses to be quite concealed. With all the strength of his conviction and all the fire of his zeal the author fights on behalf of the liberties of the nation. Prince and beggar, he reminds us, spring of one clay; yet he grants that government has a divine sanction, and is necessary and inevitable. Ay, but to whom does government belong? Not to a royal James or Charles, but to the men and women of their realm. They are the true rulers. They can delegate their authority to this representative or to that, selecting whom they please. They may measure it by ounce-weight or by pound-weight. They may limit and moderate and set banks and marches to its exercise. They can take it to themselves again, if the conditions on which they bestowed it are disregarded and broken. The king, beyond dispute, has his special dignity and stately privilege; but, when all is said and done, the commonwealth is more excellent than the king; and he is ordained to serve it as its shepherd, its captain, its leader. Is not the pilot less than the passengers, the tutor less than the children, the physician less than the patients, the master less than the scholars? He who by his very office is obliged to expend himself and, in the last resort, to sacrifice his life, for the safety of those who are denominated his subjects, must in reality be inferior to them. If they invest him with politic honours and prerogatives, they keep to themselves natural prerogatives and honours which they never can surrender. These are axioms of the *Lex Rex*: "The law is not the king's own, but is given to him in trust"; "Power is a birthright of the people borrowed from them; they may let it out for their good, and resume it when a man is drunk with it"; "A limited and mixed monarchy hath glory, order, unity from a monarch; from the government of the most and wisest it hath safety of counsel, stability, strength; from the influence of the Commons it hath liberty, privileges, promptitude of obedience." They are the axioms on which our regulated freedom of to-day is broad-based. Looking back to Rutherfurd, we see his forehead lighted with the prophecy of the better era, and we know that, almost three centuries since, he recognised

what health there is
In the frank Dawn's delighted eyes.

In the autumn of 1660 the book received its martyrdom, and in the early spring of 1661 the Privy Council and the Parliament were eager to have its author martyred too. He had been denuded of his offices in the University of St. Andrews, and deprived of his pastoral charge; but these confiscations were not enough. He was cited to appear at the bar of the House on a charge of treason. The messengers carried the citation across the Firth of Forth. But God had forestalled them. For weeks, as Rutherfurd wrote in a letter, "a daily menacing disease" had been hanging over him; and he lay now on his deathbed. It was a wasted hand which received the document the emissaries brought; but the voice had parted with none of its fire. "Tell them," he said, "that I have a summons already from a superior Judge and judicatory, and I behove to answer my first summons; and, ere your day arrives, I will be where few kings and great folks come." When they reported his condition, the Council declared with feeble malice that he must not be permitted to die within the College walls; but, even in the hostile court, one member had grace and fortitude to befriend him. Lord Burleigh rose and said, "Ye have voted that honest man out of his College, but ye cannot vote him out of heaven." Nothing could be truer than the courageous word.

While he waited till it was time to "answer his first summons," Samuel Rutherfurd must have been visited by moving memories. He was one of the most extraordinary men in an age of heroes; and he had many marvels to recall, as he tarried immediately outside the joys of what he loved to delineate as the Upper Garden of God.

He saw himself in the unprofitable half of his life—the little child in the Border village of Nisbet or Crailing, surrounded even then by miracles; the student and boyish Professor of Latin in Edinburgh; the offender, with whom the University officials quarrelled because of some irregularity in his youthful marriage, the nature of which it is not easy now to unravel. These were the acid ingredients in the cup of recollection. For it was the sorrow of his later years, as it was St. Augustine's, that he allowed himself to reach manhood before he yielded his heart to God. "Like a fool as I was," he says, "I suffered my sun to be high in the heaven, and near afternoon." Few things in the *Letters* are more beautiful than the earnestness with which he beseeches the young to consecrate their freshest hours to eternity. "It were a sweet and glorious thing for your daughter Grissel to give herself up to Christ, that He may write upon her His Father's name and His own new name." "I desire Patrick to give Christ the flower of his love; it were good to start soon to the way." To Earlston, when he was leaving boyhood behind, he writes: "There is not such a glassy, icy, and slippery piece of way betwixt you and heaven as youth; the devil findeth in youth dry sticks and dry coals and a hot hearthstone; and how soon can he with his flint cast fire, and with his bellows blow it up!" He is as vivid and as solicitous, when he addresses Lord Boyd: "It is easy to master an arrow and to set it right ere the string be drawn; but, when once it is shot and in the air and the flight begun, then ye have no more power at all to command it. And therefore O what a sweet couple are Christ and a young man! This is a meeting not to be found in every town." Was it the thought of his own delays which stirred this yearning over others? He would have no one imitate him, "loitering on the road too long, and trifling at the gate."

But this vision passed, and the dying man saw himself the minister of Anwoth. For nine years, from 1627 to 1636, he was the spiritual father of the quiet parish, lying round the Water of Fleet, among the soft green hills of Galloway. There was his manse, the Bush o' Bield, where he rose each morning at three, to spend the day's commencement in prayer and study. To its door, one unforgotten Saturday, Archbishop Ussher turned aside in the disguise of a traveller, to be hospitably entertained, and catechised, and reproved for his seeming ignorance of a fact so elementary as the number of statutes written by God's finger on the Tables of Stone—an ignorance explained when he spoke, next morning, in the Presbyterian kirk, on the new commandment of Jesus, *That ye love one another*. From the rooms of the Anwoth manse, the mistress of the home and more than one of the children went to God; "an afflicted life," the husband and father wrote, "looks very like the way that leads to the Kingdom." Close to the Bush o' Bield stood the tiny sanctuary, as tiny as George Herbert's in Bemerton; the visitor may still walk round its ivied and ruined walls. What a centre of zealous labour it was! "For such a piece of clay as Mr. Rutherfurd," said James Urquhart, minister in Kinloss, "I never knew one in Scotland like him. He seemed to be always praying, always preaching, always visiting the sick, always teaching in the schools, always writing treatises, always reading and studying." The Sabbath was his crowning day. He had a "strange utterance, a kind of a skreigh." But the shrillness of the voice could not hide the heart's fervours, and the hearers hung upon him listening. Often, one of them confessed, he fancied

the minister "would have flown out of the pulpit, when he
came to speak of Christ, the Rose of Sharon"; then, indeed,
he was "as a fish in the ocean, never in his right element
but when he was commending" his Lord.   In Anwoth the
sermons were prepared and spoken, which afterwards were
given to the world under the title of *The Trial and Triumph
of Faith*—a retelling and expansion of the immortal story of
that pleading and prevailing mother from the coasts of Tyre
and Sidon, who enmeshed Jesus in the net of His Own
promises, and clung about His feet until she had obtained all
her desire; those other sermons too, which were to be known
in their printed form as *Christ Dying and Drawing Sinners to
Himself*.   Both volumes, in spite of the dull yellow paper
and the dim and faded ink, palpitate still with their author's
affection for his divine Master.   "We but play," he protests
in the preface to one of them, "about the 'borders and
margent of knowledge of Christ, as children do with the
golden covering and silken ribbons of an Arabic Bible that
they cannot read."   Even the Middle Ages, he thinks,
encrusted with superstition as they were, put their more
prosaic and less exuberant successors to shame.   "O, how
rarely do the needle-eyed schoolmen write of Christ!   O,
how subtle and eagle-eyed seem they to be in speculations—
grave-deep, or rather hell-deep, touching His grave-linens,
what became of them when He rose from the dead, and the
chestnut colour of His hair, and the wood of His Cross, and
the three nails that wedged Him to the Tree, and the adoring
of anything that touched His body!"   But the glow of the
saint and singer who poured forth his soul in the *Jesu! dulcis
memoria* influenced every look and tone and gesture of the
Covenanting preacher, and no mediæval recluse was more
rapt in his devotion.   His parishioners, the herd boys as well
as the Viscount Kenmure, revered the "little fair man."
They recounted his untiring charities.   In his very gait they
detected his communion with God; "when he walked, it was
observed he held aye his face upward and heavenward."   The
home, the church, the "blessed birds" of Anwoth, the path
among the trees which he paced talking with his unseen

Friend—he beheld them again in dying, and thanked God for them.

Then, once more, his dream changed. He was a prisoner in Aberdeen. Thomas Sydserff, who had come from the northern diocese of Brechin to be Bishop of Galloway, was no lover of Samuel Rutherfurd; and his repugnance was heightened when the preacher published his book against the Arminians: *Exercitationes pro Divina Gratia* he called it. He haled him before the High Commission Court, in Wigtown and in Edinburgh, and had him deposed and exiled to the northern city, far enough distant from the familiar hills and tides. "I go," the banished man said, "to my King's palace at Aberdeen; tongue, pen, and wit cannot express my joy." But, if he carried music in his heart, he had his experiences of depression during his eighteen months of seclusion. It was hard for the impassioned servitor of Jesus to maintain silence. "I had but one eye," he mourned, "and they have put it out." Yet, long before he came to his deathbed, he saw that God's purpose was one of purest grace. A new field of work had been disclosed. If his lips were shut, his pen was busy. Two hundred and twenty of the *Letters*, those amaranthine Letters, whose glow and tenderness and pungency are the best demonstration of his spiritual genius, were sent from Aberdeen. It is easy doubtless to deride the tropical luxuriance which marks the style of "Joshua Redivivus." The clever, but supercilious, author of *A Literary History of Scotland* is only amused by the faults of taste and tact and discretion which the Letters reveal. Rutherfurd, we are assured, "must needs ride every metaphor, vinous or otherwise, to death." "Not even Burke in his wildest flights had less sense of proportion, less perception of the fitting"; but many of us would be glad if, in our very errors, we suggested Edmund Burke. "It would be difficult," the censor declares, "to extract a passage of any length which is not disfigured by something ludicrous or vulgar, to the point of gross irreverence." "The odd thing is," he adds, "that this jargon is sprinkled every now and then with the technical phrases of the Law of Scotland, and the effect of the mixture is indescribable." The sarcasm is cheap and shallow. Few will question that there are faults in the Letters, when they are appraised by literary canons alone. But, even before this tribunal, their grandeurs and sublimities are as conspicuous as their mistakes. And they have spoken to ten thousand souls, in the rhythm and cadence of the better country which is the heavenly. In "the little flock named after God's own heart" their writer needs no defence; for its members crowned him long ago. This, therefore, was the divine necessity for the loneliness and hatred to which Rutherfurd was subjected. The poet Wordsworth spent the winter of 1798 in North Germany. It was the bleakest of seasons, and the village of Goslar where he lived had no attractiveness. But these four months, Mr. Frederic Myers assures us, were the bloom of his career. Through the verses written then the loveliness of English scenery and English childhood shines most delicately. Lucy Gray, "the sweetest thing that ever grew beside a human door," and Ruth, who "at her will went wandering over dale and hill," had their birth in the desolate German town. The same happy compensation was given to the Covenanting minister. He lived himself in a land of brooks of water; and, not content with the personal enjoyment of it, he has guided thousands of pilgrims to the wealthy place.

Perhaps another dream followed. He was in the Jerusalem Chamber at Westminster, one of the Scottish commissioners to the Assembly of Divines. "For the great parts God had given him," wrote Robert Baillie with the pride of a countryman, "Mr. Samuel's presence was very necessary." Again, in his thoughts, he debated the doctrine of the Church's freedom against those captains of Erastianism, Lightfoot and Selden. Again he argued with the Independents; although now, more than ever, he felt that they were "gracious men," and, "of all that differed from us, came nearest to walking with God." Again he busied himself in writing his *Peaceable and Temperate Plea for Paul's Presbytery* and his *Divine Right of Church Government and Excommunication.* Again he did his emphatic part in framing the

Confession, and the Directory, and the Catechisms. Did he recall, too, the fresh and poignant home-griefs of these London years? "I had two children," so he had related the sorrow when it was new, "and both are dead since I came hither. The good Husbandman may pluck His roses and gather His lilies in the beginning of the first summer months. What is that to you or to me? The Creator of time and of winds did a merciful injury, if I may borrow the words, in landing the passenger so early." Samuel Rutherfurd was at Westminster from the middle of 1643 to the end of 1647; and he was glad when, at length, he could set his face northward to his students and congregation and childless home—glad with that emotion which the poet calls a "sour-sweet" delight.

To his students he returned; for, since the close of the Anwoth ministry in 1639, he had been Professor in St. Andrews. And there, in labours more abundant than any of his compeers, he lived the remainder of his life. They made him Principal of the New College and Rector of the University. Since Alexander Henderson had gone, he was the doyen of Scottish thinkers and teachers. Edinburgh tried, in 1649, to secure him for its own; and other lands coveted him. Twice Utrecht sent him a call to occupy its chair of theology. But the tempest-driven Kirk, with its unhappy controversies and those dangers that loomed ahead, had thrown its hoops of steel about his soul. He could not go away. "I had rather be in Scotland with angry Jesus Christ," he said, "than in any Eden or garden in the earth." So he continued in St. Andrews, until the Earl of Middleton bade him answer for his fearless witness against all arbitrary power in Church and State.

In that tumultuous Scotland which tugged so constrainingly at his heart-strings, he had, from the early days in Anwoth to the last hours in St. Andrews, made every class and rank in the community his debtors. We are surprised not by the number only but by the variety of his friends. There are godly women, like Marion M'Naught, the wife of William Fullerton, Provost of Kirkcudbright, to whom, because

of her rare insight, he could lay open his very soul; or like
Lady Jane Campbell, the Viscountess Kenmure, whom in her
illnesses and depressions he comforted with many words of
cheer; or like the mother of John Brown of Wamphray, most
redoubtable of Calvinists and most learned of theologians.
There are Churchmen famous in the transactions of the
General Assembly, and humbler ministers scattered throughout the land, and young students of divinity to whom he
commends not so much the erudition of the schools as the
practice of personal sanctification. Congregations appeal to
him in their perplexities, and he never fails to send them a
message as shrewd and penetrating as it is high-pitched and
spiritual. The nobles of Scotland, some of them headstrong
and turbulent, others temporising and disposed to halt between
two opinions, are often in his thought and prayer; and he has
for each a discriminating advice and a definite command. To
Lord Lothian he says, " To want temptations is the greatest
temptation of all "; to Lord Loudoun, " Events are God's; let
Him sit at His own helm "; to Cassillis, " The Earldom of
Cassillis is but a shadow in comparison of the city not made
with hands; it is no wisdom to be silent, when they are casting lots for a better thing than Christ's coat "; to Craighall,
" Fear your light, stand in awe of it, for it is from God.
Kings cannot heal broken consciences; it is common for men
to make doubts when they have a mind to desert the truth."
He passes through life, giving to every one who crosses his
path a word in season and a veritable pronouncement from
the King of kings.

　　Yet Rutherfurd was not himself a perfect man. There
were defects both in his creed and in his character. His
temper was fiery, and too frequently he made no serious effort
to moderate its energy; " I am made of extremes," he wrote
to his friend, David Dickson. Dialectician and polemic all
his days, he had scant mercy for those who saw the truth
from other angles than his own. Towards the Resolutioners
he showed, on many occasions, an acrimoniousness which was
far from admirable. Perhaps it was inevitable that it should
be so. " The intellectual gladiator, the rejoicing and remorse-

less logician, the divider of words, the distinguisher of thoughts, the hater of doubt and ambiguity, the scorner of compromise and concession, the incessant and determined disputant, the passionate admirer of sequence and system and order in small things as in great—in the corner of an argument as in the mighty world outside ": thus Dr. Taylor Innes paints him in a portrait as masterly as any of Mr. Sargent's ; and so intent and vehement an ecclesiastic forgets at times the urbanities of thought and the courtesies of speech. But, when these deductions are made, he still rises to a stature attained by only the select few in Christ's dazzling host—by a St. Bernard, a Madame Guyon, a Brainerd. Dr. Taylor Innes is as felicitous in depicting the more celestial side. This man, he says, was "impatient of earth, intolerant of sin, rapt into the continual contemplation of one unseen Face, finding his history in its changing aspect and his happiness in its returning smile."

That is Rutherfurd's glory, his absorption in Christ—Christ, whom he lauds as " the outset, the master-flower, the uncreated garland of heaven, the love and joy of men and angels." Many temperaments, many goals ; but for him there is only one Goal, and no other is worth the mentioning. Madame Duclaux, whom we know better as Miss Mary Robinson, tells us in an exquisite sonnet about the ideal which enthrals her—

> For in my heaven both sun and moon is he,
>   To my bare life a fruitful-flooding Nile,
>   His voice like April airs that in our isle
> Wake sap in trees that slept since autumn went.
>   His words are all caresses, and his smile
> The relic of some Eden ravishment ;
> And he that loves me so I call : Content.

But Samuel Rutherfurd's Content is a living Person and not an abstract quality, and His name is Jesus Christ. Again, Mr. Stevenson in a wonderful letter unfolds his supreme affection : " O the height and depth of novelty and worth in art ! and O that I am privileged to swim through such oceans ! What a great space and a great air there is ! An art is a fine fortune, a palace, a band of music, health, and beauty. I sleep upon my art for a pillow ; I waken in my art. I love my wife,

I do not know how much, nor can, nor shall unless I lost her; but, while I can conceive my being widowed, I refuse the offering of life without my art.   I *am* not but in my art; it is me; I am the body of it merely."   If one reads the passage a second time, deleting the word Art and substituting the word Christ, it is what Rutherfurd would have written.   He went to sleep with Christ for his pillow; he awoke in Christ. Doubtless he loved both the girl-wife of his youth and the home-companion of his riper years, although in him, as in others of his Covenanting kin, we note a certain detachment from the ties and tendernesses of the family; but, while he could endure widowhood, he would have refused the offering of life without his Christ.   His heart, as he said, was not his own; Jesus had run away to heaven with it.

Christ had been near him in infancy, though he was a man before he confessed his Lover's grace.   Playing once with the boys of Crailing, the child stumbled into a deep well; and his frightened comrades ran to acquaint his father and mother. They hurried out, fearing that they would not see their Samuel alive.   But they discovered him "sitting on a hillock, a little from the well, all wet and cold," but unharmed and safe. How had he got there? they asked, and he answered, "A bonnie white Man drew me forth and set me down."   The old story-teller adds, "It is thought it was an angel."   But we may surmise that, in later years, the boy ascribed his deliverance to One more excellent than the angels, their Lord, who had "come riding on the rainbow and clouds" to rescue him.

And, if Christ was the Beginning, the End was Christ, beheld with clearest intelligence and firmest faith and consuming love.   The *Analecta* preserves some "words that dropped from him at several times," as, in that March of 1661, Rutherfurd lay in his room and looked for his Master. "I shall shine; I shall see Him as He is.   I shall see Him reigne, and all the fair company with Him, and I shall have my large share.   Mine eyes shall see my Redeemer, and noe other forme.   This seems to be a wide word; but it's noe fancy nor delusion: it's treu, it's treu!"   These, too, were his exultations: "My blessed Master!   My kingly King!   Let

SAMUEL RUTHERFURD.

From a Portrait probably by Robert Walker.

my Lord's name be exalted; and, if He will, let my name be ground to peices, that He may be all and in all. If He should slay me ten thousand times ten thousand times, I'll trust." Often he repeated the text, *Thy Word was found, and I did eat it, and it was to me the joy and rejoicing of my heart.* " It's noe easy thing to be a Christian," he said to one; " but, for me, I have gotten the victory, and Christ is holding out both His armes to embrace me." "At the beginning of my suffering," he told some friends, " I had my fears that I might have my faintings, and not be caryed creditably throu; and I laid this before the Lord; and as sure as ever He spoke to me in His Word, as sure His Spirit witnessed in my heart, *Fear not*; and the outgate shall not be simply matter of prayer but matter of praise." " Fedd on manna "—it was one of his ejaculations. When the end drew near, Robert Blair asked, " What think you now of Christ ? " " I shall live and adore Him," he replied; and in whispers he was heard saying again and again, " Glory to Him in Emanuell's land ! " That One Face was more and more his Universe. Some one alluded to his own work of faith; but he was quick to interrupt : " I disclaim all. The port I would be in at is redemption and salvation through His blood." To four of his brethren who visited him, he gave the counsel : " Pray for Christ; preach for Christ; do all for Christ; beware of men-pleasing." Once or twice he cried for " a well-tuned harp," as if already he would participate in the strains of the worshippers within the veil. On the afternoon before he died, he predicted : " This night will close the door, and fasten my anchor; and I shall go away in a sleep by five in the morning." And thus it happened; for at that hour on the morning of the 29th of March—the daybreak hour which, as Henry Vaughan sings, " best doth chime " with the glory of the divine Bridegroom, and in which all things throughout the creation " expect some sudden matter "—God hid Samuel Rutherfurd with Himself from the wrangling and cruelty of wicked men.

Between the Parliament in Edinburgh and the deathbed in St. Andrews there is more than the distance which separates earth from heaven.

CHAPTER IV.

MARQUIS AND MARTYR.

ABOUT Archibald Campbell, the eighth Earl and the first Marquis of Argyll, there clings the fascination with which mystery and manysidedness invest a man. His nature is complex, involved, and difficult at times to read. It is not as straight as the flight of an arrow, nor as clear as the landscape which the noonday sun explains. Two portraits of him live in fiction, one nearly a century old, the other limned but a year or two since. The earlier, that of *The Legend of Montrose*, is the more unfavourable. "His dark complexion, furrowed forehead, and downcast look, gave him the appearance of one frequently engaged in the consideration of important affairs, who has acquired by long habit an air of gravity, which he cannot shake off even where there is nothing to be concealed. The cast with his eyes, which had procured him in the Highlands the nickname of Gillespie Grumach, or the Grim, was less perceptible when he looked downward, which perhaps was one cause of his having adopted that habit. In person he was tall and thin, but not without that dignity of deportment and manners which became his high rank. Something there was cold in his address and sinister in his look. He was adored by his own clan, whose advancement he had greatly studied, while others conceived themselves in danger from his future schemes, and all dreaded the height to which he was elevated." The later picture, drawn by Mr. Neil Munro, is more psychological and discriminating than Scott's rougher and rapider sketch. "Had our Lordship in-bye," says John

Splendid, " been sent a-fostering in the old style, brought up
to the chase and the sword and manly comportment, he
would not have that wan cheek this day, and that swithering
about what he would be at next." Or we may hearken to
Archibald the Grim himself, as this most recent chronicler
reports his confessions: " There is, I allow, a kind of man
whom strife sets off, a middling good man in his way perhaps,
with a call to the sword whose justice he has never
questioned. I have studied the philosophies; I have
reflected on life, the unfathomable problem ; and, before
God, I begin to doubt my very right to wear a breastplate
against the poignard of fate. Dubiety plays on me like a
flute." Here is a personality not to be interpreted by any
short and easy method—one which may present bewildering
and opposing aspects, and which is sure to be familiar with
conflicting moods.

Let us admit that Argyll's greatness was not that of the
soldier. He had moral courage; but he knew little about
the warrior's stern joy in the clash of conflicting foes. On
the fatal February day in 1645, when at Inverlochy they
faced Montrose, the men who wore the Campbell tartan were
" hewn down on the edge of the tide till its waves ran red."
And their chief left the scene of carnage in his barge, the
Dubhlinnseach—the *Black Sail*—before the battle he lost
had well commenced. Perhaps he would have come through
it honourably enough ; but it was one of the critical moments
when " dubiety played on him like a flute." He listened to
the advice of others, who pleaded that his life was much too
precious to the cause of the Covenant to be exposed to
needless danger—listened to them until his own directness
of vision and power of initiative were forfeited : and the
failure followed, and by and by the remorse. Others of the
Campbells, as Bishop Wishart, Montrose's eulogist, is ready
to admit, showed themselves " stout and gallant " in the
early hours of the fight which resulted so disastrously ; and
of the seventeen hundred who perished on the field the
majority belonged to the clan. But its overlord, whom the
Estates of Parliament were soon to thank for behaving

"painfully, wisely, and diligently in his late expedition against the rebels," did nothing by his own example to avert the rout of his friends. Gillespie Grumach—although, after all, that unflattering sobriquet is not his own but his father's —was not among the generals whose very presence brings exhilaration and victory.

Let us admit, too, that, like Cæsar, he was ambitious. He had no liking for the subordinate place. But it is hard for the man who aspires to primacy to be always consistent, to keep the unswerving course, and to steer right onward. Biting adjectives are often affixed to Argyll's name; Lord Morley has said that in his politics he was "a shifty and astute opportunist." Surely they are draconian judges who write in this style. He had his compromises and conceal-ments; it was not easy, in those years of turmoil, for the leaders in opinion and action to avoid accepting at times, instead of the prize on which their own hearts were set, some poorer substitute. If it must be granted that he appeared variable, the sudden surprises, the strange turnings and windings, of the history in which he was so outstanding a figure, are accountable for most of the changes in his tactics. In 1648, in the days of the Whiggamore Raid, when Preston had plunged the promoters of the Engagement into humiliation, and when the stricter Covenanters were supreme, he supped with Cromwell at Moray House, in the Canongate of Edinburgh. Six months later he cherished thoughts the reverse of friendly towards the English captain and his army. But the revolution in feeling had a sufficient cause. In the interval the scaffold at Whitehall had been erected. The Scots, who abhorred the tyrannies of the King, held his person and his office inextinguishably dear; and Argyll shared to the full both their hates and their loves. It was in his blood, it was a necessity of birth and tempera-ment, that he should set himself against the less emotional and more thoroughgoing Roundheads. But we could wish that, in the recoil of soul, he had been saved from espousing the quarrel of Charles the Second with such entire abandon-ment. "He used all possible address," writes Clarendon, "to make himself gracious to the King." He "entertained him with very pleasant discourses, and with such insinuations that His Majesty did not only very well like his conversation but often believed that he had a mind to please and gratify him." It is true that, through it all, he was pedagogue as much as subject. He established a watchful control over his sovereign. If Charles hinted at plans of which he did not approve, he "gathered up his countenance and retired," abruptly terminating the inconvenient discussion by leaving the room and shutting the door. But he lost favour for a while with the stricter Covenanters, a Colonel Strachan and a Colonel Ker, because there seemed to be no boundaries to his endeavours on behalf of the chief Malignant. He was principal performer in the coronation scene at Scone. There were even proposals that the prince should marry the eldest of his four daughters, the Lady Anne Campbell, "a gentlewoman of rare parts and education." The scheme came to nothing, for Queen Henrietta Maria would not tolerate it, and Charles was not himself a passionate wooer; but the disenchantment brought sore grief to poor Lady Anne, who "lossed her spirit and turned absolutely distracted," and probably the indiscreet plan was remembered at a later time to her father's discredit and undoing. Yet, short of becoming his son-in-law, the King of 1650 and 1651 was prepared to lavish every favour on the powerful noble, whose support he was so keen to win. "Particularly, I doe promis," he wrote in a letter from "St. Johnston," as the city of Perth used to be called, "that I will mak him Duk of Argyll, and Knight of the Garter, and one of the gentlemen of my bedchamber; and this to be performed when he shall think it fitt. And I doe further promis him to hearken to his counsels; and, whensoever it shall pleas God to restor me to my just rights in England, I shall see him payed the forty thousand pounds sterling, which is due to him. All which I doe promis to mak good, upon the word of a King." Imagination could not have guessed, when this letter was sent, the tragedy which the future was keeping for its recipient; but frequently Charles's smiles were auguries of disaster as sure as his frowns. Having travelled so far in Royalism, the Marquis needed to behave himself with wariness and circumspection through Cromwell's tenure of power.   To Major-General Deane he gave his formal submission to the Commonwealth; but there was little love on either side.   In the Newsletters written by the soldiers of the Parliamentary army, one reads their distrust of the man whom they dreaded most in Scotland: " It's said Argyll hath sent a Letter with several addresses to the titular King; what the effect of it is, as yet we know not. He is a subtle Fox, but, if he close not quickly, it is not the rockie Earths he hath amongst the Mountains that can secure him."   First and last, the politician trod a difficult path; and, more than once or twice, his feet were besmirched with its mire, and were trapped and entangled in its thorns.

Yet Scotland would have fared happily, if she had been permitted to keep his hand on the helm of affairs.   Within her borders he was the one man of his time, Professor Hume Brown has said with truth, who can be regarded as a states-man; and the eulogy is only a modern version of the older testimony that, in the hour of crisis, he " did give most and best advice in every purpose."   We recall what Catherine de Medici told the Huguenots about Gaspard de Coligny: " If the Admiral were dead, I would not offer you a cup of cold water."   Archibald Campbell was equally indispensable to the men who trusted him; and good John Howie of Lochgoin is as true as he is epigrammatic, when he declares that he had " piety for a Christian, sense for a counsellor, courage for a martyr, and a soul for a king."

Piety for a Christian: that is Argyll's enduring diadem. His Protestantism had always been beyond dispute.   While he was quite young—just approaching his majority, if we adopt the conclusion, arrived at by Mr. Willcock in his exhaustive biography, that he was born in 1607—his father, going over to the Roman Catholic Church, had been com-pelled to surrender to his eldest son the family inheritance and more than one public office.   But a man may be a zealous Protestant who has no vital faith; and it was not for ten years more that the new ruler of western Scotland from

Ben Cruachan to the Mull of Kintyre bowed, in lowliness of trust and obedience, before the Master who is greater than he. In the *Analecta*, that voluminous and delectable note-book, we read that he owed his soul to Alexander Henderson. "During the Assembly at Glasgow, Mr. Henderson and other ministers spent many nights in prayer with the Marquis of Argyll; and he dated either his conversion or the knowledge of it from these times." It was at the epoch-making Assembly, moreover, that he first confessed his ecclesiastical predilections. When the King's Commissioner left the High Church and the resolute ministers, Argyll advised them to persevere as if nothing had happened. His sympathy with them had been secret too long, he avowed; henceforward he would espouse their cause in the light of day and against all challengers. The Moderator could not refrain from giving open expression to his gladness over so notable a recruit. "Though we had not a nobleman to assist us," he said, and there was no braggadocio in the valiant words, "our cause were not the worse nor the weaker; but occasion is given us to bless God that they are coming in daily."

Scotland's first citizen never withdrew his championship of the Covenanters, and never became lukewarm in their defence. In the warfare of religion he was free from the uncertainties and reserves which weakened his influence, and cast some doubts over his fortitude, in the campaigns of the clans; "his authority and wise courage," Baillie says, "has much stopped the mouths of our enemies." The chivalry was to cost him dear. It made him adversaries among the men whose season of holiday and lordship began when Charles Stuart returned from vagabondage to the throne. "Underhand Argayll," Rothes dubs him in a letter written a month before the Restoration—Rothes, the degenerate son of the old Earl who figured in the Greyfriars at the swearing of the Covenant. Middleton, too, coveted for himself some of the Marquis's estates and prerogatives. But, what was worst of all, the sequel showed that the monarch was determined to crush the strongest of his Scottish lieges. There were to be no Dukedoms and decorations for Archibald

Campbell, although they had been promised him on the word of a king.

No, but something very different. Six weeks after Charles entered London, the Marquis went south to congratulate him. He had been warned of the danger of the journey; there were observant friends who saw the storm impending. But he would not admit a doubt of his royal master's constancy; he steadfastly set his face to go up to his Jerusalem. "That is a fatal man," Lord Chancellor Clarendon whispered to his son when he caught sight of him in London streets; and the ill-omened adjective meant that Argyll's execution was already fixed and that the blow would soon descend. The sovereign never allowed him to come nearer his presence than the precincts of Whitehall; as soon as his arrival was known, he commanded Sir William Fleming to imprison him in the Tower. There, through summer and autumn and early winter, he lay in chains, relieving to some extent the monotony of the long confinement by composing a little book of *Instructions to a Son.* "'Tis better to trust in valour than in policy," he affirmed in one of its brief essays; and if the sentence stirs a certain astonishment, as coming from one whose statecraft had been more conspicuous than his hardihood where the swords clash and fire leaps from the muskets, it was to summarise his own splendid steadfastness of soul during the supreme weeks in front of him. In December he was sent back to Scotland by sea, to stand his trial before the Parliament in Edinburgh. It was a trial which might have been omitted altogether, no process of justice, but a travesty of righteous procedure. The judges had decided from the commencement what the end was to be. "The M. of Argyl," wrote James Sharp on the 7th of February 1661, "is to be arraigned upon Moonday nixt; the most able advocats cannot be induced to plead for him, concluding him a gone man."

Judges and advocates understood the wishes of Charles, and they were unvexed by scruples of conscience. All sorts of obstacles were thrown in the prisoner's way. The young lawyers who at length were persuaded to defend him—

ARCHIBALD CAMPBELL, FIRST MARQUIS OF ARGYLL.

Robert Sinclair, and John Cunningham, and George Mackenzie, the last the "Bluidy Mackenzie" of later decades —were shamefully threatened and bullied. He had insufficient time allotted him to prepare any vindication of himself. He was hurried from examination to examination. Yet, although there were no fewer than fourteen counts in the elaborate indictment; although now his Covenanting, and now his harassing of Montrose, and then his compliance with Cromwell, and again his questioning of the divine right of kings, was the charge which he had to rebut; although the weary debates dragged their slow length along from January until the latter part of May: he did not once lose heart, and he succeeded in making his essential innocence so incontrovertible that even the venal tribunal before which he stood began to feel itself perplexed and baffled. Could it be that the victim, who had been marked for the scaffold, was to escape its toils and to regain his liberty? Here and there he found his sympathisers, who had nerve enough to range themselves on his side; there is no flock of black sheep but shows one or two snowy fleeces. One day the leader of this gallant minority was speaking on his friend's behalf, when suddenly a peremptory knocking was heard at the door. It was a messenger who had ridden post-haste from London, from the Duke of Albemarle, the Duke whom the country knew as General Monck, and who brought from his Grace a packet of old letters which the Marquis had written years before. They were opened. They supplied the one argument for which the unjust arbiters in the Parliament House were searching, to excuse the crime which they were pledged to commit. On the evidence of a turncoat they condemned the truer man at their bar.

In the packet were six letters, the earliest dated in July 1653 and the latest in September 1654, the first three being addressed to Colonel Lilburn and the others to Monck himself. It was the time when, in the North country, the Earls of Middleton and Glencairn were leading their futile military insurrection in support of Charles. As best he could, Argyll had to steer his course between the beetling crag of Scylla and the roaring pool of Charybdis. He was himself Royalist at heart; but, with the prudence which was always so dominant a trait in his character, he had no desire, in those days of Cromwell's supremacy, to show frankly his attachment to the exiled Stuart prince. The men of his own house, however, were the foes of this neutral and carefully balanced policy. His son, Lord Lorne, with whom indeed he had more than one sharp quarrel, had, in opposition to his wishes, openly joined Charles's lieutenants in the Highlands. Here, then, was the father's dilemma: If he stayed behind, in Inverary or Edinburgh, his fealty to the King would be called in question, while, if he disclosed in any unequivocal way his sympathies with the insurrection, he broke the troth he had sworn a few months previously to the Commonwealth, and violated promises which had been very definitely given. It was a cruel perplexity; but, in the end, he decided that he must keep faith with Oliver, and, to prove the genuineness of his goodwill, he offered to send to headquarters what information he could glean regarding the movements of the royal forces. In the first letter, he bewails the conduct of his son: "I put it to him to declare unto me if he was free from engagements with those people now stirring. He declared that he was not resolved to engage with them"—an exceedingly guarded negative; "howsoever, immediately after his going out of my sight, he took horse and went to Glenorquhy, where it seems he had appointed a meeting with Auchinbreck, M'Naughton, Sir Arthur Forbes, and such as are of that crew." The second letter adds new details of Lord Lorne's proceedings, and sets down the names of some who were prominent in the revolt. In the third, the writer makes fervent profession of his own sincerity: "I trust in the Lord, whatsoever the malice of men shall either openly calumniate me in or privately suggest against me, my way shall be found straight, and that in His strength alone who is only able to sustain His own." The fourth recounts his efforts to procure the payment of Cess to the English Government. The fifth tells how he has succeeded in intercepting some of the enemy's papers.

The last is another eager *apologia pro vita sua*: "Though I shall not go about to excuse my ignorance or weakness, yet upon the exactest trial that can be, which I beg may be taken, if your Honor"—it is Monck whom he is addressing—"find any want in me either of honesty or affection to the service your Honor is about, I shall be content to be accoumpted and used as a most unworthy person." These were the fateful letters which secured the Marquis's destruction. It will be granted at once that they were sufficient for the purpose. So strongly was this realised that, whenever they had been read, the friends of Argyll left the court; they confessed that nothing could avail him now. But, at the bar of history, what condemnation is heavy enough for General Monck? If his victim had, through stress of circumstances, parleyed with the Commonwealth and rendered it some slight assistance, he had himself been one of its most signal and indefatigable captains, forgetting nothing which might establish its rule and promote its prosperity. He had changed camps and causes just in time to gain high rank among Charles's courtiers; but his must have been a conscience hardened to adamant, and seared as with a hot iron, when he could pursue to death one whose offences were a thousandfold smaller than his own.

The sentence was relentless. The prisoner was bidden kneel down. "I will, in all humility," he replied, and suited the action to the word. Then the verdict was read: "That Archibald Campbell, Marquis of Argyll, is found guilty of high treason, and is adjudged to be execute to the death as a traitor, his head to be severed from his body at the Cross of Edinburgh, upon Monday, the twenty-seventh instant, and to be affixed in the same place where the Marquis of Montrose's head was formerly." He craved a respite of ten days, that he might address a last petition to his King; probably he anticipated the curt and pitiless refusal with which the trifling boon was vetoed. But no shadow of misgiving darkened his spirit; whatever had been frail and faulty and crooked in his nature appeared to fall from him in his closing hours, and the inner dignity of the man—the

piety of the Christian—shone forth unmistakably. "I had
the honour to set the crown on the King's head," he said,
"and now he hastens me to a better crown than his own."
Then, looking round on the crowded benches, he spoke his
final message to his persecutors. "You have the indemnity
of an earthly King in your hands, and have denied me a
share in that; but you cannot hinder me from the indemnity
of the King of kings. Shortly you must be before His
tribunal. I pray He mete not out such measure to you as
you have done to me." It is not too much to say that this
sufferer seemed to be baptized into the forgiving ruth of
Calvary, and that the younger brother reminds us in his
more finite measure of the Elder and His exceeding grace.

It was Saturday, the 25th of May 1661; within two days
his fight would be over. He employed the brief pause very
nobly. In the Tolbooth he found the Marchioness waiting
for him—the Lady Margaret Douglas she had been, until
she was wedded to Lord Lorne five-and-thirty summers past
and gone. "They have given me," he told her with quiet
gentleness, "till Monday to be with you, my dear"; and she
flung herself into his arms in an agony of weeping, crying
out, "The Lord will require it! The Lord will require it!"
But it was not on this Saturday for the first time that she
felt the sharpness of the heartbreak; through ten long years
the doom awaiting her husband had risen with her every
morning. "After King Charles's Coronation," Wodrow says,
"when he was in Stirling, the Marquis waited long for an
opportunity to deal freely with the King anent his going
contrary to the Covenant, and favouring the Malignants, and
other sins. And Sabbath night, after supper, he went in
with him to his closet, and there used a great deal of freedom
with him, and the King was seemingly sensible, and they
came that length as to pray and mourn together till two or
three in the morning. And when at that time he came
home to his Lady, she was surprised, and told him she never
knew him so untimeous. He said, he had never had such a
sweet night in the world, and told her all—what liberty they
had in prayer, and how much concerned the King was. She

said plainly, they were 'crocodile tears,' and that night would cost him his head." Thus it is that love purges the vision as with euphrasy and rue, and lays heavy burdens on the soul; and now, the predestined hour having come, its gloomiests forecasts were proving all too true.

But in his breast her husband wore the Flower of Peace, "the rose that cannot wither." All his life the Marquis had reproached himself, not wholly without reason, for his nervousness and timidity; even in prison, he confessed, he had hitherto been somewhat inclined to fear. But, since he hearkened to the death-warrant, these alarms, like birds of bad omen, had spread their dusky wings and flown away. "For my part," he said, "I am as content to be here," among the felons in the common gaol, "as in the Castle, and I was as content in the Castle as in the Tower of London, and there I was as content as when at liberty; and I hope to be as content upon the scaffold as in any of them all." He could ascribe the surgeless calm to nothing else than the special mercy of God. Both nights he slept soundly, as his bedfellow, David Dickson, could testify. On the Monday morning he rose early; for he had papers to subscribe, and letters to compose, and many friends to see. But it was no longer possible to hide that mystic gladness of the Holy Ghost which possessed him. "I thought to have concealed the Lord's goodness," he broke out; "but it will not do. I am ordering my affairs, and God is sealing my charter to a better inheritance. He is just now saying to me, *Son, be of good cheer, thy sins are forgiven.*" Argyll was tasting no draught of death, but an elixir of life.

To the end the brave equanimity was maintained. He forewarned the ministers who visited him that, in the years which were impending, they must "either suffer much or sin much"; for there would be no neutral zone, where they could denude themselves of their responsibilities. He wrote King Charles who had pursued him to his doom, and there was not a syllable of querulous complaint in the letter to his "Most Sacred Sovereign"; there was nothing else than the assertion of his freedom from every misdemeanour except that of a forced acquiescence in Cromwell's domination, "which was an epidemic disease and fault of the time"; this assertion, and the entreaty that his widow and children should not suffer on his account; and then the prayer that "your Majesty and your successors may always sway the sceptre of these nations, and that they may be a blessed people under your government." It was now almost two o'clock, the time which had been fixed for the execution; and the officer told him that they must hasten. He rose at once, and moved towards the door, taking farewell of one and another in the room. "I could die like a Roman," he said, in words which have never been forgotten; "but I choose rather to die like a Christian. Come away, gentlemen; he that goes first goes cleanliest." On the way down the stair, he called James Guthrie to him—James Guthrie who, within a week, was to follow him along the road of martyrdom. The two bondmen and freemen of Christ embraced each other. "My Lord," Guthrie assured him, "God has been with you, He is with you, and He will be with you. Such is my respect for your Lordship that, if I were not under the sentence of death myself, I could cheerfully die for your Lordship." So those who were ready to be offered up greeted one another, as they went joyously to the altar-fires.

On the scaffold he bore himself as a courteous gentleman. He bowed with grave serenity to those whom he found waiting for him. Then, after one of the ministers had prayed, he spoke his farewell words to the crowd. He would say nothing, he declared, regarding the hardness of the sentence; "I bless the Lord," he added, "I pardon all men, as I desire to be pardoned myself." He professed again his devotion to His Majesty's person and government; "I was real and cordial in my desires to bring the King home, and in my endeavours for him when he was at home." His regard for the earthly monarch was secondary only to his more consuming affection for the Heavenly. "It is the duty of every Christian to be loyal; yet I think the order of things is to be observed as well as their nature. Religion must not be in the cockboat, but in the ship. God must have what is His, as well as Cæsar what is his. Those are the best subjects that are the best Christians." Indeed, no Roman of them all, not Marcus Regulus in the splendour of his captivity and sacrifice in Carthage, had a grander ending than this. "I stayed and saw him die," says Elrigmore in Mr. Munro's story; "I saw his head up and his chin in the air as behoved his quality, the day he went through that noisy, crowded, causied Edinburgh—Edinburgh of the doleful memories, Edinburgh whose ports I never enter but I feel a tickling at the nape of my neck, as where a wooden collar should lie before the shear fall."

When the last speech was done, another of the ministers prayed; and afterwards the Marquis carried the requests of his own soul to God in petitions which lingered in the memories of those who heard them. This was the time when Cunningham, his physician, as the doctor himself told Bishop Burnet, touched his patron's pulse, and discovered that it was beating at the usual rate, unhurried and strong. And now he went forward to the Maiden. "My Lord," said George Hutcheson the preacher, "hold your grip sicker"— keep your grasp unshaken on Him who is Faithful and True. "Mr. Hutcheson," Argyll answered, "you know what I said in the chamber; I am not afraid to be surprised with fear." Once more, in a clear voice, "as one entering on eternity and about to appear before his Judge," he proclaimed himself innocent of the accusations brought against him. Then he kneeled down, and, having prayed in silence, he gave the signal, the lifting up of his hand. The knife descended. Archibald Campbell of Argyll was with his Master Christ, where the saints are fully and eternally liberated not from their adversaries merely but from themselves.

CHAPTER V.

THE SHORT MAN WHO COULD NOT BOW.

ONE of John Bunyan's Minor Prophets is Mr. Standfast. When the Pilgrims come on him, they and he are near the termination of their journey. In the Enchanted Ground, "one of the last refuges that the enemy has," they find their new comrade on his knees, speaking earnestly to One who is above. He has been tempted by Madam Bubble, who has offered to make him great and happy; "she is never weary of commending her commodities," says Greatheart the guide. Not until Mr. Standfast gave himself to wrestling with God did the "tall comely dame," with her swarthy complexion, and a smile at the end of every sentence, and a great purse at her side into which her fingers were perpetually straying, go her ways and leave him victor on the field.

Among the Covenanters James Guthrie is Mr. Standfast's counterpart. The son of the Laird of Guthrie in Forfarshire, he might have claimed Madam Bubble's treasures. His father coveted Episcopal preferment for him, and at first his own wishes ran the same courtly road; in his youth he was "prelatic and strong for the ceremonies." There was one of his Bishop's daughters, too, whose face stole into his boyish heart, and he would joyfully have been her lover and knight. But other transports were moving him soon. He went from Brechin Grammar School to St. Andrews, where he gained repute for scholarship, and was made regent, or professor, of philosophy. And in the College cloisters his soul awoke no less than his mind. Samuel Rutherfurd's friendship was partly responsible for the change; and the weekly meetings

THE MONUMENT TO THE MARQUIS OF ARGYLL,
IN ST. GILES' CATHEDRAL.

E

which teachers and students held for prayer, where "Christ was in the midst, their Friend," did the rest. When James Guthrie left the University, it was to accept a call to a humble Presbyterian church. He had chosen the path which should lead him, not to a mitre, but to a crown of sharp cactus thorns. "I am not ashamed to give glory to God," he told the Parliament two months before he died, "that, until the year 1638, I was treading other steps; and the Lord did then graciously recover me out of the snare of Prelacy, Ceremonies, and the Service Book." Mr. Standfast had shaken off the allurements of the Enchanted Ground.

Just before he was ordained, he had an opportunity of showing the side which he had espoused. He signed the National Covenant. The act had a portentous accompaniment. On his way to inscribe his name, he encountered the town's hangman, "which did move him somewhat, and made him walk up and down a little before he went forward." There was in him, as in the best men of his age, a touch of old-world credulousness. This was a prophecy, he said to his beating heart. But, let the issues be what they might, there was no thought of swerving. With the vision of death in his eyes, he wrote his autograph.

He was minister of Christ's Gospel for two-and-twenty years, the time being divided between his two charges of Lauder and Stirling. By 1650, he had transferred his home from the Berwickshire village to the town which is "the grey bulwark of the North." It is with Stirling that we associate Guthrie's name. Here he spoke those sermons which "proved him a great master of reason." Here he lived out that character whose Christianity was never blurred and vague. Busy as he was in the government of the Church, James Cowie, his precentor and beadle and amanuensis, maintained that he kept his personal religion as newborn as if "he had been but a young convert"; and is it not a tribute to be envied? Nothing filled this *fidus Achates* with deeper awe than the prayers of his master at family worship. They chased and seized and condemned every besetting iniquity; and the listener felt that he was

himself being exposed and scourged. At last he could endure the poignant slings and arrows no longer. " Tell me
freely," he begged, " in what I have grieved you." But
James Guthrie disabused him. It was his own wicked heart,
the minister said, which he was humiliating, and they were
his own errors which he tracked with the sleuth-hounds of
self-scrutiny. It is an incident which casts the vividest
light on the strength of his convictions of sin, and on his
intimacy with the abysses of the soul. Once again we think
of Mr. Standfast, importuning for his life.

The manse at Stirling was an *ecclesiola Dei*, if one may
steal Philip Melanchthon's Latin—a little church of God.
We can cite another witness to the fact besides James Cowie.
To the minister and his wife—for Guthrie had won a better
helpmate than the Bishop's daughter after whom his green love
hankered—Isabel Dougal was maidservant, a maidservant who
was an " elect lady " also. She had much to relate in after
years of her experiences. Once her master caught her contra-
dicting her mistress. " Isabel," he said, " I thought you had
learned that which is enjoined you by the Spirit of God,
Not answering again "; and the reproof did its work. No
weak place could she detect in Mr. Guthrie's armour, unless
it were his carelessness about money, an infirmity with which
many of the saints have been touched. " My heart," he
would say to Mrs. Guthrie, " I am going a journey on the
affairs of the Church, and you must get me fifty merks ";
though where the silver merks were to come from neither
mistress nor maid could divine. It is heartsome reading that,
when Isabel and the precentor were married, Guthrie insisted,
gentleman that he was, that he must give the bride away.
And very touching is the ultimate record of his affection for
those true helpers. In the Tolbooth James Cowie was
writing as his clerk. " I have one other letter," the prisoner
said, " for choice Christian friends, although I know not who
they are." The secretary set down the glowing sentences;
and the mystery flashed on their author's mind. " James ! "
he cried, " it is to your wife and you that I must send this
letter." There must have been an aroma of the better

country haunting ever afterwards the latest bequest of the man these two revered.

Everything in the Stirling home is " holy, happy, healthy," as the good Silurist portrays the home above. There was a time when, in one of the rooms, James Guthrie lay at the gates of death. His attendant was at the bedside, and the sick man bade him read the ninth chapter of the Epistle to the Romans. But at the words, *I will have mercy on whom I will have mercy*, the listener burst into tears. " I have nothing else to lippen to," he said—no sentence to lean upon, so stable as this pronouncement of Sovereignty and Love. In those anxious days his friends literally prayed him back to life. Most peremptory among them was Johnston of Wariston. " Lord," he wept, " Thou knowest the Church cannot want him."

Wariston was right. The Church could not spare the leader in Synod and Assembly. He drew up a shrewd little treatise on Elders and Deacons, which sometimes has been ascribed in mistake to his cousin, the writer of *The Christian's Great Interest*. His fingers, too, helped to pen the pamphlet on *The Causes of the Lord's Wrath against Scotland*, which was to furnish his opponents with a weapon they would use to his hurt. That was in September and October 1651, when the leaders of the Remonstrant party in the Church met, first in Glasgow and then in Edinburgh, to consider their domestic troubles, and to arrive at the conclusion that sin, personal and ministerial and official and national, was the spring and origin of these—the sin of crowning Charles Stuart at Scone being greatest and chief. Hugh Kennedy had something to do with the composition of the manifesto, and probably Archibald Johnston suggested a sentence here and there. But Guthrie's was the principal hand in preparing it for Christopher Higgins, the printer ; and the crime was not forgotten when he came to thole his last assize. Yet, built of oak and iron as he seemed to be, he carried an inexhaustible sweetness of temper into the debates of the Kirk. If he found any heat of passion bubbling up, and the patience of Christ being forgotten, he would say, " We must give over now." Stoutest of the Protesters although he was, he had rather lose the battle in logic than offend against the royal law. Beneath the life spent in a hundred conflicts, there lay and brooded and sang a spirit attuned to melody.

It is time, however, to make fuller acquaintance with Mr. Standfast in his soldier's dress: Mr. "Sickerfoot" was the very name the Malignants of Stirling devised for him. Some episodes in his career—episodes ten years older than the Restoration—provide us with unanswerable proof of his boldness.

We see him, at eight of a May morning, in company with Robert Trail,—Robert Trail, who, for this and similar misdemeanours, was yet to spend many years of his life in exile at Rotterdam,—going by order of the Assembly to the Tolbooth, to speak to the Marquis of Montrose. It is the proud chieftain's time of dolour, and to-morrow is his execution day. But he is as intrepid as he has always been. Will James Guthrie quail before him? Far from that. He will do his duty, without harshness and without compromise. He tells Montrose that his natural temper is "too aspiring and lofty"; that he did wrong to enlist Irish rebels among his followers; that he ought not to have violated the Covenant. And the Marquis, being a poet and a scholar, is playsome and eloquent. He mixes his discourse with "many Latin apothegms." He argues with the ministers that they are chargeable with the death of Charles the First. "Error is infinite"—that is his sententious axiom. "I am very sorry that any actions of mine have been offensive to the Church of Scotland": it is the one concession which he makes. There must have been yearning and regret in Guthrie's heart, when he took good-bye of the imperious cavalier.

Or let us look at him as he deals with the Earl of Middleton. There is a plot to coax the younger Charles to forsake the Committee of Estates, and to trust himself to the easy-going soldier and his friends. The prince is willing enough; but the conspiracy is unmasked. Then the Commission of Assembly appoints the minister of Stirling to read in his own church sentence of excommunication on Middleton. Going to worship on the Sabbath, he is met by a stranger who hands him a letter. It contains a request from

the King, the Committee of Estates, and the Commission re-
pentant now of its venturesomeness and zeal, that the
excommunication may be delayed.   The bell has rung out
its last note, and the minister can scarcely decide how to
act.   " Dear Heart," his wife counsels, " what the Lord gives
you clearness to do, that do."   And, after sermon, the em-
barrassment has vanished.   Let whoever will be angry, the
Assembly's verdict, Guthrie feels, must be proclaimed.   Proclaimed it is, and the country learns of it, and, although the ban
is lifted from his head three months later in Dundee, John
Middleton never forgives the man who has denounced him.

And he crosses swords with Charles himself.   Being unable to bow acquiescently in any house of Rimmon, he has
preached against the Public Resolutions " as involving ane
conjunctione with the malignant partie in the land."   The
King summons him, and his colleague, David Bennet, who is
of one mind with him, to Perth, where in the days before
Worcester he holds his court.   But if he fancies that he will
overawe so undaunted a fighter, he learns his miscalculation
immediately.   James Guthrie is King's man to the core of
his nature, and will render to Cæsar every penny that is
Cæsar's.   But, first and last and midst, he is Christ's man.
He informs his prince that, while he owns his authority in
civil affairs, he must not meddle with matters of religion ;
and for this recalcitrance he is ordered to remain in ward in
Perth for a time.   It is Andrew Melville risen to life once more.

Most notable of all, were his two encounters with Cromwell.   The first took place in the late autumn of 1648, when
the commander of the Ironsides was lodged in the house of
the Earl of Moray in the Canongate of Edinburgh.   Three
Presbyterian ministers went to visit him—Robert Blair,
David Dickson, and James Guthrie.   With " a fair flourish
of words," as they reported afterwards, the leader of the
Sectaries talked with them, punctuating his conversation
with tears and with fervent appeals to God to bear witness
to his sincerity.   They asked him a triplet of questions.   To
begin with, what did he think of monarchical government ?
and he replied that it pleased him well.   Then, did he

approve of religious toleration? and from such lips the answer amazes us, for they understood him to say "No." Finally, what was his opinion concerning the rule and direction of the Church of Christ? should it be Episcopal or Independent or Presbyterian? but now he complained that he was being pressed too severely, and that he must have time to deliberate. As they turned from the room, Dickson avowed his gladness in having heard "this man speak as he did." But Robert Blair, like too many of his Covenanting kinsfolk, had come to the colloquy predisposed against Mr. Carlyle's blameless paladin, and pronounced his very emotion false and feigned. "He is a dissembler," he retorted impatiently. "Away with him! he is a greeting devil." Guthrie's second interview with Cromwell was in April 1651, when the Lord General was in Glasgow. There, "on Sunday forenoon," as Principal Baillie reports, Oliver heard "Mr. Robert Ramsay preach a very honest sermon"; and, in the afternoon, the commander and his staff still being auditors, Mr. John Carstares lectured, and Mr. James Durham "gave a fair enough testimony against the Sectaries"—the iron warrior and his friends seated in the pews of the High Kirk. The Englishmen had their own thoughts about the plain-spoken theology; and, next day, Cromwell invited the ministers to a conference. Guthrie and Patrick Gillespie were the advocates of the Covenanters; the Puritan leader himself, with Major-General Lambert, upheld the tenets of the mailed and helmeted saints. One longs to read the minutes of the discussion; but the record has not survived. "We had no disadvantage in the thing," Baillie asserts with Presbyterian pertinacity; but one of his rivals is as positive that victory lay with the other party—"Sure I am there was no such weight in their arguments as might in the least discourage us." This is certain, that Oliver kept the figure of one of his antagonists enshrined in his recollection. When he told the story, or when James Guthrie's name was mentioned, he had his significant epithet for the preacher. "That short man who could not bow" was what he called him.

Thus steadily Mr. Sickerfoot walked to the grim consummation of his pilgrimage. A man of his calibre could not look for any favours, when the reign of riot and misrule was inaugurated. He had never wished to escape the confessor's garland; like Ignatius of Antioch, who dissuaded his fellow-Christians from asking God to spare his life, he hungered for it rather. Once, in Stirling, he was talking with some brother-ministers about "predominant sins"; and he owned that his was a too "masterful desire to suffer a public and violent death for Christ and His cause." The swift exodus, he said, was greatly better than protracted sickness. Imprisoned by disease, a man might lose his senses, and might renounce the vigour of his trust. But from the scaffold, if he was reproached for the Name's sake, he "stepped into eternity with the utmost distinctness and in the immediate exercise of prayer and faith." Was it a "predominant sin"—this solicitude for the bitterness and the blessedness of the Cross? Only the suppliant who knew its intensity could brand it so; and, too soon for those who drew strength from his communion, his prayer was fulfilled, and from the gallows he leaped in a moment to the breast of God.

At the close of August in the Restoration year, he, with some of his spiritual kinsfolk, drew up an address to the King. They prayed for the safety of His Majesty's person. With bowed knees and bended affections, they besought him to employ his power for the conservation of the Reformed religion. They told him of their anxiety that he should prosecute the ends of the Covenants he had sworn. "It is the desire of our souls," they concluded, "that your Majesty may be like unto David, a man after God's own heart; like unto Solomon, of an understanding heart to discern betwixt good and bad; like unto Jehoshaphat, whose heart was lifted up in the ways of the Lord; like unto Josias, who was of a tender heart, and did humble himself before God." The annals of Britain would have been less gleeful and sprightly, but more august, if the King's ambitions had harmonised in one detail with the purposes of this little band of his Scottish subjects.

But Charles did not dream of a theocracy. Before many hours had gone, the ten preachers, and one of the two lay-

men, who framed the exacting and ethereal address, were
prisoners in Edinburgh Castle.   James Guthrie was never to
be free again.   He was transferred to Stirling, and, afterwards,
to Dundee; and then was brought back to Edinburgh; but
his confinement was not once relaxed.   Sharp hated the
whole-hearted Protester,—a "hairbrain rebel," he called him,
who " though less criminous than others," deserved " because
of his pertinatiousnes to be the only sacrifice of our coat";
and Middleton was eager to punish the man who had excommunicated him.   The indictment charged Guthrie with the
authorship of *The Causes of the Lord's Wrath*, with writing
the petition which led to his apprehension, with denying the
King's power over the Church, and with utterances which
savoured of treason.   The net was drawn fast round the victim.

In February 1661, and again in April, he spoke in
his defence before the Drunken Parliament.   One of his
lawyers—was it Cunningham or Nisbet ?—bore frank witness
to the skill he displayed.   Not merely did he outwit the
advocates in questions of divinity, but he surpassed them in
their own fields; he might almost have been President of
the Court.   But better than his cleverness was his courage.
"Throughout the whole course of my life," he boasted
humbly, "I have studied to be serious, and not to deal with
a slack hand in what I did look upon as my duty."   "My
Lord," he said, as he drew the April speech to its conclusion,
"my conscience I cannot submit; but this old crazy body
and mortal flesh I do submit, to do with it whatsoever you
will, whether by death or banishment or imprisonment or
anything else."   *My conscience I cannot submit*: it is the
creed in five words of all good soldiers of Jesus Christ, the
Iliad of the martyrs in a nutshell.

In a thin house sentence was pronounced; for, after they
had heard him, members slipped away, unwilling to be responsible for his bloodshedding.   He was to be hanged at
the Cross on Saturday, the 1st of June; his head was to be
fixed on the Netherbow; his estate was to be confiscated:
so the decision ran.   While the Clerk was entering it on his
parchments, they put him out from the chamber, among

JAMES GUTHRIE.

the rude pikemen crowded at the door; but they could not mar his tranquillity; he thought he had never enjoyed more of Christ's consolations than then. Soon he was recalled, to hear the doom; and, when James Cowie saw him next, his master had a sort of majesty about him, and his features shone, as Stephen's did, when the Pharisees stoned him and "God's glory smote him on the face." Guthrie had his wish, and was going home to the wealthy place by the straightest path. Everything seemed to befriend him. He told his wife that he was more fortunate than the Marquis of Argyll; "for my lord was beheaded, but I am to be hanged on a Tree as my Saviour was." One is sorrier for wife than for husband. "I but trouble you," she wept as she went away; "I must now part from you." And he replied, already a tenant of the Heavenlies, "Henceforth I know no one after the flesh." He panted to be clear of the happiest entanglements, and to answer the welcome of his Redeemer.

On the Friday evening he dictated a number of letters, with Robert Wodrow's father for his scribe. He signed and sealed them himself, the seal bearing the family crest; but instantly he turned it round, and drew it over the new-made impression, and thus obliterated the heraldry. "I have no more to do with coats of arms," he explained. He supped heartily, though generally he was very abstemious; and then he slept an unbroken sleep, until four o'clock in the morning, when he sat up, and poured out his longings in prayer. The sunlight came streaming in, and James Cowie asked how he did. "Very well," he answered; "*this is the day which the Lord hath made; let us be glad and rejoice in it.*" And now "the best was at hand," as a friend had written—now, while his adversaries "got the foil," he was to "get the victory." He would have walked unbound to the gallows; but they tied his hands, as if he were a common thief. Along with him, to share his death, went Captain William Govan, a blunt Protester soldier. Two or three steps up the ladder, where he could be seen easily by the crowd, Guthrie halted to make his last speech. "I durst not redeem my life with the loss of my integrity," he said; "I did judge it better to suffer

than to sin." And, again: "My corruptions have been
strong and many, and have made me a sinner in all things,
yea, even in following my duty; and therefore righteousness
have I none of my own. But I do believe that *Jesus Christ
came into the world to save sinners, whereof I am chief.*" And,
yet again: " I take God to record, I would not exchange this
scaffold with the palace or mitre of the greatest prelate in
Britain." There was a dignity about his features as he
spoke, and onlookers thought they had "not seen more of
God at the most solemn Communion." When at last the
executioner was ready, James Guthrie's voice was heard once
more. " *Art Thou not from everlasting,*" he called in far-
carrying tones, " *O Lord my God, my Holy One? I shall
not die.*" Then, just before the end, he lifted the napkin
from his face, and cried, "The Covenants, the Covenants
shall yet be Scotland's reviving!"

" Now there was a great calm at that time in the River;
wherefore Mr. Standfast, when he was about half-way in,
stood awhile and talked to his companions. 'I see myself
at the end of my journey,' he said; 'my toilsome days are
ended. I have formerly lived by hearsay and faith; but
now I go where I shall live by sight, and shall be with Him
in whose company I delight myself. I have loved to hear
my Lord spoken of, and, wherever I have seen the print of
His shoe in the earth, there I have coveted to set my foot
too. He has held me, and I have kept me from mine
iniquities; yea, my steps hath He strengthened in His way.'"

They had kept Guthrie's soldier-friend waiting meantime
on the scaffold. He saw the martyr's body suspended lifeless
in the air, but the spectacle had no terrors for him; it was
a remembrancer of the Hill of the Cross, and of the victory
which the Saviour of men had won through the endurance
of sorrow and shame. "It is sweet! it is sweet!" he
exclaimed; "otherwise how durst I look upon the corpse of
him who hangs there, and smile upon these sticks and that
gibbet as the gates of heaven?" When Perpetua went out
into the amphitheatre at Carthage to face the wild bull which
was to toss and gore her to death, she spoke of it as her

"day of coronation"; and William Govan had learned the same proud and jubilant dialect. He was no more than thirty-eight years old, but he had been a Christian since he was a boy of fourteen; and he uttered now his good confession, "Sin and suffering have been presented to me, and I have chosen the suffering part." Eight or nine summers before, he had been a private in Middleton's army; and he recalled their former association, that he might emphasise the contrast which separated them by more than the difference of East and West: "The Commissioner and I were in the fields together for one cause; but I have the cord about my neck, and he is promoted to be His Majesty's Commissioner. Yet for a thousand worlds I would not change lots with him—praise and glory be to Christ for ever!" The two who died on this first of June were well-matched, and which was the more indomitable it would be hard to determine.

Guthrie's mutilated body was piously cared for. While some friends were dressing it in one of the town churches, a young gentleman came in—George Stirling his name was found to be—and poured on it a bottle of rich perfume; and the place, like Simon's house in Bethany, was filled with the odour of the ointment. "God bless you, sir, for your labour of love!" one of the ministering ladies said. And as for the head up on the arch between the High Street and the Canongate, there is a pathetic memory attaching to it. Not that weird legend of the ruddy drops of blood, which it let fall on the Earl of Middleton's coach, and which all the nobleman's acids could not wash away. But the homelier tale of little William Guthrie, the martyr's four-year-old boy, in later years "a most serious seeker of God," who must run out to stand and study his father's face high on the city port, and then would return and tell his mother what he had been doing, and forthwith would lock himself into a room from which all her efforts could not draw him for many hours. It was a sore and heavy thing to be a Covenanter's child; but, for Mr. Sickerfoot's Willie, there was no head in the wide world so wreathed with beauty as the head which the soldiers had fastened on the Netherbow.

CHAPTER VI.

SHARP OF THAT ILK.

LORD MIDDLETON and the nobles who abetted him were not the only foes of the Church in the months that succeeded the Restoration. Bad as they were, they were not the worst foes. They had for prompter a man about whom a modern historian has written that, "in the most comprehensive sense of the word, he was a knave, *pur sang*"—a man whose life of calculating meanness happily has few parallels. "Sharp of that Ilk," Cromwell denominated him in a shrewd phrase: Sharp, of the clan and family of the Sharps; Sharp, whose name corresponded with his nature, cunning, clever in the baser forms of cleverness, owning only "as good a heart as can be made out of brains," governed consistently by self-interest and self-regard. Oliver was a discerner of spirits. He saw into James Sharp's soul as he saw into James Guthrie's; and he distrusted the one as thoroughly as he honoured the other.

Probably no one, in the long story of the Scottish Church, bears an uglier repute; and the scrutiny of scholars has rather blackened than brightened his record. His very handwriting, as it may be seen in the hundreds of letters he has left, is "small, paltry, niggling, and exceptionally annoying"; his style of composition is self-conceited and pedantic. We have his portrait, painted by Sir Peter Lely; few of his brother-Presbyters had the gold which could procure such immortality. The face is not repulsive; it has not the bold and coarse brutality of Lauderdale's. But it is not a spiritual face. The forehead is low. The eyes are furtive and yet alert; nothing escapes them; they have little pity and little patience; one does not associate them with "droppings of warm tears." The lips are thin and firmly closed. If the features do not excite actual disrelish, neither do they attract. They remind us of the man of the world much more than of the ambassador of Christ.

Sharp was born about the year 1613, in Banffshire, where his father was Sheriff-clerk and factor to the Earl of Findlater, his mother being "a gentlewoman of the name of Leslie." Neither at school nor at the University was he in any way distinguished; his intellect never climbed very high or plunged very deep. James Kirkton, in his *Secret and True History*, preserves a curious tale of his college days, perhaps apocryphal, certainly coloured by the hatred he aroused in later years. In bed one night with his comrade, he fell into loud laughter, which continued until the other awoke him and asked why he was so merry. He had been dreaming, he answered, that the Earl of Crawford appointed him minister of Crail—the height of his ambition in his wholesomer youth. Again he fell asleep, and again he laughed, more loudly than before; and now, when his companion recalled him to the solid earth, he was offended, for, said he, "I thought I was in a paradise, because the King had made me Archbishop of St. Andrews." "Then," rejoined his fellow, "I hope you will remember old friends." But soon he was dreaming once more, and to different purpose; for he "wept most lamentably for a long time." Being asked the cause of the alteration, he gave a reply which was tragic enough. "I dreamed that I was driving in a coach to hell, and that very fast." "What way he drove," adds Kirkton with grim brevity, "I shall not say."

Uncertainty hangs over his movements after he was done with the University. Apparently he was absent from Scotland for awhile, in Oxford and probably in London; because, when he returned to the metropolis, he was familiar with its streets and townsfolk. It is unlikely that he swore the Covenant in 1638; but, if he felt any aversion to subscribing the stringent deed, he managed to disguise it; when

we meet him next, it is, as his dream predicted, in the church
and manse of the Fifeshire village of Crail. One fears that
the breath of heaven did not blow through his sermons.
His letters, except when he denounces an opponent, are grey
and hard as the whinstone and cheerless as "the cold light
of stars." He never was an Evangelical; he never was
vanquished by the Cross; he had nothing more fundamental
to recommend than those *deeds of the law* by which, an
apostle says, *a man is not justified.* "Mr. Warner tells me,"
Wodrow relates, "that he was, before Archbishop Sharp's
death, in conversation with two ladies of good sense and very
serious. They told him that the bishop, when he and they
were talking about religion, and one in the company said
somewhat of the insufficiency of blamelessness and morality
for salvation, returned the reply, 'Be you good moralists,
and I'll warrant you!'" Our hearts are forced to compassionate the parishioners of Crail.

From the *Analecta*, too, a second anecdote may be
gleaned, which brings another impeachment against him.
In the manse of Kingsbarns, at no great distance from Crail,
lived a young lady whom Sharp wished to win for wife.
But, one Sabbath, being desirous to listen to a sermon from
his lips, and equally desirous that she should not be
recognised, Margaret Bruce contrived to veil her genuine
self, and took the road that ran to Crail. Her wooer
preached so well that all her hesitancies were swept away,
and she resolved to be his bride. But between cup and lip
much may intervene. For, going soon after into her father's
study, she found on the table a volume of sermons, freshly
come from England; and, turning its pages, she saw that one
was based on the text which she had heard James Sharp
expound with such ingenuity. She read it, and discovered
that it was the original which he had copied with a faithfulness too literal and undeviating. He stood before her for
what he was, no individual explorer of the realm of truth,
but a mere plagiarist. "Which providence opened her eyes
so clearly that, when he came again to renew his proposal,
she utterly rejected his offer."

The clergyman was much away from his parish. He was a man to whom the machinery and diplomacy of the Church were more interesting than its doctrine and its life. "I remember you have sometimes merrily called me a politician," he wrote to Patrick Drummond in the December of 1660; and Drummond's jest told the truth. A politician, and one who loved the underground passages of politics more than the breezier uplands, Sharp of that Ilk was from first to last. He fought for the Resolutioners; but we shall wrong his brethren if we conceive of them as animated by his spirit; David Dickson and Robert Douglas were severed from him, like sunshine from midnight. He was simply their indefatigable agent, a schemer with endless perseverance and secrecy and *savoir faire*. Many a time, and for months at a stretch, Crail would see nothing of him; he was busily occupied in London. Thus it happened in 1657 and 1658, when Wariston and Patrick Gillespie and James Guthrie enjoyed Cromwell's regard, and when "the great instrument of God to cross their evill designes," says Baillie in one of his letters to his cousin, "has been that very worthie, pious, wise, and diligent young man, Mr. James Sharp." Poor Baillie! he thinks it necessary to counsel so gracious an emissary to supplement the harmlessness of the dove with the wisdom of the serpent. "I pray God help you and guide you; you had need of a long spoon; trust no words nor faces; for all men are liars." The advice was superfluous, and the Church's messenger returned to Edinburgh to report a substantial victory. "He had gotten all the designes of the exceeding busie and bold Remonstrants defeat; and the Protector had dismissed him with very good words, assuring he should be loath to grant anything to our prejudice." And, therefore, "we blessed God that, by Mr. Sharp's labours, was keeped off us for a tyme a much feared storme." The blindness of Christian men is occasionally excessive. And nothing helps it more potently than the false and unworthy heat of party zeal.

The moment for Sharp's supreme treachery, and for the bitter awakening of his friends, was at hand. When

it was evident that events in England preluded the reinstate-
ment of the Stuarts, "our caynd honist Sherp frend"—the
characterisation and the spelling are those of the Earl of
Rothes—was again sent up to London as envoy of the
Kirk.   He was to take care that, when Charles did recross
the narrow seas, it should be as a Covenanted and Presbyterian monarch.   From the middle of February 1660 until
long after the King was in Whitehall, he remained in the
centre of intrigue and activity; and there were few of the
plots of those hurrying weeks in which he did not have a
finger.   "So knowing a bearer, whose usefulness in your
service sets him far above my recommendation": it was
with this benison that Lord Lauderdale introduced him to
his royal master.   But the Church had need of a truer
knight.   His succour meant humiliation and calamity for
the men who confided in his good faith.

    We require no evidence to condemn him beyond that
which he has himself supplied.   He had three correspondents during 1660 and 1661; and we are allowed to read
the letters he sent to them.   The first was Robert Douglas,
the brave minister.   The second was Patrick Drummond,
one of the Presbyterian clergymen in England.   The third
was the Earl of Middleton.   It might be hard at the time
for those who hoped against hope to abjure their trusted
agent; but, in what he says to these three, there is no difficulty now in tracing his "juggling, prevarication, and betrayal."

    On the 1st of March 1660, he writes Douglas from
London that "the Cavaliers point him out as the Scottish
Presbyter"; ten days later, that "Moderate Episcopacy is
setting up its head"; in the same week, that, along with
Calamy and Ash, the representatives of English Nonconformity, he has "convinced General Monck that a Commonwealth is unpracticable," and has "beaten him off that sconce
he hath hitherto maintained."   When April comes, he "sees
not full ground of hope that Covenant terms will be rigidly
stuck to"; by the middle of the month, he is sure that
"the business of religion will be altogether waived in the
treaty" with the King; before the end of it, he "smells

JAMES SHARP.

After a painting by Sir Peter Lely.

that Moderate Episcopacy is the fairest accommodation." And,
all this while, Douglas is encouraging him to keep unshaken
his loyalty. "It is best that Presbyterian government be
settled simply; for we know by experience that Moderate
Episcopacy — what can it be other than Bishops with
cautions?—is the next step to Episcopal tyranny, which
will appear very soon above board if that ground once be
laid. You know the old saying, *Perpetua dictatura via ad
imperium.*" But the wise words were spoken in vain. In
May, Sharp was over in Breda at Charles's court; and
afterwards Robert Douglas confessed that now he began
to have his suspicions: "The first thing that gave me a
dislike at him was that, when he was in Holland, he wrote
to me in commendation of Hyde, an enemy to our nation
and Presbyterial government." Yet the delegate of the
Covenanters continued to assert his fidelity in unequivocal
terms. He told how, when he met the King—the King,
"who surpasseth all ever I heard or expected of him"—
he found him very affectionate to Scotland, and resolved
not to wrong the settled worship and discipline of the
Church. He assured his correspondent that, while Presbytery was a lost cause in England, he could not believe that
the Service Book was to be forced on the Scots; "you
know," he added, "I am against Episcopacy, root and
branch." Again, on the 16th of June, when Charles had
been three weeks in London, this was his diagnosis of events:
"The present posture of affairs looks like a ship foundered
with the waves from all corners, so that it is not known
what course will be steered; but discerning men see that
the gale is like to blow for the Prelatic party; and those
who are sober will yield to a Liturgy and Moderate
Episcopacy, which they phrase to be Effectual Presbytery;
and, by this salvo, they think they guard against breach
of Covenant. But I know," our Bayard asserts, "this
purpose is not pleasing to you, neither to me." And so
things went on, until his return to Scotland in autumn,
when he carried with him a letter from the King, promising
to protect and defend the Church, "as it was settled by

law." Some ambiguity hung about the stipulation; but the ministers of Edinburgh interpreted it as their wishes impelled, and read it as a gracious manifesto in vindication of the Covenanted cause. " They thought it not enough," Kirkton narrates, " to praise it in their pulpits, but bought for it a silver box, a shrine for such a precious relic."

The letters to Patrick Drummond take up the tale after Sharp is again in the north; probably, although they were addressed to this Presbyterian minister, they were intended mainly for the eyes of Lauderdale, Secretary at Court for Scottish business, and all-powerful with His Majesty. In them are the same tones of injured innocency, the same protestations that the writer has not deflected by a hairbreadth from his principles. " The course of my life, I bless the Lord, will not give evidence of my ambition and covetousness; I have served the interests of others more than my own; I never did seek anything of any; whatever lot I may meet with, I scorn to prostitute my conscience and honesty to base unbecoming allurements ":— there surely speaks an unsullied captain. If his friend asks his creed in a sentence, "well, I am a Scot and a Presbyter." If he desires a glimpse of his bulwark and fortress, "my fence is in God, who knoweth that my regard to my country and this Kirk doth preponder any selfish consideration." But, by and by, the hidden man of the heart discloses himself more freely. " I do cheyn my affection to that stream of providence which may make it to be well with the King, and your master, my lord; I am no phanatick, nor a lover of their way under whatsoever refyned form ": the accents of the opportunist rise to the surface in such words. Yet how weary he was of logomachies! If he could not have leave to retire amongst his books and to bewail there the evils which folly and pride had brought on his native land, then

> Waft me from the harbour-mouth,   ·
> Wild wind! I seek a warmer sky—

" I must think *de mutando solo*, and breathing in an aire where I may be without the reach of the noyse and

pressoures of the confusions coming." Ah, but we hear
the snarl of the tiger sometimes. In the end of 1660,
there is a message through no intermediary but direct to
Lauderdale. It is a revelation of the genuine James Sharp.
In it his hate of the Protesters has frank avowal, and we
learn whose the malice was which inspired the worst excesses of the persecution. "I fear there can be no remedy
against this malady without exercising severity upon the
leading impostors, Guthiree, Gillespy, Rutherford, which will
daunt the rest of the hottheads, who in time may be beat
into sound minds and sober practises." We are permitted, at
last, to hearken to the utterance of candour and veraciousness.

Most damning of all, however, is a letter to Middleton.
It is dated on the 21st of May 1661, and is written from
London. What has it to say? This, that Sharp was then
holding constant interviews with Lord Clarendon and the
English Bishops; that the subject of their discussions was
the establishment of Episcopacy in Scotland; and that the
project had his hearty approval. This, also, that, before he
travelled south he and the Commissioner in Edinburgh had
conferred on the same topic, and that he was aware of the
Commissioner's intention to humble the Kirk. And this,
finally, that, in his judgment, "the superstructure for which
Middleton has laid the foundation will render his name
precious to the succeeding generations." Let us remember
that, only two months before, he had boasted that "thrice
a week at least Mr. Douglas" was with him; that there
was no public matter he could learn which he did not
impart to his friend; and that he had joined the Presbyterian leader in beseeching Lord Middleton to call a General
Assembly, and to refrain from rescinding the Acts of
Parliament which favoured the Covenanters. Let us remember, too, his asseveration to Patrick Drummond that
he was resolved "not to meddle any more in these stormy
and bespattering entanglements." He has one language
for the old associates whom he befools, and a contradictory
language for the new masters whom he courts with a
sycophant's assiduity. His circumlocutions and artifices,

when he conversed with Drummond and Douglas, were the courtesy of Gawain, courtesy "with a touch of traitor in it." Even Robert Baillie, stung into what for him is unwonted courage, speaks some plain truths to Lord Lauderdale: "If you or Mr. Sharp, whom we trusted as our own soules, have swerved towards Chancellor Hyde's principles, as now we see many doe, you have much to answer for." Twelve months later, in May 1662, the Principal wrote his last letter, and in it he said his final word about the distasteful subject: "Had we but petitioned for Presbytrie at Breda, it had been, as was thought, granted; but, fearing what the least delay of the King's coming over might have produced, and trusting fully to the King's goodness, we hastened him over without any provision for our safetie. At that time it was that Dr. Sheldon, now Bishop of London, and Dr. Morley, did poyson Mr. Sharp, our agent, whom we trusted; who, peice and peice, in so cunning a way has trepanned us as we have never win so much as to petition either King, Parliament, or Councell." Troy was surrendered now; the citadel of Presbyterianism was overthrown. And a Sinon within the gates deceived the townsmen and wrought the ruin.

The Church, "as it was settled by law," was not to be the Church of the Covenants; when the Rescissory Act blotted out the legislation of two decades, and when Sharp pronounced his benediction on the superstructure of which Middleton laid the foundations, the phrase could only mean the Church established by James the Sixth and confirmed by his son. So, in the harvest of 1661, the Privy Council announced that Bishops were to be restored. On the sixth of September, at the Cross of Edinburgh, Charles's decree was proclaimed. It intimated the abolition of Presbytery, "because of the unsuitableness thereof to His Majesty's monarchical estate," declared Episcopal government to be again in force, forbade the meetings of clerical courts, and enjoined the magistrates to commit all Nonconformists to prison. In December, four men were sent up to London, to be consecrated by Anglican dignitaries, and thus qualified to impart similar

sanctities to their Scottish brethren. James Hamilton, brother
of Lord Belhaven, and once active in the service of the Kirk,
received the diocese of Galloway; his tergiversation was
complete, for, some years previously, he had been a Presbyterian of so rigorous a type that he had compelled the communicants in the churches where he ministered to renew the
Covenant before he permitted them to sit down at the Lord's
Supper. Andrew Fairfoul, a humorist whose life was not
over-strict—"Yes," said Lord Rothes, "he has learning and
sharpness enough, but he has no more sanctification than my
grey horse!"—became the Archbishop of Glasgow. Robert
Leighton was sent to Dunblane: Robert Leighton, the one
holy man of the four, of whom Burnet writes in a beautiful
sentence that he "seemed to be in a perpetual meditation,"
but who lacked altogether the foresight and the purposeful-
ness which mark the trustworthy guide of public opinion,
so that the satirists of the hour made merry over his too
notorious mutability of temper—

> Reporting thy compliancie
>   With each prevailing partie:
> That whatsoever change fell out
>   Thou wast to it most heartie.
> Light heart, light head, light feet, light facts,
>   Thy true name is Lightbody:
> Is this a pretty game to play
>   So oft the Palinody?

And James Sharp had the reward of his craft and tireless
time-serving in being made their titular head; the minister
of Crail was now Archbishop of St. Andrews. The patent
which nominated him to the Metropolitan See, and bestowed
on him all the rights and privileges which his predecessor,
Spottiswood, had held, proclaimed at the same time his
absolute subservience to the Crown: it declared that he was
thus exalted *ex auctoritate regali et potestate regia*. There
was a friend of John Bunyan's—John Burton by name—
who, in the early days of the tinker's conversion, when he
went through the villages of Bedfordshire preaching the
Gospel, and when his call to the ministry was disputed by
some of the wise and prudent, came chivalrously to his succour

and defence. "This man," he said, "hath been chosen not out of an earthly but out of an heavenly university, where he hath by grace taken these three degrees, to wit, union with Christ, the anointing of the Spirit, and experience of the temptations of Satan." But they were no such valid and holy compulsions which lifted James Sharp to his high position. His summons was not from the Celestial City but only from Whitehall, an entirely different fountain of inspiration—Whitehall, with its *auctoritas regalis* and *potestas regia*.

A few weeks before he received consecration in West-minster Abbey from the Bishops of London, Worcester, Llandaff, and Carlisle, he had ventured once again to visit Douglas in his house in Edinburgh. He told him of the King's purpose to settle the Church under Bishops, and how Charles desired Douglas to accept the primacy. But the true man answered curtly that he would have nothing to do with it. His guest insisted, only to receive a second No; and then Sharp rose to take his leave. Robert Douglas convoyed him to the door; but, after he had passed through it, he called him back, and said, "James, I see *you* will engage; I perceive you are clear; *you* will be the Bishop of St. Andrews. Take it, and the curse of God with it." And instantly clapping him on the shoulder, he shut the door. It was a dramatic parting between those who had been as brothers. Perhaps even this man, perverted as his conscience was, felt a tremor of awe as he went down the stair, with the good minister's anathema resting on his head. Another of the leaders of the Kirk, Robert Blair, had dealt in equal faithfulness with the recreant a month or two previously, urging him before it was quite too late to continue a simple Presbyter and to reject the glittering bribe of the Arch-bishopric. But Blair gained nothing by his truth-speaking except deposition from his pulpit in St. Andrews and the hostility of the Privy Council. Through the five years of life that were left to him, he had to keep himself in strictest retirement, in Edinburgh or in Inveresk or in Kirkcaldy. One day, when death was near, and when he lay looking out from the window of his room over the Firth of Forth, his eyes following the fishing-boats as they contended against wind and tide, the memory of James Sharp rose up unbidden to his mind. "O Sharp! Sharp!" he exclaimed involuntarily, "there is no rowing with thee." And then he thought how much better, through the mercy of God, it was with himself, rudely silenced although he had been and exposed to many an unmerited indignity. "I would not exchange my condition with thee, James Sharp," he went on, "for thy mitres and all thy riches and revenues—nay, though all that's betwixt thee and me were red gold to the boot."

We shall meet Sharp sufficiently often in the future; but we know now why his contemporaries recoiled from him with a shuddering abhorrence. The uncanniest stories were current among them regarding their arch-enemy. They whispered that he was in league with Satan, and that, more than once or twice, his ghostly coadjutor was closeted with him, in visible shape. "My lord," queried a poor creature whom the Archbishop, presiding over the Privy Council, wished to banish for witchcraft to the King's plantations in the West Indies—"My lord, who was Yon with you in your chamber on Saturday night, betwixt twelve and one o'clock?" And the Archbishop's face turned both black and pale, and the prisoner was dismissed incontinently from the bar. It seemed as if no diablerie were too hideous for the betrayer of the Church.

Mr. Whittier, the tenderest of American poets, has some terrible verses which he entitles *Ichabod*—verses that pillory a statesman, who, for a time, proved recreant to the cause of emancipation—

> Of all we loved and honoured, naught
> Save power remains,—
> A fallen angel's pride of thought,
> Still strong in chains.

> All else is gone; from those great eyes
> The soul has fled;
> When faith is lost, when honour dies,
> The man is dead.

They are verses which, if it were not that they invest him with too much intellectual strength, might have been written about James Sharp, who persecuted that which formerly he preached.

CHAPTER VII.

THEIR GRACES ENTER AND HIS GRACE DEPARTS.

THE second session of the Earl of Middleton's Parliament was commenced in May of 1662. It has not been garlanded in history with the luxuriant infamy which encircles its predecessor; but it was zealous in following up the work so emphatically begun. It brought back the Bishops to the benches of the House. It restored to them their accustomed dignities, privileges, and jurisdictions. It went further. Thirteen years before, patronage had been abolished in the Presbyterian Church, and congregations had been given the right to call ministers of their own choosing. But Parliament decreed that popular election must cease; and, not content with this provision for the future, the legislators enacted that the preachers ordained since 1649 must receive presentation from the lawful patron and sanction from the Bishop of the diocese, or else must vacate their charges. The law was as spiteful as it was retrograde.

But, if Parliament fashioned the bullets, the Privy Council fired them. The west of Scotland was the head-quarters of the Covenanters; and in the opening week of October Lord Middleton was in Glasgow. He listened to the complaint of the Archbishop, Andrew Fairfoul, that not one of the younger ministers under his superintendence would acknowledge his authority in the manner enjoined by the senators in Edinburgh. Their recalcitrancy is not strange; Fairfoul's character did not add weight to his fiats among religious men. "He used to go out to a gentleman's house, and there, all the Sabbath, play at cards and drink. One

THE PARISH CHURCH OF CRAIL.

day, one of the servants came into the room. 'Have you been at sermon?' says the Archbishop. 'Yes,' says he. 'Where was the text?' '*Remember the Sabbath day to keep it holy,*' says the servant." But the King's Commissioner, angrier and more impatient than ever because for weeks he had been in a state of intoxication, was enraged at what the Churchman told him. He vowed that he should bring the transgressors to a humbler mind. Gathering round him as many of the members of Council as were within reach, he framed an Act to enforce the submission of the ministers. Not one of those present, with the solitary exception of Sir James Lockhart of the Lee, was sober. "Duke Hamilton told me," Gilbert Burnet testifies, "they were all so drunk that day that they were not capable of considering anything that was laid before them, and would hear of nothing but executing the law without any relenting or delay." Sir James protested strenuously against their decision; but the protest was futile. His colleagues were in no mood to welcome the monitions of saving commonsense.

This was what the Glasgow meeting of the Privy Council did: it declared that all the ministers who should have failed, by the first of November, to obtain the authorisation of patron and bishop must leave their parishes. There would not be ten, Fairfoul asserted loudly, of such incorruptible faith and constancy that they would be unwilling to retain their salaries and their comforts by compliance. He was quickly and startlingly undeceived. In the depth of winter between three and four hundred Scottish clergymen, rather than wound conscience by accepting their holy office from any but Jesus Christ, abandoned stipend and parish and home. Middleton himself was astounded. "What will these mad fellows do?" he cried. James Sharp, who was keenly desirous to have the work accomplished, but who would have gone about it with more deliberation and finesse, was in a paroxysm of rage; he protested that by his fatal precipitancy Fairfoul had spoiled everything. The members of the Council, returning to an evanescent thoughtfulness and penitence, realised that they had committed a palpable error

F

in tactics, and extended the day of grace until the first of February in the following year. But the deed was done; and neither allurement nor threatening could persuade the outed ministers to come back.

Perforce their empty places must be filled; but with whom? It is now that we meet with the men, who, if they did not rouse our indignation by their arrant hypocrisy, would supply the missing element of gaiety in the sorrows of the time. The curates, "their graceless graces," were the laughing-stock of the country. Most of them were Highlanders, who had no comprehension of Lowland notions and ways. Many were beardless boys of seventeen or eighteen, "a sort of young lads," Kirkton says, "unstudied and unbred, who had all the properties of Jeroboam's priests, and who went to their churches with the same intention and resolution a shepherd contracts for herding a flock of cattle." So entirely bucolic the poor fellows were that landlords in the north were heard cursing the Presbyterian pastors, because, since they forsook their parishes, not a boy could be got to watch the cows: everywhere the farm-lads were smitten with an insatiable hunger to reap the profits of the pulpit. There were cases in which the lay patron, alive in some measure to the necessities of the people, disdained to present the ridiculous applicant; but the Bishop did not fail in his duty, and, if the curate went without the imprimatur of the secular overlord, he was sure of his appointment from his spiritual superior. "They were the worst preachers I ever saw," Burnet confesses, "ignorant to a reproach, and many of them openly vicious, the dregs and refuse of the northern parts." Sir Robert Moray, one of the fairest-minded among the rulers of the time, is as positive in his dislike. "They were such a set of men," he declares, "so ignorant and so scandalous, that it was not possible to support them, unless the greatest part of them could be turned out and better men put in their places. But it was not easy to know how this could be done. The clergy were so linked together that none of them could be got to concur in getting proofs of crimes brought against their brethren, and the people of the country said to accuse a minister before a bishop was a homologating his power." The reception which those feckless substitutes had from incensed parishioners, who longed after their own banished teachers, was in a hundred instances more testy and waspish than urbane. " Well, when they came about the end of the spring, in some places they were welcomed with tears and requests to be gone, and not to ruin the poor congregation and their own soul; in some places they were entertained with reasonings and disputes, in other places with threatenings and curses, and in others with strange affronts and indignities. Some stole the bell-tongue, that the people's absence from sermon might be excusable; some barricadoed the door, to oblige the curate to enter by the window literally. A shepherd boy, finding in the field a nest of pismires, fills a box with them; this he empties in the curate's bootheads as he is going to pulpit. The poor man began his exercise, but was quickly obliged to interrupt, the miserable insects gave him so much pain and disturbance." From which it appears that the hireling does more than stain himself with sin; he becomes an inevitable mark for derision and jest.

It was in vain that the directors of Church and country strove to secure auditors for these absurd priestlings. The Privy Council, in July 1663, devised " the Bishops' Drag Net," a measure which sought, by imposing heavy fines, to enforce attendance in the deserted churches. But the people stolidly and steadily refused to be coerced. Then, in August, the Council passed " the Scots' Mile Act," which required the recusant ministers not to reside within twenty miles of their former homes, nor within six miles of Edinburgh, nor within three miles of any royal burgh. It scarcely mattered, however, how far the loved and familiar preachers might be driven away; like their Master, they *could not be hid* from men and women who knew the value of their words and works. This was the time when the religious services began, at first in private houses and soon in the open fields, which we call the Conventicles, and which are so famous in the chequered story of the Covenant.

It was the time, too, when a career, sufficiently boastful and overbearing, was to be quenched in night. The Earl of Middleton, " who carried more high while he was in Scotland than ever any of our one hundred and eight sober limited kings had done," dared, in the blind infatuation of his confidence, to risk an encounter with one who was mightier than himself; and in the contest he was routed beyond remedy. He was filled with envy of Lauderdale, and boldly attempted to effect his rival's downfall. The history of how he tried to compass his purpose is a curious one. An Act of Indemnity had at last been given to Charles's northern kingdom, exempting from troublesome consequences those of His Majesty's subjects who had been over-friendly with Oliver and the Commonwealth. But Middleton determined that from the benefits of this Indemnity he would exclude twelve persons who were especially obnoxious to himself : he would have them disqualified, so that they could not occupy any place of public honour and trust. He arranged that the members of Parliament should write on slips of papers—" Billets " was the term he used—the names of this ostracised and unforgiven dozen ; and he cajoled and bribed and bullied them to set Lauderdale in the forefront of the catalogue of culprits. It was done as he demanded. " Viceroy hath been Roy in his word," William Sharp, the Archbishop's brother, wrote in sympathetic ink to the blackened and castigated statesman. But the intriguer had overreached himself. Lauderdale received from his own agents in Scotland a narrative of the whole transaction, before the envoys of the Parliament could get from Edinburgh to Whitehall, to report it to the King, and to gain the royal consent to the billeting of the twelve. He had endless stores of wit, wit of which Charles never wearied. He covered Middleton's bungling scheme with sarcasm and scorn. He laughed it into shreds and tatters, until even Clarendon, who was the Commissioner's friend, admitted its impossibility, and the King, when at length the messengers from the north arrived, flung their parchment unopened into his cabinet. Then Lauderdale became serious in his revenge. He dwelt on the iniquity of a plan, "whereby any man's honour, his life, his posterity, may be destroyed without the trouble of calling him or hearing his answer." He had never known, he said, that the ballot was abused to draw down disgrace and punishment on the head of a political adversary, "except among the Athenians, who were governed by that cursed sovereign lord, the People." He begged his master to take every step to undo the affront.

When things had gone so far, the last scene of the play could not be distant. Lauderdale's triumph was complete. He went down to Edinburgh, to fight the battle out in person against his less resourceful foe. In May 1663, Middleton lost the Commissionership. By and by the successful diplomatist could send joking letters to the King: "By yesterday's Act," he says, "you will see that Billeting is dead, buried, and descended." In January 1664, new disasters overtook the ruler whose folly had undermined his proud estate. Here is a document almost pathetic in its confession of defeat: "May yt pleas Your Majestie, I Jhon Earle of Middleton doe by these freelie and heartilie resigne upgive and overgive in and to Yr. Majestie's hands the offices of Captain generall of Yr. Majestie's Kingdome of Scotland, and of captain and keeper of Yr. Majestie's Castle of Edinbrogh, granted to me by two severall guifts and letters patent under Yr. Majestie's great seale of the said kingdome, to be disposed upon at Yr. Majestie's pleasour in all tyme commyng. In wittnes whereof the presents are written and signed by, May it pleas Yr. Majestie, Yr. Majestie's most faithfull most humble and most obedient subject and servant, Middleton." The Scottish nation saw the rough soldier, who had wrought its best citizens much injury, driven ignominiously from its coasts.

"It is reported that, as he passed Tweed, a poor country woman at Coldstream told him, since he had been so busy to destroy their ministers, he should never have more power in Scotland." The vaticination came to pass. Charles, indeed, felt a kind of pity for the discredited magnate. He made him Governor of Tangier. In that remote outpost of

English dominion, which the King's marriage with Catharine of Bragança had brought him, Middleton lived for a few years, until his self-indulgence was the cause of his death. Riding one day in a half-drunken state, he fell from his saddle and broke some bones, one of which penetrated his heart. "Such an end," as James Kirkton tells us in a magnanimous phrase, " had this valiant unhappy man."

CHAPTER VIII.

JOHN LIVINGSTON TELLS HIS OWN STORY.

"MY Lord Middleton's journey into the western shires," wrote the Earl of Lauderdale to Sir Robert Moray, "was only a flaunting and a feasting journey; many ministers were put out in those parts, but no further done." The achievement in expulsion, to Lauderdale so paltry, was grievous to the western shires themselves. Nor was it the west alone which suffered. The preachers were ejected in other districts of Scotland. In the Border country lies the village of Ancrum; and Ancrum in those years was happy in having John Livingston for its minister. He was compelled to go. At the Monday service after his Sacramental Sabbath, in October 1662, he spoke to his people for the last time. His gentle and modest spirit revealed itself in his farewells. "We have been labouring among you these fourteen years," he said, "and have that conviction we have not taken the pains, in private or public, which we ought; yet in some sort, we hope we may say it without pride, we have not sought yours but you. We cared not to be rich and great in this world. In as far as we have given offence, less or more, to any in this congregation, or any that have interest in it, or any round about it, or any that are here present, or any of the people of God elsewhere, we crave God's pardon, and crave also your forgiveness." Bravely John Livingston laid down the work he loved, concealing the sharpness of the pain. But his hearers could not suppress their tears. As on the seashore at Miletus, so in Ancrum Kirk, elders and folk sorrowed that they should see their apostle's face no more.

In December he appeared before the Privy Council, accused of "turbulency and sedition"—a strange indictment for one who esteemed it "better to walk the realm unseen than watch the hour's event." "I have carried myself," he pleaded, "with all moderation and peaceableness, and have lived so obscurely that I wonder how I am taken notice of." He had, he told the Chancellor, acknowledged the Lord's mercy in restoring the King. He was prepared to admit His Majesty's civil supremacy over all persons and in all causes. But he was not free to take the Oath of Allegiance in the terms in which it was proposed to him. The Chancellor offered to adjourn the court, that he might reconsider his refusal. "I humbly thank your Lordship," he replied; "it is a favour which, if I had any doubt, I would willingly accept. But if, after seeking God and advising anent the matter, I should take time, it would import that I have unclearness or hesitation; which I have not." So the Council passed sentence. Within two months the prisoner was to leave His Majesty's dominions. Within forty-eight hours he was to remove from Edinburgh, and go to the north side of the Tay. He solicited permission to pay a short visit to his home, that he might have some talk with wife and children. But the favour was withheld. There must be no more intercourse with Ancrum; the sooner its minister was in exile, the better pleased his judges would be.

John Livingston has written "a brief historical relation" of his life, so that we can look into his eyes, and can learn his motives, and can see how human and how godly he was. The land was in evil case whose governors sent such a citizen across the seas.

He was a son of the manse, born at Kilsyth in 1603, his father "all his days straight and zealous in the work of reformation," his mother "a rare pattern of piety and meekness." He could not remember the time or the mode of his own conversion; from the outset his life had belonged to our God and His Christ. While he was yet a schoolboy in Stirling, he was a member of the Church; and never could

JOHN LIVINGSTON, OF ANCRUM.

After the Portrait in Gosford House.

he forget the first occasion when he sat down at the Holy Table: "There came such a trembling upon me that all my body shook, yet thereafter the fear departed, and I got some comfort and assurance."   His earliest inclination was to the profession of medicine; but, spending a day in solitary communion with God, in a cave on the banks of the Mouse Water, over against the Cleghorn woods, he had it made out to him that he behoved to preach Jesus Christ.   Thenceforward Livingston had "one passion, and it was He, He alone."

When Glasgow College was left behind, and in 1625 he began to speak for his Master, he had his first taste of persecution.   Congregations in different parts—Torphichen, Linlithgow, Leith, Kirkcaldy—were eager to claim him; but in each case the Bishops prevented the settlement.   For five years he had no sphere of work peculiarly his own. But God's blessing went with him through the period of waiting.   Sometimes the preaching of the Covenanters is condemned as cold and hard; but Livingston's words had the flame of the Holy Ghost glowing in them, and they conquered and captivated the souls of men.   One of the great revivals in the annals of the Church is linked with the name of the young probationer whom the Bishops pursued with their hate.   It happened at the Kirk of Shotts, on the 21st of June 1630.   Like that day of good-byes at Ancrum, it was the Monday after a Sabbath of Communion.   With some friends he had spent the night before in laying fast hold upon the promise and the grace of Heaven.   When the midsummer morning broke, the preacher wanted to escape from the responsibilities in front of him.   Alone in the fields, between eight and nine, he felt such misgivings, such a burden of unworthiness, such dread of the multitude and the expectation of the people, that he was consulting with himself to have stolen away; but he "durst not so far distrust God, and so went to sermon, and got good assistance."   Good assistance indeed; for, after he had spoken for an hour and a half from the text, *Then will I sprinkle clean water upon you, and ye shall be clean,* and was thinking that now he must close, he was constrained by his Lord Himself to continue. " I was led on about ane hour's time in ane strain of exhortation and warning, with such liberty and melting of heart as I never had the like in publick all my life." No fewer than five hundred men and women, some of them ladies of high estate, and others poor wastrels and beggars, traced the dawn of the undying life to John Livingston's words that day.

Healthful as his fellowship would be, we cannot accompany him through the changeful experiences of his ministry. His first parish was an Irish one, that of Killinchy in County Down, to which the Bishop of Raphoe, more liberal than most of the prelates, ordained him. In 1638, the expatriated Scot recrossed the Channel, to Stranraer, his residence for ten years, where, if the town was " but little and poor," the people were " very tractable and respectful," and their teacher was " sometimes well-satisfied and refreshed." Then came the fourteen summers in Ancrum; and then the ejection by the Privy Council. Stirring incidents broke in on the quiet usefulness of Livingston's career in his various homes. In Ireland he and others like him were so harassed by the ill-will of Church potentates more intolerant than his Grace of Raphoe, or than Dr. Ussher, Primate of Armagh, " ane godly man although ane Bishop," that they built a ship near Belfast of one hundred and fifty tons' burden, and called it *The Eagle Wing*, and were minded in the spring of 1636 to start for the New England of the Pilgrim Fathers. It was September before they did set sail; and then, when they were about four hundred leagues away from the Irish coast, such pitiless storms overtook them that they concluded God meant them to return. It was a perilous voyage back to Ulster; but the days were vocal with social prayer and thanksgiving, and every heart felt a confidence which nothing could damp: " yea, some expressed the hope that, rather than the Lord would suffer such an companie to perish if the ship should break, He would put wings to all our shoulders and carry us safe ashoare." On board the vessel a baby-boy came to

Michael Coltheard and his wife, and, on the succeeding Sabbath, he was baptized by John Livingston, who named him Seaborn; one is tempted to think that Seaborn Coltheard must be younger brother of Oceanus Hopkins, who had his wave-rocked cradle in the cabin of the *Mayflower* sixteen autumns before.

At the Hague, in 1650, the preacher wrestled with worse billows than those of the Atlantic. He was among the commissioners who treated with Charles "for security to religion and the liberties of the country, before his admission to the exercise of the Government." He did not covet the errand. He had some scruple that ministers meddled too frequently in State matters. He knew his own "unacquaintedness and inability," and how he was "ready to condescend too easily to anything having any show of reason," so that he feared he "should be a grief and shame" to those who sent him. He would even have preferred, if it had been the will of God, to be drowned in the waters by the way. But the Church insisted that he and James Wood and George Hutcheson, with the Earl of Cassillis and Alexander Brodie, must be her representatives. To his last hour he had regretful memories of the episode. He soon saw the frivolity of the King; "many nights he was balling and dancing till near day." He could not approve the treaty which was made; "it seemed rather like ane merchant's bargain of prigging somewhat higher or lower than ingenuous dealing." He tried to avoid returning to Scotland in the retinue of the Prince, and was only enticed on board by a trick. Altogether it was a humbling reminiscence. "So dangerous it is for a man of a simple disposition to be yoked with these who, by wit, authority, and boldness, can overmaster him."

We begin to understand John Livingston's character. He was a Protester, but a Protester in whom resided the New Testament grace of *epieikeia*, moderation and sweet reasonableness. He suspected at times that those with whom he allied himself "kept too many meetings," and thus rendered the Church's divisions wider and more mournful than they need have been. Pre-eminent among his gracious features is his invincible modesty. He took the lowest room. He was a proficient in the humility of which he wrote to a friend, that "it fitteth the back for every burden, and maketh the tree sickerest at the root when it standeth upon the top of the windy hill." His gladness is unfeigned when he recalls how the parishes, which wished to have him, but from which he had been held back, were "far better provided." On one occasion, when competing calls came, "his own mind inclined most to Straiton, because it was an obscure place, and the people landwart simple people." "I think," he said, "every minister of my acquaintance gets his work done better than I; yet I would not desire to be another than myself, nor to have other manner of dealing than the Lord uses, for His power is made perfect in weakness." Yet Livingston had ample cause for an honourable pride. He was a cultured scholar. He knew Hebrew and Chaldee and "somewhat also of the Syriack." He longed to add an understanding of Arabic to his other Semitic conquests; but "the vastness of it" gave pause even to his indomitable spirit. He was familiar with French and Italian and Dutch, and read the Bible in Spanish and German. In the noble army of book-lovers our Covenanter stands well to the front. Like Richard de Bury, he "valued codices more than florins"; and he would have sympathised with Thomas Hearne's quaint and particular thanksgiving when unexpectedly he lighted on three manuscripts of venerable age. Listen to him: "I had a kind of coveting, when I got leisure and opportunity, to read much and of different subjects; and I was oft challenged"—that is to say, my wideawake conscience upbraided me—"that my way of reading was like some men's lust after play." But he was no Dryasdust, abjuring for his folios all less stringent joys. He had a melodious voice, and, in his younger days, he was fond of using it. When he was a student at Glasgow, the Principal, John Boyd of Trochrigg, "of an austere-like carriage but of a most tender heart," would now and then call him and three or four others, and would lay

down books before them, and would have them sing those
"setts of musick" in which he and they took delight.   In
later and more troublous years, Livingston did not sing so
often in concert with his friends, "wherein I had some little
skill"; just as he denied himself the other recreation of
hunting, which once he had found "very bewitching."   But
no distresses could quite silence the song in his soul.   "A
line of praises" he thought "worth a leaf of prayer"; and,
growing more rapturous, he would break forth: "O, what a
massy piece of glory on earth is it, to have praises looking
as it were out at the eyes, praises written upon the forebrow;
to have the very breath smelling of praises, to have praises
engraven on the palms of the hands, and the impression of
praises on every footstep of the walk: although this be that
day, if ever, wherein the Lord calleth to mourning and
fasting!"   He was one of those delineated in the old verse,
My people shall dwell in a peaceable habitation.

There were two places where John Livingston was seen
at his best.   One was his home.   It might be very poor.
In Killinchy—the record is almost incredible—his stipend
was £4 a year.   But the household was always rich in love.
His wife was the eldest daughter of Bartholomew Fleming,
an Edinburgh merchant.   Before he married her, in 1635,
many had told him of her gracious disposition; but for nine
months he had no clearness of mind to speak to her.   But,
going with her one Friday to a meeting, he found her
"conference so judicious and spiritual" that his scruples
were scattered to the winds.   Yet it was another month
before he "got marriage affection to her, although she was
for personal enduements beyond many."   On his knees he
asked it from God, and, when it came, there were no limits
to its fulness: "thereafter I had greater difficulty to
moderate it."   Livingston has none of that aloofness from
the gladnesses of the hearth which we note in some of his
fellows.   And his wife was worthy of him.   Years after,
when he was gone, and when the skies hung still more
thunderously over Presbyterian Scotland, she faced the Earl
of Rothes, and sought liberty for the ill-treated ministers.

It was the summer of 1674.   After the fleeting tranquillity
of "the Blink," the hurricane of persecution had risen again
into fury.   On the 4th of June the Privy Council was to
meet, to consider a letter from the King, requiring his
Councillors to use more diligent endeavours for the apprehension and trial of the field preachers and of those heritors
and landlords who were ringleaders in the conventicles.
Mrs. Livingston, and fourteen other ladies with sympathies
akin to her own, had drawn up a petition to the Lord
Chancellor, asking him to grant liberty to the threatened
ministers, through the land and in the city of Edinburgh,
that they might "lawfully and without molestation exercise
their holy function, as the people should in an orderly way
call them."   In the Parliament Close they waited for his
Grace's coach, which soon made its appearance.   Rothes
alighted, and beside him Archbishop Sharp, who was, says
John Row, "as flyed as a fox," and "clave close to the
Chancellor's back."   The Earl, doffing his hat, listened with
patience to Janet Livingston, as she read her petition
through, and then jested with the unconquerable lady after
his facetious fashion, entertaining her, Sir George Mackenzie
tells us, "with insinuating speeches," until the Council
Chamber was reached and he was safe from further importunities.   But, for six months thereafter, he and his
Lords "were very hot upon the chase against the women";
and their leader was banished from Edinburgh for awhile.
Manifestly her husband's heart could trust in her.   She was,
to quote Robert MacWard's favourite salutation of one with
whom he was well-acquainted, "a mother indeed in Israel."

The other place where Livingston showed at his worthiest
was the pulpit.   He would not acknowledge it himself,
girdled as he was with the cincture of lowliness.   "As concerning my gift of preaching," he wrote penitently, "I never
attained to any accuracie therein, and, through laziness, did
not much endeavour it."   His custom was to put down
some notes beforehand, and to leave the enlargement of them
to the time of delivery.   His style, he insists, was suited
only to the common people, and not to scholarly listeners.

Yet he has clear and shrewd ideas about the architecture of a sermon. If he would not have too few doctrines, neither would he reckon too many particular points, as "eighthly," "tenthly," "thirteenthly." The matter should not be over-exquisite, with the abstruse learning which savours of affectation; but it ought not to be childishly rudimentary, for that procures careless hearing and contempt of the gift. There should not be an excess of similitudes and pictures; but the absence of them altogether will impoverish rather than help. In his utterance, the speaker ought not to sing his sentences, not to draw out his words to an inordinate length, nor to assume a weeping-like voice, nor to shout too loud, nor to sink too low. John Livingston understood the technical side of his sacred calling. And, despite his self-depreciation, he was an ambassador who seldom failed to transact vital business for his Master; as we should expect, when we know that his chief care, before entering the pulpit, was to be in a spiritual frame, and that, in it, he was aided most by "the hunger of the hearers." The man to whom, under God, the awakening at the Kirk of Shotts was due possessed that gift of gifts in the herald of Christ—the quality which old French writers denominate *onction*. Edward Gibbon, with his clever and scornful cynicism, insists that the proper translation of the word is "cant"; and, no doubt, everything that is true has its counterfeit on which the sceptics can fasten as if by instinct. The falsetto of reason is quibbling, of sublimity is bombast, of beauty is tinsel, of learning is pedantry, and of *onction* is probably that unreality to which the author of *The Decline and Fall* has pointed us. But there is no mistaking the genuine endowment, the supernatural breath and inspiration, the *ointment of the right hand which bewrayeth itself*, the throbbing affection for the heavenly Lord and for the souls of men, the eloquence not so much of the lips as of the spirit. Livingston had it in an unwonted degree. On his deathbed these were his words: "I cannot say much of great services; yet, if ever my heart was lifted up, it was in preaching of Jesus Christ." There were multitudes who could corroborate the witness.

Mr. Lowell pays to the naturalist Agassiz the fine tribute that, "where'er he met a stranger, there he left a friend." It is a coronet which might gleam on Livingston's brow. He had a genius for friendship. To the end of life he won new sisters and brothers in the family of God. One of our debts to him is the series of portraits he has bequeathed to us of his intimates. Miniatures these portraits are, but miniatures done by a painter who has put both intellect and affection into his work. There are ladies in his gallery: like Lady Robertland, who said to him, "With God the most of mosts is lighter than nothing, and without Him the least of leasts is heavier than any burden"; and like Elizabeth Melvill, the Lady Culross, who would write, "Ye must be hewin and hamerd down and drest and prepaired, before ye be a Leving Ston fitt for His building"; and like Margaret Scott of Stranraer, who was "but in a mean condition," and yet contributed for the Covenanting army "seven twenty-two shilling sterling pieces and one eleven shillings' piece of gold," and, when her minister asked how she could part with so much, made the tender reply, "I was gathering, and had laid up this to be a portion to a young daughter I had; and, whereas the Lord lately hath pleased to take my daughter to Himself, I thought I would give Him her tocher also." There are Christian laymen among the artist's subjects: Cathcart of Carleton, who came out to family worship from the place of secret communion, and, having prayed earnestly and confidently, ran back to his chamber as soon as he had done; and John Mein, the merchant, who always sang some psalms as he put on his clothes in the morning, and who could point to a room where he had spent a whole night in fellowship with God, and where he had seen a light greater than ever was the light of the sun. But the ministers are the favourite themes. They pass before us, an inspiriting company of great-hearted gentlemen. Robert Bruce, who was short in prayer with others, but then "every sentence was like a strong bolt shot up to heaven"; John Smith of Maxtone, who, whenever he met a youth studying for the Church, would

MRS. JOHN LIVINGSTON, OF ANCRUM.

From the Portrait in Gosford House.

draw him aside, and "seriously and gravely exhort him, and heartily bless him"; David Dickson, who told Livingston with his latest breath, "I have taken all my good deeds and all my bad deeds, and cast them in a heap before the Lord, and have betaken me to Jesus Christ, in whom I have full and sweet peace"; Robert Blair, "of a majestick, awfull, yet amiable countenance," who was "seldom ever brangled in his assurance of salvation"; Robert Cunningham, "the one man to my discerning who resembled most the meekness of Jesus Christ," who, when his wife sat by his deathbed, prayed for the whole Church, and for his parish, and for his brethren in the ministry, and for his children, and in the end said, "And last, O Lord, I recommend to Thee this gentlewoman, who is no more my wife," and, with that saying, he softly loosed his hand from hers, and gently thrust her hand a little from him:—we would not miss one in the priestly and kingly succession. And his must have been a rich and roomy nature, who could gather such friends around him.

But Middleton and the Council had no place for him in Scotland. "At last, on the 9th of Aprile 1663, I went aboarde in old John Allan's ship, and, in eight dayes, came to Rotterdam." There was not an indolent fibre in his constitution, and through the years of his banishment he was almost as busy as he had been in his home. It was not merely that every morning brought him a noble chance of doing good to the citizens of the foreign town; but he found new fields of exercise for his erudition. Wishing to accomplish something "whereby the knowledge of the only true God might be more plentifully had out of the Original," he set himself to revise the Latin version of the Old Testament, comparing it throughout with the Hebrew, and meaning by and by to have both printed in parallel columns. Adverse circumstances hindered the publication of his book; but the scholar himself had the joy of "mastering learning's crabbed text" and of pursuing to the end his lofty designs. In such fruitful avocations as these, the exiled preacher tarried his Lord's leisure until the August of 1672, and then the earthly service was sublimed into the heavenly. In Ancrum or in Holland, in honour and dishonour, it fared well with the man who could write: "If it were given to my option, God knows I would rather serve Him on earth and then endure the torments of the lost, than live a life of sin on earth and then have for ever the bliss of the ransomed."

CHAPTER IX.

A NONSUCH FOR A CLERK.

"IT is clear," writes Professor Rendel Harris of a nineteenth-century saint, "that we must begin our reminiscences by constructing for him what the Jews call a *Sepher Toldoth*, or Book of Generations." There is a peculiar appropriateness in so beginning any sketch of Archibald Johnston, Lord Wariston, the Lawyer of the Covenant. He owed much to the men and women of his house, who had travelled the high-road of life before him. A bad heredity is a woeful burden; and they are much to be pitied against whom "from the cradle fate and their fathers fight." But there is a good heredity which is a strong shelter to the soul, and an incalculable aid to holy living. Archibald Johnston, like numbers more, had many reasons to be thankful for his Book of Generations.

He could hardly have been anything else than a learned advocate. His grandfather, Sir Thomas Craig, was a renowned pleader, and the author of a treatise on Feudal Law. One aunt was wife of the first Lord Durie, and mother of the second; another aunt was married to Sir James Skene, President of the Court of Session. Merchant burgess of Edinburgh as his father was, the boy who was born, in March 1611, to a career so stormy was predestined to a lawyer's ambitions and victories. The *Sepher Toldoth* prophesied his eminence in the Courts.

But, if the God of parents is the God of children, there was as much likelihood that he would be a Covenanter and a Christian. He had a grandmother, Rachel Arnot, who was a princess in the aristocracy of the Kirk. She had hidden Robert Bruce within her walls—Robert Bruce, the minister

of St. Giles, who was often at cross purposes with James the
Sixth. In the same house, too, in the Sciennes, when the
Five Articles of Perth were ratified by the Black Parliament,
those Edinburgh preachers who objected to such Episcopal
law-making, and whom the magistrates had commanded to
leave the city, spent an entire day in prayer. Archibald
Johnston was fifteen before white-haired Rachel Arnot died;
and from her lips he must have heard many a history of
heroism and godliness. This will be a lawyer, we predict, as
familiar with "Heaven's bribeless hall," and with "Christ, the
King's Attorney," as with the Court of Session and the
General Assembly of the Church.

Having taken his degree in Glasgow, he passed as an
advocate in the winter of 1633, and settled in an Edinburgh
home. Soon he married, finding his bride in a Judge's
daughter, and so forging a fresh and delightful chain to bind
him closer to his profession. Helen Hay could have no dis-
turbing presentiment, in the joyousness of her wedding
morning, of that tragic hour, seven-and-twenty years later,
when she should beg the forgiveness of her husband from an
obdurate King, and should urge him in vain to pity her twelve
children, "reduced to a poor and desolate condition." At
first all went prosperously; and the town house in the High
Street, and the country house of Wariston, seven miles from
the Mercat Cross, were palaces of content and hope. But,
indeed, let it be merry June or bleak-nighted December in
his calendar, Lord Foresterseat's daughter had only a proud
love to bestow on her husband.

He was young when he thirled himself to the cause of the
Covenant. We have seen him, still some years under thirty,
reading the great parchment to the crowd in the Greyfriars.

And now, with tone distinct and clear, as one whose word is power,
Johnston of Wariston stood forth—God's gift in danger's hour.

But, before 1638, he had been in conflict with Charles and
Laud, and had proved himself their superior in wit as well
as in piety. For example, when the Scots were busy framing
Supplications and Protestations against the tyrannous actings
of Whitehall and Canterbury, who was more enthusiastic than

he? They devised four permanent committees of their best and ablest men—Tables they called them—the first composed of the nobles, the second of representatives from the counties, the third of members of the Presbyteries, the last of burghers and townsmen. Then, out of these, they constructed a Central Table, made up of four deputies from each of the others, which sat constantly in Edinburgh, and conducted all negotiations with the Privy Council. But this effective instrument of scrutiny and criticism, this popular and vigilant Opposition, was really of Johnston's planning; and in the Central Table he was Clerk and Secretary. "Canny, lynx-eyed lawyer" he might be—it is Thomas Carlyle's portrait; but nevertheless "full of fire, of heavy energy and gloom: a very notable character." And ere long he will be "a Lord Register of whom all the world has heard."

The Glasgow Assembly set him, more conspicuously than ever, in the van of the Church's fighters. He was the man who framed its enactments, and put them into proper shape. For when, on Friday, the 23rd of November, the ministers and elders proceeded to the election of a Clerk, all of them, with one solitary exception, voted that no one else must be chosen. They understood what they were doing. The young advocate stumbled once, we are told, when he had a singularly difficult paper to write; but that was at the very commencement. There was no subsequent failure, nor semblance of it. Early in the proceedings, he was able to do the Assembly a notable service. The Church had in its safe-keeping its records from 1590 onwards; but all trace had been lost of the minutes of the previous thirty years, since John Knox and his coadjutors had by the grace of the King of kings managed to dethrone Popery and to set Presbytery in its room. The Bishops were supposed to have obtained possession of the priceless volumes; and it was feared that, in such unfriendly custodianship, they must have been either mutilated or utterly destroyed. The members mourned the disappearance of their archives as a calamity not now to be retrieved. But they were mistaken; for "the new Clerk," as the minister of Kilwinning reports, "declared that, by the good providence of God, these books they spake of were come to his hands, which there he produced to all our great joy." Five closely-written folios there were, and they made the history of the Kirk complete. A committee was appointed to scrutinise their authenticity, and it pronounced them "true registers," and Archibald Johnston was thanked with enthusiasm for what he had done. It was but a sample of his indispensable usefulness to the Assembly. When we paint a mental picture of the Cathedral in those dark wintry days, and of its thronging and eager and sometimes noisy auditory, we must see that "a little table is set in the midst, foreanent the Commissioner"—so long at least as it pleases his Grace to remain in such troublesome company; and behind the little table are sitting side by side Henderson and Wariston. "Mr. Johnestoun to us all," Baillie says, "was a Nonsuch for a Clerk."

Charles was in choleric mood when he knew what was done in Glasgow. In the summer of 1639, one must think of the Royalist soldiers, with the King at their head, embarked on the Bishops' War. They have assembled at the Birks near Berwick, whilst the Covenanters are encamped on Duns Law. No pages in Robert Baillie's three volumes are more graphic than those which depict the scene. "It would have done you good to have casten your eyes athort our brave and rich Hill, as oft I did with great contentment and joy; for I, quoth the wren, was there among the rest." The regiments had noble-men for their officers, the captains were landed proprietors, the lieutenants experienced troopers, some of whom had stood "ankle-deep in Lutzen's blood with the brave Gustavus." The colours, flying at each captain's tent, bore the Scottish arms, with the motto in letters of gold, "For Christ's Crown and Covenant." There were some companies of Highlanders, "souple fellows, with their playds, targes, and dorlachs." But most of the soldiers were staunch young ploughmen, whose capacity increased with every hour. "The good sermons and prayers, morning and even, under the roof of heaven, to which their drums did call them for bells; the remonstrances verie frequent of the goodness of their cause, of their conduct hitherto by Hand clearlie divine; also Leslie, his skill and fortoun—made them all so resolute for battell as could be wished." In Alexander Leslie they had indeed the best of commanders. "Such was the wisdome and authoritie of that old, little, crooked soldier, that all, with ane incredible submission, gave themselves over to be guided by him, as if he had been Great Solyman." And in the tents Baillie heard "the sound of some singing psalms, some praying, and some reading Scripture." Such battalions would not readily have been put to flight; and Charles did wisely when he concluded the Pacification of Berwick, and ceased for awhile from hostilities.

It was Archibald Johnston who took the main part in bringing the King to terms. In his Diary, for one month of his life, from May 21st to June 25th, 1639—a precious fragment which the Scottish History Society has published—we see him at this war-time in his virile quality, his impetuosity and heat. He asks the Edinburgh Committee and the various counties for men and material in letters which, like Cromwell's, "are like the firing of some two hundred shot." "They are not worthy to be freemen that will neglect their country, which is now ready to bleed for their neglect. Be not wanting to yourselves, and be confident God will send an outgate to all these difficulties." "Shall our enemies be more forward for invasion against the truth and for our slaverie, than we for our defence, for the truth, and for our libertie? In the end they have neither Christian nor Scottish hearts who will expose their religion, their countrie, their neighbours and themselves to this present danger, without taking part." These are clarion calls. But Wariston's devoutness is as apparent as his patriotism. On Monday, June 3rd, he spends the whole afternoon in conference with Alexander Henderson and David Dickson and Robert Meldrum, the secretary of General Leslie. They have bethought, and better bethought, on the necessities of the army, the want of money and munition and order and discipline, the natural impossibility of retiring or of remaining or of going forward. They have been "forfoghten with the consideration." But then the sun breaks through the clouds. Despairing of secondary causes and human helpers, they look up to heaven. David Dickson

attests that, when God delivers them, they, who have been
emptied and annihilated of all their wits and judgment, shall
admire and adore Him alone, for building so high an edifice on
so low a foundation, for bringing so great an ebb to so great
a tide, for drawing so rich an abundance out of so vast a want.
And "in despyte of the devill and all our straites," Archibald
Johnston goes from his Council of War with a quiet heart; he
has seen the Aurora in the eastern sky. But how rapier-like
and stinging his speech could be! It leaves goads in the minds
of others, and sometimes pangs in his own. He bears the
brunt of the negotiations with Charles, and His Majesty resents
the pithiness of his utterance. "The King answered that the
devil himself could not make a more uncharitable construction
or give a more bitter expression." Again: "The King commanded me silence, and said he would speak to more reasonable
men." And, yet again: "When we rose, he gave to every
one of us a kiss of his hand, bidding me walk more circum-
spectly in time coming." There are no half-measures in the
Covenanting lawyer's soul.

The years went on. In 1641, he was knighted, and became
a Lord of Session. Later in the decade, he was one of the
eight Scottish commissioners to the Westminster Assembly.
The Jerusalem Chamber did not see so much of him as of
Rutherfurd and Gillespie; but, when he was present, he gave
good help with "the sharp point of his manifold arguments."
Once, in March of 1646, he made a speech which was long
remembered. The House of Commons had proposed to create
a civil tribunal which should revise the verdicts of the Church
courts; and Archibald Johnston expressed the convictions of
the majority in the Assembly, when he said that there must be
no headship over the spiritual realm bequeathed to Pope or
King or Parliament. "We must not edge away an hem of
Christ's robe royal." His decisive sentences, except for their
antique dialect, might have come from the lips of Thomas
Chalmers during the Ten Years' Conflict of a later century.

There are toilers who surprise us by the amount and the
diligence of their labours; and this man was of their company.
He was seldom able to sleep more than three hours out of the

ARCHIBALD JOHNSTON, LORD WARRISTON.

After a Portrait by George Jamesone.

twenty-four, such a restless mind he had, and such a perpetual anxiety to do "a shear darg" for the Commonweal. He could have appreciated both clauses in the advice given, in a subsequent age, by one of the most famous of his countrymen: "Fear God, and work hard." And, in the midst of his multiform tasks, he strove to keep the mirror of conscience unsullied. Greatly as he distrusted the policy of Charles I.,—opposed as he was to the authors of the Engagement and to their attempts to relieve His Majesty when his sky was overcast and threatening—he made generous efforts to save him from the consequences of his own perversity. But, when the axe of the headsman ended the King's arrogances and ambiguities, Wariston was not of those who approved of treating with his son; he is clear from the stigma which clings in this connection to some saintly names. Probably this was why the Second Charles had no shadow of compunction afterwards in sending him to his doom. Even to James Guthrie the Merry Monarch could give a passing sigh when he was informed that all was over; but for Lord Wariston there were no repentances, however easy: there were only the hate of hate and the scorn of scorn.

Charles had another cause for dislike. Johnston had accepted office and emolument from Cromwell. He was among the Judges—four of them Englishmen, the other three of native birth — whom the Puritan ruler appointed to superintend the administration of the law in Scotland. Aliens although the majority of these senators were, they soon made themselves very popular in the northern Kingdom; for under their direction the Courts were cleansed from the corrupt practices which had stolen away their good name and had led all lovers of fair-play to deride their jurisprudence. "Purity and rigour"—they are Sir Walter Scott's epithets—began once more to distinguish the conduct of legal affairs; how could it be otherwise when Andrew Ker sat on the bench, who "used to say that many times he had as sweet and as great communion with God," when he was robed in his judicial scarlet and ermine, "as ever he had in secret"? and when, side by side with Andrew Ker, sat Lord Wariston, *vir justus et tenax propositi?* Later, Sir Archibald was one of the sixty-three members of Oliver's House of Peers; and James Sharp heard gossiping stories, and repeated them, of "his declarations against valentines and a stage-play lately acted by Sir William Davenant." Finally, in 1657, he was reinstated by the Protector in the dignity of Lord Clerk Register of Scotland— a dignity which, a few years before, he had been compelled to forgo. These were sanctions of the Usurpation such as no other Covenanter had supplied, and the King might point to them in justification of his severity. To-day, when Cromwell's moral grandeur is as patent to us as his military genius, we do not dream of blaming Archibald Johnston for what he did. His procedure, too, was almost pathetically necessary. He had lost all his means in promoting the great aims of his life. He had no income to provide for the boys and girls crowding the house in the High Street; and the salary of the Judge or the Lord Clerk Register was sorely required. The *lacrimæ rerum* which the incident stirs we discover elsewhere, in his own agony afterwards that he had "made himself a trespasser." In his dying speech he bewailed his misdeed in moving words: "It doth not a little trouble me, and lies heavy on my spirit, and will bring me down with sorrow to the grave, that I suffered myself, through the power of temptations, and the too much fear anent the straits that my numerous family might be brought into, to be carried unto so great a length of compliance with the late usurpers, which did much grieve the hearts of the godly, and did give no small occasion to the adversary to reproach and blaspheme." "Scruple," says Jeremy Taylor, "is a little stone in the foot; if you set it upon the ground, it hurts you." Lord Wariston's foot, we surmise, was fevered and vexed by a little stone.

But it was his habit to scourge and afflict himself, prince in Israel although he was. His hasty temper was a poignant distress to him: did it not mar his best pieces of work that he was "subject to many excesses of heat, and thereby to some precipitations, which have offended standers-by and lookers-on"? Perhaps, on occasion, his eloquence was a trifle vehement and exasperating. But his personal religion was of no slipshod kind. He was an ardent lover of the secret place. Kirkton says that he gave more time to prayer and reading and meditation than any man he ever knew. It was a common thing for him to be on his knees, alone in his room, for three consecutive hours. Again and again he lost consciousness of what was passing round him. Once, intending to spend the beginning of the day in fellowship with God, he continued his intercessions and studies from six in the morning till, to his own amazement, the town bells rang at eight in the evening. We comprehend now why his heart was garrisoned by peace, while the noise of the archers was seldom intermitted outside. He believed that he saw God face to face; and, the night before his execution, he could tell a friend that not once, for a long period, had he known a doubt regarding his salvation. Those streams from the uplands fed the courage which never flagged, and nourished until the end his wisdom and his stature.

On the 14th of July 1660, a warrant was issued for the apprehension of Sir James Stewart, Lord Provost of Edinburgh, Sir John Chiesly of Kerswall, and Sir Archibald Johnston. The first two were arrested; but Wariston had some inkling of what was coming, and escaped to the Continent. Enraged at missing him, his enemies proclaimed his offices vacant and his estates forfeit; on a February day in 1661, at the Mercat Cross, the scene of many of his triumphs, the Lyon King denounced him as a traitor, and tore his Arms asunder, and trampled them under foot; but meanwhile his life was secure. In Hamburg, some months after leaving Scotland, he fell into serious illness. He was bled by a Dr. Bates, whose creed was not that of the Covenanters; and there were reports that the physician did not deal fairly with his patient. It is certain that he never recovered either his robustness of body or his clearness of memory; he was broken and old before his time. When he had been two years in Hamburg, he ventured to France to meet his wife; but the spies of Charles found him at Rouen. It is characteristic of him that, when they entered his lodging, he was kneeling in prayer; from the audience-chamber of God they hastened him to imprisonment. In

G

January 1663, he was confined within the Tower of London, where he lay for six months; and then, in the summer, he was transferred to the Tolbooth of Edinburgh.

It was a feeble invalid who was led before the Scottish Parliament; there was no risk that the persecutors would be assailed by the indignation which once might have leaped from his tongue. Everybody compassionated him, everybody except the Bishops and the Earl of Lauderdale, once his brother-deputy at the Assembly of Divines. Lauderdale's spiteful and bitter antipathy we can read in his own letters. Thus, on the 23rd of June, he writes that there is "a petition from that wretches children, shewing that he hath lost his memorie and almost his sence, and praying for delay till he may be in a fitter condition to dye." But the Council, he adds, and his own was the most potent voice in the Council, "wold not meddle in giving any respite." On the 2nd of July, after the prisoner's case has been discussed again, he describes how "divers voted for delay," but not his Grace himself—"I confess, thogh I thinke I be as farr from a cruell disposition as any bodie, yet, considering the justice of the sentence, and that, if it had come to a delay, it must have broght the trouble of it to His Majestie, who onely can grant pardon, I did cleirly vote, Presently." Again, on the 9th, "very late," he has more news to send from "Halyrude hous." On the previous day Wariston had been at the bar once more. "Yet I must needs tell you something there was of compassion in the Parliament, when they granted fourteen dayes time for the prisoner to prepare himself to dye. And he receaved the sentence to be hanged and to have his head affixed, with much more composedness of spirit than I did expect. He sate on his knees according to the custome; and then prayed God to bless the King, to bless the Parliament, to keep every one from his condition; and againe he prayed for the King, for the Church, and for the kingdome, and without one word for himself he went out." So Lauderdale, who voted "Presently," was not balked of his wish. On the 22nd of July, Archibald Johnston was to finish his course and to receive his enduring crown.

If the fire of his nature was less fervid, the faith was as firm. His young daughter had, at her request and his, been his companion in the Tower, and she remained with him in the Tolbooth; and always afterwards the prison was to her a gracious recollection. Her father's great concern was that he might "not faint in the hour of trial"; and the nearer the end approached, the more unassailable became his tranquillity, until, on the morning of his death, he spoke with assurance "of his being clothed in a long white robe," before another night should descend on his Margaret and himself. Through all that forenoon she heard him ejaculating, *Abba, Father!*—he would have understood and rejoiced in William Canton's verses—

> Thou'st seen how closely, Abba, when at rest,
> My child's head nestles to my breast;
> And how my arm her little form enfolds,
> Lest in the darkness she should feel alone;
> And how she holds
> My hands, my hands, my two hands in her own?
> > A little easeful sighing,
> > And restful turning round,
> > And I too, on Thy love relying,
> > Shall slumber sound.

Indeed, Wariston's *Abba* was long remembered; it became a gracious tradition which was instinctively associated with his name. Sixty years later, a minister of the Scottish Church recalled it, and wrote of it in his *Diary* that it was "uttered in such a manner as was most pleasant, ravishing, and refreshing to all" who heard the martyr, "although he was so low and weak that sometimes he fainted." At two o'clock he was called from his cell, for the scaffold was waiting him at the Mercat Cross.

Well he knew the spot. It was directly opposite the windows of his own house. They had made the gallows unusually high, to be in keeping with the offences which were to be expiated on it. Round the place were the King's Life Guards on horseback, "with their carabynes and naiket swords," and there was also "ane gaird of the toun of Edinburgh with their cullouris displayed." On the way to

the Cross, Wariston often turned to the people and asked
their prayers. When he reached it, he read his dying
testimony, first to those on the north and thereafter to
those on the south, speaking in a distinct voice, the old voice
of the Greyfriars given back again. Having finished, he
prayed twice, with the deepest contrition, but then in a
kind of rapture. At the head of the ladder he cried, " I
beseech you all who are the people of God not to scar at
sufferings for the interests of Christ; for I assure you, in
the name of the Lord, He will bear your charges." The
moment after he was heard to say, " The Lord hath graciously
comforted me." Then, asking the executioner if he was
ready, he gave the signal, exclaiming, " O pray, pray, praise,
praise!" It was with arms uplifted to the summer skies,
spectators remarked, that Archibald Johnston, who had
lived in familiarity with the better world, passed to see its
glories.

In *Naphtali*, that fine old Covenanting book, his last
speech may be read. There are the advocate's accent in it,
and the patriot's accent, but, best of all, the Christian's
accent, the discourse of the townsfolk in the city of God.
He grieved that it was "weak and short," for it had to be
written in his dungeon; but it stands in no need of apology.
These are its closing sentences: "I do here now submit and
commit my soul and body, wife and children and children's
children, with all others, His friends and followers—all His
doing and suffering, witnessing and sympathising ones, in
the present and subsequent generations—unto the Lord's
choice mercies, graces, favours, services, employments,
empowerments, enjoyments, improvements, and inheritments,
on earth and in heaven, in time and eternity. All which
suits, with all others which He hath at any time by His
Spirit moved and assisted me to make and put up according
to His will, I leave before and upon the Father's merciful
bowels and the Son's mediating merits and the Holy Spirit's
compassionate groans, for now and evermore. Amen."

Something there is in such language—a colour, a music,
an intimacy—beyond Greek and Roman fame.

CHAPTER X

SABBATH MORNING IN FENWICK.

A T Fenwick, close by Kilmarnock, stands one of the
historical parish churches of the west of Scotland.
The building is unassuming and simple, shaped like a Greek
cross, with a small tower and belfry. Inside are three
galleries, each with oaken front. Beside the pulpit the
visitor discovers a quaint relic of the older time—a bracket
on which is fixed a half-hour sand-glass, once employed to
regulate the duration of the sermon. In the green grass of
the churchyard there are the graves of martyrs—Robert
Buntine and James Blackwood, executed in 1666; James
White, shot at one of the moorland farms; John Fergushill
and George Woodburn and Peter Gemmill, killed in 1685.
These were parishioners of Fenwick at its most notable epoch;
and their deaths witness what strength as of steel the
preaching they heard breathed into their hearts. There
were other hearers too, better known than these: the Howies
of Lochgoin, and Captain John Paton of Meadowhead, who
sleeps in the Greyfriars, but to whose bravery and religion
a monument has been raised in the humbler God's acre in
Ayrshire. To the Scot who reverences what is best in the
story of his country, this is holy ground.

The first minister of Fenwick was William Guthrie, cousin
of " the short man who could not bow."

Eldest son in a Forfarshire family, he was born in his
father's house of Pitforthy, near Brechin, in 1620. No fewer
than four out of the five boys in Pitforthy mansion became
Covenanting preachers—Robert, and Alexander, and John,

as well as William; not many homes in Scotland did so much for the harassed and danger-driven Kirk. In his student years at St. Andrews William Guthrie found two treasures, in addition to the classical and philosophical learning which came to him there, and better still than it. One was the intimate friendship of his cousin James, his senior by some half a dozen summers, who took the lad to lodge with him in his own rooms. From the first he had his premonitions of the goal to which his cousin was travelling, and he envied him the crown he saw waiting for his brow. "You will have the better of me," he said; "for you will die honourably before many witnesses, with a rope about your neck; and I will die whining on a pickle straw." But, in the divinity school, a still profounder happiness was in store. Samuel Rutherfurd had recently been sent, much against his desire, to the University town, to fill the chair of theology in St. Mary's College. It was through Rutherfurd that the Spirit of God spoke to William Guthrie in those accents which are at once irresistible and sweet. Lovable, high-minded, "naturally Christian" as he had been from boyhood, he received now that touch of the glowing coal from the Altar which cleanses the lips and sets the heart on fire. He was equipped for the ministry of the Gospel.

Before the ministry began, however, he proved his devotion to Christ. That nothing might wean him from his calling, he surrendered his right of succession to the Pitforthy estate. There was one brother in the household who was not destined for the pulpit, and to him the heir to the property made over his possessions. He had an overflowing reward, even in this life, in his freedom from worldly entanglements, in the geniality and joyousness of his temperament, and, most of all, in that marvellous and victorious power with which his Master endowed his preaching. He was one of the men, whom some count mad, "who, the more they cast away, the more they have."

William Guthrie was ready for his lifework. He went westward, to the county of Ayr, that he might be tutor to Lord Mauchline, eldest son of the Earl of Loudoun. But he

CHARLES I.

After a Portrait by Van Dyck.

had not been long in Loudoun Castle, until he was called
to undertake his coveted task of proclaiming the Evangel.
Preaching on a Fast-day in the neighbouring town of Galston,
he had among his listeners some Covenanters from Fenwick—
Fenwick which had but lately been endowed with a church
and congregation of its own. They felt that the young
licentiate was the minister whom God had appointed for
them. But there were difficulties in the way. Lord Boyd,
the superior, was an unbending Royalist, and he mistrusted
any one who came commended by the Earl of Loudoun. For
a time the settlement was postponed. But the disappointments and hindrances, while they made the people of Fenwick
angry with the man who was the author of them, only served
to reveal the winsome Christianity of their minister-elect.
His temper was never ruffled. One reads his essential sweetness in the letters he wrote, during the months of waiting,
to his bosom-friend, the younger Sir William Mure of
Rowallan. "As for that business which hath put so many
to trouble," he says, "wisest Providence keeps a princely
way in it. The present stop, if it be not an offence to you,
it shall not be grievous to me. Lay aside these nothings,
and detain the King in the galleries in the behalf of Zion."
William Guthrie's spirit held "no draught of bitter dew."

And meanwhile, though his lips were closed, he could
preach by his pen. Sir William Mure's lady, Dame Elizabeth
Hamilton, daughter of the Provost of Glasgow, like so many
of her high-born sisters in that earnest age, was anxious
above all things to have some seal of her "calling and
election": was she Christ's, or was she not? She could not
have consulted a safer spiritual director than young Mr.
Guthrie. He told her husband how she should "know if
her work were thorough." If her conscience were only
eased, not cured, then she would be quickly satisfied, and
"no place of Scripture would be made lively to her which
she dared call her own," and she would see no more to be
sin than she saw before, and she would be possessed with
no deeper awe at the performance of religious duties, and
she would hold the Bible in no loftier esteem than had been

her custom. But if conscience really was healed, Lady Mure would find herself the tenant of a new world. No poppy or mandragora or drowsy syrup would be permitted to lull her into sleep. She would look for her charter in the Word of Life itself. She would regard faults, which the world counted nothings, "to be as offensive to God as gross out-breakings." She would dread especially that searching sentence, *Cursed is he who doeth the work of the Lord negligently*, and would fear much in the time of service, and would remember that "the iniquity of holy things will damn, if God cover not shortcomings." Do we not feel that we are in the company of a skilled and faithful and tender physician of the soul? Here, already, are fore-glimpses of what will be the good minister's chief concern and passion. Lord Boyd's objections were overcome in the end; and, in November 1644, the preacher was ordained over the parish which was determined to have no one else for its instructor and shepherd. Often in succeeding years the attempt was made to draw Guthrie from his secluded countryside to busier and more prominent spheres; but nothing could coax him to forsake his early love. To the last, until the summer morning twenty years distant when the bishops and dragoons drove him out, he was loyal to Fenwick.

To his manse, in the August after his ordination, he brought his wife, Agnes Campbell, who was related in some distant way to Lord Loudoun. She was a woman of a gracious spirit. In after years, when death had snatched him from her only too soon, she wrote letters instinct with good cheer to the captives and sufferers of the Covenant whom she knew. But, from the outset, the mistress of the home had sharp experience of the trials that invaded Presbyterian households in those distracted times. In 1648, her husband was present, with six other ministers, at the skirmish on Mauchline Moor. In 1650, he was with the defeated army at Dunbar. Agnes Guthrie had an anxious heart during these seasons of absence. At first, indeed, she declared that he must not leave her to encounter such hazards; but illness brought him, beneath his own rooftree, to the brink of death, and she saw that, by the hearth or in the field, she must intrust him to the safe-keeping of God. It would have been a bootless enterprise—the attempt to limit his participation in his country's affairs. Like his spiritual kinsfolk, he could not understand a piety which was divorced from patriotism and good citizenship.

The minister of Fenwick, says James Stirling, preacher in the subsequent generation in the Barony Church of Glasgow, was a "great melancholian," one of the sensitive and reflective and brooding souls, whose thoughts plunge deep down, and whose eyes are accustomed to look out on men and the world through a mist of weeping. His frail body had much to do with the pensiveness of his mind; all his life long he bore about with him a tormenting sickness; and it would have been strange if one who never knew robust health had not sometimes been grave and sad. Yet, despite his serious moods, a blither heart than William Guthrie's never beat. He laughs out of court the caricature that the Covenanters were men jaundiced and fault-finding: he is a Covenanter full of merriment. His talk sparkled with humour. His nature delighted in friendliness. There were moments, he confessed, when his love of fun carried him too far; and then he shed salt tears in secret over his quips and jests in company. But that was seldom. One day he and James Durham were together, in a gentleman's house, at dinner; and he was so mirthful and vivacious that Durham, the most composed of men, caught the infection, and laughed again and again. Immediately after dinner, in accordance with the custom of the family, Guthrie was asked to pray. And such a prayer it was, burning with divine fire, opening the gates of heaven, and melting the spirits of the auditors. "O Will!" Durham cried, as they rose from their knees, "you are a happy man. If I had been so daft, I could not have been in any frame for eight-and-forty hours." "It was often observed," Wodrow says, "that, let Mr. Guthrie be never so merry, he was presently fit for the most spiritual duty; and the only account I can give of it," continues the minister of Eastwood, " is that he acted from spiritual principles in all he did, and even in his relaxations." It is the true solution. There was no profane territory anywhere in this laughing and weeping man.

He was a great angler. He knew the spots, and resorted to them frequently, where

> trout below the blossomed tree
> Plashed in the golden stream.

To carry a rod, and to cast a line, and to land a fish, were among his chief pleasures. He could have subscribed prattling Izaak Walton's confession that "angling, after tedious study, is a rest to the mind, a cheerer of the spirits, a diversion of sadness, a calmer of unquiet thoughts, a moderator of passions, a procurer of contentedness." But his supreme work was that of fishing for men. When, he went to Fenwick, the spiritual condition of the place was as low as it could be. Some of his people lived six or seven miles distant; the country was full of morasses; there were no proper roads; the majority never dreamed of attending the New Kirk, as it was named. They gave the Sabbath to amusement. They were rude enough, here and there, to close their doors in their minister's face. But he refused to be discouraged. In the cause of Christ he would not own the possibility of defeat.

Stories are recorded of his ingenuity and strategy in compelling men, however stubborn they might be, to look the eternal things fairly in the face. He would disguise himself, and would get a night's lodging in a cottage, and would talk with the inmates. Once he transformed a poacher into an elder and a saint. The man said that, abroad in the fields with his gun, he had his best sport when his neighbours were safely shut within the church, and that, each Monday morning, he earned half a crown by the sale of his moorfowl and hares. " I will pay you the half-crown," Guthrie replied, "if you will come to the New Kirk next Sabbath." The bargain was struck; but, when the offer was repeated, the bribe was refused. In God's house the poacher had heard what was of greater value than a bushel of half-crowns. He was never absent afterwards, and ere long, with the goodwill of all, he was enrolled an office-bearer. There was another time when the minister persuaded a household into the observance of family worship. Dressed as a traveller, he found admission to the home, and was bidden stay. The hour came when "the Books" should be brought out; but there was no sign of them. The stranger inquired whether he might not join his hosts in their evening devotions; but the goodman asserted that he had no gift in prayer, and must not essay a task so high. "Nay, but you ought," the pertinacious guest insisted; and soon he had them all kneeling on the kitchen floor. "O Lord," cried the abashed and stammering suppliant, "this man would have me to pray; but Thou knowest that I cannot pray." It was a hopeful beginning, the confession of ignorance, the bewailing of the heart's penury and the mouth's cowardice. And afterwards, in this house, the altar of God was kept in good repair.

William Guthrie had his recompense. Soon his parish became—what Jewish tradition calls the home of Obed-Edom, where God's Ark sojourned—the Field of the Blessed Man. The people turned his glebe into a little town, so desirous they were to live in the vicinity of the church. From every district of the west—from Glasgow, from Paisley, from Hamilton, from Lanark—crowds trooped to hear him. "The lobbies of Fenwick Kirk," writes Dr. Alexander Whyte, "were like the porches of Bethesda, with all the blind, halt, and withered from the whole country round." And in the lowly meeting-place, as in Bethesda, the power of the Lord was present to heal. "A very exercised woman," Agnes Biggart, told the minister of the Barony "that Mr. Guthrie would in one sermon have gone over a great part of the spiritual exercises of a true Christian." He had "a strange way of persuading sinners to close with Christ, and answering all objections that might be proposed." Then, too, he possessed "a gift, peculiar to himself, of speaking to the common people in their own dialect." And the Sacramental Sabbaths in the New Kirk were preludes of heaven itself. James Hutcheson of Killellan was assistant on one of them; and, over and over, he would avow that, "if there was a kirk full of saints in the world, it was the Kirk of Fenwick that day"; the shining faces he had seen, and the ecstasies he had shared, were never forgotten while life lasted. We do not wonder that men high in rank said that they "would have been heartily content to have lived under Mr. Guthrie's ministry, though they had been but in the station of poor ploughmen." It would have been a wise exchange, and they must have gained more than they lost.

The fruitful ministry had its headquarters in Fenwick; but its beneficence was widely diffused. The preacher travelled up and down all the western shires; and, wherever he spoke, souls born into the liberties of the New Jerusalem followed him with gratitude. Wodrow has a tale of a Glasgow merchant, who, coming from Ireland, was forced to spend a Sabbath in Arran, and was annoyed with the misgiving that he would hear no sermon except in Gaelic. But, when he went to the church, Guthrie was in the pulpit. It was a day when the wind of the Spirit carried everything before its invincible onset. "There was scarce a hearer without tears, and many old people, in particular, weeping." Christ's footfall accompanied His ambassador on all his pilgrimages. Thus it happened once, north in Angus, when he was journeying to the old home in Pitforthy. In the darkness he lost his way, and, after some hours, discovered himself in the policies of a gentleman whom he knew to be unrelentingly opposed to the Covenanters. He knocked at the door of the mansion, and was invited to enter. Soon he had to confess himself a minister; and then he craved permission to pray. It was granted, although the master of the house "carried pretty abstractedly." But the prayer moved the three daughters of the home as they had never been moved before. Next day the curate had to stand aside, that the unexpected guest might preach in his stead; "and these three young gentlewomen were converted at that sermon." Cures flowed from this man, as the clear water bubbles from the mountain-spring and refuses to be held back.

And many, then and since, who never heard him speak, but have read his gracious and golden little book, *The Christian's*

Great Interest, are undyingly in his debt.   It was published in 1659, and it is not obsolete even now.   It is a guide to the heart which asks the road to God, or which wishes to be assured that the road it has been walking is the right one—a guide which does not leave the wayfarer in the least uncertainty. There are no mists in its pages, no ambiguities, no needless verbiage : all is plain and simple.   First and last, it is marked by a crystal clearness of thought, an unfailing sanity of state-ment, a rich pithiness of phrase.   " It is my *vade-mecum*," John Owen said ; " I carry it and the Sedan New Testament still about with me.   I have written several folios ; but there is more divinity in it than in them all."   The greatest are ever the humblest, and contemporaries and successors are better able to rate John Owen at his proper worth than he was himself ; but the chapters in which one of the princes of scholars and saints found such surpassing merit cannot but deserve our remembrance and study.   What memorable sentences they contain !   " It is a work and business which cannot be done sleeping," cries the watchman who is too kind to let us fall into heedlessness.   The robber on the Cross was " nobly daring," he declares, " to throw himself upon the Covenant."   The soul smitten with hunger for the living bread in the Saviour's house " resolves to die if He command so, yet at His door and facing towards Him."   The man who prizes redemption as it should be prized " carefully gathers and treasures up his Michtams or Golden Scriptures," in order that, through the comfort they bring, his doubts may be scattered.   " If you will, you are welcome," the envoy of the King assures our hearts, which have a hundred difficulties to suggest.   " He turns all ways in which He can be useful to poor man "—it is his commendation of the Healer who is at such pains to induce us to make trial of His grace.   But Jesus has a holy jealousy too ; He " will never clout the old garment of hypocrites with His fine new linen."   Our belief, William Guthrie warns us, " must not swim only in the head " ; indeed it is not enough that it should be " a business in the outer court of the affections " ; it must be found " in the innermost cabinet of the soul."   A man, he says too, who is determined to seek and find, will close with Christ not in some fit of emotional excitement but in calmness of spirit, "and, as it were, in his cold blood." The Christian has such an intimacy and familiarity in prayer, it is explained in another place, that he does not "use a number of compliments in his addresses" to his Father in heaven, and does not speak to God "as one who has His acquaintance to make every hour." And, almost at the end of the book, we are admonished against the folly of expecting our harvests while it is still our changeable and boisterous spring; the ripe fruit and the full assurance can scarcely be ours immediately after we have fled to our Redeemer's arms; nay, "these things will keep a man in work all his days." It is seldom that we meet such a sentCentious, axiomatic, wise-hearted teacher. He brings us *apples of gold in baskets of silver*.

But the storm gathered. Guthrie never had reposed much faith in Charles Stuart. Visiting, in 1660, in the house of Sir Daniel Carmichael, the Treasurer Depute of the Kingdom, he found every one jubilant over the homecoming of the sovereign; but, when he led the family in their devotions, this was his ominous forecast, "Lord, Thou knowest how soon this man may welter in the best blood of Scotland." Sir Daniel complained that his guest would "put them all in hazard to be hanged"; he was "a little roughsome" over the half-treasonable speech; but, no doubt, he recalled it in the later months when its prophecy was receiving a fulfilment only too complete and tragic. For the minister himself there was a short respite. It was due in part to that beautiful courtesy which won for him, Protester as he was, a kindlier consideration than was extended to his fellows. "They that made Mr. Guthrie a minister," one of his elders said, "spoiled a good Malignant." Then he had two friends at Court, the Earl of Eglintoun and the Earl of Glencairn, the latter of whom could not forget his helpfulness when his own fortunes were at their lowest. For four years after the Restoration Fenwick kept the man whom it revered. They were years of notable usefulness. More and more the people trooped to hear him, hundreds sometimes standing outside the open doors

WILLIAM GUTHRIE, OF FENWICK.

A Portrait prefixed to some Editions of "The Christian's Great Interest."

in the churchyard. Crowned with favour as his labours had
been from their outset, God kept the best for the last, and,
as His servant stepped Westward, it was towards a region
bright and a heavenly destiny. He was active, also, in the
meetings of the Glasgow Synod, and strove hard to induce
his brethren to send a plain-spoken address to the godless
Parliament in Edinburgh; but the majority of them were not
as dauntless as he was himself, and, much to his chagrin, a less
uncompromising deliverance was adopted. For some Synods
and Assemblies, it may be feared, he felt small reverence.
"Mr. James Stirling tells me," writes Robert Wodrow, "that
Mr. William Guthrie and Mr. John Durie used to divide the
members of Assembly into *Vocales* and *Consonantes* and *Mutæ*
and *Liquidæ* and *Diphthongæ*. The application of these, to
most part of numerous meetings, is pretty obvious." Prophets
and apostles, one learns from manifold sources, are not always
the most successful ecclesiastics.

Glencairn and Eglintoun postponed the blow; but they
could not avert it. The patience of Archbishop Fairfoul was
at length exhausted; "he is a ringleader of sedition in my
diocese," he answered when the noblemen appealed to him.
In July 1664, the familiar voice was heard in Fenwick for the
last time. It was a Sabbath morning. On the preceding
Wednesday Guthrie had held a congregational Fast, preaching
from the regretful cry of Hosea, *O Israel, thou hast destroyed
thyself!* Now, for his final message, he chose a softer word,
the word of hope which follows, *But in Me is thine help.* At
four o'clock, in the cool and clear summer dawn, the congregation assembled. Twice over their minister mounted the
pulpit, making an interval between his sermons, and in the
end dismissing the people before nine. Sorrow and anger
were within them as they turned away.

At noon the curate of Calder, the one man willing to
perform the ungracious task, arrived with an escort of twelve
soldiers, to suspend William Guthrie from his office, and to
declare his church vacant. There was some conversation in
the manse. The curate spoke of the leniency shown to the
Covenanting leader; and he received the reply, "I take the

Lord for party to that, and thank Him for it; I look upon it as a door which God opened to me for preaching the Gospel." "I bless the Lord," this true bishop continued, "He hath given me some success and a seal of my ministry upon the consciences of not a few that are gone to heaven, and of some hat are yet in the way to it." By and by he turned to the soldiers. "As for you, gentlemen," he said, "I wish the Lord may pardon you for countenancing this man in this business." One of them retorted, "I trust we may never do a graver fault." "Well," was the response, an arrow shot at a venture, "a little sin may damn a man's soul." Then a blessing was asked, and refreshments were served by the persecuted to the persecutors; and curate and horsemen went to announce to an empty church the eviction of its minister.

But, though he could no more speak in his Master's name, he lived on in Fenwick for a few months longer. Nothing jangled the melodiousness of his disposition. It is a quaint and quickening incident which John Howie recounts, in *The Scots Worthies*, of this period. The silenced minister and some friends had gone to the village of Stewarton, to hear a young man preach. Coming home again, they told him of their dissatisfaction with the sermon. "Ah!" he said, "you are mistaken; it was an admirable sermon." And then he proposed that they should sit down on the grass, and he would rehearse it to them. So, "in a good summer night, about the sun-setting," they "put up at God's green caravanserai," finding their sanctuary under the open sky; and a second time the sermon was preached that day. But with what a different result! "They thought it a wonderfully great one, because of his good delivery and their amazing love to him." We are enamoured of the man, who, instead of repining over his own misfortunes, took such pains to gain for a beginner the charity of judges disposed to be censorious.

The end of life was at hand now. Pursued by ill health, he did not grow stronger with the revolving seasons; he needed a draught from the river of healing in the Paradise of God. In 1665, the brother to whom he had bequeathed Pitforthy died; and he went north to help in the arrangement of the family affairs. But his disease returned in an aggravated form. The pain was agonising; again and again it made him delirious; "but," he said, "though I should die mad, I know I shall die in the Lord." On the 10th of October, in the house of his brother-in-law, Laurence Skinner, one of the ministers of Brechin, he got his release from the troublesome world; the faith was kept and the crown attained. William Guthrie was only forty-five, when he laid down his task and fell asleep.

CHAPTER XI.

HOW COLONEL WALLACE FOUGHT AT PENTLAND.

THE Earl of Middleton had gone, and the Earl of Rothes ruled Scotland in his stead. But to the Covenanters the change brought no escape from tyranny and no help for pain. On the contrary, they were plunged into rougher waters and sent through fiercer fires. The new Commissioner had his better qualities. His judgment was clear, Bishop Burnet says, and his apprehension quick. Occasionally an evanescent mood of compassion prompted him to show a little tenderness to the persecuted men—a mood to be traced largely to the influence of his wife, who had been Lady Anne Lindsay, a woman "discreet, wise, virtuous, and good." " I would advise you, my Lady, to keep your chickens in about, else I may pick up some of them," he would tell her, if he caught sight of any of the outed ministers in the neighbourhood of his mansion-house of Leslie. But such penitences were rare, and they vanished speedily. His administration was to be marked by a violence even ruder and more vulgar than that of his pre-decessor. In personal character he can only be described as a thorough-paced debauchee; the bracing grace of self-mastery was unknown to him; and his godly wife must have wept in secret over the unabashed scandals of her husband's conduct. He was illiterate too, in spite of that clear judgment and quick apprehension of his, " barely able to do more than make his mark"; when he wrote, he formed each letter singly, and between the several letters in a word he would put as great a distance as that between the words themselves. The Church and its defenders had nothing to hope for, and much to dread, from the ascendancy of the Earl of Rothes.

It was significant that, from the first, his chief adviser was the Archbishop of St. Andrews. If he was himself keen to amass plunder, James Sharp was as eager to inflict punishment on men whose constancy was a stinging rebuke to his own faithlessness. Rothes was extortionate and brutal; the Prelate was revengeful and persistent in his enmities; with this duumvirate in authority the prospect for the friends of the Covenant was gloomy as midnight. When Parliament broke up in the autumn of 1663—a Parliament which, like one of the Kings of Judah, *departed without being desired*—it was well understood that its members were not to be called together again; henceforward Scotland was to be managed by the Privy Council, a body more limited, more homogeneous, more unpitying; and in the Privy Council Sharp and Rothes were supreme. It was at the instigation of the Primate that a new step in oppression was now taken. No congregations could be found for the curates; in the west, especially, it seemed that the Church buildings were to be forsaken; more and more the spirit of resistance was abroad. The Archbishop resolved to crush the daring spirit with an arbitrary hand. He went up to London; and, on the plea that the Council must be relieved of some of its business, he persuaded the King to bring back the obsolete Court of High Commission, for the summary trial and conviction of all recusants. Of the re-established Court he was to be President; associated with him were nine prelates and thirty-five laymen; and the tribunal had almost absolute powers bestowed on it. It could summon to its bar the "obstinate contemners of the discipline of the Church," the "keepers of conventicles," those who "preached in private houses or elsewhere without licence from the bishop." Its verdicts were final; frequently they were pronounced without evidence being adduced. It imposed exorbitant fines on men and women of rank who attended the field-preachings, or permitted them to be held in any corner of their estates. It imprisoned and banished the ejected ministers. Sometimes it ordered women to be whipped publicly through the streets. Sometimes it would have young boys scourged, and branded on the face with a hot iron, and sold as slaves, to labour at the forts in Shetland, or to till the plantations in Virginia and Barbadoes, where, as Governor Willoughby testified, they were the best workmen he had. It declared that it was sedition to give a morsel of bread to one of the hunted preachers. These were the frightful prerogatives of the High Commission Court, and its members felt no scruples about exercising them. The Covenanters were entering on that long and winding Valley of the Shadow of Death, from which they were not to emerge for a quarter of a century.

For a time they submitted in silence, although there were flying rumours that the chiefs of the party were treating with the Government of Presbyterian Holland. It only required a spark, and the conflagration would be kindled; but the spark was furnished neither by sympathisers in the Netherlands nor by the nobles at home. The insurrection had a humbler origin. What we know as the Pentland Rising was a movement unpremeditated and simple in its beginnings. From its sudden inception to its grievous close only two weeks elapsed. It was like the outbreak of a volcano in a West Indian island, unexpected, brief-lived, but leaving red ruin behind. Spontaneous and unsuggested, it was the protest of downtrodden men against taskmasters whose cruelties had become intolerable.

For eight or nine months Sir James Turner had commanded the King's troops in the district of Galloway, having his headquarters in Dumfries. Dugald Dalgetty is familiar to most; and Turner sat for the portrait of the roving and loud-voiced soldier of fortune. He has written his own *Memoirs*, to clear his name from the reproaches which besmirched its lustre, and we can see him as he saw himself: the scholar, who "allways tooke delight in the studie of humane letters and historie," and who had "read the controversies of religion betweene us and the Roman Catholickes"; the adventurer, who had fought, now on one side and then on the other, in the wars of Gustavus and Wallenstein, having "swallowed without chewing, in Germanie, a very dangerous maxime, that, so as we serve our master honnestlie, it is no matter what master we serve"; the lover and husband, who found in Ireland what he valued more than worldly riches, his "deare wife, Mary White," with whom he was "first acquainted and then enamourd at the Neurie." But the more impartial pages of history are scarcely so gentle towards his reputation. In Galloway, "a place and a people fatall to me," he harried the Covenanters. He protests his clemency, insisting that he was far from going to those excesses in extortion which were sanctioned by his instructions; but the truth remains that hundreds of families were beggared by the fines he exacted. Some years later, the Privy Council itself forced him to answer for his high-handed procedure; and matters must have been undisguisedly and flagrantly bad when a Court so friendly saw reason to interpose. "Proud, passionate, hastie, and furieous" he was "caractered to be," in Royalist as in Whiggish coteries. Before his accusers he acknowledged that he had been more grasping than there was any need: "to ease their Lordships of further trouble, and show them my oune ingenuitie, I wold charge myselfe with threttie thousand pounds Scots"—a sum which must be multiplied by three, or even by five, if the real condition of things would be known. Is it very extraordinary that the people, farmers and cottars, were goaded into revolt?

It was near the middle of November in 1666. From the Galloway hills four Covenanters, one of them the Laird of Barscobe—gaunt men who had been hiding among the mosses —came stealing down, seeking food and the shelter for one night of a kindly roof, to the clachan of Dalry, not far from Loch Ken. But it happened that some of Sir James Turner's troopers were quartered there; and, when they entered the village, these soldiers were ill-treating an old man, who declared himself unable to pay the heavy fine exacted from him because of absence from the parish church. In their frank barbarity they threatened to strip him and set him on a red-hot gridiron. This was more than the four "honest men" could endure. Daring the troopers to do the wicked deed, they found that the villagers seconded their defiance. "Why do you bind the old man?" Maclellan of Barscobe demanded. "How dare you challenge us?" was the retort. The quarrel became fiercer every minute. The thongs which tied the captive were loosed. Then the soldiers drew their swords, and, with the gleaming steel confronting them, one of the Covenanters discharged his pistol, "loaden with a great many pieces of tobacco pipes." A corporal, George Deanes by name, belonging to Sir Alexander Thomson's company, was wounded. "This," Wodrow says, "quickly made the rest yield, and the countrymen disarmed them and took them prisoners, and the poor old man was happily delivered." Out of the petty scuffle sprang unplanned a Rising, which had crowded into it a world of heroism and pathos and pain.

The men, to whom pity and anger had called imperiously, realised that they must expect the vengeance of Government. They determined to continue in arms. With the aid of others they captured one or two little groups of soldiers. Then one of the landlords, John Neilson of Corsock, joined them; and they resolved on a bold experiment. They would march rapidly on Dumfries, where Turner was living. There were now "above ninescore men, more than the halfe wherof consisted of horsemen, indifferently weill mounted, with suords, pistolls, and carabines; the rest were afoot armed with muskets, pikes, suords, sithes, and forkes." On the morning of the 15th of November, between eight and nine, they entered the town. Their enemy, as it happened, was at their mercy. A few months before, the half of his infantry had been withdrawn from him, to help in the campaign against the Dutch. In October, the most of his cavalry had gone. Only seventy men remained under his command, and of these no more than twelve or thirteen were at that moment in Dumfries itself. Moreover, Sir James was unwell and in bed. Hearing the noise, he sprang up, and went to a window, and inquired of the intruders what they wanted. He was told to surrender, and he should have fair quarter. But he needed no quarter, he replied, and he could not be a prisoner, for the country was not in a state of war. "Prisoner you must be, or die," came the inexorable answer from the street. There was nothing for it but to let

SIR JAMES TURNER.

From the Engraving by Robert White.
Through the kindness of Messrs. T. C. & E. C. Jack.

the ninescore invaders have their will, and King Charles's officer rode out of Dumfries their thrall. At first he was clothed only in his night-gear, and was mounted on " a little beast barebacked with a halter on its head "; but his own dress and his horse's trappings were more adequate soon.   For the next fortnight, through all their marchings, he continued with them.   He had, as Gabriel Sempill, one of their number, said, " been lifted up in pride, with insolency and cruelty over the poor people "; yet his captors treated him well.   If a few of the wilder spirits muttered that he ought to be put to death, they were always overruled.   His worst sorrow was the Covenanting grace before and after meat: he was " more over-wearied with the tediousness and impertinencies of their graces " than he was with " the scarceness or badness " of his food and drink.   Sometimes, too, Sempill, or young Robertson the probationer, or John Welsh himself, would deal seriously with him, assuring him that they sought the salvation of his soul.   John Welsh prayed with him, " and honord me with the title of God's servant who was then in bonds, and asked for my conversion."   But the soil was sterile and impervious. " To what they spoke of my conversion I said, it wold be hard to turne a Turner."   From first to last, there was never a rough hand laid on the persecuting soldier.

The heather was on fire now.   News of the insurrection came to the Privy Council with a shock of surprise—to the Earl of Rothes more than any.   So recently as September, he had sent to Lauderdale a rose-coloured picture.   "All is offer," he wrote, in his egregious spelling, " as to anie other teumult or ffurdier trubell."   This was the roughest of awakenings; and in a few days an army of two thousand foot and five hundred horse left Edinburgh in haste.   Its commander is a grim figure, a man with a lust for slaughter, whose " every sentence scents of blood."   Thomas Dalzell's features have been depicted by Captain John Creichton, who was among his intimates, and himself, as Dr. Jonathan Swift certifies, " of the old Stamp "; and they are features to awaken astonishment rather than liking.

"Among many other Officers, he was taken Prisoner at

the unfortunate Defeat at *Worcester*, and sent to the Tower;
from whence, I know not by what Means, he made his Escape,
and went to *Muscovy*, where the *Czar* made him his General.
But, some Time after the Restoration of the Royal Family,
repairing to King *Charles* the Second, he was constituted
Commander-in-Chief of his Majesty's Forces in *Scotland*.   He
was bred up very hardy from his Youth, both in Dyet and
Cloathing.   He never wore Boots, nor above one Coat, which
was close to his Body, with close Sleeves, like those we call
Jockey-Coats.   He never wore a Peruke; nor did he shave
his Beard since the Murder of King *Charles* the First.   In my
Time, his Head was bald, which he covered only with a Beaver
Hat.   His Beard was white and bushy, and reached down
almost to his Girdle.   He went to *London* once or twice in a
Year, only to kiss the King's Hand, who had a great Esteem
for his Worth and Valour.   His unusual Dress and Figure
never failed to draw after him a Crowd of Boys, and other
young People, who constantly attended at his Lodgings, and
followed him with Huzzas, as he went to Court or returned
from it.   As he was a Man of Humour, he would always thank
them for their Civilities, when he left them at the Door to go
in to the King; and would let them know exactly at what
Hour he intended to come out again.   When the King walked
in the Park, and *Dalzell* in his Company, his Majesty bid the
Devil take *Dalzell* for bringing such a Rabble of Boys together,
to have their Guts squeezed out, whilst they gaped at his long
Beard and antick Habit; requesting him to shave and dress
like other Christians, to keep the poor Bairns out of Danger.
In Compliance, he went once to Court in the very Height of
the Fashion; but, as soon as the King had laughed sufficiently
at the strange Figure he made, he reassumed his usual Habit,
to the great Joy of the Boys, who had not discovered him in
his fashionable Dress."   We are thankful to Captain Creichton
for the lifelike portrait, even if it amuses more than edifies.
But Scottish Whigs could not laugh like London gamins at
the "long Beard and antick Habit," for they were worn by a
man who scourged them with a lash more merciless than
the *flagellum* of a Roman lictor.   "In Muscovia," Kirkton

says, Dalzell "saw nothing but tyranny and slavery"; and tyranny and slavery filled the cup he mixed for his countrymen.

Out from Edinburgh Thomas Dalzell marched towards Glasgow, and up through Galloway came the insurgents into Ayrshire. Despite "the great rains and coldness of the weather," they increased as they came. At the town of Ayr Turner estimated that there were seven hundred; in Lanark, he believes, they "are in their greatest strength, which never exceeded eleven hundred horse and foot, if they were so many." Their first leader, meantime, deserted the camp; Andrew Gray was scarcely of the stuff of which campaigners are made. There is something mysterious about him, and about his participation in the adventure. He seems to have presented a commission or recommendation from those in authority; but no one knew exactly who he was, or whether he had come from "a Generall, or a councell, or a committee, or a junto." Now, however, having begun to realise the dangers of the proceeding on which he had embarked, or having "taken the pett," he vanished unexpectedly, and "was never seene since by any of his oune partie." But at the Bridge of Doon they found a true captain, James Wallace of Auchans, a good man and a skilled soldier, who had fought for the Parliament in the Civil Wars. We can see him still, in his long cloak, with his montero, or huntsman's cap, drawn well over his brow, and his beard very rough. To his Royalist prisoner his deportment was always courteous; he is a gentleman to the core. Along with him other trained officers joined the tiny army—Major Learmont, and Captain Arnot, and Captain Paton of Meadowhead, all three men who, at Worcester, had stood shoulder to shoulder with Dalzell himself. Under the tuition of such instructors the undisciplined crowd was lifted into a company of capable foemen, so that, against his will, Sir James Turner was driven into admiration. At Lesmahagow they were put through their exercises; and even "the ranks of Tuscany can scarce forbear to cheer." "I saw tuo of their troopes skirmish against other tuo, which I confesse they did handsomelie. I wonderd at the agilitie of both horse and rider, and how they had come to that perfection in so short a time." The force was small; but it was far from being despicable.

The Covenanters were at Lanark on the evening of the 25th of November; and, next day, crowding round the Tolbooth stairs, they renewed the Covenant "with as much joy and cheerfulness as may be supposed in such a condition," and published a Declaration. It asserted their unchanged regard for the King; but it enumerated, too, their reasons for taking up arms. Had not the Solemn League been burned by the Government? Had not Episcopacy been established? Were there not fines, imprisonments, the quartering of soldiers, the inquisitions of the High Commission Court? Unforeseen and impulsive as the uprising was, it could justify itself.

But it was ordained to failure. Perhaps those were wisest, from the military viewpoint, who would have tempted Dalzell to fight at Lanark, more numerous as his soldiers were. For then the army of the Covenant was at its best; and every day that succeeded drained its vigour and diminished its hope. But the wish of the majority was to push on to Edinburgh, where friends, it was thought, waited to welcome them. Forward they went, to disappointment after disappointment. Two hundred turned back, alleging as excuse their disapproval of the course which had been adopted. Comrades, whose help was counted on, lingered at home. Envoys came from Dalzell, suggesting questions and apprehensions, Lowrie of Blackwood, himself with strong Whiggish leanings, being most active amongst these mediators. More formidable still was the pitiless weather; nothing could be wilder; the stars in their courses seemed to fight against the saints. "To Bathgate they came through pitifull broken moores in ane extraordinary dark and rainy night, and two houres after daylight was gone. No accommodation can they find there to men wett, weary, and spent; and, about twelve o'clock at night, upon ane alarm from the enemy, they are constrained to begin their march toward the New-bridge, whither, when they were come in the morning, they looked rather like dying men than souldiers going to conquer. It would have pitied a heart to see so many faint, half-drowned, half-starved

creatures betwixt their enemies behind and their enemies
before." To complete their sorrows, they found no help in
the Lothians. When, late on the 27th, they were within five
miles of Edinburgh, they discovered that the city was arming
to resist them, and that the Provost, Sir Andrew Ramsay,
had devised a new oath, binding the townsfolk to defend the
King's authority. The cannon from the Castle ramparts had
been removed to the gates of the town. The strictest watch
was kept, and no one was allowed to pass in or out. A large
supply of lances and pole-axes had been hastily ordered from
Culross and Dunfermline. The dirge had deepened every
hour. But, in scorn of the torrents of rain, the cold, the
fatigue, the hostile town, the regiments of Dalzell, James
Wallace's soldiers kept unshaken their courage. We may
compare them to that statue of Fortitude, which Botticelli
fashioned, and which Mr. Ruskin described, not announcing
themselves clearly and proudly, with tower-like shields and
lion-like helmets, nor standing confidently ready for all
comers; no, but they are worn somewhat, and not a little
weary, and their fingers play restlessly and even nervously
about the hilt of their swords; and yet how swiftly and gladly
the playing fingers will close on the sword-hilt, when the far-
off trumpet blows!

Their hearts might be unafraid; but their eyes were
opened. They saw clearly enough now that there was no
hope. There were some fresh negotiations; but these came
to nothing, because the Privy Council was "no ways satisfied."
The insurgents, having chosen their path, must travel on over
its stones and thorns to the inevitable close; and they were
not unwilling to die, they said, for the cause of religion and
liberty. Meantime, however, a retreat, if retreat were yet
possible, seemed the advisable course. So, early on the
morning of Wednesday, November 28th, "a fair, frosty day"
at last, Colonel Wallace led his men round the eastern front
of the Pentland Hills, and then along their southern slope,
until they crossed a narrow defile which intersects the range.
Here, on the incline, at a spot which Turner calls Gallow Law
—"ane ominous name"—but which we know as Rullion

H

Green, he posted them, either that they might rest for a little, or that he might ascertain what Dalzell's intentions were. He was soon enlightened. Through the pass, on the opposite side of the glen, the three thousand of the enemy appeared, the horsemen leading the way. A skirmish of the cavalry followed, King's men and Covenant men firing at first across the ravine through which Glencorse Burn runs; but, coming to a level place, they discarded musket for sword, and grappled closely with each other. The Covenanters had the best of it, although they lost two of their band, John Crookshank and Andrew M'Cormick, ministers from Ulster with militant souls. But now General Dalzell's entire forces had been got into position. It was no child's task set them to fulfil. The nine hundred Whigs could not be easily dislodged from their vantage-ground; they had been drawn up with strategy and foresight. Twice over, the Royalist commander saw his Guardsmen turn and flee; his opponents had resolved "never to break until He who brought them together should Himself break them." But when, in the quickly descending dusk of the short winter day, the whole strength of the King's troops was led into action, the Covenanters were overwhelmed by the sheer weight of numbers. "Being oppressed with multitude," Colonel Wallace says, "we were beaten back, and the enemy came in so full a body, and with so fresh a charge, that, having us once running, they carried it strongly home, and put us in such confusion that there was no rallying." The marvel is that, ill-armed and exhausted, they had behaved with such gallantry and had maintained their ground so long. Forty or fifty were killed, seventy or eighty taken; but the larger proportion, favoured by the gathering twilight, made their escape over the hills.

John Howie has a Rembrandtesque story of the flight of Captain Paton. Dalzell saw him go, and, knowing his prowess, ordered three troopers to follow him. They came up with their quarry in front of a marshy pool, out of which, on the farther bank, three Galloway men were with difficulty pulling their horses. Turning, these Covenanters saw the plight of their captain. "What will you do?" they cried.

He answered gaily that he had but three antagonists with whom to reckon. Urging his horse forward, he leaped the pool, and then, with sword drawn, faced about and waited for his enemies. One of them came close behind, but "his doom was writ." The captain's naked brand swept down on his head, and cleft it in two. The poor cavalier's steed stumbled backwards into the morass, and carried along with it the other men who had leaped behind their comrade. "Take my compliments to your master," John Paton said to them, struggling there in the mire, "and tell him that I cannot sup with him to-night." Howie adds that he had himself seen the famous sword. "It was then counted to have twenty-eight gaps, which made his children observe that there were just as many years of the persecution as there were broken pieces in its edge."

And as for the brave commander who would have transmuted Pentland into a victory, if that had not been "an undertaking for a man of miracles"—his native land saw him no more. James Wallace fled to the Continent, where he wandered from place to place, chased by the vindictive rage of Charles's ministers. In the end of 1678, twelve winters after he had demeaned himself so valorously on Rullion Green, he died in Rotterdam, "lamented of all the serious English and Dutch of his acquaintance." It is a fine picture which Robert MacWard gives us of the closing moments [of "the most faithful, feckful, compassionate, diligent, and indefatigable elder in the work of the Lord" that ever he knew at home or abroad. Writing to his friend, John Blackader, "I forgot," he says, "to tell you that, if the cause for which he had suffered was mentioned, when it was scarce believed he understood or could speak, there was a sunshine of serene joy looked out of his countenance, and a raising of hands on high as to receive the confessor's crown, together with a lifting up of the voice with an Aha! as to sing the conqueror's song of victory." It was the crossing of a true knight, for whom all the trumpets sounded on the other side.

The leader escaped the sadder griefs which were reserved

for some of those humble warriors who had followed him.
The prisoners, the majority of whom were crowded into the
"Haddock's Hole," a portion of the High Church of Edinburgh,
had surrendered on a promise of mercy. But James Sharp
presided at the Council; and mercy was not a word in his
vocabulary. Eleven men were dragged before the Criminal
Court; they pleaded the engagement that their lives should
be spared. "You were pardoned as soldiers," the casuistic
answer ran, "but you are not acquitted as subjects." They
were condemned to be hanged at the Cross. After death,
their heads and right arms were to be cut off; the former to
be placed above the City gates, the latter—the arms which
a few days previously were lifted to swear the Covenant—to
be fixed to the prison doors at Lanark. The barbarous sentence
was borne with unweeping eyes. And that was but the beginning. In Ayr seven others were led to the scaffold; for
Dalzell had gone west to "settle that country," a work which,
he declared, "I am confident is not possible to do without the
inhabetens be remouet or destroiet": he, at least, was always
consistent in ferocity. In Glasgow the prisons overflowed
with "meane beggarlie fellowes, but stubborn in their wicked
and rebeleous way." Rothes wrote despairingly about them,
and their kith and kin, that "the Barbadoes does not in the
least terrify them, damn'd ffulls!" He too, as his letters to
Lauderdale prove, had been angered by the revolt into a
revenge which was pitiless. "It is not possibell sum of us
can be more vayolent aganst those dogs than I am and has
been alredie," he boasted, and he added that he was employing
a "perffit severatie and spearing non." On the 17th of
December he informed the Secretary of State that "upon
tyousday nixt four of the villands will be heangied"; and he
continued, "Godcnous it is not my inclinasione to be crouall,
ispeseallie as to the teacking of layffs, bot I ashour you all
thir persons and all that ar of ther opinion ar abshulatlie
incorigabell in ther uay, and for teror to them heanging must
not be sun giffin over; . . . and remember, I tell it you, thir
pipill will never be quayiett till thay be totallie reuined."
Three days later, having travelled in the interval from

THE TOLBOOTH OF GLASGOW.

Glasgow to Ayr, his mood was in no degree softened: " Altho I thought this cuntrie uer‾ all phanoticks, yett I never did expeckt to have found them so perverse in their prinsapells. . . . Befor the Lord I beliff thay wold joayn with turcks to feaght aganst the King and his guffernment; bot I hoip severatie agaynst them, and carfull uatching over them, will prevent all dangier, which I am shur I shall go about with all the phaculties of my soull." Rothes was as unforgiving as he was uneducated. In ruddy lifeblood, the blood of men who asked nothing except freedom to worship God as their consciences bade, the Pentland Rising was choked and quenched.

CHAPTER XII.

EPHRAIM MACBRIAR OR SIR GALAHAD?

" WHEN great talents are abused,"—it is Dr. Thomas M'Crie who criticises Sir Walter Scott—"when they are exerted to confound the distinctions between virtue and vice, to varnish over oppression and injustice, and to throw ridicule upon those who resist these scourges of society, they ought not to screen the possessor from condemnation and censure. He is doubly criminal: he sins in patronising a bad cause; and he sins in prostituting to its support those talents which, by the very law of his nature, he was bound to use for an opposite purpose."

The verdict is sharp and heavy; and through the whole *Review of the Tales of My Landlord* the fencer uses a foil without the dulling button on its point. He has a complete mastery of his keen-edged weapon. The great magician, " whose worst," as William Hazlitt says, " is better than any other person's best," and whom it is not a joy merely but a liberal education to follow, stands convicted of partialities and prejudices which have sometimes warped his judgment and made him an advocate rather than an historian. He has allowed his antipathies to turn him from the straight road into devious bypaths, and the castigation he received is not unmerited. If we may believe trustworthy witnesses, he winced under it, and was half-ashamed of some of the things he had written. The swordsman whom he had encountered was, in this instance, more perfectly equipped than himself.

In the pages of *Old Mortality*—and, despite the injustice which marks its portraiture of the blue-bonneted Whigs, it

ranks among the supreme books of literature—there are three
incidents in which the Rev. Ephraim Macbriar is chief figure.
He, with those ridiculous brethren of his, Gabriel Kettle-
drummle and Peter Poundtext and Habakkuk Mucklewrath,
comes before the reader as Scott's impersonation of what
the ministers of the poor and disagreeable Covenanters must
have been like. Poor and disagreeable indeed! For, says
John Graham of Claverhouse to Henry Morton, "there is a
difference, I trust, between the blood of learned and reverend
prelates and scholars, of gallant soldiers and noble gentlemen,
and the red puddle that stagnates in the veins of psalm-singing
mechanics, crack-brained demagogues, and sullen boors."
Among the demagogues Ephraim Macbriar has the place of
honour; and Ephraim Macbriar is Sir Walter's delineation
of Hugh Mackail. No doubt, Mackail had run his brief race
thirteen winters before Drumclog and Bothwell Brig were
fought; and it is round Drumclog and Bothwell that the
persons and events of *Old Mortality* are grouped. But we
offend against the liberties of the realm of imagination, if we
demand strict chronology in the chapters of a romance. Hugh
Mackail, there can be little question, was the original of the
young preacher who pursues his active and dogmatic and
eloquent way through the engrossing and misleading tale.

We are confronted first with Ephraim Macbriar after the
Covenanters have gained the day at Drumclog. Hardly twenty
years old he is; but already, though he is half an invalid, he
has gone through the vigils, the rigours, the imprisonments
of a veteran. He throws his faded eyes over the multitude
and across the scene of battle; and a light of triumph rises
in his glance. His hands are folded, his face is raised to
heaven, and he is lost in mental prayer before he addresses
the people. His sermon follows, a sermon outlined not
ungraciously. If he is not free from the coarseness of his
sect, he is an orator who understands how to compel masses
of men. He paints the desolation of the Church. She is like
Hagar, watching the waning life of her boy in the fountainless
desert; like Judah, mourning the ruin of her Temple; like
Rachel, weeping for her children. He fans into new heat the

souls of the men who have just returned from pursuing
Claverhouse. Every one's heart is to be as the heart of
Maccabæus, every one's hand as the hand of Samson, every
one's sword as the sword of Gideon which turned not back
from the slaughter. There are false notes here and there;
but there is no deliberate injustice. We see the wounded
forgetting their pain, the hungry their privations, as they listen
to truths which identify their cause with that of God Himself.

It is different when we meet Macbriar again. He is a
murderer, in effect and purpose, although his wicked intention
is happily frustrated. We are in the house at Drumshinnel,
after the rout at Bothwell; and "the pale-eyed and ferocious
zealots" are gathered in conclave; and Henry Morton has
unwittingly placed himself in their power—Henry Morton,
who fought for them a few hours before, but whom they regard
as a man spurning the light. There is no relenting, no gentleness, in their souls. It is Macbriar who pronounces the
Laodicean's doom. "This is the Sabbath, and our hand shall
not be on thee to spill thy blood upon this day; but, when
the twelfth hour shall strike, it is a token that thy time on
earth hath run." Dr. M'Crie grants that a scene so gruesome
might happen in connection with those less religious spirits
who sometimes forced themselves into the battalions of the
Covenant—men hurried by suffering into desperation and
madness. But it is a perverse caricature to ascribe such
revenges to the Presbyterian ministers. The extremists among
them would not have dreamed of staining their hands with
Henry Morton's blood. Least of all, would Hugh Mackail
have stooped to the atrocity, for he was as humane as he was
earnest.

One other glimpse of Ephraim Macbriar is given us. No
fault can be found with it; for now the painter reproduces the
facts of the history. It is the terrible and yet splendid recital
of how Mackail was tortured, and bore his intrepid testimony,
before the Privy Council in Edinburgh. When the scene
becomes so lofty and so woeful, Sir Walter is a partisan no
more; none can be honester or more generous; and we see
him at his best.

But we linger, when we ought to be cultivating the friendship of the young Covenanter himself.

The men who went to the scaffold for their share in the Pentland Rising are all worth knowing. Their courage was fed from a personal religion of the most vital sort. There is a kind of unstudied melody too, a rhythm and a cadence, in their last utterances. Thus Captain Andrew Arnot, one of ten executed on the 7th of December, sang his swan-song: "I confess that unexpectedly I am come to this place, though sometimes I have had some small thoughts of it; and I do account myself highly honoured to be reckoned amongst the witnesses of Jesus Christ, to suffer for His name, truth, and cause; and this day I esteem it my glory, garland, crown, and royal dignity to fill up a part of His sufferings." Or let us listen to Alexander Robertson, probationer for the ministry, who ended his battle seven days later: "I bless Him that gave me a life to lose and a body to lay down for Him; and, although the market and price of truth may appear to many very high, yet I reckon it low, and all that I have or can do little and too little for Him who gave Himself for me and to me." Or this is how a Glasgow merchant, John Wodrow, who is to fight his last fight side by side with Mackail, writes on his dying day to his wife: "O my heart, come and see, I beseech you! I thought I had known something of my dearest Lord before. But never was it so with me as since I came within the walls of this prison. He is without all comparison. O, love, love Him! O, taste and see! and that shall resolve the question best." Or it is John Wilson, who lauds his Friend of friends ere he goes to look into His face: "I assure you Christ is a good Master to serve; if ye knew Him rightly and His Cross, it is sweet and easy; for He maketh death to be life, and bringeth light out of darkness. I desire to follow the blessed Captain of my salvation through weal and woe." In a famous passage, Joubert contrasts Jansenist and Jesuit. "Les Jansénistes," he says, "semblent aimer Dieu sans amour, et seulement par raison, par devoir, par justice. Les Jésuites semblent aimer Dieu par pure inclination, par admiration, par tendresse, enfin par plaisir."

If the antithesis is to be accepted, the men who suffered for what they had done at Rullion Green were of the family of the Jesuits in one respect—in the glowing ardours of their affection for their divine King. They were poets in the moment and article of death. Every one of them sang unto the Lord a new song.

But Hugh Mackail was prince of the little company. He was the son of Matthew Mackail, who was parish minister of Bothwell, until he had to leave his pulpit in 1662. From the first the boy had been an exceptional child. There was a delicate beauty about his looks, which he never lost, and which stirred the compassion of the spectators as he passed along the High Street to die. He had the instincts of the scholar. While he was only a lad, he could speak with a warm eloquence which touched those who heard him. Better still, he was consecrated to God from the beginning; "all his heart was drawn above." There was about him the indescribable gift of charm. When he was taken all too early from the Church and land, verses were written in praise of this Lycidas of the Covenant.

> Some great thing sparkled in the blushing face ;
> Integrity that lovely brow did grace.

And, behind forehead and features, the mourners had descried endowments more desirable—

> A sprightly mind, and unacquaint with guile,
> Which with no baseness did itself defile ;
> A divine soul, not made to vice a drudge,
> A palace where the graces chose to lodge.

Young Lycidas indeed, who "hath not left his peer."

In 1661, when he was twenty, the Presbytery licensed him to preach. Previously he had been tutor, and he still continued chaplain, in the household of Sir James Stewart of Coltness, one of the laymen to whom the cause of the Covenant was dear. The boy-preacher was not to have many opportunities of public address. His last sermon was spoken in St. Giles, in September 1662. In it he denounced the statesmen and prelates, who were robbing Christ's sheep of the shepherds in whom they trusted. Some of his words were never forgotten by his friends, and never forgiven by his adversaries. "The fountain," he said, "whence violence flows, may be great power, which the Church cannot reach. The Scripture doth abundantly evidence that the people of God have been persecuted, sometimes by a Pharaoh upon the Throne, sometimes by a Haman in the State, sometimes by a Judas in the Church." Men and women were not tardy in assigning the names to the persons whom they fitted; and that of Judas was instantaneously apportioned to James Sharp. But Sharp was an antagonist who, when he was angered, knew how to bide his time, and then struck his blow with fatal effect and once for all.

Whether or no Hugh Mackail had in his mind such special applications of his words, he learned quickly that he must suffer the consequences of his temerity. A party of horsemen was sent to Goodtrees, Sir James Stewart's house near Edinburgh, to apprehend the chaplain. He escaped, "upon almost no more than a moment's advertisement"; and, after hiding for a time with his father, he managed to cross the seas to the Continent. We have no certain information of his whereabouts for three years; but one may guess that his home was in Rotterdam, the city of Erasmus, and the shelter for most of the refugees from the moss-hags of Clydesdale and Galloway. Here he would be able to converse with John Livingston, and with Robert MacWard, exiled for a sermon preached in the Tron Kirk of Glasgow, and with John Brown of Wamphray, whose writings form a library in themselves. Here, too, he could worship on Sabbaths in the Scots church, with the congregation to which, twenty years before, Alexander Petrie had come from his Perthshire manse. These months were a growing time in Mackail's history. "During all this space," the quaint old *Memoir* avers, "he was most seriously exercised in the study of piety and true knowledge, wherein, as he greatly advanced above all his equals, so at length he became most eminent and exemplary." As St. Paul did in Arabia, and as St. John did in Patmos, he climbed steadily upward.

He is back in Scotland, when next we light on him.

Somewhere in the west, he joined the insurgents who were marching to disaster in the wet November of 1666. He was physically weak. There was always that hectic flush on his cheek which the victors at Drumclog saw on Ephraim Macbriar's; and of late it had grown brighter and more prophetic. In Ayr, William Veitch says, "the worthy Hugh Mackail would have fallen off his horse, if one had not laid hold of him and kept him up." But on he pressed with the fated army, through the pelting rains, over the miry roads and sodden fields, when he should have been resting in some Chamber of Peace. At Colinton, however, before the battle began, he was compelled to give in; the strain on his sensitive constitution had proved too terrible. Leaving the encampment, he was making his way across the open country to Liberton, where his father had found a temporary home. But on the road he was taken prisoner. It looked as if, had he been desirous, he might have avoided the danger. " It is indisputable that, had he but retained and observed the least of that advertency and caution wherein at other times he was known to be both ready and very happy, he might, without either hazard or trouble, have escaped." Doubtless there were heavenly reasons for another issue. " God did thus, by his simplicity and folly, prepare the way for His own glory and His servant's joy and victory." It was the faith of the Covenanters that nothing can fall out by chance.

But they were scorching fires into which Hugh Mackail was cast. His friends had fought at Pentland, and had lost the day. The Earl of Rothes was beside himself with rage. The insurrection, he concluded, was part of a cunningly planned scheme of rebellion; he shared the opinion which Dalzell expressed in a letter to Lauderdale that, if the rising "had not bein mystimd," it would have " bein much moir terible "; and he swore that he would probe the conspiracy to its roots. So, when the preacher was brought before the Council, he had recourse to a horrible expedient. He examined Mackail under the torture of the Boot. " The executioner," says Sir Walter Scott, " enclosed the leg and knee within the tight iron case, and then, placing a wedge of the same metal between the knee and the edge of the machine, took a mallet in his hand, and stood waiting for further orders. A surgeon placed himself by the other side of the prisoner's chair, bared the prisoner's arm, and applied his thumb to the pulse in order to regulate the torture according to the strength of the patient. When these preparations were made, the President glanced his eye around the Council as if to collect their suffrages, and, judging from their mute signs, gave a nod to the executioner, whose mallet instantly descended on the wedge, and, forcing it between the knee and the iron boot, occasioned the most exquisite pain, as was evident from the flush on the brow and the cheeks of the sufferer." Although it happened two centuries and a half ago, we read the record with almost a cry of indignation.

It was not once only that the awful wedge was driven down. Displeased that he did not receive the information he wanted, Rothes kept demanding "one touch more." Eleven times the mallet descended, until the poor limb was shattered and shapeless. "I protest solemnly in the sight of God," the martyr cried, "I can say no more, though all the joints in my body were in as great anguish as my leg." Then they carried him, bleeding and spent, to his dungeon.

Endeavour after endeavour was made to secure his release. Highborn ladies interceded for him with tongue and pen. His cousin, Dr. Matthew Mackail, sought out Archbishop Sharp, first in Edinburgh and then in St. Andrews, to entreat his pity for a life so young, so innocent, so full of promise. But the Archbishop recollected who had spoken about a Judas in the Church; and, when he had read the letters which the doctor brought, he looked up and answered callously, "The business is now in the hands of the Justiciaries, and I can do nothing." "Can!" Matthew Mackail might have retorted; "nay, not can, my lord, but will! I will do nothing."

Technically his Grace of St. Andrews was right. After the infliction of the torture, the prisoner had been ordered to the Court of Justiciary, which ratified the decisions of the Privy Council; but he was prostrated by his sufferings, and begged for delay. "I am," he wrote, "in a great distemper and fever, and am wholly unable to walk or stand." This was on the 11th of December. A week later, on the 18th, "being indifferently recovered," he was examined by Lord Renton, the Justice Clerk, and by Sir William Murray. He admitted that he was "one of that afflicted party and persuasion called Presbyterians"; that he had been with the insurgents, in Ayr and Ochiltree and Lanark; that, when he was captured, he had a sword in his hand. It helped him nothing to urge that he had left the armed men before the actual fighting took place. The Lord Advocate, Sir John Nisbet, retorted that, even though he was absent from the battle, his treason was indisputable; for all keeping company with those in revolt against His Majesty, although it were "only for the space of half an hour," was a capital crime. He was pronounced a rebel, and was sentenced to be executed at the Mercat Cross on Saturday, the 22nd. "The Lord giveth life, and the Lord taketh," he exclaimed when he heard the verdict; "blessed be the name of the Lord!" Through the lines of the Guards he was borne back to the Tolbooth, the people weeping over the pathos of his fate. But his own face shone. "Trust in God!" he said—"Trust in God!" Then, catching a glimpse of a dear friend, "How good news it is," he cried, "to be within four days' journey of enjoying the sight of Jesus Christ!"

Yet during these four days he was visited by two different griefs. One arose from an overscrupulous conscience. Had he not done wrongly, when he abandoned the wayworn troops for whom calamity was waiting? And was it not doubly criminal that he should press his pusillanimous departure as an argument why he ought to be pardoned by his judges? The "ayenbite of inwyt," as the old English has it, was poignant and troublesome; but the self-accusations were wholly undeserved. The other pain was child of the affections rather than of the conscience. His father came to see him. The two loved without reserve. "Hugo," the older man sobbed, "I called thee a good olive-tree of fair fruits, and now a storm hath destroyed my tree and its fruits. I have sinned; but thou—what hast thou done?" But the son could not hear the father charge himself with fault without bewailing his own misdeeds. "Through coming short of the fifth commandment," he confessed, "I have come short of the promise that my days should be prolonged in the land of the living. And God's controversy with thee," he added, "is for overvaluing thy children, especially myself." It is an instance of how the saints deal most unsparingly with their own white and royal souls.

These, however, were passing shadows. Before he listened to the death-sentence, Hugh Mackail had amused himself in his prison by composing Latin verses; his were the recreations of the student. In epigrammatic lines he had portrayed the uncertainties and embarrassments of his position—

> Distrahor ambigui dubio discrimine fati:
> Aeger enim jaceo; sin revalesco, cado.

Now that he knew the worst that men could do, his speech rippled with humour. Some one asked how the outraged leg was faring. "Oh!" he responded merrily, "the fear of my neck makes me forget my leg." "I am not so cumbered about dying," he protested, "as I have often been about preaching a sermon." On the Friday night he went to bed a little after eleven, and his cousin the physician lay beside him, and related afterwards how well he slept. At five in the morning he rose, and awoke his comrade, John Wodrow, saying with a smile, "Up, John! You and I look not like men going this day to be hanged, seeing we lie so long." Yet there were serious thoughts too. "Now, Lord," he prayed, "we come to Thy Throne, a place we have not hitherto been acquainted with. Earthly kings' thrones have advocates against poor men; but Thy Throne hath Jesus Christ an Advocate for us. Our supplication this day is not to be free of death, nor of pain in death, but that we may witness before many witnesses a good confession."

The prayer had an abundant answer. Scottish martyr-ology can point to a hundred glorious deaths, but to none more glorious than the exodus of this confessor and conqueror of twenty-six years. When he reached the spot, "he appeared, to the conviction of all that formerly knew him, with a fairer, better, and more staid countenance than ever they had before observed." The sorrow was not on his side; it was on that of his friends: "scarce was there a dry cheek in the whole street or windows at the Cross of Edinburgh." To the last he bore his testimony with a kind of glad defiance; the persecutors might arrest the life of the body, but they could not modify by a hairbreadth the convictions of the soul. "Although I be judged as a rebel among men," he said, "yet I hope to be accepted as loyal before God. Nay"—and the trumpet became more remonstrant as it proceeded—"nay, there can be no greater act of loyalty to the King, as the times now go, than for every man to do his utmost for the extinction of that abominable plant of Prelacy, which is the bane of the throne and of the country." But soon the note was gentler. "I praise God for this fatherly chastisement, whereby He hath made me in part, and will make me perfectly, partaker of His holiness." Then, after prayer, he raised himself to his full height; and, lifting the napkin from his face, he continued, "I hope you perceive no alteration or discouragement in my countenance and carriage; and, as it may be to your wonder, so I profess it is a wonder to myself, and I will tell you the reason of it. As there is a great solemnity here, of a confluence of people, a scaffold, a gallows, and people looking out at windows, so there is a greater and more solemn preparation in heaven of angels to carry my soul to Christ's bosom. Again, this is my comfort, that it is to come into Christ's hands, and He will present it blameless and faultless to the Father, and then shall I be ever with the Lord." Mr. Edmund Gosse has described what he calls "the Renaissance attitude towards death." In the best men of that time, he says, dying was boldly picturesque; it was a piece of public tragedy, performed with an intention half-chivalrous and half-hortatory. So Philip Sidney died at Arnheim, with the musicians playing his own poems at his bedside. So Bernard Palissy died in the Bastille, dramatically defending his beliefs against Henry the Third. So John Donne died in his deanery of St. Paul's, with the portrait of himself in his shroud keeping him company for weeks. So holy George Herbert died at Bemerton, singing to his lute such hymns and anthems as he hoped to sing in heaven. Splendid captains in God's army these were; but there seems something too elaborate and self-conscious in their home-going. Hugh Mackail had the better of them. His death was as powerful a sermon and as veritable a triumph; but there was nothing in it deliberately decorative—its victory was spontaneous, natural, irrepressible, complete.

His final words are famous. They were the Farewell and the Welcome which, in varying versions, the later martyrs frequently repeated. "Now I leave off to speak any more to creatures, and turn my speech to Thee, O Lord. Now I begin my intercourse with God, which shall never be broken off. Farewell, father and mother, friends and relations! Farewell, the world and all delights! Farewell, meat and drink! Farewell, sun, moon, and stars! Welcome, God and Father! Welcome, sweet Lord Jesus, the Mediator of the new covenant! Welcome, blessed Spirit of grace, God of all consolation! Welcome, glory! Welcome, eternal life! Welcome, death!"

Is this the Ephraim Macbriar of that hateful conclave in Drumshinnel? Ah no, we must crown him with another name—

> He looked as young and pure and glad,
> As ever looked Sir Galahad.

CHAPTER XIII.

BLOT OUT HIS NAME THEN.

COMMISSIONER ROTHES and Sir Thomas Dalzell, with James Sharp to instigate and encourage, had established their reign of violence and avarice. They followed Rullion Green with wickednesses which proved how strong their wish was to exterminate "the wandering and weather-beaten flock of Christ." Not only were the fines doubled and trebled, and not only were there in Edinburgh and Glasgow and Ayr the public executions of the ringleaders, but, up and down the country, when the survivors of the unhappy rising were caught by the troopers, they were shot at their own doors. There was many a pathetic incident in connection with "the evils, extortions, cruelties, and exactions" of the time. Thus we read, in *Naphtali*, of a country boy of sixteen, who was bidden renounce the Covenant which he had taken at Lanark. He had no skill in spiritual matters, no wisdom such as the more advanced scholars of Christ have reached, and no full assurance of his personal salvation. He fell into great anxiety, for he was not prepared to die, and yet he could not redeem his life with the price which the persecutors proposed. But, before the end, all the windows of his heart were opened to the day. After the prayers and conference of some who saw him in his prison at Irvine, he went to his doom "leaping and praising God." Through all the west, and over most of the Lowlands during the winter of 1666 and 1667, the Covenanters could never tell from what lurking-place swift death might spring out on them.

But the tormentors went too far. The man who broke

the power of Middleton three years before, and to whom
Rothes protested an unchangeable affection, was watching
them. Lauderdale saw that, if he would keep his credit, the
blundering policy of a merciless severity must be modified
in Scotland. He detected, too, a movement against his own
supremacy—a movement in which the Commissioner, despite
his fervent assurances, and the Archbishop, who avowed his
loyalty in obsequious terms, and Dalzell, and the Duke of
Hamilton, all had their share. The prelates—for Alexander
Burnet of Glasgow had his finger in the matter as well as
his Grace of St. Andrews—and the military party both alike
wanted to humble the lordly statesman, who meant to be
the Grand Vizier of an autocratic King. Evidently it was
time for Lauderdale to bestir himself.

He did it with much effect. First he brought James
Sharp in cringing humility to his feet. Aided by Sir Robert
Moray and the Earl of Tweeddale, men of honour in whom
he could absolutely trust, and men of compassion who hated
the unmitigated brutalities which had been in vogue, he
frightened the domineering Churchman into abject submission. So completely did Sharp desert his ally Dalzell, that
one day, the "Muscovian beast" turned on him with a growl:
"Whensoever the Bishops are stoned, you deserve to be the
first." There were no limits either to the Primate's recanta-
tions or to his misgivings; he was sure that the end of his
pomps and plots had come. On a July afternoon in 1667,
Tweeddale had gone to him, and had spoken some unpalatable
truths about the sore displeasure of His Majesty's Secretary
at Whitehall. In his eyes, as he heard the distasteful
message, "stood a bak watter"; and then his apologies began,
and he "reflected upon all the kindnes and faivours he had
receaved from you," and affirmed his conviction that from
the first "you had dealt generously and nobely with him,"
and protested that "you and your frinds wold doe mor for
the settlement of the Church than those they had trusted
mor." And as for those troublesome people in the west, he
feared nothing now from them, for they were quite broken,
and it would be sufficient to secure their peace-keeping in

the future to have one or two persons of influence stationed among them who should be responsible for their behaviour. A few days after Tweeddale's visit, Sharp, apprehensive that his star was setting never to rise again, addressed the lowliest of entreaties to Lauderdale himself. " I shall yet more presume upon your Lordship's patience," he wrote, " by saying that, as I doe lament that unhappie breach betwixt your Lordship and me, which I beleeve mistake and false suggestions have caused, so I am most desirous, and it would be very acceptable to me, to find that I am restored to and rightly stated in your Lordship's good opinion and friendship, which shall be preserved on my part with all inviolable fidelity and devotion to your service." But his patron did not see fit to release him immediately from his solicitudes; the Archbishop's perturbation was too satisfactory and too amusing, and he kept him waiting through six weeks for his answer. When it was sent, it was an answer which was partly a rebuke—" I expect yow will no more suffer grundles jealousies nor clatters to draw yow off"—and partly a restoration—" If bygones may be bygones, and faire play in time to come, I am sure we shall continue good friends." At length, when the humiliation had been carried sufficiently far, and the knave had " gotten the second sight through experience and not for nought," Lauderdale became more explicit still, and ordered him to rise from his knees. But even yet he was scared. Sir Robert Moray pleads laughingly that his master will induce the King to " write two lines to him with his own hand"; for nothing less will " raise his heart, which is bemisted and lodged in his hose." So Charles, at his minister's prompting, writes the two lines; and then the winter of the Archbishop's discontent becomes glorious summer. " His Majesty's hand," he says, " with the diamond seal, was to me as a resurrection from the dead." The whole transaction flashes a searchlight into the dispositions of the men who were principals in it: Lauderdale, with quiet masterfulness, with perfect temper, with ready unscrupulousness; and Sharp, who can be bullied and cajoled with ease, and who is certain to be found on that side which promises

JOHN MAITLAND, DUKE OF LAUDERDALE.

After Sir Peter Lely.

success to himself. Among the Church's oppressors, none is
more to be dreaded than the first, and none more to be despised
than the second.

Rothes, with his coarse and glaring sins, had not the
Primate's craven spirit. Yet Lauderdale had decided that he,
too, must be rendered harmless. He persuaded the King to
transfer the Earl from the position of Royal Commissioner to
that of Lord Chancellor, vacant since the death of Glencairn
three years previously. In his new office he would have a
dignity quite as stately as in the old; but his opportunities
of working mischief would be at an end. Rothes himself was
frankly averse to the change. When Sir Robert Moray went
to tell him about it, he had to talk for hours—"it was 8 a
clock ere wee parted"; and, even then, the negotiation had
made meagre progress. He had no ability, the Earl declared,
for such work as the Chancellor's; he was not a lawyer; he
knew little Latin; he was ignorant of statutes and precedents;
how could he state a question as it should be stated? He
"opposed his youth, his humour, his way." And always, like
the needle quivering back to the pole, he returned to his
unwillingness, "which hee expressed to be high and insuper-
able." Moray had need that day of all the cleverness and
patience with which he was dowered: "to every point hee
said I found replyes, that still enervate them to my thinking."
What purpose, he asked in the end, could there be in prolonging the resistance? The King's resolution was fixed, and it
were much handsomer that Rothes should yield at the first
than at the last. Of course, there was but one termination
to the debate, though it was resumed again and again. Rothes
had to surrender, and Lauderdale's agents were determined
that he should do so without undue delay. Especially was
it necessary, they believed, that the Earl's dignities should be
demitted before he went up himself to Court. For he was a
prime favourite with the monarch, and "had a soft and
insinuating address," and who could tell what seductive
influences he might exert over His Majesty?—"You know it
is not easy for the King to say bleak things," Moray explains,
"even though there may be sweetening prefaces made to

them." The conclusion of the unequal struggle came on the 24th of September 1667, when Rothes wrote to Lauderdale, laying down his Commissionership, and requesting the all-powerful Secretary to express to King Charles his "pasionat desayr to cis his hands."

And who was to be the new Commissioner? Who, but Lauderdale in his own person. He would take the reins himself, and would vanquish the mettlesome and recalcitrant steed. Or let' us adopt Lord Tweeddale's metaphor. "The news pleas me well," he said, "that the keyes shall hang at the right belt." For nearly a decade and a half Lauderdale governed Scotland with a proconsul's absolutism; from Galloway to the Grampians his wish was law. We must look, a little more carefully, at the man who wielded a sceptre so potent.

John Maitland, the Earl of Lauderdale, was a "lost leader." He deserted the allies of his early years. In the old days, none had seemed more zealous than he. When the Kirk had its highest honours to confer, he was one of its chosen. Back in the December of 1643, when he was in his gracious youth, Robert Baillie wrote with emphasis of "the very great sufficiency and happiness of good Maitland" as a Commissioner to the Westminster Assembly. It is true that he never had been a Protester, like his fellow-delegates, Rutherfurd and Wariston. He brought away the Engagement from the Isle of Wight; but only mournful necessity, he explained, led him to meddle with such compromises; he told his Covenanting associates "how sore against his heart he went the road now he was in." By and by, when the moderate men were broken at Preston, he expressed before the courts of the Church his penitence for having lowered that flag which he should have been proud to carry aloft. The leaders of Presbytery took him unquestioningly into their confidence again, and he remained their "loving friend." He was so, when, after Worcester, the English Government threw him into confinement, first in the Tower, and then in other southern gaols; and, during the years of his incarceration, there was never a suspicion of his lealheartedness. From prison he sent to

Scotland letters which spoke the dialect of Zion, letters full of tranquil courage and acquiescence in the will of God. His correspondents rejoiced in a helper so convinced and ardent. Was it a long drawn-out imposture? Dr. Osmund Airy, who is at home in the Second Charles's reign as a man is at home in the house where he has lived for years, says Yes. Lauderdale, he believes, assumed this zeal, like a player putting on his stage accoutrements; he hoodwinked the Kirk he disliked, until the opportunity came for escaping from the meshes of its net; he was a conscious hypocrite. One wonders whether that is the only solution of this problem in personality with its "abysmal deeps." Perhaps there is another answer. John Maitland may have deceived himself as well as his brethren in the camp of the Covenant. Shrewd and sagacious men have sometimes misread their own souls, and he may have been of their fellowship. He may have dreamed that his Presbyterian comrades were right, when they assured him, in the plenitude of their faith and hope and love, that he would " go to the saints."

But, however we interpret the early section of his biography, the Restoration awakened Lauderdale, and led him out from the world of illusions to the world which was his own. The true man had full play now. There was nobody who enjoyed such intimacy with Charles, and nobody who kept the friendship unshaken through so long a period. Clarendon, to whom the King's debt was deepest, was disgraced; but Lauderdale, of whom Clarendon felt an invincible distrust, remained to glory over his rival's abasement. An uncouth-looking favourite he was. "He made a very ill appearance," Bishop Burnet says; "he was very big; his hair red, hanging oddly about him; his tongue was too big for his mouth, which made him bedew all that he talked to; and his whole manner was rough and boisterous." His portrait, although Lely's consummate art has done for it everything which could be done, attests the accuracy of the gossiping Bishop's delineation. The forehead is low; the cheeks are loose; the lips are thick and insatiable; the body is huge and brutish. The sovereign, well aware of his own ugliness, felt some satisfaction, it may be surmised, in the reflection that his confidant and boon-companion was uglier than himself. But, concealed behind the unlovely features, there was an alert brain. We are told that, in all companies, Lauderdale had much to say; he was full of ideas and expedients. Buckingham's epigram, "He is a man of a blundering understanding," may have had its side of truth; but his was an intellect capacious and fertile and resourceful. He matured his plans with calm coolness, and he never lacked the courage required to carry them into effect. He was utterly cynical in his judgments of men and things, as hopelessly cynical as his royal patron. Year in and year out his selfishness kept watch, and no fair words or plausible professions lulled it into slumber. "He was," his Grace of Salisbury bears witness, "the coldest friend and the violentest enemy that I ever knew." In his treatment of Middleton, and in his victory over Sharp and Rothes, we have seen how he could choose the psychological moment for winning a personal triumph. He showed keen penetration, also, in the agents whom he gathered about him; he knew, an intimate said, "how to make use of a knave." But yet there was a magnetism, which men higher in the moral scale than himself were forced to own; he was helped by public servants who were "very perfit gentil knights." Bad or good, they found him a despotic master. He employed them just so long as they furthered his interests; but, if they should contradict, he bade them good-bye without a regret and with no thanks. His King and himself—these were Lauderdale's deities, the Great Twin Brethren; and they occupied thrones of equal dignity. He would take a cartload of oaths, he declared, as irreconcilable as it was possible to conceive, rather than forget His Majesty or forfeit his own power.

The man is a medley, a bundle of opposing qualities. There were few scholars in Britain more versatile; there was none in the precincts of the Court. To his "deare Robin"— that Robert Moray who, if he had allowed it, would have been his good angel—he writes from Holyrood in July 1663, and this is a sentence in the letter: "Send with him," with Lord

Dunfermline, "my little octavo hebrew bible without points, which lyes in my little closet at Whitehall." Other things are to be despatched, too, which have a different aroma—" the glasses of spirit of roses which yow will finde in the middle drawer of my walnut-tree cabinet"; but' here is a student who shares John Milton's partiality for the Old Testament in the original tongue. He was as conversant with the Greek and Latin classics, and with ancient and modern history. He had a Scotsman's delight in theological discussion and speculation. His weary imprisonment assisted him to accumulate these stores of learning; but not one captive in a hundred would have compelled the years of durance to yield so rich a harvest. And yet, side by side with the culture, what spiritual degeneracy there was! Lauderdale was as rank a sensualist as could be found in Charles's palace of misrule. His vices were notorious. It was difficult for him to speak without an oath or a lie. A frequent exercise of his humour was to make puns on the verses of Scripture, or to mimic the accents and gestures of the Covenanting preachers to whom he had listened in his more honourable youth. There was, moreover, an element of superstition, which all the intellectual attainment could not banish. He never liked James Sharp. He said to Lord Melville once, Wodrow relates, that he knew the Archbishop would come to a violent end. Asked why, he answered that he had detected infallible tokens of catastrophe in little tricks of gait and demeanour which he observed about the obnoxious priest—"happing, when he walked, like a pyet; and winking with one eye; and keeping the thumb in his fingers when he spoke." "My lord," added the King's Secretary of State, "I never saw one that had these signs who died an ordinary death." Is he not a marvellous conglomerate— scholarly, capable above nine-tenths of his contemporaries, familiar with the truth, and yet the slave of passion and profaneness and credulity? There is a word of the divine Teacher which is peculiarly applicable to John, Earl of Lauderdale. It is that word which smites like a sword and saddens like the Arctic winter, *If the light that is in thee be darkness, how great is that darkness!*

The friends of the older time were aghast at the change. A few months before his own death, Robert Baillie, once so assured of Lauderdale's devotion, sent him a letter of brave and touching reproof. " My Lord, you ar the nobleman in the world I love best and esteem most. I think I may say and writ to you what I lyk. If you have gone with your hert to forsak your Covenant, to countenance the Reintroduction of bishops and books, and strengthening the King by your advyse in thes things, I think you a prime transgressor and liable among the first to answer to God for that grit sin, and opening a door which in hast will no be closit, for persecution of a multitud of the best persons and most loyal subjects that ar in the thrie dominions." It is certain, indeed, that the quondam member of the Westminster Assembly did not approve of the bringing back of Episcopacy. People said that to the close of his life he was a Presbyterian at heart ; and Burnet depicts him accurately when he tells us that privately the Secretary urged Charles against the treachery. But in public he interposed no obstacle. If he " would never have advised, he forbore to curb "; and that, in a man with his antecedents and his influence, was a crime. And, besides Baillie, there was another friend 'whom his evil behaviour cut to the quick. Richard Baxter had hoped great things of him. His were among the books which the captive studied in his various dungeons, " reading them all, and taking notes of them, and earnestly commending them to his kinsman, the Earl of Balcarres." In fact, when his hour of glory came, Lauderdale, as we learn from the *Reliquiæ Baxterianæ*, had desired to carry the author of *The Saint's Rest* north to Scotland, and to give him a bishopric there; and the great Puritan had difficulty in evading his importunities. But now the preacher was filled with pity and indignation and fear. A noble letter survives, written about 1670, in which he begs the recreant to turn and live. " God forbid that you should lose in prosperity that which you gained in adversity ! and that He who was near you in a prison should be put far from you in a Court ! If our hearts once say to Him, *Depart from us*, it's a sad prognostick that we may hear from Him at last,

Depart from Me." . . . "My Lord, I am not persuading you
for the securing of your soul to leave the Court, that you may
escape temptations. I know, if all good men should do so on
that pretence, they would but desert their trust and the
commonwealth and the interest of Christ; as cowardly soldiers
that will quit the field for fear of being wounded, or slothful
workmen that will quit the vineyard for fear of doing their
work amiss. This were to give up all as deplorate. But, I
beseech you, Watch, and Walk with God!" . . . "It were a
miserable life that should imprison your soul in smoky vanity,
and shut you out from your communion with God. This were
to be debased below those poorest Christians, that in a cottage
and in rags have daily access to Him in prayer and holy
meditation. It were a miserable honour that should depress
you, and a miserable gain that should bring upon you so great
a loss." These are among the yearning sentences in an appeal,
a *concio ad cor*, remarkable for its fidelity and its love. Lauderdale could not allege that he had received no warning of his
declension and danger. The best men whom he knew followed
him, as he went deeper and deeper down, with regretful eyes
and with prayers that he would bethink himself before it was
too late.

But he never did. He was determined to be indispensable
to Charles. He was as drunken and vicious as the Earl of
Rochester. His wit, if it was heavier, was more mordant.
He could talk in Latin, in Italian, in French, even in Hebrew.
All these were endowments which commended him to the King.
In London, from 1660 to 1667, he courted his master with
such assiduity that no presence was so essential as his; and by
1667 he was the real ruler of Scotland. Thus John Maitland,
once the hope of the Presbyterians, mounted higher and
higher in magnificence, and sank lower and lower in manhood
and grace.

CHAPTER XIV.

THE BLINK.

LORD LAUDERDALE had taken the control of Scottish affairs, because Rothes and his colleagues were spoiling everything by their vulgar violence. Odd as it seems to find any relaxation of their sorrows coming from such a source, it was to be expected, therefore, that the Covenanters would have something of a breathing-space. And so it happened. The three or four years which followed are known in the literature of the persecuted by the quaint title of *The Blink*. Through the brooding clouds a few rays of sunshine forced their way, and the hearts of the downtrodden folk were warmed. In greater numbers than ever they met for worship on the hillsides and in the fields, crowding to hear the preachers who gave them the living bread and the water which has "refreshment for all thirst." The mercy, we shall see, was mingled with new misery; and fresh causes of contention sprang up among the faithful. But, for the time, there was an easing of their burden.

One improvement was the removal from military command of two officers who had gained an undesirable repute. Of the two Sir William Ballantyne was the more savage; he "hath all this time," wrote Moray to Lauderdale, "been exacting monney and bonds, driving cattle, and harassing the innocent as well as the guilty." His reign of extortion was terminated. He was fined and ordered to withdraw from the country. From Paris he sent an angry little letter to the King's Commissioner. "I intend to som place where I may have the occasion to ffollow arms till yowr Lordship's displeasor be removed; hoping such is yowr justice yow will not desire without cawse utterlie to rowine a poore gentleman." But death met him before he saw Scotland again. He was at the siege of a beleaguered town in the Netherlands; and, as he walked one day too near the hostile guns, a comrade called out to warn him of his risk. "Cannon-balls kill none but fey folk," was his contemptuous answer. The word had just crossed his lips, when a ball shot him through the heart; and his bravadoes were ended for ever. The other officer, whose tyrannies had a summary conclusion, was Sir James Turner, the author of the Pentland Rising and its attendant wretchedness. He protested eloquently that a punishment which he did not deserve was being inflicted on him; he was "pre-condemned," he told Lord Tweeddale, who presided over the Committee of Inquiry, "with vigour enough, yet with very much discretion and civilitie," which sweetened the bitter pill the culprit knew he was to swallow. He marvelled, moreover, that any complaint about him should have gone directly to London, since none had been lodged with the Privy Council in Edinburgh, to whose jurisdiction it belonged to take notice of such affairs: It was "not ordinaire to runne to the King *per saltum*, in contempt of that authoritie which he had established in Scotland." But he was answered that in these things the Sovereign did as he pleased. There was ample cause for his degradation. Sir Robert Moray has an illuminating tale of one of his "feats of warr." He had ten horsemen, who helped him to levy his Church fines. They rode forth in twos, and in every place where they halted the two exacted quartering for themselves and for eight cavaliers more, threatening loudly that, if their demands should be refused, they would send instantaneously for this octave of desperate companions, although the octave had an existence as unsubstantial as the riches of Alnaschar in the fable. "Thus by a more solide kind of arithmetick than the scholear reckoned 2 eys to be 3," Sir James Turner had the skill to "multiply ten horse to fifty —*egregie quidem!*" But, added Moray in a sentence as shattering as the reckless foot which dissipated Alnaschar's visionary store, "there are more ways than one taken to

I

bring all such pranks to a hearing." Turner. lost his place in the army; and, if he escaped exile, he had to live in privacy for the rest of his days.

But the chief feature of these years of the Blink, when milder men and milder measures were uppermost, was the granting of the two Indulgences—the earlier in June 1669, the later in 1672. The Indulgences had a kindly look; but they added immeasurably to the troubles of the Church. What was it that they did?

The parish churches, abandoned to the lifeless curates, were almost empty. The people discovered methods of listening to their own ministers, the friends whose adoption they had tried. But, if this state of things continued, one of three consequences must ensue: either the worship of God in the ecclesiastical buildings of the land would become obsolete; or a system of persecution must be inaugurated, more unsparing in its sternness and more prolific in its results; or else some degree of toleration must be extended to the Presbyterian preachers, and a way of return must be devised for them to the offices they had filled before Middleton's black Act of Glasgow drove them to proclaim their message under the open sky. The last was the course preferred by the governors of the country; and thus the Indulgences came into being.

They were a permission to the outed ministers to reoccupy their charges. Those who declined to go for sanction to the Bishops were not to have the stipend, but only the manse, and were to receive an annuity from the nation. The ministry of those who refused to attend the Episcopal Synods was to be restricted to the parishes over which they were set. None was to admit to the sacrament of Baptism or of the Lord's Supper any one from a congregation outside his own parochial boundary. The Indulgences were thus the King's authorisation to Covenanting ministers to take up afresh, under certain stringent conditions, their dearly loved work of preaching the Gospel of Christ. Again, if they chose, their voices might be heard within the walls of those houses of prayer that were hallowed by innumerable sacred recollections. But the Government would watch, would

superintend, would control their language and their action.
How thoroughly it did so we may gather from a letter written
by the Earl of Kincardine, in the August of 1669. He
pictures with shrewd humour a little ceremony enacted
before the Privy Council, in which he had himself some share.
Twelve ministers were ushered in, to "receave their orders."
Every one had his warrant read over to him by the Clerk,
before it was delivered into his own keeping; and it was "a
peece of pagentry" to see them make their bow. Then they
had to listen to the Act that detailed the pains and penalties
to which they would be subject in case of misbehaviour.
" And when all this was done, Mr. Hutchesone made a very
discreet and pertinent little speech in their names; telling
that he was desyrd by them to returne their most humble and
most hearty thankes, to His Majestie in the first place, and
then to the Councell that hade remembered them in their
low condition, and hade granted them a libertie to preach the
gospell." So, praying God in handsome terms to bless King
Charles and their Lordships, he left the room with his train,
"which some rogues, because they were twelve in number,
cald the Twelve Apostles of the Councell." One feels that
Kincardine himself, although he approved of the new policy,
and had played an active part in initiating it, cherished only
a modified respect for the subservient souls that welcomed
its provisions. And this State regulation was the fatal blot
on the scheme, in the judgment of the majority of the men
for whom it was designed. They had cause, they felt, to fear
the Greeks, *et dona ferentes*. To their authors the Indulgences
appeared politically wise, and they were granted with some
graciousness; but a freedom so cabined and guarded, a virtue
so cloistered, was not what the Covenanters had suffered in
order to secure. If they accepted it, they would allow to
civic dignitaries the right of interference in the thrice-holy
region of the Church: they would yield up to an external
power the prerogatives which pertain to Jesus Christ alone.

Nor was this likely to be the only melancholy result.
Other harvests of mischief lay in the perilous seed. For
example, who could prophesy to what lengths the intrusion

of the State might go? Having once invaded the spiritual
realm, she would return with a demand for new benefactions,
and would assert her domination in yet more offensive ways.
Moreover, the Indulgences could not be welcomed without
dividing the adherents of the Covenant. It was useless to
expect that every one would see in their niggardly promises
a boon so rich that at any cost it must be coveted and
grasped. There would be many soldiers of Christ too jealous
of their Master's honour to reap comforts for themselves at
His expense. And thus those who took the liberty proffered
them would put a sundering chasm between themselves and
their brethren. It was a contingency to be contemplated
with dismay. There was yet another evil which could be
foreseen. Compliance with the King's proposals would only
prove an incitement to Charles and his advisers to afflict the
conventicles more mercilessly than before. What justification was there for conventicles at all, the statesmen would ask,
when the doors of the churches had been thrown open, and
Presbyterians were in the pulpits again? Look at it in what
light they would, most of the Covenanters saw something
ensnaring in the bribe held out to them ; and they declined
to profit by it.

Singularly enough, Lauderdale found his first Indulgence
vigorously condemned from the opposite side of the ecclesiastical world. Alexander Burnet, the Archbishop of Glasgow,
was a resolute High Churchman, much more zealous than
James Sharp for the independence of the spiritual realm.
That the Privy Council should arrogate to itself the power
of admitting the ejected ministers to their old places was in
his eyes a wound inflicted on the Church ; for it was she who
ought to be intrusted with such duties, and no Court of the
nation could lawfully trespass on her domain. He did not
conceal his convictions. He ventured to prepare and to
publish a formal Remonstrance—a paper whose strong and
militant words could not be misunderstood. "Wee cannot
forbeare to Resent," so the contumacious words ran, "that
some have entred to preach publickly and avouchedly, who
were before censured with deposition by us upon weighty

grounds agreeable to the standing lawes of the Kingdome."
The offenders had been cleared from blame, and restored to
duty, "yea, and exempted from the jurisdiction which Wee
should have over them." This was an Erastianism, his Grace
declared, which must not be endured in silence, and from
which a flood-tide of harm would proceed. "Thus the
authority of an Archbishop and Synod, once venerable, is
become despicable." It was the favourite argument of the
Protesters, the quick-sighted Commissioner averred, enunciated
by a man to whom the Protesters were as the abomination of
desolation. "Nor was the Archbishop of Glasgow more
innocent," said Sir George Mackenzie, "than James Guthrie,
for both equally designed to debar the King from interposing
any way in the affairs of the Church." But Burnet—*Longi-
facies* is the nickname by which he is known in the coterie of
Lauderdale's bosom-friends—won nothing but a mitigated
martyrdom from his attachment to principle. Charles himself
decreed his doom in a document of State inscribed to the
monarch's "Right Trusty and Right entirely beloved Cousin,"
John Maitland. The transgressor was to be summoned before
the Council, and there he was to be publicly informed of the
King's "resentments," felt against him on account of many
misdemeanours, but especially because of "his accession to
that paper so dangerous in nature and consequence." His
Majesty, he was to be told, might reasonably have accused
him of guilt which merited the severest dealing; but, in his
royal clemency, he would be "content to accept of a Dimission
and Resignation of his Bishoprick." Yet there must be no
reluctance or postponement, and, if there were, the King's
Advocate was forthwith to institute a process before the
judges of the land. So, at the Christmas of 1669, the too
plain-spoken diocesan was compelled to retire from his see.
"I, Alexander, Archbishop of Glasgow," he wrote, "being
sensible that my service in that province hath not beene so
acceptable to His Majestie as I could have wished, and that
I cannot expect my continuance therein can be so usefull to
the Church as the necessities thereof at this tyme require;
and intimation of His Majestie's displeasure being made to

me by My Lord Commissioner, his grace the Earl of Lauderdaill; I doe in all humility make a surrender thereof." Whether it were prelate or peer or presbyter who stood in the dictator's path, he was overtaken soon by chastisement; and the autocrat went on his regal way undisturbed.

There were forty-two of the banished ministers who availed themselves of the gate provided by the Indulgence back into the churches from which they had been expelled. If, to borrow a phrase from Samuel Rutherfurd, they preferred the lower road of the valleys to the higher road of the mountains, it would be easy to speak too harshly of men who were swayed towards compromise and concession by many appealing arguments. But the issues of pain and strife which their braver-spirited friends had predicted revealed themselves only too speedily. Their conduct was condemned by the bulk of Presbyterian people, as an acceptance of conditions ruinous to the privileges of the Church and to the headship of Christ. Kirkton sums up the more consistent view in a single pregnant sentence; the Indulgence, he says, being derived from the King's authority, "was judged a bitter fruit from a bitter tree." Henceforward there was a new breach in the Covenanting host. It was sore enough to have Resolutioner and Protester regarding one another with suspicion, and winging their controversial arrows at each other instead of 'at the common foe. But now a second cause of heart-burning had arisen. Indulged and Non-indulged manifested a too scanty affection, and were frequently engaged in verbal strife, during the years to come.

A fatality clung, one sees, to Lauderdale's gifts, and the boon became a bane. But probably the intention was not unfriendly. For, during the Blink, he had for advisers three men, whose names it is a gladness to recall, and who stand out in bright relief from the sordid crowd of needy nobles and ruthless soldiers and haughty churchmen. They lent character and refinement, for one or two quickly fleeting years, to the cause of absolutism. And they had within them what Middleton and Rothes and Sharp never had, or else had killed and lost—a heart of compassionateness and magnanimity.

One of them was the Earl of Tweeddale. In the Parliament which condemned James Guthrie to die, he had the courage to vote against the capital sentence; "not but that I thought he deserved it, but some circumstances—as the disorders of the times, the general distractions of men's minds, and the fact that the restraining power of the laws was too sadly abated and the execution of them loosed—did incline me to another punishment." For his boldness and humanity he was thrown into prison in Edinburgh; and for nine months, from September in 1661 until May in 1662, the dungeon shut him in. Ordinarily a man is seen either at his best or at his worst in his own home; and, if we subject Lord Tweeddale to this test, our liking for him is increased. In a delightful letter written to Lauderdale, whose one daughter was married to his son, he discloses most naturally and winningly his affection for children and grandchildren. He has returned to Yester after a period of absence—to Yester, "wher I found them all weal, and was qwikly encompassed with children striving who should be most mead of. Charles is grouen ane mighty kind child, and left all his frowardnes, and, I think, squints noe mor then he did. I asked Jhon if he knew me; he said 'Ay, ay,' and clapid my cheek, and kissid both of them, and asked for his grandfather at London. Ann is grouen a pleasant and bewtiful child. My littel dawghter Jean, when she saw me mak mor, as she thought, of the rest than hir, said, 'I am a bairn too.'" Such a letter opens a window into Tweeddale's nature; and, when we look through the window-panes, we see what is inviting and tender.

Another of Lauderdale's counsellors was Alexander Bruce, second Earl of Kincardine, a statesman of insight and of integrity. It was his wish from the first to deal liberally with the Kirk; and if clemency could be shown, without seeming to be extorted through the alarm of the Government and the acknowledged strength of the Covenanters, he was prepared to show it. "I am, in my privat opinion, for a qualified toleration," he declared, "but I wold have it given and not taken; and I thinke it is not to be given so long as they thinke themselves so considerable as to oblidge the grantting of it." It would have been a rich benefit to the distracted country if Kincardine, with his rectitude and forbearance, had remained longer in office. He did continue with Lauderdale, from whose guidance of affairs he hoped for many reforms, after the other two had been forced to go. But at length his patience was worn out, and he broke with the Commissioner, whose despotic exercise of authority and gross personal sins had grown repugnant to his own purer mind and sweeter temper.

But the most attractive of the trio is Sir Robert Moray. The wonder is that so chivalrous a gentleman, Evelyn's " deare and excellent friend," and the comrade of comrades to whom Thomas Vaughan, the Silurist's philosophic brother, left all his papers, because he knew no one else whom he could trust with such fidelity—the wonder is that he should be found in conjunction with the persecutors at all. In truth, it was against his will that he engaged in the drudgery of politics, and was dragged away from employments and companionships more congenial. He loved his books, his chemical retorts, his music, his medical researches, and those familiar intimates to whom he could unbosom his heart with none of the diplomatist's concealments and equivocations. He was happier in his Presidency of the Royal Society than in his toils and worries and disappointments as Privy Councillor. The Earl of Kincardine knew him well; the two had been as brothers during their season of exile before the Restoration; and no speck of cloud ever crept over the serene sky of the fellowship. One may read the beautiful letters which Moray sent to Alexander Bruce, while the one was in Maestricht and the other in Bremen; and whoever reads them will become a thrall to the enchantments of the fascinating scribe—they are luminous with wisdom, with humour, with wide literary culture, with unassuming religion. Experiment and scientific study are much more to the writer than all the intrigues of princes and parliaments. " Here I stopt," he says, breaking off in the middle of a story, " to blow the coals in the stove under my feet, though I be sitting at the cheek of a furnace will gar your eyn reel when you see it." He describes, with the

enthusiast's devotion, his "three fiddles hanging on the wall";
but there, in the foreign country, he can extract little satisfaction from their melody : "to tell you truly, I am not much
for cultivating of musick till God send me dayes of joy and
mirth, if at least He hath markt out any such for us." He
has unspeakable rest and comfort in his knowledge that there
is not a jar, not a jealousy, not a disquieting element, in that
most satisfying alliance between his companion and himself.
"I find it in my heart," he owns, "to set every word I get
from you in diamonds." Even although his eyes do not
meantime look into Bruce's, and although many miles of land
and water may separate them, "you little think how long
your armes are, and how exquisite my physical skill is grown.
I feel your pulse here as well as if I were sitting at your
elbow, and know as well what temper you are in when you
write as if I had seen you." Does his correspondent entertain the slightest doubt of it ? Then let him survey himself
in his mirror after listening to Moray's description of him,
and he will admit the correctness of the portrait and the clair-
voyance of the man who has painted it. "I can see your
cheeks beginning to get a little palish crimson again, your eyes
their wonted vivacity, your legs their vigor, and everything
fairly advanced towards your recovery. Nay, by a new science
you do not yet know a name for, I find, by your beginning to
crow, it is not far from day, and that the thaw is begun at
Bremen, and I would almost think it were May instead of
April." This was penned when his friend had been lying
ill of ague ; and how he busied himself in the effort to keep
the sufferer amused, and to banish brooding thoughts ! But
he could be serious too, and climb to ethereal heights, and
pass like a spy into the Land of Promise, that he might carry
out some of its grapes of Eshcol to refresh the sojourner in
the wilderness. He bade him remember the truest secret of
consolation : "you know whatsoever your kind, wise, good,
and powerful Father sends to you, or does with you, is the
very best that can befall you, how dark soever His ways be to
your grief, or His touches to your relish." Occasionally he
would draw aside the curtain of the Temple, and would talk

of his own spiritual longings and strivings : "I shall tell you it hath been my study now thirty-one years to understand and regulate my passions; the whole story of my progress in this, and God's dealings with me in it, will be as open to you as you would have it." Dr. Osmund Airy writes with fine generosity, but yet not too generously, of Robert Moray. "We do not wish," he says, "to describe him as a man of heroic rank; he reminds us rather of the advice in *The Betrothed*: he sat still while kings were arming, he spake not when the people listened, and he kept his fingers from the red gold. In the midst of social depravity he led a life such as is led by men of pure and lofty mind, and such as he led while in exile. Where, all around him, men schemed and lied for place, he went on his way 'placidly and securely.' When bribery and flattery and supremacy in evil living were the usual passports to success, this Scottish gentleman kept himself, so far as can be told, unspotted from the world. He touched pitch, and was not defiled." If further proof of it were needed, there is the fact that a correspondent as cherished and reverenced as Alexander Bruce was his sister-in-law, Anna Mackenzie, Lady Balcarres, "exquisite alike in person and in mind." The man who could bind such friends to himself, and could hold them unchanged to the end, must have carried in him a crystalline soul. When 1660 came, and Charles and Lauderdale leaped from poverty to power, they compelled Moray, unambitious as he was, to give them his help. Let us record it to His Majesty's praise, when the witnesses to his discredit are legion, that he felt an extraordinary regard for one who had nothing in common with himself, except the pleasure in chemistry and the brilliance in conversation which they both shared. As for the nobleman, he made Bruce's companion his own Secretary, and consulted him always. In the summer of the Restoration year he sent him across to France, to secure from the French Presbyterians an opinion in favour of moderate Episcopacy. And now, in his personal rule over Scotland, there was none on whom he leaned more confidingly, or who better deserved his trust.

So long as such men got their will, there was little likelihood of excessive tyranny. But the Blink, after all, was but a blink; it was not confirmed and abiding summer. Charles's prerogatives, sufficiently haughty and far-stretching already, were being steadily enlarged, in spite of the apparent mildness which prevailed. A new statute enunciated, with greater emphasis than ever, his ecclesiastical supremacy; and, side by side with it, another statute gave him a militia of twenty thousand men. Lauderdale was proud of the double achievement. "The first makes you Soveraigne in the Church; you may now dispose of Bishops and Ministers, and remove and transplant them as you please—which, I doubt, you cannot doe in England. The other setles you 20 thousand men to make good that power. Never was King soe absolute as you are in poor old Scotland." And, as early as 1670, there was a fresh bit of savagery, the outcome of the Indulgence of the previous year, to which Tweeddale and Kincardine and Moray were somehow constrained to yield their consent. This was the Act against conventicles. The ministers who persisted in remaining without the Church were forbidden to pray and preach except in their own houses and among the members of their own families. If they dared to conduct a service of religion in a home not their own, they were imprisoned until they gave proof of their willingness not to offend in the like fashion again, and, if the proof were not forthcoming, they were compelled to leave the country. Those who had attended the service were heavily fined, the master or mistress of the house being required to pay a sum the double of that exacted from others. But the full weight of severity fell on the meetings held in the fields. The preacher there, or even in a building so crowded that some were standing out of doors, was to be punished with death and with the confiscation of his goods. Any one arresting him was to receive a reward of thirty pounds, and to have a free pardon if, in performing his disagreeable duty, he had killed the minister or some of the obstinate and misguided listeners. Those who had been present at a field-preaching were liable to fines extravagant and crushing in their amount. And, under the terror of these exorbitant dues, the people were commanded to repair regularly to the worship conducted by the curates or by the indulged preachers inside the churches. It was the advent of winter once more—"no roses but only thorns to-day"; and again the sons and daughters of the Covenant were out under a frowning heaven.

It is almost inexplicable that high-minded and gracious men, like the three into whose faces we have looked, should have stained their consciences and tarnished their fame by agreeing to the unjust Act. We can only account for it by remembering the stronger will behind them, which employed them as its exponents and agents. In fact, their brief and clement mastership was soon to be ended. Lord Lauderdale and they were to part company and go their separate ways. It was a woman's hand which sundered the ruler of Scotland from his best friends. His first wife, poor Anne Hume, died in 1671. He had sent her to France, ostensibly for the benefit of her health, but more probably that he might enjoy the freedom which her absence would afford. Her last letter to him was written from Paris. It is a pathetic little epistle, asking him to see that a house which she owned in Highgate should be repaired, before it fell in ruins to the ground. He had filled the upper rooms with those multitudinous books of his, and it was unable to sustain so great a load; for what was it but a slim and paltry erection of paper? If he would not do so trifling a service for her sake, let him do it, she begs, for his own; for the place would belong to his family when she was gone. "I have wreiten menei leters to you," she concludes mournfully enough; "I shal deseir an anseur." Death came to rescue the Earl of Hume's daughter from the slights and sorrows of years, and to liberate her ungentle husband from the trammels of a union of which he was tired. In 1672 he married again. His new bride was Elizabeth, Countess of Dysart, a woman with plenty of brains but without any heart, who had a bad history behind her, and who for the future was to act Herodias to his Herod. She did not love him; she used him as a convenient tool to bring her money and applause. If he had been overbearing before, he became tenfold more so under his wife's evil influence.

He "lowered to her level day by day," until, as she was destitute of all that is holiest in woman, he lost all that is strongest and most righteous in man. It was a pitiful degeneracy; but there seemed no chance of checking its progress. Lady Dysart's jealousy drove Moray from Lauderdale's side—Moray who had known how to touch pitch without being defiled. In a dignified little note, whose very brevity contrasts with his franker and more unfettered confidences— a note dated from Whitehall in January 1671, before the wedding had taken place, but after the lady's supremacy was firmly established—he closed the correspondence of years. The construction he had put on the Earl's last messages to him was, he said, "very natural"; and he went on, "As I was sorry to be forced, for my own sake, to such a returne as then made, soe am I willing not to reply upon the answeres you here give, least it might continue a Dispute which I doe not desire to intertaine with your Grace." That was all, and Robert Moray "gave his bridle-reins a shake," and rode away. By and by there was a hopeless quarrel with Tweeddale. In a few years more, Kincardine, too, said his farewells. Then, with these ministers of conciliation and worth removed from the councils of the nation, "hard came to hard," and the Covenanters passed anew into an era of "boots, thumbikins, and fire-matches, the bloody rope to the neck, and bullets to the head." But the wise student of the time will be sorrier for their oppressor than he is for them.

CHAPTER XV.

A FIELD PREACHER.

IT is a foolish, but not an uncommon, mistake—the notion that the men of the Covenant were all of lowly and plebeian birth. The dedicated army, with its banner of blue and its passion for the kingly rights of Christ, may have drawn most of its recruits from the peasants and shepherds of the countryside and from the traders in the towns; and these homely warriors, as they fought their spiritual battle, showed as fine a courage as any paladins of the Court. But there were men and women of higher degree proud to associate themselves with the cause of Presbytery. Some of the wise and mighty were called, and with promptitude they answered the call.

John Blackader is one of the gentlefolks who rallied to the defence of the Kirk. He was the scion of a famous family. The original home of his kindred was in Berwickshire; and among his forebears there were figures valorous and picturesque. In the middle of the fifteenth century, "the Black Band of the Blackaders," father and seven sons, each of them swarthy in complexion, had, time and again, beaten back the invading English; "weakness was not in their word, weariness not on their brow." They did not restrict their exploits to Scottish soil and to the defence of their own castles and crofts. Like Job's warhorse, they scented the battle from afar. Those were the days when the southern kingdom was rent by the contentions of York and Lancaster; and Cuthbert Blackader with his dauntless seven marshalled themselves under the standard of the

Red Rose. But, if they reaped renown in England, they found dule and death waiting for them too. On Bosworth field the veteran and three of his Black Band were slain; and the survivors came home grieved for the flowers of the forest that blossomed at their side no longer. Yet, because they had been so brave, James of Scotland granted them and their heirs the privilege of carrying on their shields the two Roses, Red and White. Their crest was a right hand holding aloft a broadsword, and their motto ran, "Courage helps Fortune."

In later years a sea of troubles overtook the Blackaders. The Homes of Wedderburn were at feud with them, and in the strife they fared badly. Ultimately the Berwickshire branch lost its commanding position, and the honour of maintaining the household name passed to younger sons who had come by marriage into the estate of Tulliallan in Perthshire. Our field preacher is of the Tulliallan stock. He was born in the December of 1615. But, although he had "some claim to distinction," as his *Memoirs* say, because he was "the representative of an ancient and once opulent house," his was to be a different and a holier fame. He was, his student son Robert wrote in 1686, when his father's race was run, "a good soldier and servant of Jesus Christ, who esteemed his Master's reproaches greater riches than all the treasures and pleasures of this Egyptian world." Old Cuthbert Blackader, trusty as a tree, was not more unbending than John Blackader, the minister of the Covenant.

After being trained under his uncle, William Strang, Principal of Glasgow College, where "Sion became the rival of Athens and Rome," he went up and down the country preaching the Gospel. One is at some loss to understand why he was so long in finding a charge of his own; not until 1653, when he was a man of thirty-seven, was he ordained over the parish of Troqueer, in the Presbytery of Dumfries. But it was well that he came to his work in the maturity of his powers. His parish was sadly backward. The people were ignorant, some of them living in scandalous sin, many inclined to popish beliefs and ways. He had an uphill road to travel, and it took time to gain the topmost ridge. First he reformed the eldership, and then gradually changed the face of the congregation and of the whole neighbourhood. Twice every Sabbath he preached, and once, too, every Tuesday, "except in the throng of seedtime and harvest." In his sermons he explored and explained the whole territory of saving knowledge. All who could read he exhorted to provide themselves with Bibles, and those who could not were enjoined to seek out some family where, round the altar set up on the hearth, they might listen to the Word of God. In spring, and again in autumn, he catechised his parishioners. It was a duty performed in no perfunctory style. He "took inspection into their behaviour." He had many a searching question. Did they remember secret prayer? Morning and evening, did they kneel together at the throne of their Father and King? Was the Sabbath a delight? Did the parents instruct their children in the truth? If they had servants, did they "curb profanity in any whom they found to miscarry"? Somewhat rigid the old-time oversight of the flock may seem; but it bore a salutary harvest. Troqueer and its minister and session may have been one of the places which Bishop Burnet had in his thoughts, when he penned his tribute to the Presbyterians of the Commonwealth: "They had brought the people to such a degree of knowledge that cottagers and servants would have prayed extempore; they had a comprehension of matters of religion greater than I have seen among people of that sort anywhere."

For nine years John Blackader pursued his calling, till the advent of Middleton's Glasgow Act; and, as we should expect, he was among the faithful who could not bow the knee. On a November Sabbath, with the noise of sobbing heard through the church, he took his farewell. The dragoons from Dumfries were there; but meantime they did not meddle him. During the week which succeeded, from sunrise until far in the night, he moved from family to family, praying in each farm-kitchen and cottage, and commending to God every separate soul. Then, on Saturday,

THE MARKET CROSS OF MENNIHYVIE OR MONIAIVE.

he rode away to Glencairn, to seek a place of safety
beyond the bounds of his presbytery. His wife and
children were to follow. But no sooner was he gone than
the soldiers returned. They attacked the manse, and
behaved with cruelty and insolence to its defenceless
inmates. One of the boys never forgot the wild "Blew-
benders," nor the adventures of the critical day. "Bag
and baggatch, we who were the children were put into
cadgers' creels, where one of us cried out, coming throw
the Brigend of Dumfries, 'I'm banisht! I'm banisht!'"
The Troqueer ministry had an ending both sudden and sore.

John Blackader did not commence at once to preach
in the fields. If he was fervent of soul, he was cautious
in action; the epitaph on his tomb celebrates the balance
and equipoise of his nature—

> Zeal warmed his breast, and reason cooled his head.

As long as might be, he refrained from giving provocation
to the authorities. And so there were some who held
conventicles before he went out to hillside and glen. There
was Gabriel Sempill, for instance, also the son of a noble
house. And there was John Welsh of Irongray.

We must tarry over Welsh's name; he is one of the
kings of the time. His father and his grandfather were
ministers before him; he was himself the great-grandson of
John Knox; and he inherited the godliness and the manli-
ness of his progenitors. He had been a co-presbyter with
Blackader, and, like him, had been driven out by
Middleton's folly. In his case, too, the importunity and
the affection of the parish pursued the preacher, and
would scarcely let him go. His horse waited for him at
the Water of Cluden, and he had to dash into the stream
and gallop rapidly away. Even then, through the wintry
little river, men and women followed him, not turning
back while he remained in sight. It makes us think of
a similar scene in a different place and time. When Sir
Henry Lawrence left the government of the Punjab in 1853,

grief was written on every face. Old and young, rich and
poor, soldiers and civilians, Englishmen and natives, felt
that they were losing a friend. Strong men, like Sir
Herbert Edwardes, might be seen weeping like children.
A cavalcade of Sikh chiefs accompanied the departing ruler,
some for five, others for ten, others for twenty or twenty-
five miles. It was a long, living funeral procession from
Lahore nearly to Umritsur. None knew Sir Henry Lawrence
but to love him. And it was the same with John Welsh.

In one respect the members of his flock were happier
than their neighbours at Troqueer. He continued their
pastor in a sense, although he was not allowed to speak
within the church walls. In defiance of every hostile edict,
he returned again and again; sometimes he was back, in
valley or in wood or in meadow, once a week for successive
months; there was not a child whom he did not baptize;
often the familiar voice was heard proclaiming the familiar
message. But now it might be said that he had taken all
the Lowlands for his diocese. Summer and winter he was
engaged in field meetings. "The boldest undertaker"—the
most audacious lion-heart—"that ever I knew a minister
in Christ's Church": it is James Kirkton's tribute. "For,
notwithstanding the threatenings of the State, the great
price of £500 set upon his head, the spite of bishops, the
diligence of all bloodhounds, he maintained his difficult task
of preaching upon the mountains of Scotland, many times
to many thousands, for near twenty years." "I have
known," his biographer adds, " Mr. Welsh ride three days
and two nights without sleep, and preach upon a mountain
at midnight on one of the nights. He had for some time
a dwelling-house near Tweedside; and, when Tweed was
strongly frozen, he preached in the middle of the river, that
either he might shun the offence of both nations, or that two
Kingdoms might dispute his crime." We catch glimpses of
him too, with a bodyguard of twelve gentlemen in scarlet,
whom he had bound to himself in a loyalty as devoted as
that of the Gittites to David, journeying hither and thither
on horseback, through the green trees of the woods, and

among the fields of the Lothians and Fife. There were the
vivid colours of romance, and the charm of mystery, and
the poetry of peril, about a minister's life two hundred and
fifty years ago.

John Welsh's word was with power. Once, when he was
chased unrelentingly, he hardly knew where to flee; but,
relying on Scottish hospitality, he knocked at the door of a
landlord, bitterly opposed to the field preachers and to himself
in particular, although he had never actually set eyes on him.
The stranger, being unrecognised, was received with kindness.
In the evening's talk reference was made to Welsh, and the
host complained of the difficulty of capturing him. "I am
sent," the visitor said, "to apprehend rebels; I know where he
is to preach to-morrow; I will put his hand into yours."
Overjoyed, the gentleman agreed to accompany his informant
on the next morning. When they arrived at the appointed
spot, the congregation had assembled. The people made way
for the minister whom they trusted and for his comrade.
Welsh desired his entertainer to sit down on the solitary
chair which had been provided for himself, and, to his
companion's utter bewilderment, took his own stand beside it,
and rang out the story of sin and salvation. The Spirit of
God was there; and the landlord was heart-broken. When at
the close, Welsh, fulfilling his promise, gave him his hand,
that he might do with him whatever he wished, he said:
"You told me that you were sent to apprehend rebels; and I,
a rebellious sinner, have been apprehended this day."

But let us return to John Blackader. He continued in his
Galloway retreat, until, by a fresh onslaught of persecution, he
was driven forth into the wider sphere of work. Early in the
winter of 1666, Sir James Turner and a party of soldiers came
looking for him. Happily he was himself absent in Edinburgh;
but again wife and bairns suffered at the hands of the " rascally
ruffians"; and, again, we have the best account of what
happened in the artless words of one of the children. He tells
how, about two o'clock in the morning, the dragoons surrounded the house, "cursing on the Whigs to open the door";

how, when they got in, they went to stools and chairs, and
demolished them with their swords, to make a fire; how they
"stabbed through beds and bed-clothes," to find the man for
whom they were in search; how they "threw down his books
from the press upon the floor, and caused poor me hold the
candle till they had examined them; and all they thought
whiggish, as they termed it—and brave judges they were!—
they put into a great horse-creel, and took away"; how they
"climbed up to the hen-bauks, where the cocks and hens were,
and, as they came to one, threw about its neck, and down to
the floor wi't, and so on, till they had destroyed them all."
Glad at heart the boy of ten was, when he managed to elude
his tormentors. "Naked to the shirt," he ran through the
darkness to "the Brigend of Mennihyvie"; and there, discovering that the inhabitants were still deep in slumber, he
climbed to the uppermost step of the village Cross, and fell
fast asleep. "Between five and six, a door opens, and an old
woman comes out; and, seeing a white thing upon the Cross,
comes near it; and, when she found it was a little boy, cries
out, 'Save us! what art thou?' With that I awaked, and
answered her, 'I'm Mr. Blackader's son.' 'O, my puir bairn!
what brought thee here?' I answers, 'There's a hantle of
fearful men with red coats has burnt all our house.' 'O, puir
thing!' says she, 'come in, and lye down in my warm bed.'"
And the child did as he was bidden, and it was the sweetest
bed ever he met with.

It was this rude visitation of Turner's soldiery which
compelled Blackader into his larger bishopric. He tried no
longer to conciliate masters who were so barbarous. He
became one of the chiefs in the great conventicles of the time;
John Welsh and Gabriel Sempill and he were "the Three First
Worthies." "He was another indefatigable Paul," says his
soldier son, Colonel Blackader, "travelling through most parts
of Scotland, except among the Highlanders, whose case he
sadly regretted; for I heard him many a time say he would
be content to go a thousand miles on foot to have had the
Highland language." The "intolerable craving" to save
shivered through him, like a trumpet-call.

We must think of him, in the years which ensued, having his headquarters in Edinburgh, but hastening everywhere on his divine errands. Through trustworthy channels messages were sent to him, to inform him that a crowd of those who were hungering for the Bread of Life proposed to meet at this selected spot or that other; and then he and his good horse would sally forth in time for the gathering. Thus, in September 1668, "there came a man from Dunlop parish" to Newmilns, where the preacher was lodged for a few days. "So he rode about nine miles of very bad road, and came to the place very weary, expecting to have gotten rest that night. But the people had trysted the parents with their children, so he behoved to address himself to the work, and went about eleven o'clock at night to a great meeting; where he preached an hour and a half; and thereafter baptized forty-two children, dividing them, the one half at one time, the other afterwards, because they could not get all conveniently stood together; and, after this was done, it was hard on break of day." In January 1669, he is at Fenwick, with its memories of William Guthrie, where there has been no Presbyterian preaching since the defeat at Pentland. But, by his too abundant toils, he has made himself ill; and for sixteen weeks he is imprisoned in the sick-room. No sooner is health restored than the work is resumed. At Bo'ness he establishes a new congregation. At Paisley he has a multitude of twelve hundred listeners. At a burnside, in the moors near Livingstone, where his text was the tender word, *The Son of Man is come to seek and to save that which is lost*, an assemblage from many parishes hangs on his lips. "The people seemed to smell him out in spite of his caution"; like his King and Friend, he *could not be hid*. Living so much in the sun and the keen air, facing the weather in heat and cold, he discovered that his sight, employed hitherto in quiet reading and study, was being much impaired. But he did not grieve over the loss. "The eye in the heart that lies" grew clearer with every year.

Some of the conventicles in which he played a principal part were very noteworthy. There was, for example, the gathering on the Hill of Beath, near Dunfermline, in the midsummer of 1670. It was a district where ignorance and profanity were prevalent; and, "for the more solemnity and upstirring of a barbarous people," the preacher took a colleague with him. John Dickson was his companion. Having crossed the Firth of Forth on Saturday night, and having slept for a few hours at Inverkeithing without putting off his clothes, Blackader rose early, and went in quest of the meeting-place. Already the congregation was there, for worship was to begin at eight o'clock. First Dickson lectured, standing in the mouth of the tent, and addressing the crowd which thronged the braeside. Then John Blackader preached from that favourite text of Covenanting ministers, *He must reign till He hath put all enemies under His feet.* It was eleven o'clock ere he finished; and there was to be an interval of rest before the work of the afternoon. But there had been signs that those present were not all friends; and now, when the preacher started anew, things looked threatening. A lieutenant of militia dismounted from his horse, and came in among the people massed on the minister's left hand. Fortunately Blackader's second discourse had the wooing note in it. It was " composing and gaining, holding forth the great design of the Gospel, to invite and make welcome all sorts of sinners without exception." The lieutenant could find no fault; he "stood a space, and heard peaceably." Yet there might easily have been a conflagration. For, when the officer lifted his foot to the stirrup to ride off, some tried to prevent him, and he thrust them back; and there was prospect of tumult, and perhaps of bloodshed. But Blackader saw it, and interrupted his sermon, and went to the soldier's assistance. Calming the angry men with wise words, he spoke to the officer: "Let me see, sir, who will offer to wrong you. They shall as soon wrong myself; for we came here to do violence to no man, but to proclaim the Gospel of peace. If you be pleased to stay, you shall be as welcome as any; but, if you will not, you are free to go." The lieutenant escaped scathless, and the services proceeded until late in the day. Very tired the minister was, before he reached his Edinburgh home next

morning. At Queensferry he could not induce a boatman to
row him over the Firth, and he had perforce to ride the long
way round by Stirling. He was seven hours in the saddle,
after all the mental and spiritual exertion of the memorable
Sabbath. Were not his campaigns as exacting as those of his
fighting ancestors ?

The Dunfermline conventicle is worth remembering for
another reason. It was one of the first to which many of the
worshippers came armed. In 1670 the Blink was almost over,
and Lauderdale's administration was again becoming pitiless.
So the Covenanters did what they had not done before, but
what they repeated frequently in subsequent months—they
carried sword and pistol with them to the hill where they sang
their psalms and presented their prayers and hearkened to the
Evangel of Christ. We cannot blame them for a precaution to
which they were forced in self-defence, even if this conjunction
of the weapons of a carnal warfare with " the melodies of the
everlasting chime " should seem in some degree incongruous.
In desperate times the men are guiltless who resort to
desperate measures.

But more remarkable and more beautiful than the ordinary
conventicle was a Communion in the fields. John Blackader
will describe to us one of these, which he, in company with
" Mr. Welsh and Mr. Riddell," superintended and enjoyed at
East Nisbet in the Border country. After relating what
means were adopted to shield from interruption and alarm
those whose rendezvous, however fit it might be, was " by the
lions' dens and the mountains of leopards," he goes on with
his tale—

" We entered on the administration of the holy ordinance,
committing it and ourselves to the invisible protection of the
Lord of Hosts, in whose name we were met together. The
place where we convened was every way commodious, and
seemed to have been formed on purpose. It was a green and
pleasant haugh, fast by the waterside. On either hand, there
was a spacious brae, in form of a half round, covered with
delightful pasture, and rising with a gentle slope to a goodly
height. Above us was the clear blue sky, for it was a sweet

and calm Sabbath morning, promising to be indeed one of the days of the Son of Man. The Communion tables were spread on the green by the water, and around them the people had arranged themselves in decent order. But the far greater multitude sat on the brae face, which was crowded from top to bottom.

"Each day, at the congregation's dismissing, the ministers with their guards, and as many of the people as could, retired to their quarters in three several country towns, where they might be provided with necessaries. The horsemen drew up in a body, and then marched in goodly array behind the people, until all were safely lodged. In the morning, when they returned, the horsemen accompanied them. All the three parties met a mile from the spot, and marched in a full body to the consecrated ground. The congregation being fairly settled, the guardsmen took their stations as formerly. They secured the peace and quiet of the audience; for from Saturday morning, when the work began, until Monday afternoon, we suffered not the least affront or molestation from enemies: which appeared wonderful. The whole was closed in as orderly a way as it had been in the time of Scotland's brightest noon. And, truly, the spectacle of so many grave, composed, and devout faces must have struck the adversaries with awe, and been more formidable than any outward ability of fierce looks and warlike array. We desired not the countenance of earthly kings; there was a spiritual and divine Majesty shining on the work. Amidst the lonely mountains we remembered the words of our Lord, that true worship was not peculiar to Jerusalem or Samaria—that the beauty of holiness consisted not in material temples. We remembered the Ark of the Israelites, which had sojourned for years in the desert, with no dwelling but the tabernacle of the plain. We thought of Abraham and the ancient patriarchs, who laid their victims on the rocks for an altar, and burned sweet incense under the shade of the green tree.

"The ordinance of the Last Supper was signally backed with refreshing influence from above. Few such days were seen in the desolate Church of Scotland, and few will ever

OBELISK ON SKEOCH HILL, NEAR IRONGRAY.

witness the like. There was a rich effusion of the Spirit shed abroad in many; their souls breathed in a diviner element, and burned upwards as with the fire of a pure and holy devotion. The ministers were visibly assisted to speak home to the conscience of the hearers; they who witnessed declared, they carried more like ambassadors from the court of heaven than men cast in earthly mould. The tables were served by some gentlemen and persons of the gravest deportment. The communicants entered at one end, and retired at the other, a way being kept clear to take their seats again on the hillside. Solemn it was and edifying, to see the composure of all present; and it was pleasant, as the night fell, to hear their melody swelling in full unison along the hill, the whole congregation joining with one accord. There were two long tables, and one short—across the head—with seats on each side. About a hundred sat at every table. There were sixteen tables in all, so that about three thousand two hundred communicated that day."

It is a long quotation; but it portrays a noble scene in noble words. The preacher, who could delineate the solemnity so fittingly, never halted in his missionary journeys; for some fifteen years, except when illness chained him to his house, he expounded the counsel of God. We meet him and his pony in Fifeshire, in the Lothians, in Lanarkshire, in Carrick and Cunningham, in Annandale, among the hills of Galloway. Once he halts to baptize a poor man's child by the moss-side, and a crowd collects, and, as they appear to be poor innocents, who rarely hear his sort of preaching, he accompanies the ceremony with a short lecture. Once, in his old parish of Troqueer, he intends holding the meeting on a knoll amongst the trees; but the day is windy, and there is such commotion of leaves and branches that the people cannot hear, and so they go to a green and open expanse near the Laird of Dalscarth's house. Once, at Dunscore, it is a time of deep snow; and among the white snow a chair is set for the minister; and the men and women pull bunches of heather, and sit hearkening on the moor. There are a hundred exhilarating incidents which cluster round the name of John Blackader.

He missed no fruitful chance that came to him; until, early on an April morning in 1681, his enemies seized him in Edinburgh, and sent him to close his toiling and suffering and rejoicing days in the prison on the Bass Rock.

His fathers fought for the Red Rose, and won it for their crest. But surely his own crest was not the Red Rose so much as the White—the White Rose not, indeed, of York, but of Heaven. We recollect Martin Luther's words: "I took for the symbol of my theology a seal on which I had engraven a Cross, with a Heart in its centre. The Cross is black, to indicate the sorrows, even unto death, through which the Christian must pass. But the Heart preserves its natural colour, for the Cross does not extinguish nature—it does not kill but give life. The Heart is placed in the midst of a White Rose, which signifies the joy, peace, and consolation that faith brings. But the Rose is white and not red, because it is not the joy and peace of the world but that of spirits."

This was the flower, supernal and undying, which John Blackader carried on his shield and in his soul.

CHAPTER XVI.

HE SEEMED IN A PERPETUAL MEDITATION.

TWEEDDALE and Kincardine and Sir Robert Moray had all helped to usher in the broken sunlight of the Blink. But there was another agent whose part must not be forgotten. He was not a statesman but a churchman, one of those churchmen who are innocent of craft, and round whose brows the halo of heavenliness shines. Robert Leighton's name is already familiar, as one of the four bishops consecrated at Westminster in the last days of 1661. Being always most humble—did he not sign himself "one of the unworthiest caitiffs in the world"? —he had selected the diocese of Dunblane, the smallest and quietest of the four. But about 1670, when Alexander Burnet had been compelled to resign his high position in Glasgow, it seemed desirable that Leighton should be sent to the west. The Covenanters had their headquarters there, and there the most vigorous spiritual life was found; and who was likelier to wield an effective influence in these surroundings than the Episcopalian leader who was a scholar and a gentleman and a saint? This was the time, too, of Archbishop Leighton's Accommodation, as the peace-making and amiable scheme was called.

He had ever been a lover of concord, and a friend at heart to the Presbyterians whom he had left. In Dunblane he had preserved the old machinery of the Kirk, and had opposed innovations in ritual. He would not permit any to address him as "My Lord"; no right reverend father was he, but a brother perpetually aware of his shortcomings. He resembled one of John Knox's Superintendents rather than a diocesan ruler and prince.　The same conciliatory temper governed him in Glasgow.　No doubt, the politicians urged him to draw together the sundered factions; but he needed no urging: this was the goal of all his prayer and labour.　The Accommodation simply gave embodiment to the yearnings of its author's charitable spirit.　It proposed that the Church courts of former days should be retained, and that in them bishops and ministers should act in concert, the bishops having no dignity beyond that of constant presidents or moderators; that the Covenanting members should have liberty to declare that they tolerated the bishop merely for peace's sake; that ordinations should not take place without the concurrence of the Presbytery; that, in every third year, provincial Synods should be held, before which the bishops might be arraigned and censured, if their administration had been negligent or arrogant or unworthy.　That these Synods, with the spear of Ithuriel in their hands, were not unnecessary was Leighton's persuasion; he knew that some of his brethren had little title to respect. " The truth is," he wrote to Lauderdale, " I am greatly ashamed that wee have occasioned so much trouble, and done so litle or no good, now these seven or eight years since your restitution of our order, and after so many favours heapt upon us by His Majesty's Royal goodnesse. . . . Hee that can sit down content with honour and revenue without doing good, especially in so sacred a function, hath, I think, a low and servile soul."　The Accommodation was a genuine effort to reconcile those who were drifting more and more apart.

But it failed.　It could only fail, although an angel from heaven preached its value.　Conferences were held with the ministers, whom Leighton was desirous to gain.　Six of the leading men amongst them were summoned to Holyrood House, to meet several of the Members of the Council and Gilbert Burnet and the Archbishop of Glasgow.　Sharp would not come in person; but he sent one of his subordinates to watch the proceedings.　Lauderdale was there, and spoke of the King's great condescension and His Majesty's wishes for a complete unity and harmony.　Leighton appealed to his hearers in both armies to work together for the peace of the

Church. But George Hutcheson replied for the Presbyterians that they must have time to consider propositions fraught with so much significance, and to consult with their brethren about their answer. Lauderdale, with his hot and imperious temper, was angry. "He made us all dine together," says the author of the *History of My Own Time*, "and came to us after dinner; but could scarce restrain himself from flying out" against the Covenanting preachers, "for their behaviour seemed both rude and crafty." The parleyings went on during the five last months of 1670; but, a few days after the New Year, the end came. The ministers would have none of Leighton's charming. In the constant moderatorship they saw the embryo of all Prelacy. And they remembered that his colleagues on the Episcopal bench were wholly different from the dove-like man who brought the olive-branch; they knew that most of them disapproved of the overtures of friendship. "No," they said, "we cannot receive your Accommodation. It is a cloak under which tyranny will pursue its way unsuspected. It is a drug to bewitch our own vigilance into sleep." Their intractableness may appear too dogged and a trifle discourteous; but, unless they had been willing to sacrifice the convictions of a lifetime, a negative reply was unavoidable. Burnet acknowledges that even Leighton, whom that unbending Presbyterian, Sir James Stewart of Goodtrees, once called a "Nathaniell" without guile, scarcely meant his concessions to be permanent. "He went very far to the extenuating episcopal authority; but he thought it would be easy afterwards to recover what seemed necessary to be yielded at present." It was a wise distrust which prevented the Covenanters from entangling themselves in the net.

Even yet Leighton did not lose hope. He chose six of the best preachers among his clergy, and sent them to the parishes whose Whiggism appeared most pronounced and stubborn— "the Bishop's Evangelists" men dubbed them. Gilbert Burnet, formerly minister of Saltoun, now Professor of Divinity in Glasgow, by and by chaplain to William of Orange and diocesan of Salisbury, was one of them. James Nairn, of the Abbey Church in Edinburgh, was another, who "read the

K

moral philosophers much and turned it all into melting devotion," but who "pitied the Presbyterians as men of low notions and ill tempers." Laurence Charteris, of Yester, was a third—Laurence Charteris, who "loved the mystical divines," and "hated controversies and disputes as dry and lifeless things," and was himself "a very perfect friend and a sublime Christian." And a fourth was James Aird, of Torryburn, "commonly called 'Mr. Leighton's ape,'" as Kirkton mischievously reports, "because he could imitate his shrug and grimace, but never more of him"; and yet, surely, there must have been something spiritual and fine in James Aird's soul, for Leighton could address to him the most beautiful letters he ever penned:—once, for instance, he sends him "two little pieces of history" which he thinks his correspondent will relish, Paulus Nolanus and his Life of Martin of Tours, and Valerius Maximus and his selected examples; and then he goes on, "But, when all is done, there is only one blessed story, wherein our souls must dwell and take up their rest; for amongst all the others we shall not read, *Come unto Me, ye that are weary and heavy laden.* And never any yet that tried Him, but found Him as good as His word. To Whose sweet embraces I recommend you, and desire to meet you there." The Bishop's Evangelists were the flower and crown of the Episcopalians. But either the people refused to hear them, or showed that they understood their Bibles too well to be moved by their pleadings. "We were indeed amazed," the most famous of them admits, "to see so poor a communality so capable to argue upon points of government, and on the bounds to be set to the power of princes in matters of religion. Upon all these topics they had texts of Scripture at hand, and were ready with their answers to anything that was said to them. This measure of knowledge was spread amongst even the meanest of them, their cottagers and their servants." It was a case of the bruised reed proving itself "amply tough to pierce the shield of error through"; and thus, although his missionaries "stayed about three months in the country," and witnessed a momentary "stand in the frequency of conventicles," the peacemaker had again been

defeated, and his heart was sadder than ever : he spoke of it
as filled with the "peevish humors of a melancholy monk."
Less and less had he any faith in his fellow-prelates.   "I
beleev," he said, "'twere litle damage either to Church or
State, possibly some advantage to both, if wee should all
retire."   In a few years, worn out by what he described
pathetically as "a drunken scuffle in the dark," he gave up
his own archbishopric, and withdrew to spend "the remnant
of his time in a private and retired life."   The strife of
tongues was abhorrent to Robert Leighton.

"Over all that noble face lay somewhat of soft pensiveness"; and let us look into its gracious features.   Bishop
Burnet, who does not usually pierce far beneath the surface,
kindles into the eloquence of the heart when Leighton is his
theme.   "He seemed to have the lowest thoughts of himself
possible, and to desire that all other persons should think as
meanly of him as he did himself."   "He had so subdued the
natural heat of his temper that, in a great variety of accidents,
and in a course of twenty-two years' intimate conversation
with him, I never observed the least sign of passion, but upon
one single occasion."   "He brought himself into so composed
a gravity, that I never saw him laugh, and but seldom smile."
"And he kept himself in such a constant recollection, that I
do not remember that ever I heard him say one idle word."
"His thoughts were lively, oft out of the way and surprising,
yet just and genuine.   And he had laid together in his
memory the greatest treasure of the best and wisest of all
the ancient sayings of the heathens as well as Christians, that
I have known any man master of ; and he used them in the
aptest manner possible."   Thus the panegyric passes from
point to point, doing honour to him who penned its enthusiastic sentences, but investing with yet higher glories him
who could inspire a reverence so deep.

In Leighton's soul the master-power was the hunger for
holiness.   "Reverend brethren," he wrote to his curates in
Dunblane, "truly I think it were our best and wisest reflection, upon the many difficulties and discouragements without
us, to be driven to live more within ; as they observe of the

bees that, when it is foul weather outside, they are busy in their hives. If the power of external discipline be enervated in our hands, yet who can hinder us to try and judge and censure ourselves, and to purge the inner temples, our own hearts, with the more severity and exactness? And, if we be dashed and bespattered with reproaches abroad, to study to be the cleaner at home?" A passage like this discloses at once his defects and his grandeurs. It was his weakness that, in the confusions of the time, he felt himself paralysed; he could wrestle with God in his chamber, but not with men on the fierce-fought battlefield; the summons to energise and die in the conflict was too hard a counsel for his neutral heart. But, on the other hand, there have not been many who, with Leighton's simplicity and continuousness, beheld the Father's face. The little notes, axioms and quotations and prayers, which he jotted on the margins of his books, are proofs that he never wandered more than a mile or two from his first Love. Now it is: *Suavissima vita est quotidie sentire se fieri meliorem*, "This is the sweetest life, to feel that daily I am becoming a better man." And now: *Leve est sua relinquere, seipsum relinquere gravissimum*, "It is easy to leave one's things, most arduous to leave oneself." And again: *Qui veut vivre après la mort, faut qu'il meure devant la mort*, "Who wishes to live after death must die before death comes." Here we have all Professor James's visible and practical marks of saintliness: the asceticism, which prompts to self-immolation; the strength, which lifts the man above personal motives; the purity, which keeps character and conduct unspotted; and the charity, which has shifted the emotional centre away from self to others.

That Robert Leighton was an expert in the science and art of holiness may be learned from the influence wielded by his writings. It would be vain to seek to enumerate the readers, whom his books have led into those ivory palaces which are redolent with the perfume of aloes and myrrh and cassia. The dialect of absolute sincerity is heard in every sentence. He praises Christ, because the King has bound his own soul with unbreakable fetters. He bids us long for heaven, because

ROBERT LEIGHTON.

all his nature is domiciled within it. He commands us to forget and forgive, and we are left in no dubiety about the thoroughness with which he forgives and forgets. If we are not permitted to think of him as having already surmounted the white and rosy Alps, we see him pressing to them with a patience which never flags. It was his meat and drink, his business and pleasure, to do the will of God; and he awakens in men and women who hearken to him the same absorbing purpose. One instance of his success will be remembered. Henry Martyn burned out for God with the intenseness and the rapid blaze of phosphorus. Each prayer of his soul was, what he said prayer ought ever to be, a visit to the invisible world. During the six brief years of his residence in the East, he was an unresting missionary, a translator of the Bible, a follower of Christ without rebuke. When, after his death, his portrait was sent to Charles Simeon, the preacher declared that, whenever he saw it, it said to him, "Be in earnest! Don't trifle! Don't trifle!" And, next to God, there were two teachers who moulded Henry Martyn into his spiritual greatness. They were David Brainerd and Archbishop Leighton. To Leighton's *Rules and Instructions for Devout Exercises*, he confessed that he owed a debt which he could neither compute nor repay. We may comprehend the older man's consecration, when we stand afar off and marvel at that of his son in the faith.

Those books of his, with their vision of the Unseen, their subjection of the temporal to the eternal, their mystical heights and ardours, their moderate and gentle Calvinism, were the product of the Presbyterian period of his life. It was then that he preached the sermons which compose his Commentary on St. Peter. It was then that he drew up the *Devout Exercises*, for which Henry Martyn gave him untiring thanks. Mr. West, the latest and best of his editors, comments upon the strangeness of the phenomenon —this exposition of the broadest and deepest and sweetest truth proceeding from the heart of the stern-featured and sorely molested Kirk. Perhaps the apparent anomaly has part of its explanation in the fact that Leighton, who in his youth had resided at Douai and made many friends "among the quiet priests that pray in chapel low or chancel dim," was always a lover of the devotional literature of the Roman Catholic Church. "When Mr. Dickson was Professor at Edinburgh," Wodrow says, "and Mr. R. Leighton was Principall there, the Principall urged that the Professor might either teach, or, at least, recommend Thomas à Kempis to his students; and told him he regarded it one of the best books that ever was writt, next to the inspired writers." We have frequent echoes of *The Imitation* in *The Rules and Instructions*. Here is the old familiar accent: "Whoever thou be, let this voice of God be still in thine ear, My son, return inwardly to thy heart, abstract thyself from all things, and mind Me only." Here, too, speaks a disciple of the recluse of Mount St. Agnes: "Fix thy mind on thy crucified Saviour, and remember continually His great meekness, love, and obedience, His pure chastity, His unspeakable patience, and all the holy virtues of His humanity." And this, again, might have come from the little corner where Thomas Hämerken sat and brooded and wrote: "Draw thy mind, therefore, from all creatures unto a certain silence and rest from the jangling and company of all things below God; and, when thou canst come to this, then is thy heart a place meet and ready for thy Lord God to abide in, there to talk with thy soul." But the anomaly is only apparent, after all. Within many a Covenanting breast, in spite of the serious and iron words the lips might have to utter, and the steep mountain-sides the feet climbed unflinchingly, there dwelt from January to December an unruffled peace. Men who, unlike him, were keen controversialists carried as truly as Leighton the secret of God; and one or two were able to unfold that secret as musically as he did. Professor Flint certainly goes too far, when he declares that "his works are worth many times over all the writings of all his Scottish contemporaries." They are fragrant with more than Sabæan odours. They are beautiful "as if a fair flower of Paradise had dropped amidst the thorn and thistle." But so are the Letters of Samuel Rutherfurd, and so are some of the paragraphs in *The Christian's Great Interest* of William Guthrie. Leighton is not the single and solitary Presbyterian who, in those grim and ill-conditioned years, spoke as if he lived habitually in the third heaven.

There is a vexatious mystery in his biography. He became a traitor to the Church which for years he had been content to serve. His father was the unswerving Puritan on whom the Star Chamber inflicted horrors, the bare recital of which makes us shiver; we might have imagined that filial loyalty would prevent him from conforming to Episcopacy. He had himself been minister for eleven summers of the Kirk of Newbattle; and, if he preferred to preach to eternity rather than to the times, he swore the Covenant with his own lips, and he imposed it on his people. When the Midlothian parish was left, he had been Presbyterian Principal of the University of Edinburgh, prelecting once a week to the students in Latin, and imparting as much spiritual blessing as intellectual stimulus. Then, with the Restoration, he turned his back on the traditions bequeathed to him by his parent, on the Kirk whose spokesman he had been, on the Leagues and Covenants he had vowed to defend. He was in some respects more pliable than James Sharp, although he could have no intimacy with a man so worldly and sordid. For, when Sharp was disposed to stand out against the ceremony of ordination as a deacon and a priest, Leighton gave way, salving conscience with the verbal protest that, if he accepted such prelatic sanctions, the orders he had formerly received from his fellow-presbyters were not thereby annulled. It is a backsliding which puzzles us—a disappointment to rouse unappeasable regrets.

We have found him kindly to the last towards the comrades whom he had forsaken; perhaps, after a season, there were compunctions in his soul that he had severed his path from theirs. But why did he take the false turning? Why, as the poet of *The Bishop's Walk* states the question, "should a servant of God range himself on the devil's side, in the great conflict of the age?" We cannot unriddle the problem; but some of his reasons we may surmise. There was the sinister influence of his brother, Sir Ellis Leighton, the Mephistopheles in his life-drama—Sir Ellis, the courtier, the pervert to Roman Catholicism, the schemer who wished to promote his private ends when he introduced his relative to the King. There was in Leighton himself an inclination towards the outward beauty of Episcopalian worship—its liturgy, its ornate service, its seemliness. Deeper still was his recoil from the din of ecclesiastical strife, his craving for a place of rest and room. Probably, too, he had the hope, a hope which those rugged Presbyters were to shatter, that he might prove a reconciler, persuading the contending parties into goodwill. Then, also, being high-strung and cultured, he was apt to distrust the common people, and to look askance on their activity in the affairs of the Kirk; he had none of Rutherfurd's brave confidence in the democracy. Dr. Dugald Butler thinks, moreover, that, as the years went on, he came round to the position which the Marquis of Montrose had assumed in 1643: that, while he never resiled from his approval of the National Covenant of Scotland, he began to regard the Solemn League and Covenant as unconstitutional and rebellious—"rashly entered into and now to be repented of." Putting these things together, we discern some of the causes for conduct which, viewed from the vantage-ground of the later day, seems mistaken and wrong.

Robert Leighton realised soon that, in a Church which James Sharp ruled, he could have no congenial home. It is related that, on the journey from London, at Morpeth, he left the coach which was carrying the four prelates to Edinburgh. Already he was wearied of the earthliness and the unspirituality of his comrades, and he had no desire for the pomps which they anticipated with childish avidity. The breach widened with the years, until, in 1674, he laid down all his offices, and went away to live in the manor-house of Broadhurst, in Sussex, the dwelling of his sister, Mrs. Light-maker, and of her son Edward. It was a hostelry on the road to Jerusalem; but Jerusalem itself was the magnet which allured his eyes and his spirit. "Therefore Good-night is all I add," he said at the ending of a letter; "for, whatsoever hour it comes to your hand, I believe you are as sensible as I that it is still night; but the comfort is, it draws nigh towards that bright morning that shall make amends." Years before he retired to Broadhurst, death had entered the mansion in spite of the struggles of love to keep him out, and had called away a child altogether dear. Nothing could be tenderer than his words of solace to his brother-in-law, words which uttered the home-sickness in his own breast. "Indeed it was a sharp stroke of a pen that told me your little Johnny was dead. Sweet thing, and is he so quickly laid to sleep? Happy he! Though we shall have no more the pleasure of his lisping and laughing, he shall have no more the pain of crying, nor of being sick, nor of dying, and hath wholly escaped the trouble of schooling and all the sufferings of boys, and the riper and deeper griefs of upper years, this poor life being all along but a linked chain of many sorrows and of many deaths. Tell my dear sister she is now so much more akin to the other world, and this will quickly be past to us all. John is but gone an hour or two sooner to bed as children used to do, and we are undressing to follow." There and not here, Leighton confessed, is the morning without clouds, and the perfect day, and the life which is life indeed; and our Father unclothes us that He may deck body and brain with the better garment of ever-lastingness.

In June 1684, he was persuaded to come to London on an errand of mercy. Lord Perth, as virulent a persecutor as any of the tribe, had arrived in the capital, to be invested with the dignity of Chancellor of Scotland, and, being troubled in mind, had spoken of his longing for an interview with one well-fitted to communicate the consolations of God. Bishop Burnet arranged the meeting. "I was amazed," he writes, "to see the angelic man look so fresh that age seemed as it might stand still with him. His hair was still black, and all his motions were lively. He had the same quickness of thought and strength of memory, but, above all, the same heat and life i devotion." But, when his friend and disciple spoke of his own great joy at these appearances of unabated health, he was warned not to build his hopes on so unsubstantial a foundation. "He told me he was near his end for all that, and his work and journey both were now almost done." The forecast was strangely accurate. Pleurisy set in that very night, and within two days Leighton was dead. He had been accustomed to say that, if he could have the choosing of a place in which to die, he should select an inn, for that seemed most appropriate to a wayfarer hastening to his true home. God allowed the predilection to be fulfilled. In the Bell Inn, in Warwick Lane, the pilgrim parted with staff and wallet and sandals, and awoke from the dreams of the present within the City to whose light and love he had panted for many a year.

"When there was any overture or hope of peace"—few will forget the sentences in which Lord Clarendon depicts Lucius Cary, the young Viscount Falkland—"he would be more erect and vigorous, and exceedingly solicitous to press anything which he thought might promote it; and, sitting among his friends, often after a deep silence and frequent sighs would, with a shrill and sad accent, ingeminate the word, *Peace, Peace*; and would passionately protest that the very agony of the war, and the view of the calamities and desolation the kingdom did and must endure, took his sleep from him and would shortly break his heart." The enviable tribute is as applicable to Robert Leighton as to the good knight who fell at Newbury. *Peace! Peace!* was the word he ingeminated as he looked across the distractions of Church and land, and none was more solicitous to press what might promote it: he seemed to carry concession to the verge of surrender. He was baffled in his enterprise, and he erred in his public career. But, when we gaze backward on those evil times, we see him moving through them "attired in brightness like a man inspired."

CHAPTER XVII.

SPOKESMEN OF CHRIST.

ROBERT WODROW tells a story which has many a time been filched from his entertaining pages. Let us read it again in his own words: "I hear there was a certain merchant came from London to Saint Andrews in Fife, where he heard first the great and worthy Mr. Blair preach; next he heard the great Rutherfurd preach. Next Lord's day he came to Irvine, and heard Mr. Dickson preach. When he came back to London, his friends asked him what news he had from Scotland. He answered, he had very great and good news to tell them. They wondered much what they could be, for he was before that time a man altogether a stranger to true religion. He told them he heard one Mr. Blair preach at Saint Andrews; and, describing his features and the stature of his body, he said, 'That man showed me the majesty of God'—which was Mr. Robert Blair's peculiar talent. 'Then,' added he, 'I afterwards heard a little fair man preach'—Mr. Rutherfurd—'and that man showed me the loveliness of Christ. Then I came and heard at Irvine a well-favoured proper old man, with a long beard'—which was famous Mr. Dickson—'and that man showed me all my heart'; for he was most famed of any man of his time to speak to cases of conscience. And they say that Englishman became an excellent Christian. The whole General Assembly of the Church of Scotland could not have given a better character of these three men than that man gave."

And perhaps we could not give a better character of the preaching of the Covenanters, first and last, than by contenting ourselves with the repetition of Wodrow's anecdote. The majesty of God, the loveliness of Christ, and the sins and sorrows of the human heart : these were the central and commanding themes unfolded by the ministers of the Kirk in the seventeenth century. Whether they lived and died and got away home to their Master's presence during the happier years of Cromwell's ascendancy, or were driven from their parishes after King Charles returned to change the face of everything, or must be counted amongst the hunted and perfervid Hillmen of the Killing Time, their sermons express a wondering and worshipful adoration of the Lord Who is high and lifted up, and mount into perpetual praise of the beauty and sufficiency of the Saviour, and bewail the poverty and condemn the disobedience of the soul of man. And he who has such subjects, and can speak of them with lips which God Himself has opened, now sounding a blast of warning, and then appealing with urgency and tenderness to the conscience of his hearers, and by and by soaring into strains of reverent thanksgiving and delighted rapture—surely he scarcely needs any other topic ; he has a message of tremendous moment, of perennial interest, and of abundant variety.

But, for a little, we may linger among the auditors of the old preachers, and may try to gain a somewhat fuller understanding of their teaching. We must not expect too much from them. It is easy to ridicule the quaintnesses of their style, a style of homespun rather than of broadcloth. They rise, every now and then, into genuine eloquence; and their sentences, leaving "the pains of prose," become psalms and hymns and spiritual songs. But, even in their loftiest moods, all is unstudied, spontaneous, unelaborated. As John Howie of Lochgoin says, with a tang of sarcasm in his remark : "Their language was never designed for the reflections of critics, nor calculated to please the taste of those who affect scholastic phrases and grammatical oratory, with flights of fancy and terms of art, pronounced in a South British accent." Unquestionably there is nothing of the Oxford manner about the ambassadors of the Covenant; one cannot rightfully demand it from men who had " no well-furnished rooms and

THE CATHEDRAL OF DUNBLANE.

large assortments of authors"—men "with little time to study anything, and ofttimes less to deliver what they had premeditated, being alarmed by the approach of a fierce, cruel, and bloody enemy." Surroundings such as theirs may impart an extraordinary intensity to the preacher's words. They will compel his admonitions and entreaties to blaze and burn. It "reminds us of rugged heart of oak, not a chip of white wood left on it," Thomas Carlyle declares of an Oliverian letter; and the homilies of the field-preachers are not undeserving of the eulogy. But the environment was unfavourable to the graces of diction and prettinesses of rhetoric; these are plants which refuse to blossom where the tropical sun of persecution is glaring its hottest overhead.

Yet, if there is no South British accent, we catch many a pithy and axiomatic phrase; the sermons are armouries filled with those *kentra*, sharp-pointed goads, which it was the aim of Pericles to leave rankling in the hearts of his Athenian listeners. In 1692, when King William was firmly established on the throne, and when there was toleration alike for prelate and presbyter, Randal Taylor, near the Stationers' Hall in London, printed without its author's name that scurrilous satire of Robert Calder's, which is eagerly sought after nowadays by the collectors of rare editions. *The Scotch Presbyterian Eloquence*, it was entitled, *Or, The Foolishness of their Teaching Discovered from their Books, Sermons, and Prayers.* It is the purpose of the vicious pamphlet, in which the reader has, packed into the space of one hundred and sixteen pages, the amplest quantity of mocking laughter and spiteful venom, to discredit in all possible ways the ministers of the Kirk—that " Proud, Sour, Inconversable Tribe, looking perfectly like the Pharisees, having Faces like their horrid Decree of Reprobation." Of course, this Lucian and Juvenal of the Covenanters derides unsparingly the homely nature of their public speech. We may believe that many of his instances are purely mythical; but, no doubt, there is a proportion which is authentic enough. Yet one does not find that they are so excessively amusing and so barbarously uncouth. The illustrations are chosen from among the " familiar matters of to-day"; but when the speaker who desires some floweret of imagery to brighten his argument is given the opportunity of selection between the daisy and the clematis, does he not, in nine cases out of ten, prove his wisdom by preferring the daisy? So, when Mr. Wedderburn, preaching in Irvine, says, "Lord, we have overfoul feet to come so far ben as heaven; but yet as broken a ship has come to land," we acknowledge the bitter truth of the condemning simile, and we are thankful for the consolation of the comforting one. Or when Samuel Rutherfurd, speaking in the Border town near which he was born, cries in sorrow, "These years the grass is grown long betwixt Jedburgh and heaven," it is probable that other obstructed thoroughfares will forthwith present themselves to our minds. Once, in the Tron Church of Edinburgh, writes this scourge of the Presbyterians, Henry Erskine, the father of Ebenezer and Ralph, took for his text the words, *Cry aloud, and spare not*. He told the people that there were three sorts of cries: that of the mouth; that of the feet, as when it is said, *I will run the way of Thy commandments*; and that of the eye, as in the assurance, *They looked unto Him, and were lightened*. "If we would go to Heaven," Henry Erskine maintained, "we must not only cry with our Mouth, but likewise with our Hands, Feet, and Eyes." But the bold and pictorial figure creates an impression which no commonplace statement of the truth could have made. A critic has said of Raphael's wonderful cartoon, that the blind Elymas, whom the painter delineates, is not merely blind in the eyes, but blind in the hand, blind in the foot, and blind all over. We shall best escape the all-inclusive and fatal blindness by crying after that imperious and persevering and invincible fashion to which the Covenanting minister summons us.

Leaving the preacher's manner, however, we may turn to the substance of his discourses. It is but a hasty survey, superficial and imperfect, which we can take of a subject both large and interesting.

Face to face with his congregation the Covenanter was a soldier. There was the ring of battle, the stern joy of the warrior, in his utterances. He felt that he was struggling for a momentous cause, and for a Monarch peerless in His majesty and grace. The crown-rights of Jesus Christ—that was his watchword as he pressed into the strife; and it is as good a watchword as any which has breathed bravery and patience into the fighter's heart. It was the distinctive, peculiar, and pre-eminent glory of the Scottish minister of that bygone century, that he was prepared to assert against all comers the claims of his heavenly Lord. In opposition to the sacerdotalists, eager to bring the Church under the thraldom of a haughty prelacy, he pealed forth his conviction that the only Ruler in the spiritual realm is He Who died to win His subjects, and Who lives and reigns to perfect their well-being. In opposition to the courtiers and King's-men, protesting that Charles Stuart was supreme arbiter in all causes civil and ecclesiastical, he advocated the sublimer royalty of Jesus over synagogue and senate alike. There was one Bishop of the soul, One only, to Whom he swore allegiance. There was one Sovereign, Who led him in triumph behind His chariot, and under Whose benignant sway he longed to see all his countrymen enrolled. In Whitehall and in Edinburgh he found potentates usurping the throne of Christ, and imposing their laws and ceremonies where His statutes should be paramount. That must not be, the preacher said. In things both national and sacred, Jesus is the real King, governing with an authority as undeniable as that of David, when he directed the affairs of the chosen people from his palace on Mount Zion. And, in the sphere of religion, Jesus is the solitary King; over the conscience of man, and over the house of God, there can be no depute headship, of pope or primate or magistrate. These were truths for which the Covenanter contended through good report and bad—truths on behalf of which he was glad and proud to die.

Andrew Melville belongs to the First Reformation, and not to the Second; but the men of the Second were his sons, agreeing with his fearless announcement of a principle to which they were always ready to witness. What Scot does not feel the blood move more rapidly in his veins, when he reads the narrative of the interview in Falkland Palace in September 1596, at which Melville used such manly freedom with King James?—it ranks in moral impressiveness and dramatic intensity with the greatest scenes in history. "Mr. Andro brak af upon the King in sa zealus, powerfull, and unresistable a maner, that, whowbeit the King used his authoritie in maist crabbit and colerik maner, yit Mr. Andro bure him down, and outtered the Commission as from the mightie God, calling the King but 'God's sillie vassall'; and, taking him be the sleive, says this in effect, throw mikle hot reasoning and manie interruptiones: 'Sir, we will humblie reverence your Majestie alwayes, namlie in publick, but, sen we have this occasioun to be with your Majestie in privat, and the countrey and Kirk of Chryst is lyk to wrak, for nocht telling yow the treuthe, and giffen of yow a faithfull counsall, we maun discharge our dewtie thairin, or els be trators bathe to Chryst and yow. And thairfor, Sir, as dyvers tymes befor, sa now again I mon tell yow, thair is twa Kings and twa kingdomes in Scotland. Thair is Chryst Jesus the King, and His kingdome the Kirk, whase subject King James the Saxt is, and of whase kingdome nocht a king nor a lord nor a heid, bot a member. And, Sir, when yie war in your swadling-cloutes, Chryst Jesus rang friely in this land in spyt of all His enemies.'" Melville had many descendants prepared to echo these words, through which the cannons seem to blaze and boom; and they were not ordained ministers alone, but shepherds from the fields, and struggling shopkeepers in the towns, and young girls from quiet cottages in the country. Covenanting Scotland shared his jealousy of any diminution in the dignities of Christ.

We encounter the same note in one of the sermons of William Guthrie of Fenwick. Speaking in the August of 1662, he said: "Always I thought it had been true loyalty to the Prince to have kept him in his own room, and given him his own due; to have kept him subordinate to Christ, and his laws subordinate to the laws of Christ. *Fear God and honour the King*, I judged that had stood well in all the world; but there is a generation now that has turned it even contrary, *Fear the King and then honour God.* I never thought that that was true loyalty yet. They make the rule all wrong that put the King in the first place; he will never stand well there." Those are avowals throbbing with magnificent courage; and they are as true as they are courageous.

It is when we listen to such clear-sounding calls that we appreciate the lofty patriotism of the Covenanters. They would have been scrupulous in their fealty to the Stuarts, if the Stuarts had allowed them. But when the earthly laws clashed with the heavenly; when Charles's road deviated from the highway of another King, one Jesus; they vindicated at any cost the prerogatives of the better Monarch. They hungered to see the country which was dear to them bound about the feet of Christ. Sovereign, nobleman, merchant, farmer, student, the lady in the hall, and the servant in the kitchen: they would have every one kneel before Him, Whose kingdom is not of this world, yet Who must be followed through the world's throngs and temptations and vicissitudes and cares.

> Best by remembering God, say some,
> We keep our high imperial lot;
> Fortune, I fear, hath oftenest come,
> When we forgot—when we forgot:

the creed of the modern poet gained no countenance from them; they clung to the "lovelier faith" that, whether fortune comes or goes, Jesus Christ is to be obeyed by the commonwealth no less than by the individual. At its core, and in its essence, the Covenant was simply the linking of the nation, fast and firm, with the Throne of the Lord of lords.

But the covenanting preacher was Temple-warden as well as soldier. One recalls the lofty boast of ancient Ephesus that she was Neokoros to Artemis, the sweeper of the floors in the shrine which was the city's ornament and glory. The minister of the persecuted Kirk was Neokoros too, not to Diana but to Christ. Every stone of the Temple which he served was the object of his fervent affection. The

Church was often in his thoughts. Again and again he would explain to his hearers what the Church is in itself, and who those are whom it embraces.

On two truths he was accustomed to lay special emphasis. One bulked more largely in the public speech of the Scottish ministry in the earlier part of the Covenanting period. The other rose into prominence in the later and sadder section of the history, when the fightings without were fiercer and the fears and debates within had been redoubled.

The former is the inspiriting truth of the unity of the Church. The thinkers and defenders of the Covenant were not narrow in their sympathies. They were large-hearted. They took wide views of the range and scope of that empire whose affairs are guided by Christ. It appeared to them to be a vast spiritual region, within which separate congregations and national religious bodies were like so many townships and provinces: over the whole region one blood-red banner flew, and throughout its various communities the statute-book of the same incomparable Ruler was sole authority. The Reformed Church in Scotland had its own characteristics, which distinguished it from the Churches in France and the Netherlands and Germany; but, for all that, it must not be conceived as pursuing its course in isolation, and, still less, did it stand in opposition to its neighbours; it and they had *one Lord, one faith, one baptism.* This conception, as Dr. James Walker writes in his memorable lectures on *Scottish Theology*, enabled these preachers to " meet the Church idealism of Rome, in many ways so grand and attractive, with a nobler Church idealism. They could throw back the charge that Protestantism dismembers and breaks up the Kingdom of God upon earth, with the reply that Protestant unity is as much a reality as Roman unity, only that the centre of it is in heaven, not on the banks of the Tiber." None prayed more earnestly than the Covenanter for the golden hour when, as there is one Flockmaster, so there shall be but one flock. For demonstration of it, we may hearken to young George Gillespie, who died, as we have seen, at thirty-five, twelve years before Charles came

back, but who has left behind him an unforgotten name.
His brothers would have said Amen to his short, decisive,
wholesome affirmations. "There is but one Christ," he
declares. "Is there so much as a seam in all His garment?
Is it not woven throughout, from the top to the bottom?
Will you have one half of Israel to follow Tibni, and another
half to follow Omri? We shall be one in heaven; let us
pack up differences in this place of our pilgrimage the best
way we can. Brethren, it is not impossible. Pray for it.
Endeavour it."

The other truth is that of the purity of the Church.
There is no reason why it should not be maintained simultaneously with the doctrine of the Church's unity. But the
pitiful fact is that frequently the two have appeared contradictory, and that those most zealous for the white stainlessness
of the family of God have thought themselves compelled to
forget, in theory and in practice, the brotherhood of the
saints. It was so in Covenanting story. With revolving
years and darkening skies divergences entered, suspicions
crept in, strifes sprang up in the camp where there was
utmost need for co-operation. The enemy offered the outed
ministers the Indulgence, permitting them to return on
certain conditions to the pulpits from which they had been
expelled. But the Indulgence was an apple of discord. A
few accepted it. And then, amongst the faithful who
refused the bribe, the question arose: Was it right to have
intercourse with men who had lapsed from the perfect
standard? Some chose the method of kindliness; but others
thought and said that fidelity must keep them apart from
those who had parleyed with the foe. The melancholy
divisions multiplied; for soon the enthusiasts for the Church's
sanctity shrank from fellowship with the brethren of gentler
spirit who could not wholly excommunicate the Indulged. The
adoption of such positions indicates a change of view. The idea
of purity has been exalted, while that of unity is correspond-
ingly lowered. There must be no slightest discord in the
orchestral music, no speck of dark in all the firmament of blue.

It ought to be possible so to publish the Church's

catholicity that no hurt shall be inflicted on her holiness, and so to insist on her holiness that her catholicity shall yet remain unimpaired. The men who can give its due place to each of these essentials will be the best wardens of the Temple.

The minister in Covenanting times was a teacher also. And it was a great field of truth, whose treasures, when he had first found them for himself, he displayed and commended to others. He led his people through the spacious country of the Bible, going down before them into its shadowy ravines and climbing its towering heights, shepherding the flock in the green pastures and by the side of the waters of quietness.

Nothing, indeed, is more noticeable about these preachers, although it is a feature as marked in their Puritan contemporaries in England, than their anxiety that the congregation should understand the Word of God, in the breadth of it and the length of it. They were expositors. They delighted to move patiently and leisurely through entire books of Scripture, chapter by chapter, paragraph by paragraph, verse by verse. They missed nothing. *The stones thereof are the place of sapphires*, they would have confessed with the miner of whom Job speaks, *and it hath dust of gold*. There are Scottish libraries in which the favoured visitor may see whole sets of portly volumes in closely written manuscript, five of them or six, containing the pulpit commentary of a Covenanting divine on a single Gospel. It was a liberal education for the listeners to travel thus intelligently and carefully through some section of the Holy Land of revealed truth. Dr. George Adam Smith was right in saying that such expository lectures, for which the pulpit of Scotland has been renowned ever since Reformation times, " could be sustained only upon a continuous tradition and habit of scholarship"; and the instruction communicated by the preacher made the auditors in the rough unpainted pews men and women who loved to grapple with the profoundest problems, and who, if they knew nothing of the fairy tales of science, were at home among the deep things of God. Much was necessarily wanting—the results of modern

ALEXANDER HENDERSON'S CHURCH, LEUCHARS.

research, and the conclusions of a believing and reverent criticism. But, according to the standard of their day, the spokesmen of Presbytery were students and exegetes; and they trained a generation whose members were well able to give a reason for the hope that was in them. This regular and prolonged search into the contents of the Bible could not, of course, be carried forward when the fires of the Persecution were blazing most warmly. It would be foolish to look for it at the conventicles and through the agonies of the Killing Time. Then the word of the preacher had to be swift as a flash of lightning, sharp as a two-edged sword, and sweet as the dropping honey in the forest which Jonathan sipped when he and his were fainting in the day of battle. But, ere those sifting years arrived, the people had been braced to meet their demands and sorrows by the wisdom and the strength they had accumulated from the Book of God.

Calvinism was the system of truth which speaker and hearers found in the Scriptures they explored together, the Calvinism which teaches that the high decree and the regal sceptre and the majestic dominion of the Lord God Almighty extend to everything that happens in the universe. They made less of His Fatherhood than we do, and they lost by the omission; but they made more of His Sovereignty, and they were energised by the remembrance. Calvinism, it has been said by one who is an impartial witness, "is a theory that might have been expected to sink men, crouching and paralysed, into the blackest abysses of despair; and it has in fact been answerable for much anguish in many a human heart. Still it has proved itself a famous soil for rearing heroic natures. On the black granite of Fate, Predestination, and Foreknowledge absolute, the strongest of the Protestant fortresses all over the world were founded. Well might it have been anticipated that fatalism as unflinching as this of St. Paul, Augustine, and Calvin would have driven men headlong into 'desperation, and wretchlessness of most unclean living.' On the contrary, it exalted its votaries to a pitch of moral energy that has never been surpassed; and those who were bound to suppose themselves moving in chains inexorably riveted, along a track ordained by an unseen Will before time began, have yet exhibited an active courage, a resolute endurance, a cheerful self-restraint, an exulting self-sacrifice, that men count among the highest glories of the human conscience." Little needs to be added to Lord Morley's eloquent tribute, except this, that the Calvinistic training of the Covenanters helped them not only to heroism but to beauty of character. The theology which ascribes all good in man to the grace of God, which reveals the measureless distance between that which is born of the flesh and that which is born of the Spirit, and which bids us sing, "Thou must save, and Thou alone," has certainly been the parent of princely and winsome lives. It did more than gird the souls that believed in it for Drumclog and the Grassmarket; it clothed them in the splendid garments of children in the household of that King Who is eternal and immortal and invisible.

The preacher was bondman too—bondman of a Master without spot. We do him injustice if we denounce his religion as one of dry speculation, of metaphysical dogma, of mere political and ecclesiastical controversy. He was smitten with reverence for the Son of God. He bent low before the matchlessness of Christ. He was of one mind with Christina Rossetti: "O Jesu! better than Thy gifts art Thou Thine only Self to us." His language winged its flight into the empyrean of rapture and poetry, when his Lord was his theme. Among the books of the Old Testament, *The Song of Solomon* had a singular fascination for him, because he spiritualised its vehement and affectionate verses, and saw in them, as in a mirror, the consummate face of Jesus. "When they speak of Christ," says the railing scribe of *The Scotch Presbyterian Eloquence*, "they represent him as a Gallant, Courting and Kissing, by their Fulsome Amorous Discourses of the mysterious Parables of the *Canticles*." But the castigator had not that satisfying vision of the divine-human Lover which had captured the hearts of the ministers he ridiculed; if it had dawned on him, he would have understood them better, and would have sat humbly at their feet.

" Christ's absence," cried John Welwood, "is so bitter that no earthly thing can comfort folk; no corn and wine and company. Nay, not only so, but duties and the fellowship of the godly can do no good. No, till He come, angels and apostles cannot comfort." Samuel Rutherfurd, the devotee of the " white and red " in the one only Rose of Sharon, tells us the same. "The wife of youth, that wants her husband some years, and expects he shall return to her from over-sea lands, is often on the shore; every ship coming near shore is her new joy; her heart loves the wind that shall bring him home. She asks at every passenger news: 'O, saw ye my husband? What is he doing? When shall he come? Is he shipped for a return?' Every ship that carrieth not her husband is the breaking of her heart. The bride, the Lamb's wife, blesseth the feet of the messengers that preach such tidings, *Rejoice, O Zion, put on thy beautiful garments; thy King is coming.* Yea, she loveth that quarter of the sky that, being rent asunder and cloven, shall yield to her Husband, when He shall put through His glorious hand, and shall come riding on the rainbow and clouds to receive her to Himself." This plenitude of joy in Christ, this thirst of yearning for Him, may require to be expressed in other phrases in our time; but the preaching is dead, through which the kingly King does not move continually with pierced and shining feet.

The Covenanter boasted in Christ because of His own unparagoned perfection. But he never forgot that the beginning of acquaintanceship with the sufficient Lord is at the Cross. The Atonement, rather than the Incarnation, to which later thinkers have inclined to give the foremost place, was the centre of his preaching. He taught its necessity: how God, being so invincibly just and holy, could not pardon sin until satisfaction had been rendered to His broken law. He taught its efficacy and completeness: how believing men were condemned and crucified, when their Substitute was condemned and judged and crucified; how they have paid all, because their Surety has paid all. He taught its unbounded value: how, even if the testament of the dying Saviour actually takes effect in the case only of a limited number, the

legatees are sinners without exception, and every one is
entitled to put in his claim. Never did he allow the vessel
of the Church to lose sight of "the red light of Golgotha, and
shining lamp of the Holy Sepulchre of Him Who was delivered
for our offences and raised again for our justification"; he
knew that she would drift to ruin and wreck if she did. Long
ago, as Sir Thomas Malory relates, when Bors de Ganis was
riding through the woods, "he looked up into a tree, and there
he saw a passing great bird upon an old tree, and it was
passing dry, without leaves; and the bird sat above, and had
little birds, the which were dead for hunger. So smote he
himself with his beak, the which was great and sharp. And
so the great bird bled till that he died among his birds. And
the young birds took the life by the blood of the great bird.
When Bors saw this, he wist well that it was great tokening."
The spectacle of the One Who bleeds and dies for the many—
the knights of the Covenant wist well that it was great
tokening, and that no other spectacle so merits attention and
praise. There was one of the *Gude and Godlie Ballates* of the
previous century which, we may believe, must have been
particularly dear to them—

> All my Lufe, leif me not,
>   Leif me not, leif me not;
> All my Lufe, leif me not,
>   Thus myne allone:
> With ane burding on my bak,
> I may not beir it I am sa waik;
> Lufe, this burding fra me tak,
>   Or ellis I am gone.
>
> With sinnis I am laidnit soir,
>   Leif me not, leif me not;
> With sinnis I am laidnit soir,
>   Leif me not allone.
> I pray thé, Lord, thairfoir
> Keip nocht my sinnis in stoir,
> Lowse me or I be forloir,
>   And heir my mone.
>
> With thy handis thow hes me wrocht,
>   Leif me not, leif me not;
> With thy handis thow hes me wrocht,
>   Leif me not allone.

I was sauld, and thow me bocht,
With thy blude thow hes me coft,
Now am I hidder socht
    To thé, Lord, allone.

I cry, and I call to thé,
    To leif me not, to leif me not;
I cry, and I call to thé,
    To leif me not allone.
All thay that laidnit be,
Thow biddis thame cum to thé;
Then sall they savit be
    Throw thy mercy allone.

At the preacher in one other aspect we may glance. He
was a fisher of men, filled with consuming eagerness to catch
souls for life and not for death.

He was solicitous to enlarge and deepen the consecration
of the Christian. It was no slipshod godliness which he
inculcated; he urged his hearers to rise to something better
than the conventional religion of the crowd. On the evening
of a Sacramental Sabbath in the Maytime of 1659, John
Livingston spoke from that pregnant command, *Remember Lot's
wife*. She had been brought up and educated in good
company, he said. Moreover, she was half-way to Zoar, and
had left Sodom burning behind her. And her sin might be
accounted but a little fault; for she did nothing more heinous
than look back with curious eyes and with thoughts of her
old and bad companions. Yet let every one who reckoned
himself a pilgrim to heaven remember her, let him see this
woman turned into a pillar of salt, " whereby God made one
stone of another; because her heart was growing hard as a
stone, and so must the other parts of her body become stone-
like too." Three days before he was killed at Ayrsmoss, in
the summer of 1680, Richard Cameron preached his last
sermon on the banks of the Kype Water. "The Word of God
by Cameron thundered," James Grahame writes; and the
young Elijah of the Covenant could thunder when he chose.
But he left the world with a message of exceeding gentleness
on his lips. His text was, *Be still, and know that I am God*.
He might have been one of the Mystics proclaiming the need

for stillness—for that which Madame Guyon described as the Prayer of Silence. "Are ye not in love with this, *Be still! Be still?* . . . Without being still, there is no right going about duty. Without it, we cannot wrestle, pray, or praise. How can ministers preach, or people hear? How can there be reading or praying aright, without being still? The man that is disquieted is unfit for any duty. He is a prey to every temptation. There is a proverb, 'It is good fishing in troubled waters.' The devil labours to confuse men, and then he easily catches them. He busks his hook, and takes by one temptation or another. So that the thing to be understood is, to be patiently waiting on God." Thus the watchmen on the walls of the Church were alert in scrutiny, and vigorous in rebuke of what was wrong, and anxious to rouse the listless into purer aspiration and more diligent effort. They would have no disciple sacrifice the delicate bloom of his Christliness.

But even more controlling was their desire to lead dying men to the Good Physician. Of one of their number it is written that "he would have stolen folk off their feet to his Lord before ever they were aware." It was not that he made the gate into life too accommodating and elastic. He iterated and reiterated the terrible risks of self-deception. Esau "grat his fill, but he never grat himself into repentance." Judas "was admitted to come far ben, before he betrayed his Master." Even into Peter's faith "Satan sought to put a skail-wind"—a wind which should disperse all Peter's trust and hope. And yet men must not linger, before subjecting the Deliverer to trial, until their own feelings and frames are everything they could wish. "The business is not desperate or past remedy, so long as there is so much softness of heart as to perceive or take up the hardness of our hearts, and to be capable of regretting it before God. Hard softness, as we may call it, is not the worst kind of hardness." Indeed, the motive may be far from high, and yet the seeker will not be sent away; he will be loaded with a largess for which he has never asked. The sick, who appealed to Jesus in Galilee for physical health, found that He enriched their spirits as willingly as He cured their bodies. "Some came, as it were, to buy a needle. 'But stay,' said He, 'I will tell you that there is not a whole shirt upon your back.' In this way He made many a bargain with poor souls." Any one, far off or near, publican or Pharisee, might "lippen for a good turn at the hand" of One so bountiful. Only let bankrupt men "threep it on Him"—press the sorrowfulness of their case with pertinacity—and, soon or late, they must know "His blinking in upon their conscience," the lovelight in the Bridegroom's eyes; and then, ere long, they would enjoy "approven homeliness" with the very King of heaven. Again and again the ministers protested that the subtlest and worst unbelief is that which pronounces sin too dark and heavy to be condoned by the merciful Lord. "What!" they exclaimed, in amazement and almost in anger, "will you dare to say that you durst not adventure on His perfect righteousness for your everlasting relief?" With a persistence which never flagged they besought all who heard them to make peace with their Prince Emmanuel, whose friendship is the chiefest good. "For," they said, "they have small skill that seek after a greater ferlie," a more astonishing wonder, "in all the world, than Christ."

It is the crowning distinction of the preachers of the Covenant that there quivered through them the passion to redeem, and that they could themselves have perished for the saving of others. "Let me beseech you," each of them would have cried, as a prince in their company did cry, "draw aside the lap of time's curtain, and look in through the window to great and endless eternity, and consider if a worldly price—suppose this round clay globe were all your own—can be given for one smile of Christ's godlike and ravishing countenance." To allure sinners to the Saviour they had almost been content, with St. Paul, to forfeit the meed of saints and to be counted *Anathema* for ever.

But the spokesmen themselves were often their own most persuasive and victorious sermons. Their lives, quickening and enlivening and prevailing, illustrated and confirmed their words. It does not matter where or how we meet them, robed in the

L

crimson and purple grandeurs of the scaffold or within their
homes and amongst their intimates;—everywhere and always
they followed those things which are true and honourable and
just and pure and lovely and of good report. They were not
flawless, indeed; and their religion erred both on the side of
defect and on the side of excess. But they lived as worthily
as they knew how to die; and is it possible to say more in their
praise ?

One cannot fail to remark that their piety had little
asceticism in it. They were free at least from those unnatural
developments of creed and practice, which we witness in saints
whose surrender to one aim and end rebukes our desultoriness,
but whose crucifixion of self was pushed to an abnormal and
unrighteous extreme. They would have honoured Blaise
Pascal, and learned much from him; but they would have
refused to wear the girdle of iron, which he kept next to his
skin, and the sharp points of which he pressed closely whenever he thought himself in any spiritual danger. They did
not scourge and lacerate their flesh, as Henri Lacordaire did
after his triumphs in the pulpit. They could never have
snapped and destroyed the tenderest ties of family and kin as
unshrinkingly as Francis Xavier, who went away to his distant
apostolate without so much as a farewell to his father in
Navarre. The fires of domestic love were not damped by their
devotion, but were fanned into a warmer flame. Their household affections were strong, and they made no attempt to
repress and thwart them. And they were themselves men
not angular and gloomy, but human and genial and sometimes
full of laughter. Their faith was marked by a dogmatic unyieldingness, and their worship by a steadfast stringency;
but, along with these, went a brotherliness, an abundant
sympathy, even a rippling humour, which are beautiful to
see.

We shall meet no better gentlemen than some of the
preachers of the Scottish Covenant. Is it Mr. John Carstares ?
"He was nobly well-bred towards every person he had to do
with. He was very neat in wearing his cloaths. Ye would
have knouen him to be weel-born by his courteouse carriage."

WILLIAM GUTHRIE'S CHURCH, AT FENWICK.

Is it Mr. John Baird, "of a thin small body, with little flesh"?
Yet how "great a spirit" inhabits the fragile frame!—"a man
eminent for piety, gravity, and learning, and a man of a rare
gift of popular discourse." He is happy, like many of his
compeers, in his wife. God "took Margaret Bruce by the
heart" when she was but six years old, and, in her matron-
hood, she is "a most proper, comely, tall woman, and can
converse with the greatest and with the meanest in a nation."
Is it Rutherfurd, so fierce in controversy and so seraphic in
aspiration? There could not be a faithfuller or more helpful
friend. James Guthrie and he would examine one another
how they spent their time; and "Mr. Rutherfurd would say
to Mr. Guthrie, 'I think it would be a good recreation after
dinner for you to go out and visit three or four families in the
toun.'" Is it Guthrie himself, the fearless confessor who
could not bow? His was the merriest heart up to the last.
At midday, on that first of June when the gallows waited for
him at the Mercat Cross, he dined as composedly as if he had
been in his Stirling manse; and seeing the cheese at the end
of the table, a delicacy which his doubtful health had compelled him to abjure, he said, "Ye may give me a good piece
this day, for *it* will not now be my death." Or is it his cousin,
William Guthrie? There is no surer shot on the Ayrshire
moors, or cleverer fisherman by the side of a burn where the
trout leap and dart and hide. Occasionally his amusements
exposed him to the criticism of the godly. In East Lothian,
under the shadow of the Abbey of Haddington, he once spent
a night and a day with a poor man, rich in faith, "who had
been under great depths and distress and was got out of
them." He listened to his host's experience, and thanked
him for the history; and then, the following morning, so soon
as breakfast was over, he "proposed to go to the fishing."
The mistress of the cottage would have restrained him by a
discouraging text; "Solomon says," she ventured to remind
the minister, "*He that loveth pleasure shall be in poverty.*"
But, notwithstanding the reproof, her guest and her husband
set forth for the tempting stream; and, when they came in
again, William Guthrie was so far from showing any penitence

that he was "very facetious in conversation." In a few minutes, however, they sat down to family worship; and at once the angling and the argument and the banter and the plain little house were forgotten, and they were in the secret place of the Most High. To men such as these both earth and heaven seemed dear and pleasant; and their souls were stiff and perdurable and "dour," only if conscience was threatened, and if the rights of Christ were denied.

Or, if we wish to know the tendernesses of their homes, where shall we read a more gracious and touching story than this, which has James Wodrow for its hero, the father of the annalist of the Sufferings, and himself a sufferer? "He was much affected with his worthy son, Mr. Alexander Wodrow's, death, it being somewhat suddain and surprising. Yet he carried very Christianly under that sharp dispensation; for one day, when he was sitting alone and musing, they asked him, What he was doing. 'I am even,' says he, 'adoring holy, spotless, and absolute Soveraignity.' He went down to the place where his son's corpse was. He stayed some time there. They enquired at him, What he had been doing there. 'I was,' says he, 'thanking God for thretty-one years' loan of Sandie, my dear son.'" The Stoic's impassiveness, and the aloofness of the hermit from the joys and sorrows of our chequered life, were far removed from James Wodrow's broken and comforted heart.

The messengers were themselves the best commendation of their message. "As the night-wind brings up the stream murmurs and scents of the infinite sea," the dangers and conflicts of their histories kept them always close to the solemnities of eternity. Yet they were strangers to moroseness and melancholy. They enjoyed their lives, if they were willing to let them go. For they understood the great secret which Augustine unfolds in an exquisite sentence, "*Habet omnia qui habet Habentem omnia.*"

CHAPTER XVIII.

ARE WINDLE-STRAWS AND SAND-LAVEROCKS BETTER THAN MEN?

WE left the Earl of Lauderdale wedded to the Countess of Dysart, and severed through the mischief of her influence from his wisest friends. But now we must speak of him as Duke, and not as Earl; for, by the favour of his Sovereign, he had mounted higher in the peerage. It would be hard to say to what extravagant heights his Duchess and he aspired. In their progresses through Scotland they were liker royalties than subjects. They demanded pomps and splendours, a deference and a dignity, with which the monarch himself would have been content. They imposed taxes which grew more abnormal with every year. The country groaned under their rapacity, but could find no road out into the free air. Always the chains were fastened more tightly, and the emancipation day seemed to retreat into a more hopeless distance. In truth, if Lauderdale himself had been disposed to manifest any compunctions, these would have been instantly and rudely negatived by Elizabeth Dysart.

> For men at most differ as heaven and earth,
> But women, worst and best, as heaven and hell.

There was nothing that concerned his government in which she did not claim to participate. Many of those who had hitherto corresponded with him began to direct their letters now to her, as if recognising that she wielded the more potent sceptre. For example, we find the Earl of Atholl writing to her in the last week of August in 1674. He is amazed at the temerity of the Convention of Burghs in Edinburgh. "Those silly insignificant fellowes" have dared to make complaint to His Majesty of the Duke who dominates Scotland, and is dominated in turn by his Duchess—"such vermine" as they are. He can only hope that the King will resent their boldness as he ought, and will signify his royal displeasure in a manner that "may reduce them to ther first principles, which is worse than nothing." He has some additional gossip for her Grace. From Lord Ross, as honest a gentleman as lives, he has heard recently concerning "that rogue Welsh." There are six men in disguise, "taking all the paines that can be to aprehend the vilaine"; pity it is that the rascal should give such a world of trouble, and should still succeed in foiling all the cleverness and diligence of his would-be captors. Finally, his Lordship longs mightily to know how the Duke does "after the watters," and trusts in God that they have brought much good to him and to his Lady. It is an illustration of how, after his second marriage, the nation which Lauderdale misruled had to reckon with two despots instead of one.

Efforts were made, indeed, to shake off the tyranny. In November 1673, Lauderdale opened one of his Parliaments in Edinburgh; and then, more distinctly than before, he became aware of the opposition to his policy and himself, which had quietly been gathering strength, and which was never to cease so long as he continued master of Scotland. It was an opposition which filled him with displeasure. The leader was the Duke of Hamilton, a tactician, as it proved, of no little skill. When the Parliament assembled, he declared that the King's letter ought not to be answered until the sorrows of the country were redressed. The Earl of Morton rose and said that he adhered to this motion. The same short speech was made by the Earls of Eglintoun, Cassillis, Roxburgh, and Queensberry. The Earl of Dumfries delivered a longer and more emphatic address; he wished a Committee for Grievances to be named there and then. Sir Francis Scott had "a formall wise set speech," in which he maintained that Scotsmen were treated worse than strangers. The Laird of Polwarth was most wrothful of all; he would have it put to the vote whether they were a free Parliament or a herd of dumb, driven cattle. An experience like this, Lauderdale confesses, "tempted my patience." It was often to be tempted anew in the years that succeeded. "The Party," as it was known in the politics of the time—"the Faction," as he styled it somewhat more contemptuously—established itself more and more firmly; and the repression and cruelty of his dictatorship constantly added fuel to the persistent fires of the revolt. Lord Tweeddale, once his familiar counsellor, joined the malcontents soon; Lord Kincardine was to follow after a time. The heavens, one perceives, were beginning to threaten and gloom over the Duke's head.

But, for many a day, the antagonism was to end in the defeat of the assailants and in the increase of his own prestige. The reason was that, through good report and bad, the King stood by him. Charles found him essential to his schemes, and never failed in his support. In January 1674, when an onslaught was made in the House of Commons on Lauderdale's extortion and high-handedness, His Majesty hastened to comfort the harassed minister. He wrote him an autograph letter, which begins: "You may easily beleeve that I do not want businesse at this time, but yett I could not lett this expresse go to you without a line under my oune hand, to assure you of the continuance of my kindnesse to you, which nothing shall alter." A few years later, there was proof of attachment more significant yet. The distrust of the Duke was profounder, and the hostility to his person and methods more outspoken. A new attack had been directed against him in the House. Now it was that, for the only time in his life, Charles, who could always disguise the tempests of his soul under smiling looks and polite phrases, lost his temper outright. Henry Saville, one of the Gentlemen of the Bedchamber, had presumed to give his vote against Lauderdale. He was the solitary man in the royal household who showed this independence. There were those, of course, who immediately reported the matter to the King. At night, Saville entered his master's room. But, "upon the first sight of him," Charles "fell into such a passion that his face and lipps became as pale almost as death, his cheeks and armes trembled, and then he sayd to Saville, 'You Villayne! how dare you have the impudence to come into my presence, when you are guilty of such basenes as you have showne this day? I doe now and from henceforth discharge you from my service, commanding you never to come any more to any place where I shall happen to be.'" So the courageous gentleman "was sent a-packing, with a vengeance to him"; and Lauderdale has the singular honour of being the one man in Britain for whom the loveless monarch cared enough to flame forth in hot defence.

In those dreary years the iron was driven deeper into the bleeding Church. More sadly than ever, the conventicle became the target for the fiercest darts of those in authority. Let a Covenanter absent himself from the homily of the ignorant curate, and immediately he was reduced to beggary by the fines exacted from him. Let him go out to the open air to listen to the Gospel preached in the accent of his fathers, and he was assisting at a conventicle; and for such complicity he must be thrown into a prison at home, or sold as a bond-slave in the far-off plantations. No master might engage a servant suspected of Whig ideas. No landlord might keep, in farm or cottage, a tenant who held the beliefs of the hunted folk. Worst of all was it to be a minister. If pride in Christ and pity for men forced any to speak to the people in the fields, the crime was capital and the sentence was death. Preacher or hearer, his movements were dogged by spies. In the smallest company an informer was perhaps present, the wolf in sheep's clothing. The offender might be dragged before the Secret Committee of the Privy Council, a Committee responsible to no superior Court, and swayed neither by mercy nor by justice. What was more odious still, men and women were shut out, by the penalties pronounced against Intercommuning, from the common hospitalities and relationships of life. Neighbours must shun them. Their next-of-kin must close the door in their faces. They were as much isolated as the leper was under the old Jewish law. And their only leprosy was their love for an unseen Master, Who had bound them by His vows, and to Whom they must be true although the firmament should fall.

George, Lord Ross of Hawkhead, of whom the Earl of Atholl has told us something already—one of those needy nobles who "fished best in troubled waters"—was particularly active in scattering the field meetings and in hunting and punishing the field preachers. He never appeared to relax his wakefulness, or to dream of tempering his severities with mercy. At one time it is to Charles Maitland that he pours out his complaint: how "yesterday at the house of one Simion Pickerscalls in Glasgow, the which he holds of the toune, and which he has disposed in forme of a Church, ther wes ane nomerows conventickell wher ther wes publicke colections and all the ordinary marks of ther contempt to King's awthoritey." Again, about nine months later, he goes directly to Lauderdale himself with a narrative of the zeal displayed by his troop in suppressing one of the obnoxious gatherings. The scene was a meadow in the parish of Bathgate, the time the last Sabbath in February 1675. A large company had assembled for worship; but, when the soldiers approached, the congregation broke up, and its members retreated to a marshy piece of ground, whither the cavalry could not follow them. A few, however, had lingered behind, and these the horsemen surrounded, hoping to discover and entrap their minister. The sight of the danger to which their brethren were exposed immediately brought many of the others hurrying from the marsh; and, when the King's officer charged them to disperse, two or three of the more venturesome among them fired their pistols by way of defiant answer. They did no harm; but their bravado provoked the Royalists into retaliation. The soldiers fired back on the crowd. One Covenanter was killed, and the rest turned and fled. Fifteen were taken prisoners, and were securely lodged very soon in the Tolbooth of Edinburgh. And thus, unceasingly and unpityingly, Lord Ross, wedded although he was to one of the Cochranes of Dundonald, some of whom were in friendly intercourse with the Whigs, did his endeavour to terrorise the Kirk.

Through such arbitrary dealings as these, things had come to a sad pass towards the end of 1676. In so great a fight of afflictions, the Covenanters might have been forgiven if they had imagined that

God is gone,
And some dark spirit sitteth in His seat.

For a few months the conventicles were abandoned; and Lauderdale enjoyed the satisfaction of looking over a Scotland stricken and silent. In *Eothen*, Mr. Kinglake relates a surprising thing which befell him in the desert between Palestine and Egypt. On the fifth day of his journey, the air lay dead, and all the earth that he could reach with his keenest sight and keenest listening was still and lifeless. The sun shone fiercely down. He dropped his head under the glare, and fell asleep for how many minutes or moments he could not tell. But soon he was gently awakened by a peal of church bells, his native bells, the bells of the village of Marlen, which never previously had sent their music beyond the neighbouring hills. His first thought was that he re- mained under the spell of a dream. He roused himself by a determined effort. But still the Marlen bells rang on, steadily, tenderly, till slowly their tones died away. It was a peculiar experience, which he ascribed to the great heat of the sun, and the perfect dryness of the air, and the deep stillness all around—causes which rendered the hearing organs liable to tingle under a passing touch of memory in that interval of sleep. We may say that, in their deserts, the Covenanters had until now been attended by the grave, sweet melodies of the churches they had loved in happier times. For them the old bells rang in moorland spots and among lonely hills, where such music had never been heard before. But, for a season, Lauderdale frightened even these chimes into muteness; and there is no testimony to his unholy power more unequivocal and surprising.

But "the panting, huddled flock whose crime was Christ" quickly recovered itself. The King's Commissioner had returned from Whitehall to Edinburgh, in the summer of 1677. In October, Lord Dundonald reported to him that

JOHN MAITLAND, DUKE OF LAUDERDALE.

again there were field-preachings in Carrick, and that their
former practices were being resumed by the Presbyterians of
the west. In November, the Duke wrote to the English Prime
Minister, the Earl of Danby, for whom at first he had entertained a cordial dislike, but with whom now he lived on terms
of apparent friendship, informing him of a momentous step
which he had just taken. We have come, in fact, to the
darkest of his many sins against the Church in whose bosom
he was nurtured.

The news which he communicated to Lord Danby was
this, that he had given orders to assemble a Highland force,
"in case the phanaticks should rise in arms," and, moreover,
that the gentry of the disaffected shires had been called
together: "not that we expect much from them, but to try
their puls and render them inexcusable." The two Highland
lords, Atholl and Murray, he went on, had already mustered
fourteen hundred men, and tidings were looked for from other
chieftains in the north. Some ominous sentences follow:
"In the meantime they doe not rise in armes in the west.
How soone they may take armes no man can tell; for, as I
have often said, they are perfitely fifth-monarchy men, and no
judgment can be made upon the grounds of reason what they
may attempt; and therefore all preparations possible are to
be made in case they rise. For the game is not to be played
by halfes; we must take this opportunity to crush them, so
as they may not trouble us any more in hast, or else we are
to expect to be thus threatened by them next year." Lauderdale was positively setting himself to foment disturbance in
the western counties. He desired a pretext for letting slip
the dogs of war, and for sending ruin on the men whom he
hated; and, in order to awaken the rebellious spirit in them,
he took the initiative, and quartered his rough Highlanders on
a peaceful country. It was nothing short of an atrocity in
the man entrusted with the guardianship of the realm.

He found too many ready to encourage him. There were
necessitous and half-bankrupt noblemen in the north, who
expected to be generously paid for lending their clansmen to
the King's Commissioner, and who were full of eagerness to

abet him in his wicked purpose. James, Earl of Perth, was one of these. Before twelve months were past, he would be enrolled amongst Lauderdale's fieriest antagonists, but just now he saw an opportunity of winning favour and gold by compliance; and, as personal advantage was the chief motive by which his actions were controlled, he professed himself ready and anxious to assist. He had only waited, he said, to notify his Grace of the anxiety, until he should have sounded his followers on the subject; but at length he could promise for them, for they were as willing as he was himself " to complye with a thing so much tending to ther honor, and so necissarly ther duty." The sole regret he felt was that he could not contribute a more numerous band. " If my pouer were equall to my zeal for the advancement of the Royall Interest, I should yeeld to no mortall." But at the moment the family fortunes were at a low ebb, and great matters were out of his reach; and yet " A mite in charitie, if it be all one's living, outvies the largest sums of the richer offerers." Lord Perth's letter, sent from Drummond Castle in December 1677, is a singularly instructive document, in its sycophancy, its outspoken and unblushing selfishness, and its frank and contemptuous disregard of the public weal. It will not prosper with Scotland, one may confidently predict, when he becomes Lord Justice General in her courts, and by and by Chancellor of the kingdom.

The battalions were raised; but through all the suspected parts no signs of revolt were visible. This new army, turbulent and ill-disciplined, must be employed; to keep it standing idle would endanger the peace of the State. It was marched forthwith into the districts where the Whigs had their stronghold. Our anger burns at the whole transaction, and not least at the help given to it by the Bishops. The lords over God's heritage had their "suggestions" to make. This is one: "That the forces setle first at Aire, having rested some few days at Glasgow, Aire being the centre of a great circle of the disaffected; and after having reduced Carrick, and censured the conventiclers in those parishes which are served by Indulged ministers, they may goe to

Lanerick and Clidsdale, and so forward to the stewartrie of
Kirkcudbright and the shyre of Galloway; in which places,
since the forces are to have free quarters, particular care wold
be taken that the burthen thereof may be upon the guiltie,
and thus the innocent and orderlie people will find themselves
eased and encoraged to continue in their orderlines and
obedience." The kindness of ecclesiastics has sometimes a
cutting edge and a wolfish bite.

Some six thousand Highlanders ˉthere were, and some
three thousand of the militia from other parts. In February
1678 they entered Ayrshire. For many of the Gaels it was
a first excursion beyond their native glens. In those days
Celtic and Lowland Scotland were separated, as if the sea,
dissociabilis Oceanus, rolled between them. The Highlander
had no sympathy with the character and pursuits of the
Sassenach. He was himself as untutored as his own Garry,
the river which comes roaring down over its rocky bed. In
most cases his heart was no less savage than his looks.
Numbers of the clansmen were armed, not with sword and
matchlock, but with spades and picks. Their leaders,
rumour averred, although here she probably lied, brought
the shackles with which they meant to fetter their prisoners,
after they had once succeeded in extorting some incriminating confession. But in one sense the invaders were completely disappointed. They met no enemies anywhere;
their weapons, they found, were unneeded; the impetuous rush with which they carried so many of their battles
was never to be practised in this strange and gratuitous
campaign. On every side they were amongst farmers and
ploughmen and shepherds, not one of whom offered to oppose
their advance. In their hearts they must have resented the
insults to which they were subjected; but they refused to be
tempted into an insurrection like that of eleven years before.
They took the spoiling of their goods, if not joyfully, at least
with meekness and patience.

But if the visitors from beyond the Grampians were
denied the sterner delights of the warrior, there remained the
satisfaction of the reiver and bandit. Their sojourn was a

carnival of robbery. Not pleased with the simple food placed before them, they compelled the people to bring them brandy and tobacco. They fell upon the travellers whom they met on the country roads. They considered themselves authorised to enter every house. They bullied and overawed any whom they supposed to be hiding money from them. There were worse rudenesses, too, as we should anticipate from men a century behind their victims in the decencies and delicacies of life. Their pillage enriched them marvellously. "When the Highlanders went back," Robert Wodrow says, "one would have thought they had been at the sacking of some besieged town, by their baggage and luggage. They were loaded with spoil. They carried away a great many horses, and no small quantity of goods out of merchants' shops, whole webs of linen and woollen cloth, some silver-plate bearing the names and arms of gentlemen. You would have seen them with loads of bedclothes, carpets, men's and women's clothes, pots, pans, gridirons, shoes, and other furniture." One suspects that the caterans, like the Cretans, whom Epimenides and St. Paul stigmatise, were "evil beasts" and "idle gluttons."

All this was disgraceful enough; but there was more. Lauderdale's Government put in force, against those Covenanters in the west who were of higher rank, an old Scottish enactment known as the "Letters of Law-burrows." If a person feared that some one else meant to injure him, he could guard himself against his dangerous neighbour by procuring these Letters. They bound the troubler to keep the peace. They threatened him with pains and penalties if he caused any annoyance. But, in this instance, it was the executive of the country which posed as the aggrieved and terror-haunted party. The rulers feigned themselves to be plunged in alarm by the subjects, and from the subjects they demanded security by means of the Law-burrows. Were the landlords in Ayrshire and Lanark and Galloway prepared to sign a bond that every one resident on their estates would conform to His Majesty's wishes in Church affairs? If they were not, if they pleaded that the promise was extravagant and impossible, then the King's ministers and Privy Council were imperilled, and must take legal steps to shelter themselves. Up in London, the Duke of Monmouth was amazed when he heard of the remarkable expedient. Many affirmed, he said, that it was against all equity to hold a master responsible for the opinions of his tenants, and against all generous dealing to command him to part with them, and so to forfeit the rental which they brought, even if he understood that their tenets did not square with what the legislature expected these to be. Moreover, the Duke added, he was persuaded that "the Law-burrows did not meet or quadrate with this affair." But Lauderdale's friends at Whitehall, Sir James Fowler and Sir George Mackenzie,—Sir George Mackenzie, who had not always been so obsequious in his attitude towards the Secretary of State,—argued with passion on the other side. And, as usual, Charles championed his proconsul. He said that "there was much reason for the bond for securing the peace, and that the alternatives were easy for the masters, and nothing hard in it." "You have in Scotland," he went on, "the best laws of any people in the world." Good laws, certainly, for a monarch heedless about the welfare of his citizens, if he contrived to get his own way.

But the King, though he was as indifferent as an Epicurean god to the doleful song which steamed up to him, had at last to listen. In the closing days of March, a paper of protest was handed to him by the Earl of Cassillis, a nobleman whose sympathies were with the Covenant, as his father's had been before him. Even yet Charles, seeing everything through Lauderdale's eyes, was indisposed to grant relief. Calling to him the Earl of Arran, he told him that, "for his part, he thoght it a very silly paper, and that he could make a shift to answere it himself, althogh he was no lawer, yet he knew Scotland pritty well." It was a strange thing, he said, "that he had been tormented for severall weeks with horrible complaints of the creulety and outrages done in the west; yet he had done them faire play; and that he had now receaved a full account of the wholl proceedings, and that it was from persons he wold trust; that he found all to be false as hell.

and that things were not pushed so farr as the law allowed; that, as he was a Christian, he did not see what els could be done, and that he thoght himself obliged in duety not to fall in a snare a second tyme, that he was now resolved to be beforehand with the Phanaticks, that he was sure they made use of religion as a pretence only, that he understood their desseins"; and so on, and so on. Unhappy Phanaticks! when will there be an ending to their contumelies and tears? But, in April, the Duke of Hamilton and some of his allies came to London, to renew their attempt to undermine Lauderdale's autocracy.   Between the Party, backed as it was by Monmouth and the Opposition in the House of Commons, and the root-and-branch apologists for the tyrant—the English Government, the English Bishops, the Duke of York, and the King—a daily and desperate wrestle went on.   Charles managed again to snatch his favourite from disaster; but he saw that something must be yielded.   Not for the sake of the downtrodden west, but that he might steal from Lauderdale's foes the arguments they were plying too powerfully, he gave orders, on the 15th of April 1678, that within a fortnight the Highland troops must leave the countryside which they had laid waste.   Once more the Covenanters could breathe more freely.

That such devastation should have been the work of a man, who had been "the good Maitland" of Principal Baillie, and a candidate in the belief of Richard Baxter for the saint's everlasting rest, is one of the most impressive proofs that history can furnish of the unstableness of human nature.   "Better," Lauderdale cried, "that the west bore nothing but windle-straws and sand-laverocks"—dog-grass and larks—"than that it should bear rebels to the King!"   Thirty years previously, his tone had been different, more patriotic and more godly.

CHAPTER XIX.

A MAY DAY ON MAGUS MOOR.

JAMES SHARP has fallen for some time out of our story.
But through all the twelve years of Lauderdale's
administration he had been fighting busily his evil fight.
The statesman, determined to suffer no plotters against his
individual ascendancy, had humbled the Prelate's pride when
he began his own reign. Sharp's submission was abject.
With some verbal protests, for the sake of shielding himself
among his episcopal brethren, he even helped Lauderdale to
pass the Act of Supremacy, by which "the clogs laid upon
the King were knocked off," and His Majesty was endowed
with absolute control over all ecclesiastical persons and
meetings and matters. "Four lines in the Act," Sharp
asserted at the outset, "were more comprehensive than a
hundred and odd sheets of King Henry the Eighth"; yet,
when the Commissioner and he "had a sound bout, and I
dealt freely with him," all his scruples vanished into thin air,
and he riveted the chains round the wrists and ankles of his
Church. The Bishop of Ross would have fought for some
small limitation of this all-embracing Royal prerogative; but
his Grace of St. Andrews "snapt him up, and said how foolish
such a jealousie would be." He could always be relied on to
second the plans of those who showed themselves possessed of
sufficient power, and with whom it was hazardous for his
comfort and prosperity to quarrel.

No doubt, they had perpetually to watch him, although
they used his crafty diplomacy in their own interest. He was
so apt to lift his head overweeningly. "St. Andrews brags

mightily," the Earl of Kincardine wrote, in the July of 1671, " and even grows insolent. You know cajoling looseth him, and that he is never right but when he is keept under." But a little astute management would sober his arrogance, and would transmute him once more into a serviceable tool. Nobody detested the conventicles with such virulence, or meted out such punishment to the men and women who frequented them. " Most of all that were at these rendez-vouses," one of the members of the Privy Council said, " catched violent colds, in so much as they may be tryed and found out by coughing." Some pity might have been extended to those for whom the road of the Cross was thus thorny and steep; but James Sharp had none. In the spring of 1679, a year after the Highlanders had left the west, he brought before his fellow-Councillors the draft of a new edict, more deadly even than those which had been formerly devised. It gave liberty to kill any man who went armed to or from a meeting in the fields. No trial was necessary. The meanest officer who wore the King's uniform might shoot the suspected person on the spot. This was the culmination of the Archbishop's endeavours to stifle the Presbyterianism which he had once professed. But, before it received the Sovereign's consent, his race was run, and he had met with terrible death.

Before now, there had been warnings given him of the burning hatred engendered by his presence. Back in 1668, James Mitchell, a man whose brain was touched with madness, had tried to assassinate him in the streets of Edinburgh. For six years the would-be murderer escaped; but, at the end of that time, Sharp recognised him one day, and had him apprehended and led before the Privy Council. The Council, knowing that he was scarcely responsible for his actions, persuaded him to confess the crime under a solemn promise that his life should be spared. He was sent to the Bass Rock. But if the poor man reckoned himself safe from the scaffold because of the explicit stipulation made to him, he had not fathomed the unrighteousness of his judges. In 1678, ten winters after he fired his shot into the Primate's coach, he was haled before the Justiciary Court. It seems

THE TOWERS OF ST. ANDREWS.

incredible, but it is true, that the Earl of Rothes, who was
Lord High Chancellor of Scotland, Charles Maitland of
Hatton, who was Lord Treasurer Depute, the Duke of
Lauderdale, and the Archbishop of St. Andrews himself, one
after another entered the witness-box, and swore that no
promise of pardon had ever been given by the Privy Council.
It did not matter that a copy was instantly produced by
Mitchell's advocate ; mere copies of documents are without
legal value, and the Council's register was itself deliberately
withheld. Even Lauderdale had his dubieties and regrets
about the transaction which, writes Mr. Lang, leaves "an in-
delible stain upon the ermine of Scottish justice"; he would
have been content to see the prisoner consigned again to the
dungeon on the Bass. It was Sharp who showed no relenting.
He meant that, at long length, the capital sentence should be
inflicted ; and James Mitchell, in the mocking language of the
day, was sent to "glorify God at the Grassmarket."

Sixteen months after his execution, the Archbishop was
face to face with his own doom. Predictions of it, if some
of the Covenanting writers may be credited, had gone to him
in advance, awesome forerunners of the awesome event.
John Welwood, whom God took in youth from the evil to
come, preached one Sabbath at Boulter Hall, in the parish
of Forgan, not far from St. Andrews. His text was that
levelling word of St. Paul, *Not many wise, not many mighty,
not many noble are called*; and he bade Christ's people who
were in stations of distinction rejoice in the initial M.; for
what had befallen them if the apostle had said, *Not any* ?
In the congregation he saw a lad wearing the Archbishop's
livery, a servant from his Grace's palace. Calling him when
the sermon was ended, he commanded him to carry a grievous
message to his master. "Tell him from me that his wicked
life is now near an end, and that his death shall be sudden,
surprising, and bloody." The young man went home, and,
being questioned in the evening where he had been, announced
the preacher's augury of terror. His lord made sport of it.
But James Sharp's wife, poor lady, was not disposed to be
merry. "I hear," she said, "that these men's words are not

vain words." And thus the premonitory shadows, harbingers of dread, had fallen across his path. Now Sharp was on the eve of starting from Edinburgh for London, that he might secure Charles's signature to his new law against the conventicles. First, however, he went northward to St. Andrews. It was Friday, the 2nd of May 1679. He rode in his carriage of state, drawn by six horses. With him was his eldest daughter, and he had an escort of four or five servants. Having crossed the Forth, he travelled as far as Kennoway, some twenty miles from his destination, where he spent the night. On the morning of the 3rd, about nine o'clock, he left the house of his host, Captain Seatoun. Twelve miles on, he came to the manse of Ceres, where he "smoked a pipe with the Episcopal incumbent." Meantime he sent one of the servants with his salutations to Lord Crawford, whose mansion was near at hand.

We must leave him in Ceres for a few moments, that we may learn what has been transpiring at no great distance. On the Friday evening, thirteen men had met on one of the Fifeshire moors, to carry out a scheme which they had been discussing for some weeks. One of the thirteen was dismissed, the rest not being clear that they could admit him to their confidence. The twelve who remained were David Hackston, of Rathillet; John Balfour, of Kinloch, better known by the erroneous and mistaken designation of "Burley"; James Russel, in Kettle; George Fleming; two Hendersons, Andrew and Alexander; William Daniel; three Balfours, James, Alexander, and George; Thomas Ness; and Andrew Gillan, a handloom weaver, who had already suffered for his stubborn refusal to listen to the curates in Dundee, and who, four years after this memorable Maytime, was to be hanged at the Gallow-Lee. What was their scheme? It was to chastise William Carmichael, a drunken and insolvent magistrate, whom Sharp had appointed Sheriff-depute of Fife, and who had gleaned a harvest of obloquy by his brutal energy in putting into force the statutes against the Covenanters. It is not certain that they intended to kill Carmichael; probably they would be satisfied if they succeeded in frightening him from the district. That night, they went to Robert Black's in Baldinnie, who, being a prudent and wary man, had absented himself from his own homestead, leaving his guests in possession. They slept in the barn, having first sent one of their number to try and discover Carmichael's whereabouts. He returned from Cupar, about seven o'clock on Saturday morning, with the information that the Sheriff, along with three or four friends, was to spend the day in hunting. At once they prepared themselves for the pursuit. But one mishap followed another. First, Rathillet's horse stumbled, and, when it had recovered its footing, took fright and fled; and time was lost in recapturing the nervous animal. Then Russel, and one of the Hendersons, and Fleming, and George Balfour, catching sight of a rider not far off, and hoping that this was the man of whom they were in search, chased him for miles, only to find to their mortification that he was an innocuous laird of their own acquaintance. By and by, one of the band reported that he had seen Carmichael hastening to Cupar with all speed, some hint having reached him of the risks by which he was beset. "God," they began to conclude, "had remarkably kept them back, and him out of their hand." Wearied and chagrined, they gathered about midday at a part of the moor close to Ceres—all of them, except James and Alexander Balfour and Thomas Ness, who had turned their horses' heads homeward. Here they halted, and stood talking, before they said their farewells and separated on their various roads.

But, just then, a farm-boy from Baldinnie came running to them. He gave them the startling news that the Archbishop's carriage would pass in a few minutes. They were thunderstruck. They had planned the castigation of a subordinate; could it be that God was surrendering to them the prime author of their troubles? John Balfour said so in as many words—John Balfour, the Jehu of the Covenant, "a little man, squint-eyed, and of a very fierce aspect," who had been invested with his nickname of "Burley" because in physical appearance he was "laigh and broad." And Russel, afterwards one of the most irreconcilable of the Hillmen, was equally convinced. "Having more than ordinary outlettings of the Spirit for a fortnight together at Leslie," he had felt it borne in upon him that the Lord would employ him in some piece of service, and that there would be some great man, who was an enemy to the Kirk of God, cut off; and he could not be quit of the thoughts of Nero, and asked "where he could find that Scripture, for he could not get it":—a somewhat nebulous revelation of the will of Heaven, one is tempted to think. But his comrades listened approvingly. They mounted their horses, and moved in the direction which the carriage must take. Again, for an instant, they paused, to select their commander. With one consent David Hackston was chosen—a man of fearlessness, of principle, of honour, of compassion too, although he was strictest of the strict. But he declined the responsibility. "The Lord is my witness," he said, "that I am willing to venture all I have for the cause of Christ; yet I dare not lead you on to this action. For there is a known private quarrel betwixt the Bishop and me, so that what I should do would be imputed to my personal revenge and would mar my testimony. But, as you are determined to go forward, I will not leave you." When Rathillet refused, "Burley" cried in loud tones, as he spurred on his horse, "Gentlemen, follow me!" He, at least, was without scruples, without questions, without visitations of regret.

The carriage had gained the rising ground of Magus Moor; and now, for the first time, its coachman saw the men on horseback. Sharp himself saw them. "Drive! Drive!" he shouted, in an access of terror; for, whether he remembered John Welwood or no, ever since Mitchell's attack he had been dogged by fears of violent death. The carriage bounded on; but Russel, who was ahead of his companions, came up with it. Firing in at the window, he exclaimed, "Judas, be taken!" The others were but a few seconds behind. Some of them held the servants, and, severing the traces, let the horses go free. Then Russel went to the door. "Come out," they commanded; for they were anxious that Isabel Sharp should receive no harm. Again and again the old man refused; and Fleming and George Balfour shot at him seated within, and another of the group thrust at him with a sword. Strangely enough, amid such a throng of dangers, he was not wounded; but they believed him killed, and would have remounted and ridden off. But the Prelate's distracted daughter was heard sobbing, "There's life yet." It was a sorrowful and fatal indiscretion. Once again the remorseless men, with the single exception of Rathillet, gathered round her father.

They found that he was "safe and whole." Kinloch told him their purpose—to slay him, not from personal malice, but because he had shed like water the blood of the saints. "Gentlemen, gentlemen, save my life!" he begged, still from within the carriage, "and I will see to the saving of yours." But the sole answer he had was the stern one that nothing could shake their resolution; for they were spokesmen and swordsmen of God that day. Then he offered them money. "Thy money perish with thee!" they retorted impatiently. As he continued to crouch within the shelter of the carriage, they fired again, and one of them stabbed him. He was wounded now, but not mortally. Trembling, he came out at last. They urged him to devote his last moments to prayer; but he would only pray to his assailants to have pity. Soon he caught sight of Hackston, "standing at a distance with his cloak about his mouth, all the time on horseback"—standing, "revolving his case of conscience": a figure which fascinated Robert Louis Stevenson. He crept on hand and foot towards him. "Sir," he besought him, "you are a gentleman; you will protect me." But Hackston, although he had his doubts, could not interfere. "I shall lay no hand upon you," was all that he said. Meanwhile the others, unable to induce their victim to pray, were growing tired. They fired simultaneously. Perhaps in their excitement they did not take proper aim; for Sharp was still alive. Wild thoughts of sorcery seized them; Satan, they fancied, had rendered his servant proof against their bullets; nothing but cold steel would accomplish their end. Their swords were drawn, and he saw the blades gleam in the sun, and knew at length that his fate was sealed. He was not a brave man, although in such an hour of horror and anguish the very bravest might have quailed; he abandoned himself to despair. His daughter, saddest of all the participants in the frightful scene, sprang desperately between her father and the avengers of blood. Hackston could not remain longer at a distance. Hurrying to his friends, he entreated them to "spare these grey hairs." But daughter and intercessor were both too late. The swords which deal death were plunged into the body of the man who, for twenty years, had striven with might and main to destroy the Church of Scotland. An examination afterwards showed a great gash over the left eye, many cuts on the back of the head, a gun-shot wound near the collar-bone from Kinloch's "brazen blunderbus," the scar left by a dagger-thrust in the region of the kidneys, three gaping slits on the left hand and one on the right. The assassins had done their part with terrible zest, and there was a wound for every outlaw present. "They took nothing from him but his tobacco-box and Bible, and a few papers. With these they went to a barn near by. Upon the opening of his tobacco-box, a living humming-bee flew out. This either Rathillet or Balfour called his familiar; and, some in the company not understanding the term, they explained it to be a devil. In the box were a pair of pistoll-ball, parings of nails, some worsit or silk, and, some say, a paper with some characters, but that is uncertain." The odour of wizardry hung about the miserable Archbishop to the close. "Go!" James Russel said to the servants, when all was over, "go, take up your *priest*!"

History repeats itself. Three-and-twenty years later, in July 1702, a party of fifty men met in the wood of Altefage in south-eastern France, a score carrying fowling-pieces, the others armed with scythes and axes. They were Camisards, and their leaders were the Prophets, Pierre Séguier and Salomon Couderc and Abraham Mazel. After a harangue from Séguier, and a blessing in the name of the Lord of Hosts, they started their march, at sunset, through the forest and across the wastelands, to the little town of Pont-de-Montvert. It was where their arch-enemy, the Abbé du Chaila, had his home. They burst open his doors, and loosed their fellow-Huguenots lying in the cellars with stiff and swollen limbs, and fired the house. Du Chaila, twisting some sheets into a rope, attempted to escape to the garden ; but, falling in the descent, he broke his thigh. He crept painfully to the concealment of a hedge ; but the blaze disclosed him crouching in his thicket. " Ah, here thou art !" Séguier cried, " the persecutor of the Enfants de Dieu. The Spirit wills that thou shouldst die." He dealt him the first blow ; and, afterwards, the others struck him one by one. " Take this for my father broken on the wheel," one said ; and a second, " And this for my brother sent to the galleys " ; and a third, " And this for my mother dead of a bleeding heart " ; and a fourth, a fifth, a sixth, " And these for our friends imprisoned, exiled, beggared." He received, the curé declared who buried him, " fifty-two wounds, twenty-four of which were mortal." And all that night the Camisards, on their knees beside the dead body, sang the psalms of Marot and Beza, the grim chant mingling with the sound of the flames and the rush of the torrents close by.

What judgment shall we pass on the tragedies of Pont-de-Montvert and Magus Moor ? Infamous as Du Chaila and James Sharp were, this must be our verdict, " The deeds were foully done." Sharp's character was despicable. His presence was a menace and a blight. But these facts do not excuse his murder. There are, of course, elements of extenuation. The act, unlike that of Séguier and Couderc and Mazel, was unpremeditated, committed by those who had come out to scare an inferior antagonist, and who had not a thought, when they started, of dealing with their chief enemy. It was condemned, soon and utterly, by the responsible leaders in the army of the Covenant. The captain of the band, moreover, that ferocious and iron-hearted John Balfour of Kinloch, was scarcely a religious man ; he was an enthusiast, whose enthusiasm darkened into the bigotry of the fanatic ; but he showed few signs of personal godliness, and, even before this sanguinary third of May, he was kept back from sitting down at the Sacramental Table : his was not a nature sensitive to the highest and holiest things. In Walter Smith's verses we hear him speak in his own tongue—

> I killed the Archbishop, while Hackston stood by,
> And he was as much in the deed as I ;
> But, for they had a quarrel, his mind was not clear,
> Our nice punctilious cavalier !
> O, we must not sully the end we seek
> With a personal grudge or a private pique !
> So we stand aside, in the noonday sun,
> Like a stern old Roman, and see the deed done.
> Was he better than I, with my dirk to the hilt
> In the old man's heart, when his blood was spilt ?
> He had scruples, forsooth—and the priest's head was grey—
> And he did not the deed, nor yet said it nay.
> Bah ! give me a conscience that rules with a will,
> Or one that can hold its peace and be still ;
> But neither the Lord nor the devil will care
> For your conscience that scruples and splits on a hair.

It is an accurate portrait of one whose co-operation was no blessing to the Covenanters, but a weakness and a reproach.

Yes, there are extenuations; but the old word is the right word : *Dearly beloved avenge not yourselves, but rather give place unto wrath : for it is written, Vengeance is Mine, I will repay, saith the Lord.*

CHAPTER XX.

THE LORD ADVOCATE.

ARCHBISHOP SHARP, had gone to his account. But the
winds blew as unkindly, and the hail smote as bitingly,
on the men and women who loved Kirk and Covenant. In
the ranks of the Royalist party new figures come into
prominence about this time; and the succession of persecutors was not yet exhausted. One of the keenest and most
active of these opponents of Presbytery was Sir George
Mackenzie of Rosehaugh, who stood second only to Sir George
Lockhart among the lawyers of his day, and who in the
September of 1677 had been made King's Advocate.

He was a man versatile, cultured, and liberal in his ideas,
beyond most of his contemporaries. His treatises fill two
stately folios; and they are far from being concerned
exclusively with codes and statutes, with pleadings and
litigations and verdicts. He was author and stylist as well as
barrister and politician. Sometimes we meet him in the
singing-robes of the poet, and again in the teacher's gown as
philosopher and moralist. Mr. Omond, the annalist of the
Lord Advocates of Scotland, and Mr. Lang, Mackenzie's most
recent biographer, give an account of his boyish romance of
Aretina, published when he was five-and-twenty, and probably the earliest novel to be written north of the Tweed;
and, if the story is bombastic in its diction and tame and
tedious in its plot, it has the interest which attaches to the
performance of a pioneer, breaking in advance of his neighbours
into territory hitherto untrodden. The youthful venture was
followed quickly by literary work of a more serious kind.

M

Two years after recounting the tale of the Egyptian princess, whose thoughts were the only stars by which her lover Philarites could cast his horoscope, Mackenzie, in a book that he entitled *The Religious Stoic*, unfolded those principles of belief and action by which he desired to regulate his own conduct. They are tolerant and kindly principles, though he declared that he meant the volume to be an exposure of "the madcap zealots of this bigot age." Never was there a gentler Stoic. "My heart bleeds," he wrote, "when I consider how scaffolds were dyed with Christian blood, and fields covered with the carcases of murthered Christians." "It fares with heretics," he argued, "as with tops, which, how long they are scourged, keep foot and run pleasantly; but fall, how soon they are neglected and left to themselves." And on another page he inscribed a freedom-loving sentence which the author of the *Areopagitica* need not have disavowed: "Opinion, kept within its own proper bounds, is a pure act of the mind; and so it would appear that to punish the body for that which is a guilt of the soul is as unjust as to punish one relative for another." We can but marvel that a theorist, so frankly generous in sentiment, and apparently so sincere in his comprehensiveness and charity, should as he grew older have degenerated and hardened into the prejudiced and unrelenting partisan, whose professional violence was to contradict in almost every particular the nobler creed of the study; the end in this life-story was not better than the beginning. Sir George Mackenzie had his academic debate, too, with John Evelyn—a debate which was singular enough. For, absorbed in affairs as he was, and entertaining no thought of abjuring his strenuous toils, he constituted himself the panegyrist of solitude and retirement; while his rival, always enamoured of the "havens dumb, out of the swing of the sea," came forward to laud the virtues of active citizenship and public service: each was depreciating and controverting his truer self. The Lord Advocate was historian, also, of the law of Scotland, and stout defender of the hoary antiquity of its regal line, adding one nebulous and imposing monarch to another, as Merlin conjured up roof by roof, tower after tower, spire beyond spire, to dignify the sacred mount of Camelot and all the dim rich city. If we could judge him by his books alone, we should think of Sir George Mackenzie as an erudite, reasonable, gracious and lenient man, who was likely to be as indubitable a peacemaker in the State as Robert Leighton had striven to prove himself in the Church.

Moreover, the Covenanters had a right to expect his friend-ship. In his first years at the bar, he threw much zeal into their defence. Again and again they counted themselves fortunate in having for their exponent and champion the brilliant nephew of the Earl of Seaforth, the rising hope of the Courts, who had received his training in jurisprudence not only in Aberdeen and St. Andrews, but in Bourges, the great Continental school of law. We have seen him already as one of the counsellors for the Marquis of Argyll. He did the work with a vigour and courage which filled those who listened to him with wonderment. "What is so desirable," he had asked in an essay on the advocate's calling, "as to be a sanctuary to such as are afflicted, and to pull the innocent from the claws of his accuser?"—and this was the spirit in which he sought to shield the incriminated chieftain. It was his one regret, he affirmed, that his client should have a pleader so unripe both in years and in experience. Was the Marquis blamed for acquiescing in Cromwell's usurpation?— but few indeed were guiltless of that crime. It was an un-avoidable fault, a weakness to which the strongest and stablest had succumbed, during those unhappy years of His Majesty's exile: "this only kept men from starving, and by it only could men preserve their ancient estates and satisfy their debts." The very Judges whom he addressed, and who had the life or the death of the prisoner in their gift, had complied with the Lord Protector's demands; and was it conceivable that they should punish in another an error into which they had fallen themselves? Not their duty merely, but their interest, might persuade them to acquit his Lordship of Argyll; for "who in this kingdom can sleep securely this night, if this noble person be condemned?" The vindication could scarcely have been more boldly uttered; and, when men shook their heads over its rashness and told him of the risk he was running, the young lawyer smiled that they should be so timorous, and gloried impenitently in what he had done. "It is impossible to speak for a traitor," he laughed, "without speaking treason." Or let us pass on for a few years. After the Pentland Rising, the King's Advocate of the day, Sir John Nisbet of Dirleton, "who, at a time when bad men were common, was one of the worst," determined that no one implicated in the ill-starred movement should escape the sorest penalties the law could inflict. It was not sufficient, he thought, to send to the scaffold those who had been captured by the Royalist troops and who appeared for trial. He went much farther. He moved that certain other delinquents, who had played their part in the fight on Rullion Green, but who had not yet been caught by Dalzell's soldiery, should be tried in their absence and, with no opportunity to say a word in their defence, should be sentenced to death. It was a new procedure; there had been no instance of its adoption in the Scottish Courts before; and the judges hesitated. But Nisbet, appealing to Roman law, to the reason of the thing itself, to the practice of Parliament, and to the analogy found in those investigations into the conduct of a rebel which had followed the actual endurance of the death-penalty, browbeat the occupants of the bench into agreement with his proposal. Yet, though he had his way, the popular voice was raised loudly against him; and Sir George Mackenzie coincided with the people. He distrusted, he said, this excessive increase in the powers of the public prosecutor. The innovation, he was sure, carried concealed in it the seeds and possibilities of grave danger; and, had it been reckoned safe for the representatives of the Crown to possess these huge prerogatives, they would have been dowered with them long ago. "Let us not make snares in place of laws," he exclaimed; "and whilst we study to punish such as are traitors, let us not hazard the innocence of such as are loyal subjects." Again he had come to the help of the Covenanters in their season of stress and suffering.

It must be set down to his praise, also, that, in the enunciation of his personal convictions, he had not been afraid to encounter the suspicion and enmity of those who stood highest in the Councils of King Charles. As member for Ross-shire in the Scottish Parliament, he was more than once a troublesome thorn in the side of the Duke of Lauderdale. In October 1669, the dictator wished the House to adopt a resolution in favour of the Union of the Kingdoms—perhaps the solitary ambition cherished by Oliver Cromwell to which his successors had served themselves heirs. There and then, being no friend at any time to a Fabian policy, he would have forced the matter through to its conclusion. But Sir George Mackenzie intervened. He bade his fellow-legislators pause. If they were to approve a project of such far-reaching importance, he advised them to give it first the calmest and most dispassionate consideration: "What is got cheaply is little valued, and in these affairs wherein we can do but once we should deliberate long." The scheme ultimately fell to the ground; and the antagonism of the member for Ross-shire was one of the main reasons for its dismissal from current politics. That is but an illustration of a refusal repeated on various occasions; Mackenzie was not prepared to surrender to Lauderdale the unfettered and arrogant autocracy which the Secretary of State coveted. At last, the King's minister became so angry at the inconvenient and persevering criticism, that with an oath he vowed he would "remove that factious young man from Parliament." But Sir Archibald Primrose, whose diplomacy made many rough places smooth, contrived to pacify the indignant consul, and a truce was declared between the disputants. It raises Sir George in our esteem that, in those years when Lauderdale's nod was as fateful as a Moorish sultan's, and when brave men were dumb for fear of offending the tyrant, he kept his private judgment clear, and continued to steer right onward in the course which he had marked out for himself.

So, if here and there, the adherents of the Covenant ventured to predict a more peaceful era when he received the reins of power, they could adduce reasons in support of their anticipation. For a long time the Lord Advocates had chastised them with scorpions. The older men and women

could recall the Saturnian reign of Sir Thomas Hope, as great a
statesman as he was a lawyer, who had always rendered to
Cæsar the things which are Cæsar's, but who had been an
ardent lover of Presbytery and a convinced opponent of every
one that interfered unrighteously with its simplicities and
sanctities.   But Hope had been dead for one-and-thirty years;
and since the Restoration the office, to which his character
and endowments lent so notable a lustre, had been filled by
men entirely different in disposition and aim.   Sir John
Fletcher, the Earl of Middleton's friend, was as rude in speech
and as devoid of mildness and conciliation as his superior;
and he surpassed him in shameless greed.   His unconscionable
rapacity led in the end to his downfall; for it reached such
lengths that the Privy Council in Edinburgh and the Government in London—neither of them a tribunal disposed to exact
any stringent and taintless morality from its agents—having
expostulated with him in vain, were driven to denude him of
his title.   Sir John Nisbet, who succeeded, was not a whit
better.   Kirkton insists, indeed, that he was worse.   He
portrays him as a man of " more dangerous temper; for money
might sometimes have hired Fletcher to spare blood, but
Nisbet was always so sore afraid of losing his own great estate,
he could never be officious enough to serve his cruel masters."
It was in connection with his régime that the laws against
conventicles were enacted, that the Court of High Commission
was set up, and that the poor refugees from the rout at Pentland were hunted to their doom.   Well might Lord Fountainhall quote of Nisbet's unwearying misdeeds the significant
and scathing Latin hexameter,

> Flectere si nequeo Superos, Acheronta movebo.

But, in 1677, he, too, was forced to resign; and " it does not
appear," says a modern writer, " that, in the course of his
public career, he ever did one deed which lightens the darkness
of his mercenary and servile life."   When Sir George Mackenzie stepped into the vacant place, onlookers, remembering
the new Advocate's past, and supposing that the tireless
ingenuity of his predecessors in abusing their opportunities

and degrading their office could not be rivalled by another, may have indulged the hope that now the "old shapes of foul disease" were gone, and that a larger heart and a kindlier hand had come to govern Scotland in their room.

But these visions were speedily and roughly shattered. The Lord Advocate was not the George Mackenzie of former years, who had befriended the Whigs in their extremity, and had striven to shield the liberties of the people from despotic infringement. His face was turned in the opposite direction. In the heyday of his success he revealed himself as a thorough-going Episcopalian and King's-man, to whom the Covenant and its allies were nothing else than anathema. The biography of a curious and fitful wandering scholar of the nineteenth century delineates its subject as discarding, in his later life, every one of the friendships of his youth. His comrades, as one of them expressed it, were more than mortal, when he gave himself to them at first; he painted them in the beautiful colours of fancy, and worshipped them. But he had not only the poet's temperament: he had the insight of a man of science. He came soon to understand that his idols had feet of clay; and then he flamed into indignation against them for having, as he thought, deceived him. It was an extravagant idealism, which robbed himself of desirable wealth, and which was both ungenerous and unjust in its strictures on his companions. Sir George Mackenzie was no idealist of this super-sensitive kind. It was not because the associates of his opening manhood had disappointed his requirements, and fallen short of the too lofty standard to which he would have had them aspire, that he forsook them and passed over to the side of their adversaries. The motives that prompted him were, as Mr. Omond shows, less austere and rigorous. One was his lifelong jealousy of Sir George Lockhart, a more accomplished lawyer if not a cleverer man, whom he had a chance now of outstripping in the race for preferment and influence. And the other was that, at length, he was discovering his own true sentiments. A quarrel that had recently set the Scottish bar in sharp conflict against the corrupt bench, and, as a consequence, against the King whose creatures the unworthy and

venal judges were, had helped him to realise that he was
much more of a Royalist than he had dreamed.   At the outset
of the duel he was, heart and soul, with his brother-advocates ;
but as it went forward—for it was prolonged through more
than two years—he gradually lost faith in their cause, and so
complete the revolution became that, employing all his skill
in argument, he persuaded them to abandon it also.   He told
them that they were martyrs by mistake ; that "it was no
dishonour to submit to their Prince"; and that "all such
tumults tended to sedition, and sedition to war." It was the commencement of another epoch in Mackenzie's life—an epoch less
attractive, less hospitable and free-hearted, more arbitrary and
truculent.   He who had been accustomed to plead for popular
rights was henceforward to be an aristocrat to his finger-tips,
an upholder than whom none was more immoderate of the
absolutism of the Stuart kings.   "No Advocate," he boasted
towards the close of his career, " has ever screwed the prerogative
higher than I have.   I deserve to have my statue placed riding
behind Charles the Second in the Parliament Close." He ceased
to give the soldiers of the Church any countenance ; he pur-
sured them with a logic, a satire, a ridicule, an oratory, which
were consistent in the antipathy they disclosed ; he became
the "Bluidy Mackenzie," whose imposing tomb may be visited
in the Greyfriars, and over whom, as he lay low and silent
under its adornments, the Edinburgh schoolboys gloried in a
triumphant jingle :

> Bluidy Mackenzie, come out if ye daur ;
> Lift the sneck, and draw the bar !

His term of office has its own assured title to an
honourable remembrance ; for it was during its continuance,
and at his express instigation, that the Advocates' Library was
founded. But its brand-mark of disgrace is more incontrovertible than its wreath of fame. It was crowded with the
pains and wrongs which he visited on the Covenanters. Even
Mr. Lang, who fain would bless, is often driven by his sense of
historical fairness to criticise and condemn. "The times," he
acknowledges, " brought to the surface of Mackenzie's nature

SIR GEORGE MACKENZIE.

After the Portrait by Sir Godfrey Kneller, in the
Parliament House, Edinburgh.

elements which, in a more settled age, would have lain dormant and unsuspected by himself." "We wish," he adds, "that, like Archbishop Leighton, he had early abandoned a position which could not be held without smirches on the reputation." During the nine years when he was at the helm of affairs, there was hardly a prosecution, of nonconforming nobleman or westland farmer or humble servant-girl, in which he was not active. He had "a violent temper, an insolent manner, a cutting tongue"; the prisoners had meagre chance of escape, when he examined them and then bade the judges do their duty. "That excommunicate tyrant, George Mackenzie, the Advocate," Marion Harvie was to call him tersely and fiercely in her Testimony from "the women-house on the East side" of the Tolbooth-prison in the High Street; and there was too much justification for the immitigable words. At times the scenes in his Court-room were frightful; as when Alexander Gordon, the Bull of Earlston, was led in, and went raving mad on seeing the pitiless looks of his judges and the instruments of torture which the King's Advocate had provided for him; or when a poor working-man, his strength spent by his privations on the hills and moors, was ordered by his ruthless inquisitor to the Boots, and was saved from the agony simply because the surgeon found his legs so weak that a single blow of the hammer would have broken them beyond possibility of cure. It is among the strangest paradoxes of history that the author of *The Religious Stoic*, with the homage which it pays to the quality of mercy, should have lived to practise those iniquities; we compare him in our minds with Maximilien Robespierre, "nearly weeping" for one slain innocent in the September Massacre, and yet directing the Reign of Terror and sending the tumbrils to the guillotine. John Dryden salutes Sir George Mackenzie as "that noble wit of Scotland," and the greeting is accurate for one aspect of his personality. But James Beattie, who is a lesser poet, is perhaps a better authority on the matter at issue: he gives us the Lord Advocate's other side, when he writes that his "hollow promise helped the princely hand to screw confession from the tortured lips."

CHAPTER XXI.

CLAVERS IN A' HIS PRIDE.

MACKENZIE, writes Mr. Francis Watt, "seemed the brain that plotted"; but Claverhouse "was the hand that struck." In the Council Room the Lord Advocate planned his oppressions, and in the field John Graham translated them into intense and piercing facts. We have reached the moment when one of those men whose very name separates the lookers-on into contending factions, kindling either a flame of enthusiasm or a brooding fire of repugnance, comes to the forefront in Covenanting story; and we must try, if we can, to understand his personality. He has often been painted in colours which are entirely dark and forbidding; and that is not surprising, when we recall the vigour which he threw into the fulfilment of an ugly task. Yet he had his virtues. His own private life was pitched on a worthier key than that of most of his Royalist compeers; and the garland of the soldier whose courage is beyond debate has belonged to him ever since the triumph and the tragedy of Killiecrankie. The tartan of the Grahams, with its green and white and azure, is an inviolate and heroic tartan. It "kissed the death-wound of Dundee"—the death-wound of a loyal gentleman, and a warrior who fought even more bravely for a losing cause than ever he had done when the sun was shining on his banners. The pity is that he espoused the wrong side, and that, having espoused it, he strove for its maintenance and supremacy with an energy which was merciless and which never dreamed of giving quarter to its opponents.

To look at his portraits, one would not imagine that he

was flint-hearted. No doubt, Dr. Hewison, in his masterly history of the period, more than disputes their accuracy. He quotes John Dick, the student-martyr of 1684, who describes Claverhouse as " the pitiful thing," escaping in hot haste from Drumclog, " where there fell prettier men on either side than himself "; and John Morrison, of Terregles, who told Sir Walter Scott that the persecutor's " arms were long and reached to his knees," that his " hair was red or frizzly," and that his features were " altogether diabolical "; and Thomas Brownlee, laird of Torfoot, who wrote, after seeing Dundee, that he " had a complexion unusually dark," that " his irregular and large teeth were presented through a smile which was very unnatural," and that, in fine, the whole countenance suggested to his view " the image of the Emperor Julian the Apostate." But it is hard to believe that the evidence of the Leven and Glamis pictures is absolutely misleading. They show us a face which is high-bred in every line and curve. There are some haughtiness and some superciliousness in it, the hints of a proud and peremptory character lying behind. But, especially in the more youthful delineation, it is a winning face. It is boyish in its smoothness. There is a kind of womanly loveliness about it. If it were humbler, and illuminated by the grace of God, it might be the face of a Monica, or a Catharine of Siena, or a Mary Sidney—" the subject of all verse, Sidney's sister, Pembroke's mother." As it is, we may be nearer the mark if we compare it with

> the face that launched a thousand ships,
> And burnt the topless towers of Ilium.

The eyes are large and full and dark. The brow and cheeks are framed in the long love-locks of the seventeenth century, the curling hair of which its owner was so careful, attaching small leaden weights to it at nights to keep the tresses in their place. The hands, too, are small and fine; are they capable of shooting John Brown, while his wife stands by with her baby in her arms? We survey the outward aspect of Graham of Claverhouse, and we remember the two Florimells whom Edmund Spenser sings. One of them was invested with every attraction, for she was formed of purest snow in massy mould congealed. But she was an enchanted damsel. A spirit full of guile inhabited her; and, set beside the true Florimell, she vanished into nought. Beside some of the humble folk whom he pursued to death, God's little and hidden ones, the surface beauty of the persecutor is dissipated and forgotten.

He came of a noble family. His father was William Graham, of Claverhouse, in the shire of Angus, a few miles north of Dundee, who was in a distant way related to the great Marquis of Montrose. His mother was Lady Magdalene Carnegie, youngest daughter of the first Earl of Northesk. She survived her husband for many years, and must have had a more important share in the upbringing of her famous son; but no tradition remains to tell us what manner of woman she was. Uncertainty hangs about the date of the boy's entrance into the world where he was to run so swift and memorable a race. It used to be given as 1643, the year when the Solemn League was subscribed in Westminster; but, a quarter of a century ago, the *Dictionary of National Biography* argued for 1649, and, more recently still, Professor Sanford Terry has written that, "with a narrow margin on either side, Claverhouse's birth may be placed in July 1648." If this conclusion be accepted, he went to St. Andrews soon after passing his eleventh birthday; and, indeed, the Scottish Universities of the time were little else than the advanced classes of the parish schools. In 1661, before he was fourteen, he was a graduate. He had not dallied, therefore, on the road to the activities of life; but it may be surmised that his tutors in St. Salvator's College did not find him very eager to learn. It is true that, in the Memoirs of his friend, Sir Ewen Cameron of Lochiel, his attainments in various directions are depicted as more than creditable. He had made, we are told, " a considerable progress in the Mathematics, especially in those parts of it that related to military capacity"; and there was no section " of the Belles Lettres which he had not studied with care and exactness"; and he was "much master in the epistolary way of writeing," and "expressed himself with ease and plaineness, and argued well, and had a great art in giving his thoughts in few words." The last encomium is well-deserved; for Claverhouse was always clear and forceful, practical and pungent, in his style of speech. But, in their other commendations, Sir Ewen, and Sir Ewen's biographer, Drummond of Balhaldy, are too partial witnesses; or else, in the rovings and fightings of his later years, John Graham must have lost his relish for the exhilarating waters of the Pierian spring. His letters, despite their pithiness, are poor productions in composition and in orthography. He "vainly struggled after grammar," Mr. Hill Burton says; and, in an epoch when the idiosyncrasies of every individual appeared to be reflected in his spelling, he "spelled with rare originality." It may be feared that, at St. Andrews, books had no commanding charm for him. Already "his eyes were with his heart, and that was far away," on the battlefields where swords are crossed and the drum summons the combatants to action. "I am young, and thinkis til pas til France," he might have confessed with the militant parson in Sir David Lindsay's satire. Not, however, until quite ten years had elapsed after his graduation—years about which little information has descended to us—did his governing desire bear the fruit he craved.

Then, probably in 1672, he enrolled himself in one of the two Scottish regiments serving in France. Over these regiments, and over the others that were composed of Englishmen, the Duke of Monmouth was commanding general; and thus Claverhouse would gain some insight into the character of one whom he was to meet a few years later at Bothwell Bridge. But his French experiences were brief-lived. Charles was shamed by his people's displeasure into dissolving his compact with Louis. Monmouth went back to England. John Graham, and the man who was to be his antagonist in his last campaign, Hugh Mackay of Scourie, transferred themselves to the army of Holland. Strangely enough, Claverhouse came soon to be a favourite with William Henry, the young Prince of Orange and Stadtholder of the Netherlands, against whom by and by he was to contend to the death. He was made a cornet in William's bodyguard. In a note to one of the pages of his

History, Lord Macaulay rejects the tale, once received without disbelief, that on a critical occasion he saved his master from a violent end. It was the August of 1674. At Seneffe, near Mons, William was fighting the Prince of Condé. It was a weary and indecisive battle; but it added to the Stadtholder's fame for bravery and calmness. "The Prince of Orange," Condé exclaimed, "has acted in everything like an old captain, except in venturing his life too like a young soldier." In the heat of the struggle his horse plunged with him into a treacherous marsh. Immediately his enemies closed round, and it appeared as if his daring and his wisdom were both to be prematurely quenched. But Cornet Graham saw his commander's peril. Without the delay of a minute, he galloped to him, and, leaping from his horse, bade the Prince seat himself in the saddle. Little by little the two fought their way through the ring of their adversaries, back to the firmer ground. The cornet received a captain's commission for his courage, and his leader was loud in his praise. Such is the story; and if its dramatic fitness stirs in us Macaulay's scepticism, we must remember, too, that it is a legacy bequeathed to us from Claverhouse's own time. At the New Year of 1683, one of his admirers addressed some verses to him—verses which recalled his "conduct, prowess, martial gallantry" on the day when he wore his "white plumash" at Seneffe. And there is an old Latin poem written in his honour by his standard-bearer at Killiecrankie. It pictures "bonnie Dundee" musing over his camp-fire on the thanklessness of the Prince whose life he once had preserved:

> Ipse mei impositum dorso salientis equi te
> Hostibus eripui, salvumque in castra reduxi.

John Graham could never have spoken in hexameters; but there remains the shadow of a possibility that, after all, he did something like the feat which the hexameters commemorate. Had it not been for his luckless aid, says that extraordinary Jacobite, Mr. Charles Kirkpatrick Sharpe, "the persecutor of his family, the evil genius of the unfortunate James, the fiend of Glencoe, might have sunk innocuous, and comparatively unknown, in the depths of a Batavian marsh." It is

curious to think of the last and stoutest defender of the Stuarts
helping to bring about the Revolution of 1688.

In the late winter of 1677 Captain Graham was back in
Scotland. He was still under thirty, handsome, fearless, a
soldier of repute. Some knowledge of his Continental exploits
had preceded him, and from the first he was in favour in
high quarters. William, who had come to England to marry
the Princess Mary, spoke well of him to his father-in-law, the
Duke of York; and the Duke in turn commended him to the
young Marquis of Montrose, grandson of "the finest gallant
in the realm"; and at once the Marquis offered him a
lieutenancy in his troop of cavalry. "I pretend that non
bot gentlemen should ride in it," Montrose wrote, being eager
to induce his kinsman to join him. But the offer was declined,
perhaps because the troop had been raised for foreign duty;
and Claverhouse, newly arrived from the Netherlands, had no
wish to recross the seas so soon. He did not have to wait long
for an appointment more to his mind. In September 1678,
three regiments of horse were added to the King's army on
the north of the Cheviots and the Solway. The Earl of Airlie
received the command of one of them, the Earl of Home of
another; and John Graham, as it seems by the express desire
of Charles, was placed over the third. The money required
for the maintenance of these regiments was procured by means
of the odious tax which the country people called the
Cess—an impost which they paid to provide the Government
with the opportunity of overriding and spoiling themselves.
The Cess was expressly devoted to the upkeep of a military
force whose work was the repression of the field-meetings. We
do not marvel that it brought into the Covenanting camp—
that wind-smitten camp weakened from within as well as from
without—a new subject of debate. Many submitted to the
outrageous tax, as in the early ages of Christianity the saints
had yielded to Tiberius and Diocletian the tribute they asked.
But the sterner spirits rebelled. They reasoned that, if they
paid an unjust exaction, they connived at the injustice. Our
hearts bleed for them, beset by enemies, and vexed by the
questions which inflame friend against friend.

This was the state of things to which Claverhouse had returned; and in it he was taking soon a principal's share. In charge of his company of dragoons, he was sent to Dumfriesshire and Annandale, to deal in all rigour with the dogged people who persisted in attending the conventicles. It was not the most honourable employment for one who had carried his white plume so proudly; but he girded himself for its performance with promptitude: already he was learning, as he phrased it in a letter to the Earl of Linlithgow, his Commander-in-Chief, that "this contry has been very loose." At first, indeed, he was a precisian; he would not transgress by an inch the limits which had been mapped out for him. "They tell me," he went on, "that the one end of the bridge of Dumbfrich is in Galaua"—on that side of the Nith where his commission had no validity; and thus, he complained, "they may hold conventicles at our nose, and we not dare to dissipat them." He begged Linlithgow to see that the difficulty was rectified. "Such ane insult as that would not please me, and, on the other hand, I am unwilling to exceed orders." Two or three months later, he was Sheriff-depute of Dumfries, Annandale, Kirkcudbright, and Wigtown; and then he could use more freedom. But the bestowment of these fresh powers angered Lord Queensberry, one of the great landowners in the district; and the jealousy between Claverhouse and the influential nobleman had its commencement—a jealousy which increased in sharpness and rancour as the years ran on. The young officer's perplexities were of many sorts.

So we see him, in this south and south-west of Scotland, devoting himself with unremitting zeal to the execution of the Government's policy of extirpation, and heartily endorsing the policy. Sometimes it is a little building that has been raised, "upon the expence of the comon purse of the disaffected," to be a meeting-place for the men and women of the Covenant; and this he levels to the ground, writing its memorial afterwards in his despatch to headquarters—"So perished the charity of many ladys." Sometimes it is a capture he makes of those who have been foremost among

JOHN GRAHAM, OF CLAVERHOUSE.

After the Leven Portrait.

the irreconcilables. He wishes to seize six of them; but after galloping forty miles—"which is the most can be riden in one night"—he finds only two. The womenfolk have outwitted him, and have concealed their husbands safely where, with all his prying, he cannot discover them; and they themselves, like hospitable housewives, have "great candles lighted" in expectation of the arrival which he meant to be a profound secret. It is a frequent source of chagrin and disappointment that the enemy's scouting is much more effectively done than his own: "Mr. Welch and others preach securely with in twenty or thretty myles of us, but we can doe nothing for want of spays." Yet he may be trusted to strain every nerve and to apply every possible method of restraint and punishment. Because "those rogues run over to Yrland," he stations his sentinels at Portpatrick and Ballantrae. He apprehends wandering ministers, and all others whose seizure will be welcomed by the Privy Council. He cites before him those who have attended any gathering for worship in the fields, or who have had a child baptized by the outlawed preachers. He deals summarily with the obstinate people who will not frequent the parish Churches, and will not give heed to their discipline. The fines of all who are not landowners he is allowed to retain for himself and for his troop; half of the money extorted from Covenanting proprietors he sends to the Commissioner for the district, while the other half is the property of the King. As Sheriff-depute he holds his court "once every week at least, and oftener as he thinks fit." These were John Graham's occupations during the first five months of 1679.

Then he found himself suddenly confronted by one of the outstanding episodes of his history, although an episode on which he could not dwell with any pride. But, before we describe it, let us leave the strict chronology of the narrative, to glance at some events which help to unravel the character of the man. It has been said that he had two controlling. motives, that of a vaulting and quenchless personal ambition, and that of undeviating loyalty to the Stuart monarch. The analysis does him no injustice. These were the "fountain-light of all his day," the "master-light of all his seeing." And the events, to which we are to refer, are proof of it.

One was his courtship of Helen Graham. There is no evidence that, when he proposed to wed the lady, he had himself ever seen her. But the union, as he perceived with clear-sighted eyes, would be an immense material gain, lifting him upward on the social ladder, and making more sure and rapid his advance in the army and in the State. Helen Graham was heiress to the Earldom of Menteith, her cousin, the present wearer of the title, being a childless man. Him Claverhouse conciliated and won over, writing him with the skill and pertinaciousness and self-satisfaction of a practised diplomatist. "Who ever you mak choyse of," he protested, "will be in place of a sonne," perhaps, indeed, much better than a son. "You know that Julius Caesar had no need to regrait the want of isseu, having adopted Augustus, for he knew certenly that he had secured to himself a thankfull and usefull friend as well as a wyse successor, neither of which he could have promised himself by having childring; for nobody knows whether they begit wyse men or fooles, beseids that the tays of gratitud and friendship ar stronger in generous mynds than those of natur." Is not the advocate sententious as well as vehement? And he has an abundant confidence in himself. "And then, my Lord, I may say without vanity that I will doe your family no dishonor, seing there is nobody you could mak choyse of has toyld so much for honor as I have don, though it has been my misfortun to atteen but a small shear." But, although Menteith himself was wholly favourable, and although the suitor never abandoned the hope of success until, in the spring of 1682, the lady was finally denied to him and betrothed to the nephew of the Earl of Conway, one hindrance after another obstructed his path. First, my Lord Montrose threatened to be a rival in the race; and, at a later stage in the story, the mother of Helen Graham, "a very cunning woman," interposed to thwart the persevering wooer. He had become more ardent as the quest became more troublesome and desperate. "I will asseur you," he told the Earl of Menteith, "I need nothing to perswad me

to take that young laidy. I would take her in her smoak."
Possibly there was less of self-interest and more of genuine
affection in the closing than in the earlier chapters of the
adventure; but to the end Claverhouse preserved undiminished
his sanguine faith in his star. "When my affaires goe wrong,"
he wrote, "I remember that saying of Loucan, *Tam mala
Pompeii quam prospera mundus adoret.* On has ocasion to
shou ther vigeur after a wrong stape to make a nimble
recovery." There never was any deficiency of vigour about
John Graham.

The tenacity he had revealed in courtship with such small
result was displayed, a few years subsequently, in his acquisi-
tion of the estate of Dudhope—"ane extraordinare pleasant
and sweet place, with a good house, excellent yards, much
planting, and fyne parks," which "lyes on the syde of the
hill of Dundie, and is as of purpose built there to command
the town." No one will blame him for desiring to add
Dudhope to the ancestral acres of Claverhouse; but the
negotiations through which it was transferred to him illustrate
unpleasantly the strain of selfishness and greed in his
disposition. The property belonged to Charles Maitland,
Lord Hatton, Lauderdale's brother and heir. For twenty
years he had been Master of the Mint in Scotland; and
through all that time, though his criminality was not
suspected at first, he had been guilty of peculation. At length
he was tried and condemned, was fined £20,000—it had
originally been £72,000, but the King reduced the tremendous
sum—and was forced to submit to the loss of many of his
possessions. John Graham wished the lands which lay so
near to his own, and the Constableship of Dundee which went
with these lands; but how was he to obtain the coveted
treasure? He knew that Queensberry hankered after a
Dukedom; and, although there was no particle of love
between them, he journeyed up to London, to interview his
patron, James of York, and Charles himself on the subject.
"All here," he wrote to the Marquis with a deft and complaisant pen, "magnify what you doe, and says it is a good
copie for them, and the noyse of it helps to keep there affaires

right." His importunities were incessant, and he had his way; the King bestowed the longed-for title; and thus one powerful ally was gained. He knew, moreover, that the Earl of Aberdeen, President of the Court of Session, was in need of money; and he took care that his Lordship's wants were supplied. Of Maitland's fine of £20,000, four-fifths were allotted to the President, and the remaining fifth to Claverhouse himself. So a second henchman was won. The goal was not reached without the intrigues and labours of a year and a half; but at last it was attained, and, in April 1684, "the King's familiar Councillor, Colonel John Graham of Claverhouse, and his heirs and assignees" received a Crown Charter of Dudhope Castle. When we follow its turnings and windings, the incident is scarcely one which enhances our respect for him.

Still more characteristic is the tale of his marriage. It is marred by none of that self-seeking which was too conspicuous in his endeavour to capture Helen Graham, and which tainted his ownership of his new estate; there is rather, says Mr. Terry, "a touch of sporting recklessness in it." But, before the tale had got to the conclusion of its opening chapter, his conduct was to furnish fresh evidence that he valued no one and nothing half so much as his sovereign prince in London, and that Charles's errands were infinitely more important than weddings and honeymoons. The marriage-contract was signed on Monday, the 9th of June, in the same year which brought him the lordship of Dudhope. The bride was the Honourable Jean Cochrane, of the famous Ayrshire house of Dundonald. She had a widowed mother, Catherine, daughter of the Earl of Cassillis, who was staunch and stieve in her adhesion to the Covenant—"the she-dragon" Sheriff Napier designates her, abhorring as he does this too Whiggish union into which his immaculate hero was entering. We do not wonder that the mother was violent in her opposition to the match; nor yet that it excited surprise and suspicion among many of the Royalists, who marvelled that their champion should seek a spouse in a quarter so unexpected. But difficulties were merely an incentive to the Laird of Claver-

house. He went determinedly forward, encouraged, one can
but hope, by the fealty of his high-spirited sweetheart, who
had to navigate a sea of troubles as convulsed as his own.
" For my pairt," he declared, " I look on myself as a cleanger.
I may cur people guilty of that plaigue of presbitry be
conversing with them, but cannot be infected. And for the
yong ladie herself, I shall answer for her. Had she been
right principled "—this is the bridegroom's irony—" she would
never, in despyt of her mother and relations, made choyse of
a persicutor, as they call me." So, on the Tuesday, the
curious union was consummated ; and Jean Cochrane—

> It seems the gods design'd her outward form,
> Their masterpiece and standart uniforme—

was mated with " the wicked-witted bloodthirsty Graham,"
a husband of whom, in the hurried and feverish years which
ensued, she was to see comparatively little. But the benediction had hardly been spoken, when the best-man, the Master
of Ross, son of the Lord of Hawkhead, informed Claverhouse
of a new conventicle, at Black Loch near Slamannan, of which
he had heard from General Dalzell ; and the husband, who
had boasted a day or two before that he would " lait the world
see that it is not in the pouer of love, nor any other folly, to
alter my loyalty," rode away immediately from his wife to
chase the " dogs " across the moors. All that night, and all
the next day, he prosecuted his bootless search after men who
were too well hidden in the hour of their peril. On the 12th
of June, he was again with Lady Jean ; but, by noon on the
13th, he had flung himself into the saddle once more, to urge
his horse southward. He sent four parallel columns to scour
every yard of a far-stretching countryside. It was a futile
enterprise. " We were at the head of Douglas. We were
round and over Cairntable. We were at Greenock-head,
Cummer-head, and through all the mosses, hills, glens, woods ;
and spread in small parties, and ranged as if we had been at
hunting, and down to Blackwood, but could learn nothing of
those rogues." Was there ever a marriage so strangely
celebrated ? " They might have let Tuesday pass," the chief

actor in the ceremony wrote to the Lord President. But, in truth, he preferred his fighting gear, and the following of the Covenanters up the braes and down the ravines and over the heather, to the quieter joys which home could offer him. His bride must not expect the allegiance he kept for his King. For five short years she was to claim her broken fraction of his heart; their one boy was to die, an infant of eight months old; seven years after Killiecrankie, she and the child of her second husband, William Livingstone, Viscount Kilsyth, were killed by the falling of a roof in an inn at Utrecht. Sorrow heaped on sorrow was the "tocher," the wedding-portion, of Lady Claverhouse.

If John Graham thought less of his wife than of his prince, his God fared no better at his hands. Yet, although Charles Stuart was first and last, God had His inferior place. Claverhouse was scrupulous in his religious observances. After his death, an old Presbyterian lady, who had lodged below him in Edinburgh, told one of his friends of her astonishment to discover that a man of his reputation and profession was regular in the practice of his devotions. Doubtless there was cause for surprise; but the vagaries and contradictions of our humanity are infinite. Robert Burton discusses, in one of his captivating chapters, the "divers symptoms and occasions" of hypocrisy. "Some deny there is any God; some confess, yet believe it not; a third sort confess and believe, but will not live after His laws, worship and obey Him; others allow God and gods subordinate." One shrinks from using the word "hypocrisy" in reference to a personality not merely virile and emphatic, but apparently direct and sincere in its various manifestations. But sincerity in the cult of self, in obedience to the arbitrary commandments of a tyrant, and in the routine and punctilio of ritual, is not a quality in which Heaven takes any delight. And we do not break the queenly rule of charity, if we classify Graham of Claverhouse in Robert Burton's "third sort," who at once confess and disobey.

CHAPTER XXII.

THOSE THAT WERE STOUT OF HEART ARE SPOILED.

SINCE his return to Scotland, Claverhouse had accomplished nothing very notable. But, in the beginning of May 1679, the Archbishop was assassinated; and now stirring events were crowded thick and fast—events in which Graham was a prominent actor. On the 29th of the month, the town of Rutherglen witnessed one of them. A body of armed men, numbering seventy or eighty, entered the streets. Their leader was Sir Robert Hamilton, of whom we shall hear more soon; with him rode John Balfour of Kinloch and James Russel, two of the instigators of the deed of blood done on Magus Moor. It was the King's Restoration Day, and a bonfire blazed in the main thoroughfare. The visitors extinguished the flames; and then, proceeding to the Town Cross, they read a Declaration which condemned the conduct of the Government since 1660. Lighting a fire of their own, they burned the Acts of Parliament and Privy Council, which for nineteen years had been launched against the Covenanted Reformation; and, having finished the task for which they came, they withdrew. Honest men many of them were, though driven to extremity by the excesses of the hour. But they could not hope that their daring deed would escape the notice of the civil and military rulers of the land. John Graham was at Falkirk; and, as soon as the rumour of what had happened reached his ears, he set out to avenge the affront. On the road he seized John King, Presbyterian chaplain to Lord Cardross, and, along with him, some fourteen others. Two and two he tied them together, and drove them on before his troop of horse.

But affairs took a turn which he had not anticipated. Having halted for the night at Strathaven, and finding that there were stories in the air about a field preaching to be held not far away, " I thought,"—he wrote to the Earl of Linlithgow —" that wee might mak a litle tour to see if we could fall upon a conventicle ": which, he adds shamefacedly enough, " we did, litle to our advantadge." The place of meeting was a gentle slope, overlooked by the larger mass of Loudoun Hill. At the foot of the slope the moorland became a swamp, through which a stream made its way, its sides fringed with stunted bushes. It was Sabbath morning, the first of June ; and from different districts of the west the crowd had gathered, to hear God's Word. Thomas Douglas was to be preacher ; but scarcely had he commenced the services of the day, when the signal gun, the token of alarm, was fired by a watchman on a neighbouring height. Claverhouse was approaching from the east, and listening had to yield meanwhile to the ruder work of fighting. " I have done," Douglas said. " You have got the theory; now for the practice. You know your duty ; self-defence is always lawful." There was no disorder. Those who had weapons separated themselves quietly from the rest, counselling their friends to secure their own safety as best they could. " When we came in sight of them," their enemy says, spelling his words with eccentric individuality, " we found them drawen up in batell upon a most advantagious ground, to which there was no coming but throgh moses and lotkess "—mosses and lochs, the captain means. " They wer not preaching, and had sat away all their weomen and shildring." In fine, the Cove-nanters were girding themselves, soldier-like, for the duty in front.

Sir Robert Hamilton was there with his Rutherglen body-guard. The other officers were the veteran Henry Hall of Haughhead, and the young William Cleland of Douglas, and two men whom we have met before, John Balfour with his oblique eyes and fierce aspect, and David Hackston of Rathillet. How many had they under their command ? Royalist writers, anxious to condone the rout of their hero, have numbered them by thousands ; and it is certain that, within a few weeks, the

THE BATTLEFIELD OF DRUMCLOG.

army grew to considerable proportions. But there is no real
reason for questioning the accuracy of Wodrow's figures—
figures which Dr. Hill Burton and Professor Hume Brown have
accepted. Forty horsemen, fifty footmen who carried guns,
and one hundred and fifty equipped with antiquated halberts
or with the long pitchforks used in the labours of the farm:
that, we may believe, was the extent of the tiny force. The
other side was no larger—may, indeed, have been somewhat
smaller. Yet, man for man, the two parties would have
appeared to an onlooker to be almost equally matched. The
King's troops had the advantage in arms and ammunition, in
discipline and equipment. But the defenders of the Covenant
had the better preparation of religion and faith and the
assurance that they fought for the honour of Jesus Christ.

While the combatants face each other, we may make the
acquaintance of one of the captains of the Whigs. William
Cleland is little more than a boy, having been born, where
the Douglas Water comes down from Cairntable, in the year
after His Majesty's Restoration. But such confidence have
the older men in his skill and bravery that, on this day of
battle, they have given him the direction of the best of their
foot-soldiers. An interesting figure he is, student of St.
Andrews, bosom-friend of the young Lord Angus, Christian
whom the field meetings that he loves have made " very sober
and pious," and poet to boot, writing verses which sometimes
scintillate with humour and sometimes peal and flash with
indignation. In his rhymes, as in everything else, he is the
patriot through and through. He will not drink of Castaly,
nor set himself to learn " Æolian charms and Dorian lyric
odes."

> For I am very apt to think
> There's as much virtue, sense, and pith
> In Annan or the Water of Nith,
> Which quietly slips by Dumfries,
> As any water in all Greece.

You perceive William Cleland in his imaginative mood, light-
hearted, with eyes awake to all the sights and happenings
around him, in lines like these—

Fain would I know
  If beasts have any reason,
If falcons, killing eagles,
  Do commit a treason,
If fear of winter's want
  Makes swallows fly the season.
      Hollo, my fancy! whither wilt thou go?

You discover him serious, sarcastic and angry, a keen watcher
of public events, a born warrior who can appraise the fighting
qualities of others, in his Hudibrastic recital of the "Expedition of the Highland Host." He draws, with caustic force,
the portrait of this persecutor and of that. There is Lauderdale, who is the more fatal a foe to Presbytery because he was
bred within its walls : "He kens weel how to loose their knots,
for he was once in all their plots." There is her Grace the
Duchess, who has tied her husband to her apron-strings, so
that they are never apart—

        To leave her east would not be right;
        She'll weary on a winter night.
        To bring her west would mend but little;
        For Hielant lairds are very kittle.

There, too, is Sharp, eager to "cleanse the Kirk with sword
and dagger" — Sharp, who never has any leisure: "he's
troubled with so many cases of conscience, which he's still
dissecting." William Cleland is only a lad in years; but the
perils of the time have made a man of him, in shrewdness, in
insight, in courage. We are not surprised to see him in
command of his troop, on the first of June, when the Covenanters have resolved, "for the relief of the prisoners, their
own defence, and the defence of the Gospel, to put their lives
in venture, and, through the Lord's assistance, to go to meet
the enemy."

     The contest had a dramatic prelude. Down the face of
the slope the Covenanters advanced, singing the familiar
verses of one of the Scottish metrical psalms, the seventy-
sixth, to the fine old tune, as tradition relates, of *Martyrs*.
They were kindling words which rang out in the resonant bass
of two hundred and forty strong-throated and strong-souled
men—

In Judah's land God is well known,
  His name's in Israel great;
In Salem is His tabernacle,
  In Sion is His seat.
There arrows of the bow He brake,
  The shield, the sword, the war.
More glorious Thou than hills of prey,
  More excellent art far.

Those that were stout of heart are spoiled,
  They slept their sleep outright;
And none of those their hands did find
  .That were the men of might.

The battle was half-won which could be introduced by a song
so confident and unafraid.

At the foot of the rising ground was the morass, and just
on the other side Claverhouse was ranged with his troopers.
The Royalists fired first, and from across the swamp the
Covenanters answered. But the skirmish of musketry was a
mere preliminary. Graham was resolved to lead his followers
over the marshy ground, and to engage the adversary at close
quarters. He sent some horsemen to discover a shallow and
well-bottomed place, where a passage might be effected. It
was a mistaken move. The horses staggered and stumbled in
the treacherous bog, and a volley from the enemy emptied
many saddles. Then the men of the Covenant had their
opportunity. They knew the morass better than their
opponents. Though " Clavers was tooming the shot all the
time on them," Kinloch with his cavalry, Cleland with his
homely infantry, were through the swamp and grappling with
their foes, almost before the dragoons understood what they
meant to be at. Their fire brought down Cornet Robert
Graham, Corporal Crawford, and Captain Blyth. The sudden-
ness of their onset overwhelmed the others. Claverhouse saw
his soldiers reel and turn and flee. His own charger, a gallant
sorrel, was hurt fatally with a pitchfork, so that, in the rider's
forcible language, " his guts hung out half an elle, yet he
caryed me af an myl," before he sank exhausted and dead.
The day was lost for the persecutor, and was gained by the
persecuted. " They perseud us so hotly," the discomfited

N

commander reports, "that we got no tym to ragly. I saved
the standarts, but lost on the place about aight ord ten men,
beseids wounded; but the dragoons lost many mor."   Sir
Robert Hamilton was responsible for the death of one of the
captured cavaliers; and, if he had been allowed to have his
way, other five, who had received quarter without his knowledge, would have shared the same fate.   Happily he had
colleagues more merciful than he was, and the triumph of
Drumclog was not sullied by needless acts of barbarity.

Across hill and moor King Charles's troopers fled, followed
by those who had achieved a success so amazing over "the
shield, the sword, the war."   The chase was kept up for miles.
Passing the spot where Lord Cardross's chaplain sat, Claverhouse was invited by his prisoner of the morning to tarry for
the afternoon sermon.   But neither captain nor guardsmen had
any thought of lingering.   At Strathaven the inhabitants,
whose sympathies were with the victors, would fain have
stopped the progress of the Royalists; but most of the men
of the place, able to bear sword and gun, were away; and the
flying soldiers went galloping at great speed up the village
street, and out at the farther end.   On they clattered, a
chafed and dispirited band, who had renounced every trace of
the bravery with which they had ridden along the same roads
some hours earlier.   At length they reached Glasgow, where
Lord Ross, whom we met five years back as the scourge and
hammer of the worshippers in the fields, and whose son
William was, five years after Drumclog, to be the young
groomsman at John Graham's wedding, gave them the protection of his regiment.   There at their leisure they could
rehearse to their friends their surprising experience.

Six or seven of the Covenanters received their death-
wound in the sharp, short struggle under Loudoun Hill.
Among them was William Daniel, one of those unappeasable
men who, a month before, had helped in the slaughter of the
Archbishop.   He lived for twenty-four hours after the battle,
and "was in a rapture of joy all that day."   Before the fight
began, he had "freely offered himself in prayer to seal the
truth, but especially the controverted truth, with his blood;

and, after prayer, he was made to praise in the time of action."
As fast as he could himself return from pursuing the enemy,
James Russel hurried back to him, where he lay on the
margin of those waters which are " to the palate bitter and to
the stomach cold." " Dear brother Will," he asked, " ye have
many times told me ye was sure enough of heaven ; have ye
any doubts now ? " The dying man could scarcely speak ; in
a whisper he replied, " No doubts, but fully assured—fully
assured ! " We think of the French enthusiast who, on the
very edge of shameful death, declared that his soul was " a
garden, full of shelter and of fountains." He and his brother
of Magus Moor and Drumclog did unwarrantable things ; but
who will deny that they knew the secret of the Lord ?

CHAPTER XXIII.

GLOOM AFTER GLEAM.

IN *The Grammar of Assent*, Newman, speaking of the magic of Virgil's style, refers to "his pathetic half-lines," which give expression to that sense of pain and weariness experienced by men in every age and land. *O passi graviora—; Dis aliter visum—; Di, si qua est cœlo pietas—; Heu vatum ignarœ mentes—:* in such broken utterances, charged with emotion through their brevity, the great Mantuan shows how clearly he perceived, and how profoundly he felt, the burdens and mysteries and toils of our human life. It is as if he could not enlarge on the theme, nor unfold more leisurely the thoughts which arise in him. He is choked by an intensity of sorrow, and is compelled to stop midway.

There are pathetic half-lines in history as well as in literature. A career from which we hoped much is suddenly checked; its passion leaves the ground to lose itself in the sky; and, although the music may be God's more unreservedly than before, the conviction of loss, and the disappointment which the conviction brings, abide with us. Or a movement, after momentary success, is overtaken by catastrophe. We were interested in its prosperity. We pictured it going from strength to strength. But *noctes atque dies patet atri janua Ditis*, and the eclipse comes, and at noon the sun goes down. There are tears in our souls for the shattered hope, and the irretrievable blow, and the enterprise snapped and left in ruins.

After the Sabbath-day on which they sent Claverhouse flying at Drumclog, the Covenanters knew that they must hold

302

together, because their enemies would muster soon to punish them. They grew rapidly in numbers; for there is a contagion in victory. Within three weeks the two hundred and fifty had multiplied into a legion of between five and six thousand, an army with which memorable feats might easily have been accomplished. Probably the ultimate issues of the campaign were never in doubt; the soldiers of the Kirk could not vanquish the overwhelming forces which the King was able to send against them. But, for months, they might have maintained a guerilla war, and, in the end, have extorted from their persecutors terms which were not unfavourable. The radiance which broke over them at Loudoun Hill, like a gleam of light bursting through a bank of cloud, might have increased until the cloud was dispelled. They were themselves to blame that the result was mournfully different. Their foes on this occasion were not Charles Stuart, and the Duke of Lauderdale, and General Dalzell, and John Graham; they were the men of their own household.

The little band of fighters had pursued their adversaries till they were within sight of the gates of Glasgow, and then, calling a halt, had returned to the friends whom they left at Drumclog. They had allies within the walls; and, if they could have effected an entrance, the likelihood is that Claverhouse must have prolonged his flight towards Edinburgh and the east. But they were few, and worn with the battle and the chase; and the King had a considerable garrison in the town. So they withdrew for the meantime; and yet they came back soon: Glasgow was a prize worth making an effort to win. In anticipation of their decision Lord Ross hurriedly threw up barricades in the four principal streets, and stationed his musketeers at certain coigns of vantage, bidding them watch for the approach of the enemy. It was still early on the morning of Monday when the Covenanters appeared; they had not allowed the grass to grow beneath their feet. They broke into two parties, one going towards the Gallowgate, the other towards the High Kirk and the College. But their assault was badly managed and futile. From behind the barricades the guns of the Royal troops flashed out flame and death. At least seven were killed, and their comrades were compelled to beat a retreat. "Thes wes the warmest day I saw the yeare," Ross reported in a message written the same evening to his superior, the Earl of Linlithgow. Tuesday, Wednesday, and Thursday were spent by the Whigs in marchings to and fro; they encamped now in one place and now in another. But in this interval the men who had repulsed them were ordered by the somewhat bewildered and inconclusive Linlithgow, who had led his army from Edinburgh to the west but shrank from the risk of striking a blow, to leave their quarters within the gates and to join his regiments outside. The Covenanters were quickly apprised of this change in the tactics of their foe, and, having sent a search party in advance of their main body to reconnoitre and bring them tidings of how the land lay, they marched again to Glasgow, and stationed themselves in and around the place: it was in their hands now. This was on Friday, the 6th of June; and the midsummer sun seemed for a little to be shining at its brightest on their desperate cause. For, ever since their success on the Sabbath, they had been gathering new recruits. From Ayrshire, from Renfrew, from Lanark, from Stirling in the north and Galloway in the south, companions hastened to join them. Already they were so formidable, that the rebellion began to trouble the authorities not only in Holyrood but in Whitehall. But they kept Sir Robert Hamilton in the chief command—Sir Robert Hamilton of Preston and Fingalton, a young man whose thirtieth birthday was still in front of him. Gilbert Burnet, when he was Professor of Divinity in Glasgow, had been his tutor, and understood him well. He was not without his "lively and hopeful" traits, the Professor said, but his fondness for dissent in its most intransigent varieties would soon, he predicted, turn him into "a crackbrained enthusiast." Events were to prove the correctness of the forecast. In the fact of his presidency lay the presage of calamity and gloom for the soldiers whom Hamilton captained and irritated and devoted to destruction.

It is time that we studied the spiritual features of this man. The witnesses to the reality and depth of his personal

THE KIRK OF IRONGRAY.

Christianity are many and trustworthy. Plainly, One was his Master, even Christ. He gives himself an involuntary testimony to his citizenship in the Heavenlies, in those private letters of consolation that he wrote to friends in trouble. They tell us, as Mr. Hill Burton says, that he "had his tendernesses," and that these were "peculiarly rich and overflowing." But he had his narrownesses and antipathies as well, and they travelled beyond the boundaries both of charity and of reason. He could not brook the presence of any one, who failed to see each of the many facets of truth from the same angle as himself. He was willing to suffer rather than swerve from this morbid conscientiousness. At a later period, he would not return from exile in Holland to take possession of his estate of Preston, simply because he could swear no oath of loyalty to William and Mary. Thus his scrupulosity inflicted injury on himself. But it was more mournful that an exclusiveness so rigid did infinite harm to others, and wrecked the army of the Covenant.

The Indulgence was the trouble. Sir Robert Hamilton, purist as he was, abhorred it and its authors and the consequences it had brought about. But, if this had been all, nobody among the six thousand Covenanters would have quarrelled with him. He pushed his contention to extremer lengths. Not only did he refuse to hold intercourse with the ministers who had gone back to their parishes, and with the congregations tolerant enough to hearken to them, but he shut out from his fellowship those who, while themselves disapproving of the Indulgence, were not prepared to ostracise the weaker brethren to whom it had seemed a boon. He insisted that these mediating and forgiving souls were guilty of laxity and sin. God, he held and proclaimed, could never give His benediction to a fighting force, which embraced within its ranks men who would deal gently with unfaithfulness, and would eat and drink with traitors. They must be clean who carried His vessels and wrestled for His truth. Such was Hamilton's untenable creed. For its justification, he would point back to the example of the Protesters in denouncing the Public Resolutions. But he went far beyond Rutherfurd

and Guthrie. It was against the participation in the work
of the Lord of actual Malignants, King's votaries without
admixture, that the Protesters lifted their voices; they said
no word against bearing and forbearing with brothers who
fell short of their own standard. It is difficult to imagine
that they would have commended a strictness to which theirs
was as moonlight unto sunlight.

Sir Robert Hamilton was head and chief of this old Hard
Church, if one may borrow Mr. R. H. Hutton's pregnant
phrase: the Hard Church, which "believes in a Hard Master,"
which "thinks that it is not the endurance, but the infliction
of hardness that makes a true soldier of Christ," which walks
about like "a theological detective, without any care or compassion for the sins of the defaulters it arrests." Yet there
were other leaders whose opinions agreed with his. Hackston
and Henry Hall and William Cleland, Thomas Douglas the
preacher too, were, almost but not altogether, of one mind with
their unbending captain. Perhaps Major Learmont and John
Paton of Meadowhead, those stout soldiers who had fought
with such spirit at Pentland, leaned to the same drastic side;
but, if they did—and there is doubt about the former—they
were not loud-tongued and insistent in promulgating their
tenets. And there were good men, ready to contend to the
death for Christ's Crown and Covenant, whose sympathies
were wider. There was James Ure of Shargarton, for instance,
a gentleman of Perthshire, who, prompted by deep conviction,
had left Episcopacy for Presbytery, and who now brought to
the aid of the blue banner a troop of volunteers from the
northern counties. And there was John Welsh, our brave
field-preacher, who came from Dumfriesshire to the camp.
He had never tampered with the Indulgence. Dear as were
the memories of the kirk of Irongray, he would not wound
conscience by re-entering it through the favour and patronage
of Government. But yet he could not find it in his heart to
excommunicate those who were not so stalwart as he was
himself; he would not say that they had erred unpardonably
when they returned to the pulpits for which they felt an
ineradicable affection. Because these were the thoughts he

cherished and avowed, Sir Robert Hamilton and his disciples
were angry with John Welsh, and would have sent him away.
Like Tertullian and the Montanists, they would have no
association, however indirect, with heresy and lapse and
compromise.

For weeks the wretched debate went on between men who
should have been of one spirit and one step. Every new
band of helpers, as it arrived, was compelled to declare itself
for the party of rigour or for that of comprehension; there
was no neutral zone, no golden mean, no permission to see
the truth on both sides. The army determined, at one stage,
to draw up a manifesto—a "Declaration" was the word of the
time. But over this the leaders quarrelled: Hamilton and
his intimates demanding that the document should contain a
definite repudiation of the Indulgence; the others answering
that "neither were we a Parliament nor a General Assembly"
to judge such matters, and that, "if we meddled with them,
it would hinder many to come who would be as willing as we,
and would make friends to become enemies." There were
moments when the strife grew acrimonious, and hot words
were spoken. "We told them," says James Ure in his
narrative, "they were more taken up with other men's sins
than they were with their own, and that it was our duty first
to begin with ourselves." Again, on Sabbath the 15th, when
on Hamilton Moor the ministers were about to preach to the
soldiers, and when Sir Robert required that in the sermons
the Indulgence should be condemned with no bated breath,
"we told them that it was the height of supremacy to give
instructions to ministers what to preach; we would hear no
such doctrine." More than once the moderate men were on
the eve of leaving; it needed John Welsh's eloquence and
the near approach of the common enemy to prevent them
from departing in heartache and despair. "For aught that
we saw," they complained, "we were come here to fight
among ourselves." What a sorrow's crown of sorrow it is!

And, all the while, their doom drew closer to them. From
London a large force had been despatched; and, when this was
added to the Scottish contingents, the Royalists numbered

about fifteen thousand horse and foot. The young Duke of Monmouth, Charles's son and, meantime at least, Charles's favourite, had the principal command. He was popular for his good looks, his courtesy, his Protestantism, although the Protestantism was neither very intelligent nor very ardent. He was disposed, too, to lenient courses; it was an encouraging omen for the Covenanters that he received the first place, and that Dalzell had to be content with standing second. Many of them were inclined to negotiate with Monmouth; and, though the extremists resisted the proposal, the moderate men managed to carry their point. Another Sabbath had come round, the third since Drumclog. Soon after daybreak two envoys went to interview the Duke—David Hume and a Galloway landlord named Murdoch. He gave them a not unkindly welcome, and listened while they read the Declaration of some days before. Then he answered that their petition ought to have been worded in humbler terms, but that, if they were willing to lay down their arms, he had no intention to deal harshly. They returned to their comrades, to report how they had fared. But the proviso about disarming was a fatal obstacle. Sir Robert Hamilton laughed loudly when he heard it. "Yes, and hang next!" he said. Manifestly the strife must be fought out to the end. Yet there was another pause before the artillery began to play. Hume and his friend had something more to ask, and Major Maine went over from the King's lines to ascertain what it was. Had not Monmouth brought with him, they inquired, "terms of accommodation from England"? and would he acquaint them with their purport? But these were questions to which the General was not prepared to give any reply. The parleyings were over, and the time for decisive action had arrived.

The combatants confronted each other on opposite banks of the Clyde. Between them was the old and steep and narrow Bridge of Bothwell, not more than twelve feet wide, and guarded in the centre with a gatehouse. The King's army was much the larger. It was well officered. The Duke of Montrose led the cavalry, the Earl of Linlithgow the infantry. Claverhouse rode at the head of his dragoons, and the Earls

of Home and Airlie were in charge of their respective troops;
Lord Mar held a command of foot. Dalzell's commission,
much to his annoyance, was late in arriving from London;
and he did not get to the scene of action until everything was
over. That the Covenanters should succeed in beating back
opponents so disciplined and so superior in strength was
improbable; but history records exploits more arduous. The
advantages of position were with the Presbyterians. If they
could only have abandoned their controversies, and gone to
work singing the Drumclog Psalm, a new victory might have
been theirs. But at Bothwell they were without unity, without buoyancy, without competent generalship. Let us listen
again to James Ure: "We were not concerned with an enemy,
as if there had not been one within a thousand miles of us.
There were none went through the army, to see if we wanted
powder and ball. I do really think there were few or none
that had both powder and ball, to shoot twice." From such
infatuation nothing could result but defeat. The Covenanters
had predestined themselves to failure and shame.

There were some who did their best. Ure was one, and
Henry Hall was another; but the honours of the lamentable
day are with David Hackston of Rathillet. For hours, with
three hundred men of Galloway to aid him, the genuine and
great-hearted soldier held the bridge. After awhile, the
three hundred, wearied with their vigil and struggle, begged,
not to be withdrawn, but to have reinforcements from the
larger mass behind them; but no reinforcements were sent.
Then they asked for ammunition, and were told that the
ammunition was at an end. At last Hamilton gave them
the order to fall back upon the main body. They obeyed
"with sore hearts," as Hackston writes; for they felt that the
order was the last folly of this black and bitter Sabbath, and
that now their fate was sealed. The barrier which hitherto
had hindered its advance having been removed, the Royal
artillery slowly and steadily crossed the Clyde; and soon,
from the same bank as that on which they stood themselves,
the Duke's cannon poured death into the lines of the Whigs.
Even yet the Royalist triumph might have been postponed.

But a panic seized the Covenanters. Numbers of them fled recklessly and at random. Only Rathillet and his companions maintained their ground, until they too, seeing that all was over, retired from the moor in sullen silence. The rout was complete. By ten o'clock in the morning, every hope was extinguished; and from the King's side a messenger took horse for Edinburgh, bearing news of the victory. "Never," Wodrow moralises, "was a good cause and a gallant army, generally speaking hearty and bold, worse managed; and never will a cause, though never so good, be better managed when divisions, dis- jointings, and self creep in among the managers."

No fewer than four hundred perished in the death-chase; some accounts, indeed, would double that number. Twelve hundred were taken prisoners; and very many of these would have been massacred in cold blood, if Monmouth had not interposed. He declared emphatically that they must be spared, and he refused to modify his injunction, although Dalzell, hurrying to Bothwell Brig some hours too late for the battle, rated him soundly for it. We may doubt, however, whether the captives did not suffer worse pains than their brothers emancipated by the swift anguish of death. Bound two and two, they were dragged eastward to Edinburgh. No one on the wearisome road dared extend to them a hand of succour. When the capital was reached, the mob greeted them with the taunt, "Where's your God? where's your God?"—the glib interrogation of that shallow atheism which has no hardihood of faith to penetrate into *the thick darkness where God is*. Two of the ministers, adherents of Welsh rather than of Robert Hamilton, were executed at the Mercat Cross: John Kid one of them, and the other John King—the same John King whom Claverhouse had captured immediately before Drumclog, and who had enjoyed three weeks of liberty only to fall again into the enemy's clutches. Five Covenanters were hanged on Magus Moor, though not one of them had a personal share in the death of the Archbishop. As the Edin- burgh gaols could not hold the crowd of other prisoners, a part of Greyfriars churchyard was transmuted into a place of confinement; and into it they were penned like sheep.

Sentinels guarded them day and night. They were exposed to sun and rain, wind and weather; for there was no covering above their heads—none at least until, with the approach of winter, some wooden huts were erected, " which was mightily boasted as a great favour." Their bed was the bare ground. They were poorly fed, and it was next to impossible for friends to convey any comfort to them. In this plight they lived, like Samson in Gaza, " a life half dead, a living death, and buried," until the dreary weeks of November. A few hundreds had been freed on giving their pledge to desist in the future from armed resistance ; here and there one, more fortunate than his comrades, had gained the goodwill of his gaolers; some had contrived to escape across the churchyard walls; some were dead. Only two hundred and fifty-seven remained out of the twelve hundred.

For these two hundred and fifty-seven, new distresses and ignominies were kept. Early one November morning, they were marched by a party of soldiers from the Greyfriars to a vessel, the *Crown*, lying in Leith Roads ; the Privy Council had decreed that they should be banished to the West Indies, and sold for slaves. On board the ship their pains came to a climax. They were crowded under deck in a space not sufficient to hold one hundred people. Those with some health were forced to continue standing, that the sick and dying might lie down on the hard boards. Hour after hour, in the poisonous air, many fainted away. Their meat was stinted, and water was doled out with a niggardly hand. "All the troubles we met since Bothwell," one of them, James Corson, wrote to his wife, " were not to be compared to one day in our present circumstances. Our uneasiness is beyond words. Yet the consolations of God overbalance all; and I hope we are near our port, and heaven is open for us."

Most of them were nearer their port than they surmised, and that port the best; their sails " were set to reach Jerusalem." Off the coast of Orkney, in a night of tempest, the captain ran his vessel close inshore and cast anchor, locking and chaining the hatches over the prisoners in the hold. In the darkness, at ten o'clock, the ship was dashed against the rocks, and was broken in two. The sailors made a bridge of the mast and escaped to the rough beach; nearly sixty of the Covenanters were able, in one way or in another, to follow their example. But the other two hundred were drowned, only a few of their bodies being washed to the land, to be buried at a place called Scarvating, where one may see the graves to-day. Was it a pitiful death? Was it not a happy enfranchisement? As once before in a night of storm, Jesus went unto them, walking on the sea, and saying, *It is I; be not afraid.*

AT DEERNESS, ORKNEY.
THE MONUMENT TO THE COVENANTERS DROWNED IN
THE *CROWN*.

CHAPTER XXIV.

A TEMPORARY.

A TEMPORARY—one who tries year in and year out to "carry his dish level," and adjusts his sails to catch the changing winds, and on his own confession feels much "fear of exposing himself to suffering": such was Alexander Brodie of Brodie, the representative in Covenanting times of an old Scottish family, with properties lying in the northern shires of Moray and Nairn. A Temporary, whose reservations and compliances and abatements are written with painful clearness in his voluminous Diary; but yet, at heart, a man of conscience and of true and warm religion. When he died, in the April of 1680, his son bore touching testimony to his worth. "I have had the benefit of instruction, warning, means of knowledge." "I have seen the godlie conversation, holy and Christian walk of a father—his watchfulnes, fruitfulnes, his secret communion with God." "Alas! what an emptie roum and place will all men find heir!" "This day"—it was the 22nd of April—"my wyffe and Alexander Finlater and I put the bodie of my dear Father in his cerecloth, and caus anoint with oyls and pouders and spices. The bodie was the cask which keipd a nobl jewal." But, when we read the self-accusing Diary, how earnestly we wish that this "gentleman of shining piety" had been less timorous, more independent, caring only for the approval of God, and paying smaller heed to the favour and the censure of men! Alexander Brodie stands inside the spiritual realm; there is not a doubt of his faith and hope and love; but mountains and seas separate him from those more immovable kinsfolk of his in the Kirk, of whom it could be said, as the soldiers in Scarborough said of George Fox, that they were " as stiff as a tree and as pure as a bell."

He was a man of much repute. Born in 1617, and by and by a student in the King's College of Aberdeen, he entered on the possession of his ancestral lands as soon as he came of age, for his father had died when he was himself a boy in his sixteenth year. In 1643, he was chosen to represent the county of Elgin in the Scottish Parliament; and, season after season, he went up as ruling elder to the General Assembly. In 1649, ànd again in 1650, he was one of the little band of Commissioners sent across the water to Holland, to treat with Charles the Second. Twice over, in 1649 and once more in 1658, he took his seat on the bench of the Court of Session, and was greeted everywhere as Lord Brodie ; although, on the latter occasion, the office was accepted " after much Resistance and Reluctance." Indeed, he was afraid of such lofty employments, for he was " naturally a venturous undertaking creature," and he dreaded the harm which ambition and presumption might inflict on his inner life. Once, when he " got Oliver Cromwell's letter, or rather a citation and summons to come to London," his soul cried out in alarm, " O Lord ! I have met with the lion and the bear before ; but this is the Goliath—the strongest and greatest temptation is last." But altogether, even if he liked best to live quietly in his northern home, riding out daily through his ample fields, and adding acre after acre to the family inheritance, Brodie of Brodie was a conspicuous figure in his stormy and perplexing time.

A figure too, in very many of its characteristics, not conspicuous merely, but admirable. In the portrait which he paints for us of himself, we read, for one thing, of the depth and permanence of his affections. A crushing sorrow fell on him in his opening manhood. When he was twenty-three, his young wife, Elizabeth Innes, the granddaughter of " the bonny Earl of Moray," was snatched from him by death, after they had enjoyed but five summers of unalloyed happiness together. " I asked at the Lord iff He could strick anie mor," he wrote, fifteen years after the blow had descended; "for I did not esteem anie thing behind." And on a much later day, he draws on the margin of the Diary an admonitory finger pointing significantly to one of the entries, and it moves us greatly to encounter a fresh record of the heartbreak which is both old and new: "August 12, 1673.—This day 33 years my beloved wife was removed from me by death. I desir to be humbld under the Lord's hand, and to acknowledg His holines and justice." Alexander Brodie did not marry a second time; he reverenced one woman supremely, and was faithful to her while life lasted. And in this he is a kind of far-off relation of Raphael, leaving his pictures to make a century of sonnets for the peerless lady of his choice, and of Dante, forsaking his poetry to paint an angel for Beatrice: each mastered by the longing,

> Once, and only once, and for one only,
> (Ah, the prize!) to find his love a language
> Fit and fair and simple and sufficient.

Then, also, we mark with pleasure how open-eyed and wakeful the intellect was which the Morayshire laird carried about with him. He went to London in the summer of the Restoration; and everything interested him. "I saw a mighti citi, numerous, manie souls in it, great plentis of all things, and thoght him a great king that had soe manie at command; yet how much greater is He that has all the cities of the world, persons, nations, things created in erth and heauen!" In the gardens beyond Bishopsgate he marvelled at the variety of trees and plants and flowers, and was "apt to be inordinat about thes earthli delights." Towards the end of October he was a witness of "the Lord Maior of London his solemnities," and was amazed by "the witt and invention of men," and, still more, by the strangeness of "the Lord's creatures on other parts of this earth," for some quaint and portentous monsters had had a place in the show. Ten days later he dined at Billingsgate, and inspected "the prison of the King's Bench in Southrick, and the workers of glass; in all which I saw the manifold wisdom of

God in the gifts and faculties which He has given to men."
He missed nothing. And there was no necessity for him to
make his pilgrimage to London, that he might know himself
the denizen of a significant and surprising realm. The fields
round his house at Brodie were filled both with astonishments
and with admonitions. On a May day in 1656, George
Stewart came to him, "and we traveld throgh the wood of
Darnaway. We saw and kild an adder; wherein I saw, as
the Lord's providenc, so my natur; how lyk was I to that
beast that was ful of poison, and ther teeth did cutt unto
death. I considerd ther cace in the wildernes that wer
stung, and adord the Lord for the brazen serpent. Lord
Jesus! then said I, Thou art that serpent: I desir to look
to Thee and be heald." Later in the same summer, his eyes
and his heart were arrested by the leaves of the holly tree,
and he thought that their bright and glittering lustre
represented the beauty of the world: "green was it, but
full of pricks, and hurt them that did cleave most to it.
O then!"—he cried, as conscience spoke to him of his own
feeblenesses and perils—"guard my hart against this." The
landscape round him was all symbolic and mystical; the
acacia-bush was aflame with the presence of God. Two
centuries subsequently, John Ker, writing of Thomas Guthrie
in his Highland home at Lochlee, had a similar story to
tell : "A splintered rock, with an adder he had seen lurking
below it, became the emblem of man's ruined nature, with
the poison and the sting beneath. A single tree that crowns
the top of a crag, amid the wreck of a fallen mountain,
shows where grace can rear its trophies. The reeds by the
lochside bending to the sudden breeze call up the stir of
the heart under the Spirit's breath. The wild ducks starting
from the rushing covert, and in a moment out of reach, are
the riches that fly away on wings. The walls of a forsaken
shieling at the foot of Craig Maskeldie give a glimpse of
patriarchal life gone by, and take up the lament for the
exile. The little ruined church seen at the lower end of
the lake is a symbol of the deserted shrine of the soul, on
which 'Ichabod' may be written." Two worlds belonged to

Thomas Guthrie, and to Alexander Brodie before him; and for both of them nature was impregnated with spiritual meanings and lessons.

He was a book-lover, too; and he counted no product of brain and imagination foreign territory. Now we catch him reading "something of the romance of Cassandra," and bewailing the fact that his affections were wrought on more by these fictions than by the truth. Again, he is deep in "the Turk's Alcoran," but finds nothing in its pages to stagger him or to seduce. Or he is exceedingly desirous to buy an Atlas; but he dreads lest he should trespass—cautious Scot as he is—by extravagant and unnecessary expense, or by an undue contentment and comfort in the use of the creatures. He draws out a list of the books he has purchased during his sojourn in the capital in 1660 and 1661. There is a Bible in quarto. There are "Sir Walter Raleigh," and "Alex. Ross his Continuation," and "Heylyn's Geographie." There are Tacitus, and Lucan, and Dionysius of Halicarnassus, and Thucydides, and Livy, and Polybius. He was often distressed in mind, because in his studies he was so strongly tempted to travel far afield, leaving the sacred hill of Zion out of sight, and forgetting the themes which are of supremest moment. "I am feard," he confesses, "that the pleasur of profane Histori should expel the loue of Scriptur and that which is diuin. I besoght the Lord against this snare." Ten days afterwards the hazard has recurred: "I found my inordinatnes in reading Lucan." Within a fortnight he is chastising himself anew for yielding to the fascinating and entangling delight: "I boght som histori books, but nothing of diuinitie. This feard me that I was withering, and I desird to search. Oh! the studi and knouledg of the one thing necessar, and the use of al means to that end, is that which should be cheife." But just as he found sermons in stones, and in all the voices and happenings of the natural world, so he could take no excursion up the slopes and through the fields of literature without gleaning some spiritual harvest. Through a long and dark November evening, he reads "Charles 5th, his laying down the imperial croun, and taking him to a cloister or monasteri in Castil, near Placentia. He caused celebrat his funeral befor himself ere he died. This did affoord me matter of exercise." Few men in the Scotland of his day were better informed than Brodie of Brodie.

A profounder trait still, and a more spiritual, was his anxiety about the godliness of the home. When his wife went from him, he was left with two little children, James and Grissel. Year after year he observed their growth, omitting no means of grace, catechising, reproving, encouraging, taking care that his bairns made their personal covenants with God, directing them habitually to the hill and house of holiness. On many a Sabbath evening, he would call for his son, and "exhort and admonish him to self-trial, and to more exactness, sincerity, and watchfulness over his heart and thoughts." Or it was the daughter, who, after sad and grave warning, would dedicate herself to Christ in a new engagement after this sort : " This night my Father carried me before God for my forgetting the former resolutions which I made lately. I did confess and take with my hainous guiltiness, and promised yet again to bewail it and mourn for it ; and I will beseech the Lord not to forsake me, but to forgive and heal for His Own name's sake." Afterwards, when they married, and boys and girls of theirs began to gather round his knees, he was as concerned for the piety of the new generation. Only nine months before the close of his life, we meet this sentence in the Diary : " I did speak to Ann, Cath., and Elz., my poor grandchildren, and asked if they were content to enter in covenant with Him, and they consented, and gave themselves to the Lord to be His for ever, and tuk on His bands." Alexander Brodie had no wish to pass empty-handed to the Sacred Presence and the Gracious Face ; he would fain lead others along with him to the splendid goal.

Yet, with so many laudable features of mind and heart, he was a Temporary. It was not that he cherished a scintilla of doubt as to which was the cause of righteousness. It was not that, by conviction and preference, he was a trimmer, determined to remain lukewarm in so brisk and peremptory a world, where almost everybody was vociferously supporting one side of each question. An American essayist describes a students' society at Harvard which was intended to represent the tepid and neutral spirit of Laodicea—a spirit which the members esteemed no peril to be shunned, but a *summum bonum* to be sought and won. Moral heat or moral cold in any applicant was a reason for his rejection. The word "But" was suggested as a motto, because it contains a subtle hint that something can always be said from the opposite point of view. Lord Brodie never could have belonged to the ranks of this society. His soul had its ascertained and definite beliefs, and they led him to sympathise with the stricter Covenanters. But the sympathy was sedulously repressed, and held in check with constant vigilance, and kept in the cellar instead of being set on the housetop. It was a whisper rather than a flag. He was afraid to avow it. His name was Mistrust, and not Proteus or Janus. He refused to put out on the vast seas, where the risks of sinking are great, even if there are the Happy Isles to be reached. His faint and nervous temper led him to hug the shore and to engage in a timid coasting trade. He compromised his own ideals, and was content with what he knew to be the second-best.

One learns where his real predilections lay from many of his confessions, and, not least, from what he narrates about Robert Leighton. The two were fast friends; and we think the better of the laird because of his love for the saintly theologian. But, when Leighton proposed to conform to Episcopacy, nobody grieved more than the northern squire. "Mr. Lighton din'd with me," he notes on the 25th of October 1661. "I perceaved he was not averss from taking on him to be a Bishop; all was clear to him; civil places free from censurs; he approv'd the orgains, antheams, musick in ther worship. He said the greatest error among papists was ther persecution and want of charitie to us. His intention was to doe good in that place, and not for ambition. He was against defensive arms : men in poprie holding all ther tenets might be sav'd. He had no scruple in anie thing which they did, repeating oft this word, Religion did not consist in thes external things, but in righteousness, peace, and joy. I pray'd for him, as for myself, and was feard that his charitie misguided might be a snare to him." A month afterwards, when the consecration of the four Bishops was not far off, he had another meeting with the good man. "Anent his undertaking I did express myself freelie to him. He shewd that he retaind the same tendernes and bowels to thes that feard God. I desird him to use his libertie not to stumble but to edifie others. He said, he thoght he was bound to use his libertie to the utmost; and, if he did forbear to use his libertie in things quherein he had freedom, he thoght he sinn'd. I exhorted him to guard against Poprie. He said, he had not anie thing he mor desird than that they might have libertie also, and not for ther consciences to be prest; he would indulge them, and Anabaptists, and Quakers: he lykd the Liturgie and som of thes things best. Thes opinions wer dangerous. I besoght him to watch, and prayd the Lord for him. I desird him to use his credit that the Ceremonies might not be broght in upon us. He said, he wishd soe; but he hop'd they should be prest on none. Alace! efter introducing, force will soon ensew. But he does not perceave or suspect it." Here is the scrupulous Presbyter face to face with the apostle of sweetness and light, the advocate of breadth and comprehension. He is eager to save him from the coils of fatal concession. He sees the serpents which are sure to sting and kill, if once the protective hedges are broken down. He urges his friend to pause, ere he has committed himself and the mischief is beyond repair. Leighton had not travelled far on the new road, before he discovered that Brodie's prevision was not wholly at fault. "I spoke with B. Dumblain," the record runs on the 27th of January 1662. "He told me he feard he shold be disappointed in them he was to be joind with; and he exprest his desir and purpos to know and doe the will of God. O, let the Lord grant him and me also this mercie!" These are colloquies out of which the Covenanter comes a victor; he seems to have chosen the breezier uplands and the better road.

Ah, but has he? We are compelled to doubt it soon;

THOMAS DALZELL.

From a Contemporary Print.
Through the kindness of Messrs. T. C. & E. C. Jack.

and, long before we reach the latest entry in the Diary, our
verdict is reversed, and eulogy is exchanged for lament. So
soon as King Charles's policy had revealed its bitter issues for
the men of the Covenant, Lord Brodie toned down the vivid
blue of his banner into a more indeterminate tint. The fear
of man held him in constant vacillation and trouble of mind.
He would not risk his position, he would not forfeit a farm or
a field, in defence of his beliefs; "the trash and hagg," as in a
moment of candour he designates his goods and gear, were too
priceless to lose for the sake of intangible truth. The narrative
becomes pitiful in the extreme. "O my dulnes, blindnes,
barrennes, fleshlines!" the surgeon sobbed, as he thrust the
scalpel into his own flesh; but, in spite of his self-knowledge,
there was no attempt to heal his wounds—he hated his
unworthinesses, and he clung to them. Even while he expostulated with Leighton, he was perjuring himself to win the
grace of a meaner man. "Dr. Sharp din'd with me. I movd
to him to speak to the King, and to my Lord Rothes, for me
and my freinds. Let not his favour be a snare to me; for his
principls are full of danger; neither let anie stumble at it."
And, again: "I did purpos not to mak mickle use of Mr. Ja.
Sharp; albeit I thoght I might doe it lawfulie, and, through
the grace of God asisting, not sin or necessarlie fal in anie
snare. But I perceave ther is small tendernes in me. O help,
Lord, quhen tendernes fail!" And, more noteworthy still: "I
call'd Sharp Lord. I desir to examin if I sin'd in it." Dr.
Mozley writes of the New Testament Pharisee that he
succeeded in "taming and domesticating" his conscience, in
vulgarising and humiliating and chaining it; and it was what
Alexander Brodie had set himself to do. But, when Mozley
adds that the Pharisee contrived in the end to make conscience
"a manageable and applauding companion," we feel that the
Covenanter is no longer in alliance with him. The Lord of
Session might rein in his convictions, so that they had no
liberty; but they kept him always in turmoil of spirit. He
was for ever labouring in the deep mid-ocean, for ever climbing
up the climbing wave.

For things did not mend as years went on. He was well

aware that, if he followed the inner light, he must listen to the field-preachers; but it was as manifest that, if he consulted his interest, he must attend the parish church, and hearken to the curate whose "dead ministrie" he deplored and despised. He selected the ignobler course; and thus the Sabbath, the *Dies Dominica* of the Diary, instead of being a delight and honourable, brought him nothing else than self-accusation and pain. Sometimes, to extricate himself from his spiritual toils, he remained in his own room; and there are frequently recurring admissions after the fashion of this: "Decr. 24.—Die Dom. I staid at hom becaus of the tym, and the observation, and the danger of the Earle of Murray." The unhappy tenant of the Debateable Land was tossed from difficulty to difficulty, from the swords of the Douglas to the arrows of the Percy. He is told about some poor men who are fined at Inverness, for not hearing the present ministers; and "whatever be ther errour or darknes," he owns that "they hav mor affection, simplicitie, and honestie than I." Or the curate complains to him of those who are disconform, and alleges that they have the doctrine and ways of the Donatists and Cathari; but "I did deny this, and said that they had nothing common with them, but wer sound and orthodox, excep in the maiter of government"; and then, carrying the war into the enemy's country, "I said, I feard manie preachd for love of ther stipends, and could be content to quit preaching so that they had ther livlihood." The leaders in the north of the more unswerving party, James Fraser of Brea and Thomas Hog of Kiltearn, were now and then in Brodie's society; and they did not fail to reprove his tergiversations and excuses. "He had an argument"—Thomas Hog is the logician— "That they who want the qualifications which by Christ's institution should be in a minister, they are noe ministers. I scrupld at this, and broght the example of Judas. I said, A man might be a calld lawful minister in some respects, and yet want these qualifications of grace that's needful. He said, That I could be a curat or anie thing." Indeed, there was cause for the anger of the preacher who was "steel-true and blade-straight"; but the other who felt its edge did not like it. "My woful heart kindl'd "—this was on a subsequent day —"and I said I did noe less dislyk his severitie in censuring the condition and estate of others, and that he took the keys, and judgd rashlie and rigidlie, and that I could not embrace the opinion becaus Mr. Tho. Hog said it, and if he stumbld at me, he might forbear me." The reader becomes more and more sorry for a man whose faith and love journey one road, and his advantages and gains precisely the opposite ; and who prefers the easier going in Bypath Meadow, even when he knows that he should be out on the King's Highway.

But at times sorrow deepens into indignation. From the northern districts some troops of militia were summoned to contend against the Whigs at Bothwell Bridge. We could not have dreamed that Alexander Brodie, himself a Covenanter, would contribute his band of retainers to fight those with whom he was in sympathy. But he did. There was, of course, the customary inward debate, the swaying back and forward of the reed shaken with the wind. "This morning I had wrestlings" whether "I should go against these in the west." And then the turns of the mental discussion are recounted: "1. I did not allow their rising. 2. There is mickle rashnes. 3. They seim not to have a call to it. 4. They have no rational grounds to expect that they can prevail against these that ar against them, being the armies of three Kingdoms. Yet it is not the question, is it safest ? but, is it most acceptable to God, will it get approbation, and hav peace ? On the one hand, I sie if I draw back there is unavoidable danger of destruction to me, my poor children, and familie. On the other hand, I have onlie to ponder what God utters, and, being clear in that, to take Him for all, and cast dangers, fears, power, malice, lust of men, upon His all-sufficiencie, truth, providence, wisdom, sovereigntie, power." But he shut his eyes to these legions of angels, and again he was compliant and timeserving, although with not a whit more of satisfaction to himself. "June 21, 1679.—I reflected on my putting out the foot, and promoving and strengthening ther hands that were goeing against the handful, and was shaken, and doubted if

God did allow." Three months later, when all was over with
"the handful," peace had not returned to him. "Septr. 4.—
The last night I was exercis'd much with greif and had
chalendg for asisting the levies." And, again: "Septr. 20.—
I found great disorder in my heart, brain, mind, and temper,
apprehensions and imaginations disquieting me." The Diary
supplies us with an object-lesson of the remediless misery
that keeps gnawing, with eagle's beak and talons, at the
vitals of the man who sins against his own soul.

To the last the wavering and irresolute heart was without
the sunshine which rewards a stouter trust. Two days before
he escaped from his "confusions and heaviness," this was his
cry, "Quhen will mercie find a way to overtake a poor
rebell?" Yet, when the end was but three or four hours
distant, his son testifies that he had "some blink of reviving,"
and that those round his bed heard from his lips "sweit,
savorie, seasonable words." One is glad that there was a
beam of light in the evening of that cloudy day. "Above
all, believe it," said Lord Bacon, "the sweetest canticle is
Nunc Dimittis"; and Alexander Brodie could have confirmed
the truth.

His autobiography, with its introspections and self-
scourgings, is a human document, in which perhaps some of
us may find delineated our own frailty and unfaithfulness.
But it has its value, too, because it emphasises a contrast.
We lift our thoughts from it to the life-histories of the men
and women who stood unshaken, unseduced, unterrified; and
we understand, more clearly than ever, against what persistent temptations from without and within they needed to
battle, and how glorious the patience and hardihood were
which enabled them to overcome.

CHAPTER XXV.

THE LION OF THE COVENANT.

THE year of Drumclog and Bothwell had serious consequences for others than the Covenanters. There was
the Duke of Lauderdale, for example. That such grievous
rebellions should perturb the country was not to the credit
of the man who was the country's overlord; and he had
enemies who were quick to use them against him. Yet he
had triumphed over similar antagonisms before, and he might
have asserted his supremacy again. The King was still his
friend; and he needed only to manifest the old arrogance,
and most of the governing class in Scotland would cringe
before their master. But now his own health was breaking.
Much of his time was spent in drinking the waters at Bath
and Tunbridge Wells. He had not the physical vitality
which would enable him to combat his adversaries; and they
gained on him little by little. In November 1680, we find
the Scottish Bishops sending him a farewell address; for he
has resigned his great office of "sole Secretarie of State for
this kingdom," handing over its dignities to the Earl of
Moray. They avow themselves most grateful to their
imperious benefactor. "For the eminent appearances and
actings of your Grace for our Religion, our Order, and our
Church, as wee offer to your Grace our most humble and
heartie thanks, so sall wee offer unto God our most fervent
Prayers for your Grace's honor, interest, and Glorie in both
worlds." Queensberry's star was in the ascendant, the
Queensberry whom Claverhouse flattered, though there was
neither trust nor liking between the two. And another

O

personage—foreboding, sinister, intolerant, even if in Holy-rood he cultivated the good opinion of Scottish lords and ladies by routs and gaieties—began in those years to figure prominently in the guidance of affairs.

This was the Duke of York. In London and throughout England he was suspected on account of his Papistry; and it was judged prudent that he should go to the north for a time. Through the closing months of 1679 and the early ones of 1680, he had his home in Edinburgh. In the Privy Council he took his seat without swearing any Oath of Allegiance; laws which were iron for Presbyterians became elastic for a Roman Catholic so imposing and powerful. Indeed, he did very much what he pleased. When, in the spring, he returned to Whitehall, twenty-six of the Councillors wrote to the King an epistle of commendation as fulsome in its tone as it was daring in its chronology. "May it please your sacred Majesty," the first sentence ran, "the remem-brance of having been under the protection of your Royall family above two thowsand years; of having been preserved by their valour from the slavery to which others were so often reduced; and of having receaved from their bounty the lands wee possess: Hath been very much refresh'd and renew'd by having your Royall Brother among us, in whom wee have seen that moderation of spirit and equality of Justice, that is so remarkable in your sacred Race." Charles, whose humour never failed, and who was shrewd in his under-standing of men, must have been amused by the singular tribute. Sixteen months later, the Duke was back in Edinburgh, on this occasion as King's Commissioner; and at length the reign of Lauderdale was at an end.

By August 1682, John Maitland was dead. Step by step he went down his tragic descent. His body was shaken by gross self-indulgence. He was denied the affections of home; for his wife, who had cared only for the pomp and wealth her husband brought her, now neglected him openly. One wonders what his thoughts were as he looked before and after. If he felt any penitences, any misgivings, any yearnings after Heaven's forgiveness, no record of these remains. "O, my lord," Richard Baxter had pleaded with tearful importunity, "do I need to tell you that all this glory will quickly set in the shadows of death, and that all this sweeting will turn soure? And how little it will comfort a departing soule to look back on prosperity, and how terrible it will be to reflect on a life of covenant-breaking and unfaithfullnes to God!" But Lauderdale passed, and gave no sign. Seven months after he breathed his last in Kent, he had a stately burial in Haddington. At Inveresk Kirk Bishop Paterson of Edinburgh preached very learnedly; and, at one of the clock, the funeral —the body being in the hearse covered with the pall or canopy—went in procession to the Abbey Church in the East Lothian town. By and by, at five o'clock, "that noble and extraordinary person" was placed in his tomb, next to his father's, but raised higher upon a base of stone made of purpose. There were present two thousand horse, insomuch that they filled the highway for full four miles in length; and there were twenty-five coaches. So they "led out the pageant, sad and slow." But there were poor men, whom he had sent to glorify God in the Grassmarket, who had an exodus more impressive and victorious.

When Bothwell had been fought and lost, silence fell on the Kirk. The silence would have been unbroken, if it had not been for the voices of two or three in the straitest sect of the Covenant. Their testimony increased in determination and vehemence. We have seen what the debates were which divided Presbyterians. There were the Indulgences. Was it permissible, or was it unlawful, to receive the measure of liberty which these offered? There was the Cess. It was a tax applied to the persecution of the faithful; but, if payment should be refused, the dragoons had their commission to plunder and kill. Might one submit at the bayonet's point; or, let the worst come to the worst, ought the Covenanter to say No? It is impossible to condemn outright the good men who chose the path of least resistance; even for them the road was thorny enough. But their brethren, who would bend to no wind that blew, were more consistent. They maintained untorn the independence of the Church. They vindicated the subject's right of protest against the arbitrariness of overbearing rulers. They carried to their proper issue the principles of the Covenant.

They were sometimes unreasonable. When Sir Robert Hamilton and his staff wasted time and temper in unbrotherly debate with John Welsh, there is no justification for the folly. Instead of distilling like the dew, they riddled like hailstones those with whom they should have been friends. But, had they spoken it in love, they had truth on their side. And, allied with them, there were some as undismayed but more admirable, men to kindle in their fellows the uttermost of devotion. Richard Cameron was one of these, "the Lion of the Covenant," as he has been called. He was in no sense responsible for the miserable bickerings which preceded Bothwell; he was absent in Holland on that mournful Sabbath. But he, too, is among the stalwarts, who hold all temporising policies in abhorrence. To the Committee on Military Education a British General of the twentieth century said, "It is not form to show keenness." The opposite was Cameron's faith. He believed in keenness, in convictions inwoven into the texture of the soul, in confessions proclaimed by lips that are clear-toned, in the scorn of consequence, in obedience to God although the heavens should fall. "A detestable indifferency and neutrality" had no lodging in his heart.

Like Hugh Mackail and James Renwick, Richard Cameron remains always young. When death came, sharp and red and kind, he was but a year or two above thirty. The date of his birth is uncertain; but, if we fix it for 1648, we cannot be far from the mark. He was a native of the old Fifeshire town of Falkland, where the Stuart kings had a famous palace; he grew up, as we may say, under the very shadow of the autocracy and prelacy against which he waged war à outrance. His father, Allan Cameron, merchant in Falkland, and his mother, Margaret Paterson, were Scots of the sober, "bien," diligent middle-class which, first and last, has done so much for the country. There were two younger sons: Michael, to be linked inseparably with Richard in the supreme moments of his history, and Alexander, who became a Covenanting minister, but of whose biography little is discernible. In the spring of 1680, six months before Ayrsmoss, he went to study theology in Holland, being then over twenty-one years of age, and having wrought for a time as a handloom weaver. He possessed only "some smack of Humanity," his father said in a letter to MacWard, apologising for the absence of classical attainment on the ground that it would have been dangerous to send the lad to a Scottish university, now that his brother's antagonism to the ruling powers was notorious. For a good few summers and winters this youngest son of the house must have remained in the Low Countries, for we detect his presence in Utrecht when the Revolution of 1688 took place; but then he fades into a mist of indistinctness, and soon we lose sight of him altogether. There seems to have been a daughter also, Marion Cameron—a fearless girl, whom tradition reports to have suffered death at the hands of the troopers. The little family gave overflowing proof of its affection for the persecuted Church.

But, in the outset, Richard was not the Lionheart he afterwards became. When he had taken his University degree, he was precentor and schoolmaster in Falkland under the Episcopal curate. Occasionally, however, in the fields, he listened to a Covenanting minister; and, by the grace of God, these stolen opportunities made all things new. "In that sun-blink day of power," writes Patrick Walker, "when the net of the Gospel was let down at the right side of the ship, then a great draught of perishing souls was effectually caught." One of the enmeshed and happy souls was Cameron's; and nothing could be more radical than the change he underwent. It was not simply that he found his spiritual home henceforward amongst Presbyterians, but immediately he showed himself a root-and-branch man. Now, and to the close, he stood among the most inflexible of his fresh-found comrades. But Falkland was no residence for an enthusiast, and he left his native town. For a time he was tutor in the family of Sir William Scot, of Harden, in the county of Roxburgh—a gentleman who, in a later

year, was sentenced both to imprisonment and to a fine of
£4000 because of his love for the Covenant. Yet even Sir
William Scot and his lady were not sufficiently decisive for
the young tutor. It was to the preaching of one of the
Indulged ministers that the Harden household went; and
Richard Cameron's conscience would not permit him to
accompany them. Once more he forsook home, to join
himself with John Welsh, who was then holding meetings
in Teviotdale. It was Welsh who prevailed on him, against
his own desire, to receive licence as a preacher; he was sure,
he said, that, with his peremptory beliefs, he would only be
a root of bitterness in the camp. But his objections were
repelled; and in the house of Henry Hall of Haughhead,
the captain who fought at Drumclog and Bothwell, the hands
of a little company of outed ministers were laid on his fair
hair, and he was set apart to publish to a convulsed nation the
Evangel of peace.

They had gauged the quality of the new recruit; and, at
once, they bade him repair to a difficult portion of the field.
"The first place they sent him to"—Mr. Welsh and Mr.
Sempill and the others—"was Annandale. He said, How
could he go there? for he knew not what sort of people they
were. Mr. Welsh said, 'Go your way, Ritchie; set the fire
of hell to their tail.' The first day he preached upon that
text, *How shall I put thee among the children?* In the application he said, 'Put you among the children, the offspring
of robbers and thieves!' Many have heard of Annandale
thieves. Some of them, who got a merciful cast that day,
told it afterwards that it was the first field-preaching that
ever they heard, and that they went out of curiosity, to see
how a minister would preach in a tent and people sit on the
ground; but, if many of them went without an errand,
they got one that day." From the commencement, his Lord
honoured the ministry of Richard Cameron.

But his outspokenness, as he had dreaded, brought him
an inheritance of distrust. He could not refrain from condemning the Indulgence; until some even of those who
confided in him began to doubt his wisdom, and to find

fault with sentences which burned like a flame and smote like a hammer. At Dunscore in Nithsdale, a parish with memories both of Robert Burns and of Thomas Carlyle, a meeting of ministers was held. John Welsh attended, and Gabriel Sempill, and Thomas Douglas, and David Williamson. They reproved, though surely with all gentleness, the eager young preacher who had won their love. If they rejoiced in his zeal, they would have it tempered by a more long-suffering spirit. It would seem, although his latest biographer doubts it, that he gave them a promise of increased watchful-ness and moderation; he would try to hold in check the ardencies of his heart and tongue, and would deal more exclusively with those rich evangelical themes on which all the prophets of the Covenant were agreed. Was it because afterwards he regretted the promise and fell into trouble of spirit on account of his fancied backsliding, or was it simply that he might receive abroad the ordination which in so distressful a time it was difficult to get in Scotland, that, a few months subsequently, he crossed the North Sea to Holland? Whatever the motive might be— and this is but one of the unsettled questions in Cameron's life-story—we meet him erelong in the company of the exiles, John Brown and Robert MacWard. In May 1679, as Pro-fessor Herkless and Dr. Hay Fleming conclude, he left his own country for the Continent. And so he was hundreds of miles away when, in the following month, victory waited on the flag of the Covenant, and then defeat trailed it shame-fully in the mire.

He made an instant impression on those among whom he had gone. "I crave leave to tell you," writes MacWard " that the common report of poor Mr. Cameron was, that not only he did preach nothing but babble against the Indulgence, but that he could do no other thing. And this was so confidently and commonly talked, that I was not in case to contradict it upon knowledge. But, by his coming hither, the reporters have lost their credit of being so easily believed for the future; and many who heard him were convinced that prejudice, heightened to malice, had given men liberty to talk so. For here he was found a man of a savoury Gospel-spirit; the bias of his heart lying towards the proposing of Christ, and persuading to a closing with Him." In the Scots Kirk at Rotterdam, he delivered a "satisfying and delightsome" sermon, refreshing to many, on that appealing cry of the Lover of men, *Come unto Me, all ye that labour and are heavy-laden, and I will give you rest.* He was far removed from the ordinary type of controversialist; there was the note of affectionateness in his utterance. In public prayer he would still bewail the tyrannies and defections in the homeland; but, when he stood up to speak, he was the herald of the King of grace who died to redeem the lost.

So entirely were Brown and MacWard united in community of thought with Richard Cameron that they gladly gave him ordination. In Rotterdam, with a Dutch divine, Pastor James Koelman, to assist them, the ceremony took place. Immediately before it, MacWard addressed the young man. "Richard," he said, "the publick standard of the Gospel is fallen in Scotland; and, if I know anything of the mind of the Lord, ye are called to undergo your trials before us, and go home and lift the fallen standard, and display it before the world. But, before ye put your hand to it, ye shall go to as many of the field ministers as ye can find, and give them your hearty invitation to go with you; and if they will not go, go your lone, and the Lord will go with you." When Brown and Koelman had lifted their hands from the head bent in consecration beneath them, MacWard left his resting on the light-brown locks. "Behold!" he cried, "all ye spectators. Here is the head of a faithful minister and servant of Jesus Christ, who shall lose the same for his Master's interest; and it shall be set up before sun and moon in the public view of the world." Those were days when old experience, and sanctified sorrow, and brooding meditation, and daily communion with God, endowed men with the insight of the saint and the foresight of the seer.

Robert MacWard's prediction did not tarry long for its realisation. In the October of 1679, Cameron was again in

Scotland, resolved, even if he had to essay the enterprise in loneliness, that he would "lift the fallen standard and display it publicly before the world." Within nine months his race was completed; but so marvellously had he succeeded in his work that only three or four names in the annals of the Covenant are better remembered than his. Not many stood by him during these fateful months; he had need of the boldness and the faith which can dispense with human helpers. Sometimes old Donald Cargill would assist him in preaching on hillside or moor, and sometimes Thomas Douglas; but generally he hurried in solitude on his Master's errands. John Welwood would have been his true yokefellow had he lived; but, in the same year of 1679, worn with labour and sickness, he betook himself to the joys of heaven; that morning on which he died, when he saw the first streaks of the dawn, he said, "Now, eternal light! no more night nor darkness to me!" In Clydesdale and Ayrshire Richard Cameron carried his burden, and made full proof of his ministry; and the succours he had were spiritual and unseen.

He was a preacher who knew how to persuade his hearers. Usually, as in Holland, his discourses treated of the perennial verities. Once, on a knowe in New Monkland, he had that great text, *A Man shall be as an hiding-place from the wind*; and the people enjoyed "a desirable, confirming, and comforting day." Again, somewhere between the shires of Ayr and Lanark, he spoke on the wistful words of Jesus, *Ye will not come to Me that ye might have life*. In the heart of the sermon he paused; and in the pause he prayed for the restoration of the Jews, for the fall of Antichrist, and for the hastening of the hour when the Stuarts should be swept from the throne. Then he went back to his theme, mounting into a sublimer strain as he proceeded. " 'I have had a profession for many years,' say ye, 'and yet, I fear, I have never yet come to Christ.' But I say, Our Lord is here this day, saying, 'Will ye take Me, ye that have a lie so long in your right hand?' . . . There may be some saying, 'If I get or take Him, I shall get a cross also.' Well, that is true; but ye will get a sweet

cross. Thus we offer Him unto you in the parishes of Auchinleck, Douglas, Crawfordjohn, and all ye that live thereabout.
And what say ye? Will ye take Him? Tell us what ye say;
for we take instruments before these hills and mountains
around us that we have offered Him unto you this day. . . .
Angels are wondering at this offer; they stand beholding with
admiration that our Lord is giving you such an offer this day.
The angels will go up to report at the Throne what is every
one's choice.'" The hunger to catch souls drove him on; he
could not let his listeners go without learning how matters
stood between them and his Lord. As he closed, again he
paused, compelled to do so now by the depth of his emotion.
He fell into "a rap of calm weeping," and the congregation
wept along with him. It was a conventicle never forgotten.
And there were others like it—at Mungo Hill, to the south of
Eaglesham; at Kirkmahoe; at the Shawhead; at Quarryholes
on the Duneaton; at Kype Water in Evandale; and at
Carluke. In *Heathercat*, that short fragment of Covenanting
story which he left behind him—would that it had been a
perfect round and not a broken arc!—Stevenson describes
such an open-air gathering as Cameron often addressed. It
was an assembly of the last of the faithful. "God, who had
averted His face from all other countries of the world, still
leaned from Heaven to observe, with swelling sympathy, the
doings of His moorland remnant. Christ was by them with
His eternal wounds, with dropping tears. The Holy Ghost
was dimly supposed to be in the heart of each and on the lips
of the minister." And over against them was the army of the
hierarchies, "from the men Charles and James Stuart, on to
King Lewie and the Emperor; and the scarlet Pope, and the
muckle black devil himself, peering out the red mouth of hell
in an ecstasy of hate and hope. 'One pull more!' he seemed
to cry; 'one pull more, and it's done! There's only Clydesdale, and the Stewartry, and the three Bailieries of Ayr, left
for God.'" There might be three hundred to four hundred
present—with long, serious, strongly marked faces, the cheeks
lean and brown, the mouth set, the eyes shining with a fierce
enthusiasm; shepherds, labouring men, and here and there a

laird, in their broad blue bonnets or laced hats. A 'squall came up, with a great volley of flying mist, and a stormy wind, and a pitiless rain. Men and women panted aloud in the shock of the violent shower-bath; plaids, mantles, and riding-coats gave them no shelter; the worshippers felt the water stream on their naked flesh. But the minister's voice triumphed over it all. His were the metaphors characteristic of the hill preachers. "Their images scarce ranged beyond the red horizon of the moor and the rainy hilltop, the shepherd and his sheep, a fowling-piece, a spade, a pipe, a dunghill, a crowing cock, the shining and the withdrawal of the sun. An occasional pathos of simple humanity, and frequent patches of big Biblical words, relieved the homely tissue. It was a poetry apart; bleak, austere, but genuine, and redolent of the soil." Many a time Cameron must have looked on such a scene. Many a time he was himself such a speaker and poet.

But Richard Cameron lives in Scottish history in another character, as the man who denounced and abjured the despotism of the Royal house. After his home-coming from the Continent, he had little to say regarding the Indulgence and the Indulged. He disapproved them still; but, in these eventful weeks when he travelled so swiftly to the sight of Christ's face, his witness was directed against the worst evils in the land and the chief offenders. He became a rebel, but a glorious rebel whom our consciences justify and our hearts revere. It was the 22nd of June 1680, just twelve months since the calamity of Bothwell Brig. On that day the ancient burgh of Sanquhar was startled by the appearance of twenty men on horseback, who rode slowly up the main street, with swords drawn and pistols in their hands. When they arrived at the market, two of them dismounted and walked to the Cross, while the rest formed a circle round, and the inhabitants flocked to the spot. The two who had dismounted were Richard Cameron and his brother Michael. A psalm was sung; a prayer was offered; after which Michael read a paper amid the breathless attention of the crowd. It was the Sanquhar Declaration—a meaningful and momentous Declaration.

"Although we be for government and governors, such as the Word of God and our Covenant allows, yet we for ourselves, and all that will adhere to us, as the representative of the true Presbyterian Kirk and Covenant nation of Scotland, considering the great hazard of lying under such a sin any longer, do by this present disown Charles Stuart, that has been reigning—or rather tyrannising, as we may say—on the throne of Britain these years bygone, as having any right, title to, or interest in the crown of Scotland. We declare that, several years since, he should have been denuded of being king, ruler or magistrate, or of having any power to act, or to be obeyed as such. As also we, being under the standard of our Lord Jesus Christ, Captain of Salvation, do declare war with such a tyrant and usurper, and all the men of his practices, as enemies to our Lord Jesus Christ and His cause and Covenants ; and against all such as have strengthened him, sided with, or anywise acknowledged him in his tyranny, civil or ecclesiastic." These were the cardinal sentences. When the document had been read, Michael Cameron affixed it to the Cross. Another prayer was presented to God. And then the twenty horsemen formed again in rank, and, their mission fulfilled, returned to the hills and caves from which they had come.

What had they done ? They had cast off the authority of their monarch. But they had not done it in mischievous anarchy and blatant revolt. They made their abjuration a religious act. They prefaced and followed the oath of insurrection by the worship of God. Moreover, they had disavowed King Charles in the interest of King Jesus. They disobeyed the unworthy ruler, that they might obey the Ruler who is incomparable. They set aside a despotism, in order to establish a theocracy. "Think ye," asked Queen Mary of John Knox, "that subjects, having power, may resist their princes ? " "If their princes exceed their bounds," quoth he, "Madam, and do against that wherefore they should be obeyed, it is no doubt but they may be resisted." "Well, then," she continued, "I perceive that my subjects shall obey you and not me." "God forbid," he rejoined, "that ever I

RICHARD CAMERON'S MONUMENT AT AYRSMOSS.

take upon me to command any to obey me, or yet to set
subjects at liberty to do what pleaseth them. But my travail
is that both princes and subjects obey God." The Cameronians, the men who assented to the daring deed done in
Sanquhar, were simply translating into act the wholesome
patriotism of John Knox. We may not approve every phrase
in their Declaration. We may not like its revengeful conclusion : " And we hope, after this, none will blame us for, or
offend at, our rewarding those that are against us as they have
done to us, as the Lord gives opportunity." But it contends
for the essentials, for a free Parliament and an unshackled
Church. Its principles triumphed in 1688. What was
treason, when the Hillmen proclaimed it, was the Revolution
Settlement, when William of Orange drove James from
Whitehall. The rebels were the forerunners of the happier
era. Others entered into their labours. The nation reaped
the harvest which, in a boisterous spring, twenty adventurous men had sown.

After Sanquhar, the death of the chief participant in the
drama could not be distant. One of the seals of the Moravian
Church is the picture of an ox, and on this side of it a plough,
and on that an altar, so that it is prepared either for labour
or for sacrifice. It might have been Cameron's crest. Now
we hear him longing for the incorruptible inheritance, but yet
praying for patience; at another moment we see him busy to
the last in his ministry in his fields. On the latest Sabbath
of his life, when Cargill was with him, his sermon was on the
text, *Be still, and know that I am God.* When the service was
over, he arranged with his friend that, a fortnight afterwards,
they should preach together once more. But, before the
fortnight was ended, he had got his discharge from earth and
his entrance into heaven.

On the night of the 21st of July, he slept in the farmhouse
of William Mitchel in Meadowhead at the Water of Ayr.
Out on a slope of the moor, under the sky, his bodyguard
snatched what rest they could; for, during that week, he was
attended by about forty foot and twenty horse. "They were
of one heart and soul," says Patrick Walker, "their company

and converse being so edifying and sweet; and, having no
certain dwelling-place, they stayed together, waiting for
further light in that nonsuch juncture of time." In the
morning, at his request, the farmer's young daughter gave
him water to wash his hands; and, when he had dried them
with a towel, he looked to them, and laid them on his face,
and said, "This is their last washing; I have need to make
them clean, for there are many to see them." Her mother
wept; but, like his Lord before him, he bade her, "Weep not
for me, but ·for yourself and yours, and for the sins of a sinful
land; for ye have many melancholy, sorrowful, weary days
before you." Bruce of Earlshall, a Fifeshire proprietor, was
in command of the soldiers—Lord Airlie's troop and Strachan's
dragoons—who had been sent by Dalzell to seek for Cameron.
The pitiful ingredient in the story is that they seem to have
been informed of his whereabouts by Sir John Cochrane, who
himself claimed to be of one mind with the Covenanters, but
whom the stricter party would have described as among the
"dumb dogs" that did not bark. At four o'clock in the
afternoon of the 22nd—it was a Thursday—the pursuers came
on the little band, lying in the east end of Ayrsmoss, a bleak
stretch of mossy ground extending through part of the three
parishes of Sorn, Auchinleck, and Muirkirk. When Richard
Cameron saw the enemy advancing, he gathered his men round
him, and led them in prayer. There was no leisure for a
multitude of words, no space for anything but one of those
swift and strong ejaculations which carry the Kingdom of
Heaven by force. Three times he cried, "Lord, spare the
green, and take the ripe!" Then he looked to his brother,
brother by spiritual as by natural ties. "Michael," he said,
"come, let us fight it out to the last! For this is the day that
I have longed for, and the death that I have prayed for, to die
fighting against our Lord's enemies; and this is the day that
we will get the crown." To the rest he cried, "Be encouraged,
all of you, to fight it out valiantly; for all of you that shall
fall this day, I see Heaven's gates cast wide open to receive
them." It was an encounter of cavalry, the foot soldiers
scarcely needing to do anything. The Covenanters strove like

heroes; but they were out-numbered, and the end was sure. Nine of their horsemen lay dead; and one of the nine was Richard Cameron.

> When the righteous had fallen, and the combat was ended,
> A chariot of fire through the dark cloud descended;
> Its drivers were angels on horses of whiteness,
> And its burning wheels turned on axles of brightness.
>
> A seraph unfolded its doors bright and shining,
> All dazzling like gold of the seventh refining:
> And the souls that came forth out of great tribulation
> Have mounted the chariot and steeds of salvation.

So he whom men named the Lion of the Covenant sped to God, and laid down in His breast that fiery spirit of his; he was no more than thirty-two years of age. Michael, too, fought his last fight on the lonely Ayrsmoss. They took Richard's head and hands to Edinburgh; and the man who had cut them off declared, as he delivered them to the Privy Council, "There's the head and hands that lived praying and preaching, and died praying and fighting"—no mean panegyric to be spoken by the lips of an enemy. Old Allan Cameron, the father, was a prisoner in the Tolbooth, incarcerated because of the help he had given the conventicles near his own town of Falkland. On their way to the Netherbow, where they meant to fix them up, they carried head and hands to him, "to add grief to his sorrow." "Do you know them?" they asked. And he took them upon his knee, and bent over them, and kissed them, and said, "I know them! I know them! They are my son's, my dear son's." And then, weeping and yet praising, he went on, "It is the Lord! Good is the will of the Lord, who cannot wrong me nor mine, but has made goodness and mercy to follow us all our days."

One of the prisoners who was taken, bleeding and almost lifeless, at Ayrsmoss was reserved for a fearful doom. It was Hackston of Rathillet. In the fight he had inflicted many wounds; for he was a deft swordsman. He was assailed from right and left, and maintained the battle as if its issue depended on himself alone. At last his horse was trapped in the marshy ground, and so was that of one of the foremost of

the troopers, David Ramsay—a man "of my acquaintance,"
as Hackston relates, grimly enough, in the narrative which he
drew up in the Tolbooth.   The two fought awhile on foot, very
evenly matched ; but three dragoons from behind, taking a
dishonourable advantage, struck Hackston on the head.   He
fell, and surrendered as Ramsay's prisoner.   "They gave us all
testimony," he says, and his soldierly heart was proud of the
confession extorted from his foes—"they gave us all testimony
of being brave, resolute men."   He had need of every particle
of the bravery and resolution.   In Edinburgh, eight days after,
they meted out to him an awful death.   We are horrified as
we read the sentence in the minutes of the Council: "That
his body be drawn backward on a hurdle to the Mercat Cross ;
that there be an high scaffold erected a little above the Cross,
where, in the first place, his right hand is to be struck off, and,
after some time, his left hand ; then he is to be hanged up,
and cut down alive, his bowels to be taken out, and his heart
shown to the people by the hangman ; then his heart and his
bowels to be burned in a fire prepared for that purpose on the
scaffold ; that, afterwards, his head be cut off, and his body
divided into four quarters ; his head to be fixed on the
Netherbow ; one of his quarters with both his hands to be
affixed at St. Andrews, another quarter at Glasgow, a third at
Leith, a fourth at Burntisland ; that none presume to be in
mourning for him, or any coffin brought ; that no person be
suffered to be on the scaffold with him, save the two bailies,
the executioner and his servants ; that he be allowed to pray
to God Almighty, but not to speak to the people ; that
Hackston's and Cameron's heads be fixed on higher poles than
the rest."   The permission to pray, Professor Herkless says,
is the one human thing in this devilish verdict, devised by the
Privy Council which governed Scotland in the name of Charles
Stuart, King by the grace of God and Defender of the Faith.
Through flame and through flood, a flame seven times intensi-
fied, a flood swelling to the brim, David Hackston of Rathillet
went to the land where the sun does not light on the citizens
nor any heat, and where there is no more sea of tumult and
peril.

CHAPTER XXVI.

BREAKER AND BUILDER OF THE ETERNAL LAW.

THE Sabbath after Ayrsmoss, preaching in the parish of Shotts, Donald Cargill chose for his text, *Know ye not that there is a prince and a great man fallen this day in Israel?* It was Richard Cameron's funeral sermon that he preached, the elegy for the young soldier of Christ on whom he had himself leaned as on a staff that would not fail. For "that blest singular Christian, Mr. Cargill," was thirty summers older than the Timothy who had none of Timothy's fearfulness in his temperament; and it would have been a joy to retain by his side a friend who, with the strength of Roland, could "hew a chasm sheer into the barrier rock, and bring the army of the faithful through." One of the most attractive among the leaders of the Covenant is Donald Cargill. His nature was timid and shrinking, and yet he learned for his Master's sake to trample his alarms under foot. He was disposed to depreciate himself, and nevertheless he kept the flag flying when others were too panic-stricken to unfurl its folds. The son of Laurence Cargill, notary and gentleman, he was born in the Perthshire town of Rattray, probably in 1619; but it was not until 1655, when he was leaving his youth behind, that he was ordained minister of the Barony Church in Glasgow—the Church which met then in the crypt of the Cathedral. His father, indeed, had experienced much difficulty in persuading him to undertake the study of divinity, and to dedicate his life to the preacher's work; who was he, he thought with himself, that he should aspire to a calling so sacred? And, when the call to the Barony was presented to him, he determined to decline it as something too lofty and high; he was in the act of leaving the town, that he might shake himself clear from further importunities. But a woman saw him mounting his horse, and said to him, " Sir, you have promised to preach on Thursday; have you appointed a meal for poor hungry people, and will ye go away and not give it? If you do, the curse of God will go with you." It recalls William Farel, laying the ban of Heaven on young John Calvin, if he should turn away from the Geneva which needed him so sorely: " After having learned that my heart was set upon devoting myself to private studies, and finding that he gained nothing by entreaties, he proceeded to utter an imprecation that God would blast my retirement and the tranquillity which I sought, if I should withdraw and refuse assistance when the necessity was so urgent." And Cargill, like Calvin, relinquished his purpose of flight and remained at the post of duty, asking his reprover to pray for him that he might be faithful unto death. But, having once put his hand to the plough, he never turned back.

For only seven years did he speak on behalf of Christ within the shelter of sanctuary walls; he was ejected by the Earl of Middleton's Act in the winter of 1662. "And for avoiding the inconveniences that might follow by his residing at Glasgow or places near adjacent," the Lords of Council "commanded and charged Mr. Donald Cargill not to live in any place on the south side of the river Tay, and to cause transport his family and what belonged to him out of the town before the first of November; with certification that, if he chose to contravene the decree, he should be apprehended, imprisoned, and proceeded against as a seditious person." It was after his expulsion that his effective ministry began. In private houses and in the conventicles of the fields, when "the Lord had pity on this weather-beaten Church, and sent forth a thaw-wind and spring-tide day of the Gospel," there was none more untiring than he. With the exception of a short time spent in Holland, he never was away from the place of duty and jeopardy; other and quieter surroundings would not have satisfied his heart; he was ready to subscribe to Alexander

Shields's dictum that "the ill of Scotland he found everywhere, but the good of Scotland he found nowhere." There were no family ties to place restraint on his activities; within a year and a day of their marriage, God's finger had beckoned from him his wife, Margaret Brown; Cargill was lonely, except for the affection of the hill-folk who loved him for the messages he brought, and for the unfailing presence of Father and Son and Holy Ghost. But, like one of his Covenanting friends, he scarcely missed the sweet endearments of home. "I have been taken up in meditating on heavenly things," he, too, could say; "I have been upon the banks of Ulai, plucking an apple here and there."

Timorous although he was in his disposition, he could do things as audacious as the Lion of the Covenant himself. The Queensferry Paper, the precursor of the Sanquhar Declaration, was one proof of his courage. Perhaps Cameron helped in its composition; but it is generally ascribed to the older man. It was a bond strong in its affirmations and denials. It made solemn confession of religious faith, and just as frankly it disavowed the sinful rulers. Proceeding further yet, it boldly declared in favour of a Republic. "We shall no more commit the government of ourselves, and the making of laws for us, to any one single person, or lineal successor, we not being by God, as the Jews were, bound to one single family; and this kind of government by a single person being most liable to inconveniences, and aptest to degenerate into tyranny, as long and sad experience hath taught us." The document is the most advanced of all the Covenanting manifestoes. But it was never published by the Covenanters themselves; it was stolen from them by their enemies; and, when that happened, Donald Cargill came near meeting his death. It was the 3rd of June 1680; and he was in Queensferry, with Henry Hall, who had been much with him in his many wanderings. Hearing of their presence, the Governor of Blackness Castle took a single servant, and discovered them in an inn. He hoped that soon his soldiers would come up to his assistance; but, when they procrastinated, he threw off all disguises, and told the two that they must regard themselves as his prisoners.

They demurred, and a struggle followed. In the confusion Cargill escaped; but Hall was wounded and made captive. By and by, on the road to Edinburgh, he died; and it was when his clothes were searched that the compromising and uncompromising Paper was found.

But " blest Cargill " was in no wise deterred from pressing on in his crusade. Two months after Cameron, in James Hyslop's vivid phrase, had " mounted the chariot and steeds of salvation," the Covenanting minister did what some of his friends condemned. At a great gathering at Torwood, on the road between Larbert and Stirling, he preached from that tremendous oracle of the prophet Ezekiel, *Thus saith the Lord God, Remove the diadem and take off the crown*; and, when the sermon was finished, he went on, in well-weighed words, to excommunicate Charles Stuart, King of England; James, Duke of York; James, Duke of Monmouth; John, Duke of Lauderdale; John, Duke of Rothes; the King's Advocate, Sir George Mackenzie; and Thomas Dalzell, of Binns. " And, as the causes are just, so, being done by a minister of the Gospel, and in such a way as the present persecution would admit of, the sentence is just; and there are no kings or ministers on earth who, without repentance of the persons, can reverse these sentences. God, who is their Author, is the more engaged to the ratifying of them; and all that acknow-ledge the Scriptures ought to acknowledge them." In a letter which the Bishop of Edinburgh, on the 18th of September, wrote to Lauderdale, we can read the amazement and rage of the prelates at the deed of the humble preacher. He sends, Bishop Paterson says, " a copie of that treasonable and sacriligious sentence pronunced last Lord's day by Mr. Donald Cargill in a numerous field conventicle at the Torwood, where manie were in armes. Your Grace wes forgotten by him in the fornoon; but uncanonicallie he brought you up in the afternoon, and, after ane scurrilous apologie for his ommission, he proceeded with his blunt thunder against you. This spirit of profannes and blood hath here arrived to the height of dementation and maddnes, and is ane verie angrie dispensation of God's judgement upon that ungodlie and

TORWOOD CASTLE.

ungovernable tribe." But, although the ferocity of enemies was only enhanced, and even brothers in the faith were more than dubious, and in the clear dry light of prudence and sagacity we may decide that Cargill did a reckless thing, there is something august and magnificent in the spectacle of a poor, ageing, hunted minister announcing the displeasure of high Heaven against the powers and principalities that swayed the destiny of the country.

In all likelihood, however, most of us will prefer to recall Donald Cargill in his softer and more purely spiritual moods. In many of his sermons he never touched on the misdoings of the King and the guiltiness of the land; he was the votary of nobler thoughts. "I have followed holiness," he said, when he came to die; "I have taught truth; I have been most in the main things; not that I esteemed the things concerning our times little." His sermons were briefer than those of the majority of his brethren. "Some spoke to him that he preached and prayed short, saying, 'O, sir, 'tis long betwixt meals, and we are in a starving condition. All is good, sweet, and wholesome, which ye deliver; but why do you straiten us so much for shortness?'" He returned a wise as well as a self-abnegating answer. "Ever since I bowed a knee in good earnest to pray, I never durst pray and preach with my gifts; and where my heart is not affected, and comes not up with my mouth, I always thought it time for me to quit it. What comes not from my heart, I have little hope that it will go to the heart of others." *Cor ad cor:* the motto of a man, who stood at the opposite pole in the world of theologians and saints, was his motto too; and, because it was, the power of his Lord was present with him to heal very many. We are sure that, now and then, as with another of the conventiclers, there was during the sermon "a small dissle of warm rain"; but he would be "as sensible of a dissle of the dew of heaven upon his own soul and the souls of that people"; the years of hot persecution were also years of God's right hand. He did not pray at much length in public, Cargill said, lest he should be praying with his own gifts and not with the divine Spirit's graces; but he never wearied of private devotion. From his youth he loved the solitary place; and more than once he continued whole nights in fellowship with his Father. He had his distinctive attitude when he talked to God. "It was observed by some, both in families and when in secret, he always sat straight upon his knees, without resting upon anything, with his hands lifted up; and some took notice he died the same way, with the bloody rope about his neck." Happy man, to live and to die in perfect familiarity of trust with his King and Friend!

It has been said that Scottish religion walks among shadows and doubts. Its children, we are told, have not a stable and gladsome conviction of salvation; they cling at best to a solicitous hope; they are seldom fully persuaded that they have passed from death to life. The author of the *Travels with a Donkey in the Cevennes,* who should speak with some authority, contrasts Camisard and Covenanter, not to the advantage of the latter. "Those who took to the hills for conscience' sake in Scotland had all gloomy and bedevilled thoughts; for once that they received God's comfort they would be twice engaged with Satan; but the Camisards had only bright and supporting visions. They knew they were on God's side, with a knowledge that has no parallel among the Scots; for the Scots, although they might be certain of the cause, could never rest confident of the person." But, as one dips deeper into Covenanting story, the conclusion grows irresistible that the antithesis is exaggerated; and that Whig preachers and listeners, if outwardly they often wintered on hills of snow, "summered high in bliss upon the hills of God." Cargill, at least, once the great transaction was done, had no annoying visitations from the spectres of the mind. One day he gave Robert Wodrow's father a scrap of autobiography. In his youth, he said, he fell under deep soul-exercise, and no relief came, and the trouble increased, until he determined to make away with his life. But when he was standing, in the early morning before anybody was about, on the brink of the coal-pit into whose darkness he meant to throw himself, he heard an unmistakable voice from the skies, *Son, be of good cheer, thy sins be forgiven thee!* It was not only the advent

of deliverance, when deliverance was needed most; it was the
beginning of an inward peace which never faltered nor fled
from the recipient. At the end, with the scaffold waiting, he
wrote that he had not been "without an assurance of his
interest in Christ these thirty years," and that he "never
durst undertake to preach salvation to others until he was
sure of his own." The Delectable Mountains were Donald
Cargill's home.

But he was always willing to descend from their heights
and raptures, to cure what was ailing and set right what was
wrong. In the later years of the Persecution, there arose
among the Covenanters, to the grief of all wise and godly
men, a little sect of fanatics with "demented enthusiastical
delusions." They were known as the Sweet Singers, or, more
frequently, as the Gibbites, from the sailor, John Gib, who
was their leader and prophet. They held that a metrical
Psalter was a wicked thing, a meddling of man with the text
of Scripture, and ought therefore to be torn from the Bible
and burned; that Catechisms and Confessions, Acts of Assembly,
Covenants and Declarations, were all devices of the evil one,
to be ignored and trodden under foot; that every one in
authority—the minister of religion as well as the minister
of State—must be resisted and disobeyed by the freemen
of the Lord: they hated "steeple-houses" and "hireling
shepherds" as fervently as George Fox. None of the field
preachers but was in their stringent eyes a backslider and
enemy. They would pay no taxes. They left house and
family and occupation for the desert places, where, as they
imagined, they should be free from snares and sins; some
of them repairing to the Pentland Hills, with the resolution
to remain there until they saw the smoke and ruin of the
bloody city of Edinburgh. They were continually fasting,
and continually chanting their penitential and dirge-like
Psalms—the 74th, the 79th, the 80th, the 83rd, the 137th.
To these poor Gibbites, four men and six-and-twenty women,
Cargill made a pilgrimage of faithfulness and love, finding
them in the midst of a great flow-moss betwixt Clydesdale and
Lothian, and striving to bring them to a better mind. Out

on the moor he stayed, through a night of cold, easterly, wet fog, trying every device to effect their rescue from the phantasms which had mastered them. But the hour of penitence had not yet arrived, although to most of them it was to come ere very long; and the messenger of pity had to take his departure with disappointment in his soul.

For twenty years Donald Cargill, feeble in himself, but strengthened with might by God's Spirit in the inner man, pursued his hazardous vocation. "We think, sir," said his friends to him one night, "praying and preaching go best with you, when your danger and distress is greatest." He answered that it had been so, and he hoped that it would be so: that, the more adversaries thrust at him that he might fall, the more sensibly and discernibly his Lord had helped. And then, as his custom was, he repeated quietly, as if to himself, a few exultant words of his favourite Psalm, *The Lord is my strength and song, and is become my salvation.* William Vilant, one of the ministers who had welcomed the screen and ease of the Indulgence, having heard of Cargill's patient and cheerful endurance, asked, a trifle petulantly, "What needs all this ado? We will get heaven, and they will get no more." But when the retort was repeated to the man of whom it had been uttered, he replied—and the reply is singularly noble— "Yes, we will get more; we will get God glorified on earth, which is more than heaven."

It was the good fortune of Patrick Walker to hear blest Mr. Cargill preach his last sermon. The place was Dunsyre Common. The text was Isaiah's counsel, *Come, My people, enter into your chambers.* He was short, marrowy, and sententious, as his ordinary was. Nothing could exceed his overwhelming sense of the urgency of God's Word, or his eager anxiety to win men; nothing could be greater than his indignation at the unconcernedness of hearers. He spoke out of experience, and he touched a responsive chord in the experience of every one who had tasted that God is gracious. "He insisted what kind of chambers these were of protection and safety, and exhorted us all earnestly to dwell in the clefts of the Rock, to hide ourselves in the wounds of Christ, and to wrap ourselves in the believing application of the promises flowing therefrom: thus to make our refuge under the shadow of His wings, until these sad calamities pass over, and the Dove come back with the olive branch in her mouth. These were the last words of his last sermon." Musical and most tender words they are.

The Dove with the olive branch, the Holy Ghost who is the earnest of supersensual bliss, was brooding over Donald Cargill while he spoke. Early next morning, in Covington Mill, where he had rested overnight, he was captured by James Irvine of Bonshaw, who held a commission from General Dalzell, and who was set on gaining the prize of 5000 merks placed on the preacher's head. He and the friends who were seized with him, Walter Smith and James Boig, were hurried to Glasgow, and from Glasgow to Edinburgh. They soon listened to their sentence. "God knows," Cargill said, as he mounted the ladder, "I go up this ladder with less fear, confusion, or perturbation of mind, than ever I entered a pulpit to preach." On its topmost step he spoke again, addressing himself to the auditors below the scaffold, though the drums were kept beating to drown his voice. "Now," he declared, "I am near to the possession of my crown, which shall be sure; for I bless the Lord that He hath brought me here, and makes me triumph over devils and men and sin: they shall wound me no more. I forgive all men the wrongs they have done me; and I pray the Lord to forgive the elect the wrongs they have done against Him." Then he took his farewells of "reading and preaching, praying and believing, wanderings, reproaches, sufferings"; he was leaving the shadow for the reality and the storm for the Sabbatism of the people of God. They fixed his head on the Netherbow, beside Richard Cameron's, the old saint in communion once more with the young. It was the 27th of July 1681, just a year since Cameron had been "honourably and rightly carried through."

The coincidences and contrasts of life are more remarkable than those of romance. When Donald Cargill was a student in St. Andrews, he had for one of his comrades the young Earl of Rothes. There is still preserved in the University Library the copy of the Solemn League and Covenant which

was signed in the Fifeshire town. The first column of the
names of undergraduates in St. Salvator's College is headed by
Rothes; and not far from this signature stands the autograph
of the Rattray notary's son. The two had started on their
course together. But how soon they diverged, and how completely! In an age of license, the profligacy and the
drunkenness of the Earl were notorious; he "gave himself,"
Lord Fountainhall says, "great liberty in all sorts of pleasures
and debaucheries." He threw his energy too, with peculiar
violence, into the work of persecution. And, all this while,
his fellow-student was, as Cargill phrased it, getting God
glorified on earth, and commending those things which are
true and venerable and lovely. No separation could be better
defined or more thorough. But once again, in their deaths,
the former associates were brought strangely near. On the
26th of July, the very night before Cargill witnessed his good
confession, the Duke of Rothes, his strength sapped by his
intemperance, found himself in the grip of the last enemy.
He called out that some of his wife's ministers should be
summoned to Holyrood to talk with him; for his own
ministers were "good to live with but not to die with." So
Lady Anne's counsellors were sent for ; and John Carstares
and George Johnston came. They spoke to the nobleman of
his sins, and told him of the mercy which even at the last
was within his reach. The comfortable word was the medicine
he required; but he could not believe that it was designed
for him. "We all thought little," he said to John Carstares,
"of what Cargill did in excommunicating us; but I find that
sentence binding upon me now, and it will bind to eternity."
Thus Lord Rothes went out into the night; and the Duke of
Hamilton, standing near, exclaimed, "we banish these men
from us, and yet when dying we call for them: this is
melancholy work!" The ending at the Mercat Cross, when
"the hangman hashed and hagged off" the martyr's head with
an axe—was it not more glorious than that other ending
within the walls of His Majesty's palace of Holyrood ?

High up in the Alps are two small lakes, which lie in such
proximity that it is possible to throw a stone from one to the

other. The one is Lago Bianco, the White Loch, because its
waters are light green in their colour; its neighbour is Lago
Nero, or the Black Loch, for its appearance is gloomy and
forbidding. But, although they are so close, they are on
different inclines of the watershed. Lago Bianco sends its
overflow to the Adriatic, while Lago Nero is connected with
the Black Sea. We look at the one, and think about the
sunshine of Italy; at the other, and are transported to the
wintry Crimea. So men whose lives begin in intimate union,
with the same aspirations and opportunities, pursue their
sundered courses, " breaker and builder of the eternal law "—

> One to long darkness and the frozen tide,
> One to the peaceful sea.

CHAPTER XXVII.

TWO OCTOBERS.

CAMERON and Cargill were captains of the unbending Covenanters. But captains must have followers; and the two chiefs, *sans peur et sans reproche,* had the support of soldiers who were at times even more defiant than themselves. It is impossible to approve always what was said by these representatives of the Extreme Right, although they had provocation for every biting word, and we know how hard it is for the victim to measure his language when he speaks of those who pursue him to the death, or of the others who fail him in the hour of need. Still we could wish that "the dreadless angels" of the Church had been gentler in their verdicts against "silent and unwatchful ministers"—ministers who "are become light and treacherous persons," and "ravening wolves," and "men of Shechem" trusting in the Abimelech who will beguile them to their undoing. Even Charles Stuart and "that Popish Duke" might have been disowned, we are prone to fancy, in more gracious terms. It was true, as one of the Cameronians declared, that subjects "might as well tie their consciences to the devil and their own corruptions" as to the iniquitous laws of an evil Court; but the very truth loses pith and pungency when it is published in accents which are scolding and strident. Yet, after all, it is an easy exercise, in times vastly tolerant, to sit at home and criticise the forefathers, marching sternly through the merciless hurricane; and one is almost angry with one's self for engaging in an occupation so cheap.

And they comprehended the secret of dying, the rank and

THE NETHERBOW PORT, EDINBURGH.

From the East, as it appeared in the Seventeenth century.

file no less than the officers with their far-flashing virtues.
Half-way between Edinburgh and Leith was the Gallow-Lee,
a slightly rising ground formed of sand, near the spot where
the old tollhouse stood, and on the west side of the road. To
the Gallow-Lee many of the martyrs of the persecution were
taken to be hanged. It was a place of execution less public
than the Cross or the Grassmarket, where the deaths of the
Covenanters drew together great crowds, and where their
farewell speeches made a deep impression. It was a place,
too, reserved for the punishment of the worst criminals;
so that not only was a measure of quietness secured by its
adoption, but a new stigma of reproach was branded on the
sufferers. On Monday, the 10th of October 1681, five humble
men fought their last fight for Christ's Crown and Covenant
on the malefactors' scaffold at the Gallow-Lee. Patrick
Forman was one of them, a native of the parish of Alloa, and
an adherent, as he said, "of that poor persecuted remnant, that
are yet left as berries on the top of the outmost branches."
At a fast-day service, which Cargill had held on Loudoun Hill
six months before, Patrick had well-nigh attained the consummation of his battle. For the dragoons appeared, and shot at
the preacher; but the musket-ball, missing him, ploughed its
way through the listener's hair. He had escaped then; but
to-day, beyond dispute, there was "the king of terrors to
grapple with" and to triumph over. David Farrie climbed
the shameful and delightsome steps along with him—David
Farrie, who had sat at the "devil's fireside" until about four
years previous to his martyrdom, but who could bid his friends
now "walk in the sight of God and man both, without offence;
and then, if men will be offended, let it be for your duty and
not for your sin." He was one of the dourest of Cameronians,
asserting openly that it was lawful to kill murderers, and that
the King was a murderer; but he had a fatherly heart, pulsing
with a peculiar love for the children. "O!" he cried, "invite
one another to prayer, especially young folk; for I think, if
the Lord do good to this generation, it will be to young folk."
Then there was James Stewart, of whom Wodrow writes that
he might almost be termed a boy, a boy of serious inclinations,

who never had been engaged in anything for which the law should have molested him; the blood boils when we read that, on his refusal to answer some questions put to him on his trial, Sir George Mackenzie threatened to take out his tongue with a pair of pincers. And Alexander Russel died on the same autumn Monday. For fourteen years he had listened to the curates, and had been addicted to drinking and profaneness and Sabbath-breaking; but at the first field-preaching ever he heard, to which he went merely out of idle inquisitiveness, it pleased the Lord to convert him. Alexander Russel, also, was prepared to seal his faith with the sacrifice of his life.

But the most interesting among the five witnesses of the Gallow-Lee is Robert Garnock, whose story as the slave and friend of Christ may be studied in the pages of *The Scots Worthies*. He was born in Stirling, and had been baptized by James Guthrie; he esteemed it a singular honour, he said, to follow the good shepherd of his boyhood to the scaffold, although, for many days after the shepherd's lifetime was finished, he had himself been a wayward member of the flock. His was a remarkable spiritual experience; he was a perse-cuted man long before he felt the majesty and the intimacy of divine grace. A blacksmith in his trade, he was forced to abandon his work in Stirling, and to wander from hiding-place to hiding-place, because of his perseverance in attending the conventicles; and, all these months, as he confessed in the later and better time, "the hidden things of godliness were yet a mystery to me, and I did not know anything of the new birth." It reminds us of John Bunyan, confident that he pleased God as much as any man in England, because he had given up swearing and taken to reading the historical parts of the Bible, and was striving to keep the commandments; and yet there was no heartbreak, no revolution of soul, until the brisk talker overheard three or four poor women in Bedford streets conversing of heavenly matters, as they sat at a door in the sunshine, and realised that their speech was far above him, and was compelled to remain silent. The same revelation of his own poverty and of Christ's measureless supply was granted to Robert Garnock — granted when he was seventeen or

eighteen years of age, at one of those Communions in the open
air where Welsh and Blackader preached. "The 20th, 21st,
and 22nd of April 1677," he wrote, with a joy he could not
conceal, "were the three most wonderful days with the Lord's
presence that ever I saw on earth. O, but His power was
wonderfully seen, and great to all the assembly, especially to
me." Then began a brief Christian life of which, so far as
this world was concerned, the old words are true—

Love is the fire, and sighs the smoke, the ashes shame and scorns.

Garnock was captured at Stirling in the May of 1679, after
a skirmish between sixty soldiers and a small company who
had met for the worship of God. He lay in prison untried for
more than two years; and many an effort was made to wean
him to an easier and less assertive devotion to the Covenants.
But every attempt failed ; and at length, like Robert Browning's
martyr, his "own release was earned," and he was sent to
coronation and victory at the Gallow-Lee.

What strikes the reader of his dying testimony is his
fullness of delight in the burden he was permitted to carry,
the agonies he was honoured to undergo, for Jesus' sake.
Now that he was "come to have his head cut off and put upon
a port," it seemed the day of days to him. Had he a thousand
lives, he said, he must think them all too little to be martyrs
for the truth. That night he would indeed get his fill of
gladness, for he should be with his Lord in paradise. "O
sirs !" he sang, mounting into a chant of ecstasy, "His cross
hath been all paved over with love to me all along, and it is
sweeter now than ever. O, will ye be persuaded to fall in
love with the cross of royal Jesus? Will ye be entreated to
come and taste of His love? O, sweet lot this day ! for me
to go to a gibbet for Christ and His cause. I think the thoughts
of this do ravish my heart and soul, and make me to fall out
in wondering." Long before, and in different surroundings,
the author of *The Imitation* had written: "Jesus hath many
lovers of His heavenly Kingdom, but few bearers of His Cross.
He hath many desirous of consolation, but few of tribulation.
He findeth many companions at His table, but few of His

abstinence. Many follow Him unto the breaking of bread, but few to the drinking of the cup of His passion. . . . Yet, if thou hadst the choice, thou oughtest rather to wish to suffer adversities for Christ than to be refreshed with many consolations; because thou wouldest thus be more like unto Christ, and conformable to all the saints." Robert Garnock, once hammerman in Stirling, had never so much as heard of Thomas à Kempis, and would have counted his name anathema if some chance wind had blown the rumour of it his way; but the cross-bearers speak the same dialect, whether they are monks brooding in cloisters over their books or Cameronian recusants dying in the face of the sun.

So these five suffered at the Gallow-Lee, and their bodies were buried below the scaffold; but not until the heads had been stricken off, and put upon five pikes, and conveyed to the Pleasance Port, and there fastened in a high and ghastly publicity. There were those, however, whose reverence for the martyred men was only enhanced by all these ignominies. In the night the abused and mangled bodies were lifted by faithful friends, and decently interred in the West Kirkyard. A short time afterwards, others dared in the boldness of love to take down the heads from their too prominent throne, and laid them in one chest, and hid it in Alexander Tweedie's garden at the south-west corner of the city wall. There they rested through many revolving seasons, and in summer the dews dropped cool above them, and the snow in winter lay lightly and warmly on their garden grave. Over the spot the owner planted two rose trees, one with white blossoms, the other with red; and never did rose trees anywhere bloom into such richness and fragrance. They became the marvel of the neighbourhood, although only a few, who could be trusted not to betray it, understood the secret of their splendour. There was a treasure, Alexander Tweedie was wont to say, concealed within his yard, but not of gold or silver.

Forty-five years ran on. The Persecution was little else than a piercing and loathsome memory. Except by one here and another there, the sufferers of the Gallow-Lee were forgotten. Again it was the month of October—the 7th of

October 1726. A gardener was busy in the old place of flowers and fruit, which must have been situated at the upper end of what afterwards was Lauriston Lane. Suddenly his spade turned up the five skulls, the box which once had covered them having in the interval rotted completely away. Alarmed by the disconcerting spectacle, he hurried to Mr. Shaw, the new owner of the garden. But his employer had some knowledge of what had happened nearly half a century back, and he lifted the heads of Forman and Farrie and Stewart and Russel and Garnock, and placed them side by side on a table in his summer-house. And then, on the 19th of October, the slaughtered confessors had the honourable burial withheld from them formerly; as Patrick Walker, himself a leading actor in the curious incident, is eager to inform us. " We caused make a complete coffin for them in black, with four yards of fine linen, the way our martyr-corpses were managed. And having the happiness of friendly magistrates at the time, we went to the present Provost Drummond and Bailie Nimmo, and acquainted them with our conclusions anent them; with which they were pleased, and said, If we were sure that they were our martyrs' heads, we might bury them decently and orderly. . . . Some pressed hard to go through the chief parts of the city, as was done at the Revolution. But this we refused, considering that it looked airy and frothy to make such show, and inconsistent with the solid, serious observing of such an affecting, surprising, unheard-of dispensation; but took the ordinary way of other burials from that place, to wit, we went east by the back of the Wall, and in at Bristo Port, and down the way to the head of the Cowgate, and turned up to the Greyfriars Churchyard; where they were interred close to the Martyrs' Tomb, with the greatest multitude of people, old and young, men and women, ministers and others, that ever I saw together."

Those whom men defraud unrighteously of their dues sometimes come to their heritage at long last, not simply before the Great White Throne, but in the lower world where waters of a full cup are wrung out by the people of God.

CHAPTER XXVIII.

FOR A GENTLEMAN THERE IS MR. BAILLIE.

THERE are two methods of fighting tyrants. One is open, and the other is secret. One courts the blaze of noonday, and boldly proclaims its purpose; the other, for a time, prefers to haunt the shadows, and matures its plans in hidden places. When the tyranny has become intolerable, both methods have their justification, and demand little apology among those who assent to old John Barbour's creed that " freedom is a noble thing."

The Cameronians chose the open way. It was in the sun that they unfolded their banner. Richard Cameron at Sanquhar, and Donald Cargill at Torwood, published in the country's hearing their stupendous ultimatum. They were determined that, let the issues be what they might, men should know where they stood. And this gallant recklessness had its reward. To themselves it brought the great prize of death in battle or on the martyr's scaffold. Into many others it breathed new heart and hope, making the final deliverance more certain. Never let us forget that the Hillmen only antedated, by a few years, the better age of the Revolution.

But there were Whig politicians and patriots, who, seeking the same ends, took the quieter road. It seemed premature and rash to depose the King and his minions in the audience of the world. In their judgment, just as in that of their outspoken allies, resistance to the Crown was now a religious duty. They were worn out by the long continuance of misrule. They believed that, before many months had passed, the hour of reckoning must strike. They were convinced of

the necessity of bestirring themselves, if they would save the
cause of liberty and check the leprosy of corruption which was
spreading everywhere. But they wished to postpone the
explicit avowal of their schemes. Until their friends had
gathered and the propitious moment had arrived, it appeared
the part of wisdom to cultivate a cautious and reticent spirit.
These Whig statesmen held that there are enterprises which,
like mosses and ferns, thrive at first in the twilight, and may
wither if they are exposed too soon to the glare of day.

In July 1681, James, Duke of York, the King's brother,
who had come down to Edinburgh at the close of the previous
year, was invested with the tasks and pomps of Royal Commissioner in succession to Lauderdale. He was not unknown
in Scotland, which he had visited more than once, and where
he had many friends. But now he seemed to have undergone
a change for the worse. Savage as Lauderdale had been, the
old lion who was dying at Tunbridge Wells, the King's heir
was not a whit more merciful. He showed himself bigoted,
saturnine, hard as the nether millstone. Lord Fountainhall
relates an incident of the time, which many did not like.
Shortly after James's arrival, he visited the Castle. By the
advice of "an English canoneer," the great gun that was
known as Mons Meg was employed to fire a *feu de joie*, and
was burst in the process; and the Englishman was regarded
as having deliberately destroyed a piece of ordnance bigger
than any in his own country. There were graver destructions,
people said, on which the Duke appeared to be bent. At once
he initiated a policy, the trend of which could not be mistaken.
Having called a Parliament, the first that had been convened
for many a day, he compelled it to sanction two measures
which were a significant index of his character. One was the
Act of Succession, declaring that "no difference in religion
can divert the lineal descent of the Crown." He was himself
an unconcealed Romanist, and the design of the Act was
patent; it was intended to throw the shield of the law over a
Popish king. The other measure struck a blow even more
crushing. It was a Test, which all persons aspiring to any
office in Church or State must take. So stringent it was, so

long-winded, and at the same time so contradictory,—inferring
"an obligation upon those who took it to conform to any
religion the King pleased, and yet to adhere to the Presbyterian religion; to oppose prelacy, and yet to maintain the
present constitution of the Church, which was prelacy; to
renounce and yet to affirm the doctrine of non-resistance"—
that eighty of the Episcopal clergymen of the country refused
to be bound by it, and, resigning their benefices, withdrew to
England. Sir James Dalrymple, the President of the Court
of Session, and afterwards the first Viscount Stair, gave up his
dignities rather than pledge himself to obligations which were
impossible to fulfil. And the Earl of Argyll, son of the great
Marquis, and a man who had striven to maintain his loyalty
under immense difficulties, said that he would swear the Test
only in so far as it was consistent with itself, and in so far,
too, as it did not engage him to do anything against the
Protestant faith. For this explication, as it was styled, he was
thrown into "sure firmance"—into the inner prison—in the
Castle of Edinburgh; and was charged with "leasing-making
and depraving of laws," with treason and perjury. His
fortunes and his life were both threatened. On the 12th of
December he was tried before the Court of Justiciary, with
Lord Queensberry as its President. "Whether I live publicly
or in obscurity," he said, "my head, my heart, and my hand
shall never be wanting when I can be useful to His Majesty's
service; and while I live, and when I die, I shall pray that
God Almighty would bless His Majesty with a long, happy,
and prosperous reign; and that the lineal loyal successors of
the Crown may continue monarchs of all His Majesty's
dominions, and be defenders of the true, primitive, Christian,
apostolic, catholic, protestant religion, while sun and moon
endure." Sir George Lauder affirmed on his behalf that a
man's clearing his own conscience had no affinity with those
actions which "beget discord between the King and his
subjects" and "tend to the reproach and dislike of his government." But, though two of the Judges, Lord Collington and
Lord Kirkhouse, were brave enough to vote for acquittal,
three sentenced the culprit to death. They knew that the

JAMES, DUKE OF YORK.

After the Portrait by Sir Godfrey Kneller.

Duke of York was eager to denude Argyll of influence and
property and privilege, if not also to consign him to the
scaffold. "Whether James designed," writes Macaulay, "as
his enemies suspected, to commit murder, or only, as his
friends affirmed, to commit extortion by threatening to commit
murder, cannot now be known." The blackness of night
descended on the Earl, and the omens for his future were as
unfavourable as they could be. He determined to risk everything on the bold endeavour to escape from his cell in the
Castle. His step-daughter, Lady Sophia Lindsay, came, on his
invitation, to see him. A servant with a lantern attended her,
and a page bore her train. The latter was "a tall, awkward,
country-lad, with a fair wig and his head tied up as if he had
been engaged in a fray." He and Argyll exchanged clothes;
and, in a short time, the party set out through the darkness,
leaving the country-lad behind. The first sentry questioned
them "pretty warmly," but allowed them to pass. At the
outer gate "one of the guard took Argyll by the arm and
viewed him." But the lantern-bearer exclaimed in well-
affected anger, "What ails the fellow at the page?" and the
curious soldier let him go. At the foot of the Castle Hill the
Earl took good-bye of his clever and fearless daughter, and
went on with the servant to Bristo Port, where horses were
waiting. He was free. Some weeks later, from his English
retreat, he wrote in rhyme to Lady Sophia :—

> You came an angel in the case to me,
> Expressly sent to guide and set me free.
> The great gate opened of its own accord—
> That word came in my mind, I praise the Lord.
>
> When I was out, I knew not where I went;
> I cried to God, and He new angels sent.
> If ye desire what passèd since to me,
> Read through the book of psalms, and think on me.

Things were serious enough in the Scotland which the
Duke of York ruled, although gleams of humour shot through
the Egyptian darkness. This was the time when the boys of
Heriot's Hospital resolved to administer the Test to their
watchdog. Greatly daring, they turned into a jest the

rambling and illogical and terrible oath. The dog sensibly refused to eat the paper on which they had written out the enactment. Even when they had smeared it with butter, that the vexatious sentences might be more palatable, the sagacious animal licked the butter off, and then discarded the essential parchment. So, having gone through such a mock-trial as had been given to his Grace of Argyll, they gravely hanged the nonjuror for his obstinacy. One may be permitted a sigh over the sufferer's undeserved fate; but is it not good to hear the children's laughter pealing through the cheerless season? Men and women could not laugh. They feared for themselves and for their friends, whenever they caught sight of the King's Commissioner. Bishop Burnet tells us how, when the other members of the Privy Council used to leave the chamber if a prisoner was to be tortured in the Boots, unable to look on at the excruciating process, the Duke remained and took note of all that was done, as if he were watching a curious experiment in science. Under the morose face there seemed to be a heart of stone.

We do not wonder that righteous men became conspirators. In England, through the whole of 1682, the great Whig plot had been moving forward. It aimed at accomplishing a revolution, but a revolution which should leave a constitutional monarchy behind, and which should simply exclude James from the throne. The leaders were the Duke of Monmouth, Lord William Russell, Lord Essex, and Sir Algernon Sidney. Monmouth, the illegitimate son of Charles, and the commander of the Royal troops at Bothwell Bridge, had no genuine moral strength, and was governed mainly by his fondness for popularity and position; but the others were patriots of a purer kind. They were anxious to gain and keep the goodwill of the malcontents among the gentlemen of Scotland. They corresponded with the Earl of Argyll, a fugitive now on the friendly shores of Holland. And in London they had the advice of William Carstares, and Fletcher of Saltoun, and Baillie of Jerviswood. Carstares, a born diplomatist, had his shining virtues, if sometimes he reached his goal by circuitous paths; he was afterwards to be King William's astute coadjutor in everything relating to the northern parts of the realm. Baillie's was a simpler and higher nature, and he would have welcomed the frankest and manfullest opposition to the royal encroachments. When Carstares, finding that the English were somewhat languid in carrying out the common purpose, insisted that the Scots should stay their preparations and walk with wariness, Robert Baillie stoutly maintained the contrary opinion. That their allies were laggards was no reason, he argued, why the Scots should not immediately unfurl the standard of the people's rights. It might be more arduous and more beset with fateful consequences to risk the under-taking alone, but it was also more glorious. If they should succeed, as he believed they could succeed, it would not be the first time, since the Stuarts inherited the Sceptre of Henry the Eighth and Elizabeth, that Englishmen owed to Scotland their enfranchisement from tyranny. But politic Carstares —Cardinal Carstares, as he was dubbed in subsequent days— prevailed with his counsels of moderation; and before an aggressive step was taken, the secret was out and the retribution fell.

Now, side by side with this great conspiracy, in which some of the finest spirits in the two countries were engaged, and which desired nothing but a beneficent change of government, there was being matured an unworthier plot whose intention was the assassination of the King and the Duke of York. The confederates who hatched the bloodthirsty project nick-named the royal brothers " Slavery " and " Popery "; or some-times they gave them sobriquets borrowed from their personal appearance: Charles, a dusky monarch, was the " Blackbird," while the Duke, who was blonde, was the " Goldfinch." Many were the debates as to where and when they should be killed. With one or two the proposal was to shoot at them from Bow Steeple; others would have them attacked in St. James's Park or in their barge on the river. The road between Hampton Court and Windsor, and that between London and Winchester, highways in which King and Duke were often seen, were suggested too. At last Rumbold, who had been a fearless officer among the Ironsides, but who was irreconcilably Re-publican in his political creed, invited the conspirators to meet at his house, the Rye, about eighteen miles from London, in Hertfordshire.   Near it ran a narrow lane which Charles was in the habit of using as he travelled to and from Newmarket. On one side of the lane grew a thick hedge, on the other was an outhouse with several windows; men bent on desperate deeds could not have wished a spot more suitable for the execution of their plan.   The mansion itself stood hard by; it was surrounded by a moat, and could easily be defended by a few determined fighters.   The offer of the advantageous place was instantly accepted, and therefore we speak of the Ryehouse Plot.   But the plot came to nothing, for the King left Newmarket on an earlier day than was expected, and there were no antagonists to intercept him as he drove rapidly home to Whitehall.   And then one of the band, after "much conflict with himself," uneasy in mind about so ugly a business, resolved to "discharge his conscience of the hellish secret."   The disclosure had far-reaching issues.   Some of the Ryehouse men were aware of the existence of the other scheme.   They had hoped to secure the help of the Whig gentlemen in their own wilder enterprise; but they had been indignantly repelled.   Now, when they were examined by the lawyers of the King, they revealed what they knew of the doings of Monmouth and Russell and Sidney and Baillie.

We need not linger over the sequel so far as it concerned England.   Few pages in British history are more touching and impressive than those which narrate how Lord William Russell underwent his trial; how he parted with his children and his wife, his eyes following her as she left his cell, and then turned to Gilbert Burnet and said, "The bitterness of death is past"; how calmly he moved through the crowded streets to the scaffold, and prayed his last prayer, and died. And Algernon Sidney ranks among the most heroic in "our rough island story."   "In his imprisonment he sent for some Independent preachers, and expressed to them a deep remorse for his past sins and great confidence in the mercies of God. And indeed he met death with an unconcernedness that became one who had set up Marcus Brutus for his pattern.

He was but a very few minutes on the scaffold at Tower Hill; he spoke little, and prayed very short, and his head was cut off at one blow."

It is round the Scottish victim, Robert Baillie of Jerviswood, that our interest gathers.

James Stirling of Paisley, Wodrow's friend, will introduce us to him. " He was a man of great natural parts, and learned, and well-travelled, and very pious from his very youth. He said, as I heard, that God had begun to work upon him when he was about ten years of age—that Christ crucified had been his daily study and constant delight. He was a man that had a sort of majesty in his face and stateliness in his carriage." There are other witnesses who confirm James Stirling. Burnet photographs the Laird of Jerviswood in one happy line: " A gentleman of great parts, but of much greater virtue." And John Owen, the massive Puritan, is unstinted in his admiration. "You have truly men of great spirits in Scotland," he said once; " there is for a gentleman Mr. Baillie, a person of the greatest abilities I almost ever met with." We are to think of a country proprietor of the best type, with estates in Lanark and Berwickshire. He is a great-grandson of John Knox. He has married one of the daughters of Archibald Johnston, Lord Wariston. He is a just and kindly landlord. He is a man, moreover, who thoroughly deserves Dr. Owen's tribute— a man of vigorous intellect, who can read various languages, who has a liking for mathematics, and who dabbles in scientific speculation and experiment. Better still, he is a little child in the household of faith, walking in humility and in friendship with his God. Let us hear Mr. Stirling again: " He owned himself a true Presbyterian, and a son of the Church of Scotland in her purest and best times. He was a great lover of public ordinances and Communion occasions; he was frequently present at several Communions in Cam'nethan, and he went to the Table there with a great measure of seriousness and devotion, greatly trembling, and yet sweetly coming forward with a holy boldness." Robert Baillie was wealthy, and scholarly, and saintly; and it is not often that we can apply the three adjectives to one man.

And what a good citizen he was! He had thought much about the problems of the State. His opinions were carefully weighed and wise. If King Charles had understood his own opportunity, he would have summoned him to the Council-board instead of hurrying him to the public executioner. "As for my principles with relation to Government," he wrote, "they are such as I ought not to be ashamed of, being con-sonant to the Word of God, the Confessions of Faith of the Reformed Churches, the rules of policy, reason, and humanity." He was, in fact, a gifted and devout champion of freedom in every department of the nation's life. Only the direst necessity drove such a man into the comradeship of con-spirators; loyalty was his native soil and air, but then it was loyalty to the righteousness and the clemency and the kingli-ness of soul which invest the ruler with his true sovereignty. He had been associated with those nobles and burgesses who, in these dreary months at home, were promoting a scheme of emigration from Britain to South Carolina; but it cut him to the quick that in the land he loved religion and justice should be standing "on tiptoe, ready to pass to the American strand." We have seen him taking his share in the negotiations by which honest and courageous statesmen hoped to inaugurate a change—such a change as would harmonise the liberties of the subject with the prerogatives of the Crown; but he was no extremist and leveller. If his inquisitors in Edinburgh tried to link him with the Ryehouse Plot, they did not succeed; he wished an end of tyranny, but he held tyrannicide in abhor-rence. It is certain that his affection for Church and Covenant had an emphasis about it which was missing from that of Argyll and Fletcher and Carstares; but it is as certain that he outstripped them in the intelligence and steadfastness of his attachment to the institutions of the State. Robert Baillie's chivalrous patriotism should have been beyond suspicion.

He was captured in London, in the summer of 1683. For some months he lay in prison there, so heavily loaded with irons that his health broke down. On different occasions he was examined by the King's Judges, and, once at least, by the

King himself. But they could not extort from him the information which they were eager to gain. They determined that, in company with the other Scottish prisoners, he should be sent to Edinburgh, where the laws were more arbitrary, and where torture could be applied to compel confession. On the first of November the royal yacht, the *Kitchin*, sailed from London. It was a protracted and stormy voyage of a fortnight's duration. On the fourteenth of the month Baillie, with William Carstares and the Campbells of Cessnock and Mure of Rowallan and the rest of the accused men, was carried from Leith up to Edinburgh, and was lodged in the Tolbooth.

He was in the lowest state of weakness now. His wife, the child of one good soldier of Christ and the helpmate of another, begged that she might be admitted to his dungeon, and declared her readiness to be laid in irons at his side, if the Council feared that she meant to aid him to escape; but her petition was roughly rejected. His little daughter, who longed to comfort him in his sore sickness, was denied access to her father. At length, when his bodily frailties had increased so alarmingly that death seemed close at hand, Mrs. Baillie and his sister-in-law, Lady Graden, received a grudging permission to attend upon him. For his enemies were by no means desirous that he should slip from them so quietly and so soon. This would both disappoint them of their revenge and rob them of the legal power to forfeit the prisoner's estates. That they might make sure of profiting to some extent, they imposed on him a great fine of £6000 for harbouring the outlawed preachers; the common feelings of humanity had deserted judges whose tender mercies were so cruel. "Yet," we learn from one who knew him, "he was so composed, and even so cheerful, that his behaviour looked like the reviving of the spirit of the noblest of the old Greeks or Romans, or rather of the primitive Christians and first martyrs in those best days of the Church."

Meanwhile, in the September of 1684—for the Edinburgh imprisonment lasted through a long time—the authorities had been torturing Carstares. The King's smith accompanied His Majesty's Privy Councillors, bringing with him a new pair of thumbkins, which were warranted to do their gruesome work in the deadliest fashion. The prisoner's thumbs were inserted, and screwed down, until the sweat of his anguish streamed over forehead and cheeks. The Dukes of Hamilton and Queensberry rose after a few minutes and left the room, finding the horrible scene too much for their nerves to bear. But Lord Perth, who presided, ordered the executioner to give the instrument another turn; and General Dalzell in a rage came up to Carstares, and vowed that he would roast him alive if he did not divulge whatever he knew. It was in vain. The sufferer continued firm, although the cruelty was prolonged for "near an hour and a half." Some days later, however, when he was threatened with a repetition of the frightful experience, or with the still worse agonies of the Boot, he promised to answer the questions which might be put to him, first making the stipulation that nothing he said should be brought, directly or indirectly, against any man who was on trial. The condition was acquiesced in; he was told that his replies would be matters of confidence. In these replies Robert Baillie's name was mentioned more than once. It was what the Privy Council had been seeking for; and, when they had the information, they did not scruple to break their engagement with Carstares. They determined to use every syllable which they had drawn from his unwilling lips.

Late in December, when his life was hanging by a thread, and he was so feeble that he was brought to the bar wrapt in his nightgown, Baillie confronted his judges. Because of her ill-health, his wife was absent; but Lady Graden sat by his side, and supported him, and had often to give him cordials to prevent him from fainting away. Sir George Mackenzie recited his crimes. He dwelt on the relationships of the accused man: "Remember you that he is nephew and son-in-law to the late Wariston, bred up in his family and under his tutory." He was at pains to identify the Ryehouse Plot with the larger designs of Lord William Russell and the Earl of Argyll, and he charged the prisoner with having a pre-eminent part in the less defensible scheme. Then he described how

ROBERT BAILLIE, OF JERVISWOOD.

After a Miniature of 1660.

Carstares, a "chief conspirator," had incriminated Robert
Baillie. With the deft and unlovely cleverness of a Machiavelli,
he connected the Presbyterian minister's unwillingness to give
his evidence with his knowledge that the information was to
be employed against his comrade; and he deduced Baillie's
guilt from that "scrupulosity" which the Privy Council had
at last discovered how to overcome. "Mr. Carstares knew,"
he said, "when he was to depone, that his deposition was to
be used against Jerviswood; and he stood more in awe of his
love to his friend than of the fear of the torture, and hazarded
rather to die for Jerviswood than that Jerviswood should die
by him. How can it then be imagined that this kindness,
which we all admired in him, would have suffered him to
forget anything which might have been advantageous in the
least to his friend? They understand ill this height of friendship, who think that it would not have been more nice and
careful than any advocate could have been." It is disin-
genuous reasoning; and, when one wants to study the sacred
subject of friendship, one turns to other teachers than Sir
George Mackenzie.

But Robert Baillie listened undismayed. When the
advocate finished, he had his opportunity. In his physical
frailty he was compelled to lean on the bar in front of him;
but there was no lessening of his spiritual nerve and force.
He addressed the President of the Court. "My lord," he
said, "the sickness now upon me, in all human appearance,
will soon prove mortal, and I cannot live many days. I find
I am intended for a public sacrifice in my life and estate; and
my doom being predetermined, I am only sorry, under such
circumstances, that my trial has given the Court so much and
so long trouble." Then, turning to the jury, he went on: "As
to the witnesses who have appeared against me, I do most
heartily forgive them: but"—and now there were fire and
energy in his words—"there is one thing where I am injured
to the last degree, that is, to be charged with a plot to cut off
the King and the Duke of York. I am in all probability to
appear in a few hours before the tribunal of the Great Judge.
In His omniscient presence, I solemnly declare that never was

I prompted or privy to any such thing, and that I abhor and
detest all thoughts and principles that would lead to touching
the life and blood of His Majesty, or of his royal brother, or
of any person whatever.   I was ever for monarchical government, and I designed nothing in all my public appearances,
which have been few, but the preservation of the Protestant
religion, the safety of His Majesty's person, the redressing
of our grievances by King and Parliament, the relieving of the
oppressed, and putting a stop to the shedding of blood."   The
freedom, for which so true and wise a reformer hungered,
must broaden slowly down.

A dramatic incident followed.   With a sudden movement,
he forsook the President and the jury, and fixed his eyes
straight and full on Sir George Mackenzie.   "My Lord
Advocate," the brave voice rang, as if before death its strength
were being renewed, " I think it strange that you accuse me of
such abominable things.   When you came to me in the prison,
you told me that such things were laid to my charge, but that
you did not believe them.   Are you convinced in your
conscience that I am more guilty now than I was at the
interview where you acquitted me of guilt ?   Do you remember
what passed betwixt us in the prison ? "   At once the gaze of
the court was fixed on Mackenzie.   He rose, annoyed and em-
barrassed.   " Jerviswood," he replied, " I own what you say.
My thoughts were then as a private man ; but what I say
here is by special direction of the Privy Council.   He "—
pointing to Sir William Paterson, the Clerk of the Justices—
" *he* knows my orders."   " Well, my lord," came the stinging
and unanswerable response, " if your lordship has one
conscience for yourself and another for the Council, I pray
God to forgive you: I do.   My lords, I trouble your lordships
no further."

The trial lasted until three o'clock in the morning of the 24th
of December.   The same day, six hours later, the jury found
him guilty.   It was plain that he was sick unto death, and,
says Lauder of Fountainhall, who had been Mackenzie's
junior at the memorable assize, " the holy days of Yule were
approaching "; so the Government, " at once bloodthirsty and

pious," must not delay the sacrifice. The Doomster declared the verdict. That very afternoon, between two and four of the clock, the convicted man must die. His head was to be placed on the Netherbow; his limbs were to be scattered throughout Scotland; his possessions were forfeit; his blood was tainted. Another degradation was added. The King's heralds came forward, and, having sounded their trumpets, they tore asunder the Jerviswood coat of arms, and trampled it under their feet, and proclaimed the martyr's family humiliated and abased. It was malediction heaped on male-diction, one ban treading fast and hard on the heels of a preceding ban. When he had heard it all, he drew himself up. "My lords," he said, in words which never were forgotten, "the time is short; the sentence is sharp; but I thank my God who hath made me as fit to die as ye are to live." He was the conqueror in the evil and yet glorious scene.

With Lady Graden's arm to sustain him, he left the court for his prison. As they passed Lord Wariston's house, he looked up to a well-known window, and, smiling, said to Helen Johnston, "Many a sweet day and night with God had your now glorified father in that chamber." He was himself a Christian whose unceasing joy had been to maintain communion with the heavenly place. We have learned how solitary his confinement was, and how his tormentors were reluctant to allow him the solace of intercourse with a single human friend. But in the cell next to his own lay some others bound, as he was, with a chain for the Hope of Israel; and "when they went together about worship, he brought his chair hard to their door, and laboured thus to join with them as far as he could." Now, for a brief hour or two, he was back in the Tolbooth for the last time. So soon as he entered the dungeon, we are told, he threw himself on his bed, and broke into a prayer which "soared like incense to the skies." He was in a rapture; there was a shining light about his looks; the tears of gladness refused to be held in check. He spoke like one who was already in his Father's house. Rising from his knees, he assured those beside him that, long ago, God had begun the good work in him, that He had carried it steadfastly on, and that now He was putting the copestone upon it. "Within a few hours," he said, "I shall be beyond conception inexpressibly well." Afterwards, when the moment had come for departure, he kissed his wife, his son George, a lad of nineteen, who was to be a statesman in King William's time, and the little daughter—kissed them, and blessed them, and pleaded earnestly that God might be with them. "And," he added, "within a little we shall have a cheerful and blithe meeting." "So pleasantly," good James Stirling writes, "he parted with them all."

Lady Graden, strengthened inwardly by the Spirit of God, went with him to the scaffold. She had to help him up the ladder, his body was so worn. When he had reached the topmost step, he cast his glance over the crowd. "My faint zeal for the Protestant religion," he said, "has brought me to this end." But it was not the wish of his adversaries that he should address a multitude in which he had many sympathisers, and immediately the drums began to beat. There was no reason, he continued, why the rulers should trouble themselves; for he had not intended to speak any more. Then he gave himself anew to prayer, and, as he prayed, the executioner did his work; and Robert Baillie had fought his last fight and his best.

The Whig movement for reform, like the Cameronian movement, was baptized in blood. But the baptism of blood very often is the preface of deliverance and the avenue to victory. A Hebrew psalm declares that through fire and water men are conducted to the wealthy place; and the doctrine of the psalm has been illustrated in many another epoch than the Old Testament era, and in many another land than Palestine.

CHAPTER XXIX.

LE ROI EST MORT.

CLOUD and grief had encompassed the Scottish Church for wearisome years. Yet, now and then, there were alleviations of the gloom—faint streaks of promise and hope in the heavy sky. Eight days after the sorrow of Bothwell Bridge, through the exertions of the Duke of Monmouth, whose heart was not so wholly unfamiliar with melting charity as were those of most of his contemporaries, the Third Indulgence had been published. While it still pronounced traitors the ministers who took any part in the field meetings, it permitted house conventicles, save in the towns of Edinburgh, St. Andrews, Glasgow, and Stirling. It granted liberty, too, to some of the imprisoned preachers. Was there in it, men asked themselves, the faltering prophecy, which might become more articulate soon, of a brighter time? But the feeble flicker of apparent dawn was very quickly obscured and quenched. Monmouth's influence with the King diminished within a few months, the Duke of York ousting him from his position of favour. The breathing-space was over, Wodrow says, before numbers of the Presbyterians knew of it at all. The Third Indulgence had disappeared, and the measures of repression were again enforced with unpitying rigour.

But occasionally a glint of sunshine came from an unexpected quarter. One of the friends of the Laird of Jerviswood was Sir Hugh Campbell of Cessnock. In the spring of 1684 he was on his trial in Edinburgh for high treason. It looked as if little fault could have been found with his behaviour; he was not one of the root-and-branch men; Jerviswood was

373

prepared to fight a much more unyielding battle than he.
Before the Court he pleaded that he had allowed no conventicles to be held on his ground, that neither he himself
nor his children and servants had been present at any, and
that he worshipped regularly within the walls of his own
parish church. But it was well enough understood that his
sympathies were with the friends of civil and religious
freedom; and, moreover, his estates were coveted by some
who stood in lofty place. So, while Baillie was lying in his
dungeon in the Tolbooth, Sir Hugh Campbell, "of very ancient
and honourable family," was arraigned before the Judges on
a capital charge, and the signs were that he would share his
comrade's death. Sir George Mackenzie and Sir George
Lockhart, the leaders of the bar, conducted the prosecution;
and the majority of the Lords on the bench were hostile to
the prisoner. The indictment was that, when two of his
retainers had left Sir Robert Hamilton's army and returned
to their master, he had sent them back to carry on the quarrel
of the Covenant, and had assured them that they should not
lack assistance from himself. But the one witness who told
this story, Thomas Ingram of Borlands, was a perjurer, a man
with a personal grudge against Campbell. When he was put
upon "the great oath," and when the prisoner, looking him
full in the face, bade him beware of making eternal shipwreck
of his soul, his courage failed. "Being interrogate upon the
rest of the libel"—that incriminating speech which he had
ascribed to Cessnock—he "deponed he knew nothing of it;
and this was the truth, as he should answer." Immediately
there arose a great shout of joy in the crowded court, and
hands were clapped; and the King's Advocate, Bloody Mackenzie, was beside himself with fury : he believed, he said,
that Campbell had hired his friends to make the unseemly
acclamation, and never, except in the trial of Shaftesbury,
had he heard "such a Protestant rore." The most disgraceful
feature of the proceedings was yet to be disclosed. The Lord
Justice General, the Earl of Perth, set himself from his place
on the bench to bully Ingram into supplying the evidence
which might condemn the prisoner. He took the task of

prosecution out of the hands of the advocates. But Sir Hugh
discovered allies on whose succour he scarcely had reckoned.
The jury was composed of men with beliefs which were not
those of the Covenanters; but they were men who kept in
their hearts the love of righteous dealing. First one of them,
and then another, and afterwards the whole of their company,
rose and bravely protested against the unjustifiable conduct
of the President of the Court. Lord Perth scolded and
stormed. "It is not I whom you contemn," he exclaimed,
"it is His Majesty's authority." His passion had no result.
The verdict was one of Not Guilty; and the Laird of Cessnock
owed his life to political and ecclesiastical antagonists, who
refused to be browbeaten out of fair-mindedness and chivalry.
No doubt, his bitterer enemies contrived an excuse for holding
him still in durance and for confiscating his property. But
more than that they dared not do.

An encouragement of a different sort, to be dated in July
or August of 1684, was the rescue at the Enterkin, the famous
pass between Lanarkshire and Dumfries, of which Dr. John
Brown has written: "We know nothing more noticeable,
more unlike any other place, more impressive, than this short,
deep, narrow, and sudden glen." Wodrow has one version of
the rescue, Defoe another, which varies somewhat, and which,
as we should expect from the creator of Robinson Crusoe, is
told in language at once more homely and more picturesque.
According to this narrative, some of Claverhouse's dragoons
had entered the gorge, dragging with them as prisoners a
Covenanting minister and five blue-bonneted countrymen.
They were slowly climbing the hill, when they heard a voice
call to them from the heights on their left. Then, through
the mist, twelve men came into view who, from a certain
distance, demanded the release of the minister. The officer
in command refused with an oath, but instantly he was shot
through the head; and, ever since, the wild cascade half-way
down the ravine has borne his name, and been called Kelte's
Linn. From the side of the dragoons, now conquered by
panic, which was all the more complete and paralysing that
there seemed to be a second body of armed men stationed on

the hill in front, a truce was asked. The prisoners were at once liberated—all of them, avers Defoe; all except John M'Kechnie, "a singularly pious man of Galloway," corrects Wodrow. "Go, Sir," said the captain to the preacher, "You owe your Life to this Damn'd Mountain." "Rather, Sir," replied the minister, "to that God that made this mountain." "Well, but," cried the soldier to the leader of the gallant peasants who had got the better of him, "I expect you call off those Fellows you have posted at the Head of the Way." "'They belong not to us,' says the honest Man, 'they are unarm'd People, waiting till you pass by.' 'Say you so?' said the Officer; 'Had I known that, you had not gotten your Men so cheap, or have come off so free.' Says the Country-man, 'An ye are for Battle, Sir, We are ready for you still. If you think you are able for us, ye may trye your Hands; we'll quit the Truce, if you like.' 'No,' says the Officer, 'I think ye be brave Fellows; e'en gang your Gate.'" Thus, from the Enterkin and its guardian hills, Thirstane and Stey Gail—hills which, Defoe is compelled to confess, are "as high as the Monument"—the Covenanters bore away rejoicingly their precious booty, and the troopers rode crestfallen towards Edinburgh.

For months before young James Renwick, having returned from Holland, held his first conventicle in the winter of 1683, the voices of the public preachers were stilled and hushed. But amongst the Cameronians there continued to be an un-broken and thriving spiritual life; as he comprehends who reads that interesting old book which Michael Shields penned, and which carries on its opening page the expressive title of *Faithful Contendings Displayed*. It is the story of the Societies —the meetings of those who owned the testimony of Cargill and Cameron, holding themselves apart from their fellow-Presbyterians because they judged them lax and latitudinarian on the subject of the Indulgence and the Indulged, and separating themselves as emphatically from all acknowledg-ments of the governance of a persecuting State. These men and women, to whom the declarations of Sanquhar and Torwood were dear, *spake often one with another*. They strengthened

CHARLES II.

After the Portrait by Sir Peter Lely.

each other's hands in God. Over the whole of the South of
Scotland their gatherings for prayer and mutual counsel were
held. The gatherings in every county were under the supervision of a District Society or Correspondence. And, once in
three months, the Correspondences sent commissioners to the
General Meeting, to which matters of difficulty were remitted
for debate and settlement. In 1683, as Gordon of Earlston
informs us, there were no fewer than eighty societies, with seven
thousand men in their membership, men who would not bow
the knee to Baal, and many of whom had wives and children
as steadfast as themselves. And so the holy fire was kept
blazing on the altar of Christ, even when the love of multitudes
had waxed cold.

With Michael Shields for our guide, we have the
opportunity of entering a Society meeting. There may be
sixty or seventy persons present. They have assembled
probably under cover of the night, and there is a friendly
farmhouse close at hand. Everything is done in quietness
and order. A president is chosen; and by and by he states
the special question to be discussed. Perhaps it is: Must we
decline to pay bridge-dues and market-dues as well as the
cess and the militia-money? Some insist on the extremer
position; but they are overruled by the larger number, who
are not prepared to go so far in non-compliance. Or it may
be: How shall we help our brothers, who are reduced to
poverty by their refusal to submit to the tyrannous demands
of Government? Then those who have not been fined and
stripped to the same sad extent promise their aid; for the
Society men have learned to bear one another's burdens, and
so to fulfil the law of Christ. Or it is: If there should be a
Popish rising, must we refrain from assisting our country in
the moment of its dire distress? And the decision is a
patriotic one: there must not be any intimate association with
Royalists; but the Cameronians may organise by themselves
their fighting forces, and may strike hard against Jesuitry and
all its works; ere many years have passed, they will actually
be doing it to good purpose. Often, in the General Meeting,
the talk would turn on the crying need for ministers of the

Q

Gospel, who should preserve their garments unspotted and their witness unshaken and full; and it was agreed that the only method of obtaining these was to send some of their own young men to Holland, to be educated and ordained by the exiled Covenanters there. But, in the midst of those anxious colloquies over the practical difficulties of the time, the Societies never forgot the perpetual claims of the individual soul. Their meetings were homes of earnest prayer and patient study of the Scriptures; and the worshippers who went to them would come away with their faces transfigured and their spirits empowered with new and heavenly strength.

The very children were imbued with the dauntlessness of their elders. To this year of 1683 belongs a Bond subscribed by fifteen girls in the village of Pentland, who had their own little gathering for purposes of devotion. "This is a Covenant between the Lord and us," it begins, "to give up ourselves freely to Him, without reserve, soul and body, hearts and affections, to be His children, and Him to be our God and Father, if it please the holy Lord to send His Gospel to the land again." Soon they mount from self-dedication into entreaty: "O Lord, give us real grace in our hearts to mind Zion's breaches, that is in such a low case this day; and make us to mourn with her, for Thou hast said, them that mourn with her in the time of her trouble shall rejoice when she rejoiceth." Each girl sets down her name to the fearless document: Beatrix Umpherston—she was but ten summers old; Janet Brown, Helen Moutray, Marion Swan, Janet Swan, Isobel Craig, Martha Logan, Agnes Aitken, Margaret Galloway, Helen Stratton, Helen Clark, Margaret Brown, Janet Brown, Marion M'Morren, Christian Laurie. If, as the Talmud says, Jerusalem fell because the training of the children had been neglected, the Scotland of the Covenant was manifestly doing her part to escape so sore a fate.

These were some of the straggling rays which succeeded in penetrating the thick darkness. But the times were as evil as they could be. Nor were they improved by the startling event of February 1685—the death of King Charles. We have now to say our farewells to the monarch in whose company

we have been through all these chapters, a monarch whom
Scotsmen cannot love. The end was in harmony with everything which had preceded. It came suddenly. On Sunday
night, the first of the month, he spoke to Thomas Bruce, one
of the gentlemen in attendance, about his new palace in
Winchester. "I shall be so happy this week," he said, "as
to have my house covered with lead." "And God knows,"
adds Bruce, awe-stricken, "the Saturday following he was put
into his coffin." On Monday morning he was seized with
apoplexy, and there never was any hope of recovery for one
whose frame was sapped by his own vices. An hour or two
before the last, the strange thing occurred which seemed a
fitting termination to a career full of evasion and deceit. A
Catholic priest, Father Huddleston, was brought into the
death-chamber. Charles and he had met formerly in
memorable circumstances, immediately after Worcester. "As
soon as the King saw the father come in, he cried out, ' You
that saved my body is now come to save my soul.' He made
a general confession, with a most true, hearty, and sincere
repentance, weeping and bewailing his sins, and he received
what is styled all the rites of the Church ; and, just at high
water and full moon at noon, he expired." One wonders
whether, anywhere in his dominions, there was a single citizen
who sincerely mourned his departure. The hunted folk north
of the Tweed drew a long breath of relief when they heard
that, at length, the Chief Malignant was gone.

We may be certain, too, that, with their emphatic
Presbyterian notions, they thought none the better of him for
his interview with priest Huddleston. As for us, who read
the curious tale after the lapse of more than two hundred
years—how gladly our hearts would believe in the genuineness
of the spiritual change, whether the agent employed to accomplish it were Jesuit or Cameronian ! But it may be feared
that King Charles died as he had lived, a worldling and a
libertine. It is thus, with austere dignity, that John Evelyn,
whose temper is so amiable, writes of the consummate hour :
" I can never forget the inexpressible luxury and prophaneness,
gaming, and all dissoluteness, and as it were total forgetfullness

of God—it being Sunday evening—which this day se'en-night
I was witnesse of; the King sitting and toying with his con-
cubines, Portsmouth, Cleaveland, and Mazarine; a French
boy singing love-songs in that glorious gallery; whilst about
20 of the greate courtiers and other dissolute persons were at
basset round a large table, a bank of at least £2000 in gold
before them: upon which two gentlemen who were with me
made reflexions with astonishment. Six days after, all was
in the dust!" That terribly sharp-edged word with which
Thomas Boston of Ettrick smites the loose livers of his and
every time, not to expect "the chance of a leap out of Delilah's
lap into Abraham's bosom": would it not have been well if
Charles Stuart had weighed and pondered its truth sooner
than he did?

Before we leave him, let us look at him again. He
appeared to be an incorrigible idler, a hero of the tennis-
court and the ballroom, a king of Yvetot—

> Se levant tard, se couchant tôt,
> Dormant fort bien sans gloire.

He was a hunter of moths and a friend of little dogs. He
was, says Mr. G. M. Trevelyan, "the humorist, whose thick
licentious lips were a fountain of wit, seemingly his only
defence against servants who robbed and statesmen who
opposed him." He is the Merry Monarch, laughing uproari-
ously at all Puritanism and seriousness. Yet he was
undeniably the ablest of the Stuarts, with an astute mind
and a resolute determination concealed beneath the jester's
motley of trifling and ribaldry. The ministers of State whose
boon-companion he was were more frequently his tools and
dupes than they themselves ever imagined. He listened to
them with an unconquerable politeness, while he made his
own plans and went his own way.

Recent investigation has been doing justice to the King's
cleverness and craft; and, in the fresh light which it has
thrown on his complex personality, we can detect three great
movements of policy that he adopted and prosecuted in
successive periods of his reign. Earliest among them was the

tremendous scheme which Lord Acton has described in a
remarkable essay on the *Secret History of Charles II.* It was
nothing else than the subversion of the Protestantism of the
nation and the substitution for it of a Catholic despotism,
with himself at the head of it as the irresponsible and unfettered master whom nobody should hold in check. The
treason was to be accomplished with the assistance of the
money and arms of Louis XIV. In May 1670, Charles's sister,
Henrietta of Orleans, herself gentle and affectionate but a
pupil only too apt of her priestly confessors, negotiated for
him the private Treaty of Dover, by which England and
France agreed to partition Holland, and the French King
promised his English ally active and substantial aid in the
establishment of Romanism in Great Britain. Charles had
another confidant in his plot. This was the eldest of his
illegitimate children, a son born in Jersey when he was
himself no more than sixteen years of age—a favourite son
whom he loved to call by the royal name of James Stuart.
The boy's mother was a lady of high rank whose name the
father was careful always to conceal, for even in his cynicism
there were a few vulnerable places; and a mystery clings
about the character and biography of the lad himself. In his
opening manhood he became a Jesuit; and, sometime in 1668,
Charles brought him back from Italy to London. He was
eager, through him, to make his own peace with the Pope,
and to gain the powerful help of the Jesuits for his attempt
to reinstate Catholicism. To the young man he held out the
glittering possibility of becoming one day King of Britain
and defender of the true faith. But, although James Stuart
had much intercourse with his father in those years, he was
not attracted by the dazzling bribe; he preferred to remain
a humble soldier in the ranks of the Society of Jesus. The
King's coadjutors both failed him when he required them
most. The son went back to his spiritual calling, and, a brief
month after the shameful Treaty of Dover had been concluded
and signed, Henrietta of Orleans was dead. Moreover, the
country had begun to suspect that something was wrong;
and, although men did not dream of the extent of the

treachery, they revealed their detestation of Popery in various modes and with sufficient explicitness. By 1673, Charles was convinced that the Catholic revival for which he had been hungering and intriguing was an impossibility.

Then came the second phase of his statecraft—his alliance with the unbending Toryism and Anglicanism of Sir Thomas Osborne, the Earl of Danby. If he could not compass the Romanist ascendancy which would have been after his own heart, he might still be an absolute monarch, while he veiled his individual predilections in matters of religion. He could find in the Cavaliers a convenient instrument for confirming and increasing his autocratic powers. So the King stood like a veiled figure behind his first minister, and urged Danby forward in every high-handed measure, and fought Shaftesbury and Sacheverell and the Whigs with a diplomacy whose skill was seldom at fault and whose perseverance never flagged. Gradually this antagonism to the Country Party, as the Whigs were designated—the popular and prevailing party in a succession of Parliaments—led Charles into the third supreme endeavour of his reign. Shaftesbury and his friends brought in one Exclusion Bill after another. They were resolved, if they could, to prevent the Roman Catholic Duke of York from entering upon the heritage of royalty. The bulk of the nation was on their side. But often their leaders were ill-advised, and often they were selfish and violent in the methods they followed. Their councils were divided, some of them desiring Monmouth for King, others with much greater wisdom turning to the Prince of Orange. And Charles, under the cloak of his indifference and laughter and epicureanism, never ceased watching them. He knew perfectly what he wished, that his brother, whom his people distrusted and disliked, should be his heir. He laboured unwearyingly for his end. And he achieved it, partly through the blunderings and errors of his opponents, but in large degree through his own patience, his own cunning and vigilance, his own abundant resource. It is evident that we must not picture him simply as a *roi bonhomme*, and still less as a *roi fainéant*. He could be diligent when he chose; but

the diligence was never exerted in a noble cause. He was
shrewd and sage; but the shrewdness was consistently mis-
applied, and the sagacity was malicious and disastrous. It is
hard indeed to decide whether Charles's idleness or his
activity bore the more poisonous and the more fatal fruits.

The brother, who stepped into the vacant place, and with
whose policy and methods the Covenanters were already too
fully acquainted, was as obnoxious to all right-thinking men.
James, the Seventh of Scotland, the Second of England, was
dull and narrow in understanding, stubborn in temper, cruel
and revengeful in disposition. The patriots of both countries
had planned and striven to deprive him, because of his
avowed Popery, of the supreme possession of kinghood; but
their efforts had been foiled. The political world was quiet
now; and the nation listened to assurances from the Throne
of "the innate clemency of His Majesty, a virtue which hath
shined in the whole line of his royal race." But, in the
earliest days of the Duke of York's reign, there were ominous
symptoms of impending trouble. He declined to take the
Coronation Oath for Scotland, because its terms would have
hampered him in his schemes for the re-establishment of
Roman Catholicism. An obsequious Privy Council suffered
him to have his way; but three and a half years later, when
the hour of reprisal arrived, the omission became a count in
the indictment which deprived him of his sceptre and crown.
Meanwhile, however, he was an untrammelled tyrant. He
might do what he chose; and he used his power with merci-
lessness and ferocity.

CHAPTER XXX.

THE KILLING TIME.

OCCASIONALLY we find the designation, *The Killing Time*, applied to the twenty-eight years of the Persecution, the long winter of wind and snow which lay between the home-coming of King Charles and the advent of King William. But it is a loose and slipshod employment of the phrase. What the men who survived the tempest meant, when they looked back and spoke of the Killing Time, was a shorter period—the period between 1684 and 1688. Then they entered "the gloomy cave of Desperation." Then, more than ever, they were "battered with the shocks of doom." And then, too, Christ, the Prince of sufferers and the Brother born for adversity, came nearest those who passed through innumerable trials for His Name's sake. "Not a few of us stood in this faith," wrote Cromwell to Speaker Lenthall after the battle of Dunbar, "that, because of their numbers, because of their advantage, because of their confidence, because of our weakness, because of our strait, we were in the Mount, and in the Mount the Lord would be seen." The remnant in the fields and moors were in the Mount, when their enemies gloried over them; and in the Mount they saw their Lord. They listened to the vivifying accents of His voice, and felt, as it were, the grasp of His warm hands.

While all Covenanters experienced the edge of the gale, the members of the Praying Societies were treated with sharpest severity. It became evident that nothing short of their extirpation was intended. Bloodhounds were used to ferret out their places of hiding. Spies and renegades were

hired to win their confidence and to betray them. Soldiers
had permission to shoot at once, without any pretence of
trial, suspected persons who should refuse to take the Test,
or to answer bewildering and insidious questions about the
murder of Archbishop Sharp and about the legality of the
rising at Bothwell and about the righteousness of bearing
sword and gun against the King. We do not marvel that
the Hillmen were driven to exasperation by these atrocities.
They retaliated. They turned on their oppressors, as in the last
resort the stag will turn on the baying hounds. On the night
between the 11th and the 12th of December in 1684, Peter
Peirson, the curate of Carsphairn, was shot dead by James
MacMichael, one of the Wanderers. More than most, the
unfortunate preacher had incurred their enmity. That winter
evening they went to his manse, a little company of angered
and outraged men, "the black MacMichael" their leader.
They meant to extort from the curate a written promise that
he would cease encouraging their foes; they "expressly
declared that they would do him no bodily harm." But he
came to the door armed and threatening; and, in a moment,
their captain's pistol had robbed him of life. It was a crime
against righteousness and against love. And there were
other uprisings of anger. Two months previously, in October,
the Cameronians had published their *Apologetical Declaration*
—a document which bids good-bye to meekness and gentleness. "We warn the enemies to our cause, such as bloody
militiamen, malicious troopers, soldiers and dragoons and
spies, and their aiders and abetters, all who either conspired
with bloody Doeg to shed our blood, or with the flattering
Ziphites to inform persecutors where we are to be found.
We warn you of the hazard that ye incur by following such
courses; for sinless necessity for self-preservation, accompanied with holy zeal for Christ's reigning in our land
and suppressing of profanity, will move us not to let you pass
unpunished. All that is in peril is not lost, and all that is
delayed is not forgiven."

Probably the vehement and volcanic sentences ought not
to have been penned; there is more of the Book of Judges

in them than of St. Paul's chapter on charity.   Let us
remember, in condonation of their sanguinary tone, that, like
Thomas Lodge's *Rosalynde*, they were "hatcht in the storms
of the Ocean and feathered in the surges of many perillous
seas."   Certainly they brought fresh sorrow on the heads of
their authors and of those who read them with satisfaction.
The Lords of the Privy Council decreed that any one who
owned, or who might scruple about disowning, "the late
treasonable" manifesto, whether he carried arms or not, was
immediately to be killed, care being taken simply that the
slaughter was carried out in the presence of two witnesses.
Special courts were appointed, which met in various centres
and summoned the country-people before them, to see that
they "did abhor and renounce the pretended declaration of
war lately affixed at several Parish Churches."   "All usual
forms of law," Sir Walter Scott writes, and he is no partisan
of Kirk and Covenant, "all forms by which the subjects of
a country are protected against the violence of armed power,
were broken down."   It was a reign of terror.   Lowland
Scotland lay, during the Killing Time, at the mercy of the
dragoons, and most of them did not know what the quality
of mercy is.

Who were some of their leaders?

One was Sir James Johnstone of Westerhall.   Once, *The
Cloud of Witnesses* says, he was, as others of these hot-foot
persecutors had been, "a great professor, and one who had
sworn the Covenant."   Indeed, his retractation was quite
recent.   "When the Test was framed, he bragged that he
scorned the Test; but, when he had the trial, he embraced
it, and became a bitter enemy to the work and people of
God."   There is a peculiarly lurid story with which Johnstone's
name is linked in infamy.   Andrew Hislop was a lad of
seventeen.   To the cottage home of his widowed mother
there crept one day, conquered by mortal sickness, a fugitive
from the cold hills, one of the proscribed Cameronians.   She
gave him shelter; and there, in a short time, he died.   Fearing
punishment for their hospitable deed, she and the boys who
had grown up at her knee buried the body, under the curtain·

of night, in a neighbouring field. But the grave was discovered soon; and the widow's house was stripped of all
its simple and cherished belongings, and was pulled to the
ground. While she and her sons were wandering from place
to place, Claverhouse came upon Andrew, and conveyed him
as a prisoner to Eskdale to the Laird of Westerhall.
Johnstone, there and then, passed sentence of death. But
even Claverhouse had his compunctions about this murder,
perhaps, Wodrow suggests, because conscience was speaking
to him of the wrong he had done ten days before to John
Brown of Priesthill. It was not until Westerhall insisted,
that he ordered three of his dragoons to fire. The guns were
loaded, and the boy was told to pull his bonnet over his eyes.
But he refused, and stood confronting his slayers with his
Bible in his hand. "I can look you in the face," he said;
"I have done nothing of which I need to be ashamed. But
how will you look in that day when you shall be judged by
what is written in this Book?" He fell dead, and was
buried among the Craighaugh brackens and heather. No
doubt, it was the exodus which Andrew Hislop craved; it
was euthanasia to him. His were the prayers and avowals
which a modern poet has put into the lips of another boyish
knight of the Cross—

> O give my youth, my faith, my sword,
>   Choice of the heart's desire:
> A short life in the saddle, Lord!
>   Not long life by the fire.
> The outer fray in the sun shall be,
>   The inner beneath the moon;
> And may Our Captain lend to me
>   Sight of the Dragon soon!

But Westerhall's shame is perpetual, and the blot on his
character will never be removed.

Or here is Lieutenant Douglas, brother of the Duke of
Queensberry. In 1685, in a cave at Ingliston, in the parish
of Glencairn, he surprised a little company of the Covenanters.
His soldiers, having shot into the cave, rushed in through the
smoke of their muskets. They captured five prisoners—John
Gibson, Robert Grierson, Robert Mitchell, James Bennoch,

and John Edgar. Without even the most perfunctory examination, Douglas ordered them to prepare for death. Gibson was led out first. He was allowed to pray: and so familiar and tender and appealing his prayer was that, in spite of themselves, the very dragoons were moved. He sang part of the 17th Psalm, and read aloud the sixteenth chapter of the Gospel of John. His sister and, after her, his mother —for their home was near at hand—were permitted to speak to him. He told them that it was the joyfullest day ever he had in the world. He charged them that they must not yield to tears, but must bless the Lord on his account. Then they were thrust back; and from the matchlocks death came, rapid, sweet, a boon and not a curse. His four comrades were shot together. The volley killed three; but the fourth, while he was fatally wounded, was still conscious. One of the soldiers saw it, and ran on him with his sword. Even yet the indomitable witness-bearer could give his testimony. "Though every hair of my head were a man," he cried, "I am willing to die all those deaths for Christ and His cause"; and so he went through the River singing. That is but one recital of martyrdom for which James Douglas was responsible; there are many like it.

Or there is Captain Bruce of Earlshall, who fought Richard Cameron at Ayrsmoss. The persecution of the Westland saints was like meat and drink to him. In January 1685, near Straiton in Ayrshire, his men seized Thomas M'Haffie, whom everybody in the district reverenced for his godliness. On this winter morning he was hiding in a glen adjoining the village. He was fevered and ill; exposure and rain and frost were robbing him of strength and hastening him to the sight of his Master. But he was to travel by a still speedier road to the land where the inhabitant does not say, *I am sick*. In his covert he heard the soldiers approaching, and rose, and fled. He reached the shelter of a friend's roof; but there, exhausted, he threw himself down; he could make no further effort. In a few minutes Captain Bruce and his troop entered. One or two questions—the usual ensnaring and dishonest questions—were addressed to him; but he declined to answer. And then they dragged him from the room, out to the high-road, and shot him without more ado. For Thomas M'Haffie the days of mourning were ended.

More notorious, however, than Johnstone or Douglas or Bruce was Sir Robert Grierson of Lag. Who does not know Wandering Willie's Tale in *Redgauntlet*? "I will not believe in anything to match it," Mr. Ruskin said; and Grierson is hero of the weird and piquant story. "Ye maun have heard of Sir Robert Redgauntlet of that Ilk, who lived in these parts before the dear years. The country will lang mind him; and our fathers used to draw breath thick if ever they heard him named. . . . He was knighted at Lonon court, wi' the King's ain sword; and being a red-hot prelatist, he came down here, rampaging like a lion, with commissions of lieutenancy, and of lunacy, for what I ken, to put down a' the Whigs and Covenanters in the country. Wild wark they made of it; for the Whigs were as dour as the Cavaliers were fierce, and it was aye which should first tire the other. Redgauntlet was aye for the strong hand: and his name is kenn'd as wide as Claverhouse's or Tam Dalyell's. Glen, nor dargle, nor mountain, nor cave, could hide the puir hill-folk when Redgauntlet was out with bugle and bloodhound after them, as if they had been sae mony deer. And troth when they fand them, they didna mak' muckle mair ceremony than a Hielandman wi' a roebuck. It was just, 'Will ye tak the Test?'—if not, 'Make ready; present; fire!'—and there lay the recusant."

Redgauntlet was aye for the strong hand. Yes indeed, there was no vestige of tenderness in Sir Robert Grierson. He had not even the superficial polish with which some of his brother-Royalists bedizened their cruelties. He was as ungracious in manner as he was hard of heart, a Judge Jeffreys on a smaller scale. There is an acrid pasquil of the eighteenth century which immortalises him in biting words. It takes the sinners of Scripture one by one, and asks which may "with Grier of Lag compare." Cain was bloody; but "he to Lag's latchets never came." "Doeg the Edomite did slay Fourscore and five priests in one day"; but "brave Lag did Doeg far exceed." Herod killed many "by a decree"; but he was outrun by Grierson, who "in his person went To every place where he was sent, To persecute both man and wife." To this hour, in Dumfries and Galloway, a paramount horror cleaves to his name.

We are not astonished at it, when we read such an incident as that of John Bell. He was a man well born, the only son of the heiress of Whiteside, in the parish of Anwoth, who, after his father's death, had for her second husband the Viscount Kenmure. Far and near he was held in repute, both for his religion and for his prudence and "mensefulness." Since Bothwell Brig he had borne many trials and wrongs. The horses of the dragoons had "eaten up all his meadows"; the men themselves had "broken down the very timber of his house and burned it." In February 1685 the last of his griefs arrived. With four associates, John Bell fell into Grierson's hands. Quarter had been promised, but Lag laughed at the promise; he commanded that they should be shot instantly. "Let me spend a few minutes in prayer," said Bell. "What have you been doing so many years in these hills?" Grierson retorted— "No, no! you have prayed enough." And, when the good man was dead, he would not let them bury him; his vengeance must be wreaked on the lifeless frame. Some weeks later, he met Lord Kenmure in Claverhouse's company, at Kirkcudbright. The Viscount upbraided him for his brutality to a kinsman, whom Lag knew to be of gentle blood and breeding, and especially for his churlish refusal to allow the body a resting-place. But Grierson swore at him, and made a most offensive reply. "Take him," he cried, "if you will, and salt him in your beef-barrel." In his anger the nobleman drew his sword, and would have attacked the man who had insulted him so coarsely. But Claverhouse interposed, and separated the two.

John Graham himself was foremost actor in the misdeeds of the Killing Time. His eulogists admit that he was "imbued with a disregard of individual rights," and that, himself "careless of death, he was ruthless in inflicting it upon others."

He was appointed Sheriff of Wigtown in January 1682, and was also commissioned to act as Sheriff-depute in the neighbouring districts of Dumfries, Annandale, and Kirkcudbright, inasmuch as " guilty persons do remove from one jurisdiction to another, when they are called in question and pursued, and it is necessary, in this exigent, that they be brought to justice " ; and, being both magistrate and soldier, he had special opportunities for executing the policy of the Government.   Even little children did not escape his notice. There is no reason to doubt the truthfulness of that persistent tradition which gives a grim account of his untendernesses towards them.   He would collect the girls and boys of a country hamlet, some of them no more than six years of age, and, drawing up a line of dragoons, would bid his victims pray, because he intended to put them at once to death. Sometimes, to heighten their alarm, the men were actually ordered to fire over their heads.   And then he would inform the poor innocents, terrified that the close of life had come, that he was willing to spare them, if they would show him where their fathers or elder brothers or friends were concealed. It is not easy to understand how one so cold-blooded should be exhibited to us as the mirror of chivalry.

In his Sheriffdom he showed no lack of energy.   Three weeks after his appointment he had travelled through the whole of Galloway, from Stranraer on the west to Dumfries on the east.   He wrote letter after letter to Queensberry, detailing his movements and activities.   Now and then, like the rare oasis in the hot sands of an African desert, there is a milder note : " It will be mor of consequence to punish one considerable laird than a hondred litle bodys.   Beseids, it is juster, because these only sin by the exemple of those."   But the relenting was brief-lived.   A week later, he had captured " that great villain MkClorg, the smith at Menegaff, that made all the clikys, and after whom the forces has troted so often " ; and there was to be no door of escape for this descendant of Tubal-cain, who had known too well how to cut the bridle-reins of the persecutor's cavalry.   " I am resolved to hang him, for it is necessary I make some exemple

of severity, least rebellion be thoght cheap here. There can
not be alyve a mor wiked fellou." It was his ever-recurring
regret that he had not a larger company at his disposal. "It
wer no great business for the King to send as much mony as
would mantain fyve or six hondred mor dragoons; and in
tuo or three years this contry, I am seur, would be broght to
forgett all there follys." Erelong he was in violent conflict
with one of the principal Wigtownshire families, the
Dalrymples. The father, Sir James, the Viscount Stair of
subsequent years, was absent in London, whither he had
fled when the Test Act came into operation. But Sir
John, his son, remained behind him, and continued to be
Heritable Bailie of the Regality of Glenluce. He was at heart
opposed to the repressive measures of the time; and, as far as
he could, he showed his distrust of them, and of those who,
like the vigorous master of the countryside, were zealous in
carrying them out. But Claverhouse would not tolerate such
slackness and neutrality. He formally indicted Dalrymple
before the Privy Council, accusing him of giving employment
to disloyal and disaffected persons, of imposing mock-penalties
—not the fiftieth or sixtieth part of what the law demanded—
in order that the culprits might be immune from any sorer
punishment, and of conniving at the irregularities of the
ladies of his house who had some fondness for the teachings of
the Covenant. The case, which dragged its slow length along
through several months, stirred, as Lauder of Fountainhall
tells us, "much transport, flame, and humeur"; but Claverhouse won the libel. Sir John Dalrymple lost his Bailery,
and was fined five hundred pounds sterling, and learned how
dangerous it was to thwart King Charles's Sheriff.

It is futile to contend, as has occasionally been done,
that in his persecuting zeal Claverhouse was simply the
instrument of others. For two years, from May 1683 to
March 1685, he was himself a member of the Privy
Council. He was not always present at its meetings, being
kept so busy out in the fields and on the hillsides and at
the Courts of Justiciary up and down the country. He was
not on the best of terms with some of its dominant figures,

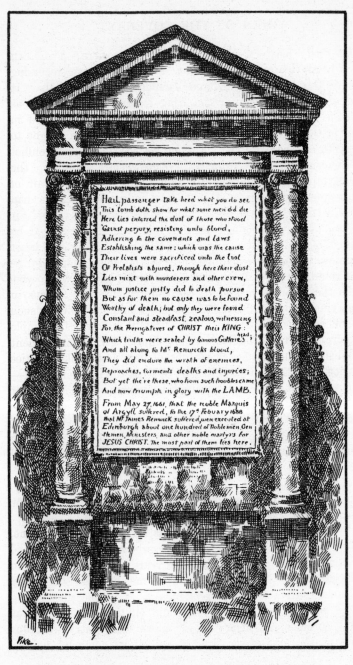

Hail, passenger, take heed what you do see.
This tomb doth show for what some men did die.
Here lies interred the dust of those who stood
'Gainst perjury, resisting unto blood;
Adhering to the covenants and laws
Establishing the same; which was the cause
Their lives were sacrificed unto the lust
Of Prelatists abjured, though here their dust
Lies mixt with murderers and other crew,
Whom justice justly did to death pursue.
But as for them no cause was to be found
Worthy of death; but only they were found
Constant and steadfast, zealous, witnessing
For the Prerogatives of CHRIST their KING:
Which truths were sealed by famous Guthrie's head;
And all along to Mr. Renwick's blood,
They did endure the wrath of enemies,
Reproaches, torments deaths and injuries;
But yet the're these, who from such troubles came
And now triumph in glory with the LAMB.

From May 27, 1661, that the noble Marquis
of Argyll suffered, to the 17ᵗʰ February 1688
that Mr. James Renwick suffered, were executed at
Edinburgh about one hundred of Noblemen Gentlemen, Ministers and other noble martyrs for
JESUS CHRIST. The most part of them lies here.

THE MARTYRS' MONUMENT IN THE GREYFRIARS
CHURCHYARD.

coming as he did into sharp collision more than once both
with Queensberry and with General Dalzell. But he played
his own part in its decisions and enterprises, and he was best
pleased when these were emphatic and thorough. " I fynd
myself worse there every day," he wrote to a friend ; " but I
take no notice of it. I goe thither as I used to doe, but only
when I have business of publik concern ; and houever things
goe am resolved to doe as a good subject oght and a man of
honor." There are papers of the Council, letters and decrees,
on which his signature may be seen ; for what it determined
and did he must bear his moiety of responsibility. The dogged
ill-will of Queensberry succeeded at last, when James II. had
mounted the throne, in humbling John Graham, with his
" hye, proud, and peremptor humor," and in expelling him
from his seat at the Council's board. But his exile lasted for
less than two months. If James had surrendered temporarily
to the machinations of his rivals, in reality he cherished no
intention of dispensing with an agent whose beliefs and
methods were entirely to his own mind ; he had him restored
to the dignity from which jealousy and hate had driven him.
It is apparent that we must amend somewhat the antithesis
which was quoted on a former page from Mr. Francis Watt :
there were years of his life in which Claverhouse was not
only " the hand that struck "—like Sir George Mackenzie, he
was also " the brain that plotted."

A specially burdensome grievance of the Killing Time was
the exorbitant fines inflicted on men who could not conform.
It was the boast of Claverhouse that he never sought " to
enrich himself " ; but the boast was ill-founded. His avarice,
if it is not so conspicuous in the earlier part of his career,
grew with the numberless chances he had of reaping a harvest
from the misfortunes of others. It is proved by the narrative
of Lord Fountainhall, who draws a picture of the soldier-
Sheriff's exactions, and of the meanness which too often disfigured his procedure. He spoiled the homes of the sufferers,
whether they were richer or poorer. He wrung from them
the last farthing of the extravagant dues which he had imposed. With all his anxiety to force the people to accept

Episcopacy, he was willing to release his prisoners if he could secure from them the promise of a thousand merks apiece. His rapacity became at last a public scandal; and the officers of the Crown compelled him to pay into the Exchequer moneys which he was appropriating to his own purposes. John, Viscount Melfort, brother of the Earl of Perth, and one of the two Secretaries of State for Scotland in King James's reign, wrote to Queensberry news which gladdened that envious nobleman's heart—how, in London, the Duke of York was observant of the "insolence" of the overweening Colonel of dragoons, and was "really angry with him"; how he had himself got orders to send him such a reprimand as would sufficiently show his Royal Highness's displeasure; how, at length, James had commanded "the fynes upheld by Claver-hous to be counted for and payed in"—so now, "without a grudge," Queensberry might call for them. "I am affrayed," Melfort added, "that gentleman has mistaken his measures, and, if he persist, I question not that he will find it so." When they had to combat greed as well as bloodthirstiness, were not the advocates of the Covenant in pitiable case?

Then there were the banishments. Let us take *The Cloud of Witnesses*, and turn to its concluding pages, with their list of those driven into strange lands for conscience' sake. In March 1684, seven were sentenced and sent to West Flanders, "never to return under pain of death." In July 1684, "were banished to Carolina thirty, who were transported in James Gibson's ship, called sometime Bailie Gibson in Glasgow, of whom it is observed that, in God's righteous judgment, he was cast away in Carolina Bay, when he commanded in the *Rising Sun*." In the same month five men are exiled to New Jersey. In the following year, we read that "in the time of Queens-berry's Parliament, of men and women were sent to Jamaica two hundred." A little later, "one Pitlochie transported to New Jersey one hundred, whereof twenty-four were women." Before 1685 has ended, "three-and-twenty men and women were sent to Barbadoes." And so the record pursues its course. What ignominies, what agonies, are hidden under the brief entries! Often the vessels were poor and unsea-

worthy. The unfortunate captives were treated with a harshness which felt no relentings of mercy. They were crowded
together under the decks. They had insufficient food, and
the scantiest supply of water, and scarcely any fresh air.
Many of them died on the voyage, and never saw the shores
of the Western world. When they landed, they were sold as
slaves ; and if they resisted, and strove to retain their freedom,
trouble upon trouble was visited on them. " Their cruelty
to us," writes John Mathieson of Closeburn, " was because we
would·not consent to our own selling or slavery; for then we
were miserably beaten, and I especially received nine great
blows upon my back very sore, so that for some days I could
not lift my head higher than my breast." Chattels rather
than persons the Covenanting bondmen seemed to their taskmasters.

In the experiences of these exiles romances are shut up,
which, if they were but deciphered, would prove as thrilling
as any adventures that the novelists give us. John Mathieson
is an instance in point. Contriving to escape, he sailed to
Virginia through a dangerous storm. Then he journeyed on
foot to Pennsylvania, and from Pennsylvania made his way
mile by mile to New England, where he knew of some
Presbyterian friends. But they had changed their soul as
well as their sky, and were no longer so faithful as they had
once been; and he could not stay among them. With a
saddened heart he turned back to New Jersey, and there
sickness fell on him. But strangers entertained him hospitably ; and, when he recovered, he bound himself of his own
accord to be their servant. " For, albeit we could not work to
them that had brought us over, yet we behoved to work for
something to bring us back again." All this while, too,. his
Lord was very gracious to him in the distant land. Twice or
thrice he covenanted with Him, " on these terms that He
would carry me and my burden both, and save His noble
truth from being wronged by me; and so I took Him for my
King, Priest, and Prophet." There were seasons when he
felt such a clearness of his interest and salvation, that the
thought of it made him leap for joy in the midst of his

travail. "For many and wonderful were His loving kind-
nesses unto me, even to me, one of the silliest things that ever
He sent such an errand; so that, as its passes my memory to
relate, I think truly it would seem incredible to many to
believe, when they heard them told, even what He hath done
for poor, insignificant, unworthy me." But the *Heimweh*, the
home-sickness, was strong; his heart hungered to be back
with the devoted remnant in Scotland. At last he had
gathered enough to pay his passage from New York to London;
and, after an absence of something over three years, he was
again among those for whom he had so quenchless a desire,
"hearing with much delight the Gospel faithfully preached,
yea, powerfully preached, by that shining light, Mr. James
Renwick." Pathos and gladness pursued John Mathieson to the
close. When he entered his own house, his wife was preparing dinner for the reapers cutting and binding the yellow corn.
She did not recognise him; he was a wayfarer, she fancied,
who had come in at the open door to rest himself. She
pressed him to take some food, and, with hands full, went out
to the workers with their portion. But, as she passed him,
he rose, and followed her at a respectful distance. Turning
her head, she saw him, and, mistaking his intention, said to
the bystanders, "The gangrel body wants a second dinner."
The words drew the eyes of the reapers towards him; when
one of his own sons whispered to his mother, "If my father is
living yet, that's him." She looked keenly into the stranger's
face for a single moment, and then ran to his arms, crying,
"My husband!" It is meeting after parting as touching, and
as bonnie, as the meeting of Penelope and Ulysses.

Two other memories of the Killing Time are worth recal-
ling. Shall we name them, The Stories of Mr. Valiant and
his Brother?

We have not forgotten Captain John Paton of Meadowhead, who fought stoutly at Rullion Green and again at
Bothwell, those twin days of struggle and flight. He was an
old man now, and the privations of a soldier's career had
added to his age. The dragoons had not much difficulty in
making him prisoner. In August of 1683, he was in a friend's

house near Kilmarnock, when a party of five troopers, moving along the road, claimed him as their prize. It happened, contrary to his practice, that he had with him neither pistol nor sword; but those under whose roof he was offered him both. Ten summers before he would have welcomed the offer, and have fought the dragoons single-handed; to-day he declined the suggested aid. He was well stricken in years, he said, and worn with fleeing from place to place; and he had no fear of death, for his portion in Christ's love and redemption was sure—it was best that he should surrender to his antagonists. But as yet they did not surmise who he was; they imagined him some venerable preacher of the Covenant. It was when they passed a farm farther on, and the farmer, standing at his door, exclaimed in amazement, " Captain Paton! are you there?" that they discovered the value of the booty they had taken. From Kilmarnock they carried him to Ayr, from Ayr to Glasgow, from Glasgow to Edinburgh. General Dalzell saw him as he was led bound into the capital. They had fought together at Worcester two-and-thirty years past and gone; and there were fragments of courtesy and com-passionateness surviving still in the rugged old persecutor. He embraced the prisoner. " John," he said, " I am both glad and sorry to see you. If I had met you on the way before you came hither, I should have set you at liberty; but now it is too late." On the impartial tablets of history, the speech must be written to the honour of the rude Muscovite bear.

Captain Paton's trial did not take place until the spring of 1684. He was condemned on his confession that he had been at Bothwell, and was sentenced to be hanged in the Grass-market on Wednesday the 23rd of April. But twice over, the first time on his own petition, the second time perhaps through the influence of Dalzell, the execution was delayed. On the later occasion the Clerk of Council noted in his books: " John Paton, in Meadowhead, sentenced to die for rebellion, and thereafter remaining in mosses and moors to the high contempt of authority, reprieved till Friday come sen'night, and to have a room by himself, that he may prepare more conveniently for death." It was an unwonted clemency; but the interval was soon ended. On Friday, the 9th of May, he was executed, dying, Wodrow relates, " most cheerfully," as indeed he had always lived. His last testimony shows how thoroughly he had appropriated the lessons William Guthrie taught him from the pulpit of Fenwick Church. " There is no safety," he declared, " but at Christ's back ; and, I beseech you, improve time, for ye know not when the Master calleth, at midnight or the cock-crowing. Seek pardon freely, and then He will come with peace. Seek all the graces of His Spirit—the grace of love, the grace of holy fear and humility." It is the dialect of *The Christian's Great Interest*.

Mr. Valiant's brother was John Nisbet of Hardhill. He too had fought at Pentland ; and not for twelve months thereafter were his wounds altogether healed. With his own right hand he sent seven of Claverhouse's troopers to death at Drumclog. At Bothwell he occupied the post of danger at the bridge, standing as long as a comrade stood beside him. After that, he was a rebel, denounced by the Privy Council, with a price set on his head, chased unceasingly from one concealment to another. He had a wife as brave as he was. With her young children she was turned adrift upon the world ; but never was she heard or seen to show the least discontentment with her lot. Through more than four years she contended against her great army of afflictions, until, on a December day, her enfranchisement came ; and she died " in a sheep's cot, where was no light nor fire but that of a candle, no bed but that of straw, no stool but the ground to sit on." It was some time before the news that she had gone from him reached her husband. As soon as he heard, he hurried to the spot, to find that her dead body had been in its grave for days, and that meanwhile new sorrows were sweeping down on his head. The first sight on which his eyes lighted was the rude coffin which some friendly hands had put together, and in which he saw his daughter lying, her short race finished and her soul flown away to God. Glancing round the hut, he discovered other troubles ; for in a corner two of his boys lay in the delirium of fever. He spoke to them, but they were unconscious of his presence ; and then he groaned, and said,

"Naked came I into this world, and naked must I go out of it; the Lord is making my passage easy." It is difficult to believe that, in all literature, one will encounter any story more bitter-sweet.

At last John Nisbet had his liberation. He was taken on a Sabbath morning in November 1685. Three friends in the family of faith had spent the preceding evening and night in his society, not sleeping much, but praying and conversing a great deal. With day-dawn the soldiers appeared. The four defended themselves for a time, Nisbet standing with his back to the wall, and caring nothing for the wounds he received. But they were overpowered. The other three were shot immediately; but, because there was a reward of three thousand merks offered for him, he was bound, and conducted across the country to the Privy Council in Edinburgh. They tried him on the 30th of November, and ordered his death in the Grassmarket four days later. The spell of respite was spent in heaven rather than on earth. Hitherto he had been a man who had never uttered much of his own soul's convictions and joys; but now *his tongue was loosed and he spake plain.* "Scar not," he wrote, "at Christ's sweet, lovely, and desirable cross; for, although I have not been able because of my wounds to lift up or lay down my head but as I was helped, yet I was never in better case all my life. He has not given me one challenge since I came to prison, for anything less or more; but, on the contrary, He has so wonderfully shined on me with the sense of His redeeming, strengthening, assisting, supporting, through-bearing, pardoning, and reconciling love, grace, and mercy, that my soul doth long to be freed of bodily infirmities and earthly organs, that so I may flee to His royal palace—even the heavenly habitation of my God, where I am sure of a crown put on my head, and a palm put in my hand, and a new song put in my mouth. . . . Welcome, welcome, welcome, our glorious and alone God! Father, Son, and Holy Ghost, into Thy hands I commit my spirit, for Thou art worthy!" Mr. Valiant's brother did not require to wait until he gained the other side to hear the trumpets sound for him. The invigorating music greeted his ears before he placed his foot in the waters; and he went through the swellings of Jordan with a high heart.

We cannot exhaust the pains and the pageants of the Killing Time. We cannot recount all its sufferers and conquerors. "It has not been possible to come at the certain number," Daniel Defoe says in a passage of notable eloquence, "there being no record kept of their prosecution in any court of justice, nor could any roll of their names be preserved in those times of confusion. But under the Altar, and about the Throne of the Lamb, where their heads are crowned and their white robes seen, an exact account will at last be found."

THE GRASSMARKET OF EDINBURGH.

CHAPTER XXXI.

HOW JOHN BROWN WON HIS DIADEM.

THE month of May in 1685 stands out with a melancholy pre-eminence, a garland of thorns, among the dark months of the Killing Time. It saw the deaths of John Brown and of the Wigtown Martyrs. The veracity of both histories has been questioned by writers whose sympathies are courtly and prelatist; but both have been proved true beyond dispute.

Here, for example, is Professor Aytoun. In the appendix to his *Lays of the Scottish Cavaliers*, lays which persist in placing the laurel on the less deserving brows, he investigates at much length "the story of John Brown," which he was "particularly anxious to expiscate." The "tale," he says, "is usually brought forward as the crowning instance of the cruelty of Claverhouse." In the course of his examination Aytoun writes : "For thirty-three years after the Revolution, the details of this atrocious murder were never revealed to the public! Nowhere in print or pamphlet, memoir, history, or declaration, published previously to Wodrow—1722—does even the name of John Brown occur, save once, in *The Cloud of Witnesses*, a work which appeared in 1714; and in that work no details are given, the narrative being comprehended in a couple of lines." But, as Dr. Hay Fleming replies, "Aytoun's search must have been perfunctorily performed." In a pamphlet by Alexander Shields, published immediately after the Revolution, the tragedy is thus told : "The said Claverhouse, in May 1685, apprehended John Brown in Priesthill, in the parish of Moorkirk, in the shire of Air, being at his work about his own house, and shot him dead before his own door, in presence of his wife." A year later, Gilbert Rule gives a brief but explicit account of the martyrdom. Two years afterwards, there is allusion to it again in one of the best-known controversial books of the time. The Royalist professor has been negligent in his scrutiny.

Claverhouse, he would have us believe, "was not present at the execution." But it is a sheer impossibility to prove an *alibi* for John Graham. His own biographer, Sheriff Mark Napier, who sees no slightest spot on the face of the sun, has published the letter which the persecutor addressed to the Duke of Queensberry on Sabbath, the 3rd of May 1685. These are its opening sentences: "on Frayday last, amongst the hills, betwixt Douglas and the Plellands, we purseued tuo fellous a great way throu the mosses, and in end seised them. They had no armes about them, and denayed they had any; but, being asked if they would take the abguration, the eldest of tuo, called John Broun, refused it, nor would he swear not to ryse in armes against the King, but said he kneu no King. Upon which, and there being found bullets and match in his house, and treasonable peapers, I caused shoot him dead: which he suffered very inconcernedly." There need be no debate in our minds either about the arbitrary conduct of Claverhouse or about the triumphant faith-keeping of the carrier of Priesthill. These are not the pathetic adornments of a skilfully constructed page of fiction. They are demonstrated facts.

In his despatch to Queensberry, Claverhouse speaks of capturing, along with John Brown himself, "a young fellow and his nephew." It is curious that neither Robert Wodrow nor Patrick Walker has a word to relate regarding this second participant in the tragedy—John Brounen or Browning. Perhaps they forbore to mention him, because they judged him unfaithful to his vows, one who had ingloriously preferred the cowardly road of compliance. For, after he had said his prayers, and the carbines had been presented, John Graham offered that, if he would reveal something which might be of importance for the King's service, he should himself plead for his life with those in authority. So the lad admitted that he had been one of an attacking party which, a day or two previously, had assailed the royal soldiers in Newmilns, and that he had come straight from this escapade to his uncle's house. Meantime, while the inquisitor and the frightened boy were engaged in their interview, the dragoons had been searching the place, and had lighted on a new piece of evidence. In a cave under the ground were concealed some swords and pistols. These they brought to their commander; and John Brown's nephew, being confronted with them, acknowledged that they were the property of his relative, the man who lay dead a few yards away. The captain thereupon bade his troopers put their carbines down, and sent the Covenanter to his Lieutenant-General, that the superior officer might dispose of him as he pleased.

No doubt it was with the view of defending himself from the accusation of barbarity in slaying John Brown, that Claverhouse was thus particular in recounting what he had learned from the younger man. Let it be confessed that the Priesthill carrier was in revolt against the rulers of the land: are there not moments when rebellion is transfigured into spiritual duty, and when the subject clothes himself with honour if he takes rank amongst insurgents? There are laws sublimer than the statutes of Government—the dictates of conscience, the requirements of patriotism, the precepts of God; and sometimes he who reverences the higher laws must resist the lower. But it may be argued that John Graham, being the emissary of those who were parents of the bad legislation, had no choice but to punish the man who set it at defiance. This fact, however, must hinder us from condoning him, that the damnatory evidence was not forthcoming until the victim had been sacrificed; the nephew was examined after the uncle's murder. In truth, there was neither justice nor mercy in all the proceeding. No real assize was held. No defence was permitted. The doom fell in an instant. But it fell on a heart which it could not impoverish, and which it was powerless to affright.

Some five miles distant from the town of Muirkirk, up among the lonely hills, was the croft of Priesthill. There is no cottage there to-day, nor any garden bright with homely flowers; but the spot may be identified by the monument which has been raised to the tenant who made it famous. In 1685 Priesthill was the abode of John Brown and his wife, Isabel Weir. Suspect and dangerous the husband might be in his politics, but in personal life none was more inoffensive: the countryside knew his religion and his uprightness. An impediment in his speech had forced him to surrender his hope of entering the office of the ministry; but his reading and shrewdness and character fitted him to be the teacher of those near the little farm who desired instruction in the truth as it is in Jesus. One evening in each week he met with "the young persons of the neighbourhood," and expounded to them the Bible and the Confession of Faith. In summer they gathered in a sheepfold out in the fields; in winter they formed a circle round the fire of peat which blazed on the kitchen floor in the carrier's house. The place was wild and solitary, and round it the heather and moss stretched for miles; but it was a training-school for theologians and heroes. Three of those who looked to John Brown as guide were afterwards put to death for their faith; and frequently their modest teacher was obliged to secrete himself in the moors of Lanarkshire and Kyle.

In 1682 he and Isabel Weir had been married. From the first there were some drops of vinegar in their chalice of joy. Within the home, trust and tenderness were perpetual guests, and Christ sat at the humble table. But to the wife's heart forebodings would come, unbidden visitors compelling her to listen to their prophecies of evil. It was Alexander Peden who pronounced the lovers one flesh. When the simple ceremony was over, "Isabel," he said, "you have got a good man; but you will not enjoy him long. Prize his company, and keep linen by you to be his winding-sheet; for you will need it when ye are not looking for it, and it will be a bloody one." Did ever bride receive so heavy a benediction? That was why there were undertones of sadness in the music of Isabel Brown's home-life, and why, when the man of God on whom she leaned was absent longer than his wont, a look

of apprehension leaped into her eyes. Just three years of
wedded gladness the two were to know; and then the hour
came when the winding-sheet had its dread use.

Again, on one of the last days of April in 1685, Alexander
Peden came to the carrier's house at Priesthill. He was
always an honoured friend, and he remained overnight—this
gaunt and yet gracious seer of the Covenant, who, for the
most part, had nowhere to lay his head. Early on May-day
morning he said his farewells ; but, passing out from the door,
he was heard repeating to himself, " Poor woman, a fearful
morning ! " These words twice over, and then—"a dark
misty morning ! " John Brown too was up betimes ; and,
having kept the worship of God with those dearest to him,
he went, with a spade in his hand, to dig some peat-ground
not far away. The mist lay thick and grey over everything.
Neither he nor his nephew dreamed that their enemies were
so near them. They " knew not until bloody, cruel Claverhouse compassed them with three troops of horses." There
was no chance of flight; they were made prisoners and led
back to the house. It was remembered afterwards by the
poor wife that, in these most poignant and blessed moments
of his life, her husband's stammering left him altogether; he
addressed Claverhouse in clear and unshaken accents. So
noticeable was this distinctness of utterance that the captain
inquired of those who had directed him through the moors
whether they ever had heard the tenant of Priesthill deliver a
sermon; but they answered, " No, no ! he was never a preacher."
" If he has not preached," Claverhouse said, " meikle has
he prayed in his time "; and then, turning to his captive,
he added, " Go to your prayers, for you shall immediately
die." So, on the grass beside the door, the carrier knelt
down, to speak to his Friend in heaven. But he had many
things to say; and John Graham, growing more and more
impatient, interrupted him three times over. It was not for
himself that the suppliant was concerned, although he was on
the threshold of death, nor yet chiefly for his wife and little
ones; it was downtrodden and afflicted Scotland which lay
like a burden on his soul. He was pleading that the Lord

R

would spare a remnant, and would not make a full end in the day of His anger. "I gave you time to pray," Claverhouse exclaimed angrily, "and ye've begun to preach." The intercessor paused to reprove the man whose ignorance was inexcusable. Looking about on his knees, he said, "Sir, you know neither the nature of preaching nor of praying, that calls this preaching." Then, for a short space longer, he continued unconfused his interview with the Father above.

And now John Brown "yielded to Fate as lambs to the eagle's pounce"; or rather, as Alexander Henderson before him and Adoniram Judson long afterwards described the sunnier side of death, he ran to God with the alacrity of a boy bounding home from school. When the prayer was done, Claverhouse spoke again. "Take good-night of your wife and children," the lips commanded which seldom had any compassion for stubborn Whigs. The woman whom the martyr loved was standing near, with a baby in her arms. Going to her he said, "Now, Isabel, the day is come that I told you would come, when I spake first to you of marrying me." She replied, with a fortitude at which probably she marvelled afterwards, "Indeed, John, I can willingly part with you." "That's all I desire," he answered; "I have no more to do but die." He kissed his wife and the bairns with whom he had both prayed and played, and begged God to multiply "purchased and promised blessings" upon them, and gave them his good-bye. Then, says Patrick Walker, "Claverhouse ordered six soldiers to shoot him, and the most part of the bullets came upon his head, which scattered his brains upon the ground." Turning to the new-made widow, the officer asked callously, "What thinkest thou of thy husband now, woman?" "I thought ever much good of him," she responded with swift loyalty, "and as much now as ever." "It were but justice," he went on, "to lay thee beside him." "If ye were permitted," she said, "I doubt not but your cruelty would go that length; but how will ye make answer for this morning's work?" His was a mocking and contemptuous retort: "To man I can be answerable, and, for God, I will take Him in my own hands." But he had no leisure to bandy more words. At this point, we may believe, the nephew's examination took place; and when it was completed, he mounted his horse, and left Isabel Weir with her loved and holy dead.

For some hours she had no human comforter, so isolated and remote the cottage was. The last sacred duties were performed without a neighbour's aid ; and, heart-breaking as the task was, she would not have wished things otherwise; what other fingers had such incontestable right to make the good confessor ready for his sleeping-place ? " She set the bairn upon the ground, and gathered his brains, and tied up his head, and straightened his body, and covered him with his plaid, and sat down and wept over him." The relief of tears had been granted at length. Then, after a time, when the news reached the nearest dwellers in that wilderness country, a mother in Israel found her way to Priesthill. " The first that came was a very fit hand, that old singular Christian woman, in the Cummerhead, named Jean Brown, who had been tried with the violent death of her husband at Pentland, and afterwards of two worthy sons killed and shot." We can see them still, these kinsfolk in grief, one with the white hair and the other with the dark, as they wept and prayed together, until the younger could thank God for the angel He had sent to minister to her in her Gethsemane.

Hitherto we have been following Walker's account of the events of that May dawn. But there is one part of the story where Wodrow gives us another version. Instead of relating how the six troopers fired simultaneously, he declares that the rough soldiers were so subdued and broken by John Brown's prayer that, " as my information bears, not one of them would shoot him or obey Claverhouse's commands, so that he was forced to turn executioner himself, and in a fret shot him with his own hand before his own door." The commander was capable of such a deed, and this is the narrative which has been commonly accepted. But, because there is some uncertainty, we may allow John Graham the benefit of the doubt.

The murder was committed between six and seven in the morning. Alexander Peden was then ten or eleven miles distant. Before eight o'clock he found himself at the gate of a friend's house, and lifted the latch, and entered the kitchen, craving permission to pray with the family. "Lord," he said, "when wilt Thou avenge Brown's blood? O, let Brown's blood be precious in Thy sight!" When the voice of yearning and entreaty had ceased, John Muirhead, the father in the home, asked Peden what he meant by Brown's blood. "What do I mean?" he answered. "Claverhouse has been at the Priesthill this morning, and has murdered John Brown. His corpse is lying at the end of his house, and his poor wife sitting weeping by his corpse, and not a soul to speak comfortably to her." And then, lifted into a kind of ecstasy, he continued, "This morning, after the sun-rising, I saw a strange apparition in the firmament, the appearance of a very bright, clear, shining star fall from heaven to the earth. And indeed there is a clear, shining light fallen this day, the greatest Christian that ever I conversed with." Into Peden's eyes "from the well of life three drops" were instilled; his heart, as the Quaker apostle said, was baptized into a sense of all conditions; and he saw, by a spiritual intuition, the sorrows which were happening in other parts of the vineyard of Christ.

One knows not whether the courage of husband or of wife is the more admirable. But hers were the loss, the cup of gall, the weighty heritage of pain. He went instantaneously from his moorland croft to the "lovely city in a lovely land," where "pleasures flow as rivers flow." She lived on in widowhood, dowered with ineffaceable memories.

> "What think you now of your braw goodman?"
>   Ah, woe is me!
> My heart was high when I began,
> My heart was high, and my answer ran,
>   "More than ever he is to me."
> But when I laid him on his bed—
>   Ah, woe is me!—
> And spread the face-cloth over his head,
> And sat me down beside my dead,
>   O, but my heart grew sair in me.
> It's well for men to be heroes grand—
>   Ah, woe is me!
> But a woman's hearth is her country, and
> A desolate home is a desolate land:
>   And he was all the world to me.

CHAPTER XXXII.

AT THE WATER OF BLADNOCH.

THE tragedies and victories of the Maytime of 1685 were not concluded. Little more than a week after Claverhouse had sent John Brown to the summer and Sabbath of the everlasting country, young Andrew Hislop refused to pull his bonnet over his eyes, and looked the death-bringers in the face without fear or shame. On the very day of his triumph, Margaret Lachlison and Margaret Wilson were drowned in the tides of the Solway, because their wills were eager and steadfast to promote the glory of Christ.

The persecutors reached the lowest depths of infamy when they made war on women. This drowning is an indictment of their methods and actions so terrible that every endeavour has been put forth to represent it as a figment of the imagination. Half a century since, Sheriff Napier stated *The Case for the Crown,* and strove hard to prove that never, except in Covenanting literature, had there been any Wigtown Martyrs. He admitted that the two Margarets—the widow of more than threescore, and the girl whose womanhood was yet in front of her—were condemned to die. But, he asked, did they not petition the Government for a reprieve? And was not the request granted? And were they not transferred from their Galloway prison to Edinburgh, that they might await the announcement of the King's pleasure? And is it not the conclusion to which probability and analogy and argument tend, that the royal pardon did actually come to them, and that they went out from their bonds to safety and freedom? The Sheriff's questions have a plausible sound, and we ought to know how they can be answered.

Over nine separate districts in the south of Scotland, James Douglas, the kinsman of the Duke of Queensberry, and a man with whom already we have some acquaintance, ruled as Commissioner for the Privy Council and for His Majesty King James. It was impossible that he should take personal cognisance of all that occurred throughout a jurisdiction so widely extended; he was compelled to intrust much of his work to subordinates. Thus he had no immediate share in trying and sentencing the two women; the ugly task fell to four of his agents—David Graham who was Claverhouse's brother, Robert Grierson of Lag, Major Winram, and Captain Strachan. They were |men to whom even so unchivalrous an exploit was not utterly repugnant; and at a court held in the little town of Wigtown, on the 13th of April, they decreed that the culprits should be consigned to the mercies of the Solway. They had, it must be acknowledged, some legal justification for their barbarity. Only a few weeks before, the Privy Council had ordained that, while a man who hesitated about disowning James Renwick's Declaration was at once to be hanged, a woman "who had been active in the said courses in a signal manner" was to be drowned in loch or stream or sea. Margaret Lachlison and Margaret Wilson, being followers of Renwick who did not scruple to avow their beliefs, had indubitably exposed themselves to the pains and penalties of this extraordinary statute.

They were sentenced, therefore; but did they not, a few days after their trial, seek a reprieve? In the Register House of Edinburgh may be seen a petition addressed to the Council by the older of the two sufferers, and authenticated by "Gulielmus Moir, notarius-publicus," the suppliant herself being unable to write. It confesses that Margaret Lachlison, prisoner in the Tolbooth of Wigtown, had been righteously condemned to death for "|not disowning that traiterous apollogetical declaration laitlie affixed at severall paroch churches within this kingdom," and for "refusing the oath of abjuration of the saymein." It declares that, having now had an opportunity of considering "the said declaratione," she realised that it conduced to "nothing but rebellione and seditione," and was "quyt contrair unto the wrytin word of God," and so she was "content to abjure the same with her whole heart and soull." It beseeches his Grace the Lord High Commissioner, and the remanent lords of His Majesty's Most Honourable Privy Council, to " take pitie and compassione " on the offender, and to "recall the foirsaid sentence so justlie pronouncet." And, finally, it promises that ".your supplicant shall leive ane good and faithful subject in tyme cuming, and shall frequent the ordinances, and shall give what other obedience your Grace and remanent Lords sall prescryve." Such was the petition; and, although no document has been found which makes these admissions and solicits these favours in the younger woman's name, the likelihood is that the authorities in Edinburgh were approached on her behalf too. For, on the 30th of April, the Privy Council granted a reprieve to both; and, once again, life and liberty seemed to lie within the grasp of the prisoners. Death had come very close; but, meanwhile, his advance was checked, and perhaps he might be routed altogether and driven away.

But no one who reads this petition with unbiassed mind will maintain that it is couched in Margaret Lachlison's own language, or that it photographs with accuracy her sentiments and thoughts. It was drawn up for her by friends, who were afflicted in her affliction and would fain have effected her escape. She was unlettered, although she was not ignorant of God's mysteries and of the secrets which Christ keeps for those whom He loves. She could not have written the craven parchment; and it appears incredible that she could have inspired its paragraphs. For, a day or two previously, she had protested before her judges her whole-hearted approval of that which she was made now to scorn and deny and trample in the dust. And when we turn to Margaret Wilson, the conviction is deepened that the recantation and the appeal did not originate directly with the sufferers. She had received that schooling which her comrade lacked, and in her prison she set herself to compose an Apologia—a defence of " her refusing to save her life by taking the Abjuration." The more we ponder the matter, the clearer it becomes that the petition for mercy proceeded not from the women themselves but from kindly neighbours, who felt, it may be, in how much discredit the execution of the sentence would involve the Government, and who were unfeignedly anxious to succour those with whom they were linked in acquaintanceship and intimacy.

The reprieve itself is curiously worded. It leaves a blank where we should expect to find inserted the date on which the days of grace were to expire. And it "discharges the Magistrates of Edinburgh," and not the Provost and Bailies of Wigtown, from carrying out the sentence which had been pronounced. The date may have been designedly kept in suspense, that time might be allowed for procuring the King's forgiveness, if the culprits should actually swear the oath that was demanded of them. It is more difficult to understand the allusion to the civic rulers of Edinburgh. On the ground of it, Sheriff Napier contended that, having satisfied the authorities in Wigtown of their penitence, the two Margarets were conveyed to the Scottish capital, and were detained there until the decision as to their ultimate fate should come from Whitehall. But there is not a shred of proof for this theory, and there are many testimonies to the fact that the women were never removed from Galloway. Probably the intention was to carry them to Edinburgh if only they had shown themselves pliable and complaisant, and to intimate to them within its walls their final pardon. The rulers were much too shrewd to liberate the delinquents in the same provincial town where they had been condemned, and among the people most deeply interested in their welfare. They would themselves have reaped a harvest of contempt, they would have been taunted with their own patent and palpable defeat, if they had done so. Prudence required that the reversal of their sentence should be accomplished at a safe distance. So the magistrates of the capital were selected instead of their municipal brothers in Wigtown, and the design was that they should be the latest actors in the drama. But the prisoners spoiled the well-planned scheme by their recalcitrancy. They refused stubbornly to take the Abjuration Oath. And thus they never saw the High Street, and the crown of St. Giles, and the Tolbooth where many of their spiritual kindred had lain. From Wigtown Gaol they were led out to die.

That neither in one part of Scotland nor in another did King James's pardon bring freedom to Margaret Lachlison and her virgin sister in Christ is as certain as any historical fact can be. Dr. Archibald Stewart, the minister of Glasserton, replied to Sheriff Napier; and the refutation is overwhelmingly complete. There are five witnesses, Dr. Stewart says, to demonstrate the truth of the Solway martyrdom. There is tradition: could there have been the persistent and undying story, the universal local belief in the reality of the execution, if "the cruel crawling foam" never crept up and up until all was over? There is the evidence of old pamphlets: in the *Informatory Vindication* of 1687 reference is found to what the persecutors had done in "drowning women, some of them very young and some of exceeding old age"; in *A Hind Let Loose*, published immediately afterwards, the indictment is reiterated—"Neither were women spared; but some were hanged, some drowned tied to stakes within the seamark, to be devoured gradually with the growing waves"; and these are but precursors of many similar reminiscences of the gruesome event. There are the unequivocal assurances of the earliest histories: Daniel Defoe, for example, came to Scotland in 1706, and gathered personally the materials for his *Memoirs of the Church*, applying to the most trustworthy sources of information; and he is visited by no doubts on the subject of the martyrdom. There are the minutes of the Church courts —the Synod of Galloway, the Presbytery of Wigtown, the Kirk-Sessions of Kirkinner and Wigtown and Penningham: for, in the commencement of the eighteenth century, the Church of Scotland enjoined its various judicatories throughout the country to collect accounts of the sufferings for religion in the troublous times which were then happily past; and, down in the south-west, as these minutes narrate, numbers came forward to tell how they had been familiar with Margaret Lachlison and Margaret Wilson, how they knew the manner of life the godly women had lived, and how their sorrowful

and yet glorious death was graven indelibly on mind and
heart. And, last of all, there is the younger confessor's tombstone in Wigtown Churchyard—a tombstone which was
erected within the lifetime of those who could remember the
occurrences of 1685, and which in rude and vivid rhyme
relates that

> Within the sea ty'd to a stake
> She suffered for Christ Jesus' sake.

It is a fivefold cord which cannot easily be broken.

Who will testify that the tragedy indubitably took place?

Bailie M'Keand will. On the 8th of July 1704, he came
to the Kirk-Session in Wigtown, a man of a broken spirit, and
begged that again he might enjoy the high privilege of partak-
ing, side by side with the members of the Church, in the
sacrament of the Lord's Supper. He spoke of "the grief of
his heart that he should have sitten on the seize of these
women who were sentenced to die in this place in the year
1685, and that it had been frequently his petition to God for
true repentance and forgiveness for that sin." And the elders,
having inquired into the carriage of the Bailie since the epoch
of his transgression, and being satisfied that his contrition was
sincere and deep, admonished him, and granted him the boon
he craved, and exhorted him to "due tenderness in such
solemn address unto God." Over in New England, in Bailie
M'Keand's day, Judge Sewall—" Samuel Sewall, the great and
wise "—rose one Sabbath in the Old South Church of Boston,
and before the minister, Mr. Willard, and in the hearing of
the congregation, avowed with downcast head and faltering
voice his heinous crime in sending the Salem witches to death
five years before. The Massachusetts lawyer and the Galloway
magistrate were brothers in their error and in their penitence.
But Bailie M'Keand's remorse would not have been so penetrating and so profound, if the saints whom he condemned had
never really been subjected to the unjust punishment which
he meted out to them.

And Elizabeth Milliken will testify. She was Margaret
Lachlison's daughter, and was already a married woman before
the month of May in 1685. It was in her husband's house at

Drumjargan that her mother was seized by the soldiers; from its threshold the prisoner was hurried to Wigtown, three miles distant, to be tried and doomed. She must have known whether one so dear, to whom she was bound by the tenderest ties, swore the oath on which such tremendous issues hinged, and was released from the dungeon, and returned to Drumjargan to close her quiet days. But what she did know seems to have been wholly different. Long afterwards, in 1718, as Robert Wodrow recounts, she still met with her martyred parent in visions of the night. She told Mr. Campbell, her minister, how she dreamed that "her mother, Margaret Lachlison, came to her at the Cross of Wigtown, with the garb, gesture, and countenance that she had five minutes before she was drowned in Bladnoch." A daughter's memories of a mother's home-going to God are not to be lightly gainsaid.

And Thomas Wilson will testify. He was the girl Margaret's brother, two years younger than she. He had shared some of his sister's conflicts, but was permitted to escape participation in that "one fight more, the best and the last," in which her brief warfare was consummated. Half a century after her death, he was an elder, much consulted and revered, in Penningham Kirk. But in the minute-book of the kirk, as he knew well, there was written a detailed and circumstantial recital of his sister's drowning on Wigtown sands. He never contradicted the recital; he allowed it to remain on the page where the minister had inscribed it as a true relation of a veritable event. Thomas Wilson, being the man he was, could not perpetrate a falsehood. He suffered the record to continue undisputed, because no one understood better than he how incontestable it was.

We have tarried sufficiently long in this "still-vexed Bermoothes." Let us get to the immortal story itself.

Of Margaret Lachlison, or Maclachlan, as the name would be spelled in our modern time, there is little to be told. She was poor in the world's gear, a widow, and at least sixty-three years of age when persecution dragged her out to fame. A Cameronian in her ecclesiastical beliefs, she was rich in faith and a princess in the court of heaven. About her companion more can be said. Margaret Wilson was the daughter of Gilbert Wilson, farmer in Glenvernock. He and his wife were unimpeachable in their adhesion to Episcopacy; "a man to ane excesse conform to the guise of the tymes," and she "without challenge for her religion"—so they are portrayed in Mr. Rowan's Penningham minute. But seldom have good Prelatists been more tried by the obstinacy of their children. Margaret, who was eighteen, Thomas, who was sixteen, even little Agnes, who had just passed her thirteenth birthday, with one consent resolutely declined to adopt the creed of their parents. "They, being required to take the Test and hear the curates, refused both; were searched for, fled, and lived in the wild mountains, bogs, and caves." Alike in the farm and on the hills, life grew harder and more severe. Little by little Gilbert Wilson's substance became the prey of those who were determined to make him suffer for the waywardness of his family. And the young people were outlawed; their friends were forbidden to give them houseroom or to supply their necessities; the cottars and shepherds were obliged to pursue them with hue and cry. There could be only one ending to such a state of things.

It came in February of 1685. Then, Thomas still keeping the mountains, Margaret and Agnes ventured to creep forth from their place of hiding and to steal down to Wigtown, compelled by the privations which they had been enduring. But they were discovered, and locked up in prison, in the Thieves' Hole, where the worst malefactors were their associates. For six or seven weeks they lay in the dismal place; and then, in April, having been charged with the guilt of Bothwell Brig and Ayrsmoss and the Apologetical Declaration—for their judges were capable of any monstrosity —they were sentenced, along with widow Lachlison—sentenced to be "ty'd to palisados fixed in the sand, within the flood-mark, and there to stand till the flood overflowed them and drowned them." Gilbert Wilson succeeded with much difficulty in saving the life of thirteen-year-old Agnes. It meant a journey to Edinburgh, and the payment of a hundred pounds sterling—no slight achievement when he had been

HERE LYES MARGRAT
WILLSON DOUGHTER
TO GILBERT WILLSON
IN GLENVERNOCH
WHO WAS DROUNED
ANNO 1685 AGED 18

LET EARTH AND STONE STILL WITNES BEARE
THEIR LYES A VIRGINE MARTYRE HERE
MURTHER'D FOR OUNING CHRIST SUPREAME
HEAD OF HIS CHURCH AND NO MORE CRIME
BUT NOT ABJURING PRESBYTRY
AND HER NOT OUNING PRELACY.
THEY HER CONDEM'D BY UNJUST LAW,
OF HEAVEN NOR HELL THEY STOOD NO AW.
WITHIN THE SEA TYD TO A STAKE
SHE SUFFERED FOR CHRIST JESUS SAKE
THE ACTORS OF HIS CRUEL CRIME
WAS LAGG STRACHAN WINRAM AND GRHAME
NEITHER YOUNG YEARES NOR YET OLD AGE
COULD STOP THE FURY OF THERE RAGE.

MARGARET WILSON'S TOMBSTONE,
IN WIGTOWN CHURCHYARD.

so impoverished by the rapacity of the dragoons. But her sister, although she had the short breathing-space secured by the reprieve, resisted steadily every attempt to shake her fidelity, and looked on with fearless eyes to the moment of death.

So, on the 11th of May, the two women, widely separated in years, but equally enamoured of what they regarded as the very truth of God, were marched from their gaol to the shore. That those who superintended the execution—Grierson was there, and Major Winram—still supposed that their prisoners might yield at the last, when they felt the approach of the merciless waters, is manifest from the efforts which were made even on the sands to weaken their resolution. With the help of the old records we can imagine the scene. The course of the little Bladnoch has been changed in subsequent times by embankments, raised with the purpose of redeeming land from the sea. But, two hundred years ago, the channel it had cut for itself was close beside the foot of the hill on which Wigtown stands, and the coasting sloops could sail almost up to where the church and the churchyard are to-day. Then, when it left the streets and houses, the stream took a bend seaward, fashioning for its progress a deep canal-like path in the soft sand. At low water the Solway recedes for miles, and it is over the naked sands that the Bladnoch trickles to its goal. But, when the tide returns, it rushes rapidly up the river's path, and by and by it overflows the banks on both sides. What the officials of the burgh did, under Lag's and Winram's directions, was to drive two stakes into the channel of the stream, at no great distance from where it leaves the houses and turns to the sea. One of the stakes was farther out, the other nearer the town. To the former they fastened Margaret Lachlison, to the latter Margaret Wilson. Meanwhile, so long as the inrushing Solway would permit them, the persecutors and some of the kinsfolk of the sufferers stood on the banks of the Bladnoch, waiting for any indication that the martyrs were wavering in their resolve, and prepared to pull them from the quickly deepening flood to the higher ground. But they could not

linger for any length of time, because soon the banks themselves would be surmounted by the advancing tide, and their
own security would be imperilled.

There are different styles in which the brave confront
and conquer death. There is what one may denominate the
French way—the way which is marked by *élan*, vivacious
gaiety, reckless and joyous abandonment. It is almost
pyrotechnic in its gallant mockery of the last enemy. It
greets the unseen with a cheer. Those as young as
Margaret Wilson, and younger still than she, have illustrated
splendidly this rash and romantic mode. At twenty, Henri
de la Rochejaquelein, fair-haired, enthusiastic, gently bred,
addressed his hastily summoned troop: "I am only a boy;
but I will prove that I desire to lead you. When I advance,
do you follow me; when I flinch, cut me down; when I fall,
avenge me!" And he had soldiers yet more boyish than
himself, and just as eager to champion King Louis against
the Revolutionaries. Beaurepaire joined the tiny army at
eighteen, and fell at Châtillon, pierced with twelve sabres.
Duchaffault, no more than eleven, having been sent back to
his mother, rode into the ranks again at Luçon, to dedicate
himself in glad sacrifice for the cause. But, over against so
merry a defiance of the adversary, there is the Scottish way
of dying. It may be as courageous, but gravity and temper-
ance mingle with the courage. It is infinitely more thoughtful,
more pensive, less exuberant. It looks in to see how things
go with the soul, and it looks on to the august presence of
God the Judge; and therefore there are the accents of
confession as well as the notes of confidence and song, and
it is with a lowly humility that faith claims her inheritance
in the skies. This was Margaret Wilson's method. Hoping
that the sight of her friend's last struggle would dismay her
into submission, they bound the old woman to the stake
which the water reached first; and, when the Solway was
doing its pitiless work, they asked the girl what she thought
of her companion now. "What do I see," she answered,
"but Christ wrestling there? Think ye that we are the
sufferers? No, it is Christ in us; for He sends none a

warfare on their own charges." Then, opening her New
Testament, she read aloud the eighth chapter of the Epistle
to the Romans—the great chapter which tells how the
condemnation of sin is cancelled by the Saviour; and how
the spirit of adoption delivers from bondage and fear; and
how nothing, neither death nor life, can separate from the
love of God which is in Christ Jesus our Lord. The chapter
finished, she sang her farewell psalm—the 25th Psalm, from
the seventh verse—

> My sins and faults of youth
> Do thou, O Lord, forget;
> After Thy mercy think on me,
> And for Thy goodness great.

It is not "Monsieur Henri's" way of facing the King of
Terrors; but perhaps it is a better way.

Even at the last she might have kept her life. Before
the end came, they pulled her from the grip of the tide;
and, holding her until she was able to speak, they inquired
if she would pray for King James. "I wish the salvation of
all men," she responded, "and the damnation of none."
Some who were related to her by ties of blood cried out,
"She is willing to conform," reading into her words the
significance which they longed to find. "Dear Margaret,"
entreated another of the bystanders, "say, God save the
King!" "God save him if He will!" she replied, "for it is
his salvation that I desire." "She has said it! she has said
it!" numbers in the crowd exclaimed. But Major Winram
was not so sure. He offered to administer the Oath of
Abjuration to her. If she accepted it, there would be no
drowning; if she spurned it as she had done formerly, she
must return to the waters. No doubt life was as sweet to
her as it is to most girls of eighteen; but, when conscience
was in hazard of being wounded, there could not be a minute's
hesitancy. "I will not," she said; "I am one of Christ's
children; let me go." They plunged her again into the tide,
which soon would be at its deepest; and, in a few seconds
more, her battle had terminated in victory. To some of us
it may seem a little matter for which she and her comrade

suffered. But to them it was not little, for it was part of the faith committed to their keeping. It was a fringe of Christ's royal robe, and in their hands no harm, however apparently trifling, must befall the seamless vesture of their Monarch. Like the Christians of the first days, they would not cast so much as a single grain of incense on the heathen altars of Diana.

Years after the crime at the Bladnoch had become a sombre incident of the past, a broken old man might be seen wandering alone through the streets of Wigtown. He was afflicted with an unquenchable thirst—a thirst so unusual that he never dared to venture abroad without carrying with him a large jar full of water. As he moved slowly forward with his singular burden, the people who met him would involuntarily shrink back. They believed that they knew the origin of his strange disease. This man had been the Town's Officer of Wigtown, who, when Margaret Wilson was raised out of the stream, and when she declared that she could not preserve her life by uttering the few words that would have sufficed, thrust her down with his halbert, saying, "Tak' anither drink, hinny!" and bidding her "clep wi' the partons"—gossip with the crabs. In his own body, his townsmen fancied, he was reaping the harvest of his misdeeds.

Salvations vary in their character. Mrs. Oliphant describes a scene which happened on Solway sands rather more than a century later than the May of 1685. While they were still children, John Irving and his younger brother Edward—"true friend and tender heart, martyr and saint"—strayed down to the shore, with the intention of meeting their uncle, George Lowther, who was expected to cross at the ebb from the Cumberland side. But in the wilderness of shingle, with its gleaming salt-water pools, full of curious creatures, the boys presently forgot their errand, and thought neither of their relative nor of the rising tide. While they were absorbed in their amusement, a horseman suddenly came up to them, seized first one and then the other, and, throwing them across the neck of his horse, galloped on without pausing to speak or even perceiving who they were. When they had safely reached the higher bank, he drew bridle, and pointed back breathless to where he had found them. The startled children saw the tawny waves pursuing almost to where they stood; and then "the happy Hercules-uncle" discovered who they were whom he had saved. They were fortunate in their deliverer; but young Margaret Wilson had a better redemption—

> the intrepid maid for whom
> Old Solway plied his waters monumental,
> And gave that glorious heart a glorious tomb
> Worth Scotia's rental.

For, when the impetuous sea had done its work, it was the strong right arm of Christ Himself which received her spirit.

CHAPTER XXXIII.

THE ADVENTURES OF GEORGE BRYSSON, MERCHANT.

MR. RUSKIN has told us that, in our intellectual life, we need not only what is sublime and vast, but what is soft and silent and small; and that we turn from the magnitudes and majesties of nature to find in a wild flower or a snowflake or a foam-bell bread enough and to spare. As we read history, it must be an exceeding comfort to many of us to see that God has innumerable servants no more imposing than foam-bells and snowflakes and wild flowers. In the annals of the Covenant an Isabel Alison figures less conspicuously but no less honourably than a Lady Balcarres, and George Brysson as well as Lord Wariston wins for himself a good degree. He was neither preacher nor lawyer nor captain; but, when we look into his face as he paints it in his own *Memoirs*, we pronounce it a face which has frankness and honesty written on every feature. It gains our trust and deserves our love.

The son of a farmer in Midlothian, born in the eventful year which beheld the death of King Charles the First, he was an apprentice-boy in Edinburgh, when, as he listened to a sermon from that "very worthy, famous, godly minister, Mr. James Kirkton," the power came along with the Word, and the Lord opened his prison doors, and he was made to wonder at God's surprising goodness towards him. Thereafter he was done with the curates and their pithless prelections; let the results be what they might, George Brysson must keep close by the ordinances which had become so sweet and refreshing. Soon he had his first taste of the troubles of noncomformity. His master, a kindly man but no enthusiast, was seized with alarm lest the imprudences of his apprentice should compromise himself and hurt his trade. He sent for the boy's father, who, when he arrived, "gave him a very sore onset," assuring him that he had expected better things than that his only son should be a follower of men forbidden by law to preach, and that, if he persisted in his obstinacy, he must disown him altogether. But the young convert's zeal was not daunted by the threat. "Father," he said, "I am sorry to hear such words coming from you. If you had found me guilty of cursing, swearing, Sabbath-breaking, stealing, or uncleanness, you would have ground to disown me. But, seeing the Lord has kept me from these things, and that the only quarrel is my hearing the Gospel when I have opportunity, I cannot help it." Bravery so outspoken was not to be resisted, and love put discretion to flight in the older man's heart. "My dear bairn," he cried, breaking into ready tears, "God forbid that ever I should hinder you from going where you may get most good for your soul !"   And thus George Brysson fought his initial battle, and came forth successful.

It preluded many similar battles. A year or two later his father died, and the lad was called away from business to take charge of the farm. But he had not been many months at home when the landlord, Sir Robert Preston, a Judge in the Court of Session, summoned the tenants, that he might compel them to sign one of the numerous bonds or engagements of the time against conventicles, and those who conducted them. Most of the farmers, overawed, meekly did as they were enjoined. But our young confessor stood staunch as a rock. "George," Sir Robert said, "I know you can write; take the pen, and subscribe this bond." But George was inflexible. "My lord," he answered, "I cannot. I durst not bind up myself from hearing the Gospel preached by the Lord's sent servants; neither durst I refuse to give them entertainment, if it lies in my power." His superior told him angrily that he was playing the fool ; but, because he had cherished a great respect for his father, he would not, he said, put him off the estate immediately; he should have until next term-day to bethink himself. So the recusant, with two others who held his uncompliant creed, was packed to the door, and "escaped that snare." And he notes it as a memorable providence that, ere the term-day dawned, Sir Robert Preston was dead; it was the laird and not the tenant who had been forced to quit the green fields of Goursnout and the barony of Craigmillar.

As years went on, there was little rest for the determined Covenanter. He had been in more than one skirmish with the dragoons before Bothwell; and, on that day of dule, he fought in the beaten army. When the prisoners had been marched to Edinburgh, the search after those who, like Brysson, were neither killed nor captured, was diligent and tireless. From one concealment to another he had to flee, making his way gradually back to the familiar homestead. Sometimes he slept in the wood beside the house, sometimes under the ripening corn; sometimes he would venture for a night into his own bed. He had friends in the ranks of the enemy. To his praise, and to the honour of foes as humane as Saladin with the Crusaders, he records how two of the proprietors of the district, one of them being Sir William Drummond of Hawthornden, the son of the poet, never wearied aiding his sister in the farm, during the weeks when he lay in hiding. They fed her sheep and cows with their own. They bade her gather everything of value in the house and send it to their mansions, where it was kept from the covetous greed of the soldiers. It is a little bit of knightliness and courtesy, which breaks like a shaft of gold through the prevailing clouds, and which it heartens us to remember.

But, although these generous opponents, and other helpers too, were his advocates, George Brysson ran perilous risks so long as he lingered near the Midlothian home. The place was attacked one night by a party of infantry, and it was by a sort of miracle that he contrived to get safely away. He felt that, until happier days came, he must turn his back on Scotland. For a while he sheltered himself in the big world of London. But the air of the town harmed his health; and the emissaries of the Government were still in pursuit of the fugitive. At length he found an asylum in a curious quarter—in the family of an English gentleman who was a thorough-going Royalist.

ARCHIBALD CAMPBELL, EARL OF ARGYLL.

The good man, who had been almost killed for his fidelity to the Stuarts when the Commonwealth was supreme, was now more than seventy, and so deaf that he could not catch a single word spoken by those about him. He had a wife as devoted to the Whigs as he was to the Tories. She filled his house with servants whose principles, had he known what they were, would have driven him to distraction—poor dissenters worried by rulers who did not understand the first elements of toleration. The exiled Scot was one. He became the cavalier's personal attendant; and we see the stiff Presbyterian in the disguise of a courtier, " mounted all new " and decorated with " a fine walking sword." His security lay, of course, in his lord's deafness; for, although the two conversed by signs, the problems of faith and Church were too recondite for so circuitous a mode of discussion. Brysson began to " build a paradise " to himself ; and the months when he was hunted like a partridge looked far enough distant. But there was a sudden awakening. His master and he were cited before the Justices, to swear some new oath. The convinced Presbyter had no liberty to perjure his soul ; and, although the astonished gentleman persuaded the magistrates to postpone their verdict to a later day, the secret was out, and his servant had to be sent off at once in order to avoid capture and punishment. Again the wandering bird managed to wing its flight from the lure up into the freedom of the skies.

And now we enter a section of George Brysson's life which links him with public history. Here and there we have had glimpses of the Earl of Argyll, son of the great Marquis. We have seen how he strove to reconcile his religion with his loyalty to his prince, but how he could not take the piebald Test, and was imprisoned, and would have suffered death, if his step-daughter had not piloted him past the sentinels on the Castle Hill. Chaperoned by William Veitch, one of his ministerial friends, and concealed under the assumed name of " Mr. Hope," he travelled to London by roads which were comparatively unfrequented. Soon he crossed to Holland, that kindly retreat of persecuted men ; and there, in conjunction with the Duke of Monmouth, he was now organising an expedition against Popish King James. The Scots Earl was much more eager than his English colleague to essay the hazardous attempt. James, he wrote to Monmouth, could not withstand their double attack ; and was not the Duke desirous to be known to posterity as the deliverer of his country ? and would not delay merely strengthen the power of the enemy ? To the last Monmouth was not sure. " To tell you my thoughts without disguise," he said, " I am now so much in love with a Retired Life that I am never like to be fond of making a Bustle in the World again." His had been a happier lot, had the bustle been more resolutely declined and the retirement more unswervingly chosen. To Argyll and to his company Brysson resolved to go. He and a friend, Major Henderson, had much difficulty in eluding the watchfulness of officials who, in these weeks of rumour and suspicion, kept a vigilant eye on ships bound for Dutch harbours. But they chose the King's Coronation Day, when everybody was engrossed with the shows and sports ; and at Gravesend no one questioned them, and so, with a very fair wind, they sailed for Amsterdam, where in due time they had the heartiest of welcomes.

But nothing except sorrow was allotted those who shared in the ill-starred enterprise of Argyll. The next two months in George Brysson's life were spent *in weariness and painfulness, in watchings often, in hunger and thirst, in fastings often, in cold and nakedness.* With three good ships—the *Anna,* the *Sophia,* and the *David*—loaded with arms and ammunition and all the necessaries of war, the Earl and his three hundred men sailed for Scotland. With him went two of his sons, Sir John Cochrane also, and Sir Patrick Hume. He had other coadjutors of a more fanatical temper—Richard Rumbold, the Oliverian soldier, who had been proprietor of the Rye House, when the plot was hatched against Charles and James ; and John Balfour of Kinloch, who led the murderers of Archbishop Sharp on Magus Moor. It was the end of April in 1685. But, although the passage was quick and easy—so quick and easy as to induce some to " think that witches had sold them a wind "—they had steered too much to the north, and, instead of sighting the mainland, they found themselves off the crags and skerries of Orkney. And now their troubles began. Two of their number—William Spence, Argyll's secretary, and William Blackader, son of the brave field-preacher—whom they put on shore to glean what information they could, were speedily apprehended by the King's officers.   Round the coasts they went, past Cape Wrath and the Hebrides, towards Argyll's territory in the west.   A raid into Islay was attended with meagre success.   At the Cross of Campbeltown, the formal Declaration was read by which they sought to justify the insurrection.   From one district and another they added to their number about a thousand men; but, in spite of all their efforts to win recruits, the force continued disappointingly small and insufficient.   In an old fortalice near the Kyles of Bute which they strengthened and equipped, the tower of Eilean Gheirrig, they stored their arms and provisions.   But the *Kingfisher*, the *Falcon*, and the *Mermaid*, three English men-of-war, were watching them; and, when they were absent in pursuit of Atholl and his Highlanders, the little magazine was rifled and its contents were lost.   It was a shattering blow, and they never rallied from the disappointment   There were marchings and counter-marchings, crossings of Loch Long and the Gareloch, debates among the officers, perplexities and privations and sleepless nights for the men.   The expedition was doomed.   It failed to attract to its ranks the reinforcements which were needed.   It was not guided with wisdom and certitude.   Sometimes Sir Patrick Hume and Sir John Cochrane would commend one course of action, whilst Argyll, gallant and kindly and candid, but impetuous and opinionative, had set his heart on another: they overruled his wish to engage the Royalists in a decisive struggle, and, again, his scheme of marching rapidly on Glasgow.   In the middle of June the crisis came.   Early on Thursday morning, the 18th, Sir Patrick, with five hundred tired and discouraged followers, entered the village of Kilpatrick; and, having eaten a morsel of bread and drunk hurriedly a cup of ale, he went in quest of his commander, the Earl.   But, instead, he met Sir John, who grasped his hand, and turned him round, and said earnestly, "My heart, go you with me."   "Go whither?" asked Sir Patrick. "Over the Clyde by boat," the other replied. "But

where is Argyll?" Hume queried, "for I must see him first."
"You cannot see him," Cochrane said; "he is gone away to his
own country." The night before, on Sir John's advice, the
Earl had started for a friend's house in Glasgow, and the army
of which he was the General was helplessly broken into two.
The calamitous issue of the luckless venture was in sight.

On Argyll himself the catastrophe fell within a few days.
Clothed in the dress of a peasant, he attempted to make his
escape on a pony. At Inchinnan, near Paisley, in the grey of
the evening, he was observed by two servants of Sir John
Shaw of Greenock, who were driving in front of them a saddle-
horse. Their beast was worn with long travel, and they
summoned him to surrender to them his own fresher animal.
He refused, and a quarrel ensued; and then, from one of the
cottages, a weaver, angered by the noise, came out, and, not
dreaming whom he assailed, struck the nobleman on the head
with a rusty broadsword. Stunned by the blow, he tottered
to the ground, and betrayed himself by an involuntary cry—
"Unfortunate Argyll!" They made him their prisoner; and
very soon he was lodged, this time not to elude his captors,
within the strong walls of Edinburgh Castle.

He left the world with the same tranquil bravery which
had illumined the last hours of his father. The old sentence,
passed upon him for seeking to qualify the Test of 1681, was
revived; since its imposition he had been legally dead, and
therefore no charge of treason was preferred against him now
because of his invasion of the realm. His final day, the 30th
of June, was the best of all his days. To one of his step-
daughters, the Lady Henrietta Lindsay, he said in the
morning, "We must not part like those not to meet again";
to the other, the Lady Sophia, who had rescued him so
fearlessly in his former strait, he wrote a little letter which
breathes the perfume of calm: "What shall I say in this great
day of the Lord, wherein, in the midst of a cloud, I find a fair
sunshine? I can wish no more for you but that the Lord may
comfort you and shine upon you as He doth upon me, and
give you the same sense of His love in staying in the world as
I have in going out of it." How he dined with appetite, and

conversed with gaiety at the table, and then lay down to take a short slumber, in order that his body and mind might be in full vigour when he should mount the scaffold, is known to every admirer of Ward's famous picture and to every reader of Macaulay's vivid page. "At this time one of the Lords of the Council, who had probably been bred a Presbyterian, and had been seduced by interest to join in oppressing the Church of which he had once been a member, came to the Castle with a message from his brethren, and demanded admittance to the Earl. It was answered that the Earl was asleep. The Privy Councillor thought that this was a subterfuge, and insisted on entering. The door of the cell was softly opened, and there lay Argyll on the bed, sleeping in his irons the placid sleep of infancy. The conscience of the renegade smote him. He turned away sick at heart, ran out of the Castle, and took refuge in the dwelling of a lady of his family who lived hard by. There he gave himself up to an agony of remorse and shame. 'I have been,' he said, 'in Argyll's prison. I have seen him, within an hour of eternity, sleeping as sweetly as ever man did.'" He awoke to go to the place of execution. There, falling on his knees, he embraced the Maiden, the guillotine which was to close his earthly life, protesting that it was the winsomest maiden ever he had kissed, "it being a mean to finish his sin and misery, and his inlet to the glory for which he longed." Then, when he had prayed, he gave the sign to the headsman; and immediately all was over. "Thus fell," wrote Lord Fountainhall, "that tall and mighty cedar in our Lebanon"—the impersonation, as a later historian has said, at once of feudal power and of freedom-loving Protestantism.

We have forgotten George Brysson in following the distresses and the joys of his leader. He stayed behind with Sir John Cochrane when Argyll had left the camp—stayed to encounter new excitements and perils. Against a troop of cavalry and two troops of militia those devoted Whigs, exhausted though they were, fought a hot skirmish at Muirdykes and came forth from it unbeaten. From within "an old stonefold, which was a little defence to us," the enemy was riddled with a furious musketry-fire, first on the right hand and then on the left; and, in the end, Lord Ross was glad to give over, and to withdraw his men from the dyke that helped the Covenanters so effectively. When they had retreated to a certain distance, though still they circled the fold round as in a ring, Sir John Cochrane bade his sharp-shooters bless God for their marvellous preservation. He took a book, and sang the 46th Psalm throughout, and after that prayed pertinently, the warriors behind the bield of the wall holding themselves in a watchful posture while they knelt to praise the Lord of battles. They were not troubled again by those whom their captain called derisively "the cowardly rogues"; and in a day or two, having heard the news of Argyll's seizure, they parted one from another.

In what direction was Brysson to turn his footsteps now? With three lads who came from London, he decided to journey south and to join the Duke of Monmouth—Monmouth, whose own rainbow-coloured bubble was in the next month to be dissipated as completely as the hopes of the Scottish con-spirators had just been. But the four wayfarers "travelling all night and derning all day," did not require to make the long and bootless pilgrimage. On a Sabbath morning, when they could perceive neither wood nor moss in which to screen themselves, one of them went up to a house near by, and confessed frankly who they were. They had difficulty in persuading the inmates to believe their tale; but, once it was credited, they were graciously received: for they had fallen among Cameronians, who, if they were not disposed to enlist under the standard of Argyll, yet wished him well. There was a brave fire burning on the hearth, and the weary men sat down and warmed themselves. They had plenty of meat given them; and, once their hunger was appeased, lest King James's dragoons should discover their place of hiding, the daughter of the home carried straw out to "an old torn house" where the sheep were accustomed to rest, and there they "slept as sound as ever they did upon a feather-bed." Their generous hosts would not permit them to face the dangers involved in pushing on towards the English border. They must remain, they said, in their fellowship. And so, for some weeks, they did, not indeed always with a roof to cover their heads, but often lying in the fields, scarcely knowing at night where they might be on the morrow, and yet through it all never tasting anything but liberal love from brothers and sisters who had tears and temptations as many as their own.

Then the pursuit slackened a little, and George Brysson crept across the country to the Midlothian farmstead he remembered so loyally. Six months afterwards — for he was still a marked and persecuted man—he stole away to Northumberland. There it was his lot to enjoy the special friendship of James Welsh, who had been minister in the Stewartry of Kirkcudbright, but who was now in exile on the English side of the Border, his name appearing in the Fugitive Roll of 1684. In the preacher's society he travelled from one serious-minded family to another, and learned from experience how warm were the hospitalities of grange and cottage in the Northumbrian dales. Once, when Welsh was in Berwick, the wife of Justice Grieve asked whether he knew of an honest man who could be overseer of her husband's affairs. He commended his comrade Brysson; and at Martinmas the wanderer entered the Justice's household. The wages, he says, were not high, " but only five pounds per year and my diet "; but here, with much satisfaction, he lived for five quiet years, until " the happy Revolution " was an accomplished fact, and he could return to Edinburgh, to build up the business of a thriving merchant, to marry that " godly wife who was a true yoke-fellow indeed," and, when age was silvering his hair, to write his *Memoirs*. Four of his nine pleasant children, with their mother, were in glory ere he took his pen in hand, and the five who were left were very comfortable to him. He desired them to read what wonderful care the Lord had lavished on their father, in the various steps of His providence: surely the record would encourage them to cleave to so good a Master. As for himself, he blessed his Guide, who had followed him with mercy all his days ; and he hoped soon to be in that inheritance where there is not a complaint amongst the redeemed company—not a complaint, but only the river of pleasure and the joy for evermore.

CHAPTER XXXIV.

THOSE WOMEN WHICH LABOURED IN THE GOSPEL.

THE women that publish the tidings are a great host: it is the tribute of an Old Testament psalm to the holy enthusiasm which throbbed in the hearts and announced itself from the lips of the daughters of Israel. In the camp of the Scottish Covenant that ancient enthusiasm had its parallel and repetition. Already, in these chapters, we have had momentary visions of various queenly figures. With a fortitude as manifest as that of their fathers and husbands and sons, we have seen the matron and the maid going out behind the banners of the Son of God and performing their part in His battle. But others in the sisterhood of valour and religion deserve to be recalled by us. The literature of seventeenth-century Presbytery, strenuous, argumentative, stained with blood, is beautified by its Legend of Good Women.

And, first of all, one is tempted to travel backward from King Charles's days to the year 1642, when the war that was to work such woe to his father was only breaking out. To that year belongs a characteristic Covenanting document penned by Mr. Archibald Porteous, himself "a pertinent, knowing, seriouse youth." It is the "edifying narration of the sad sweet exercise of soul, and blessed death, of Dame Mary Rutherfurd, Lady Hundalee." Here, indeed, the reader learns with what agonising earnestness men and women in this old seventeenth century sought for the assurance of the love of Christ, and how poor and pitiable they accounted their

THE CROWN OF ST. GILES, EDINBURGH.

condition until they were certain of their Heavenly Bride-groom's grace. It is an accent distinct from the religious dialects of to-day. It compels us to question whether we know the same sorrows of desertion, the same ardency of desire, the same triumphs of appropriation and communion.

Lady Hundalee, with her cousin and waiting-woman, Mary M'Connell, and her young chaplain, Archibald Porteous, had journeyed, sometime in 1642, from Scotland up to London. But the pestilence was raging in the town; and soon the good waiting-woman was visited by a presentiment, "a post from the Celestial City with matters of great importance," to tell her that her Master called her to stand in His presence, in clothes of immortality, within a few days. She was en-raptured at the thought. "Well is my soul!" she cried, "I shall get Christ, my Love, now." But her mistress would not be outdone; she avowed that she also was hungering and thirst-ing to be caught up immediately into Paradise. And the chaplain broke in upon them with his separate aspiration: "Madam, I could never endure strife; but I am glad to see such a strife as this. May not I, as a third, challenge my part in the bargain? I hope ye dare not envy any that come to Christ." Thus those three stretched out their eager hands to welcome Death, because in Death they saw simply the herald and apparitor of Him who governed their souls with His sceptre of gold.

Before many hours had passed, Mary M'Connell's presage was fulfilled, and she had "peaceably entered the everlasting kingdom." But, when she had gone, a darkness as of seven midnights swept over Lady Hundalee. She was "mightily discouraged," veteran soldier of the divine King although she was. Her inbred corruptions started up to slay her faith, and the temptations of Satan gathered round. It was in vain that her spiritual counsellor, wise beyond his years, strove to impart the consolations of God. "Nothing shall hinder your Lord," he said; "though your sins were as hard as a rock, and as high as mountains in the way, yet neither the height of the one nor the hardness of the other shall keep Him from you. For He would as fain be at you as ye at Him, and fainer too.

Take courage! He that shall come will come, and will not
tarry." They were strong anodynes; but they did not pluck
the rooted sorrow from the memory and spirit. She had been
but a hypocrite, the Lady mourned; and between Christ and
herself what was there except "fremmitness"—distance and
estrangement and alienation? In a day or two, however,
there appeared some little lifting of the gloom. At least she
could talk to the chaplain about the grievous lapses and
wanderings with which she was chargeable: her "deadness,
dulness, coldness in prayer, distraction and forgetfulness in
hearing, an unruly passion, and a number of such ills breaking
out." "Away! away!" she expostulated, when again he tried
to comfort, "speak not to me of any grace that I have, for I
am graceless; I feel not so much as a dram of grace." Yet, as
the needle points to its pole "and knows not why," her soul
constantly turned to Him whom she reckoned better than all
the world. One morning, after a short rest, she showed
Porteous a tiny manuscript book in which she had written a
catalogue of God's providences and Christ's special mercies.
She protested that each of these was "a dittay," an indictment,
against her thanklessness and disobedience. But the scattering
of the night-clouds had begun, and the sun was preparing to
rise.

The pestilence had caught her ere now in its fatal grasp;
but, with the return of inward peace, she could glory over the
bodily fever and pain. Once, those who attended her marked
that she sang in her sleep. "Madam," asked the chaplain,
"what did ye dream when ye smiled?" "Smile!" said she,
"how could I but smile, when I saw my Lord drawing by the
bed curtain? But He went swiftly away." Then she bade her
friend leave her for two hours. He came back at the appointed
time, to discover that there was no trace of the long-continued
combat—nothing but the ravishment of deliverance. She had
her good confession to make. "Now I see that all is not lost
that is in danger; and that God's children will have as many
troubles as twice over ten horses will bear; and yet they will
bear them all, though they seem to be sunk under them. I
see they who love Christ love Him not for nought, but shall

get as good as they brought, yea ten thousand times better.
I see God never wholly casts off those whom He once takes by
the hand, and who honestly indent with Him; and, if He
seems to cast them off, it's only in their own apprehension,
and for the trial of their grace, and only for a while; and, in
the meanwhile, His hand is under their head to support them,
though they perceive it not." Step by step she went down to
the swelling of Jordan, with a shining radiance on her face.
"Give me Hell if Thou wilt," she was heard pleading, "but
Christ with it; for He and I shall never part again." What
did she think of eternal life? the minister queried. "O, it's
the only life!" she replied. "This is but a living death. But
it's a lively, everlasting, honourable, immortal, easy, happy,
and comfortable life." And how did she like death? he
queried again. "Very well," she answered. "I think it will do
me the best that can be. It is a passage to bring me to, and
to plunge me in, the ocean of love. If I could win out of this
house, I would be content to go see my own grave made." In a
few minutes she left off speaking, although the onlookers knew
by the motion of her lips that she persevered in prayer. And,
on the next daybreak, when he saw her dissolution approaching, Mr. Porteous, as he had promised, sounded in her ears "the
love of Christ." And she, with hands uplifted and eyes fixed
and smiling countenance, did step victoriously into eternity.

Because this history, first of desolation and then of delight,
was repeated in numbers of Covenanting hearts, it is well
worth our while to remember Lady Hundalee's sore struggle
and glorious "outgate."

Isabel Alison and Marion Harvie, each a little older than
Margaret Wilson, were called to walk the road of death and
gain, four years before the opportunity came to her of
threading "the sombre boskage of the wood toward the morning
star." They suffered in the Grassmarket on the 26th of
January 1681. One of them was a maidservant from Bo'ness,
the other had "lived very privately in the town of Perth";
but their testimonies before the Council and on the scaffold
were uncompromising, like those of the Lion of the Covenant

himself. They were Cameronians, who could give a reason
for the resolute creed which they avowed. They owned the
Excommunication at the Torwood, and the papers found at
the Queensferry, and the Sanquhar Declaration. They declined
the authority of the rulers at whose bar they stood, telling
them that they had declared war against Christ, and had
usurped and taken His prerogatives, and so were carrying the
sword against Him and not for Him. They died, they
claimed, not as fools, nor as evil-doers, nor as busybodies in
other men's matters—no, but for adhering to the truths of
Jesus, and for confessing Him to be King in Zion. On the
heads of their enemies they left the guilt of their bloodshedding. It has a revengeful sound; but probably it was
only their solemn warning addressed to those who had
travelled as far as tyrants can go in unrighteousness and
oppression. There is a proud ring, an accent of finality, a
note of immovable conviction, in every answer they gave and
every sentence they spoke. To Marion Harvie the Councillors
said that "a rock, the cod, and boboons"—a distaff and a
pincushion and a bobbin of thread—would befit her better
than such high theological and ecclesiastical discourse. But,
while her fingers were familiar with the homely implements,
she knew no cause why her heart and brain should not move
among more transcendent things. She had a personal and
powerful motive for that faith which she professed with an
emphasis so assured. As she climbed the ladder to surrender
her life, she narrated a fragment of her autobiography. " At
fourteen or fifteen I was a hearer of the curates and the
indulged; and, while I was a hearer of these, I was a
blasphemer and Sabbath-breaker, and a chapter of the Bible
was a burden to me. But, since I heard this persecuted
Gospel, I durst not blaspheme nor break the Sabbath, and the
Bible became my delight." That it had regenerated her own
experience was proof sufficient that the Evangel she loved
must be the authentic Word of God.

Their burning ardour and adamantine quality are the
memories we bring away from our converse with these " two
honest, worthy lassies," Marion Harvie and Isabel Alison.

" O, be zealous, sirs ! be zealous ! be zealous ! " the latter cried from the eminence of the scaffold ; and zeal was the attribute characteristic of their firm-set souls. To both of them in their prison the judges sent Mr. Archibald Riddell, a Covenanting minister and a good man, who had his trials still to face for the kingdom of Christ, but who had blurred and enfeebled his message in the eyes of all Cameronians by accepting the Indulgence. He was to persuade them to conform ; but he might as successfully have tried to soften into velvet and silk the brute mass of the Castle Rock. " He offered to pray. We said we were not clear to join with him in prayer. He said, ' Wherefore ? ' We said, ' We know the strain of your prayers will be like your discourse.' He said, ' I shall not mention any of your principles in my prayer, but only desire the Lord to let you see the evil of your doings.' We told him we desired none of his prayers at all. The goodman of the Tolbooth and some of the gentlemen said, would we not be content to hear him ? We said, ' Forced prayers have no virtue.' " Their flag flew as boldy on the morning of their execution. Led for the last time into the Council Chamber, they were taunted by Bishop Paterson, who had none of Leighton's compassionateness and grace, " Marion, ye said 'you would never hear a curate ; now you shall be forced to hear one " ; and he commanded one of his suffragans to pray. But he was outwitted. " Come, Isabel," exclaimed the unconquerable serving-maid, " let us sing the 23rd Psalm." Line by line she repeated the calming and uplifting words which Scottish children are taught so soon as they can lisp their syllables ; and line by line these two, who were appointed to death, sang of the Lord their Shepherd, and of the Valley of the Shadow where His rod and His staff sustained them, and of God's House in which, for evermore, their dwelling-place should be. And not a petition of the curate's prayer was heard.

Amongst all Shakespeare's women there is none auguster none more heroic, than Portia—the Portia of *Julius Cæsar* and not of *The Merchant of Venice*. Cato's daughter and the spouse of Brutus, she is as stoical as her husband. Professor

Dowden points out that we read of no embrace, no touch of hands or lips, between this noble wife and her lord; but we know that their souls have met, that they are inseparably one and absolutely equal. His aims, his theories of justice, his consistent devotion to his republicanism, are hers as well. Something of the tenacity, the pure idealism, the lofty sternness of the Roman matron, lived again in the humble Scotswomen.

But they were happier than she. Diviner consolations upheld them in dying. They were executed with "some three or four wicked women, guilty of murdering their own children"; no possible insult was spared them. But they soared heavenward, as the larks soar, still singing a song instinct with certainty and gladness. "I have looked greedy-like to such a lot as this, but still I thought it was too high for me," said Isabel Alison. "O my Fair One, my Lovely One, come away!" cried Marion Harvie, for she was enraptured with the beauty of the celestial Bridegroom. Together they raised their voices in the verses of the 84th Psalm; and thus they took their flight to the Lord God who is a Sun and a Shield.

Mr. Stevenson, who held the magical key that unlocks the ivory and golden gate of their hearts, tells us that

> The children sing in far Japan,
> The children sing in Spain.

But in the experience of a Covenanting child there was little room for blithe and light-hearted song. One may surmise that, from the earliest years of life, the burden lying on the soul checked the overflow of gaiety, and made the ordinary speech preternaturally serious and grave. A proof of it is supplied in a tiny memoir published in the Glasgow of 1720. "Some Few Choice Sentences and Practices of Emilia Geddie," the booklet is named.

Emilia Geddie was the young daughter of a man of considerable note in his day, a Writer to the Signet in Edinburgh, the Clerk of the King's Stewartry of Fife, and

factor to the Marquis of Atholl. He had a liking for natural
science, and discovered a new method for "improving and
colonising bees," winning the compliments and congratulations
of the Royal Society on his ingenuity. He was rich too, and
lived on his own estate of Hilton, near the old palace of
Falkland. In 1657, John Geddie married Anna Wallace,
sister of the Provost of Glasgow, and cousin to Lord Burleigh.
Their two boys died in childhood, happy in escaping quickly
from the distractions of the hour to the City of God which is
built of crystal, pearl, and gem. Emilia, the one girl in the
home, was born in 1665, to spend fifteen years in a world over-
weighted with sorrow, and then to join her brothers in the
presence of Christ. Her parents were firmly fixed in their
affection for the cause of the Covenant, and her own feet
began very soon to walk the same thorny path.

Before her third birthday she had framed for herself a
grace before meat. One day some guests were present, and
overheard the lisping benediction, and wondered at its fresh-
ness and propriety. How had she been taught it? they
asked; and she replied that she "had learned now and then
a word from several persons, and her Lord had set the words
together, and she had made a blessing of them." She was
like the little girl whom Mr. Canton has compelled us to love,
in this, that, within the house, she was a kind of conscience in
flesh and blood, "who winnowed every sin, who tracked each
slip and fall, one of God's spies"; only she was a more
intentional, preconcerted, deliberate conscience than W. V.,
who reproved the transgressor only by those unshrinking and
deep-gazing eyes of hers. One of the lads in the farmyard
blurted out an oath, as Emilia passed with her hand linked
in her nurse's. She turned to him. "Henry," she said
reprovingly, "I'll tell God." "Go and do it, miss," the
impenitent boy retorted; and without delay she went. The
offender could not maintain his unshaken front against such
artillery, and the praying child conquered him. Seven years
afterwards, when he was surprised again by temptation, and
somebody reminded him of the incident, he fell a-weeping, and
declared that to his dying day he ought not to have forgotten

so gracious a reproof. She had invariably her pat and pertinent answer. A captain of the King's forces, busy about His Majesty's persecuting work, had halted under her father's roof, and was receiving hospitable refreshment from those who held his principles in abhorrence. "Emily," he said, "I'll marry you." Her "No" was instantaneous and decisive. "Why?" he asked in pretended amazement. "Oh!" she replied, "you have no grace." "And have you?" said he. "Whatever grace I have," was the response, "you have none; for, if you had, you would not do the King's and the Bishop's bidding, to take the honest ministers and to shoot the praying folk." But often John Geddie, like the Gaius of the New Testament, was host to an apostle. Donald Cargill preached frequently in Fife, among the Lomond Hills, at no great distance from Hilton; and then he was welcomed to the shelter and kindness of the factor's mansion. On a certain Saturday morning he was there; but, having made many unsuccessful attempts to get a message for the following day, he proposed to take his departure before the Sabbath dawned. They begged him to remain; they would leave him in quietness, they promised, that he might try once more to discover a text and a sermon. He consented, and everybody went from the room—everybody but Emily, of whose presence none seemed to be aware. Half-an-hour later she crept to the minister's side, to whisper a hope that the difficulties were disappearing. "No," he confessed, laying his hand on her head, and wondering at such solicitude in a child—"No! they are not"; and then he proposed that the two of them should kneel together, and that she should pray with him. And the little lass did so, and, after they had risen, Donald Cargill protested that his mind and spirit were both so strengthened that he could do nothing else than tarry and preach; and, next day, his power and liberty in proclaiming the Word were so manifest that all who heard him received great benefit, and Emilia Geddie herself found that the sermon "wrought mightily on her heart." Her own father was forced to marvel at her unyieldingness: she was as dreadless as Abdiel among the angels. When she was eight years of age, he once put her to the test. "Shall I take the Oath?" he asked, referring to one of those vexatious Declarations which the Government concocted and imposed. "No, no!" she entreated. "But, if I should refuse. I shall be no longer King's steward," he told her, "and they will send us out of house and home, and then how will you and I live?" She felt no qualm of anxiety. "God will provide," she said, "and we shall live by faith." "Ay!" he went on, though he was simply putting her to the proof, and had himself resolved not to conform, "but I see no means for our livelihood except I take the Declaration." "Dear father," spoke up Miss Intrepid, "I will tell you what we shall do. I shall go to service, and will get my victuals and some old clothes from persons of honour whom I know, and so I will save all my wages, and I will give them to you to live upon." She was a maiden as stout as La Pucelle herself, or as "Eleanor whose fearless breath Drew the venomed fangs of death."

But, as we read Emilia Geddie's short life-record, the conviction is driven in that her seriousness is too precocious and premature. There is an introspection which, at times, grows almost morbid. There is a tendency, too, to sit in hypercritical judgment on others, which is not a customary habit of the young. "The first fall of the snow" is more noticeable in her pathetic year than "the birds and the sunshine" and the musical ripple of the brook. Hazlitt said of the children whom the canvases of Sir Joshua have made immortal that, invariably, they are "happy, bold, and careless"; and these are the adjectives which should summarise the very religion of a child. Emilia's religion demands other epithets. It is exacting. It is severe in depreciation and sentence. It is unkind both to herself and to her companions. The iron of cruel circumstance had entered her soul. The atmosphere was unfriendly to the wholesome and joyous development of the girl's nature. There is an element of strain and excess which we would fain miss. Was it not difficult to be young in a Covenanting home? Age, and thought, and sadness, and fear came almost as soon as mind and heart awoke to the events that were transpiring round them; and childhood had

fled before ever it could be seized and held fast and gloried in.
Emily was fond of birds of all kinds. They not only amused
but "edified" her, showing her much of the wisdom of God.
Sometimes, like great St. John, she would excuse herself for
the gladsome minutes she spent among them : "my spirit
cannot be always in benzil," she would explain—always out-
stretched and bent to the utmost, like the bowstring to which
the arrow has been fitted before it wings its flight through the
air. But soon a too scrupulous and too wakeful conscience
would lift its voice in admonition, and, bowing her head in
penitence, she confessed, "I cannot altogether defend myself
from wasting time."   One Sabbath she heard a sermon against
backsliding, and afterwards was very heavy and afflicted. "I
am a great backslider," she said, when a friend asked her the
cause of so sore a trouble ; and then she related the tale of her
sin. "I had met with a wonderful deliverance ; for, as I sat
by the wall of a house, a great piece of slate fell by me,
touching only my clothes, and I was not hurt ; and yet I did
not set apart a day to praise the Lord for such a mercy." It
was an undue sensibility, a too sharp disquiet, in a disciple
whose summers did not number more than eleven or twelve ;
and we may be certain that the liberal Master had no condemning indictment to bring against her. The strict discipline
with which she ruled herself was as firmly exercised towards
other delinquents. She and her comrades—this was before
her ninth birthday—had established their own Praying Society.
To the Society a complaint was made of the conduct of one of
its members, the oldest and tallest girl among them. She
had heard a curate preach in the church at Strathmiglo ; she
had laughed once during public prayer ; she had spoken
untenderly of some godly people : such was the triple accusation. A little court was formed, and Emilia was chosen to
preside, and the culprit was placed at the bar. She admitted
meekly that there was some truth in all of the charges, though
she pleaded that in each case there were palliations of her
fault. Then the president, after a discourse to the meeting,
announced her verdict : "That the offender should not be
debarred from the Society, but allowed to be present with

them for hearing and converse; but, in regard of her blame-worthiness in this matter, she should not be permitted to pray with them for the space of a month; so that, during that time, they might have occasion to observe her deportment, and she might have access to improve herself." We smile, and yet there are tears behind the smile. It is right that the children should pray; but here is a too precise inquisition into one another's behaviour; here is a budding censoriousness; here are the echoes of those dividing conflicts and bitter pains through which their elders passed, and by which their opening souls should never have been racked and perturbed. One recalls the half-amusing, half-poignant page of a modern book, in which a delightful writer portrays the lesser crosses of the child of to-day. "Now what shall I say?" inquired Rebecca of her teacher. "'The subjunctive mood, past perfect tense, of the verb *to know.*' '*If I had known. If thou hadst known. If he had known. If we had known. If you had known. If they had known.* Oh! it is the saddest tense,' sighed Rebecca, with a little break in her voice; 'nothing but *ifs, ifs, ifs!* And it makes you feel that, if they only *had* known, things might have been better.'" If Emilia Geddie could have omitted or deferred some of the ingredients in her education, and if only she had known the vivacity proper to the young, things would surely have been better with her.

In February 1681, she went away to "the mountain of myrrh and the hill of frankincense." She had an enviable death. For, after some time in secret prayer, she broke forth into excellent and significant words in commendation of the Lord Jesus, reciting one after another of His satisfying names —the Bright and Morning Star, the Lion of the tribe of Judah, the Lamb slain from the foundation of the world, the Rock which hath followed His people, the Chief of ten thousands, "and the Chief of all to me." She enjoined her young associates, who were with her, to learn a life of holiness, and spend more of their time in seeking God, and abhor indolence and sloth, and work diligently with their hands. She interceded for the suffering Church of Christ, and for the father and mother from whom she was going away. "Only upon the blood of Jesus and the faithfulness of God," she said, "do I rest." Afterwards she "spoke a word which we could not hear, and then she closed her own eyes and lips as one falling asleep, and having stretched down her body she had no motion more." And thus she went to the Jerusalem, whose streets are filled with boys and girls at play, where the childhood of which she had caught so slight a glimpse on earth would be given her with no abatement or defect.

The lady in whose fellowship we move next was separated from these others by many sundering lines. She was great and stately. That she was no member of the Cameronian family is demonstrated by the fact that the husband of her youth breathed his last in exile because of his fealty to the Stuarts, and by the other fact that her son led King James's forlorn hope side by side with John Graham of Claverhouse. Nor was it her heritage to die young or in the Grassmarket; she lived until her years were well-nigh ninety, and passed from the earth in the quietude of her own room. But her sorrows were deeper in reality than those tasted by the girlish martyrs; and her religion, if it was roomier and more forbearing, was identical with theirs in its essence. Anna Mackenzie of Seaforth, Lady Balcarres, and afterwards Countess of Argyll, is a princess not of the Covenant alone but of that wider realm in which all love-worthy and saintly women dwell.

She was Sir Robert Moray's sister-in-law and friend; his "dear Cummer," he delights to name her in the familiarity of his letters. Abraham Cowley extolled her worth no less than that of the husband whom she lost in Holland—

> Unfortunate for ever let me be,
> If I believe that such was he,
> Whom, in the storms of bad success,
> And all that error calls unhappiness,
> His virtue, and his virtuous wife, did still accompany!

Richard Baxter was unstinted in gratitude and praise. "She is," he said, "of a solid understanding in religion, and of prudence much more than ordinary, and of great integrity and constancy, and a great hater of hypocrisy, and faithful to

Christ in an unfaithful world." They are certificates to be envied; but not one of them contains a word which transgresses the boundaries of simple verity.

We shall learn something of Lady Anna Mackenzie's goodness if we join her at Breda, in one of the saddest weeks of her life, the closing week of August in 1659. That "brave and able gentleman," Alexander Lindsay, the Earl of Balcarres, the husband to whom she had given herself nineteen years before, was dying. "The last eight days of that dear life," she wrote to her cousin, Colonel Henderson, "I may say his dear heart was always in heaven, for he was almost always praying or hearing prayer, or reading, or speaking to the praise of his blessed Maker and Redeemer." . . . "Upon the Saturday's night, he and I talking togeder alone, he said to me that there was many divines of the opinion that all who belonged to God, less or more, found that which Saint Paul speaks of in the eighth of the Romans—of the spirit of bondage: he said, he could not say that ever he found it in all his life. I remembered him what I had heard our minister, who is a most excellent man, say upon that text, that all had it less or more, but God, when He wounded some with the sight of their lost condition without Christ, applied the plaister so soon to the person wounded that the wound was not at all sensible, and he was sure there was many in heaven that never could say they felt the spirit of bondage." . . . "I sat always upon the carpet before his bedside, and often I looked up to him, and, when I found not his eyes fixed upon heaven, I spake to him. Upon the Lord's day I asked him what he was doing, and said, 'My love, have you attained to that great measure of assurance that you desire?' To which he answered, 'I cannot tell what they call full assurance; but this I can tell you, that I am as full of joy in believing that my Redeemer is mine and I am His as I can hold, and that I shall be with Him before it be long, and that He will never leave me.' 'That's good news, my dear,' said I, 'for you.' 'Aye,' said he, 'and for you also; for you will quickly follow me.' 'Aye, my dear,' said I, 'you will not think it long; for a thousand years where you are going is but as yesterday when it is past.''

. . . "At last I closed those dear eyes, and that dear mouth I never in all my life heard make a lie or take the name of God in vain. O, how Christianly that dear saint of mine lived and died it is impossible for me to tell to you as it was!" And, as we read, we feel that it is impossible to tell what abounding comforts Lord Balcarres, Royalist and Presbyterian and blameless captive of the King of kings, drew, living and dying, from the communion of his great-hearted wife.

As a mother, she demeaned herself in the same shining fashion. One grief, which came soon after her husband's death, was the conversion to Roman Catholicism of their eldest child, the Lady Anna Lindsay, a girl scarcely more than sixteen, to whose faith the Jesuits about Charles's continental court had laid too effectual a siege. Over in the Fifeshire home, another sharp-edged trial smote her in October 1662. Her boy Charles, the young Earl, just twelve years old, was summoned after a short illness from this world to that which is unseen and eternal: "upon Wednesday morning, at six o'clock, after a quiet night's rest, in a moment he found all his strength and spirits decay togeder, and called to me, and threw his arms about my neck, and prayed God to 'bless his dear lady mother,' and then he looked up and desired that the blood of Jesus Christ would clean him of all his sins, and that God would take him to be for ever with Himself, which He immediately did." Two daughters were left to her, Sophia and Henrietta, and a son, Colin, afterwards to toil and fight chivalrously in the lost cause of the Stuarts. To him, when he was on the verge of manhood, she addressed a letter which is perfect in its thought and style and as perfect in its spiritual dignity. She bade him, first of all, dedicate some certain time every day to the service of his Saviour. To his prince she inculcated loyalty and reverence; to his country, love and protection; to his friend, fidelity and patience and truth; to his bride, chastity and tender affection, for, "believe it," she declared, "no man is happy but he that is so in his own house." She would have him speak little and be silent much; but there must be no reticence when he saw an occasion to do good to his King, his fatherland, or his neighbour. In the management of his estate, she counselled him to take an hour every day for the study of the affairs of the charter-chest, until he should understand each detail for himself. "You," she concluded, "that have such a closet"—that is, so noble a library—"such gardens, and so much to do within doors and without, need not think the time tedious or be idle; it's the hand of the diligent maketh rich." Did not Lady Balcarres mingle the strength and the judgment of a father with a mother's soft gentleness and pity?

Just before this letter was written, her history had undergone an important change. In 1670, eleven years after she had been parted from the true lover and captain of her early life, she was married a second time, to the Earl of Argyll—the Earl for whom, as we have discovered, the headsman's axe was waiting at the Cross of Edinburgh. She became mistress of Inveraray Castle, although perhaps her home more frequently was in Stirling, in that "Great Lodging or Manor-place, lying upon the north side of the High Street," which then was a favourite residence of the Argylls. In the Manor-place she had her own sitting-room, into which she gathered those pretty articles of "womanly furniture" that she loved—three sweetwood boxes, two little statues of "marable," two crystal candle-sticks, two-and-twenty counterfeit porcelain dishes, a silver ink-horn, a bell of bell-metal, a case of wooden "tae-cups," and, on a fir-table in the centre of the room, her Cambridge Bible, in two large volumes in folio, with Ogleby's cuts. Many of these heirlooms had to be sacrificed at a later day, that money might be found for the supply of her husband's necessities in his banishment. And, later, there came the bitterer parting of his death. "Forgive me all my faults," he wrote from the Laigh Council House, "and now comfort thyself in Him in whom only true comfort is to be found. The Lord be with thee, and bless thee, my dearest!" On few women have the strokes of affliction rained more heavily, and few have borne them with a meeker and more trustful spirit. "Though I live in a continual storm," she had written years before 1685, "the gale will blow at last which will blow me into the haven."

Twenty-one summers and winters were still to pass over her whitened hair before that longed-for gale arose. They were full of excitement and change, of which her gallant son, Lord Colin, had his ample share; but, season after season, she carried within herself the chimes of an overcoming peace. At last the hour arrived which she had desired. She died in the old home, among the "sunward-sloping farms" of fair Balcarres; and in the chapel there they laid her body, beside her first husband and the young Earl Charles.

On a former page reference was made to William Veitch, the minister who helped Argyll so shrewdly in that venturesome pilgrimage to London which followed on his Grace's very dramatic outgoing from his Scottish dungeon. Veitch had himself a biography marked by a hundred vicissitudes and troubles. But he would scarcely have played the man as cheerfully as he did, if he had not been mated with a wife whose spiritual stature was yet taller than his own. In most of his struggles and flights and hardships she participated; and, when she could not accompany him, she wrought miracles on his behalf by her prayers. For the prayers of Marion Veitch were of the resistless kind which carry the citadel of heaven by storm, and which return to our earth laden with the bread and wine and wealth of God.

How she bore herself when her lord was separated from her, when the children were young and unfit to do for themselves, and when she was far from friends and acquaintances, is recounted in those *Memoirs* which the good minister left behind him. Then she but nestled more close to the Almighty Benefactor in the skies. He should be the Husband, and He should be the farm; He should be the stock and the crop; He should be the Provider, the food, and the raiment, the Master of the family and the Father of the bairns. "Yea, she resolved to cleave faster unto this relation than Ruth did to Naomi, for that which parted her should bring her to the greatest nearness, most inseparable and comfortable communion with her God. Thus, while deep called unto deep, she held by her compass." And what can vanquish a spirit

LADY BALCARRES.

From the Portrait in Brahan Castle.

of this temper, which casts its burdens one by one at the feet of the King its Friend, and goes its arduous road enlarged and glad? What wind can ruffle its profound tranquillity?

> It may blow north, it still is warm;
> Or south, it still is clear.

With such souls the summer lasts the whole year round.

But even better than her husband's *Memoirs* is her own *Diary*, which she intended simply for her children's eyes, and in which she commemorated her divine Lord's "gracious dealing with her and His remarkable hearing and answering her supplications." When the innate scepticism which dogs us all insinuates that it is a foolish vanity to kneel and pray, we shall act most wisely if we let Mrs. Veitch speak to us, and if we pay diligent heed to her victorious reply. She is always seeking some great suit from God, and always finding that He may be trusted to send the sufficient deliverance and the satisfying treasure. "Eternal life to me and mine"—that is her request; and He helps her to believe that He is able and willing to grant it, "as Ahasuerus was the life of Hester." That He will return in His glory to His Church, and especially to Scotland—that, too, is her entreaty; and she has this Scripture given her in response, *I have seen his ways, and will heal him; I will restore comforts unto him and to his mourners.* Perpetually she keeps dipping her pitcher down into the deep well, and perpetually she draws it up filled to its brim with the waters of salvation; until, after she has made numberless errands to the spring, and has been nine or ten years a beggar at the Father's door, she concludes that "faith and love have never an ill tale to tell of Him," and that "His promises can neither die nor drown."

We rejoice to know that both Marion Veitch and her husband survived the Revolution, and at long length found a restful home for themselves, first in the manse at Peebles and then in that of Dumfries. But the trials which tested her with most severity, compelling her to grasp God's right hand more clingingly than ever, were perhaps those which befell in this Indian summer of her life.

Two of her sons had gone to America, to take their part in the hapless scheme of colonising the Isthmus of Darien. They brought her no sorrow through any misdoing; her intercessions for the children of her house had been crowned indeed with the completest recompense; but now one of these two, her firstborn, returning to Scotland, died at sea, heart-broken with the toils and disappointments of the expedition for which he had done his best. At first, the darkness and the pain in the mother's breast were unrelieved by a ray of light. " I had never such a combat with carnal reason and misbelief. Christ appeared like a spirit and frightened me, as He did the disciples." But in her strait she went to Him Who had not failed her yet, and soon she had His medicine for her wound. " Faith told me: I must not be discouraged at the death of my son, for Moses and Aaron died both in the wilderness, and Rachel died by the way, and the saints of God were slain and got none to bury them, whereas thy son got a winding-sheet and a chest of cedar-wood; and this may be a comfort to thee, that he never gave thee cause to have a sad hour for his sinful practices, though he had been a captain of soldiers and with the King abroad." So in the bare ruined choirs Faith piped her hymn of cheer, and the sufferer listened and ceased to despond.

Even yet the discipline of her chastened soul—*pressed on every side, yet not straitened; perplexed, yet not unto despair; pursued, yet not forsaken; smitten down, yet not destroyed*—was not altogether finished. Her youngest son, her Ebenezer, just ordained minister at Ayr, sickened in Edinburgh, where he was attending a meeting of the General Assembly, and the sickness ran quickly on to death and to the ravishments of immortality. " You passengers for glory !" he cried to some ministers in the room, " how near think ye I am to the New Jerusalem ?" And when they answered, " Not far, Sir !" it was his rapturous vow, " I'll climb, until I be up amongst the innumerable company of angels and the spirits of just men." He had given his parting kiss a few minutes before to his newly wedded wife; but she could not tear herself from him, and he had to beckon her away with the whisper, half expostulatory, half tender, " No more converse with the creature ! I never, never, will look back." The story of such a translation, when his mother had it repeated to her, was as sweet as it was sharp. And, no doubt, she "desired the loss to be made up by the presence of the Lord," as, when the nails were driving into the coffin of his Ebenezer—the second of the name whom he had to bear to the grave—Thomas Boston was strengthened to do.

A captivating gaiety and an invincible brightness and a sprightly charm gleam from the features of that lady of the Covenant who, in her girlhood, was Sir Patrick Hume's daughter, and, in riper years, Sir George Baillie's wife. She had a happy issue from all Emilia Geddie's afflictions and introspections ; rebuke and reprimand were far from her soul. If one asks for the final refutation of the delusion that the Covenanter must needs be splenetic and sour-faced, he has it in Grissel Baillie, who sang—

Werena my heart light I wad die,

and who translated her song into the irrepressible lilt of her lovely and pleasant life. "Good Breeding, Good Humour, Good Sense were her daily ornaments," the epitaph says which Judge Burnet wrote for her tombstone in Mellerstain ; and it is an epitaph that tells the truth.

Born at her father's castle of Redbraes on a wintry day in 1665, she was no more than twelve when the chance came of proving her courage and wit. Sir Patrick bade her carry a letter to Edinburgh, to his bosom friend, Robert Baillie of Jerviswood. But Baillie was closely shut up in prison ; although this is not yet the captivity that was fated to terminate in the capital sentence and the martyrdom of injustice. How was his girl-helper to gain admittance to his cell without awakening the suspicion of the gaoler ? She did it somehow, and delivered her letter, and took home with her the tidings of which her father was in quest. The chapter has its fit and romantic climax. In the melancholy Tolbooth she saw for the first time young George Baillie, and the two

were lovers from that moment. It was a small distress to
Grissel Hume that she required to wait in patience through
thirteen care-crowded summers before she could be married
to the man whose eulogy she uttered long afterwards—"the
best of husbands and delight of my life for forty-eight years,
without one jar betwixt us": the flame glowed on the altar
from the minute of the encounter in the dungeon, and her
reward was sure.

In 1684 it was Sir Patrick Hume himself whose head was
endangered; and who but the high-spirited daughter of the
house was his shield and buckler? The tale has often been
told, but it bears to be repeated again and again. How, when
the troopers were in search of him, she got Jamie Winter, the
carpenter, to come to her aid; and, under the screen of the
darkness, they carried from Redbraes a bed and the bed-clothes
to the empty vault beneath Polwarth Church; and there, for
a month, she kept the hunted man in safest hiding. He had
no light to read by; but he did not dream of weariness, for
he would recite to himself George Buchanan's Latin Psalms,
which he knew from beginning to end. And, every midnight,
Grissel stole out from the castle to visit him. She could not
pretend to any eagerness for the mile of lonesome travel,
however hearty her laughter was when it was over and she sat
beside Sir Patrick in the Cimmerian gloom. The gravestones
in the churchyard gave her many a downfall; and the rustling
of a leaf suggested the redcoats in pursuit of that dear life she
was resolved to save; and the minister's dogs barked so loudly
that she imagined herself detected, until her mother coaxed
him to hang them all lest perhaps there was a mad member
in the pack. And then, the perplexity of catering for the
captive's hunger, when the servants must be told nothing of
his whereabouts, and the younger children could not be trusted
to guard the secret! Sheep's head, that homely and wholesome fare, was a favourite dish with her father; and once,
while the nine brothers and sisters were intent over their
broth, she "conveyed most of one into her lap"; but by and
by Sandy missed it, and was bewildered and horrified by such
shameless voracity. "Mother, will ye look at Grissel?" he

cried upbraidingly, "she has eaten up the whole sheep's head!"

Other devices had to be tried soon: Sir Patrick Hume's security in the cellar under Polwarth Kirk could not always be guaranteed. Again Jamie Winter was summoned into consultation, and was set now to the task of constructing a great wooden box. Meanwhile, in an unused room on the ground floor of the castle, Grissel was busy; she was digging out in the earth a hole, both wide and deep, in which the carpenter's chest was to be laid. So silently her work must be accomplished that she would not risk the employment of tools, her own lithe and shapely hands were her knife and mattock and spade; she laboured at her strange love-darg until there was not a nail left on her fingers. Then, in the night-time, the father was hurried across from the vault below the church, and within his own mansion-walls was imprisoned in the spacious casket got ready for him. Through the openings bored in its lid he breathed in the air which fed his life; and he spent some weeks in his curious resting-place. But in the hole in the earth the water deepened daily, till it was not possible for its occupant to remain. Once more he betook himself to flight, a longer flight, to London and Bordeaux and Holland.

Grissel Hume followed him, though not until her mother and most of the children had gone in advance of her; she stayed behind to take a special care of Julian, who was sick; "there is no friend like a sister, to cheer one on the tedious way, to lift one if one totters down." For three years and a half she was the angel in the little house at Utrecht. A most diligent and practical angel she showed herself. The exiles could not afford to keep a servant, and she toiled early and late, to drive the wolf from the door, and to fill the rooms with sweet content. "There was not a week," Lady Murray tells us, "in which my mother did not sit up two nights, to do the business that was necessary. She went to market, went to the mill to have the corn ground—which, it seems, is the way with good managers there—drest the linen, cleaned the house, made ready the dinner, mended the children's stockings and other cloaths, made what she could for them, and, in short, did everything." Only now and then had she leisure to con a lesson with the rest in French and Dutch, and to divert herself with the music which she loved. Among her most priceless possessions her daughter cherished a manuscript book, in which the hard-driven Cinderella had written the snatches of song which came to her in those months of banishment; and some of them were interrupted half-way, and some were broken off in the middle of a sentence; the Muse and she could not sit down for ten quiet minutes in familiar chat. It was always another's enjoyment which she consulted first; it never was her own. There was her brother Patrick, who rode in the Prince's Guards; it was her constant attention to have him appear right in his linen and dress; she would have blushed for shame if his little point cravats and cuffs had not been in as good order as those of the most fastidious cavalier of them all. Or there were the professors and men of learning who visited her father, a true scholar as well as a courteous gentleman; they must be greeted with the best entertainment, even if it were but "a glass of alabast beer, which was a better kind of ale than common." It was seldom, in this palace of frugality whose chambers were fragrant with the herb called Heart's Ease, that they went to dinner without three or four or five strangers to share the meal with them; and many a hundred times had Lady Murray heard her mother declare that she never could look back upon their manner of living in Utrecht without thinking it a miracle: they had no want, but plenty of everything. Morning, evening, noon, and night, Grissel Hume sang Theocrite's song, "Praise God!" For as her father would say to her, none had so good reason to be merry and pleased as those who served the Lord and obeyed His commandments.

But, although the load of hardships and annoyances was carried with incomparable grace, it was a fortunate hour when it could be unloosed and left behind. At last the Prince of Orange was King of England; and the exiles crossed the seas to Redbraes again; and Sir Patrick—that "thin clever man" —became Earl of Marchmont and Chancellor of Scotland; and, about two years after the Revolution, Lady Grissel could wed the lover for whom she had been proud to wait ever since she was a little maid of twelve. The river of their affection had broadened and deepened, in spite of the cataracts over which it had been tumbled, and the many miles of its progress in darkness and secrecy underground. During their banishment they did not dare to avow their engagement, "neither of them having a shilling." Even the girl's parents must not be told. And what a trouble it was "when, in the midst of their distress, there were offers pressed upon her by her mother and father, from two gentlemen, in their neighbourhood at home, of fortune and character, who had done nothing to forfeit either, and with whom they thought it would have been happy to settle their daughter at any time"! But every obstacle was surmounted when for George Baillie, as for Patrick Hume, the brighter era dawned; and never, throughout the future, did the true wife repent her constancy. To the close of his life, she felt the same wish to please him in the smallest trifle that she had had at their first acquaintance. "Indeed, her principal and sole delight was to watch and attend to everything that could give him pleasure or make him easy. He never went abroad, but she went to the window to look after him; and so she did that very day he fell ill, never taking her eyes from him so long as he was in sight." When at length God called him from her side, she lived "with but half a heart," and

> followed him with all the speed
> Desire could make or sorrows breed.

One fine day, looking round and admiring the beauties of their Scottish home, she checked herself, burst into tears, and said to her daughter, "What is all this to me, since your father does not see and enjoy it?" Neither amusement nor occupation could expel those regrets. "As I almost always put her to bed," Lady Murray relates, "I can declare I never saw her lie down but with a deep groan, and generally tears not soon to be pacified; nor could she be persuaded to take another room, choosing everything that could put her in mind of him." But they had almost half a century of trust and fellowship ere the separation came; and in her age she was as beautiful to him, without and within, as she had been in her youth. "She was middle-sized, well made, very handsome, with a life and sweetness in her eyes most uncommon and a great delicacy in all her features; her hair was chestnut, and to her last she had the finest complexion, with the clearest red in her cheeks and lips that could be seen in one of fifteen." And her husband, if he had known the words, would have applied to her a lyric of our later day—

> And oh, her happy queenly tread,
> And oh, her queenly golden head!
> But oh, her heart, when all is said,
>   Her woman's heart for me!

LADY GRISSEL BAILLIE.

After the Portrait at Mellerstain.

CHAPTER XXXV.

PUIR AULD SANDY.

WHAT is trite and customary was far removed from
Alexander Peden. A glamour clings about his person,
and we seem to be walking among enchantments and marvels
when we are in company with him. Weirdness, humour,
genius, mystery : these are the words which leap to the lips if
some one pronounces his name. Dr. John Brown, speaking of
"the round-backed, kindly, solemn hills" of Tweed, Yarrow,
and Ettrick, says that they are "too plain to be grand, too
ample and beautiful to be commonplace." But there are
Scottish mountains which are not plain—dark Lochnagar, the
wild and lonely Cuchullins, four-peaked Ben Laoghal, the
jagged Cobbler which frowns on Arrochar and Glen Croe.
Peden resembles one of these, in his imaginativeness, in his
eccentricities, in that individuality which was so marked.
Yet we may easily exaggerate the elements of wonder. Could
we know him as he actually was, we should find that he was
no wizard, but a man most devout and most lovable. If he
was a prophet, his own spiritual insight and his untiring
fellowship with God endowed him with the penetration that
others lacked. If he lived among escapes and mercies which
appear to belong to the realm of magic, that was because he
exercised the faith which laughs at impossibilities. The
heaven from which issue answers to human prayer, and
divine interpositions, and great and precious promises, and
disclosures of things unseen, was nearer to him than it is to
many; by continual trust and daily speech with the King he
accustomed himself to "climb higher than the sphery chime."

And beneath the quaint exterior there was a heart both brotherly and godly.

It surprises us to read that, lover as he was all his days of the common people—the peasants, the moorland shepherds, the dwellers in hamlet and croft—Alexander Peden was a gentleman by descent and upbringing. He was born, about the year 1626, in the house of Auchincloich—Auchincloich, which means "The Field of the Stones"—in the northern part of the parish of Sorn, in the shire of Ayr. His father was a small proprietor, and he must have been the eldest son, for he is descibed as heir to the lairdship. Gentlemen were his friends too, and, prominent among them, the Boswells of Auchinleck, forebears of that sturdy radical who gloried in the memory of Cromwell because he "garred kings ken that they had a lith in their necks," and of him who gave to the English language one of its immortal books. If for many of his sixty years Peden was homeless and outcast, his life might have been passed amongst those who want for nothing; it was of his own accord and for his Master's sake that he chose the comradeship of poverty. And he was well educated, a scholar of the University of Glasgow, who finished his college course when James Dalrymple, famous in after days as lawyer and statesman, was Professor of Philosophy. One would give much to have Peden's portrait. There would be nothing vulgar in the face, we are certain; it would be strong, but refined as well, with a starry light in the eyes. As it is, we are without information about his appearance. He was full of physical vigour, else he could never have travelled as he did from one lurking-place to another. "He laid his heavy hand upon me," one of his intimates writes; it is the solitary hint allowed us of his build and bearing. If we may construct Hercules from his foot, we may perhaps picture Alexander Peden from his "heavy hand"; and then we shall see a giant in body whom God had fitted to endure much toilsomeness and pain. But not less was he a giant in soul.

In much tribulation he began the race which was to be run through thickets of brier to the end. When he was schoolmaster and precentor in Tarbolton, a young woman charged

him with having done her grievous wrong. The accusation
was false; and his innocence was proved as if by a miracle,
on the very day when he was about to be excommunicated
from the Church. But the anguish of the experience was
terrible, and it left its scar on a nature more trustful and
friendly than most. Soon, however, the keenness of the wound
was healed; and nothing, not even this, soured Peden, or
made him ascetic, or dried up the bubbling fountain of his
cheerfulness. He never had wife and children, but there was
no vow of celibacy, as imaginative writers have surmised;
out in his wildernesses he maintained his fresh and limitless
interest in his fellow-men.

The *Diary* of Andrew Hay of Craignethan, a fragment of
autobiography which the Scottish History Society has published,
gives us a peep at the schoolmaster in the process of admission
to the ranks of the ministry. Hay was a landlord in Clydesdale, of considerable social influence, bearing a name honoured
for godliness and worth, and endowed with a wide culture; he
was acquainted with French and Italian and Dutch, and had
possessed himself of a Hebrew Grammar, that he might gain
some understanding of the language in which the Old Testament was written. In 1659 he was a member of the Presbytery of Biggar and Lanark; and before this court Peden
appeared on trial for license. No fewer than five times, Andrew
Hay relates, he was subjected to examination. In those days
ecclesiastical judges erred surely not on the side of lenience
but on that of severity. The learned elder was himself disposed at first to be critical, as one of his entries testifies:
" 25th August 1659.—About eleven a'cloak, I went into the
Presbrie, and heard Mr. Alexr. Pathen have a common head
in Latin, *De cultu divino*, which was prettie weell composed,
but not weell delivered." But this is the sole depreciatory
comment. A month later, the diarist notes with satisfaction
the chief points in a sermon of Peden's on the imprisonment
of the Apostles: "Obs. 1. That sometimes the Lord maks
His enemys first earand-bearers of His people's delivery.
2. That wicked men leav no means unessayed to embitter the
lot of the righteous. 3. That ordinarly the Lord disappoints

T

enemyes, when they think themselves most sikker. 4. That
it's a hard thing to bear home the conviction of a disappointment on the wicked. 5. That the wicked are so blind as they
cannot see the palpable proofes of God's power. 6. That God
whyles trysts His people's deliverance with impossibilities."
They were theoretical truths which were afterwards to have
abundant illustration in the sorrows and succours of him who
uttered them. By slow degrees the student exhausted the
numerous exercises prescribed to him, until at length he was
ready for the official recognition which he craved. Late in the
same year of 1659, or early in the next year, came the preacher's
ordination. New Luce in Galloway was his parish, a parish
solitary and pastoral and still, in a land of glens and hills.
Through the village the little river of the Luce runs on its
journey to the Bay, not many miles below. One grieves over
the degeneracy of to-day. "If you met a mixed company in
the King's Arms at Wigtown," Mr. Stevenson says, "it is not
likely that the talk would run on Covenanters. Nay, at
Muirkirk of Glenluce, I found the beadle's wife had not so
much as heard of Prophet Peden." It was a blameworthy
ignorance.

But the New Luce ministry was brief. Peden succeeded
in prolonging it for a few months after Middleton's Eject-
ment Act came into force; but in 1663 he had to go. His
last Sabbath was one which the youngest parishioner, even
when he was a white-headed veteran, could not forget. Night
had fallen before the minister left the church; the people
clung to him, eager to keep him still. Every little while they
broke into sobs; although he was himself shaken to the core
of his being, he entreated them to be calm. At last he opened
the door of the pulpit, and, having passed through it, closed
it fast behind him; and, knocking on the pulpit very hard
with his Bible three times, he repeated thrice these words:
"In my Master's name I arrest thee, that none ever enter
thee but such as enter as I have done, by the door!" The
hireling must not stand where the true shepherd had stood,
whose voice the flock knew and whom they followed. And
so, indeed, it happened; because none of the curates and no

minister who had accepted the Indulgence ever spoke from the place where Alexander Peden had published Christ's warnings and welcomes. Not for thirty years was the arrest lifted and the door reopened. Then, in 1693, when the Revolution was fairly established, William Kyle was ordained in New Luce, and took up the prophet's mantle, and in humbler fashion proclaimed the self-same message.

It is after his expulsion that Peden's romance commences. He is chief and monarch of those wandering heralds of God to whom, in that era of death and silence, the country owed the deepest debt. For twenty-three years the mountains and moors were his haunts; we pant in vain after his unresting footsteps. If we look out from the vantage-ground of his native county of Ayr, sometimes he is north in Lanarkshire or Renfrewshire or Linlithgowshire, sometimes south in Dumfries or Kirkcudbright or Wigtown. Here he is remembered by a grotto, which is Peden's Cave; and here by a rock, which is Peden's Pulpit; and there by a shaded hollow, which is Peden's Bed. One of his friends, James Nisbet of Hardhill, son of him round whom such agonies gathered in the Killing Time, has drawn up an inventory of his own retreats, the scenes of his dangers and deliverances; and the minister's catalogue would have been longer still. "The Lord's watchful providence," Nisbet narrates, "prevented me losing my life at all the following places—namely, when amongst the hurry of the enemy's cruel searches at my father's house of Hardhill, at the Bennet Hill, at Gelt Hill, at Garclagh Hill, at the Castle of Kyle, at Dornal, at Corsancone Hill, at Greenock Mains, at Cargilloch, at Wallaceton, at Cubb's Craigs, at Barlonochie, at the Heilsh Wood, at Hairstocks, at Carnduff Hill, at Friarmidden Moor, at Spango 'Glen, at Hoggan Burn, at Cairnscamb, at Leadloch, at Crossford, at Middton, at Burnhouse, and at Loudoun Wood." There is a wealth of movement and risk and rescue in a Covenanting hero's life.

And then Peden's adventures—how various! how significant of his dauntlessness and mother-wit and unstaggering trust! Once he showed a party of the enemy's horse the way to the ford. "You might have sent the lad," a friend expostulated. "No!" he retorted, "they would have asked questions at the lad, and he might have fainted and discovered us." Once, over among the glens of Antrim, he was pinched by hunger. He hired himself to a farmer to thresh his corn. The work was well done, and at night he had a comfortable bed in the barn. But in the dark and in the day, as his fellow-servant reported, the stranger was continually praying for the afflicted Church of Scotland, "naming a great many people who were in a furnace." So he had to confess his identity, and was received into the house as an honoured guest, and was a blessed instrument in the conversion of some of the neighbours and the civilising of others. Once, in the spring, when the rivers were big with melting snow, the troopers pursued him fast and close. Into a flood, where the current ran strong, and where it seemed that nobody could live, he plunged with his horse. The dragoons drew bridle, and watched; they did not dare to follow. He guided the horse skilfully to the farther side. Then, turning in his saddle, he saluted his baffled antagonists. "Lads," he cried, with the gleam of fun in his looks, "ye want my boat for crossing waters, and will certainly drown." But, as he galloped away, his accents were serious and wistful: "Consider where your landing would be. Ye are fighting for the devil, and riding post to him. O think of it!" Many a time the mist shrouded him, at the crisis when his capture appeared inevitable. "Cast the lap of Thy cloak," he would pray in touching anthropomorphisms—"cast the lap of Thy cloak, Lord, over puir auld Sandy"; and God covered His child with his pinions, and under His wings His servant found refuge. No wonder that an intense reality rang through his thanksgivings. Early on a certain morning, after sleeping with some others in a sheepcote, he took a walk along the margin of the stream which rippled through the moor. He was absent some time. When he returned, he saluted his associates with that bracing verse of the 32nd Psalm—

> Thou art my hiding-place; Thou shalt
> From trouble keep me free,

adding, in his picturesque dialect, "These and the following
are sweet lines. I got them at the burnside; I will get more
to-morrow; and so we shall have daily provision, and go on
in His strength." Mr. Meredith writes of the men whom he
loves, that "their aspect is an enlivenment, whatever may be
the carving of their features": and the sentence may be
snatched from its context and appropriated to "savoury Mr.
Peden." His cheerfulness made others cheerful. His might
have been the motto of another Covenanter, *Sub pondere cresco*
—I grow, and aspire, and prosper, under the loads meant to
drag me down.

Yet he did not always escape the snares so assiduously
laid. Proscribed after Pentland, though he had left the
insurgents before the decisive moment, he was captured in
June 1673, when he was holding a conventicle at Knockdow,
between Ballantrae and Colmonell, in one of the pleasantest
bits of southern Ayrshire. Brought before the Privy Council,
he was consigned to prison on the Bass, to remain there for
four years and three months; and then, for fifteen months
more, the Tolbooth of Edinburgh, that "grave for men alive,"
shut him in. Confinement had its special irksomeness for
one whose life had been so unfettered; but he did not
murmur. We have a letter written from the Bass to Patrick
Simpson, minister of Kilmacolm, who had sent him some gifts
gathered by friends—a letter full of dignity and delicacy.
He thanks the benefactors for their kindly dealings with him,
"unworthy of bonds and most unworthy to be remembered in
bonds." He portrays the sorrows of a captive: "We are
close shut up in our chambers; not permitted to converse,
diet, worship together; but conducted out by two at once in
the day, to breathe in the open air; envying, with reverence,
the birds their freedom, provoking and calling on us to bless
Him for the most common mercies. Again we are close shut
up, day and night, to hear only the sighs and groans of our
fellow-prisoners." But there is no loss of faith. "He knows
wherefore we are reserved and what is appointed for us, Who
out of the eater brings forth meat. When darkest, it will be
light; and most care, least care. O for grace to credit Him,

hitherto never cumbersome, and His Cross, in whatever piece of service, in bonds or freedom, He cuts out!" One does not find Alexander Peden sojourning of his own will in a land of sand and thorns.

In December 1678 he was out of the Tolbooth, to enter on fresh experiences of trouble. With sixty others he was sentenced to banishment. They were put on board a vessel in Leith Roads, to be conveyed to America. But he assured his brothers in the kingdom and patience of Christ that "the ship was not built that would bear them over the sea to any of the Plantations"; and thus, in fact, it turned out. For in London they were all liberated, perhaps because Lord Shaftes-bury was courting the goodwill of the Presbyterians. Peden made his way gradually back to Scotland; and, for the seven years of conflict that remained, he divided his ministry between his native country and the north of Ireland, going, as he phrased it, "from the one bloody land to the other bloody land."

If we have no portrait of the man, his friend, Sergeant Nisbet, has limned the likeness of the preacher. "Such," the Sergeant says, "was the weighty and convincing majesty that accompanied what he spoke, that it obliged the hearers both to love and fear him. I observed that, between every sentence, he paused a little, as if he had been hearkening what the Lord would say unto him, or listening to some secret whisper. And sometimes he would start, as if he had seen some surprising sight." The vivid words bring the weather-worn prophet before our eyes; and we are beholders of his native kingliness, of the awe and the affection he inspires, of his pauses and sudden starts, of his most brotherly familiarity with his Lord. Such a man was certain to be credited with supernatural powers; and, because his commerce with the Throne was unbroken and his discernment of men was shrewd and clear, the ascription was not wholly foolish. Often his forecasts were simply the convictions to which he had been led by a keen observation and an alert wisdom; Norna of the Fitful Head, if she had shared his sympathies, would have predicted as he did that, at Rullion Green and at Bothwell,

ALEXANDER PEDEN'S BIBLE.

the saints should be "broken, killed, taken, and fled." And
if, here and there, the premonitions and presentiments are
more inexplicable, what can we do but fall back on the axiom,
as true in Britain as in Israel, that *the secret of the Lord is
with them that fear Him, and He will show them His covenant*?
Peden was the friend of God, and therefore the thin veil
which hides the future became sometimes more transparent
and diaphanous.

As Nisbet hints, he could mount in preaching to great
heights—rugged, to be sure, but sublime and solemn. In
one sermon he spoke of the living who yet are dead; for
"when God comes to call the roll of Scotland He shall find
many blanks—dead ministers, dead professors, dead men and
women though going upon their feet." He instanced different
classes of the pulseless, bloodless, soulless folk. There are
those who "are plunging in the world," and who excuse
themselves by the plea that they must labour for their
livelihood. "O sirs," he cried, "will ye trust God and give
Him credit? If so, He will help you at all your work. I
will tell you what He would do for you. He would plough
your land, sow your corn, shear your corn, sell your corn,
and bring home your money. He will even, as it were, rock
the cradle, if it were necessary, for you. He will condescend
as low as ye desire Him." Then there are the others who have
a religious profession but no inward holiness. "I fear Christ
hath quitted many of you," their monitor said, "and given
you the farewell clap upon the heart, and He will reprove
you no more"; and can there be an exodus more grievous?
Peden could not speak without expressing himself in sentences
full of piquancy. "For you," he declared, "the poor broken-
hearted followers of Christ, to whom He hath given grace to
follow Him in the storm, I tell you, Grace is young Glory."
Or what better delineation of the Church can we conceive
than this?—"Where is the Church of God in Scotland at
this day? It is not amongst the great clergy. I will tell
you where the Church is. It is wherever a praying young man
or young woman is at a dykeside in Scotland: that's where the
Church is." Or again, he would encourage his hearers to talk

face to face with Christ: "If there be one of you, He will be the Second. If there be two, He will be the Third. Ye shall never want company." Frequently he drew his illustrations from what he had himself seen. "There was a poor widow in Clydesdale as I came through, that was worth many of you put together. She was asked how she did in this evil time. 'I do very well,' says she; 'I get more good of one verse of the Bible now than I did of it all lang syne. He hath cast me the keys of the pantry-door, and bidden me take my fill.' Was not that a Christian indeed?" It was no marvel that men listened to such an interpreter of the secrets of heaven.

But, as the sands of life ran out in the hour-glass, and as the thunder-clouds massed themselves threateningly over the country, it was more difficult to persuade him to expound his Lord's message. A time had come, he thought, when ministers and people must dedicate their strength solely to pleading and entreaty; they must take no rest and give God no rest. So, when they begged him still to be their teacher, he would answer, "It is praying folk alone that will get through the storm." "O John!" he said, as he laid his heavy hand on John Clerk of Muirbrook in Carrick, "there shall be dark days, such as the poor Church of Scotland never saw the like, nor ever shall see if once they were over. If a poor thing should go from the East seabank to the West seabank, seeking one to whom they might communicate their case, or that would tell them the mind of the Lord, he shall not find one. Many a conventicle has God had in thee, O Scotland! but erelong God will hold a conventicle that will make Scotland tremble. He sent forth faithful messengers to preach to thee; but erelong He shall preach to thee by fire and sword. Yet"—for Peden was an inveterate hoper, and always he saw "a rose bud in the distant East"—"yet, John, the Church shall arise from her grave; and, at the crack of her winding-sheet, as many as had a hand in her burial shall be distracted with fear. Then shall there be brave days for the Church, and she shall come forth with a bonny bairn-time at her back. O John! I shall not see these days; but you may." *A bonny bairn-time:* it is a tender metaphor. If the prophet was without little ones of his own, he had glimpses of the heaven which lies about the infants, and he knew nothing so fair and good as that the boys and girls should find their hearth and schoolroom and playground in the Jerusalem which he loved with all the passion of his soul.

In truth, there was no gentler heart. Let one story prove the sweetness of his temper. It was an age when faith in witchcraft was rife, and when, in the courts of law no less than in the ruder tribunals of the countryside, cruelties well-nigh unbelievable were inflicted on poor creatures suspected of necromancy and the evil eye. But Peden chose the better way. Once, when he was addressing a crowd, an old woman, with a name for everything uncanny, sat before him. He went to her, and, placing his two hands on her head, " I offer Christ to thee," he said in tones authoritative and kind. She had a bad master, he told her, and she would never " make a bawbee of him "; why not, then and there, renounce the devil's service, and turn to the Master whom it was the preacher's joy to obey? And the witch-wife did as he bade; and from that day the neighbours saw the change; and years after, when she waited for death, she " expressed her great thankfulness that she had the good fortune to hear Mr. Peden." To her, in her ignorance and peril, he was the mouthpiece of the King of Love.

Gladly would the Cameronians have enrolled " auld Sandy " among the captains of their tenacious soldiery. But, though his beliefs and theirs were akin, he never allied himself with them. Probably their rule was somewhat too rigid for his larger catholicity. Yet he honoured the men who were ardent to root every doubtful plant, darnel or poppy or mustard, from the cornfields of Jesus Christ; he saw in them the truest of his spiritual brothers. For a while, indeed, there was variance between him and young James Renwick. They differed in their estimates of the Earl of Argyll's ill-omened expedition, Peden welcoming a movement whose aim was to drive a Popish king from the throne, while to Renwick the enterprise seemed too exclusively political and secular. They stood apart, these leaders in one army. But, when the call came to the older man to pass within the veil, he purged mind and heart from every shred of bitterness. He sent for Renwick, who hastened to his side at once, finding him "in very low circumstances, with few to take care of him; for seldom had he unclothed himself these years, or gone to bed." Tears mount to the eyes as we read what followed. When the boy of twenty-three entered, Peden raised himself on his elbow, and looked at him. "Sir," he asked, "are ye the Mr. James Renwick that there is so much noise about?" "Father," the other answered, "my name is James Renwick; but I have given the world no ground to make any noise about me, for I have espoused no new principle or practice, but what our Reformers and Covenanters maintained." "Well, sir," commanded the dying man, "turn about your back." It was done. "I think your legs too small and your shoulders too narrow to take on the whole Church of Scotland. Sit down, sir, and give me an account of your conversion and of your call to the ministry, and the grounds of your taking such singular courses in withdrawing from all other ministers." Renwick told the sacred story—how from his childhood the Lord's voice had spoken with him; how on three successive mornings, in a retired place in the King's Park, which he used to frequent before he went abroad, he got very signal confirmations of his call to the ministry; what his reasons were for contending against tyranny and defections, and for keeping up an active testimony against all the evils of the day. And, when he ceased, Peden said, "Ye have answered me to my soul's satisfaction, and I am very sorry that I should have believed any ill reports of you. But, sir, ere you go you must pray for me; for I am old and going to leave the world." Then Renwick, "with more than ordinary enlargement," poured out his soul for the travel-worn pilgrim whose course was almost finished. The prayer ended, Peden took him by the hand, and drew him towards himself, and kissed him. "Sir," he said, his last suspicions scattered, "I find you a faithful servant to your Master. Go on in a single

dependence on the Lord, and ye shall win honestly through
and cleanly off the stage." And now it was his turn to
pray; and he pleaded that God might spirit, strengthen,
support, and comfort young James Renwick in all duties
and difficulties. Was there ever a lovelier peacemaking?
We rejoice that it was enacted on this side of death,
before Peden and Renwick reached that desirable country
where, as Francis Quarles puts it, "Martha's reconciled to
Mary."

When he felt that the end was very near, Alexander
Peden crept back to the old home at Auchincloich. But
even then there was no rest for him; the Government kept
up its constant search. He left the house, and hid himself
in a cave close at hand. Sometimes he would say, "Carry
me to Ayrsmoss, and bury me beside Richie, that I may
have quiet in my grave; for I have had little in my life."
But instantly he would add, the prophet's vision unscaling
his sight once more, that it mattered nothing where his body
might be laid, because it would immediately be lifted again.
And so it actually was. He died in January 1686, no more
than sixty years old, exhausted by his countless privations.
As soon as he was gone, the Boswells of Auchinleck, anxious
to guard from insult what remained of their friend, caused
his bones to be interred secretly in their own family vault.
But the soldiers discovered the gracious deed, and rifled
the tomb of its prey. Up to the hill above Cumnock
they took the body, and there, in spite of every remonstrance,
they suspended it on the gibbet. When it was cut down,
it was buried afresh in contempt, like a criminal's, at the
foot of the gallows-tree. In death as in life, Peden was
dowered alike with the love of love and with the scorn of
scorn.

But see how God avenges His own elect! Until these
waning years of the seventeenth century the churchyard
of Cumnock had been in the village below. But now men
and women began to carry their "unforgotten dearest dead"
out to the Hill of Reproach, that they might sleep the sufficient
sleep by the side of Alexander Peden. Little by little the

place became the hallowed graveyard of the town; and, as Professor Veitch sings,

> Hearts were drawn to the saint lifted up,
> Christlike in the glory of shame.

He does not lie alone to-day, that part of him which was mortal and corruptible. Round him on every side he has his own friends of the West Country.

CHAPTER XXXVI.

DUNNOTTAR AND THE BASS.

NEAR Stonehaven, on a huge mass of conglomerate rock which rises from the restless waters of the North Sea to a height of almost 160 feet, stand the ruins of Dunnottar Castle. The great keep had a lively history in the years when it was still roofed and inhabited, as he knows who has read Dr. John Longmuir's wise little book. Here, however, we are concerned with but one of its chambers—a chamber whose four walls, in King James's time, were witnesses of many cruelties and wrongs. The Whigs' Vault is about fifty-five feet long, fifteen and a half feet broad, and twelve feet high. It has two tiny windows, which used to be secured by strong iron bars. Cut in the stone of the walls, at an elevation which removes them to more than the height of the tallest man from the ground, are a number of horizontal niches. These have their memories of anguish and brutality. For the keepers, in the black months of which we are thinking, would force into them the hands of refractory prisoners; and there the unfortunates hung, sustaining the whole weight of their bodies, until it pleased the iron gaoler to set them free.

In eleven weeks, in the summer of 1685, the Whigs' Vault in Dunnottar was the beholder of sufferings which were more painful, and tyrannies which were less defensible, than those which the fortress of a feudal baron has seen in its long lifetime of despotism and unrighteousness.

These were the days when the authorities in London and Edinburgh were apprehensive that Argyll, and the ships and

men he was bringing from Holland, might work grievous
mischief, and might cause them a world of trouble. It was
not politic, they told themselves, to keep so many fiery-
hearted Covenanters massed together in the Tolbooths in
the High Street and the Canongate. On Monday, the 18th
of May, they hurried the captives down to Leith, to lie
overnight in open boats, and to be ferried at daybreak next
morning across the Firth to Burntisland. Dr. Hay Fleming,
who is student and lover of each pin and cord and tassel
in the tabernacle of the Covenant, has told us that there
were in all 224 of these prisoners, and that, after thirty-six
men and four women had satisfied the Laird of Gosford at
Burntisland that their Presbytery was scarcely of the
decisive sort which will make no concessions, and had in
consequence been sent back to Edinburgh, there remained
184 whose destination was the vault in Dunnottar. But
on the march through Fife and Forfar a few escaped, and,
within a short space after their arrival at the woeful ending
of their journey, some died. Thus we arrive at that catalogue
of 167—of whom forty-five were women and 122 were men
—which is preserved in the office of the Sheriff-Clerk of
Kincardineshire.

Let us try to conceive the horrors of it. Into the Whigs'
Vault all of these men and women were huddled by the
Governor of the Castle, George Keith of Whiteridge. It
was ankle-deep with mire. It was a cramped cell, where
they were without air to breathe and without room to sit
down. They were closely confined within it for days.
Although some were sick and on the verge of death, their
friends were denied a candle in the dark, to minister to
their needs. The provisions allotted them were the coarsest,
and for these they were charged an excessive price: the
soldiers compelled them to pay even for the cold water
which they drank. After a time, forty of their number were
transferred to a dungeon underneath the vault itself, a sort
of Mamertine Dungeon. It was still worse than the prison
they had left. Its inmates had no light except what reached
them through a slit in the wall. They might have been

DUNNOTTAR CASTLE.

dwellers in the grave. Then, after another interval, a real alleviation of their distresses was granted them. The Governor's wife caught a glimpse of their pitiful condition, and her gentler heart was shocked at what she saw. She induced her husband to give the women two rooms which they should have as their own; and for their brothers in tribulation she contrived to gain a few trifling privileges.

Yet their misery was only a shade less intolerable than it had been. At length twenty-five determined to make the attempt to escape. At the risk of their lives, they let themselves down to the steep rocks overhanging the sea. But fifteen were recaptured: they were so enfeebled by the degradations and pains to which they had been subjected that they could not run for anything but the shortest distance. For them more excruciating agonies were reserved. They were carried to the guard-house, where they were bound and laid on rough low benches. Between the fingers of their hands kindled matches were placed; and, lest the flame should flicker out, the soldiers, standing round, blew it into an intenser glow. For three long hours the torture was continued; until William Niven lost one of the fingers of his left hand, and Alexander Dalgleish died of his wounds and of the inflammation which resulted from them, and others had the bones of their hands reduced to ashes. In Nicholas Ferrar's Story Book—that quaint manual of interludes and discourses and dialogues recited in the Great Room at Little Gidding fifty years before the terrible wrongs of Dunnottar—there is the tale of Theodorus, a youth of Julian the Apostate's day, who for singing psalms was by the Emperor's command tormented from morning to noon. Afterwards he was asked how he had endured sufferings so great with constancy and cheerfulness. " I wanted not the sence of Paine," he said, " but there stood by mee a Young Man, that ever and anon with a fine Linen wiped away the sweat, and sprinkled my body with a most cold water, whereby not only the heat and the smart of the stripes and wounds was mitigated, but I was so refreshed and delighted as, when I was taken down from the Engine of torment, it grieved me more than before." Niven and Dalgleish and the rest had, surely, the presence of the divine Young Man—Him at whom the Jews hurled the taunt, *Thou art not yet fifty years old.* In their later age, they were able to repeat the ancient victory of Theodorus.

Many of their companions in tribulation are worth remembering. There was John Fraser, for example. From 1678 to the end of 1684 he had been the associate of Alexander Shields in London, helping him in his ministry to the Scots who had fled to the shelter of the great city from the troubles at home. On one of their meetings the King's soldiers broke in, and most of the worshippers were seized and fettered, Shields and Fraser in the number. Those who had been brothers in toil, and now were brothers in trial, were, however, to be separated in captivity, for, while Shields was sent to the Bass, Fraser became one of the inmates of the Whigs' Vault. He was among the forty transferred after a time to the deeper midnight of the dungeon below, where he contracted weaknesses and pains that never quite left him through his subsequent years. And yet he had a long and useful service still to fulfil on Christ's behalf and the Kirk's, because it was not until 1711 that he died in his Ross-shire manse at Alness. With him we may link William McMillan, a preacher from Galloway, who for many a day had been familiar with prison-cells and indignities. Before Bothwell Brig, having been apprehended on account of his assiduity in conducting the meetings in the fields, he had lain in durance through three summers and winters; and, after the Covenanting rout, the stone walls of many gaols—Dumfries and Wigtown and Edinburgh—shut him in. Now he made acquaintance with Dunnottar, although there his health was so precarious that some little relaxation of its agonies had perforce to be granted him. And the time would fail to tell of William Hannah from the parish of Tundergarth, and William Campbell from Middlewelwood in Ayrshire, and James Forsyth of Lochmaben, and Robert Goodwin of Glasgow, and Quintin Dick of Dalmellington. They had their sisters in sorrow, in courage, and in honour—Euphan Threpland, and Agnes Harestanes, and Jean Moffat, and Janet Fumerton, each of whom knew that "port of rest" which Samuel Daniel commended to the Lady Margaret, Countess of Cumberland, "a heart prepar'd that fears no ill to come."

But Patrick Walker, the biographer of the Men of the Covenant, is perhaps the best-known among the confessors of Dunnottar. It is he who has preserved for us the wonderful letter which Peden, in one of the weeks of July, sent him and his fellows, a letter of richest comfort couched in homeliest words. "If ye think Christ's house be bare and ill-provided, harder than ye looked for, assure yourselves Christ minds only to diet you and not to hunger you; our Steward kens when to spend and when to spare." ... "Grace and glory comes out of Christ's lucky hand." ... "He's the easiest Merchant ever the people of God yoked with; if ye be pleased with the wares, what of His graces makes best for you, He and ye will soon sort on the price; He'll sell good cheap, that ye may speir for His shop again, and He draws all the sale to Himself." ... "Now, when it is come to your door either to sin or suffer, I counsel you to lay your count with suffering; for an outgate coming out of any other airt will be prejudicial to your soul's interest." ... "There shall not be a pin in all your graces, but God shall know whether it be crooked or even; He will never halt until He be at the bottom of men's hearts." ... "I defy the world to steal a lamb out of Christ's flock unmissed; what is wanting at the last Day of Judgment, Christ must make them all up." ... "Christ deals tenderly with His young plants, and waters them oft, lest they go back; be painful, and lose not life for the seeking. Grace, mercy, and peace be with you." These are among the Cardiphonia of an epistle as sweet and strong as that which St. Peter sent to the Strangers of the Dispersion, when they marvelled at the fiery trial which tried them.

After the brief blaze of Argyll's insurrection had exhausted itself, the prisoners of Dunnottar were released. At Leith they were offered the Oath of Allegiance, and thirty men and seven women, their spirit gone after treading such a Dolorous Way, repeated the subservient sentences. But the majority, "stooping into a dark tremendous sea of cloud," did as

Paracelsus did—"pressed God's lamp close to their breasts."
They refused to conform. They were sent away, in a ship
which scarcely had turned Land's End before a fatal fever
broke out on board, to the King's Plantations on the American
continent.

The reader of *Catriona* is well acquaint with Andie Dale,
the Prefect of the Bass, as David Balfour jocularly called him,
the shepherd and the gamekeeper of that small and rich
estate. "Ay," Andie would say, "it's an unco place, the
Bass"; and the untranslatable Scots adjective, his whilom
captive felt, was the only one to describe the Plutonic stronghold on which he found himself detained. "It was an unco
place by night, unco by day; and these were unco sounds,
of the calling of the solans, and the splash of the sea and
the rock echoes, that hung continually in our ears." There
were Covenanters who had an experimental knowledge of the
"unco place." From 1673 to 1687 some of their number were
always there. Lauderdale had bought it, for the exorbitant
sum of £4000 sterling, from Sir Andrew Ramsay, the Provost
of Edinburgh, and had transmuted it into a state prison. To
its dreariness and isolation, for periods which ranged from a
few months to more than six years, the Privy Council sent
nine-and-thirty of the troublesome soldiers of the Kirk.

One of them, James Fraser of Brea, delineates the rock as
he saw it between the January of 1677 and the July of 1679.
In stormy weather, he tells us, it is girt about with the
thunders and reverberations of the waves, which will toss
themselves up to the fortress and pour into the court in front
of the prisoners' chambers. Round the whole circumference,
which is some three-quarters of a mile, there is but one place
of landing: every other front is too high and too steep. And
you must have a full sea when you land; for, if the tide is at
the ebb, you will need to climb on hands and knees up the
artificial steps—steps, each of which is so distant from its
neighbour that, now and then, you must get the help of some
one above you. On the south side stands the Governor's
house; and, a little higher, one comes to the gaol and the

quarters for the garrison. From these, by windings cut in
the crag, there is a path which mounts to the summit. It will
repay you to make the ascent, because on the top various
pleasant things are to be found. There is grass sufficient to
feed twenty or twenty-four sheep, which are there very fat and
good. There is a garden too, where herbs grow, and, among
the herbs, a few cherry trees, the fruit of which Fraser had
several times tasted; and, just beneath the garden, a chapel
for divine service—but, alas! the soldiers have profaned the
house of prayer into a magazine for the storing of their ammunition. In these uppermost parts, moreover, the visitor discovers
sundry walks. Of necessity, they are tantalisingly short:
threescore feet in length they may claim to have, but no more.
Yet the caged men in those dark and narrow dungeons below
are glad when they are permitted to seek them out. There
they can be solitary, musers and talkers with God, who meantime are not interrupted by the coarsenesses and mockeries of
their keepers: there, indeed, they are able to entertain themselves. A strong place the Bass is, as well as an "unco" one.
On its southern face cannon are planted; but on its other
aspects it is sufficiently defended by nature, so huge is it in its
height and so frowning in its looks. Two dozen warriors,
if they are courageous, James Fraser thinks, will defend it
against millions of men; and, in fine, it is only expugnable by
hunger.

The good man, according to his wont, makes the best of his
unlovely prison; of the martyrs it has been written that "he
who lies broyling on a Gridiron in others' eies lies in his owne
Conceit upon a Bed of Pleasure." But incarceration on the
Bass was far from being a holiday experience. Some of the
cells had only one small window, and it was placed at such a
height above the floor that the occupants could see neither
earth nor sky. Others of them looked out upon nothing but a
stone pavement between two rigid walls; and up and down
this pavement the sentry paced, watching the movements of his
cribbed and cabined victims. In the winter the rooms were
many a time full of smoke, so dense that it threatened to
suffocate those who were condemned to live under its inky

pall. And, here and there, there was a Black Hole yet loathsomer and more frightful than its companions, as Thomas Hog of Kiltearn knew. In his dungeon serious· illness overtook him, and he petitioned the Council to give him his freedom. Some of its members were disposed to grant the prayer; but Sharp said No, protesting that Hog could do them more hurt sitting in his elbow-chair than twenty others could by travelling through the country, and that, if there was one place on the Bass hatefuller than another, he ought to be consigned to it. That was the Archbishop's sentence; and, when the prisoner heard it, he declared that it was as severe as if Satan had been the penman. So they dragged him down by a subterranean alley to a dismal den, and left him there, in "a hideous cavern, arched overhead, dank and dripping, with an opening towards the sea which dashes within a few feet below." With Thomas Hog the worst had come to the worst. But then, as in kindred instances of suffering for righteousness' sake, a miracle happened. His sickness disappeared; soon he was perfectly well. When, in subsequent years, he spoke of his Grace of St. Andrews, not a syllable of resentment escaped his lips. "Commend him to me," he would say laughingly, "for a good physician."

In truth, it was the habit of the prisoners on the Bass to esteem their granite walls and iron bars a hermitage. Peden did so, and Major Joseph Learmont, and the Campbells of Cessnock, and Gilbert Rule, and Alexander Shields. Our brave field-preacher, John Blackader, was sent to the loneliness of the cliff in 1681 and died there four and a half years afterwards, every request of his friends for his release proving fruitless; but he moved always in a large place, and his epitaph in North Berwick churchyard assures us that, as an older John had found Pisgah in Patmos, so "no chains could bind his heaven-aspiring soul." Or let us hearken to John M'Gilligen, the minister of Fodderty. "Since I was a prisoner," he writes, "I dwelt at ease and lived securely. The upper springs flowed liberally when the nether springs were embittered; and I have had the experience of that saying, *Tanta est dulcedo cœlestis gaudii ut, si una guttula deflueret in*

infernum, totam amaritudinem inferni absorberet" : a saying
which is a veritable trumpet-call and pæan of victory—" Such
is the sweetness of Heaven's delight that, if one little drop of
it were to flow down into hell, it must vanquish all hell's gall
and wormwood," transfiguring this Marah of Marahs into an
Elim where we may have " rest beneath the palm tree and
joy beside the well."   Thomas Ross, taken from his Morayshire
parish to the rigorous crag, survived his release for only a few
months; but he, also, had nothing except a psalm of praise on
his lips.   " I am persuaded," he said, " and my soul has been
triumphing these three years bypast in seeing that the delivery
of the Church and people of God is coming."   " I assure you,"
he sang, as he passed from earth to heaven, " there is neither
rock nor mountain between me and Christ."   Or here is
Robert Trail, son of the minister of Greyfriars who went with
James Guthrie to interview the Marquis of Montrose, ere the
fearless soldier met his doom.   Robert Trail's sojourn on the
Bass was shorter than that of his comrades; he seems to have
had friends with influence sufficient to procure his liberation.
But, during his two months there, he learned much of that
familiarity with the Throne of Grace which he was to describe
in later years with such pleasantness and power as to make
Ebenezer Erskine his confessed and thankful debtor.   On a
Saturday in 1721, about twelve of the day, the founder of the
Secession wrote in his Diary that all the forenoon he had been
studying Mr. Trail's exposition of the verse in the Hebrews,
*Let us therefore come boldly unto the throne of grace, that we may
obtain mercy and find grace to help in time of need.*   " I bless
the Lord," he added, " who directed that honest man to
preach and write on this subject; and I bless the Lord that
brought his book to my hand.   I read some of it with tears of
joy."   And as for Fraser of Brea, no persecution could make
his heart bankrupt or could lessen his fruit-bearing.   " Every
day," he records, " I read the Scriptures, exhorted and taught
therefrom, did sing psalms, and prayed with such of our
society as our masters did permit to worship God together, and
this two times a day.   I studied Hebrew and Greek, and
gained some knowledge in these Oriental languages.   I like-

wise read some divinity, and wrote a Treatise of Faith, with some other miscellanies, and letters to Christian friends and relations." He could scarcely have done more if he had been at home in his northern manse.

Silvio Pellico, in the narrative of his imprisonment, pictures a dungeon in Milan, on the walls of which he read the legends inscribed by those who had tenanted the chamber before him. Some were mere names and dates; some, rude and degrading sketches; some, sentiments of resignation and religion; some, scoffing atheism. Those Covenanters who sojourned in the old keep on the Bass Rock, with the surging and sobbing sea beating round them, left in their cheerless rooms only the high tradition of fortitude and godliness.

CHAPTER XXXVII.

HE WAS OF OLD KNOX'S PRINCIPLES.

IF James Renwick was not absolutely the last of the Scottish
martyrs—for in the Ayrshire fields, George Boyd, a boy
of sixteen, was shot in the summer of 1688—he was the last
who died a public and judicial death in the cause of the
Covenant. The roll of witnesses, whose testimony was sealed
with blood, could not have had a nobler ending and colophon.
The very letters of his name seemed full of spiritual significance to those who loved him, and who mourned when he was
torn from their head. "I am Christ's Meek Servant," or else,
"Mine Marck is *Ever the Same*"—these were the halting
anagrams which they elicited from "Master James Rhenvick."
The art was forced and defective; but the reverence was
limitless. He was their dearest, kingliest, best, whom the
scaffold had taken; and their cup of sorrow overflowed.

Renwick was born in Nithsdale, in the village of Moniaive,
in February 1662. His parents had little worldly wealth, the
father being a weaver by trade; but, like other Scottish
peasants and toilers, they dedicated their boy from his infancy
to the ministry of Christ's Church. In the child's gracious
behaviour they began soon to see tokens that their hopes for
him were to be amply fulfilled; "by the time he was but Two
Years of Age," his biographer, Alexander Shields, says, "he
was discerned to be aiming at Prayer, even in the Cradle and
about it." There were other premonitions too—shadows in
the Dumfriesshire Nazareth of the Edinburgh Cross. His
father, dying when the lad was thirteen, was already firmly
persuaded that his son's day of life should be short—short, but

eminent and far-shining. Yet it was not without tribulation
of soul that young Renwick found himself amongst believing
men. He was a student and a graduate of the University of
Edinburgh; and, at college, he had his own agony of intellectual struggle to pass through. For awhile he wandered in
a labyrinth; he felt uncertain of the foundation-truths of
religion. Once, "being in the Fields and looking to the
Mountains, he was so strongly assaulted with Temptations of
Atheism that he said, 'If these were all devouring Furnaces of
burning Brimstone, I should be content to go through them,
if so be that thereby I could be assured that there is a God.'"
He could have sympathised with Rutherfurd, who speaks of
the sceptical questions with which the good are assailed, and
adds in a pregnant parenthesis, *Expertus loquor*. It was
through the wilderness that he entered the land flowing with
milk and honey. He faced the spectres of the mind, and laid
them, and came to find a stronger faith as his own. And
we, whom the same spectres trouble, are drawn into nearer
brotherhood with him, because he had these sharp contendings
of spirit, and because the clouds threatened to blot out his
Sun.

When peace had returned, and God was firmly enthroned
in the citadel of the soul, an incident happened which
determined the character of his future. In the July of 1681,
in the crowd at the Mercat Cross, he saw Donald Cargill done
to death, and the resolution awoke within him that he must
take up that torch which the older confessor was compelled to
lay down; he and no other should be Cargill's son in the faith.
Thus we discover him among the Mountain Men, a member of
the United Societies, as eager as any of their ranks for the
battle against the tyrannies of the time. It was they who
sent him to Holland, to Rotterdam and Groningen and
Leeuwarden, that he might complete the studies which were
preparing him for the office of preacher. There, when he was
twenty-one, he was ordained to the high and precarious
calling; and in the summer of 1683 he was again in his own
country, the "rendezvous of hell" and yet the gate of heaven.
How he had longed, during his temporary exile, for the hour

of home-going! "O, mind sweet Scotland!" he wrote to one correspondent; and to another, "I am not a little sorrowful at the very heart that I am not in Scotland, for nothing that ever I was trysted with was such an exercise to me as my being detained out of it is"; and, on still another occasion, "I think that if the Lord could be tied to any place, it is to the moors and mosses in Scotland." The fire of the patriot leaped and flamed within James Renwick.

In November 1683, at Darmead in the parish of Cambusnethan, he preached his first sermon, out under the open sky, to a great congregation. Of set purpose he selected for his text the passage from which Donald Cargill had spoken last: was he not unfurling anew the standard which had fallen from the veteran's hand? It was the invitation of the Book of Isaiah, the heavenly call to a perplexed and tortured Church to confide in the guardianship of God: *Come, My people, enter thou into thy chambers and shut thy doors about thee; hide thyself as it were for a little moment, until the indignation be overpast.* If any one imagines that Renwick was merely an ecclesiastic and a controversialist and a man of war, he needs but to read this sermon in order to be disabused of the error. It is full of evangelical tenderness and fervour. The intense desire to make his hearers acquainted with the living Saviour governs and illuminates and quickens its pleading sentences. The preacher lingers over the opening word of the verse, the word which Christ never tired addressing to labouring and heavy-laden men: "We must proclaim this word *Come* to you as long as you are here, until you be transplanted out of your spiritual warfare into celestial triumph. O sirs, come,. come! Ask what you will, and He will give it. O, come, come!" A century and a half after the Cameronian's day, over in Würtemberg, another young spokesman of the Crucified Lord carried the same message to his countrymen. He was but five years older than Renwick when he finished his course; but, as in the case of the Covenanter, the effect of his teaching was wonderful. People flocked from distances of twelve and sixteen miles to listen, and under his spiritual power their heads were bent involuntarily, so that the congregation resembled a cornfield with the grain bowing beneath the sweep of the wind. "I have but one sermon," he said: "Come, sinners, and look on Christ. I preach the Lamb that was slain; that draws hearts—O brothers, that draws hearts! It is a pity that we have so many words which do not go to Him. But I have found that he who preaches Christ never runs done. We get done with our wisdom, for it is a vessel, and a vessel has a bottom; but the love of Christ is an abyss, and out of His fulness we receive grace for grace." Ludwig Hofacker and James Renwick were close of kin.

After the conventicle at Darmead there began for Renwick, who was scarcely more than a boy, a life of unremitting effort. In four years' time he was dead; but into the brief ministry he crowded the labours of a quarter of a century. He was perpetually preaching; it was the task in which he delighted most. But this was not all. Within twelve months he is said to have baptized more than six hundred children; for fathers and mothers rejoiced to have their little ones introduced to the family of faith by a man behind whom they heard the steps of the divine Master. And he wrote Informatory Vindications, to defend his creed and his comrades and himself from the slanders which were heaped on them. Plainly he did not understand what idleness meant. It has to be remembered, moreover, that he was not physically strong, like Alexander Peden—he had no "heavy hand" to lay on the shoulder of a friend; he was delicate and fragile. In a letter written in the concluding months of his life to Sir Robert Hamilton, we catch a pathetic glimpse of the weakness against which he had to fight. "My business was never so weighty, so multiplied, and so ill to be guided, to my apprehension, as it hath been this year; and my body was never so frail. Excessive travel, night wanderings, unseasonable sleep and diet, and frequent preaching in all seasons of weather, especially in the night, have so debilitated me that I am often incapable for any work. Sometimes I fall into fits of swooning and fainting. When I use means for my recovery, I find it someways effectual; but my desire

to the work, and the necessity and importunity of people,
prompts me to do more than my natural strength will well
allow, and to undertake such toilsome business as casts my
body down again. I mention not this through any anxiety,
quarrelling, or discontent, but to show you my condition in
this respect. I may say that, under all my frailties and
distempers, I find great peace and sweetness in reflecting
upon the occasion thereof; it is a part of my glory and joy
to bear such infirmities, contracted through my poor and
small labour in my Master's vineyard." He makes us think
of David Brainerd, riding through the endless woods of New
Jersey and Pennsylvania, intent on gathering the Red men
into the kingdom of God, all the while that consumption was
eating into his frame. Indeed, he makes us think of Jesus
Christ, whom zeal for the Father's house consumed.

His flights and concealments and hairbreadth escapes were
thick as the leaves in Vallombrosa. On a July day in 1684
he was travelling, in company with other three, to a meeting.
Suddenly they espied two dragoons riding towards them;
but, because at first they saw no more than two, they continued to pursue their own way. As soon as they were
within word and shot, the enemy disclosed his real strength.
There was a company of over twenty. It was hopeless for
four men to contend against such odds, and they turned and
fled. Renwick's three companions were captured, although
one of them had received eleven wounds before he yielded.
But he himself, with the King's soldiers close behind him,
galloped to the top of a low hill called Dungavel. When he
was almost at the summit, he judged it best to dismount from
his horse; for he was too conspicuous a target for the
matchlocks of his antagonists. He threw himself on the
green grass, and crept on hands and knees to the shelter of
a little cairn that crowned the hill. Behind the cairn, on the
farther slope, where for a minute or two he would be concealed
from the troopers, he found a pit; and "it entered into my
mind," he says, "that it was ordained of God for hiding me."
He lay down within the hollow, ready for whatever the divine
will might be, even if a moorland death or a march to the

gallows were in store for him. Still the conviction was strong that the last stage of his journey had not yet arrived. Over and over to himself he repeated the verses of the psalms: this, *Depart from me, all ye workers of iniquity*, which he crooned a hundred times; and this, *He shall give His angels charge concerning thee*, a promise which came to his spirit with such conquering force that he lifted his head to see the angels; "but, considering my folly in that particular, I was made to laugh at mine own witlessness." There, in the hole on the hillside, he remained hidden and still until sunset, sometimes praying, sometimes praising, and sometimes weeping over the fate which, he was convinced, had befallen his friends. Then, when he thought that he might venture forth, but yet remembered his ignorance of the country and of the whereabouts of any house which was likely to give him welcome and shelter, he asked God to lead and guide him. And the Father heard the cry of the child; for, after he had tramped about four miles over the heather, he encountered a companion, whom he could trust implicitly, and went with him to his home, and kept a meeting there, although the militia were searching the whole district for the proscribed preacher. "The world is full of miracles," cried John Howe; "we are compassed about with such, and are such." Renwick, himself a constant miracle, moved in a realm where the miraculous was the occurrence of every day. Across the wine-red moors, and up the mountain-slopes, and down the glens, through all those western shires which he described as "flowered with martyrs," the legions of heaven accompanied him as bodyguard and retinue.

Nowhere have we such a revelation of the man himself, in his mingled bravery and gentleness, as in his letters. They may not have the "Oriental fragrancy" of Samuel Rutherfurd's, but they breathe their own aroma; if they are not garden roses, they are the violets and hyacinths of the woods. Certainly Renwick shares his forerunner's limitless enthusiasm for Christ. "Though I had ten thousand times ten thousand years," he says in the March of 1684, "yea, the faculty of angels, I could in no ways lay out mine

obligations to free grace; but behoved, when I had babbled
my fill, to seal up all with this, *Christ is matchless.*" Two
years later, "to the honourable Societies of Strangers at
Leeuwarden in Friesland," he breaks out in similar raptures:
"They that have been most ravished with His love, and most
eloquent in the praise of His comeliness, will see that they
have been but, at best, babes learning to speak. O, what
shall I say? He is the wonderful, glorious, and inestimable
Jewel; the incomparable Pearl of price. O, who would not
choice Him? who would not give away themselves to Him?
Let a man look through heaven and earth, and seek a portion
where he will, he shall not find the like of Christ." For a
Master so supremely good, in a service so desirable, one may
greet difficulty and hardship and hostility with smiling face.
"O precious Kingdom!" exclaims our pilgrim along the
highroad of the Cross; "and O noble way that He is taking
this day to enlarge it, by stretching out the borders thereof
with blood! His house is a costly house, and it is well
worthy of costly cementing." Borne for Him, reproaches
become "badges of honour," and is it not "more sweet to be
swimming in the swellings of Jordan for Christ than to
swelter in the pleasures of sin"? "Love," Renwick declares,
his prose assuming the melodies of poetry, "love is a resolute
soldier; love is an undaunted champion; love's eye is so much
taken up with contemplating the Beloved that it cannot see
dangers in the way, but runs blindly upon them, and yet not
blindly, because it knoweth for whom and for what it so
ventureth:" we might imagine that he had been reading
George Herbert—

> Love is swift of foot;
> Love's a man of warre,
>   And can shoot,
> And can hit from farre.

The race is beset with toils, as he can testify who main-
tains it "through many damps and deeps"; but nothing
will persuade him and his brothers to forsake it for the path
of dalliance and ease. "Our natures would have the way
so squared as we might travel without a rub; but it lieth

U

through many a rencounter. We would have it through a valley of roses; but it lieth through a valley of tears. We would have it so as to be travelled sleeping; but it must be travelled waking and watching and fighting. We would have it to be travelled with laughing; but it must be travelled with weeping. But, whatever folks do think, the way is pleasant to the believer, and a sight of the recompense of reward maketh bold to pass through every opposition. If they were possible, ten thousand deaths, ten thousand hells, would seem nothing to a soul who gets a sight of Christ at the other side." The world's most splendid boons cease soon to satisfy a hungering spirit; "the earth is round and the heart of man three-nooked, and therefoie this cannot be filled by that." But the poor man who walks with God, even when shadows and tempests are round about Him, fares, summer and winter, through a good land and large: "Away with scrimpit sense, which constructs aye God's heart to be as His face! Faith is a noble thing; it soars high; it can read love in God's heart when His face frowns." James Renwick has learned it from experience. Out on the hills at midnight, "when the curtains of heaven have been drawn," the quietness of all things brings to his mind the deep and silent and inexpressible ocean of joy, in which the whole family of the higher house are everlastingly drowned; each star leading him out to wonder what He must be who is the Bright and Morning Star, and who makes His people to shine as stars in the firmament. And, on such ineffable midnights, would he exchange places with Lord Perth, or Viscount Dundee, or King James in his palace of Whitehall? No, no! "Indeed, if I may term it so, I am much obliged to my enemies; for, though they purpose my misery, yet they are instrumental in covering many a fat table to me; and, while they are pining away in dusk envy and pale fear, I am feeding in peace." They are the beggars, and he is the prince.

For some years the voice of the penman of these beautiful letters was raised alone on behalf of the Covenant; even Peden, as we have seen, dismayed by the excesses of Lag and

MONUMENT TO JAMES RENWICK, MONIAIVE.

Earlshall and Claverhouse, had given himself to praying rather than to preaching. On Renwick's head, therefore, the fury of the Government was poured in its fullest flood. "We command and charge all and sundry our lieges and subjects," an edict of the Privy Council runs, which was issued in September 1684, "that they nor none of them presume, nor take upon hand to reset, supply, or intercommune with the said Mr. James Renwick, rebel aforesaid; nor furnish him with meat, drink, house, harbour, victual, nor no other thing useful or comfortable to him; or to have intelligence with him by word, writ, or message, or any other manner of way whatsoever, under the pain of being esteemed art and part with him in the crimes foresaid, and pursued therefor with all rigour to the terror of others. And we hereby require all our sheriffs and other officers to apprehend and commit to prison the person of the said Mr. James Renwick wherever they can find him." It was a pitiless proclamation; but it proves how warmly and how widely the Cameronian preacher was loved that, in spite of its threatenings, he remained secure from his persecutors for more than three years after it was promulgated. In every part of the Lowlands he could count his leal friends, who were prepared to succour him however the men in authority might rage. The slight, bright-haired stripling, from whose lips the word of God flowed in gentle stream, had twined himself about their hearts; they would willingly have suffered for him themselves. Sir Robert Stopford, who commanded one of the ships with which Nelson chased to the West Indies a fleet nearly double in number, says in a letter, "We are half-starved and otherwise inconvenienced by being so long out of port, but our reward is that we are with Nelson." It was what numbers of the Covenanters would have said: our reward is that we are with James Renwick. Yet he was misled by no illusions; day after day he told himself and others that he was marching towards his death. "I think," he wrote to a lady, "we are not yet entered our Jordan; for though we have come through a miry and thorny wilderness, yet our Jordan is before us, and it will be very deep but it will not be very broad. When the Ark of God enters it, it shall be like to drown; but it shall suddenly and admirably win to the farther side." His own Jordan was assuredly to be deep, but happily not very broad; erelong he would stand on its higher banks, the brimming floods breasted and left behind.

In May 1685, with two hundred men surrounding him, he rode into Sanquhar, and affixed to its Market Cross a Declaration couched in terms akin to those of the memorable document which Richard Cameron had fastened to the same spot five years before. In 1686 he was for some weeks in the north of England, preaching in its fields and villages whenever an opportunity was given him. In the wintry days of December he took part in the General Meeting of the United Societies, at which Alexander Shields was ordained to the ministry. In the springtime of 1687 he and Shields framed and, later in the year, published the *Informatory Vindication*. It is the apology for the stricter party among the Covenanters. It defends them from the charges brought against them, not only by undisguised foes but by those many of whose beliefs were identical with theirs. Especially it explains why they could not own all the ministers of the Kirk—why they felt constrained in conscience to hold aloof from the fellowship of their brethren; and were not on that account to be denounced as guilty of schism, and of marring needlessly the peace of Jerusalem. The argument is clearly stated and forceful, and yet the pages are not lacking in the celestial grace of charity. For, says Renwick, " we do not look upon all these ministers that we withdraw from, upon more or fewer of the foresaid grounds, to be no ministers, yea or no more ministers of the Church of Scotland, or that their pastoral acts are invalidate or null; but only that we cannot lawfully embrace them as *our* ministers, and concur with them in the public work, as they are now circumstanced." Through chapter after chapter, compactly welded and carefully reasoned, the book journeys with firm step, until it reaches this characteristic final sentence: " We add no more, but desire that this be taken as the unbosoming of the genuine thoughts, and exhibiting the mind and sentiments, as to the controversies of the present time, of a poor, wasted, wounded, afflicted, bleeding, misrepresented, and reproached Remnant and Handful of suffering people, who desire to throw down what God will throw down, and to build what He will establish when He comes: to whom be the kingdom and dominion for ever and ever. Amen." He who wishes to appreciate the ecclesiasticism of James Renwick must mark and digest the *Informatory Vindication.*

But the hour approached when he was to be delivered up. At Peebles, in the end of 1687, he had a narrow escape from capture. In Edinburgh, a month or two later, he was taken. He was lodging in the house of a friend on the Castle Hill, where his voice was overheard in prayer, and recognised. The next morning an attempt was made to arrest him; but, avoiding those who entered the room, he ran down the Castle Wynd to the head of the Cowgate. There he was seized, and given over to the City Guard. When Graham, the captain, saw him, he was astonished. "What!" he said, "is this boy that Mr. Renwick whom the nation has been so troubled with?" Hurried to prison he fell on his knees, and offered himself freely to God, asking only that the cruelty of his enemies might be so far restrained that they should do nothing more against his body than take his life. He was highly strung and sensitive, and had suffered much from the dread of torture, wondering often whether among the pains of boots and thumbscrews he could continue faithful to the last. His entreaty was answered; on the day before he died he could bear witness, "I have found Christ's Cross sweet and lovely, for I have had many joyful hours and not a fearful thought since I came hither." And when his mother spoke of how she shrank from seeing the head and hands which she had fondled set up in derision on the gates of the town, "You shall never see that," he smiled and assured her; "because I have offered my life to the Lord, and have sought that He will bind them that they may do no more; and I am much persuaded that they shall not be permitted to torture my body, nor touch one hair of my head further." Already, in the phrase of his great contemporary who wrote *The Saint's*

Everlasting Rest, Renwick had the malignant planet Saturn under his feet.

The Privy Council condemned him on three charges: that he refused to acknowledge the King's authority; that he would not pay cess to His Majesty; that he counselled his followers to come armed to their meetings—charges the truth of which he admitted at once. They reprieved him for a week after the sentence of death had been passed; and during its course they tried by every means to shake his constancy, or, at least, to persuade him to apply for pardon and release. But their endeavours were futile; he had set his face like a flint towards the consummation of his good fight. Once his mother asked him how he was, and he answered, " I am well; but, since my last examination, I can hardly pray." Then, when he saw her glance of distress, he added, " Being so much taken up with praising, and so ravished with the joy of the Lord."

Those responsible for his execution knew in what odium the crime would involve them; and, almost to his latest minute, they strove to induce him to furnish them with the pretext for setting him at liberty. But he clung to his consistency rather than to his life. He would part with no fragment of the truth, although there were accents in which at times his message had been uttered that seemed now to his scrupulous conscience over-emphatic and severe. On the morning of the day on which he suffered, he sent his last salutation to Sir Robert Hamilton: " I do still adhere unto the matter of my Testimony," he wrote, " but I think the manner of expression is in some things too tart." Love ruled him to the end—to that death of which he said that for him it was " as a bed to the weary." At length the drums beat for the guard. " Yonder," he cried with brightening looks, " is the welcome warning to my marriage. The Bridegroom is coming. I am ready! I am ready!" Round the scaffold in the Grassmarket an immense crowd was grouped; but he was permitted to say very little to the people: the rattle of the drums went on through the death-scene. He sang the 103rd Psalm, and read the nineteenth chapter of the Book of the Revelation, and prayed aloud. " By and by," he exclaimed, turning his face upwards to the bleak and wintry skies, " I shall be above those clouds; then I shall enjoy Thee and glorify Thee without intermission for ever." Once more the young preacher of twenty-six had the better of his enemies. Once more, while they pined in dusk envy and pale fear, he fed in peace.

It was the 17th of February 1688 when James Renwick was martyred. Before the year was out, the Stuarts were in exile, and the persecution was closed. He died as the herald of a more gracious day. "He was of old Knox's principles," his adversaries said, when they noted his unassailable stead-fastness. But we may take our farewell of him in words which were written by one who loved him dearly: "When I speak of him as a man, none more comely in features, none more prudent, none more heroic in spirit, yet none more meek, more humane and condescending. . . . He learned the truth and counted the cost, and so sealed it with his blood."

CHAPTER XXXVIII.

LO, THE WINTER IS PAST.

WHEN James Renwick died, the persecution had been prolonged for twenty-eight years of daily alarms and miseries. It is not easy to arrive at an accurate computation of the victims of the sorrowful and weary time. John Howie in *The Scots Worthies* may overshoot the mark, and yet he cannot be far from the truth. Eighteen thousand, he calculates, endured either death or "the utmost hardship and privation." Of these, seventeen hundred were banished to the American plantations; and, out of the seventeen, two hundred were lost in shipwreck. To the northern islands of Scotland, then almost a *terra incognita,* seven hundred and fifty were exiled, to wear out an existence which would have been forlorn enough if it had not been sweetened by supernal consolations. Those sentenced to imprisonment in the Tolbooths of the towns, and the dungeons and keeps of the country, are reckoned at two thousand eight hundred. Those killed in skirmish and insurrection were at least six hundred and eighty ; while no fewer than seven thousand sought voluntarily an asylum under milder and friendlier skies. In the fields and on the hillsides five hundred were slain in cold blood ; and three hundred and sixty were executed after some form of examination had been perfunctorily and summarily hurried through. It is impossible to count the men and women and children who succumbed to rain and frost and fatigue and hunger in their wanderings across mosses and mountains. When everything is remembered, John Howie's figure of eighteen thousand cannot be much in excess of the grim reality.

But even the long winter of the Arctic world yields place to summer and sunshine. The days lengthen. The ice melts. The flowers appear on the earth. And the end of the travail and anguish of the Scottish Church was at hand.

King James touched nothing which he did not mismanage and spoil. His policy was a curious mixture of tyranny and toleration. A Romanist himself, he was resolved to grant new liberties to his Catholic subjects. But he dared not single them out alone for the enjoyment of favour; the country, he realised, was too fervently Protestant to permit such a preference. Of necessity he embraced other excluded folk in the largess he distributed. In Scotland, the year 1687 saw no less than three Indulgences issued under the royal seal. These suspended "all penal and sanguinary laws made against any nonconformity to the religion established by law," and gave sanction to His Majesty's "loving subjects to meet and serve God after their own way and manner, be it in private houses, chapels, or places purposely hired or built for that use." Only against the Conventicler did the lightnings continue to flash forth; the Acts which Parliament had decreed for the suppression of the gatherings in the open fields were left in full force; for impenitent Cameronians it seemed that there could be no whisper of mercy and no outgate into freedom. Yet here were large measures of release, which might carry in them the promise of a hopefuller era. If the followers of Renwick denounced them, there were Presbyterian ministers, in prison or banishment or hiding, who welcomed James's Indulgences, and returned to their homes under the shelter of their provisos. But even they, profiting although they did by the altered current of affairs, had no confidence in the man who brought it about.

They could not but see that he was a despot of the purest type. The emancipation he allowed them was their birthright, to which they had an inalienable claim; they ought never to have been defrauded of it; and, now that it was restored, the acknowledgment should have been made that the King gave them merely what was their due. But there was no such admission. On the contrary, the liberty was described emphatically as a singular boon, bestowed in virtue of " Our sovereign authority, prerogative royal, and absolute power." It came from an autocrat, who might withdraw his concessions as arbitrarily as he had granted them. They must have remarked, also, how he tore down with one hand what he built up with the other. While the Indulgences preached toleration, the Killing Time ran its unhindered course, and men were still butchered on the moors or dragged to execution in the Grassmarket. There was no effective quenching of the fires of persecution, no sheathing as yet of the sword which had been dipped so deeply in Covenanting blood. And it was not a hard matter to divine the motive which underlay the surface clemency. Had there been no Roman Catholics to secure from disabilities and penalties, the bluebonnets would have been kept in the heat of the scorching furnace. Not because they were pitied, not because at length some sense of their tragic woes had touched the stony heart of the monarch, was the relaxation yielded, but solely because those who stood at the opposite pole from themselves in the religious world were in need of roomier space and an ampler air.

And Scotland dreaded nothing so profoundly as the return of Roman Catholicism. The peril crept close to her in those months. James induced many of the nobles to send their children abroad, that they might be educated in Jesuit colleges. At home, under the care of zealous priests, schools were established, where the boys and girls of the poor were taught without fees. Popish ecclesiastics, brought from the Continent, walked about the Edinburgh streets in their monkish dress. Protestant books and pamphlets were suppressed as "insulting to the King's religion." The highest honours in the country were conferred on men who had abjured the creed and Church of their youth, in order that they might insinuate themselves into the graces of their bigoted sovereign: James Drummond, the Earl of Perth, was Chancellor, and his brother, Lord Melfort, was Secretary of State—*par ignobile fratrum*. Things were much amiss when even Bluidy Mackenzie was angered into revolt, and resigned

his office rather than help James to travel farther along the
path of absolutism and priestcraft.   For nearly two years, from
May 1686 until February 1688, he ceased to be King's Advocate,
his place being filled, curiously enough, by Sir John Dalrymple,
the ally and friend of the Presbyterians.   But he, too, had soon
to go; he had no satisfaction in executing the behests of the
tyrant on the throne.   For a few brief months Sir George
Mackenzie came back, to administer the law with much less
virulence than formerly ; he realised that the catastrophe was
not far off, and that the days of the dynasty were numbered.
By and by the first mutterings of the impending storm were
heard.   The mob sacked the chapel which the Chancellor had
fitted up in his town house, and pelted the Countess with
mud ; and, when the soldiers from the Castle attempted to
disperse the rioters, they found themselves greeted with
volleys of stones.   The weather portents could not be blacker
or more ominous.

Then momentous tidings came in from England.   The
seven bishops were tried for their refusal to read the King's
proclamations, and were acquitted ; and Westminster Hall
rang with the shouts of the delighted multitude.   Anglican
and Nonconformist joined hands, Tory and Whig made
common cause against the injustice of the Throne.   In June
1688 an event took place which accelerated the crisis.   The
Prince of Wales was born.   South and north of the Tweed
the nation understood now that the fate of Protestantism was
irrevocably sealed, unless something decisive was done without delay.   If a Catholic son should succeed to the heritage of
a Catholic father, there could be but one result—the destruction of the religious liberties of the Commonwealth.   There
was no more dallying.   The fateful address was sent to the
Hague, to William Henry, Prince of Orange and Count of
Nassau, stadtholder of the republic of the United Provinces.
Shaftesbury signed it; and Danby; and Devonshire; and
Lord Lumley, who parted from James only because he loved
his honour and his country more than his King; and Edward
Russell ; and Henry Sidney, Algernon's brother ; and Compton,
the suspended Bishop of London.   They implored William to

cross the seas at once, and to constitute himself the deliverer
of the land. The rest is a familiar story. How, in the first
week of November, the Dutch fleet rode safely in the harbour
of Torbay. How all the land grew vocal with cries of "No
Popery!" and "A Free Parliament!" and "The Protestant
Religion!" How, after one abortive effort at flight, James,
between two and three o'clock in the morning of the 23rd of
December, stole through a Rochester garden to the banks of
the Medway, and boarded a frigate, which landed him at
Ambleteuse on the French coast. How, after many debates
over troublesome points of procedure, William and Mary were
proclaimed King and Queen in February 1689. The Glorious
Revolution was complete.

In Scotland there were to be tumultuous experiences before
the reign of orderliness and quiet was fairly inaugurated.
On the eve of his departure from Holland, William had sent
a Declaration to the northern kingdom. He spoke of its
lamentable condition under the arbitrary rule of the Stuarts,
of the extravagant privileges extended to men whose faith
was abhorrent to the bulk of the citizens, of the terrorism
exercised over the Judges, of the autocratic powers which
had been claimed and wielded without ruth and without limit.
He offered himself to the Scots as defender of the Protestantism
they loved, and of the civil freedom which they were in
danger of losing outright. The Privy Council forbade the
Declaration to be published; but in the western shires, always
the peculiar home and fortress of Presbytery, it was widely
disseminated. Within the walls of many a cottage, and at the
meetings for worship, its terms were read; and hearts beat
more quickly, and eyes were filled with tears. The men and
women of the Covenant knew that their redemption drew
nigh.

By the end of the year, Edinburgh was crowded with the
supporters of the Prince of Orange; and those who championed
the discredited King could make no headway in the endeavour
to retrieve his falling fortunes. A disturbance in the streets
frightened Lord Chancellor Perth into flight; after a week or

two, he was captured in the attempt to escape to the Continent; and for four years he lay in prison. The Catholic chapel at Holyrood was demolished; and the townsmen and the train-bands burned in a bonfire its ornaments and Popish books and paraphernalia of idolatry. This was the time, too, when the "rabbling" of the curates went merrily forward in the capital and over the country.

These pitiful curates had not a friend outside the threshold of their own families. Their methods of conducting the service of God had not differed very greatly from the severe simplicities of the Presbyterian order; for Scottish Episcopacy in the seventeenth century was devoid of liturgical forms and of the pomps of ceremony and ritual. But by nine-tenths of the inhabitants, alike in the burghs and the little rural villages, they had themselves been held in unmitigated dislike. They came as usurpers, the tools of a tyrannical system; and, being in most instances unacquainted with either learning or godli-ness, they had never been able to live down their initial disadvantage. Now that they were dismissed, nobody wept over their going. And yet, hirelings and intruders and "graceless graces" although they were, the wish rises in the mind that they had been handled with more forgivingness and magnanimity. No doubt, it is "matter of admiration," as Wodrow says, "that the provoked people ran not to a far greater length"; and Patrick Walker marvels much at his own leniency and that of his Cameronian kinsfolk. "How would they tremble and sweat," he asks—the miserable and obnoxious preachers—"if they were in the Grassmarket, going up the ladder, with the rope before them, and the lad with the pyoted coat at their tail?" It is a pertinent question; but, for all that, the "rabbling" was a process neither dignified nor generous. Some three hundred were ejected from church and manse. The incumbent was led to the town's Cross, or to another convenient spot where the people were accustomed to con-gregate. His indictment was solemnly recited. Not the slightest injury was done to his person, and no scrap of his property was harmed, except the fringed gown that he wore—a vestment which was viewed with special aversion. This was torn from him, and trampled ignominiously beneath a hundred protesting feet.   The ceremony finished, the disrobed man was marched to the boundaries of the parish, and there cast off without word or look of pity or regret or goodwill.   Thus, after many days and much provocation, the Earl of Middleton's puppets were, somewhat rudely, unsaddled and turned adrift.

The "rabblings," however, did not, terminate the battle. Fighting on the graver and grander scale was imminent.   In April 1689 the Convention in Edinburgh framed the Claim of Right, declaring that "King James the Seventh, being a pro-fessed Papist," had "forfaulted" his royal place, so that "the Throne was become vacant"; and, after the interval of a day, William and Mary were proclaimed at the Mercat Cross.   But, some weeks previously, one man, whose name has figured often in these pages, had determined to strike a resolute blow on behalf of the old order.   John Graham of Claverhouse, whom James had created Viscount Dundee, finding that the city was no longer a safe home for a partisan with his past history and his present sympathies, had ridden away northward. He knew that he could rely on the aid of all those Highland clansmen who hated the Campbells of Argyll.   They clustered round him in Lochaber; and, for nearly half a year, he main-tained with extraordinary daring and skill a guerilla warfare against the Government.   It is the portion of his biography on which it is possible to look back with something akin to pride. If he fought for the cause of oppression, he fought with un-flagging spirit and persistent loyalty.   Of him it may be said, as was said of another, that nothing in his life became him like the leaving it.   The end, splendid and unforgotten, came on the heights of Killiecrankie.   On the 27th of July, after sunset, his men, few in number, half-starved, weary with their toilsome campaigning, rushed down the hillside on General Mackay and the King's troops.   They threw away their guns as they ran pellmell to meet the bayonets of their enemies.   They broke into wild and unearthly cries.   They swung their broadswords and axes to right and left with terrible effect. The Royalists were panic-stricken, and fled.   Many were drowned in the foaming waters of the Garry.   Many more

were slaughtered. The rout was as thorough as it could be.
Yet the sorest loss was with the followers of James. Claverhouse had received his death-wound a few minutes after the
conflict began. A bullet pierced his side below the breastplate, as he rose in his stirrups to wave his plumed hat and to
cheer his Highlanders and Irishmen in prospect of the fray.
The bravest ally of the Stuarts, and the prime antagonist of
the Covenanters, was gone.

Three weeks later, at Dunkeld, the last scenes in the strife
were enacted. William Cleland, the young poet and captain
of Drumclog, had, in those stirring days of 1689, raised and
marshalled his regiment of Cameronians—men of character
and religion, who rejoiced to serve under such competent
command for the wage of sixpence a day. To these Cameronians the task fell of defending Dunkeld against the Highland
army, which was expected to attack the town as it swept
southward on its victorious progress towards the Lowlands.
It was an army flushed into arrogance by its recent triumph
over King William's General. It was six or seven times as
numerous as the small force which stood in its way. Its
success seemed sure. The Covenanters themselves feared that
their position was untenable. They sent a deputation to
Cleland, suggesting that they should retreat while there was
still the chance of doing so without reproach. But the word
" retreat" had no place in the dictionary of their captain.
" I have been bidden to hold Dunkeld," he said, "and for me,
I shall stay here although every man in the regiment leaves
me." " We will never do that," they replied ; " but the officers
have their horses, whereas we cannot ride for it, if it should
come to the worst." Cleland turned to his orderly. " Lead
out the horses, and let them be shot," he commanded ; "and
you will know that we shall stand by you, if you stand by us."
But all the misgivings had been dispelled. " No ! " the men
cried—" we trust our Colonel and our officers." The duel
which ensued was tremendous. The outposts of the
Cameronians were driven in ; but from dyke to dyke they
retired in good order, until they had massed themselves together in one steadfast phalanx. Against this the Highlanders

charged, with swords in hand, as they had done at Killiecrankie, only to be met by the pikes and halberts of their adversaries, and to be repulsed again and again.   After a time the bullets of the Covenanters were exhausted ; but lead was cut from the flat roof of Dunkeld House, and melted in furrows dug in the earth, and the struggle went on.   From seven in the morning until noonday it raged, and then the clansmen abandoned their onslaught and fled in disorder to the hills, while the Cameronians paused and sang their loud thanksgiving to God for His mighty acts.   After Dunkeld, William's power over Scotland was uncontested and safe.   But Colonel Cleland, like John Graham, died in the smoke and fever of the battle. At an early point in the fight he was shot through both head and body, as he went from post to post encouraging his officers and men.   " Carry me into the house behind us," he said, " that they may not lose heart when they see how I am wounded." While they obeyed his request, he breathed his last.   After the turmoil had sunk into calm and the day was won, the soldiers who loved him prepared his resting-place in the nave of the old cathedral, near the western door.   There he lies " where he longed to be," on the ground guarded so manfully against overpowering odds by those good comrades whom he had trained in the art of war.

A hundred difficulties confronted King William in his settlement of the Scottish Church.   If he was himself a Presbyterian by predilection and profession, he was surrounded in London by Anglican advisers ; and he was well aware that, in spite of the " rabblings," many northern parishes were occupied still by the curates.   Among these eddies and shoals and contrary tides, it was a perplexing problem to know in which direction to pilot the vessel.   Some of the historians have insisted that the King desired to find the solution in the establishment of a modified and carefully guarded Episcopacy ; but we look in vain for confirmation of the statement.   The fatuousness of the Scottish bishops had, surely, made such an issue an incredibility.   In the beginning of November in 1688, when the Revolution was almost an accomplished fact, thirteen of them signed and sent to James one of the most obsequious and fawning letters ever penned. They spoke of him as " the darling of Heaven." They said that his " long, illustrious, and unparalleled line was the greatest glory of this ancient realm." They avowed their intention of inculcating, more strongly than they had yet done, the duty of allegiance to His Majesty as "an essential part of religion." Having heard rumours of an invasion from Holland, they prayed with impassioned ardour that " God would still preserve and deliver " their beloved monarch " by giving him the hearts of his subjects and the necks of his enemies." It was a document as stupid as it was servile. It prevented the prelates from having any share in the ecclesiastical reconstruction of Scotland.

One most persevering pleader on behalf of Episcopacy was Sir George Mackenzie. On a winter's day, in London, he dined with the Archbishop of Canterbury and with others of the English prelates. He confessed that in his own country the bishops had done much harm ; but he added that they had now come to their senses. He implored the Primate to use his influence with William in their favour. He himself wrote an appeal to the Prince. In its sentences he argued that, while in England the Reformation had been brought about by the royal authority, in Scotland the movement had been solely the result of popular passion and violence, and that nothing was so inconsistent as Presbytery with the respect and reverence due to the sovereign. But he spoke to ears that remained unconvinced ; and soon his own public career was at an end. When, in the spring of 1689, the Scottish Convention offered the crown to William and Mary, he ceased to take an active part in the affairs of the Kingdom. There are pathetic stories of how, at this time, he would wander for hours through the Churchyard of the Greyfriars, and how men saw him there alone at midnight on the eve of his final departure from Edinburgh. Some would fain have had him punished for his severities and injustices as Lord Advocate; but the Whig government was too tolerant to encourage such reprisals. The last two years of his life—he died in 1691—were spent in quietness, sometimes in Oxford and sometimes in London.

John Evelyn, with whom he had crossed foils in one of the mock-duels of literature, met him in the former town at the table of the Bishop of St. Asaph's. He testifies to his persistent attachment to Episcopacy and as persistent dislike of the Covenants. Who was it, cried Sir George, who first introduced Presbytery to Scotland? He had his own astounding answer to the question. It was a Jesuit priest in disguise, who had done the mischief back in the spacious times of great Elizabeth. He began the system of extemporaneous prayer. He feigned himself the champion and propagandist of unliturgical devotions and evangelical sermons. And he lived for years without being discovered for what he really was!

The new Church must be modelled on the old Presbyterianism of John Knox and Andrew Melville and Alexander Henderson; but to get it done was no child's play. In July 1689 the first step was taken. Then "a lawful and free Parliament"—an institution whose face and likeness the nation had not seen for years—rescinded all those Acts which had maintained that in the Kingdom of Jesus Christ there are officers superior to the elders or Presbyters of the New Testament. The Episcopalian hierarchy was stamped with disapproval and was robbed of its diadem. In the succeeding April, when the Parliament entered on its second session, other notable decisions followed. Those Covenanting ministers who had been ejected, when Charles and his councillors upset everything which Scotsmen counted dear, were restored to the parishes they had known and taught and yearned over in the older and better era. Not more than sixty of them survived; and who will say with what thoughts, lying too deep for tears, the sixty wind-beaten men went back to the scenes where the ministries of their youth had been fulfilled? At the same time the fines and forfeitures imposed during the persecution were cancelled; and the decrees passed against Conventicles, with the tests and oaths and penalties of eight-and-twenty bitter years, were repealed. It was as when the tossing billows of a protracted storm subside at last, and again the sailors can breathe freely; or as when the dawn of an Emancipation Day releases the serfs whose vassalage has

been long-continued and humiliating; or as when the hero
Beowulf slew the Grendel with his own hand-grip, and the
helpless lands of Hrothgar awoke to a happiness as strange as
it was blessed.

The midsummer of 1690 brought the most significant
enactment of all. On the 7th of June it received the imprimatur of Parliament. It provided for the perpetual
corroboration of all laws "made against Popery and Papists,
and for the maintenance of the reformed Protestant religion."
It ratified "the Confession of Faith as the public and avowed
Confession of this Church." It established "the Presbyterian
church government and discipline," as these had been set up
in 1592; for were they not "agreeable to the Word of God
and most conducive to the advancement of true piety and
godliness"? And it appointed "the first meeting of the
General Assembly to be at Edinburgh, the third Thursday of
October next to come." In this great statute the thirty-three
chapters of the Westminster Confession were printed in full,
and so the theological fiats of the Jerusalem Chamber form to
this hour an integral portion of the law-book of the Scottish
nation. Little remained to be added when things had proceeded thus far. In the middle of July, patronage was
abolished; and, if to the heritors and elders there was con-
ceded the right to propose the fitting minister to a vacant
congregation, the parishioners themselves kept the power
either to accept him or to refuse. The Kirk had risen from
the dust, and was robing herself afresh in her beautiful
garments.

Much has been written both for and against the Revolution
Settlement. It certainly was not perfect. The mailed hand
of the State was by far too prominent. King and legislature
planned all, decided all, confirmed and approved all; and the
Church had scanty opportunity of making her voice heard;
to a large extent she was treated as a negligible quantity.
Some of the concessions, too, were granted reluctantly and
with bad grace. William, while he wrought an urgent and
marvellous deliverance for Britain, was not a man to kindle
the white heat of enthusiasm and the red glow of affection.

He was reserved and austere; and it was only in the moment
of battle and the crisis of danger, as Macaulay tells us, that
the coldness thawed and his nature took fire. Many a desirable
boon he spoiled by the grudging manner of its bestowment.
A more fundamental defect still, in the eyes of those Covenanters whose consistency was undeviating and firm, was that
the Settlement ignored some of the most memorable attainments of the past. It did not revoke the Act Rescissory, by
which the Drunken Parliament had erased in a trice much
that was brightest and worthiest in the Church's record of
achievement; it left the wicked decree untouched. For this
reason mainly, the Cameronians deliberately elected to stand
outside the General Assembly of the Revolution period.
Three of their preachers, Alexander Shields being the most
famous, did find a home within its bounds; but only three.
The inflexible majority, true to themselves and hating all
paltering and accommodation, refused to countenance arrange-
ments which were not the highest but merely the next to
the highest. Thankful as their inexorable souls were when
" the new sun rose bringing the new year," they recognised
with sadness that even this nobler and joyfuller epoch was not
that *acceptable Year of the Lord* for which they had prayed
and bled.

But, if the Settlement had unmistakable shortcomings, it
was the parent of abundant good. It put an end to the pains
and wrongs of persecution. It gave the people of Scotland
the Church for which they cherished an ineradicable love, and
the ministers whose enforced absence and silence they had
mourned. It ushered in the gladder age which still runs its
course, when conscience is freed from the hateful dictation of
palaces and consistories and unjust Courts of Justice, when
national and religious despotisms are clothed with merited
dishonour, and when men and women dwell in a wide room.
The disciples of Richard Cameron and Donald Cargill and
James Renwick, if they would fain have had the enfranchised
State and the comforted Church permeated by a still diviner
atmosphere, were to a great degree the human architects of
those liberties which the country welcomed with overflowing

gratitude, and in which she read the promise of a stable and prosperous future. They might be disappointed, as all knights and votaries of the ideal are disappointed. But tens of thousands reaped the bountiful harvest of the seed they sowed in a wild and stormy spring, and praised God for the valleys covered over with corn.

EPILOGUE.

THE GENERAL ASSEMBLY MEETS AGAIN.

THE Parliament of 1690 had invited the General Assembly of the Church to meet once more ; and, on the 16th of October, the invitation was obeyed. Thirty-seven years had come and gone since Cromwell dispersed the last gathering of Presbyterian ministers and elders—years crowded with labours and sacrifices and griefs. As the members took their places in the old Assembly Aisle of St. Giles's Church, what visions they saw ! what battles they fought anew ! what scaffolds rose, stark and yet glorious, before the eyes of the mind ! They could not forget that they had travelled to their inheritance out of the house of bondage and through a land of pits and snares. It was natural and right that they should give their earliest sessions to the exercises of solemn fasting and prayer, to meditation on the words and ways of God, and to adoring praise of Him Who had led them so wondrously to the city of habitation.

Lord John Carmichael was the Commissioner of the King —a man prudent, intelligent, of quiet and equable temper. There were present, Principal Rule says, one hundred and sixteen ministers and forty-seven ruling elders. " For the age, piety, learning, and gravity of the members," writes one who had his seat in the Assembly Aisle, " it is much to be doubted if they were not equal, if not superior, to any convocation of churchmen that ever were in Britain in our day." Men were there who had carried gun and sword at Rullion Green and Bothwell Bridge ; men who bore branded on their bodies the marks of the rack and the thumbscrew, and who could tell of the horrors of Dunnottar and the Bass; men on whose heads the Government of Charles and James had set a price, and who had been laid under the ban of intercommuning, so that it was a capital offence to let them have a morsel of food or to hide them from their pursuers. There was pathos in the meeting of these warriors of the faith, whose hair was grey and whose cheeks were furrowed. Yet there was much cheerfulness too. An old legend relates that Lazarus never smiled after he left his charnel-cave and returned to Mary's house; but, although they had passed through seven deaths, the Covenanters had not forgotten how to smile. Like the Little Brothers of Assisi, they were the merry men of the Lord.

Hugh Kennedy was chosen their Moderator. He was a Protester of the antique type, *an early disciple*, as was Mnason of Cyprus, who accompanied St. Paul from Cæsarea to act as his host in Jerusalem. Not one of the others who did not respect him for his saintly character and his well-tried attachment to the Kirk. He had been so keenly opposed to Prelacy that the Malignants nicknamed him "Bitter Beard." But they mistook the man altogether. His brethren assure us that his disposition was gentle and sweet and helpful, and that he brimmed over with pleasantry and good humour.

> It was his nature
> To blossom into song, as 'tis a tree's
> To leaf itself in April.

Round the Moderator some ministers are grouped, who have been with him in the crucible of affliction. One is old Gabriel Sempill of Jedburgh. He assisted when the Covenants were renewed at the Town Hall of Lanark, in those wintry days of 1666 which saw the insurgents on their road to defeat at Pentland. He is, we remember, a gentleman by birth, being the son of Sir Bryce and the grandson of Lord Sempill. Often he has been the comrade of John Welsh and John Blackader in their adventures and deliverances and field-preachings; but, whilst they have gone to be with Christ in the upper sanctuary, he has escaped his perils "with the skin of his teeth," and is eager to do his part in rebuilding the desolated and ruined Church. "Eminently countenanced of

God with success in the work of the Gospel" Gabriel Sempill
has been; and he stands in the Assembly of 1690 with a
vigour so unimpaired that Thomas Boston, when he hears him
speak in a yet later year, is compelled to marvel. "I was in
a manner amazed," the listener confesses, "for his words went
out through me and in through me, so that I said in my heart,
Happy are those that hear thy wisdom!" The Conventicler's
natural and supernatural force is not abated.

William Veitch sits not far away, the husband of heavenly-
hearted Marion Veitch, and the friend who did his utmost for
the Earl of Argyll. And, beside him, is his chief companion,
Gilbert Elliot, who will be Lord Minto soon and a Judge on
the Edinburgh bench. Once, when he was a young advocate,
Elliot contrived to bring about Veitch's acquittal and to save
his life. "Ah, Willie, Willie!" he whispers to him now, "had
it no' been for me, the pyots had been pyking your pate on
the Netherbow Port!" But the shrewd minister has his
retort ready. "Ah, Gibbie, Gibbie! had it no' been for me,
ye would have been writing papers yet for a plack the page!"
These are the quips and jests which enliven the Assembly's
serious toil.

There, too, one can look up into the serene face of a man
most gracious, whose name alone might fill St. Giles's Church
with odours of spikenard—devout and apostolic Thomas Hog
of Kiltearn. We have not forgotten how, on the Bass,
Archbishop Sharp was his good physician; but, indeed,
nothing and no one could hurt Thomas Hog, for his life was
hid with Christ in God. He spent whole nights in prayer;
and to this day his sanctity is recalled in the north country,
by those who love to meditate on the years of the right hand
of the Most High. Four summers before the Revolution took
place, he predicted that the change was certain to come, sending
this message to the Prince of Orange out of the distresses of
the Killing Time: "Tell him that I have assurance of the
Lord that, though the Church of Scotland is under a dark
cloud now, yet it will be over quickly, and that he shall be
the instrument of her enlarging and shall be King of these
realms." Now his prophecy was realised, and his joy was full.

The fidelity of the martyr accompanied him to the ending of his pilgrimage. He ordered his grave to be dug on the threshold of his Highland church, and on the tombstone he bade them write the admonition: "This stone shall bear witness against the parishioners of Kiltearn, if they bring ane ungodly minister in here." The mightiest transports moved and thrilled Thomas Hog.

A true spiritual brother of the saint was Henry Erskine; and he also was a participant in the debates and verdicts of the Assembly. Forty-five years later all Scotland was to ring with the words and deeds of his sons, Ebenezer and Ralph. To his preaching, too, Boston, "whose golden pen to future times will bear his name," ascribed, under God, the awakening of the new life in his soul. But Henry Erskine is worth knowing for his own sake. He had a great fortitude. When he stood before the Privy Council with the instruments of torture fastened on his hands, Sir George Mackenzie ordered him to preach no more at the meetings in the fields. But he would not be browbeaten. "My lord," he replied, "I have my commission from Christ, and, though I were within an hour of my death, I durst not lay it down at the feet of any mortal man." There spoke the stout confessor who feared his unseen Master so much that he felt no meaner fear. And he had a childlike faith. Once, in the cottage at Dryburgh, the meagre stock of provisions was consumed at supper-time, and in the night the children awoke crying for bread. Their father had none to give them, but he trusted the better Father to send the supply. So meanwhile he took down his gittern, and played to the bairns, and comforted their mother with the promises of God. And erelong some one knocked peremptorily at the door, and a stranger on horseback left a bag stocked with food, and became surly when he was asked who he was and from which quarter he had come, and rode immediately away into the dark. Above Henry Erskine's head, let the weather be fair or foul to his neighbours, the sky was always blue. In his heart, every month of the twelve, the birds sang, and the flowers bloomed, and the river of the water of life made happy music.

These men of the Covenant were saints, "first and last
and midst and without end." But there were members of
Assembly somewhat different in their temperament, more
politic and more courtly: Dr. Gilbert Rule, for example, the
Principal of the University of Edinburgh, who was to distinguish himself in after years by his writings in defence of
Presbytery; and David Blair, minister of the Old Church, son
of the famous Resolutioner of St. Andrews and parent of the
poet of *The Grave*. Rule's spirituality and Blair's was, no
doubt, genuine; and yet it was not of that masterful and
illimitable and unearthly sort which invested Hog and Erskine
with the fragrance and the glory of the sons of God. There
were threads of attachment which bound them tightly to the
world of the seen and temporal.

The prince of this party, who was in constant attendance
at the sitting in St. Giles, though he represented the Court
in London rather than any congregation or Presbytery in
Scotland, was William Carstares. "He surely," says a eulogist
in the *Coltness Collection*, "was one of the greatest clergymen
who ever embellished any church." And so, beyond question,
he was. But the greatness is not altogether of the ethereal
kind. The diplomatist was blended in Carstares with the
disciple, the statesman with the Christian. His was a potent
voice in Parliament, although he never sat in the legislative
chamber. His was a prevailing and unceasing influence with
the King, although he wore the Geneva gown of an unpretend-
ing preacher. His father, John Carstares, had shown him a
rare example of lifelong faithfulness, and he had himself
undergone the agony of the thumbkins. But he was of a
more modern school than the old Covenanter. The virtues
of the resourceful man of affairs were united in his nature
with those of the servant of Christ: courage and address,
sagacity and wit and caution, patience and conciliatoriness
and charity, moderation and tolerance. Many different
estimates of him have been bequeathed to us by his contemporaries. "He is the cunningest dissembler in the world,
with an air of sincerity," his ecclesiastical and political
antagonists maintained. "Through all the vicissitudes of

WILLIAM CARSTARES.

fortune," his friends replied, " he preserved the same humble spirit and simple worth, the same zealous piety, the same amiable and affectionate heart." " I have known him long," King William declared with a warmth which he did not often manifest, " I know him thoroughly, and I know him to be a truly honest man." One approaches a personality that bulks largely in the public view from the angle of hostility, or from the angle of reverence, or from the angle of intimate and brotherly fellowship, and how diverse the personality seems! It is a tribute to Carstares's real magnitude that he moved men to feelings so various and contradictory; a lesser soul would not have appeared so kaleidoscopic. And, doubtless, there were elements of truth in all the portraitures.

He could do fearless things. On one occasion he risked the loss not only of his master's favour but of his own head. In 1694 the King wished to impose on the Church in Scotland terms which her members could not have subscribed without forfeiting every shred of their spiritual independence. He said that, if they refused to obey his orders, the General Assembly of that year must be dissolved. Either issue—that of submission or that of resistance—meant the downfall of Presbyterianism. Carstares did not hesitate. It was late at night when he heard the character of the despatches which William was sending to his Commissioner in Edinburgh. At once he hastened to the messenger, just setting out on his journey, and in His Majesty's name required him to deliver up the royal letters. It was done. Then he hurried to the King's apartments. William was asleep. He awoke him. He told his astonished sovereign that he had come, at this untimely season and with such temerity, to beg for his own life. " Of what crime," William asked, "have you been guilty that you deserve to die ? " He produced the despatches. At first the King frowned and fumed; but Carstares craved the privilege of an interview. Before it was over, William acknowledged his error, and bade his monitor throw the fatal letters into the fire.

And he could do things most kindly and chivalrous. There is a story narrated by his first biographer, which helps us to understand how thoughtful he was and how generous. Among the ejected curates none was more scurrilous in his denunciation of Presbytery than Robert Calder. One day this accuser of the brethren visited Carstares, and the leader of the Church noticed that his clothes were worn until they were threadbare. He surveyed him narrowly from head to foot, and, as he went out, asked him to return two days afterwards. No sooner had he left than Carstares sent for his own tailor, "and desired him to make a suit of clothes that would answer himself as to length but not so wide by two or three inches." They must be ready by the hour when the curate was expected to reappear. Calder came back, to find his host scolding the tailor in angry terms for mistaking his measure. It was impossible, he cried, and his visitor was compelled to acquiesce, that ever he could wear clothes so lacking in proportion and grace. "'Then,' says he, 'they are lost if they don't fit some of my friends; and by the bye,' adds he, 'I am not sure but they may answer you: be so good as to try, for it is a pity they should be thrown away.'" After some persuasion the guest complied, and discovered, to his surprise, that they fitted as if they had been made for him; and thereupon Carstares ordered the clothes to be packed up and sent to the poor man's lodging. And this was not all; for into one of the pockets he slipped a ten-pound note, and when the curate wanted to restore it, "By no means, Calder," he protested; "it cannot belong to me; for, when you got the coat, you acquired a right to everything in it." It is seldom that the coals of fire are heaped so cleverly and so unselfishly on the head of an enemy.

When we recall such incidents as these, we do not feel very sorry that, in the Assembly of 1690 and its immediate successors, the authority of William Carstares was paramount. Though Richard Cobden's talk was of trade and tariffs, of wages, profits, rents, loans, debts, budgets, it is easy to see, writes Professor MacCunn, that there was room in him for much besides the things which were perforce most upon his lips. "Who was it, that vacant half-hour at Shrewsbury, who sighed for the knowledge of mullions and architraves that x*

INDEX

525

Argyll on his expedition, 426 ; his dangers and deliverances, 452.

Hundalee, Dame Mary Rutherfurd, Lady : her "sad sweet exercise of soul, and blessed death," 432.

Hutcheson, George : with the Marquis of Argyll on the scaffold, 87 ; with Charles II. at the Hague, 123 ; takes the Indulgence, 195 ; confers with Lauderdale and Leighton, 221.

Hutton, R. H. : quoted of the Hard Church, 306.

Hyslop, James : *The Cameronian's Dream* quoted, 339.

Imitation of Christ, The : Leighton's delight in, 226 ; a Cameronian parallel, 355.

Indulgences, The : the First and the Second, 194 *et seq.* ; an apple of discord, 239 ; the trouble before Bothwell Bridge, 305 ; the Third, 373 ; King James's Indulgences, 495.

Ingram, Thomas, of Borlands : gives information against Campbell of Cessnock, 374.

Innes, Dr. A. Taylor : quoted of the character of Samuel Rutherfurd, 71.

Innes, Elizabeth : wife of Alexander Brodie of Brodie, 314.

Irvine, James, of Bonshaw : captures Donald Cargill, 349.

James VI. of Scotland, I. of England : his interview with Andrew Melville at Falkland Palace, 236.

James VII. of Scotland, II. of England : see York, Duke of.

Johnston, Archibald, Lord Wariston : helps to frame the National Covenant, 5 ; reads it to the people in Greyfriars, 6, 132 ; marked for death by the Drunken Parliament, 61 ; prays James Guthrie back to life, 91 ; his heredity, 131 ; his bride, 132 ; Clerk at the Glasgow Assembly, 133 ; treats with Charles I. in the Bishops' War, 135 ; at the Westminster Assembly, 136 ; his scrupulous conscience, 138 ; in office under Cromwell, 138 ; his personal religion, 139 ; his flight, capture, and imprisonment, 139 ; Lauderdale's antipathy to him, 140 ; his execution, 141 ; Baillie of Jerviswood his son-in-law, 365, 368, 371.

Johnston, Margaret, daughter of the preceding : with her father in the Tower of London and the Tolbooth of Edinburgh, 141.

Johnstone, Sir James, of Westerhall : commands Andrew Hislop to be shot, 386.

Kenmure, Lady Jane Campbell, Viscountess : one of Rutherfurd's correspondents, 70.

Kennedy, Hugh : has a share in the authorship of *The Causes of the Lord's Wrath against Scotland,* 91 ; Moderator of the General Assembly of 1690, 509.

Ker, Dr. John : on Dr. Thomas Guthrie's spiritualising of the sights and sounds of nature, 316.

Kid, John : executed after the battle of Bothwell Bridge, 310.

Killiecrankie, the battle of : 500.

Killinchy, in County Down : John Livingston's ministry at, 122, 125.

Killing Time, the : 384 *et seq.*

Kilsyth, William Livingstone, Viscount : second husband of Lady Claverhouse, 294.

Kincardine, Alexander Bruce, Earl of : on the Indulged ministers, 195 ; his high character, 199 ; his friendship with Sir Robert Moray, 200 ; his withdrawal from Lauderdale, 205 ; joins "the Party," 253 ; on the insolence of Archbishop Sharp, 264.

King, John : captured by Claverhouse, 295 ; at liberty, 300 ; executed at the Mercat Cross, 310.

Kirkton, James : The *Secret and True History* quoted, of the religious condition of Scotland under the Commonwealth, 37 ; of the Drunken Parliament, 58 ; of James Sharp's dream, 101 ; of the obsequiousness of the Church to Charles, 106 ; of the curates, 114 ; of the death of the Earl of Middleton, 118 ; of Archibald Johnston's prayers, 139 ; of the Indulgences, 198 ; of John Welsh, 210 ; of James Aird, 222 ; of the dangerous temper of Sir John Nisbet, 278.

Knox, John : how the Cameronians translated his patriotism into fact and act, 336.

Koelman, Pastor James : takes part in the ordination of Richard Cameron at Rotterdam, 332.

Kyle, William : ordained in New Luce after the Revolution, 461.

had been denied him? Who was it laughed at the Paisley manufacturer who wished to exploit the classic Doon for water-power? Who was it who never ceased to yearn for the peace and simplicity of country life? Who was it stirred the heart by his tribute to the heroism of those Quakers who held life light amid the horrors of the Irish famine? Who was it declared that, had he the casting of the rôle of the actors on the world's stage, he would not suffer a cotton mill to have a place in it?" Men are less materialistic, and more mystical and friendly with the skies, than their critics and detractors are willing to admit. There are moments when their nature opens out into unexpected beauties; theirs, too, are the consecration and the poet's dream. And if there was no small infusion of worldly wisdom in Carstares's scheming, active, capacious soul, there were sublimer qualities as well. He, also, was "nigh to heaven and loved of loftiest stars."

Under the high crown of old St. Giles we may leave the fathers of the Scottish Church, as they busy themselves in deliberation over the concerns of the goodly heritage which has been restored to them. They have been conducted from midnight darkness and trouble into a region of light and peace; *hiems abiit moestaque crux.* In their hearts and on their lips are the expressive sentences of the Jewish singer, whose Babylonian captivity is past and gone—

> *If it had not been the Lord who was on our side,*
> *Let Israel now say;*
> *If it had not been the Lord who was on our side,*
> *When men rose up against us:*
> *Then they had swallowed us up alive,*
> *When their wrath was kindled against us:*
> *Then the waters had overwhelmed us,*
> *The stream had gone over our soul;*
> *Then the proud waters had gone over our soul.*
> *Blessed be the Lord,*
> *Who hath not given us as a prey to their teeth.*
> *Our soul is escaped as a bird out of the snare of the fowlers:*
> *The snare is broken, and we are escaped.*
> *Our help is in the name of the Lord,*
> *Who made heaven and earth.*

x

INDEX